TEST BANK

Mark Hirschey
University of Kansas

FUNDAMENTALS OF MANAGERIAL ECONOMICS
Sixth Edition

Mark Hirschey
University of Kansas

James L. Pappas
University of South Florida

THE DRYDEN PRESS

*Chicago   New York   San Francisco   Philadelphia
Montreal   Toronto   London   Sydney   Tokyo*

Copyright © 1998 by Harcourt Brace & Company

All rights reserved. No part of this publication may be reproduced or transmitted in any form or by any means, electronic or mechanical, including photocopy, recording or any information storage and retrieval system, without permission in writing from the publisher.

Address for Editorial Correspondence:
Harcourt Brace College Publishers, 301 Commerce Street, Suite 3700, Fort Worth, TX 76102

Address for Orders:
Harcourt Brace & Company, 6277 Sea Harbor Drive, Orlando, FL 32887-6777
1-800-782-4479, or 1-800-433-0001 (in Florida)

ISBN: 0-03-024599-0

Printed in the United States of America

7 8 9 0 1 2 3 4 5 6   023   9 8 7 6 5 4 3 2 1

The Dryden Press
Harcourt Brace & Company

PREFACE

This *Test Bank* has been prepared to accompany *Fundamentals of Managerial Economics*, Sixth Edition. It is designed to ease the instructor's burden in teaching what for many students is a difficult subject. Like the text itself, the *Test Bank* emphasizes those aspects of economic theory and analysis that are most relevant to students of business administration in an intuitive noncalculus-based format. It has been used successfully in both undergraduate and graduate courses. Typically, the *Test Bank* is relied upon for the broad range of material covered in *Fundamentals of Managerial Economics*, Sixth Edition, but it can be selectively employed to cover only specific chapters as well. Like the text, each chapter of the *Test Bank* is self-contained, and can thus be used to serve instructors who omit one or more chapters in programs where some material is covered in other classes.

At least twenty-five multiple choice questions with four answer options each have been provided for each textbook chapter; a total of over 485 multiple choice questions are included. Each of these questions is carefully structured to emphasize topics of major importance, and to test the student's basic understanding of key concepts. By using these questions, instructors are able to structure exams that focus on course material in a rigorous and intuitive, but nonmathematical, fashion.

Roughly 25 problems plus detailed solutions are provided for Chapters 2 through Chapter 16, more than 350 problems in all. Each problem in this *Test Bank* is identified in a manner consistent with the end-of-chapter problems. Like end-of-chapter problems, problems in the *Test Bank* increase in difficulty as the numerical sequence progresses, e.g., from P2.1 to P2.25. This approach allows instructors to design exams that offer problems with varying degrees of difficulty. I often adopt this approach in courses that I teach to ensure that every student in the class finds problems on each exam that provide both encouragement (easier problems) and challenge (tougher problems). Of course, detailed solutions to each problem are provided. For instructor convenience, the body of each question is shown in italics; problem solutions are shown in regular typeface.

As suggested above, multiple-choice questions are well suited for instructors who wish to test at the conceptual level where relatively little problem solving is needed. Short problems are designed for in-class tests that are 50 to 120 minutes in length. Most of these problems address a single topic and have from one to four parts to be solved. Long multi-part problems are suitable for in-class tests where students are allowed more than the usual 50 minutes to complete the test. They are perhaps best suited for "take-home" tests where additional time can be allowed for developing solutions.

The *Test Bank* is available in both printed and computerized forms for the IBM PC® and IBM® compatible computers. This allows questions, problems and solutions to be accessed very quickly. This not only makes test preparation quick and easy, it provides a means for easily making solutions available to students. In my classes, I provide students with detailed solutions immediately after the exam is taken. This is a useful instructional device, since students are presented relevant information when the material is fresh in their minds. Instructors may also wish to use the *Test Bank* as a convenient source for problem sets that can be assigned as homework or take-home exams. No matter how the *Test Bank* is used, it makes easier the task of preparing a variety of questions and problems that can be used in teaching the managerial economics course.

Please let me know if you have any suggestions for improving this *Test Bank*.

And finally, I would like to thank Karla R. Wallace for document preparation assistance, and Christine Hauschel for help with proof reading and problem checking.

Mark Hirschey
email: mhirschey@bschool.wpo.ukans.edu

October, 1997

TABLE OF CONTENTS

Preface		iii
PART ONE:	**OVERVIEW OF MANAGERIAL ECONOMICS**	
Chapter 1:	Introduction	1
Chapter 2:	Economic Optimization	8
Chapter 3:	Statistical Analysis of Economic Relations	51
PART TWO:	**DEMAND ANALYSIS**	
Chapter 4:	Demand and Supply	80
Chapter 5:	Demand Analysis	123
Chapter 6:	Forecasting	172
PART THREE:	**PRODUCTION & COST ANALYSIS**	
Chapter 7:	Production Analysis and Estimation	208
Chapter 8:	Cost Analysis and Estimation	258
Chapter 9:	Linear Programming	304
PART FOUR:	**MARKET STRUCTURE ANALYSIS & ESTIMATION**	
Chapter 10:	Perfect Competition and Monopoly	345
Chapter 11:	Monopolistic Competition and Oligopoly	390
Chapter 12:	Pricing Practices	440
PART FIVE:	**LONG-TERM INVESTMENT DECISION MAKING**	
Chapter 13:	Government Regulation of the Market Economy	480
Chapter 14:	Risk Analysis	538
Chapter 15:	Capital Budgeting	588
Chapter 16:	Public Management	639

Chapter 1

INTRODUCTION

MULTIPLE CHOICE QUESTIONS

Q1.1 In a free market economy, the optimal quality of goods and services is determined by:

    a. workers.
    b. firms.
    c. government.
>   d. customers.

Q1.2 A typical annual rate of return on invested capital is:

    a. 5%.
>   b. 10%.
    c. 15%.
    d. 20%.

Q1.3 Warren Buffett looks for "wonderful businesses" that feature:

    a. ongoing innovation.
    b. large capital investment.
>   c. consistent earnings growth.
    d. complicated business strategies.

Q1.4 Business profit is:

>   a. the residual of sales revenue minus the explicit accounting costs of doing business.
    b. a normal rate of return.
    c. economic profit.
    d. the return on stockholders' equity.

Q1.5 According to frictional profit theory, above-normal profits:

    a. are sometimes caused by barriers to entry that limit competition.
    b. arise as a result of successful invention or modernization.
    c. can sometimes be seen as a reward to efficient operations.
>   d. are observed following unanticipated changes in product demand or cost conditions.

Q1.6 The primary virtue of managerial economics lies in its:

    a. logic.
> b. usefulness.

    c. consistency.
    d. mathematical rigor.

Q1.7 The value of the firm will fall following a rise in:

> a. interest rates.

    b. profits.
    c. the time horizon.
    d. revenues.

Q1.8 Managers who seek satisfactory rather than optimal results:

> a. take actions that benefit parties other than stockholders.

    b. are insensitive to social constraints.
    c. are insensitive to self-imposed constraints.
    d. increase allocative efficiency.

Q1.9 Nonvalue-maximizing behavior is most common:

    a. in vigorously competitive markets.
> b. when shareholders are poorly informed.

    c. when managers own a significant ownership interest.
    d. in the production of goods rather than services.

Q1.10 Accounting net income divided by the book value of the firm is the:

    a. return on assets.
    b. profit margin.
> c. return on stockholders' equity.

    d. total asset turnover ratio.

Introduction

Q1.11 *Freely competitive markets:*

    a. reduce consumer choice.
    b. ignore social costs.
    c. ignore social benefits.
>   d. allocate goods via supply and demand.

Q1.12 *Managerial economics cannot be used to identify:*

    a. how macroeconomic forces affect the organization.
>   b. goals of the organization.
    c. ways to efficiently achieve the organization's goals.
    d. microeconomic consequences of managerial behavior.

Q1.13 *To maximize value, management must:*

    a. maximize short run revenue.
    b. minimize short run average profit.
>   c. maximize long run profit.
    d. maximize short run profit.

Q1.14 *Value maximization is broader than profit maximization because it considers:*

    a. total revenues.
    b. total costs.
    c. real-world constraints.
>   d. interest rates.

Q1.15 *Industry profits can be reduced by constraints on:*

    a. the number of firms in the industry.
>   b. pollution emissions.
    c. unions.
    d. price competition.

Q1.16   Industry profits can be increased by constraints on:

       a.   natural resources.
> **b.**   imports.

       c.   skilled labor.
       d.   worker health and safety.

Q1.17   Manager display satisficing behavior if they seek:

       a.   leisure.
       b.   to maximize community well-being.
       c.   to maximize employee welfare.
> **d.**   an industry-average profit rate.

Q1.18   Unfriendly takeovers have the greatest potential to enhance the market price of companies whose managers:

       a.   maximize short-run profits.
       b.   maximize the value of the firm.
> **c.**   satisfice.

       d.   maximize long-run profits.

Q1.19   Value maximization theory fails to address the problem of:

       a.   risk.
       b.   uncertainty.
       c.   sluggish growth.
> **d.**   self-serving management.

Q1.20   Constrained optimization techniques are not designed to deal with the problem of:

> **a.**   self-serving management.

       b.   contractual requirements.
       c.   scarce investment funds.
       d.   limited availability of essential inputs,

Introduction

Q1.21 *Excessive risk avoidance is consistent with:*

> a. utility maximization.
> b. growth maximization.
> c. the adaptive theory of the firm.
> d. value maximization.

Q1.22 *Business profit equals:*

   a. a normal rate of return before risk adjustment.
   b. sales revenue minus implicit costs.
> c. sales revenue minus explicit costs.
   d. a risk-adjusted normal rate of return.

Q1.23 *Economic profit equals:*

   a. normal profits plus opportunity costs.
> b. business profits minus implicit costs.
   c. business profits plus implicit costs.
   d. normal profits minus opportunity costs.

Q1.24 *The return to owner-provided inputs is an:*

> a. implicit cost.
   b. economic rent.
   c. entrepreneurial profit.
   d. explicit cost.

Q1.25 *Economic profits for cable TV companies that arise due to restrictive local licensing procedures are described by:*

   a. frictional profits theory.
   b. innovation profits theory.
   c. compensatory profits theory.
> d. monopoly profits theory.

Q1.26   Above-normal profits reward:

   a.   inefficiency.
   b.   workers.
   c.   suppliers.
> d.   innovation.

Q1.27   Below-normal profits signal a need for industry:

   a.   regulation.
> b.   contraction.
   c.   expansion.
   d.   wage increases.

Q1.28   To be useful, the theory of the firm must:

   a.   refrain from abstraction.
   b.   only consider quantitative factors.
> c.   accurately predict real-world phenomena.
   d.   rely upon realistic assumptions.

Q1.29   The value of a firm is equal to:

   a.   the present value of tangible assets.
   b.   the present value of all future revenues.
> c.   the present value of all future profits.
   d.   current revenues less current costs.

Q1.30   The value of the firm decreases with a decrease in:

> a.   total revenue.
   b.   the discount rate.
   c.   the cost of capital.
   d.   total cost.

Introduction

Q1.31 Managerial economics cannot be used to show how the imposition of auto import quotas:

    a. raises auto prices.
    b. creates the possibility of monopoly profits.
>   c. is good public policy.
    d. reduces the availability of substitutes for domestically produced cars.

Q1.32 Government regulation is important because government:

    a. regulation reduces public-sector employment.
    b. produces most of society's services output.
    c. produces most of society's material output.
>   d. uses scarce resources.

Q1.33 The share of revenues paid to suppliers does not depend upon:

    a. resource scarcity.
    b. input market competition.
>   c. output market competition.
    d. relative productivity.

Q1.34 Direct regulation of business has the potential to yield economic benefits to society when:

    a. barriers to entry are absent.
>   b. there are no good substitutes for a product.
    c. many firms serve a given market.
    d. diseconomies of scale exist.

Q1.35 Monopoly exploitation is reduced by regulation that:

>   a. enhances product-market competition.
    b. increases the bargaining power of workers.
    c. increases the bargaining power of employers.
    d. restricts output.

Chapter 2

ECONOMIC OPTIMIZATION

MULTIPLE CHOICE QUESTIONS

Q2.1 The choice alternative that produces a result most consistent with managerial objectives is the:

>   a. optimal decision.
    b. economic decision.
    c. least-cost alternative.
    d. uneconomic decision.

Q2.2 The optimal decision produces:

    a. maximum revenue.
    b. maximum profits.
    c. minimum average costs.
>   d. a result consistent with managerial objectives.

Q2.3 An equation is:

>   a. an analytical expressions of functional relationships.
    b. a visual representation of data.
    c. a table of electronically stored data.
    d. a list of economic data.

Q2.4 A dependent variable is:

    a. an X-variable determined separately from the Y-variable.
>   b. a Y-variable determined by X values.
    c. a Y-variable determined prior to X values.
    d. a Y-variable determined with X values.

Q2.5 Inflection is:

    a. a line that touches but does not intersect a given curve.
>   b. a point of maximum slope.
    c. a measure of the steepness of a line.
    d. an activity level that generates highest profit.

Economic Optimization 9

Q2.6 The comprehensive impact resulting from a decision is the:

    a.   gain or loss associated with a given managerial decision.
    b.   change in total cost.
    c.   change in total profit.
>   d.   incremental change.

Q2.7 Total revenue is maximized at the point where:

>   a.   marginal revenue equals zero.
    b.   marginal cost equals zero.
    c.   marginal revenue equals marginal cost.
    d.   marginal profit equals zero.

Q2.8 If $P = \$500 - \$2Q$,

    a. $MR = \$500 - \$2Q$.
>   b. $MR = \$500 - \$4Q$.
    c. $MR = \$500Q - \$2$.
    d. $MR = \$500 - \$4$.

Q2.9 Total cost minimization occurs at the point where:

    a. $MC = 0$.
    b. $MC = AC$.
    c. $AC = 0$.
>   d. $Q = 0$.

Q2.10 The slope of a straight line from the origin to the total profit curve indicates:

    a.   marginal profit at that point.
    b.   an inflection point.
>   c.   average profit at that point.
    d.   total profit at that point.

Q2.11 The optimal output decision:

      a. minimizes the marginal cost of production.
      b. minimizes production costs.
>   **c.** is most consistent with managerial objectives.
      d. minimizes the average cost of production.

Q2.12 Holding all else equal, the value of the firm falls with a decrease in:

      a. interest rates.
      b. average investment-project life.
      c. uncertainty.
>   **d.** total revenue.

Q2.13 Marginal profit equals:

>   **a.** the change in total profit following a one-unit change in output.
      b. the change in total profit following a managerial decision.
      c. average revenue minus average cost.
      d. total revenue minus total cost.

Q2.14 Marginal cost is:

      a. the change in output following a one-dollar change in cost.
>   **b.** the change in cost following a one-unit change in output.
      c. the change in average cost following a one-unit change in output.
      d. the change in cost following a managerial decision.

Q2.15 Total revenue increases at a constant rate as output increases when average revenue:

      a. increases as output increases.
      b. increases and then decreases as output increases.
      c. exceeds price.
>   **d.** is constant.

Economic Optimization

Q2.16 Marginal profit equals average profit when:

   a. marginal profit is maximized.
> b. average profit is maximized.
   c. marginal profit equals marginal cost.
   d. the profit maximizing output is produced.

Q2.17 If average profit increases with output marginal profit must be:

   a. decreasing.
> b. greater than average profit.
   c. less than average profit.
   d. increasing.

Q2.18 An increase in output reduces total profits if:

   a. marginal profit is less than average profit.
   b. marginal profit is greater than average profit.
   c. average profit is decreasing.
> d. marginal profit is negative.

Q2.19 At the profit-maximizing level of output:

> a. marginal revenue equals marginal cost.
   b. marginal cost equals zero.
   c. average profit equals zero.
   d. marginal profit equals average profit.

Q2.20 The breakeven level of output occurs where:

   a. marginal cost equals average cost.
   b. marginal profit equals zero.
> c. total profit equals zero.
   d. marginal cost equals marginal revenue.

Q2.21 Incremental profit is:

   a. the change in profit that results from a unitary change in output.
   b. total revenue minus total cost.
> c. the change in profit caused by a given managerial decision.
   d. the change in profits earned by the firm over a brief period of time.

Q2.22 The incremental profit earned from the production and sale of a new product will be higher if:

   a. the costs of materials needed to produce the new product increase.
> b. excess capacity can be used to produce the new product.
   c. existing facilities used to produce the new product must be modified.
   d. the revenues earned from existing products decrease.

Q2.23 Which of the following short run strategies should a manager select to obtain the highest degree of sales penetration?

> a. maximize revenues.
   b. minimize average costs.
   c. minimize total costs.
   d. maximize profits.

Q2.24 If total revenue increases at a constant rate as output increases, marginal revenue:

   a. is greater than average revenue.
   b. is less than average revenue.
   c. is greater than average revenue at low levels of output and less than average revenue at high levels of output.
> d. equals average revenue.

Q2.25 When marginal profit equals zero:

   a. the firm can increase profits by increasing output.
   b. the firm can increase profits by decreasing output.
   c. marginal revenue equals average revenue.
> d. profit is maximized.

Economic Optimization 13

Q2.26 *Geometrically, average profit is represented by:*

    a. the length of a ray running from the origin to the total profit function at each level of output.

> **b.** the slope of the ray running from the origin to the total profit function at each level of output.

    c. the slope of the line tangent to the marginal profit function at each level of output.

    d. the slope of a line tangent to the total profit function at each level of output.

Q2.27 *An optimal decision:*

    a. minimizes output cost.

    b. maximizes profits.

> **c.** produces the result most consistent with decision maker objectives.

    d. maximizes product quality.

Q2.28 *To be descriptive of managerial behavior, the process of optimization must:*

    a. consider all decision alternatives.

    b. ignore real-world constraints.

> **c.** predict observed performance.

    d. be mathematically formulated.

Q2.29 *If marginal profit is positive, as output increases:*

    a. total profit must decrease.

> **b.** total profit must increase.

    c. average and total profit must increase.

    d. average profit must increase.

Q2.30 *If profit is to rise as output expands, then marginal profit must be:*

    a. falling.

    b. constant.

> **c.** positive.

    d. rising.

PROBLEMS & SOLUTIONS

P2.1 **A.** Given the price (P) and output (Q) data in the following table, calculate the related total revenue (TR), marginal revenue (MR), and average revenue (AR) figures:

Q	P	TR	MR	AR
0	$35			
1	30			
2	25			
3	20			
4	15			
5	10			
6	5			
7	0			

B. At what output level is revenue maximized?

P2.1 **SOLUTION**

A.

Q	P	TR=P×Q	MR=ΔTR	AR=TR/Q=P
0	$35	$ 0	--	--
1	30	30	$30	$30
2	25	50	20	25
3	20	60	10	20
4	15	60	0	15
5	10	50	-10	10
6	5	30	-20	5
7	0	0	-30	0

B. Revenue is maximized at an output level 4, where MR = 0.

Economic Optimization

P2.2   **A.**   *Marginal Analysis.* Given the price (P) and the output (Q) data in the following table, calculate the related total revenue (TR), marginal revenue (MR), and average revenue (AR) figures:

Q	P	TR	MR	AR
0	$80			
1	70			
2	60			
3	50			
4	40			
5	30			
6	20			
7	10			
8	0			

   B.   At what output level is revenue maximized?

P2.2   **SOLUTION**

   A.

Q	P	TR=P×Q	MR=ΔTR	AR=TR/Q=P
0	$80	$ 0	--	--
1	70	70	$70	$70
2	60	120	50	60
3	50	150	30	50
4	40	160	10	40
5	30	150	-10	30
6	20	120	-30	20
7	10	70	-50	10
8	0	0	-70	0

   B.   Revenue is maximized at an output level slightly greater than 4, where MR = 0.

P2.3 **A.** *Graph Analysis.* Given the output (Q) and price (P) data in the following table, calculate the related total revenue (TR), marginal revenue (MR), and average revenue (AR) figures:

Q	P	TR	MR	AR
0	$50			
1	45			
2	40			
3	35			
4	30			
5	25			
6	20			
7	15			
8	10			
9	5			
10	0			

B. Graph these data using "dollars" on the vertical axis and "quantity" on the horizontal axis. At what output level is revenue maximized?

C. Why is marginal revenue less than average revenue at each price level?

Economic Optimization

P2.3 **SOLUTION**

A.

Q	P	TR=P×Q	MR=ΔTR	AR=TR/Q=P
0	$50	$ 0	--	--
1	45	45	$45	$45
2	40	80	35	40
3	35	105	25	35
4	30	120	15	30
5	25	125	5	25
6	20	120	-5	20
7	15	105	-15	15
8	10	80	-25	10
9	5	45	-35	5
10	0	0	-45	0

B. Revenue is maximized at an output level of 5.

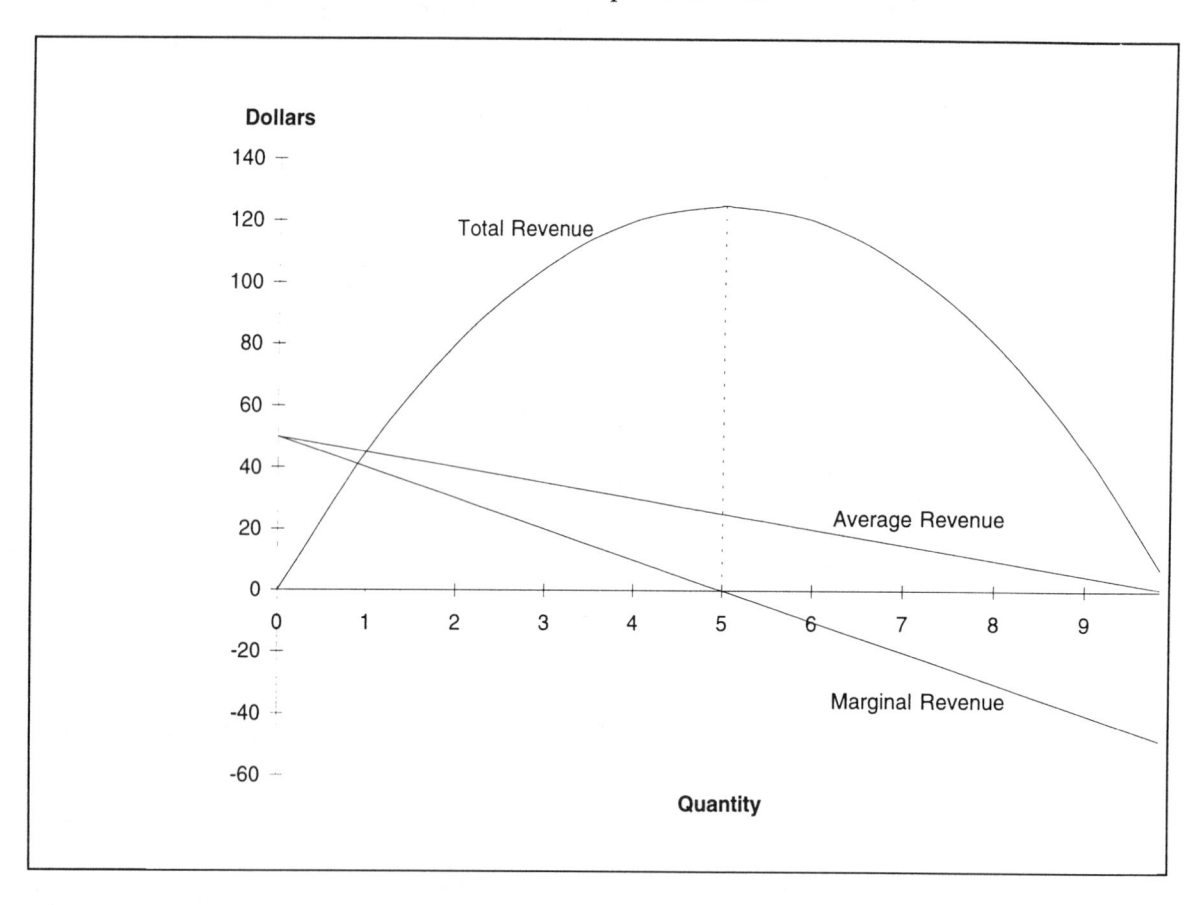

C. At every price level, price must be cut by $5 in order to increase sales by an additional unit. This means that the "benefit" of added sales from new customers is only gained at the "cost" of some loss in revenue from current customers. Thus, the net increase in revenue from added sales is always less than the change in gross revenue. Therefore, marginal revenue is always less than average revenue (or price).

P2.4 **A.** *Marginal Analysis.* Fill in the missing data for price (P), total revenue (TR), marginal revenue (MR), total cost (TC), marginal cost (MC), profit (π), and marginal profit ($M\pi$) in the following table:

Economic Optimization

Q	P	TR	MR	TC	MC	π	Mπ
0	$200	$ --	$ --	$ 0	$ --	$ 0	$ --
1	180	180	180	100	100	80	80
2	160				175	75	65
3		420	65	180	35		
4		60	295	185			
5		100	500	350			
6		480	-20	50	80		
7		420	450	50	-120		
8		40	320	505	-185		
9		65	-205				
10		100	750				

B. At what output (Q) level is profit maximized?

C. At what output (Q) level is revenue maximized?

D. Discuss any differences in your answers to Parts B and C.

P2.4 SOLUTION

A.

Q	P	TR=P×Q	MR=ΔTR	TC	MC=ΔTC	π=TR-TC	Mπ=Δπ
0	$200	$ 0	--	$ 0	--	$ 0	--
1	180	180	$180	100	$100	80	$ 80
2	160	320	140	175	75	145	65
3	140	420	100	240	65	180	35
4	120	480	60	295	55	185	5
5	100	500	20	350	55	150	-35
6	80	480	-20	400	50	80	-70
7	60	420	-60	450	50	-30	-110
8	40	320	-100	505	55	-185	-155
9	20	180	-140	570	65	-390	-205
10	10	100	-80	750	180	-650	-260

B. Profit increases so long as MR > MC and Mπ > 0. In this problem, profit is maximized at Q = 4 where π = $185 (and TR = $480).

C. Total Revenue increases so long as MR > 0. In this problem, revenue is maximized at Q = 5 where TR = $500 (and π = $150).

D. Given a downward sloping demand curve and MC > 0, as is typically the case, profits will be maximized at an output level that is less than the revenue maximizing level. Revenue maximization requires lower prices and greater output than would be true with profit maximization. The potential long-run advantage of a revenue maximizing strategy is that it might generate rapid market expansion and long-run benefits in terms of customer loyalty and future unit cost reductions. The cost is, of course, measured in terms of lost profits in the short-run (here the loss is $35 in profits).

P2.5 A. *Marginal Analysis. Fill in the missing data for price (P), total revenue (TR), marginal revenue (MR), total cost (TC), marginal cost (MC), profit (π), and marginal profit (Mπ) in the following table:*

Q	P	TR	MR	TC	MC	π	Mπ
0	$160	$ 0	$ --	$ 0	$ --	$ 0	$ --
1	150	150	150	25	25	125	125
2	140			55	30		100
3		390			35	300	75
4			90	130		350	
5	110	550		175			
6		600	50		55	370	
7		630		290	60		-30
8	80	640		355		285	
9					75		-85
10		600		525			

B. At what output (Q) level is profit maximized?

C. At what output (Q) level is revenue maximized?

D. Discuss any differences in your answers to Parts B and C.

Economic Optimization

P2.5 **SOLUTION**

A.

Q	P	TR=P×Q	MR=ΔTR	TC	MC=ΔTC	π=TR-TC	Mπ=Δπ
0	$160	$ 0	--	$ 0	--	$ 0	--
1	150	150	$150	25	$ 25	125	$125
2	140	280	130	55	30	225	100
3	130	390	110	90	35	300	75
4	120	480	90	130	40	350	50
5	110	550	70	175	45	375	25
6	110	600	50	230	55	370	-5
7	90	640	30	290	60	340	-30
8	80	640	10	355	65	285	-55
9	70	630	-10	430	75	200	-85
10	60	600	-30	525	95	75	-125

B. Profit increases so long as MR > MC and Mπ > 0. In this problem, profit is maximized at Q = 5 where π = $375 (and TR = $550).

C. Total Revenue increases so long as MR > 0. In this problem, revenue is maximized at Q = 8 where TR = $640 (and π = $285).

D. Given a downward sloping demand curve and MC > 0, as is typically the case, profits will be maximized at an output level that is less than the revenue maximizing level. Revenue maximization requires lower prices and greater output than would be true with profit maximization. The potential long-run advantage of a revenue maximizing strategy is that it might generate rapid market expansion and long-run benefits in terms of customer loyalty and future unit cost reductions. The cost is, of course, measured in terms of lost profits in the short-run (here the loss is $90 in profits).

P2.6 **A.** *Marginal Analysis*. Fill in the missing data for price (P), total revenue (TR), marginal revenue (MR), total cost (TC), marginal cost (MC), profit (π), and marginal profit (Mπ) in the following table:

Q	P	TR	MR	TC	MC	π	Mπ
0	$230	$ 0	$ --	$ 0	$ --	$ 0	$ --
1	210			10			
2		380			20		
3			130			450	
4				100			50
5	130				60		
6		660				430	
7			-30				-110
8			-70		90		

B. At what output (Q) level is profit maximized?

C. At what output (Q) level is revenue maximized?

D. Discuss any differences in your answers to Parts B and C.

P2.6 **SOLUTION**

A.

Q	P	TR=P×Q	MR=ΔTR	TC	MC=ΔTC	π=TR-TC	Mπ=Δπ
0	$230	$ 0	--	$ 0	--	$ 0	--
1	210	210	$210	10	$ 10	200	$200
2	190	380	170	30	20	350	150
3	170	510	130	60	30	450	100
4	150	600	90	100	40	500	50
5	130	650	50	160	60	490	-10
6	110	660	10	230	70	430	-60
7	90	630	-30	310	80	320	-110
8	70	560	-70	400	90	160	-160

B. Profit increases so long as MR > MC and Mπ > 0. In this problem, profit is maximized at Q = 4 where π = 500 (and TR = $600).

C. Total Revenue increases so long as MR > 0. In this problem, total revenue is maximized at Q = 6 where TR = $660 (and π = $430).

D. Given a downward sloping demand curve and MC > 0, as is typically the case, profits will be maximized at an output level that is less than the revenue maximizing

Economic Optimization

level. Revenue maximization requires lower prices and greater output than would be true with profit maximization. The potential long-run advantage of a revenue maximizing strategy is that it might generate rapid market expansion and long-run benefits in terms of customer loyalty and future unit cost reductions. The cost is, of course, measured in terms of lost profits in the short-run (here the loss is $130 in profits).

P2.7 **A.** *Marginal Analysis.* Fill in the missing data for price (P), total revenue (TR), marginal revenue (MR), total cost (TC), marginal cost (MC), profit (π), and marginal profit ($M\pi$) in the following table:

Q	P	TR	MR	TC	MC	π	$M\pi$
0	$50	$ 0	$--	$ 10	$--	$-10	$--
1			45		50		
2				115		-35	
3	35						
4		120			65	-50	
5			5	310			
6	20				75		

B. At what output (Q) level is profit maximized (or losses minimized)? Explain.

C. At what output (Q) level is revenue maximized?

P2.7 **SOLUTION**

A.

Q	P	TR=P×Q	MR=ΔTR	TC	MC=ΔTC	π=TR-TC	$M\pi$=$\Delta\pi$
0	$50	$ 0	--	$ 10	--	$-10	--
1	45	45	$45	60	$50	-15	$ -5
2	40	80	35	115	55	-35	-20
3	35	105	25	175	60	-70	-35
4	30	120	15	240	65	-120	-50
5	25	125	5	310	70	-185	-65
6	20	120	-5	385	75	-265	-80

B. At every output level given, profit is negative. In this problem, profit is maximized (loss is minimized) at Q = 0 where π = -$10 (and TR = 0).

C. Total Revenue increases so long as MR > 0. In this problem, total revenue is maximized at Q = 5 where TR = $125 (and π = -$185).

P2.8 *Marginal Analysis. Characterize each of the following statements as true or false, and explain your answer.*

A. Given a downward-sloping demand curve and positive marginal costs, profit-maximizing firms will always sell less output and at higher prices than will revenue-maximizing firms.

B. Profits will be maximized when marginal revenue equals marginal cost.

C. Total profit is the difference between total revenue and total cost and will always exceed zero at the profit-maximizing activity level.

D. Marginal cost must be less than average cost at the average cost minimizing output level.

E. The demand curve will be downward sloping if marginal revenue is less than price.

P2.8 SOLUTION

A. True. Profit maximization involves setting marginal revenue equal to marginal cost. Revenue maximization involves setting marginal revenue equal to zero. Given a downward sloping demand curve and positive marginal costs, revenue maximizing firms will charge lower prices and offer greater quantities of output than will profit maximizers.

B. True. Profits are maximized when marginal revenue equals marginal cost. Profits equal zero at the breakeven point where total revenue equals total cost.

C. False. High fixed costs or depressed demand conditions can give rise to zero or negative profits at the profit-maximizing activity level. Profit maximization only ensures that profits are as high as possible, or that losses are minimized, subject to demand and cost conditions.

D. False. Average cost falls as output expands so long as marginal cost is less than average cost. Thus, average cost is minimized at the point where average and marginal costs are equal.

Economic Optimization

       E.   True. The demand curve is the average revenue curve. Since price (average revenue) is falling along a downward sloping demand curve, marginal revenue is less than average revenue.

P2.9   ***Optimization.*** *Characterize each of the following statements as true or false, and explain your answer.*

       A.   To maximize the value of the firm, management should always produce the level of output that maximizes short run profit.

       B.   Average profit equals the slope of the line tangent to the total product function at each level of output.

       C.   Marginal profit equals zero at the profit maximizing level of output.

       D.   To maximize profit, total revenue must also be maximized.

       E.   Marginal cost equals average cost at the average cost minimizing level of output.

P2.9   **SOLUTION**

       A.   False. Value can be maximized by producing a level of output higher than that which maximizes profits in the short run if the long run future profits derived from greater market penetration and scale advantages are sufficient to overcome the disadvantage of lost short run profits.

       B.   False. Average profit is represented by the slope of the ray running from the origin to the total product function at each level of output.

       C.   True. Marginal profit equals the slope of the line tangent to the total profit function at each level of output. The slope of the line tangent to the total profit function at its maximum point equals zero. Thus, marginal profit equals zero at the profit maximizing level of output.

       D.   False. Total revenue is maximized at a level of output greater than the level of output that maximizes profit since the level of output at which $MR = 0$ is greater than the level of output at which $MR = MC > 0$ when MR is decreasing.

       E.   True. Marginal cost equals average cost at the average cost minimizing level of output.

P2.10 *Marginal Analysis: Tables.* Bud N. Starr is a regional sales representative for Snappy Tools, Inc., and sells hand tools to auto mechanics in New England states. Starr's goal is to maximize total monthly commission income, which is figured at 15% of gross sales. In reviewing monthly experience over the past year, Starr found the following relations between days spent in each state and monthly sales generated:

	Maine		New Hampshire		Vermont	
Days	Gross Sales	Days	Gross Sales	Days	Gross Sales
0	$2,000	0	$1,500	0	$1,000
1	5,000	1	3,500	1	2,600
2	7,500	2	5,300	2	3,700
3	9,500	3	6,900	3	4,300
4	11,000	4	8,300	4	4,600
5	12,000	5	9,500	5	4,800
6	12,500	6	10,500	6	4,900
7	12,500	7	11,000	7	5,000

A. Construct a table showing Starr's marginal sales per day in each state.

B. If administrative duties limit Starr to only 10 selling days per month, how should he spend them?

C. Calculate Starr's maximum monthly commission income.

P2.10 SOLUTION

A.

	Maine		New Hampshire		Vermont	
Days	Marginal Sales	Days	Marginal Sales	Days	Marginal Sales
0	--	0	--	0	--
1	$3,000	1	$2,000	1	$1,600
2	2,500	2	1,800	2	1,100
3	2,000	3	1,600	3	600
4	1,500	4	1,400	4	300
5	1,000	5	1,200	5	200
6	500	6	1,000	6	100
7	0	7	500	7	100

B. The maximum commission income is earned by allocating selling days on the basis of obtaining the largest marginal sales for each additional day of selling activity. Using the data in part a, we see that 4 days should be spent in Maine, 5 days in New Hampshire, and 1 day should be spent in Vermont.

C. Given this time allocation, Starr's maximum commission income is:

State	Sales
Maine	$11,000
New Hampshire	9,500
Vermont	2,600
Total	$23,100
× Commission rate	0.15
	$3,465 per month

P2.11 *Marginal Analysis: Tables.* Julie Branigan is a sales representative for Harper Insurance Company, and sells life insurance policies to individuals in the Phoenix area. Branigan's goal is to maximize total monthly commission income, which is figured at 10% of gross sales. In reviewing monthly experience over the past year, Branigan found the following relations between days spent in each city and monthly sales generated:

28   Chapter 2

	Tempe		Scottsdale		Paradise Valley
Days	Gross Sales	Days	Gross Sales	Days	Gross Sales
0	$1,500	0	$1,000	0	$ 500
1	2,700	1	2,600	1	2,600
2	3,500	2	4,000	2	4,400
3	4,000	3	4,900	3	5,900
4	4,400	4	5,500	4	7,100
5	4,700	5	5,900	5	8,000
6	4,900	6	6,150	6	8,600
7	5,000	7	6,300	7	8,900

A. Construct a table showing Branigan's marginal sales per day in each city.

B. If administrative duties limit Branigan to only 15 selling days per month, how should she spend them?

C. Calculate Branigan's maximum monthly commission income.

P2.11 **SOLUTION**

A.

	Tempe		Scottsdale		Paradise Valley
Days	Marginal Sales	Days	Marginal Sales	Days	Marginal Sales
0	--	0	--	0	--
1	$1,200	1	$1,600	1	$2,100
2	800	2	1,400	2	1,800
3	500	3	900	3	1,500
4	400	4	600	4	1,200
5	300	5	400	5	900
6	200	6	250	6	600
7	100	7	150	7	300

Economic Optimization

B. The maximum commission income is earned by allocating selling days on the basis of obtaining the largest marginal sales for each additional day of selling activity. Using the data in part a, we see that 4 days should be spent in Tempe, 5 days in Scottsdale, and 6 days should be spent in Paradise Valley.

C. Given this time allocation, Branigan's maximum commission income is:

City	Sales
Tempe	$4,400
Scottsdale	5,900
Paradise Valley	8,600
Total	$18,900
× Commission rate	0.10
	$1,890 per month

P2.12 *Marginal Analysis: Tables.* Jess Langston is a telemarketing manager for Laser Supply, Inc., which sells replacement chemicals to businesses with copy machines. Langston's goal is to maximize total monthly commission income, which is figured at 5% of gross sales of his telemarketers. In reviewing monthly experience over the past year, Langston found the following relations between worker-hours spent in each market segment and monthly sales generated:

Businesses with over 250 employees		Businesses with 250-500 employees		Businesses with less than 500 employees	
Worker-hours	Gross Sales	Worker-hours	Gross Sales	Worker-hours	Gross Sales
0	$6,000	0	$5,000	0	$7,000
100	8,500	100	8,000	100	9,000
200	10,700	200	10,500	200	10,500
300	12,600	300	12,500	300	11,500
400	14,200	400	14,000	400	12,300
500	15,500	500	15,000	500	12,900
600	16,500	600	15,500	600	13,400
700	17,200	700	15,500	700	13,700

A. Construct a table showing Langston's marginal sales per 100 worker-hours in each market segment.

B. Langston employs his telemarketers for 1,000 worker-hours per month, how should he allocate the hours among market segments?

C. Calculate Langston's maximum monthly commission income.

P2.12 SOLUTION

A.

Businesses with over 250 employees		Businesses with 250-500 employees		Businesses with less than 500 employees	
Worker-hours	Marginal Sales	Worker-hours	Marginal Sales	Worker-hours	Marginal Sales
0	--	0	--	0	--
100	$2,500	100	$3,000	100	$2,000
200	2,200	200	2,500	200	1,500
300	1,900	300	2,000	300	1,000
400	1,600	400	1,500	400	800
500	1,300	500	1,000	500	600
600	1,000	600	500	600	500
700	700	700	0	700	300

B. The maximum commission income is earned by allocating worker-hours on the basis of obtaining the largest marginal sales for each additional worker-hour of selling activity. Using the data in Part A, 400 worker-hours should be spent calling businesses with less than 250 employees, 400 worker-hours calling businesses with 250-500 employees, and 200 worker-hours should be spent calling business with over 500 employees.

C. Given this time allocation, Langston's maximum commission income is:

Business	Sales
Less than 250 employees	$14,200
250-500 employees	14,000
Over 500 employees	10,500
Total	$38,700
× Commission rate	0.05
	$ 1,935 per month

P2.13 Marginal Analysis: Tables. Dan Meyers is a regional sales representative for Specialty Books, Inc., and sells textbooks to universities in midwestern states. Meyers' goal is to maximize total monthly commission income, which is figured at 10% of gross sales. In reviewing monthly experience over the past year, Meyers found the following relations between days spent in each state and monthly sales generated:

Economic Optimization

	Kansas		Oklahoma		Nebraska
Days	Gross Sales	Days	Gross Sales	Days	Gross Sales
0	$2,000	0	$500	0	$1,000
1	4,000	1	1,500	1	3,500
2	5,600	2	2,300	2	5,500
3	6,800	3	2,900	3	7,000
4	7,900	4	3,300	4	8,100
5	8,500	5	3,500	5	8,900
6	8,800	6	3,600	6	9,400
7	8,900	7	3,600	7	9,600

A. Construct a table showing Meyers' marginal sales per day in each state.

B. If administrative duties limit Meyers to only 15 selling days per month, how should he spend them?

C. Calculate Meyers' maximum monthly commission income.

P2.13 SOLUTION

A.

	Kansas		Oklahoma		Nebraska
Days	Marginal Sales	Days	Marginal Sales	Days	Marginal Sales
0	--	0	--	0	--
1	$2,000	1	$1,000	1	$2,500
2	1,600	2	800	2	2,000
3	1,200	3	600	3	1,500
4	1,100	4	400	4	1,100
5	600	5	200	5	800
6	300	6	100	6	500
7	100	7	0	7	200

B. The maximum commission income is earned by allocating selling days on the basis of obtaining the largest marginal sales for each additional day of selling activity. Using the data in Part A, 5 days should be spent in Kansas, 4 days in Oklahoma, and 6 days should be spent in Nebraska.

C. Given this time allocation, Meyers' maximum commission income is:

State	Sales
Kansas	$ 8,500
Oklahoma	3,300
Nebraska	9,400
Total	$21,200
× Commission rate	0.10
	$2,120 per month

P2.14 *Profit Maximization: Equations. Woodland Instruments, Inc. operates in the highly competitive electronics industry. Prices for its R2-D2 control switches are stable at $100 each. This means that P = MR = $100 in this market. Engineering estimates indicate that relevant total and marginal cost relations for the R2-D2 model are:*

$$TC = \$500,000 + \$25Q + \$0.0025Q^2$$

$$MC = \$25 + \$0.005Q.$$

A. *Calculate the output level that will maximize R2-D2 profit.*

B. *Calculate this maximum profit.*

P2.14 SOLUTION

A. To find the profit-maximizing level of output we set MR = MC and solve for Q:

$$MR = MC$$

$$\$100 = \$25 + \$0.005Q$$

$$0.005Q = 75$$

$$Q = 15,000$$

Economic Optimization

(*Note*: Profits are decreasing for Q > 15,000.)

B. The total revenue function for Woodland is:

$$TR = PQ = \$100Q$$

Then, total profit is:

$$\pi = TR - TC$$
$$= \$100Q - \$500,000 - \$25Q - \$0.0025Q^2$$
$$= -\$0.0025Q^2 + \$75Q - \$500,000$$
$$= -\$0.0025(15,000^2) + \$75(15,000) - \$500,000$$
$$= \$62,500$$

P2.15 *Profit Maximization: Equations.* Far East Manufacturing, Inc. (FEM) operates in the highly competitive electronics industry. Prices for its pocket-sized electronic appointment minder are stable at $50 each. This means that P = MR = $50 in this market. Engineering estimates indicate that relevant total and marginal cost relations for the appointment minder are:

$$TC = \$25,000 + \$10Q + \$0.00025Q^2$$
$$MC = \$10 + \$0.0005Q.$$

A. Calculate the output level that will maximize appointment minder profit.

B. Calculate this maximum profit.

P2.15 **SOLUTION**

A. To find the profit maximizing level of output we set MR = MC and solve for Q:

$$MR = MC$$
$$\$50 = \$10 + \$0.0005Q$$
$$0.0005Q = 40$$

$$Q = 80,000$$

(*Note*: Profits are decreasing for Q > 80,000.)

B. The total revenue function for the appointment minder is:

$$TR = PQ = \$50Q$$

Then, total profit is:

$$\pi = TR - TC$$

$$= \$50Q - \$25,000 - \$10Q - \$0.00025Q^2$$

$$= -\$0.00025Q^2 + \$40Q - \$25,000$$

$$= -\$0.00025(80,000^2) + \$40(80,000) - \$25,000$$

$$= \$1,575,000$$

P2.16 *Profit Maximization: Equations.* Fujetsu, Inc. operates in the highly competitive consumer electronics industry. Prices for its budget-priced, carousel compact disk player are stable at $250 each. This means that P = MR = $250 in this market. Engineering estimates indicate that relevant total and marginal cost relations for the player are:

$$TC = \$400,000 + \$70Q + \$0.002Q^2$$

$$MC = \$70 + \$0.004Q.$$

A. Calculate the output level that will maximize carousel CD player profit.

B. Calculate this maximum profit.

P2.16 SOLUTION

A. To find the profit-maximizing level of output we set MR = MC and solve for Q:

$$MR = MC$$

$$\$250 = \$70 + \$0.004Q$$

Economic Optimization 35

$$0.004Q = 180$$

$$Q = 45,000$$

(*Note*: Profits are decreasing for Q > 45,000.)

B. The total revenue function for Fujetsu's CD player is:

$$TR = PQ = \$250Q$$

Then, total profit is:

$$\begin{aligned}\pi &= TR - TC \\ &= \$250Q - \$400,000 - \$70Q - \$0.002Q^2 \\ &= -\$0.002Q^2 + \$180Q - \$400,000 \\ &= -\$0.002(45,000^2) + \$180(45,000) - \$400,000 \\ &= \$3,650,000\end{aligned}$$

P2.17 **Profit Maximization: Equations.** *Trimex, Inc. operates in the highly competitive sports watch industry. Prices for its Q4 model with stopwatch features are stable at $30 each. This means that P = MR = $30 in this market. Engineering estimates indicate that relevant total and marginal cost relations for the Q4 model are:*

$$TC = \$750,000 + \$20Q + \$0.00002Q^2$$

$$MC = \$20 + \$0.00004Q.$$

A. *Calculate the output level that will maximize Q4 profit.*

B. *Calculate this maximum profit.*

P2.17 **SOLUTION**

A. To find the profit-maximizing level of output we set MR = MC and solve for Q:

$$MR = MC$$

$$\$30 = \$20 + \$0.00004Q$$

$$0.00004Q = 10$$

$$Q = 250,000$$

(*Note*: Profits are decreasing for Q > 250,000.)

B. The total revenue function for the Trimex Q4 is:

$$TR = PQ = \$30Q$$

Then, total profit is:

$$\begin{aligned}\pi &= TR - TC \\ &= \$30Q - \$750,000 - \$20Q - \$0.00002Q^2 \\ &= -\$0.00002Q^2 + \$10Q - \$750,000 \\ &= -\$0.00002(250,000^2) + \$10(250,000) - \$750,000 \\ &= \$500,000\end{aligned}$$

P2.18 **Profit Maximization: Equations.** Lone Star Insurance offers mail-order automobile insurance to preferred-risk drivers in the state of Texas. The company is the low-cost provider of insurance in this market with fixed costs of $18 million per year, plus variable costs of $750 for each driver insured on an annual basis. Annual demand and marginal revenue relations for the company are:

$$P = \$1,500 - \$0.005Q$$

$$MR = \$1,500 - \$0.01Q$$

A. Calculate the profit-maximizing activity level.

B. Calculate the company's optimal profit and return-on-sales levels.

P2.18 **SOLUTION**

A. Set MR = MC and solve for Q to find the profit-maximizing activity level:

Economic Optimization

$$MR = MC$$

$$\$1,500 - \$0.01Q = \$750$$

$$0.01Q = 750$$

$$Q = 75,000$$

B.
$$\pi = PQ - TC$$

$$= \$1,500(75,000) - \$0.005(75,000^2) - \$18,000,000$$

$$- \$750(75,000)$$

$$= \$10,125,000$$

$$TR = PQ$$

$$= \$1,500(75,000) - \$0.005(75,000^2)$$

$$= \$84,375,000$$

$$\text{Return on Sales} = \pi/TR$$

$$= \$10,125,000/\$84,375,000$$

$$= 12\%$$

P2.19 **Profit Maximization: Equations.** *Quilted Products, Ltd. offers mail-order storage containers for fine china to newlyweds. The company is the low-cost provider of these quilted boxes with fixed costs of $480,000 per year, plus variable costs of $30 for each box. Annual demand and marginal revenue relations for the company are:*

$$P = \$70 - \$0.0005Q$$

$$MR = \$70 - \$0.001Q$$

A. *Calculate the profit-maximizing activity level.*

B. *Calculate the company's optimal profit and return-on-sales levels.*

A. Calculate the profit-maximizing activity level.

B. Calculate the company's optimal profit and return-on-sales levels.

P2.21 SOLUTION

A. Set MR = MC and solve for Q to find the profit-maximizing activity level:

$$MR = MC$$

$$\$225 - \$0.25Q = \$25$$

$$0.25Q = 200$$

$$Q = 800$$

B.
$$\pi = PQ - TC$$

$$= \$225(800) - \$0.125(800^2) - \$10,000 - \$25(800)$$

$$= \$70,000$$

$$TR = PQ$$

$$= \$225(800) - \$0.125(800^2)$$

$$= \$100,000$$

$$\text{Return on Sales} = \pi/TR$$

$$= \$70,000/\$100,000$$

$$= 70\%$$

P2.22 *Not-for-Profit Analysis.* The Indigent Care Center, Inc. is a private, not-for-profit, medical treatment center located in Denver, Colorado. An important issue facing Jessica Nicholson, ICC's administrative director, is the determination of an appropriate patient load (level of output). To efficiently employ scarce ICC resources, the board of directors has instructed Nicholson to maximize ICC operating surplus, defined as revenues minus operating costs. They have also asked Nicholson to determine the effects of two proposals for meeting new state health care regulations. Plan A involves

Economic Optimization

an increase in costs of $100 per patient, whereas Plan B involves a $20,000 increase in fixed expenses. In her calculations, Nicholson has been asked to assume that a $3,000 fee will be received from the state for each patient treated, irrespective of whether Plan A or Plan B is adopted.

In the calculations for determining an optimal patient level, Nicholson regards price as fixed; therefore, P = MR = $3,000. Prior to considering the effects of the new regulations, Nicholson projects total and marginal cost relations of:

$$TC = \$75,000 + \$2,000Q + \$2.5Q^2$$

$$MC = \$2,000 + \$5Q$$

where Q is the number of ICC patients.

A. Before considering the effects of the proposed regulations, calculate ICC's optimal patient and operating surplus levels.

B. Calculate these levels under Plan A.

C. Calculate these levels under Plan B.

P2.22 SOLUTION

A. Set MR = MC, and solve for Q to find the operating surplus (profit) maximizing activity level:

$$MR = MC$$

$$\$3,000 = \$2,000 + \$5Q$$

$$5Q = 1,000$$

$$Q = 200$$

$$\begin{aligned}
\text{Surplus} &= PQ - TC \\
&= \$3,000(200) - \$75,000 - \$2,000(200) - \$2.5(200^2) \\
&= \$25,000
\end{aligned}$$

B. When operating costs increase by $100 per patient, the marginal cost function and optimal activity level are both affected. Under Plan A we set MR = MC + $100, and solve for Q to find the new operating surplus (profit) maximizing activity level.

$$MR = MC + \$100$$

$$\$3,000 = \$2,000 + \$5Q + \$100$$

$$5Q = 900$$

$$Q = 180$$

$$\text{Surplus} = PQ - TC - \text{Plan A cost}$$

$$= \$3,000(180) - \$75,000 - \$2,000(180) - \$2.5(180^2)$$

$$- \$100(180)$$

$$= \$6,000$$

C. When operating costs increase by a flat $20,000, the marginal cost function and operating surplus (profit) maximizing activity level are unaffected. As in Part A, Q = 200.

The new operating surplus (profit) level is:

$$\text{Operating Surplus} = PQ - TC - \text{Plan B cost}$$

$$= \$25,000 - \$20,000$$

$$= \$5,000$$

Here, the ICC would be slightly better off under Plan A. In general, a fixed-sum increase in costs will decrease the operating surplus (profit) by a like amount, but have no influence on price nor activity levels in the short-run. In the long-run, however, both price and activity levels will be affected if cost increases depress the operating surplus (profit) below a normal (or required) rate of return.

P2.23 *Average Cost Minimization.* Commercial Recording, Inc. is a manufacturer and distributor of reel-to-reel recording decks for commercial recording studios. Revenue and cost relations are:

Economic Optimization

$$TR = \$3,000Q - \$0.5Q^2$$

$$MR = \$3,000 - \$1Q$$

$$TC = \$100,000 + \$1,500Q + \$0.1Q^2$$

$$MC = \$1,500 + \$0.2Q.$$

A. Calculate output, marginal cost, average cost, price, and profit at the average cost-minimizing activity level.

B. Calculate these values at the profit-maximizing activity level.

C. Compare and discuss your answers to Parts A and B.

P2.23 SOLUTION

A. To find the average cost-minimizing level of output, set MC = AC and solve for Q:

$$\$1,500 + \$0.2Q = \frac{\$100,000 + \$1,500Q + \$0.1Q^2}{Q}$$

$$1,500 + 0.2Q = \frac{100,000}{Q} + 1,500 + 0.1Q$$

$$0.1Q = \frac{100,000}{Q}$$

$$Q^2 = \frac{100,000}{0.1}$$

$$Q = \sqrt{\frac{100,000}{0.1}}$$

$$Q = 1,000$$

Harcourt Brace & Company

And,

$$MC = \$1,500 + \$0.2(1,000)$$

$$= \$1,700$$

$$AC = \frac{\$100,000}{1,000} + \$1,500 + \$0.1(1,000)$$

$$= \$1,700$$

$$P = TR/Q$$

$$= (\$3,000Q - \$0.5Q^2)/Q$$

$$= \$3,000 - \$0.5Q$$

$$= \$3,000 - \$0.5(1,000)$$

$$= \$2,500$$

$$\pi = (P - AC)Q$$

$$= (\$2,500 - \$1,700)1,000$$

$$= \$800,000$$

(*Note*: Average cost is rising for $Q > 1,000$.)

B. To find the profit-maximizing level of output, set MR = MC and solve for Q:

$$MR = MC$$

$$\$3,000 - \$1Q = \$1,500 + \$0.2Q$$

$$1.2Q = 1,500$$

$$Q = 1,250$$

And

Economic Optimization

$$MC = \$1,500 + \$0.2(1,250)$$

$$= \$1,750$$

$$AC = \frac{\$100,000}{1,250} + \$1,500 + \$0.1(1,250)$$

$$= \$1,705$$

$$P = \$3,000 - \$0.5(1,250)$$

$$= \$2,375$$

$$\pi = (P - AC)Q$$

$$= (\$2,375 - \$1,705)1,250$$

$$= \$837,500$$

(*Note*: Profit is falling for Q > 1,250.)

C. Average cost is minimized when MC = AC = $1,700. Given P = $2,500, a $800 profit per unit of output is earned when Q = 1,000. Total profit π = $800,000.
  Profit is maximized when Q = 1,250 since MR = MC = $1,750 at that activity level. Since MC = $1,750 > AC = $1,705, average cost is rising. Given P = $2,375 and AC = $1,750, a $670 profit per unit of output is earned when Q = 1,250. Total profit π = $837,500.
  Total profit is higher at the Q = 1,250 activity level because the modest $5(= $1,705 - $1,700) increase in average cost is more than offset by the 250 unit expansion in sales from Q = 1,000 to Q = 1,250 and the resulting increase in total revenues.

P2.24 ***Average Cost Minimization.*** *Giant Screen TV, Inc. is a manufacturer and distributor of high-resolution 50-inch television monitors and consoles for individual and commercial customers. Revenue and cost relations are:*

$$TR = \$4,500Q - \$0.1Q^2$$

$$MR = \$4,500 - \$0.2Q$$

$$TC = \$2,000,000 + \$1,500Q + \$0.5Q^2$$

$$MC = \$1,500 + \$1Q.$$

A. Calculate output, marginal cost, average cost, price, and profit at the average cost-minimizing activity level.

B. Calculate these values at the profit-maximizing activity level.

C. Compare and discuss your answers to Parts A and B.

P2.24 SOLUTION

A. To find the average cost-minimizing level of output, set MC = AC and solve for Q:

$$MC = AC$$

$$\$1,500 + \$1Q = \frac{\$2,000,000 + \$1,500Q + \$0.5Q^2}{Q}$$

$$1,500 + Q = \frac{2,000,000}{Q} + 1,500 + 0.5Q$$

$$0.5Q = \frac{2,000,000}{Q}$$

$$Q^2 = \frac{2,000,000}{0.5}$$

$$Q = \sqrt{\frac{2,000,000}{0.5}}$$

$$= 2,000$$

And,

Economic Optimization

$$MC = \$1,500 + \$1(2,000)$$

$$= \$3,500$$

$$AC = \frac{\$2,000,000}{2,000} + \$1,500 + \$0.5(2,000)$$

$$= \$3,500$$

$$P = TR/Q$$

$$= (\$4,500Q - \$0.1Q^2)/Q$$

$$= \$4,500 - \$0.1Q$$

$$= \$4,500 - \$0.1(2,000)$$

$$= \$4,300$$

$$\pi = (P - AC)Q$$

$$= (\$4,300 - \$3,500)2,000$$

$$= \$1,600,000$$

(*Note*: Average cost is rising for Q > 2,000.)

B. To find the profit-maximizing level of output, set MR = MC and solve for Q:

$$MR = MC$$

$$\$4,500 - \$0.2Q = \$1,500 + \$1Q$$

$$1.2Q = 3,000$$

$$Q = 2,500$$

And

$$MC = \$1,500 + \$1(2,500)$$

$$= \$4,000$$

$$AC = \frac{2,000,000}{2,500} + \$1,500 + \$0.5(2,500)$$

$$= \$3,550$$

$$P = \$4,500 - \$0.1(2,500)$$

$$= \$4,250$$

$$\pi = (P - AC)Q$$

$$= (\$4,250 - \$3,550)2,500$$

$$= \$1,750,000$$

(*Note*: Profit is falling for Q > 2,500.)

C. Average cost is minimized when MC = AC = $3,500. Given P = $4,300, a $800 profit per unit of output is earned when Q = 2,000. Total profit π = $1.6 million.
Profit is maximized when Q = 2,500 since MR = MC = $4,000 at that activity level. Since MC = $4,000 > AC = $3,550, average cost is rising. Given P = $4,250 and AC = $3,550, a $700 profit per unit of output is earned when Q = 2,500. Total profit π = $1.75 million.
Total profit is higher at the Q = 2,500 activity level because the modest $50(= $3,550 - $3,500) increase in average cost is more than offset by the 500 unit expansion in sales from Q = 2,000 to Q = 2,500 and the resulting increase in total revenues.

P2.25   *Revenue Maximization.* Dyna-Rubber, Inc. manufactures a high-performance tire called Sport 70. Fixed development costs for the current year are $600,000. Marginal costs for manufacturing and distribution are $63 per tire. Based on recent sales experience, the estimated demand curve and marginal revenue relations for Sport 70 are:

$$P = \$130 - \$0.000125Q$$

Economic Optimization

$$MR = \$130 - \$0.00025Q$$

A. Calculate output, price, total revenue, and total profit at the revenue-maximizing activity level.

B. Calculate output, price, total revenue, and total profit at the profit-maximizing activity level.

C. Compare and discuss your answers to Parts A and B.

P2.25 SOLUTION

A. To find the revenue-maximizing level of output, set MR = 0 and solve for Q:

$$MR = 0$$

$$\$130 - \$0.00025Q = 0$$

$$0.00025Q = 130$$

$$Q = 520,000$$

$$P = \$130 - \$0.000125Q$$

$$= \$130 - \$0.000125(520,000)$$

$$= \$65$$

$$TR = PQ$$

$$= \$65(520,000)$$

$$= \$33,800,000$$

$$\pi = TR - TC$$

$$= \$33,800,000 - \$600,000 - \$63(520,000)$$

$$= \$440,000$$

(*Note*: Revenue is falling when Q > 520,000.)

B. To find the profit-maximizing level of output, set MR = MC and solve for Q:

$$MR = MC$$

$$\$130 - \$0.00025Q = \$63$$

$$0.00025Q = 67$$

$$Q = 268,000$$

$$P = \$130 - \$0.000125(268,000)$$

$$= \$96.50$$

$$TR = \$96.50(268,000)$$

$$= \$25,862,000$$

$$\pi = \$25,862,000 - \$600,000 - \$63(268,000)$$

$$= \$8,378,000$$

(*Note*: Profit is decreasing for Q > 268,000.)

C. Revenue maximization is achieved when MR = 0. Profit maximization requires MR = MC. These output levels will only be the same if MC = 0. This would be highly unusual. In this problem, as is typical, MC > 0 and profit maximization occurs at an activity level with lower output and revenue, but higher prices and profits, than the revenue maximizing activity level.

Chapter 3

STATISTICAL ANALYSIS OF ECONOMIC RELATIONS

MULTIPLE CHOICE QUESTIONS

Q3.1 *Descriptive measures of the overall population are called:*

> a. population parameters.
> b. sample statistics.
> c. summary measures.
> d. descriptive measures.

Q3.2 *Generally speaking, population parameters are not known and must be estimated by the sample:*

> a. mean.
> b. mode.
> c. median.
> d. statistics.

Q3.3 *A measure of inflation that washes out price extremes employs:*

> a. mean price changes.
> b. weighted average price changes.
> c. the standard deviation of price changes.
> d. median price changes.

Q3.4 *A multiple regression model involves two or more:*

> a. Y-variables.
> b. X-variables.
> c. intercept terms.
> d. data points.

Q3.5 *When no scatter about the regression line exists:*

> a. S.E.E. = 0.
> b. $R^2 = 0$.
> c. t = 0.
> d. F = 0.

Q3.6 High correlation among X-variables leads to:

> **a.** multicollinearity.
> **b.** high R^2.
> **c.** low R^2.
> **d.** high t-statistics.

Q3.7 Statistics are:

> **a.** descriptive measures for a sample.
> **b.** summary measures for the population.
> **c.** predetermined variables.
> **d.** endogenous variables.

Q3.8 The "middle" observation is the:
> **a.** median.
> **b.** average.
> **c.** mean.
> **d.** mode.

Q3.9 A normally distributed test statistic with zero mean and standard deviation of one is the:

> **a.** z-statistic.
> **b.** t-statistic.
> **c.** F-statistic.
> **d.** S.E.E.

Q3.10 A relation known with certainty is called a:

> **a.** statistical relation.
> **b.** multiple regression.
> **c.** deterministic relation.
> **d.** simple regression.

Statistical Analysis of Economic Relations 53

Q3.11 The standard deviation of the dependent Y-variable after controlling for all X-variables is the:

- a. correlation coefficient.
- b. coefficient of determination.
- c. F-statistic.
- > d. standard error of the estimate.

Q3.12 Statistical analysis of economic relations focuses on the estimation and interpretation of:

- > a. sample statistics.
- b. population parameters.
- c. summary measures.
- d. descriptive measures.

Q3.13 In a symmetrical sample, the median observation equals the:

- a. variance.
- b. standard deviation.
- > c. mean and the mode.
- d. number one.

Q3.14 If the greater bulk of sample observations are found to the left of the sample mean, then the sample is said to be:

- > a. skewed downward.
- b. skewed upward.
- c. skewed to the right.
- d. symmetrical.

Q3.15 Central tendency is measured by the:

- a. range.
- b. variance.
- c. standard deviation.
- > d. mode.

Q3.16 In a uniform distribution, the mode:

> **a.** equals the median.
> **b.** is less than the mean.
> **c.** is less than the median.
> **d.** is greater than the mean.

Q3.17 If a distribution is skewed upward, the median:

> **a.** is greater than the mean.
> **b.** is less than the mean.
> **c.** is greater than the average.
> **d.** equals the mean.

Q3.18 The most common sample observation is the sample:

> **a.** mean.
> **b.** median.
> **c.** mode.
> **d.** average.

Q3.19 Relative dispersion is measured by the population:

> **a.** range.
> **b.** standard deviation.
> **c.** variance.
> **d.** coefficient of variation.

Q3.20 Sample variance is the:

> **a.** square root of the average squared deviation from the sample mean.
> **b.** average squared deviation from the sample mean.
> **c.** average deviation from the sample mean.
> **d.** square root of the average deviation from the sample mean.

Statistical Analysis of Economic Relations

Q3.21 When the variance is greater than one, the standard deviation is always:

    a. less than the coefficient of variation.
    b. greater than the coefficient of variation.
>   c. less than the variance.
    d. greater than the range.

Q3.22 Incorrect rejection of a true hypothesis is called:

>   a. type I error.
    b. type II error.
    c. z-statistic error.
    d. t-statistic error.

Q3.23 Holding all else equal, the z-statistic falls as:

    a. the population mean decreases.
    b. the sample mean decreases.
>   c. sample size increases.
    d. the sample standard deviation decreases.

Q3.24 A relation known with certainty is a:

    a. cross-section relation.
>   b. deterministic relation.
    c. time-series relation.
    d. statistical relation.

Q3.25 A linear model implies:

    a. constant elasticity.
    b. a log-linear relation.
    c. a constant effect of Y on X.
>   d. a constant effect of X on Y.

Q3.26   A multiple regression model necessarily involves:

> **a.** more than one X variable.
> **b.** a multiplicative relation.
> **c.** more than one Y variable.
> **d.** a linear relation.

Q3.27   In a simple regression model, the correlation coefficient is:

a. greater than one.
b. less than one.
c. equal to one.
> **d.** the square root of the coefficient of determination.

Q3.28   Holding all else equal, the corrected coefficient of determination falls with:

a. an increase in the standard error of the estimate.
b. a decrease in the number of estimated coefficients.
c. an increase in sample size.
> **d.** a decrease in R^2.

Q3.29   High correlation among the independent X variables leads to:

> **a.** multicollinearity.
> **b.** serial correlation.
> **c.** a statistically significant Durbin-Watson statistic.
> **d.** heteroskedasticity.

Q3.30   A goodness of fit measure for a multiple regression model is provided by the:

> **a.** coefficient of determination.
> **b.** standard error of the estimate.
> **c.** correlation coefficient.
> **d.** F-statistic.

Statistical Analysis of Economic Relations

PROBLEMS & SOLUTIONS

P3.1 **Sample Data Description.** Express Mail Services, Inc., delivers small parcels to residential addresses in the Long Beach, California area. To learn more about the efficiency of a new employee, EMS has collected the following data on the number of deliveries per week for a recent six-week sample:

$$125 \quad 140 \quad 155 \quad 140 \quad 135 \quad 145$$

A. Calculate the mean, median and mode measures of central tendency for the number of deliveries per week. Which measure does the best job of describing central tendency for this variable?

B. Calculate the range, variance and standard deviation for this data series. Which measure does the best job of describing the dispersion in this variable?

P3.1 SOLUTION

A. The mean, or sample average, is 140 deliveries per week. By inspection of a rank-order from highest to lowest values, the "middle" or median value is 140 deliveries per week. The mode is also 140 deliveries per week, and is the most commonly observed value among these six customers. In this instance, the sample distribution is perfectly symmetric. As a result, either the mean, mode or median can be used as a useful measure of central tendency and the size of the typical observation.

B. The range for these six weeks is from 125 to 155 deliveries per week. The sample variance is 100 (deliveries squared), and the sample standard deviation is 10 deliveries. Given the symmetrical nature of the delivery distribution, perhaps the sample standard deviation offers the most useful indicator of the magnitude of sample dispersion.

P3.2 **Sample Data Description.** The law firm of Dewy, Cheetum & Howe is planning to offer its partners personal tax preparation and tax planning services as a fringe benefit. Lucy Ricardo, an independent tax accountant, has been asked to submit a bid on the projected cost of tax preparation services. For estimation purposes, Ricardo has run a test of tax preparations for five partner returns. The actual number of hours required to complete each return was:

$$6 \quad 8 \quad 7 \quad 9 \quad 10$$

58   Chapter 3

        A.   *Calculate the mean, median and mode measures of central tendency for the number of hours required to complete partner returns. Which measure does the best job of describing central tendency for this variable?*

        B.   *Calculate the sample range, variance and standard deviation for this data series. Which measure does the best job of describing the dispersion in this variable?*

P3.2   **SOLUTION**

        A.   The mean, or sample average, is 8 hours per return. By inspection of a rank-order from highest to lowest values, the "middle" or median value is also 8 hours per return. This is a uniform distribution, so there is no single mode or most commonly observed value among these five returns. As a result, and despite substantial variation, either the mean or median can be used as a useful measure of central tendency and the size of the typical observation.

        B.   The range for these five returns is from 6 to 10 hours per return. The sample variance is 2.5 (hours squared), and the sample standard deviation is 1.58 hours. Given the uniform nature of this distribution, perhaps the sample standard deviation, when used in conjunction with the range, offers the most useful indicator of the magnitude of sample dispersion.

P3.3   ***Sample Data Description.*** *United Package Service, Inc., delivers small parcels to business addresses in the Greater Detroit area. To learn more about the demand for its service, UPS has collected the following data on the number of deliveries per week for a sample of six customers:*

                              3   4   5   6   2   4

        A.   *Calculate the mean, median and mode measures of central tendency for the number of deliveries per week. Which measure does the best job of describing central tendency for this variable?*

        B.   *Calculate the range, variance and standard deviation for this data series. Which measure does the best job of describing the dispersion in this variable?*

P3.3   **SOLUTION**

        A.   The mean, or sample average, is 4 deliveries per week. By inspection of a rank-order from highest to lowest values, the "middle" or median value is 4 deliveries per week. The mode is also 4 deliveries per week, and is the most commonly

Harcourt Brace & Company

Statistical Analysis of Economic Relations   59

observed value among these six customers. In this instance, the sample distribution is perfectly symmetric. As a result, either the mean, mode or median can be used as a useful measure of central tendency and the size of the typical observation.

B. The range for these six customers is from 2 to 6 deliveries per week. The sample variance is 2 (deliveries squared), and the sample standard deviation is 1.41 deliveries. Given the symmetrical nature of the delivery distribution, perhaps the sample standard deviation offers the most useful indicator of the magnitude of sample dispersion.

P3.4 **Skewed Sample Distribution.** *Quality Products, Inc., is greatly concerned about the failure rate experienced for products produced on a new assembly line. Last week, the percent failure rate experience per day was:*

$$2 \quad 3 \quad 3 \quad 3 \quad 8$$

A. *Calculate the sample mean, median and mode measures of central tendency for the failure rate. Which measure does the best job of describing central tendency for this variable?*

B. *Calculate the sample range, variance and standard deviation for this data series. Which measure does the best job of describing the dispersion in this variable?*

P3.4 **SOLUTION**

A. The mean, or sample average, failure rate is 3.8%. By inspection of a rank-order from highest to lowest values, the "middle" or median value is a failure rate of 3%. The mode is also a 3% failure rate, and is the most commonly observed value. In this instance, the sample distribution is skewed upward by the very high 8% failure rate experienced on a one-time basis. As a result, the mode and median provide better measures of "typical" failure rates than does the sample average.

B. The range for failure rate is from 2 to 8%. The sample variance is 5.7 (failure rate percentage squared), and the sample standard deviation is 2.39%. Given the skewed nature of the failure rate distribution, both the sample standard deviation and the sample range measures provide useful insight concerning the magnitude of sample dispersion.

P3.5 **Skewed Sample Distribution.** *Keiretsu Manufacturing, Ltd., has asked you to characterize the typical productivity of five manufacturing plants located in* southeastern states. The following data sho output per worker horu for each plant during the past month:

$$6 \quad 9 \quad 9 \quad 10 \quad 9$$

A. Calculate the sample mean, median and mode measures of central tendency for output per worker hour. Which measure does the best job of describing central tendency for this variable?

B. Calculate the sample range, variance and standard deviation for this data series. Which measure does the best job of describing the dispersion in this variable?

P3.5   **SOLUTION**

A. The mean, or sample average, productivity is 8.6 units per worker hour. By inspection of a rank-order from highest to lowest values, the "middle" or median value is a productivity level of 9 units per hour. The mode is also 9 units per hour, and is the most commonly observed value. In this instance, the sample distribution is skewed downward by the very low productivity rate of 6 units per hour experienced in a single plant. As a result, the mode and median provide better measures of "typical" productivity than does the sample average.

B. The range for productivity is from 6 to 10 units per hour. The sample variance is 2.3 (units per hour squared), and the sample standard deviation is 1.52 units per hour. Given the skewed nature of the productivity rate distribution, both the sample standard deviation and the sample range measures provide useful insight concerning the magnitude of sample dispersion.

P3.6   ***Population Data Description.*** Friendly Ford & Mercury, Inc., recently sponsored a weekend promotion featuring a $500 rebate on the purchase of a new Mercury Villager minivan. In all, six new minivans were sold. The following data show the average annual household income for these customers:

$$\$55,000 \quad \$60,000 \quad \$60,000 \quad \$45,000 \quad \$75,000 \quad \$65,000$$

A. Calculate the population mean, median and mode measures of central tendency for the annual household income for these customers. Which measure does the best job of describing central tendency for this variable?

Statistical Analysis of Economic Relations 61

        B.   Calculate the population range, variance and standard deviation for this data series. Which measure does the best job of describing the dispersion in this variable?

P3.6   **SOLUTION**

        A.   The mean, or population average, is $60,000 per year in household income. By inspection of a rank-order from highest to lowest values, the "middle" or median value is $60,000 per year. The mode is also $60,000 per year, and is the most commonly observed value among these six customers. In this instance, the population distribution is perfectly symmetric. As a result, either the mean, mode or median can be used as a useful measure of central tendency and the size of the typical observation.

        B.   The range for these six customers is from $55,000 to $75,000 in household income. The population variance is $83,333,333 (dollars squared), and the population standard deviation is $9,129. Given the symmetrical nature of this household income distribution, the standard deviation offers perhaps the best indicator of the magnitude of population dispersion.

P3.7   **Population Data Description.** *The Office Supply Warehouse, Inc., recently offered a weekend promotion featuring a 50% discount off the regular purchase price of photoconductor units for the IBM 4216 Personal PagePrinter. The rate of growth in unit sales experienced at each of the company's five retail outlets was as follows:*

100% 80% 120% 110% 90%

        A.   Calculate the population mean, median and mode measures of central tendency for the rate of growth in unit sales. Which measure does the best job of describing central tendency for this variable?

        B.   Calculate the population range, variance and standard deviation for this data series. Which measure does the best job of describing the dispersion in this variable?

P3.7   **SOLUTION**

        A.   The mean, or population average, is 100% growth in unit sales. By inspection of a rank-order from highest to lowest values, the "middle" or median value is also 100%. Since each value is encountered but a single time, there is no mode or single most commonly observed value among these five outlets. In this instance, the population distribution is perfectly symmetric. Despite the fact that substantial dispersion is present in these data, the mean can be used as the best available measure of central tendency and the size of the typical observation.

    B. The range for these five outlets is from 80% to 120% growth in unit sales. The population variance is 200 (percent squared), and the population standard deviation is 14.1%. Given the symmetrical nature of unit growth at each retail outlet, the standard deviation offers perhaps the best indicator of the magnitude of population dispersion.

P3.8   **Skewed Population Description.** *Legal Video Client Services, Inc., provides audio-visual recreations of accident scenes to assist personal injury lawyers in civil damage lawsuit proceedings. Billable hours for LVCS's five client law firms during the past year are as follows:*

                  200   400   500   600   600

    A. *Calculate the population mean, median and mode measures of central tendency for the number of billable hours per client. Which measure does the best job of describing central tendency for this variable?*

    B. *Calculate the population range, variance and standard deviation for this data series. Which measure does the best job of describing the dispersion in this variable?*

P3.8   **SOLUTION**

    A. The mean, or population average, is 460 billable hours. By inspection of a rank-order from highest to lowest values, the "middle" or median value is 500 billable hours per year. The mode is 600 billable hours, and is the most commonly observed value among these five customers. In this instance, the population distribution is slightly skewed downward as a result of one client law firm having only 200 billable hours during the past year. As a result, either the mode or median can be used rather than the population mean as perhaps more useful measures of central tendency and the size of the typical observation.

    B. The range for these five client law firms is from 200 to 600 billable hours per year. The population variance is 22,400 (billable hours squared), and the sample standard deviation is 149.7 billable hours. Given the asymmetrical nature of the delivery distribution, each measure of dispersion offers useful insight concerning the degree of dispersion in client size, and should be used in conjunction with one another.

Statistical Analysis of Economic Relations 63

P3.9 **Skewed Population Description.** *The Sport Haus, Ltd., recently offered a weekend promotion featuring a 20% discount off the regular purchase price of a deluxe ski package including skies, boots, and poles. The rate of growth in unit sales experienced on each of five different ski packages was:*

30%   50%   60%   30%   60%

A. *Calculate the population mean, median and mode measures of central tendency for the rate of growth in unit sales. Which measure does the best job of describing central tendency for this variable?*

B. *Calculate the population range, variance and standard deviation for this data series. Which measure does the best job of describing the dispersion in this variable?*

P3.9 **SOLUTION**

A. The mean, or population average, is 46% growth in unit sales. By inspection of a rank-order from highest to lowest values, the "middle" or median value is 50%. Since both 30% and 60% growth in unit sales are encountered twice, this population has a bimodal distribution. In this instance, the population distribution is somewhat asymmetric in that the mean of 46% is slightly below the median value of 50%. Despite the fact that substantial dispersion is present in these data, both the mean and the median values offer useful measures of central tendency and the size of the typical observation.

B. The range for these five items is from 30% to 60% growth in unit sales. The population variance is 184 (percent squared), and the population standard deviation is 13.6%. Given the asymmetrical nature of unit growth of each item, both the range and standard deviation offer useful indicators of the magnitude of population dispersion.

P3.10 **Population Data Description.** *One-Hour Drycleaning Services, Inc., operates six franchise outlets in the city of Denver, Colorado. The number of hours per day that each outlet is open on weekdays is:*

12   11   10   10.5   11.5

A. *Calculate the mean, median and mode measures of central tendency for the number of hours these outlets are open. Which measure does the best job of describing central tendency for this variable?*

64   Chapter 3

B.   Calculate the population range, variance and standard deviation for this data series. Which measure does the best job of describing the dispersion in this variable?

P3.10   SOLUTION

A.   The mean, or population average, is 11 hours per day. By inspection of a rank-order from highest to lowest values, the "middle" or median value is also 11 hours per day. This is a uniform distribution, so there is no single mode or most commonly observed value among these five outlets. As a result, and despite substantial variation, either the mean or median can be used as a useful measure of central tendency and the size of the typical observation.

B.   The range for these five outlets is from 10 to 12 hours per day. The population variance is 0.5 (hours squared), and the population standard deviation is 0.71 hours. Given the uniform nature of this distribution, perhaps the population standard deviation, when used in conjunction with the range, offers the most useful indicator of the magnitude of population dispersion.

P3.11   ***Confidence Intervals: t-tests.*** *Digitized Documents, Inc., is a small but rapidly growing firm in the digitized document translation business. The company reads architectural and engineering drawings into a scanning device that translates graphic information into a digitalized format that can be manipulated on a personal computer or work station. During recent weeks, the company has added a total of five new clerical and secretarial personnel to help answer customer questions and process orders. Data on the number of years of work experience for these five new workers is as follows:*

$$5 \quad 4 \quad 3 \quad 4.5 \quad 3$$

A.   Calculate the mean, median and mode measures of central tendency for the number of years of work experience. Which measure does the best job of describing central tendency for this variable?

B.   Calculate the sample range, variance and standard deviation for this data series, and the 95% confidence interval within which you would expect to find the population's true mean.

P3.11   SOLUTION

A.   The mean, or sample average, is 3.9 years of work experience. By inspection of a rank-order from highest to lowest values, the "middle" or median value is 4 years

Statistical Analysis of Economic Relations 65

work experience. The mode is 3 years experience, enjoyed by two workers. Despite the fact that these sample data are somewhat skewed downward, each measure of central tendency offers a highly similar view of the typical observation.

B. The range for these 5 workers is from 3 to 5 years experience. The sample variance is 0.8 (years squared) with a standard deviation of 0.894 years. Given the very small sample size involved, the t-test with df = n - 1 = 5 - 1 = 4 is used to determine the 95% confidence interval within which you would expect to find the true population mean. This confidence interval is from 2.79 years to 5.01 years, and calculated as follows:

$$\bar{X} - t(s/\sqrt{n}) = 3.9 - 2.776\,(0.894/\sqrt{5}) = 2.79 \text{ years (lower bound)}$$

$$\bar{X} + t(s/\sqrt{n}) = 3.9 + 2.776\,(0.894/\sqrt{5}) = 5.01 \text{ years (upper bound)}$$

P3.12 ***Confidence Intervals: t-tests.*** *21st Century Mutual Funds, Inc., is a rapidly growing firm offering money market, bond and equity mutual funds to investors. During the past week, the company has added five new phone answering personnel to help answer investor inquiries, process orders, and so on. Data on the number of years of work experience for these five new workers is as follows:*

1   1.5   2   2.5   3

A. *Calculate the mean, median and mode measures of central tendency for the number of years of work experience. Which measure does the best job of describing central tendency for this variable?*

B. *Calculate the sample range, variance and standard deviation for this data series, and the 95% confidence interval within which you would expect to find the population's true mean.*

P3.12 **SOLUTION**

A. The mean, or sample average, work experience is 2 years. By inspection of a rank-order from highest to lowest values, the "middle" or median value is also 2 years work experience. This is a uniform distribution, so there is no mode or most common measure. As a result, and despite substantial variation, either the mean or median can be used as a useful measure of central tendency and the size of the typical observation.

B. The range for these 5 workers is from 1 to 3 years experience. The sample variance is 0.625 (years squared) with a standard deviation of 0.791 years. Given the uniform nature of this distribution, perhaps the sample standard deviation, when used in conjunction with the range, offers the most useful indicator of the magnitude of sample dispersion. In light of the very small sample size involved, the t-test with df = n - 1 = 5 - 1 = 4 is used to determine the 95% confidence interval within which you would expect to find the true population mean. This confidence interval is from 1.02 years to 2.98 years, and calculated as follows:

$$\bar{X} - t(s/\sqrt{n}) = 2 - 2.776 (0.791/\sqrt{5}) = 1.02 \text{ years (lower bound)}$$

$$\bar{X} + t(s/\sqrt{n}) = 2 + 2.776 (0.791/\sqrt{5}) = 2.98 \text{ years (upper bound)}$$

P3.13 **Confidence Intervals: t-tests.** *Recycletek, Inc., is a small firm offering precious metal recycling services to industrial firms in the Buffalo, New York area. The company takes in waste metal and chemical byproducts from industrial manufactures, removes any silver, and then disposes of remaining waste matter. To determine how much it should offer a new customer for their waste materials, Recycletek must accurately project the amount of silver to be obtained, on average, based on its study of the percentage of silver contained in a random sample of five batches of waste chemicals. The percentage of silver content obtained from each batch is:*

2%   2.25%   2%   2.5%   2.25%

A. *Calculate the mean, median and mode measures of central tendency for the percentage of silver content. Which measure does the best job of describing central tendency for this variable?*

B. *Calculate the sample range, variance and standard deviation for this data series, and the 99% confidence interval within which you would expect to find the population's true mean.*

P3.13 **SOLUTION**

A. The mean, or sample average, percent silver content is 2.2%. By inspection of a rank-order from highest to lowest values, the "middle" or median value is 2.25% silver content. This is a bimodal distribution, with modes of 2% and 2.25%. Despite some variation, either the mean or median can be used as a useful measure of central tendency and the size of the typical observation.

Statistical Analysis of Economic Relations 67

B. The range for these 5 samples is from 2% to 2.5% silver content. The sample variance is 0.044 (percent squared) with a standard deviation of 0.209%. Given the bimodal nature of this distribution, perhaps the population standard deviation, when used in conjunction with the range, offers the most useful indicator of the magnitude of population dispersion. In light of the very small sample size involved, the t-test with df = n - 1 = 5 - 1 = 4 is used to determine the 99% confidence interval within which you would expect to find the true population mean. This confidence interval is from 1.77% to 2.63%, and calculated as follows:

$$\bar{X} - t(s/\sqrt{n}) = 2.2 - 4.604\,(0.209/\sqrt{5}) = 1.77\% \text{ (lower bound)}$$

$$\bar{X} + t(s/\sqrt{n}) = 2.2 + 4.604\,(0.209/\sqrt{5}) = 2.63\% \text{ (upper bound)}$$

P3.14 *Confidence Intervals: t-tests.* Materials Management Services, Ltd., is a small firm offering precious metal recycling services to industrial firms in the Sacramento, California area. The company takes in waste metal and chemical byproducts from industrial manufactures, removes any gold, and then disposes of remaining waste matter. To determine how much it should offer a new customer for their waste materials, Materials Management must accurately project the amount of gold to be obtained, on average, based on its study of the percentage of gold contained in a random sample of five batches of waste chemicals. The percentage of gold content obtained from each batch is:

1%   1.1%   1.05%   1%   1.1%

A. Calculate the mean, median and mode measures of central tendency for the percentage of gold content. Which measure does the best job of describing central tendency for this variable?

B. Calculate the sample range, variance and standard deviation for this data series, and the 99% confidence interval within which you would expect to find the population's true mean.

P3.14 SOLUTION

A. The mean, or sample average, percent gold content is 1.05%. By inspection of a rank-order from highest to lowest values, the "middle" or median value is also 1.05% gold content. This is a bimodal distribution, with modes of 1% and 1.1%. Despite some variation, either the mean or median can be used as a useful measure of central tendency and the size of the typical observation.

B. The range for these 5 samples is from 1% to 1.1% gold content. The sample variance is 0.0025 (percent squared) with a standard deviation of 0.05%. Given the bimodal nature of this distribution, perhaps the population standard deviation, when used in conjunction with the range, offers the most useful indicator of the magnitude of population dispersion. In light of the very small sample size involved, the t-test with df = n - 1 = 5 - 1 = 4 is used to determine the 99% confidence interval within which you would expect to find the true population mean. This confidence interval is from 0.95% to 1.15%, calculated as follows:

$$\bar{X} - t(s/\sqrt{n}) = 1.05 - 4.604\,(0.05/\sqrt{5}) = 0.95\% \text{ (lower bound)}$$

$$\bar{X} + t(s/\sqrt{n}) = 1.05 + 4.604\,(0.05/\sqrt{5}) = 1.15\% \text{ (upper bound)}$$

P3.15 **Hypothesis Testing: t-tests.** *The Environmental Protection Agency routinely gathers samples of wastewater produced by industrial manufacturers to judge their compliance with guidelines concerning the permissible amount of lead discharges. Regulations require that wastewater contain no more than 4 lead parts per million (ppm). A series of five recent wastewater samples taken from Noxious Chemicals, Inc., displays the following lead content, measured in terms of lead ppm gallons of discharge:*

3.1   3.2   3.3   3.4   3.3

A. *Calculate the mean, median and mode measures of central tendency for lead content. Which measure does the best job of describing central tendency for this variable?*

B. *Calculate the sample range, variance and standard deviation for this data series, and the 99% confidence interval within which you would expect to find the population's true mean.*

C. *Is it likely that Noxious Chemicals is in compliance with regulatory guidelines with respect to lead discharges?*

P3.15 **SOLUTION**

A. The mean, or sample average, lead content is 3.26 ppm. By inspection of a rank-order from highest to lowest values, the "middle" or median value is 3.3 ppm lead content; this value also represents the sample modal observation. Based upon these data, the mode and median value of 3.3 ppm provides a good representation of the typical observation within this sample.

Statistical Analysis of Economic Relations

B. The range for these 5 samples is from 3.1 to 3.4 lead ppm. The sample variance is 0.013 (ppm squared) with a standard deviation of 0.114 ppm. Given the nature of this distribution, perhaps the population standard deviation, when used in conjunction with the range, offers the most useful indicator of the magnitude of population dispersion. In light of the very small sample size involved, the t-test with df = n - 1 = 5 - 1 = 4 is used to determine the 99% confidence interval within which you would expect to find the true population mean. This confidence interval is from 3.03 to 3.50 ppm, calculated as follows:

$$\bar{X} - t(s/\sqrt{n}) = 3.26 - 4.604\,(0.114/\sqrt{5}) = 3.03 \text{ (lower bound)}$$

$$\bar{X} + t(s/\sqrt{n}) = 3.26 + 4.604\,(0.114/\sqrt{5}) = 3.49 \text{ (upper bound)}$$

C. Based upon the 99% confidence interval estimated in Part B, there is a less than 1% chance that the true mean for lead falls outside the range from 3.03 to 3.49 ppm. From this sample information, the probability that Noxious Chemicals, Inc., has a true population average of 4 ppm is less than 1%. Therefore, one can be 99% confident that the company is in compliance with regulatory guidelines.

P3.16 *Hypothesis Testing: t-tests. The California Environmental Protection Agency (CEPA) routinely gathers samples of wastewater produced by paper companies to judge their compliance with guidelines concerning the permissible amount of mercury discharges. Regulations require that wastewater contain no more than 3 mercury parts per million (ppm). A series of five recent wastewater samples taken from the Sweetwater Paper Company displays the following mercury content, measured in terms of mercury ppm gallons of discharge:*

4.1   4.2   4.3   4.4   4.2

A. *Calculate the mean, median and mode measures of central tendency for mercury content. Which measure does the best job of describing central tendency for this variable?*

B. *Calculate the sample range, variance and standard deviation for this data series, and the 99% confidence interval within which you would expect to find the population's true mean.*

C. *Is it likely that Sweetwater Paper is in compliance with regulatory guidelines with respect to mercury discharges?*

P3.16 **SOLUTION**

A. The mean, or sample average, mercury content is 4.24 ppm. By inspection of a rank-order from highest to lowest values, the "middle" or median value is 4.2 ppm mercury content; this value also represents the sample modal observation. Based upon these data, the mode and median value of 4.2 provides a good representation of the typical observation within this sample.

B. The range for these 5 samples is from 4.1 to 4.4 mercury ppm. The sample variance is 0.013 (ppm squared) with a standard deviation of 0.114 ppm. Given the nature of this distribution, perhaps the population standard deviation, when used in conjunction with the range, offers the most useful indicator of the magnitude of population dispersion. In light of the very small sample size involved, the t-test with df = n - 1 = 5 - 1 = 4 is used to determine the 99% confidence interval within which you would expect to find the true population mean. This confidence interval is from 4.01 to 4.47 ppm, calculated as follows:

$$\bar{X} - t(s/\sqrt{n}) = 4.24 - 4.604\,(0.114/\sqrt{5}) = 4.01 \text{ (lower bound)}$$

$$\bar{X} + t(s/\sqrt{n}) = 4.24 + 4.604\,(0.114/\sqrt{5}) = 4.47 \text{ (upper bound)}$$

C. Based upon the 99% confidence interval estimated in Part B, there is a less than 1% chance that the true mean for mercury ppm falls outside the range from 4.01 to 4.47 ppm. Based upon this sample information, the probability that Sweetwater Paper has a true population average of 3 ppm is less than 1%. Therefore, one can be 99% confident that the company is *not* in compliance with regulatory guidelines.

P3.17 **Hypothesis Testing: t-tests.** *Magazine Subscription Services, Inc., offers discount rates on popular magazines using a telephone solicitation channel of distribution. Last week, the number of magazine subscriptions sold per hour by a new sales trainee were as follows:*

2   3.5   3   2.5   4

A. *Calculate the mean, median and mode measures of central tendency for the number of magazines subscriptions sold per hour. Which measure does the best job of describing central tendency for this variable?*

B. *Calculate the sample range, variance and standard deviation for this data series, and the 95% confidence interval within which you would expect to find the population's true mean.*

Statistical Analysis of Economic Relations

C. Is it likely that sales by this trainee are typical of MSS employees who enjoy an average sales rate of 4.5 subscriptions per hour?

P3.17 SOLUTION

A. The mean, or sample average, is 3 magazine subscription sales per hour. By inspection of a rank-order from highest to lowest values, the "middle" or median value is also 3 magazine subscription sales per hour. This is a uniform distribution, so there is no mode or most common measure. As a result, and despite substantial variation, either the mean or median can be used as a useful measure of central tendency and the size of the typical observation.

B. The range for these 5 observations is from 2 to 4 magazine subscription sales per hour. The sample variance is 0.625 (magazine subscription sales per hour squared) with a standard deviation of 0.791 magazine subscription sales per hour. Given the uniform nature of this distribution, perhaps the sample standard deviation, when used in conjunction with the range, offers the most useful indicator of the magnitude of sample dispersion. In light of the very small sample size involved, the t-test with df = n - 1 = 5 - 1 = 4 is used to determine the 95% confidence interval within which you would expect to find the true population mean. This confidence interval is from 2.02 to 3.98 magazine subscription sales per hour, and calculated as follows:

$$\bar{X} - t(s/\sqrt{n}) = 3 - 2.776 \, (0.791 / \sqrt{5}) = 2.02 \text{ units (lower bound)}$$

$$\bar{X} + t(s/\sqrt{n}) = 3 + 2.776 \, (0.791 / \sqrt{5}) = 3.98 \text{ units (upper bound)}$$

C. Based upon the 95% confidence interval estimated in Part B, there is a less than 5% chance that the true mean for magazine subscription sales per hour for this employee falls outside the range from 2.02 to 3.98 units. Based upon this sample information, the probability that this trainee has a true population average productivity of 4.5 units per hour is less than 5%. Therefore, one can be 95% confident that this trainee is *not* typical of MSS's employees.

P3.18 *Hypothesis Testing: t-tests.* Durable Products, Inc., has received a bid from a foreign supplier to fill the company's needs for additional mineral solution. Durable's current supplier provides material that is, on average, 99% pure. Sixteen samples provided by the foreign supplier have an average purity of 98%, with a standard deviation of 1%.

A. Calculate the 95% confidence interval within which you would expect to find the true mean purity level for solution provided by the foreign supplier.

B. Is it likely that solution provided by the foreign supplier is typical of the purity level provided by Durable's current supplier?

P3.18 SOLUTION

A. In light of the very small sample size involved, the t-test with df = n - 1 = 16 - 1 = 15 is used to determine the 95% confidence interval within which you would expect to find the true population mean. This confidence interval is from 97.47% to 98.53% purity, and calculated as follows:

$$\bar{X} - t(s/\sqrt{n}) = 98 - 2.131(1/\sqrt{16}) = 97.47\% \text{ (lower bound)}$$

$$\bar{X} + t(s/\sqrt{n}) = 98 + 2.131(1/\sqrt{16}) = 98.53\% \text{ units (upper bound)}$$

B. Based upon the 95% confidence interval estimated in Part A, there is a less than 5% chance that the true mean for product purity from the foreign supplier meets the 99% purity (quality) level obtained from the domestic supplier.

P3.19 *Confidence Intervals: z-tests.* Bright Lights! light bulbs have an advertised life of 1,500 hours. A test of products shipped from the manufacturer found a sample average life of 1,525 hours with a sample standard deviation of 10 hours when a sample of n = 81 observations was studied.

A. Calculate the range within which the population average life can be found with 95% confidence.

B. Assuming that s = 10 hours cannot be reduced, and a sample size of n = 81, what is the minimum range within which the sample average life must be found to justify with 95% confidence the advertised life of 1,500 hours?

P3.19 SOLUTION

A. Given the very large sample size, the relevant test statistic is the z-statistic, where the known sample standard deviation s = 10 is substituted for the unknown population standard deviation. For this sample, the 95% confidence interval for the population mean is from 1,523 hrs to 1,527 hours, found as follows:

$$\bar{X} - z(s/\sqrt{n}) = 1,525 - 1.96(10/\sqrt{81}) = 1,523 \text{ hrs (lower bound)}$$

$$\bar{X} + z(s/\sqrt{n}) = 1,525 + 1.96(10/\sqrt{81}) = 1,527 \text{ hrs (upper bound)}$$

B.
Given the very large sample size, the relevant test statistic is again the z-statistic, where the known sample standard deviation s = 10 is substituted for the unknown population standard deviation. To justify an advertised life of 1,500 hours, the sample mean must fall no lower than within the minimum range of 1,498 hrs to 1,502 hrs, found as follows:

$$\bar{X} - z(s/\sqrt{n}) = 1{,}500 - 1.96(10/\sqrt{81}) = 1{,}498 \text{ hrs (lower bound)}$$

$$\bar{X} + z(s/\sqrt{n}) = 1{,}500 + 1.96(10/\sqrt{81}) = 1{,}502 \text{ hrs (upper bound)}$$

P3.20 **Confidence Intervals: z-tests.** *Digital Switches, Inc., produces a product called the C3PO with an advertised 0.5% failure rate. A test of products shipped from the factory to the company's testing lab found a sample average failure rate of 0.45% with a sample standard deviation of 0.15% when a sample of n = 64 observations was studied.*

A. *Calculate the range within which the population average failure rate can be found with 95% confidence.*

B. *Assuming that s = 0.15% cannot be reduced, and a sample size of n = 64, what is the minimum range within which the sample average failure rate must be found to justify with 95% confidence the advertised failure rate of 0.5%?*

P3.20 SOLUTION

A. Given the very large sample size, the relevant test statistic is the z-statistic, where the known sample standard deviation s = 0.15% is substituted for the unknown population standard deviation. For this sample, the 95% confidence interval for the population mean is from 0.41% to 0.49% found as follows:

$$\bar{X} - z(s/\sqrt{n}) = 0.45 - 1.96(0.15/\sqrt{64}) = 0.41\% \text{ (lower bound)}$$

$$\bar{X} + z(s/\sqrt{n}) = 0.45 + 1.96(0.15/\sqrt{64}) = 0.49\% \text{ (upper bound)}$$

(*Note*: A less-than-advertised failure rate means that this product has better-than-advertised quality.)

B. Given the very large sample size, the relevant test statistic is again the z-statistic, where the known sample standard deviation s = 10 is substituted for the unknown population standard deviation. To justify an advertised life of 1,500 hours, the sample mean must fall no lower than within the minimum range of 0.46% to 0.54% found as follows:

$$\bar{X} - z(s/\sqrt{n}) = 0.5 - 1.96(0.15/\sqrt{64}) = 0.46\% \text{ (lower bound)}$$

$$\bar{X} + z(s/\sqrt{n}) = 0.5 + 1.96(0.15/\sqrt{64}) = 0.54\% \text{ (upper bound)}$$

P3.21 **Hypothesis Testing: z-tests.** *SoftSkin is a skin moisturizing product designed to treat overly dry or neglected skin. A test of products shipped from the manufacturer found a sample average product volume of 8.1 ounces per unit with a sample standard deviation of 0.16 ounces, when a sample of n = 256 observations was studied.*

    A. Calculate the range within which the population average volume can be found with 99% confidence.

    B. Assuming that s = 0.16 cannot be reduced, and a sample size of n = 256, what is the range within which the sample average volume must be found to justify with 99% confidence the advertised volume of 8 oz.?

    C. Is the company justified in claiming an advertised volume of 8 oz.?

P3.21 **SOLUTION**

    A. Given the very large sample size, the relevant test statistic is the z-statistic, where the known sample standard deviation s = 0.16 is substituted for the unknown population standard deviation. For this sample, the 99% confidence interval for the population mean is from 8.07 to 8.13 ounces, found as follows:

$$\bar{X} - z(s/\sqrt{n}) = 8.1 - 2.576(0.16/\sqrt{256}) = 8.07 \text{ oz (lower bound)}$$

$$\bar{X} + z(s/\sqrt{n}) = 8.1 + 2.576(0.16/\sqrt{256}) = 8.13 \text{ oz (upper bound)}$$

    B. Given the very large sample size, the relevant test statistic is again the z-statistic, where the known sample standard deviation s = 0.16 is substituted for the unknown population standard deviation. To justify an advertised volume of 8 ounces, the sample mean must fall no lower than within the minimum range of 7.97 to 8.03 ounces, found as follows:

$$\bar{X} - z(s/\sqrt{n}) = 8 - 2.576(0.16/\sqrt{256}) = 7.97 \text{ oz (lower bound)}$$

Statistical Analysis of Economic Relations 75

$$\bar{X} + z(s/\sqrt{n}) = 8 + 2.576\,(0.16/\sqrt{256}) = 8.03 \text{ oz (upper bound)}$$

C. Yes, based upon the 99% confidence interval estimated in Part A, there is a less than 1% chance that the true mean for product volume falls outside the range from 8.07 to 8.13 oz. In light of this sample information, the probability that this product has a true weight of less than 8 oz. is less than 1%. Therefore, one can be 99% confident in the company's advertised claim of *at least* an 8 oz. product size.

P3.22 **Hypothesis Testing: z-tests.** *Sweeties!* breakfast cereal is sold on the basis of weight, not volume. A test of products shipped from the manufacturer found a sample average product weight of 15.9 ounces per box with a sample standard deviation of 0.1 ounces, when a sample of n = 100 observations was studied.

A. Calculate the range within which the population average volume can be found with 99% confidence.

B. Assuming that s = 0.1 ounces cannot be reduced, and a sample size of n = 100, what is the minimum range within which the sample average weight must be found to justify with 99% confidence the advertised weight of 16 oz.?

C. Is the company justified in claiming an advertised product weight of 16 oz.?

P3.22 **SOLUTION**

A. Given the very large sample size, the relevant test statistic is the z-statistic, where the known sample standard deviation s = 0.1 is substituted for the unknown population standard deviation. For this sample, the 99% confidence interval for the population mean is from 15.87 ounces to 15.93 ounces, found as follows:

$$\bar{X} - z(s/\sqrt{n}) = 15.9 - 2.576\,(0.1/\sqrt{100}) = 15.87 \text{ oz (lower bound)}$$

$$\bar{X} + z(s/\sqrt{n}) = 15.9 + 2.576\,(0.1/\sqrt{100}) = 15.93 \text{ oz (upper bound)}$$

B. Given the very large sample size, the relevant test statistic is again the z-statistic, where the known sample standard deviation s = 0.1 is substituted for the unknown population standard deviation. To justify an advertised weight of 16 ounces, the sample mean must fall no lower than within the minimum range of 15.97 ounces to 16.03 ounces, found as follows:

$$\bar{X} - z(s/\sqrt{n}) = 16 - 2.576\,(0.1/\sqrt{100}) = 15.97 \text{ oz (lower bound)}$$

$$\bar{X} + z(s/\sqrt{n}) = 16 + 2.576 (0.1/\sqrt{100}) = 16.03 \text{ oz (upper bound)}$$

  C. No, based upon the 99% confidence interval estimated in Part A, there is a less than 1% chance that the true mean for product weight falls outside the range from 15.87 to 15.93 oz. In light of this sample information, the probability that this product has a true weight of as much as 16 oz. is less than 1%. Therefore, one can be 99% confident that the company is *not* meeting its advertised claim of *at least* a 16 oz. product weight.

P3.23 **Correlation and Simple Regression.** May Brothers Department Store has conducted a survey to learn the buying intentions of a sample of 62 department store customers. The survey asked each customer their household gross income(in $ thousands), and their number of shopping trips per year.

  A. Interpret the coefficient of correlation between the TRIPS and INCOME variables of 0.8.

  B. Interpret the following results for a simple regression over this sample where TRIPS is the dependent Y-variable and INCOME is the independent X-variable:

The regression equation is:

TRIPS = 0.5 + 0.1 INCOME

Predictor	Coef	Stdev	t-ratio
Constant	0.48	0.30	1.6
INCOME	0.10	0.05	2.0

S.E.E. = 0.3 R^2 = 64% $\bar{R}^2$(adj) = 63.4% F-statistic = 106.7

P3.23 **SOLUTION**

  A. A correlation coefficient r = 0.8 means that there is a strong direct relation between the TRIPS and INCOME variables. The correlation coefficient falls in the range between 1 and -1. If r = 1, there is a perfect direct linear relation between the dependent Y-variable and the independent X-variable. If r = -1, there is a perfect inverse linear relation between Y and X. In both instances, actual values for Y all fall exactly on the regression line. The regression equation explains all of the underlying variation in the dependent Y-variable in terms of variation in the independent X-variable. If r = 0, zero correlation exists between the dependent and independent variables; they are autonomous. When r = 0, there is no relation at all between actual Y observations and fitted Ŷ values.

B. The constant in such a regression typically has no meaning. Clearly, the intercept should not be used to suggest the number of planned trips for a department customer with zero income! The INCOME coefficient is statistically significant at the $\alpha = 0.05$ level with a calculated t-statistic value of 2, meaning that it is possible to be 95% confident that income affects the number of planned department store trips. The probability is less than 5% of encountering such a large t-statistic for INCOME when in fact that variable has no influence on TRIPS. The INCOME coefficient value of 0.1 implies that a one-unit (thousand dollar) increase in INCOME results in an average increase of 0.1 units in the TRIPS variable.

The $R^2 = 64\%$ means that 64% of the variation in the number of planned trips can be explained using just the INCOME independent variable. The R^2 (adj.) = 63.4 means that 63.4% of the variation in the number of planned trips can be explained using just the INCOME independent variable, when controlling for both sample size (n = 62) and the number of estimated coefficients. The F-statistic of 106.7 means that this level of explained variation is statistically significant at more than the 99% confidence level. The probability is less than 1% of encountering such a large F-statistic when in fact no relation exists between these Y and X variables. The standard error of the estimate of 0.3 can be used to indicate the range within which the actual number of planned trips might be found for a customer with a given income level. On average, the number of TRIPS equals Ŷ ± (2 × S.E.E.) with 95% confidence, and roughly Ŷ ± (3 × S.E.E.) with 99% confidence.

P3.24 **Simple Regression.** *The European Engine Company (EEC) is a multi-national manufacturer of small gasoline and diesel motors. EEC has estimated the following cost experience for a new 3.5 hp engine over a sample of 122 observations:*

COST = $8,500 + $32 OUTPUT

Predictor	Coef	Stdev	t-ratio
Constant	8,500	5,000	1.7
OUTPUT	32	8	4.0

S.E.E. = $2,500 $R^2 = 75\%$ $\bar{R}^2$(adj) = 74.8%   F-statistic = 360

where COST is the dependent Y-variable and OUTPUT is the independent X-variable.

A. *Fully interpret these simple regression results.*

B. Describe this cost category as fixed or variable based upon the simple regression results described previously

P3.24 SOLUTION

A. The constant in such a regression typically has no meaning. Clearly, the intercept should not be used to suggest the costs for a zero output level! The OUTPUT coefficient is statistically significant at the $\alpha = 0.01$ level with a calculated t-statistic value of 4, meaning that it is possible to be more than 99% confident that OUTPUT affects COST. The probability is less than 1% of encountering such a large t-statistic for OUTPUT when in fact that variable has no influence on COST. The OUTPUT coefficient value of 32 implies that a one unit increase in OUTPUT results in an average increase of $32 in the COST variable.

The $R^2 = 75\%$ means that 75% of the variation in COST can be explained using just the OUTPUT independent variable. The R^2 (adj.) = 74.8 means that 74.8% of the variation in COST can be explained using just the OUTPUT independent variable when controlling for both sample size (n = 122) and the number of estimated coefficients. The F-statistic of 360 means that this level of explained variation is statistically significant at more than the 99% confidence level. The probability is less than 1% of encountering such a large F-statistic when in fact no relation exists between these Y and X variables. The standard error of the estimate of $2,500 can be used to indicate the range within which the actual number of planned trips might be found for a customer with a given income level. On average, COST equals $\hat{Y} \pm (2 \times \text{S.E.E.})$ with 95% confidence, and roughly $\hat{Y} \pm (3 \times \text{S.E.E.})$ with 99% confidence.

B. There seems to be a very clear linear relation between this cost category and OUTPUT. This cost category can be described as variable in nature.

P3.25 *Multiple Regression.* Hawkeye Pierce, CFO at B.J. Hunnicut, Inc., finds in a simple regression analysis of product demand that demand increases with an increase in advertising, and falls as advertising expenditures are reduced. Similarly, a simple regression analysis of product demand and price reveals that demand increases with a decrease in average price, and falls as prices are raised. Coefficient estimates for each independent variable are statistically significant, as is the level of overall explanation achieved, as revealed by the coefficient of determination (R^2). However, when both advertising and price are included as independent variables in a multiple regression model, neither variable has a statistically significant coefficient estimate.

A. Explain the difference between coefficient estimates obtained using a simple regression model versus a multiple regression model.

Statistical Analysis of Economic Relations

      B.   *What is the source of the difficulty encountered here in measuring the marginal influences of advertising and price on demand? Any suggestions?*

P3.25   **SOLUTION**

      A.   Simple regression model coefficient estimates illustrate the marginal effect of a single independent X-variable on the dependent Y-variable. In the multiple regression approach, each coefficient estimate illustrates the marginal influence of each respective independent variable, *after* controlling for the influence of all other independent variables.

      B.   The difficulty encountered in measuring the marginal influences of advertising and price on demand is that advertising expenditures and product prices are themselves related. If a firm aggressively advertises price promotions, it will then be difficult to attribute the resulting increase in demand to either the increase in advertising expenditures or to the price reduction; *both* are responsible. This is sometimes referred to as the multicollinearity problem. The multiple regression model cannot attribute the change in demand to any single origin because *multiple* independent variable influences are evident, and these influences are highly correlated with one another. To discover the independent influence of advertising and price on demand, the firm might run a detailed experiment by noting the influence on demand when one variable is increased while holding the other constant. Only after such an experiment is run under a variety of different circumstances will it be possible to determine the autonomous influences of each independent variable.

Chapter 4

DEMAND AND SUPPLY

MULTIPLE CHOICE QUESTIONS

Q4.1 Holding all else equal, an unnecessary increase in federally-mandated auto safety requirements leads to a decrease in:

- a. auto demand.
- b. the quantity of autos supplied.
- > c. auto supply.
- d. the quantity of autos demanded.

Q4.2 Holding all else equal, an increase in mandatory payments by employers for universal health care coverage for workers would lead to a decrease in the:

- a. supply of workers.
- b. the quantity supplied of workers.
- c. the quantity demanded of workers.
- > d. demand for workers.

Q4.3 The demand for inputs is derived from the:

- > a. profit motive.
- b. utility of supply.
- c. utility of consumption.
- d. market demand function.

Q4.4 The effect on sales of an increase in price is a decrease in:

- > a. the quantity demanded.
- b. demand.
- c. supply.
- d. the quantity supplied.

Q4.5 The quantity of Product X supplied can be expected to rise with a fall in:

- a. prices of competing products.
- b. price of X.
- c. energy-saving technical change.
- > d. input prices.

Harcourt Brace & Company

Demand and Supply

Q4.6 *Derived demand is directly determined by:*

>
- **a.** utility.
- **b.** the profitability of using inputs to produce output.
- **c.** the ability to satisfy consumer desires.
- **d.** personal consumption.

Q4.7 *A demand curve expresses the relation between the quantity demanded and:*

- **a.** income.
- **b.** advertising.
> **c.** price.
- **d.** all of the above.

Q4.8 *Change in the quantity demanded is:*

> **a.** a movement along a single demand curve.
- **b.** an upward shift from one demand curve to another.
- **c.** a reflection of change in one or more of the nonprice variables in the product demand function.
- **d.** a downward shift from one demand curve to another.

Q4.9 *A supply curve expresses the relation between the quantity supplied and:*

- **a.** technology.
- **b.** wage rates.
> **c.** price.
- **d.** all of the above.

Q4.10 *Change in the quantity supplied reflects a:*

> **a.** change in price.
- **b.** switch from one supply curve to another.
- **c.** change in one or more nonprice variables.
- **d.** shift in supply.

Q4.11 Utility is measured by:

    a. wealth.
    b. price.
>   **c.** value or worth.
    d. income.

Q4.12 In equilibrium, the marginal utility of a product is measured by:

    a. average cost.
    b. marginal cost.
>   **c.** price.
    d. total cost.

Q4.13 Demand is the total quantity of a good or service that customers:

    a. are willing to purchase.
    b. are able to purchase.
>   **c.** are willing and able to purchase.
    d. need.

Q4.14 Demand for consumption goods and services is:

    a. derived demand.
>   **b.** direct demand.
    c. product demand.
    d. utility.

Q4.15 Derived demand is the:

>   **a.** demand for inputs used in production.
    b. demand for products other than raw materials.
    c. first derivative of the demand function.
    d. demand for consumption products.

Demand and Supply

Q4.16 The demand function for a product states the relation between the aggregate quantity demanded and:

> **a.** all factors that influence demand.
b. the aggregate quantity supplied.
c. consumer utility.
d. the market price, holding all the other factors that influence demand constant.

Q4.17 Change in the quantity demanded is caused by a change in:

a. advertising.
b. wage rates.
c. raw material costs.
> **d.** price.

Q4.18 The demand curve for automobiles will shift to the right if:

a. interest rates increase.
> **b.** advertising expenditures increase.
c. the price of steel decreases.
d. the price of automobiles decreases.

Q4.19 Change in the quantity supplied is caused by a change in:

a. income.
b. weather.
c. energy costs.
> **d.** price.

Q4.20 The supply of a product does not depend on:

a. raw material costs.
b. wage rates.
> **c.** consumer incomes.
d. technology.

84

Q4.21 If the production of two goods is complementary a decrease in the price of one will:

    a. increase supply of the other.
    b. increase the quantity supplied of the other.
    c. decrease the price of the other.
>   **d.** decrease supply of the other.

Q4.22 Farmers in certain areas of the U.S. can grow either wheat or corn. If the price of corn increases the:

    a. supply of wheat will shift to the right.
>   **b.** supply of wheat will shift to the left.
    c. supply of both corn and wheat will shift, but in opposite directions.
    d. supply of corn will shift to the right.

Q4.23 The supply curve expresses the relation between the aggregate quantity supplied and:

>   **a.** price, holding constant the effects of all other variables.
    b. aggregate quantity demanded, holding constant the effects of all other variables.
    c. profit, holding constant the effects of all other variables.
    d. each factor that affects supply.

Q4.24 The equilibrium market price of a good is the:

    a. price that buyers are willing and able to pay.
    b. price where shortages exceed surpluses.
    c. price that maximizes profit for sellers.
>   **d.** price where the quantity demanded equals the quantity supplied.

Q4.25 If the market price is higher than the equilibrium price a:

    a. shortage exists and the equilibrium price will rise until it equals the market price and the shortage is eliminated.
>   **b.** surplus exists and the market price will fall until it equals the equilibrium price and the surplus is eliminated.
    c. surplus exists and the equilibrium price will rise until it equals the market price and the surplus is eliminated.
    d. shortage exists and the market price will fall until it equals the equilibrium price and the shortage is eliminated.

Demand and Supply

Q4.26 The equilibrium market price and quantity of beef would increase if:

    a. consumers increasingly view beef as unhealthy.
    b. the price of cattle feed decreased.
> **c.** consumer income increased.
    d. herd sizes fell following a severe drought.

Q4.27 The equilibrium market price of lead pencils would decrease and the quantity of pencils produced and sold would increase if:

> **a.** the price of graphite (pencil lead) decreased.
    b. pencil workers obtained higher wages.
    c. the price of typewriters or word processors decreased.
    d. the price of pens, a substitute for pencils, increased.

Q4.28 If demand and supply both increase:

    a. its equilibrium price will decrease while the quantity produced and sold could increase, decrease or remain constant.
> **b.** the quantity produced and sold will increase while its equilibrium price could increase, decrease, or remain constant.
    c. the quantity produced and sold will decrease while its equilibrium market price could increase, decrease, or remain constant.
    d. its equilibrium price will increase while the quantity produced and sold could increase, decrease, or remain constant.

Q4.29 If demand increases while supply decreases for a particular good:

> **a.** its equilibrium price will increase while the quantity of the good produced and sold could increase, decrease, or remain constant.
    b. the quantity of the good produced and sold will decrease while its equilibrium price could increase, decrease, or remain constant.
    c. the quantity of the good produced and sold will increase while its equilibrium price could increase, decrease or remain constant.
    d. its equilibrium price will decrease while the quantity of the good produced and sold could increase, decrease, or remain constant.

Q4.30 *Shortage is a condition of:*

    a. excess supply.
    b. a deficiency in demand.
    c. market equilibrium.
>   **d.** excess demand.

Demand and Supply

PROBLEMS & SOLUTIONS

P4.1 **Demand and Supply Curves.** *The following relations describe demand and supply conditions in the lumber/forest products industry:*

$$Q_D = 75,000 - 10,000P \quad \text{(Demand)}$$

$$Q_S = -15,000 + 50,000P \quad \text{(Supply)}$$

where Q is quantity measured in thousands of board feet (one square foot of lumber, one inch thick) and P is price in dollars.

A. Complete the following table:

Price (1)	Quantity Supplied (2)	Quantity Demanded (3)	Surplus (+) or Shortage (-) (4) = (2) - (3)
$3.00			
2.50			
2.00			
1.50			
1.00			

P4.1 **SOLUTION**

A.

Price (1)	Quantity Supplied (2)	Quantity Demanded (3)	Surplus (+) or Shortage (-) (4) = (2) - (3)
$3.00	135,000	45,000	+90,000
2.50	110,000	50,000	+60,000
2.00	85,000	55,000	+30,000
1.50	60,000	60,000	0
1.00	35,000	65,000	-30,000

P4.2 **Demand and Supply Curves.** *The following relations describe demand and supply conditions in the wheat industry:*

$$Q_D = 5{,}500 - 1{,}000P \qquad \text{(Demand)}$$

$$Q_S = -4{,}500 + 1{,}500P \qquad \text{(Supply)}$$

where Q is quantity measured in millions of bushels and P is price in dollars.

A. Complete the following table:

Price (1)	Quantity Supplied (2)	Quantity Demanded (3)	Surplus (+) or Shortage (-) (4) = (2) - (3)
$4.50			
4.25			
4.00			
3.75			
3.50			

P4.2 SOLUTION

A.

Price (1)	Quantity Supplied (2)	Quantity Demanded (3)	Surplus (+) or Shortage (-) (4) = (2) - (3)
$4.50	2,250	1,000	+1,250
4.25	1,875	1,250	+ 625
4.00	1,500	1,500	0
3.75	1,125	1,750	- 625
3.50	750	2,000	-1,250

P4.3 **Demand and Supply Curves.** The following relations describe demand and supply conditions in the milk industry:

$$Q_D = 315{,}000 - 250{,}000P \qquad \text{(Demand)}$$

$$Q_S = -165{,}000 + 550{,}000P \qquad \text{(Supply)}$$

where Q is quantity measured in millions of gallons and P is price in dollars.

Demand and Supply

A. Complete the following table:

Price (1)	Quantity Supplied (2)	Quantity Demanded (3)	Surplus (+) or Shortage (-) (4) = (2) - (3)
$0.90			
0.80			
0.70			
0.60			
0.50			

P4.3 SOLUTION

A.

Price (1)	Quantity Supplied (2)	Quantity Demanded (3)	Surplus (+) or Shortage (-) (4) = (2) - (3)
$0.90	330,000	90,000	+240,000
0.80	275,000	115,000	+160,000
0.70	220,000	140,000	+80,000
0.60	165,000	165,000	0
0.50	110,000	190,000	-80,000

P4.4 Demand and Supply Curves.

The following relations describe demand and supply conditions in the oil industry:

$Q_D = 525{,}000 - 7{,}500P$ (Demand)

$Q_S = -150{,}000 + 15{,}000P$ (Supply)

where Q is quantity measured in millions of barrels and P is price in dollars.

A. Complete the following table:

Price (1)	Quantity Supplied (2)	Quantity Demanded (3)	Surplus (+) or Shortage (-) (4) = (2) - (3)
$35			
30			
25			
20			
15			

P4.4 SOLUTION

A.

Price (1)	Quantity Supplied (2)	Quantity Demanded (3)	Surplus (+) or Shortage (-) (4) = (2) - (3)
$35	375,000	262,500	+112,500
30	300,000	300,000	0
25	225,000	337,500	-112,500
20	150,000	375,000	-225,000
15	75,000	412,500	-337,500

P4.5 **Demand Analysis.** The demand for automobiles is often described as highly cyclical, and very sensitive to automobile prices and interest rates. Given these characteristics, describe the effect of each of the following in terms of whether it would increase or decrease the quantity demanded or the demand for automobiles. Moreover, when price is expressed as a function of quantity, indicate whether the effect of each of the following is an upward or downward movement along a given demand curve or instead involves an outward or inward shift in the relevant demand curve for autos. Explain your answers.

A. A decrease in auto prices

B. A fall in interest rates

C. A rise in interest rates

D. A severe economic recession

Demand and Supply

        E.   A robust economic expansion

P4.5   **SOLUTION**

        A.   A decrease in auto prices will increase the quantity demanded and involve a downward movement along the auto demand curve.

        B.   A fall in interest rates will increase the demand for autos and cause an outward shift of the auto demand curve.

        C.   A rise in interest rates will decrease the demand for autos and cause an inward shift of the auto demand curve.

        D.   A severe economic recession (fall in income) will decrease the demand for autos and result in an inward shift of the auto demand curve.

        E.   A robust economic expansion (rise in income) will increase the demand for autos and result in an outward shift of the auto demand curve.

P4.6   *Demand Analysis.* *The demand for refrigerators is often described as cyclical, and very sensitive to refrigerator prices and interest rates. Given these characteristics, describe the effect of each of the following in terms of whether it would increase or decrease the quantity demanded or the demand for refrigerators. Moreover, when price is expressed as a function of quantity, indicate whether the effect of each of the following is an upward or downward movement along a given demand curve or instead involves an outward or inward shift in the relevant demand curve for refrigerators. Explain your answers.*

        A.   An increase in refrigerator prices

        B.   A fall in interest rates

        C.   A rise in interest rates

        D.   A severe economic recession

        E.   A robust economic expansion

P4.6   SOLUTION

    A. An increase in refrigerator prices will decrease the quantity demanded and involve an upward movement along the refrigerator demand curve.

    B. A fall in interest rates will increase the demand for refrigerators and cause an outward shift of the demand curve.

    C. A rise in interest rates will decrease the demand for refrigerators and cause an inward shift of the demand curve.

    D. A severe economic recession (fall in income) will decrease the demand for refrigerators and result in an inward shift of the demand curve.

    E. A robust economic expansion (rise in income) will increase the demand for refrigerators and result in an outward shift of the demand curve.

P4.7   Demand Analysis. *The demand for big screen color TVs (BSTV) is often described as highly cyclical, and very sensitive to BSTV prices and interest rates. Given these characteristics, describe the effect of each of the following in terms of whether it would increase or decrease the quantity demanded or the demand of BSTVs. Moreover, when price is expressed as a function of quantity, indicate whether the effect of each of the following is an upward or downward movement along a given demand curve or instead involves an outward or inward shift in the relevant demand curve for BSTVs. Explain your answers.*

    A. A decrease in BSTV prices

    B. A fall in interest rates

    C. A rise in interest rates

    D. A severe economic recession

    E. A robust economic expansion

P4.7   SOLUTION

    A. A decrease in BSTV prices will increase the quantity demanded and involve a downward movement along the BSTV demand curve.

Demand and Supply 93

      B.   A fall in interest rates will increase the demand for BSTVs and cause an outward shift of the demand curve.

      C.   A rise in interest rates will decrease the demand for BSTVs and cause an inward shift of the demand curve.

      D.   A severe economic recession (fall in income) will decrease the demand for BSTVs and result in an inward shift of the demand curve.

      E.   A robust economic expansion (rise in income) will increase the demand for BSTVs and result in an outward shift of the demand curve.

P4.8   ***Comparative Statics.*** *Demand and supply conditions in the market for unskilled labor are important concerns to business and government decision makers. Consider the case of a federally mandated minimum wage set above the equilibrium or market clearing wage level. Some of the following factors have the potential to influence the demand or quantity demanded of unskilled labor. Influences on the supply or quantity supplied may also result. Holding all else equal, describe these influences as increasing or decreasing, and indicate the direction of the resulting movement along or shift in the relevant curve(s).*

      A.   *An increase in the popularity of self-service gas stations, car washes, and so on.*

      B.   *A fall in welfare benefits*

      C.   *An increase in the minimum wage*

      D.   *A rise in interest rates*

      E.   *A decrease in the quality of secondary education*

P4.8   **SOLUTION**

      A.   "Self-service" gas stations, car washes, and so on, involve a substitution of the consumer's own labor for hired unskilled labor. As self-service increases in popularity, a decrease or leftward shift in the demand for unskilled labor occurs.

      B.   A fall in welfare benefits makes working more attractive, and will cause an increase or rightward shift in the supply of unskilled labor.

C. An increase in the minimum wage will have the effect of decreasing the quantity demanded of unskilled labor, while at the same time increasing the quantity supplied. The first involves an upward movement along the demand curve, while the second involves an upward movement along the supply curve.

D. Holding all else equal, a rise in interest rates will decrease the attractiveness of capital relative to labor. Employers can be expected to substitute labor for the now relatively more expensive capital. An increase or rightward shift in the demand for unskilled labor will result. Of course, this influence can be mitigated to the extent that higher interest rates retard capital investment and thus decrease employment opportunities.

E. A decrease in the quality of secondary education has the effect of decreasing worker productivity and will cause a decrease or leftward shift in the demand for unskilled labor. To the extent that the benefits of quality education are recognized by students, fewer will stay in school and a secondary effect of an increase or rightward shift in the supply of unskilled labor will also be observed.

P4.9 ***Comparative Statics.*** *Demand and supply conditions in the steel market are important concerns to business and government decision makers. Some of the following factors have the potential to influence the demand or quantity demanded of raw steel. Influences on the supply or quantity supplied may also result. Holding all else equal, describe these influences as increasing or decreasing, and indicate the direction of the resulting movement along or shift in the relevant curve(s).*

A. Increases in the Department of Transportation's mileage requirements for car fleets.

B. Public outcry at the poor condition of the nation's interstate freeway system.

C. New alloys that increase steel's tensile strength are created.

D. A severe recession.

E. A new technology reduces the production cost of raw steel by one-third.

P4.9 SOLUTION

A. An increase in the DOT's minimum mileage requirement for the auto maker's fleets would incite auto manufacturers to substitute lighter materials for steel (e.g., plastics, high-temperature ceramics) in order to build the cars lighter, and hence,

Demand and Supply 95

        more fuel-efficient. The result would be a decrease in demand for steel, or a leftward shift in steel's demand curve.

B.   A grass-roots dissatisfaction with the poor condition of the interstate system would prompt legislation allocating more tax dollars for renovation of the freeways. Since steel is a primary component of these roads and construction equipment, a rightward shift in the demand curve for steel would occur, reflecting the increase in derived demand.

C.   Development of new alloys increasing steel's strength would have two effects: the first is a decrease in demand for steel (leftward shift) because less steel is now needed to achieve any preset structural strength; the second effect would be an increase in demand for steel (rightward shift) because the new, stronger steel may be used in applications that before were not possible due to steel's strength-to-weight ratio. The net effect is uncertain.

D.   A severe recession would lower new construction rates and thus decrease the demand for steel (leftward shift).

E.   Changes in production technology affect the supply curve of an industry. A favorable change in technology, such as this, will drop the cost of manufacturing and hence, shift the supply curve to the right (i.e., for any given price P, the quantity supplied at that price by steel manufacturers will increase).

P4.10   *Comparative Statics. Demand and supply conditions in the market for utility-generated electric power are important concerns to business and government decision makers. Some of the following factors have the potential to influence the demand or quantity demanded of electric power. Influences on the supply or quantity supplied may also result. Holding all else equal, describe these influences as increasing or decreasing, and indicate the direction of the resulting movement along or shift in the relevant curve(s).*

A.   *An increase in the strategic desirability for large manufacturers to co-generate (or self-generate) power.*

B.   *Congress mandates reduced emissions from coal combustion.*

C.   *Environmentalist groups spark a conservation effort nationwide.*

D.   *A health study finds a positive correlation between number of hours under a heat lamp and reduced risk of cancer.*

E. An advance in solar technology creates very efficient collection devices, allowing for cheap and efficient roof-top solar energy.

P4.10 SOLUTION

A. Co-generation of power by manufacturers will reduce demand for electric power, causing a leftward shift of the demand curve.

B. Reduced emission standards for nitrous oxides generated from the burning of coal will impose additional costs on the electric utilities, causing the supply curve to shift up and to the left (i.e., at every given price level, less power will be supplied).

C. Conservation efforts represent a change in consumer tastes and preferences. Such actions would reduce the demand for electric power and cause a leftward shift in the demand curve.

D. A study finding that the more time one spends under a heat lamp, the less the chance of developing a cancer will undoubtedly increase the demand of electric power, causing a rightward shift in the demand curve.

E. Cheap, efficient solar power available to homeowners as a roof-top adjunct to standard utility-supplied electric power will reduce the demand for utility-supplied electricity (leftward shift).

P4.11 ***Comparative Statics.*** *Coupon Promotions, Inc. is a coupon book publisher with markets in several southwestern states. CPI coupon books are either sold directly to the public, sold through religious and other charitable organizations, or given away as promotional items. Operating experience during the past year suggests the following demand function for its coupon books:*

$$Q = 10,000 - 5,000P + 0.02Pop + 0.4I + 0.6A$$

where Q is quantity, P is price ($), Pop is population, I is disposable income per household ($), and A is advertising expenditures ($).

A. *Determine the demand curve faced by CPI in a typical market where P = $5, Pop = 1,000,000 persons, I = $35,000 and A = $10,000. Show the demand curve with quantity expressed as a function of price, and price expressed as a function of quantity.*

B. *Calculate the quantity demanded at prices of $5, $2.50, and $0.*

Demand and Supply

C. Calculate the prices necessary to sell 10,000, 25,000, and 50,000 units.

P4.11 **SOLUTION**

A. The value for each respective non-price variable must be substituted into the demand function in order to derive the relevant demand curve:

$$Q = 10,000 - 5,000P + 0.02 \text{Pop} + 0.4I + 0.6A$$

$$= 10,000 - 5,000P + 0.02(1,000,000) + 0.4(35,000) + 0.6(10,000)$$

$$Q = 50,000 - 5,000P$$

Then, price as a function of quantity is:

$$Q = 50,000 - 5,000P$$

$$5,000P = 50,000 - Q$$

$$P = \$10 - \$0.0002Q$$

B. At,

$$P = \$5 \;:\; Q = 50,000 - 5,000(5) = 25,000$$

$$P = \$2.50 \;:\; Q = 50,000 - 5,000(2.5) = 37,500$$

$$P = \$0 \;:\; Q = 50,000 - 5,000(0) = 50,000$$

C. At,

$$Q = 10,000 \;:\; P = \$10 - \$0.0002(10,000) = \$8$$

$$Q = 25,000 \;:\; P = \$10 - \$0.0002(25,000) = \$5$$

$$Q = 50,000 \;:\; P = \$10 - \$0.0002(50,000) = \$0$$

P4.12 **Quantity Demanded.** Gurgling Springs, Inc. is a bottler of natural spring water distributed throughout the New England states. Five-gallon containers of GSI spring water are regionally promoted and distributed through grocery chains. Operating experience during the past year suggests the following demand function for its spring water:

$$Q = 250 - 100P + 0.0001Pop + 0.005I + 0.003A$$

where Q is quantity in thousands of five-gallon containers, P is price ($), Pop is population, I is disposable income per household ($), and A is advertising expenditures ($).

A. Determine the demand curve faced by CPI in a typical market where $P = \$4$, $Pop = 4,000,000$ persons, $I = \$30,000$ and $A = \$400,000$. Show the demand curve with quantity expressed as a function of price, and price expressed as a function of quantity.

B. Calculate the quantity demanded at prices of $5, $4, and $3.

C. Calculate the prices necessary to sell 1,250, 1,500, and 1,750 thousands of five gallon containers.

P4.12   SOLUTION

A. The value for each respective non-price variable must be substituted into the demand function in order to derive the relevant demand curve:

$$Q = 250 - 100P + 0.0001Pop + 0.005I + 0.003A$$

$$= 250 - 100P + 0.0001(4,000,000) + 0.005(30,000) + 0.003(400,000)$$

$$Q = 2,000 - 100P$$

Then, price as a function of quantity is:

$$Q = 2,000 - 100P$$

$$100P = 2,000 - Q$$

$$P = \$20 - \$0.01Q$$

B. At,

$$P = \$5: \quad Q = 2,000 - 100(5) = 1,500$$

Demand and Supply

$$P = \$4: \quad Q = 2{,}000 - 100(4) = 1{,}600$$

$$P = \$3: \quad Q = 2{,}000 - 100(3) = 1{,}700$$

C. At,

$$Q = 1{,}250: \quad P = \$20 - \$0.01(1{,}250) = \$7.50$$

$$Q = 1{,}500: \quad P = \$20 - \$0.01(1{,}500) = \$5$$

$$Q = 1{,}750: \quad P = \$20 - \$0.01(1{,}750) = \$2.50$$

P4.13 **Quantity Demanded.** *Sharp Edge, Inc. is a producer of Yingsu Knives, a set of kitchen cutlery, which it markets on a nationwide basis. SEI knife sets are either sold directly to the public through national television marketing programs, or given away as promotional items. Operating experience during the past year suggests the following demand function for its knife sets:*

$$Q = 4{,}000 - 4{,}000P + 10{,}000N + 0.5I + 0.4A$$

Where Q is quantity, P is the price ($), N is the average Nielson rating of television programs during which SEI advertises Yingsu Knives, I is average disposable income per household ($), and A is advertising expenditures ($).

A. *Determine the demand curve faced by SEI in a typical market where P = $35, N = 18.5, I = $22,000, and A = $500,000. Show the demand curve with quantity expressed as a function of price, and price expressed as a function of quantity.*

B. *Calculate the quantity demanded at prices of $40, $35, and $30.*

C. *Calculate the prices necessary to sell 264,000, 292,000, and 320,000 sets of knives.*

P4.13 **SOLUTION**

A. The value for each respective non-price variable must be substituted into the demand function in order to derive the relevant demand curve:

$$Q = 4{,}000 - 4{,}000P + 10{,}000N + 0.5I + 0.4A$$

$$= 4{,}000 - 4{,}000P + 10{,}000(18.5) + 0.5(22{,}000) + 0.4(500{,}000)$$

Harcourt Brace & Company

$$Q = 400{,}000 - 4{,}000P$$

Then, price as a function of quantity is:

$$Q = 400{,}000 - 4{,}000P$$

$$4{,}000P = 400{,}000 - Q$$

$$P = \$100 - \$0.00025Q$$

B. At,

$P = \$40$: $Q = 400{,}000 - 4{,}000(40) = 240{,}000$

$P = \$35$: $Q = 400{,}000 - 4{,}000(35) = 260{,}000$

$P = \$30$: $Q = 400{,}000 - 4{,}000(30) = 280{,}000$

C. At,

$Q = 264{,}000$: $P = \$100 - \$0.00025(264{,}000) = \$34$

$Q = 292{,}000$: $P = \$100 - \$0.00025(292{,}000) = \$27$

$Q = 320{,}000$: $P = \$100 - \$0.00025(320{,}000) = \$20$

P4.14 **Demand Curve Analysis.** *Air California, Inc. is a regional airline providing service between Los Angeles, California and Las Vegas, Nevada. An analysis of the monthly demand for service has revealed the following demand relation:*

$$Q = 45{,}000 - 250P - 300P_C + 250BAI + 10{,}000S$$

Where Q is quantity measured by the number of passengers per month, P is the price (\$), P_C is a price index for connecting flights (1982 = 100.), BAI is a business activity index (1982 = 100) and S, a binary or dummy variable, equals 1 in summer months, zero otherwise.

A. *Determine the demand curve facing the airline during the winter month of January if $P = \$100$, $P_C = 150$, BAI = 200, and S = 0.*

Demand and Supply 101

  B. Calculate the quantity demanded and total revenues during the summer month of July if all price-related variables are as specified above.

P4.14 **SOLUTION**

  A. The demand curve facing Air California during January can be calculated by substituting the appropriate value for each respective variable into the firm's demand function:

$$Q = 45{,}000 - 250P - 300P_C + 250BAI + 10{,}000S$$

$$= 45{,}000 - 250P - 300(150) + 250(200) + 10{,}000(0)$$

$$Q = 50{,}000 - 250P$$

With price expressed as a function of quantity, the firm demand curve can be written:

$$Q = 50{,}000 - 250P$$

$$250P = 50{,}000 - Q$$

$$P = \$200 - \$0.004Q$$

  B. During the summer month of July, the variable $S = 1$. Therefore, assuming that price-related values remain as before, the quantity demanded during July is:

$$Q = 45{,}000 - 250(100) - 300(150) + 250(200) + 10{,}000(1)$$

$$= 35{,}000 \text{ passengers}$$

Total July revenue for the company is:

$$TR = PQ$$

$$= \$100(35{,}000)$$

$$= \$3{,}500{,}000$$

P4.15 **Demand Curve Analysis.** Wisconsin Bus Company is a regional busline providing service between Milwaukee, Wisconsin and Chicago, Illinois. An analysis of the monthly demand for service has revealed the following demand relation:

$$Q = 1{,}750 - 40P - 15P_C + 30BAI - 1{,}700S$$

Where Q is quantity measured by the number of passengers per month, P is the price ($), P_C is a price index for connecting bus routes (1982 = 100.), BAI is a business activity index (1982 = 100) and S, a binary or dummy variable, equals 1 in summer months, zero otherwise.

A. Determine the demand curve facing the bus service during the winter month of February if P = $40, P_C = 120, BAI = 175, and S = 0.

B. Calculate the quantity demanded and total revenues during the summer month of August if all price-related variables are as specified above.

P4.15 SOLUTION

A. The demand curve facing Wisconsin Bus Company during February can be calculated by substituting the appropriate value for each respective variable into the firm's demand function:

$$Q = 1{,}750 - 40P - 15P_C + 30BAI - 1{,}700S$$

$$= 1{,}750 - 40P - 15(120) + 30(175) - 1{,}700(0)$$

$$Q = 5{,}200 - 40P$$

With price expressed as a function of quantity, the firm demand curve can be written:

$$Q = 5{,}200 - 40P$$

$$40P = 5{,}200 - Q$$

$$P = \$130 - \$0.025Q$$

B. During the summer month of August, the variable S = 1. Therefore, assuming that price-related values remain as before, the quantity demanded during August is:

Demand and Supply

$$Q = 1{,}750 - 40(40) - 15(120) + 30(175) - 1{,}700(1)$$

$$= 1{,}900 \text{ passengers}$$

Total August revenue for the company is:

$$TR = PQ$$

$$= \$40(1{,}900)$$

$$= \$76{,}000$$

P4.16 **Demand Curve Analysis.** Za's Pizza Company provides delivery and carryout service to the city of South Bend, Indiana. An analysis of the daily demand for pizzas has revealed the following demand relation:

$$Q = 1{,}400 - 100P - 2P_S + 0.01CSP + 750S$$

where Q is the quantity measured by the number of pizzas per day, P is the price (\$), P_S is a price index for soda pop (1982 = 100), CSP is the college student population and S, a binary or dummy variable, equals 1 on Friday, Saturday and Sunday, zero otherwise.

A. Determine the demand curve facing Za's on Tuesdays if $P = \$10$, $P_S = 125$, and $CSP = 35{,}000$, and $S = 0$.

B. Calculate the quantity demanded and total revenues on Fridays if all price-related variables are as specified above.

P4.16 SOLUTION

A. The demand curve facing Za's Pizza Company on Tuesdays can be calculated by substituting the appropriate value for each respective variable into the firm's demand function:

$$Q = 1{,}400 - 100P - 2P_S + 0.01CSP + 750S$$

$$= 1{,}400 - 100P - 2(125) + 0.01(35{,}000) + 750(0)$$

$$Q = 1{,}500 - 100P$$

With price expressed as a function of quantity, the firm demand curve can be written:

$$Q = 1{,}500 - 100P$$

$$100P = 1{,}500 - Q$$

$$P = \$150 - \$0.01Q$$

B. On Fridays, the variable $S = 1$. Therefore, assuming that price-related values remain as before, the quantity demanded on Fridays is:

$$Q = 1{,}400 - 100(10) - 2(125) + 0.01(35{,}000) + 750(1)$$

$$= 1{,}250 \text{ pizzas.}$$

Total revenue on Fridays for the firm is:

$$TR = PQ$$

$$= \$10(1{,}250)$$

$$= \$12{,}500$$

P4.17 *Supply Curve Analysis.* A review of industry-wide data for the domestic wine manufacturing industry suggests the following industry supply function:

$$Q = -7{,}000{,}000 + 400{,}000P - 2{,}000{,}000P_L$$

$$- 1{,}500{,}000P_K + 1{,}000{,}000W$$

where Q is cases supplied per year, P is the wholesale price per case (\$), P_L is the average price paid for unskilled labor (\$), P_K is the average price of capital (in percent), and W is weather measured by the average seasonal rainfall in growing areas (in inches).

A. Determine the industry supply curve for a recent year when $P = \$80$, $P_L = \$10$, $P_K = 12\%$, and $W = 25$ inches of rainfall. Show the industry supply curve with quantity expressed as a function of price and price expressed as a function of quantity.

Demand and Supply

B. Calculate the quantity supplied by the industry at prices of $50, $75 and $100 per case.

C. Calculate the prices necessary to generate a supply of 10 million, 25 million, and 50 million cases.

P4.17 SOLUTION

A. With quantity expressed as a function of price, the industry supply curve can be written:

$$Q = -7{,}000{,}000 + 400{,}000P - 2{,}000{,}000P_L - 1{,}500{,}000P_K + 1{,}000{,}000W$$

$$= -7{,}000{,}000 + 400{,}000P - 2{,}000{,}000(10) - 1{,}500{,}000(12) + 1{,}000{,}000(25)$$

$$= -20{,}000{,}000 + 400{,}000P$$

With price expressed as a function of quantity, the industry supply curve can be written:

$$Q = -20{,}000{,}000 + 400{,}000P$$

$$400{,}000P = 20{,}000{,}000 + Q$$

$$P = \$50 + \$0.0000025Q$$

B. Industry supply at each respective price is:

P = $50 : Q = -20,000,000 + 400,000(50) = 0

P = $75 : Q = -20,000,000 + 400,000(75) = 10,000,000

P = $100: Q = -20,000,000 + 400,000(100) = 20,000,000

C. The price necessary to generate each level of supply is:

Q = 10,000,000: P = $50 + $0.0000025(10,000,000) = $75

Q = 25,000,000: P = $50 + $0.0000025(25,000,000) = $112.50

Q = 50,000,000: P = $50 + $0.0000025(50,000,000) = $175

P4.18 **Supply Curve Analysis.** A review of industry-wide data for the frozen grape juice manufacturing industry suggests the following industry supply function:

$$Q = -3{,}000{,}000 + 500{,}000P - 800{,}000P_L - 1{,}000{,}000P_K + 300{,}000W$$

where Q is cases supplied per year, P is the wholesale price per case (\$), P_L is the average price paid for unskilled labor (\$), P_K is the average price of capital (in percent), and W is weather measured by the average seasonal temperature in growing areas (in fahrenheit).

A. Determine the industry supply curve for a recent year when $P = \$40$, $P_L = \$10$, $P_K = 15\%$, and $W = 70$ degrees fahrenheit. Show the industry supply curve with quantity expressed as a function of price and price expressed as a function of quantity.

B. Calculate the quantity supplied by the industry at prices of \$30, \$40 and \$50 per case.

C. Calculate the prices necessary to generate a supply of 10 million, 25 million, and 40 million cases.

P4.18 SOLUTION

A. With quantity expressed as a function of price, the industry supply curve can be written:

$$Q = -3{,}000{,}000 + 500{,}000P - 800{,}000P_L$$
$$- 1{,}000{,}000P_K + 300{,}000W$$
$$= -3{,}000{,}000 + 500{,}000P - 800{,}000(10)$$
$$- 1{,}000{,}000(15) + 300{,}000(70)$$
$$= -5{,}000{,}000 + 500{,}000P$$

With price expressed as a function of quantity, the industry supply curve can be written:

$$Q = -5{,}000{,}000 + 500{,}000P$$

Demand and Supply

$$500{,}000P = 5{,}000{,}000 + Q$$

$$P = \$10 + \$0.000002Q$$

B. Industry supply at each respective price is:

P = $30: Q = -5,000,000 + 500,000(30) = 10,000,000

P = $40: Q = -5,000,000 + 500,000(40) = 15,000,000

P = $50: Q = -5,000,000 + 500,000(50) = 20,000,000

C. The price necessary to generate each level of supply is:

Q = 10,000,000: P = $10 + $0.000002(10,000,000) = $30

Q = 25,000,000: P = $10 + $0.000002(25,000,000) = $60

Q = 40,000,000: P = $10 + $0.000002(40,000,000) = $90

P4.19 *Supply Curve Analysis.* Hi-tec, Inc. is a supplier of 4Mb memory expansion cards used to speed the processing of data on desktop workstations. Based on an analysis of monthly cost and output data, the company has estimated the following relation between its marginal cost of production and monthly output:

$$MC = \$100 + \$0.005Q$$

A. Calculate the marginal cost of production at 100,000, 200,000, and 300,000 units of output.

B. Express output as a function of marginal cost. Calculate the level of output at which MC = $1,000, $1,500 and $2,000.

C. Calculate the profit-maximizing level of output if prices are stable in the industry at $1,500 per expansion card and, therefore, P = MR = $1,500.

D. Again assuming prices are stable in the industry, derive Hi-tec's supply curve for cards. Express price as a function of quantity and quantity as a function of price.

P4.19 **SOLUTION**

A. Marginal production costs at each level of output are:

Q = 100,000: MC = $100 + $0.005(100,000) = $600

Q = 200,000: MC = $100 + $0.005(200,000) = $1,100

Q = 300,000: MC = $100 + $0.005(300,000) = $1,600

B. When output is expressed as a function of marginal cost, we find:

MC = $100 + $0.005Q

0.005Q = -100 + MC

Q = -20,000 + 200MC

The level of output at each respective level of marginal cost is:

MC = $1,000: Q = -20,000 + 200(1,000) = 180,000

MC = $1,500: Q = -20,000 + 200(1,500) = 280,000

MC = $2,000: Q = -20,000 + 200(2,000) = 380,000

C. We note from part b that MC = $1,500 when Q = 280,000. Therefore, when MR = $1,500, Q = 280,000 will be the profit maximizing level of output. More formally:

MR = MC

$1,500 = $100 + $0.005Q

0.005Q = 1,400

Q = 280,000

D. Since prices are stable in the industry, P = MR. This means that Hi-tec will supply expansion cards at the level of output where:

Demand and Supply

$$MR = MC$$

and, therefore, that:

$$P = \$100 + \$0.005Q$$

This is the supply curve for Hi-tec expansion boards, where price is expressed as a function of quantity. When quantity is expressed as a function of price, we find:

$$P = \$100 + \$0.005Q$$

$$0.005Q = -100 + P$$

$$Q = -20,000 + 200P$$

P4.20 **Supply Curve Analysis.** Binary Link, Inc. is a supplier of generic safety switches used in the doors of washing machines and dryers used to halt the turning of internal parts if the door is opened while the machine is running. Based on an analysis of monthly cost and output data, the company has estimated the following relation between its marginal cost of production and monthly output:

$$MC = \$2 + \$0.00001Q$$

A. Calculate the marginal cost of production at 400,000, 500,000, and 600,000 units of output.

B. Express output as a function of marginal cost. Calculate the level of output at which $MC = \$5, \$8$, and $\$10$.

C. Calculate the profit-maximizing level of output if prices are stable in the industry at $8 per switch and, therefore, $P = MR = \$8$.

D. Again assuming prices are stable in the industry, derive Binary Link's supply curve for switches. Express price as a function of quantity and quantity as a function of price.

P4.20 SOLUTION

A. Marginal production costs at each level of output are:

$$Q = 400,000: MC = \$2 + \$0.00001(400,000) = \$6$$

$$Q = 500{,}000: \text{ MC } = \$2 + \$0.00001(500{,}000) = \$7$$

$$Q = 600{,}000: \text{ MC } = \$2 + \$0.00001(600{,}000) = \$8$$

B. When output is expressed as a function of marginal cost, we find:

$$\text{MC} = \$2 + \$0.00001Q$$

$$0.00001Q = -2 + \text{MC}$$

$$Q = -200{,}000 + 100{,}000\text{MC}$$

The level of output at each respective level of marginal cost is:

$$\text{MC} = \$5 : Q = -200{,}000 + 100{,}000(5) = 300{,}000$$

$$\text{MC} = \$8 : Q = -200{,}000 + 100{,}000(8) = 600{,}000$$

$$\text{MC} = \$10: Q = -200{,}000 + 100{,}000(10) = 800{,}000$$

C. We note from Part B that MC = $8 when Q = 600,000. Therefore, when MR = $8, Q = 600,000 will be the profit maximizing level of output. More formally:

$$\text{MR} = \text{MC}$$

$$\$8 = \$2 + \$0.00001Q$$

$$0.00001Q = 6$$

$$Q = 600{,}000$$

D. Since prices are stable in the industry, P = MR. This means that Binary Link will supply switches at the level of output where:

$$\text{MR} = \text{MC}$$

and, therefore, that:

$$P = \$2 + \$0.00001Q$$

Demand and Supply

This is the supply curve for Binary Link switches, where price is expressed as a function of quantity. When quantity is expressed as a function of price, we find:

$$P = \$2 + \$0.00001Q$$

$$0.00001Q = -2 + P$$

$$Q = -200,000 + 100,000P$$

P4.21 **Optimal Supply.** Shake-n-Shing, Inc. is a supplier of wood shakes and shingles used in home construction. Shakes and shingles are sold by the bundle. Based on an analysis of monthly cost and output data, the company has estimated the following relation between its marginal cost of production and monthly output:

$$MC = \$50 + \$0.00005Q$$

A. Calculate the marginal cost of production at 500,000, 700,000, and 900,000 bundles of output.

B. Express output as a function of marginal cost. Calculate the level of output at which MC = $75, $100 and $125.

C. Calculate the profit-maximizing level of output if prices are stable in the industry at $100 per bundle, and, therefore, P = MR = $100.

D. Again assuming prices are stable in the industry, derive Shake-n-Shing's supply curve for bundles of shakes and shingles. Express price as a function of quantity and quantity as a function of price.

P4.21 SOLUTION

A. Marginal production costs at each level of output are:

Q = 500,000: MC = $50 + $0.00005(500,000) = $75

Q = 700,000: MC = $50 + $0.00005(700,000) = $85

Q = 900,000: MC = $50 + $0.00005(900,000) = $95

B. When output is expressed as a function of marginal cost, we find:

$$MC = \$50 + \$0.00005Q$$

$$0.00005Q = -50 + MC$$

$$Q = -1{,}000{,}000 + 20{,}000 MC$$

The level of output at each respective level of marginal cost is:

$$MC = \$75: \quad Q = -1{,}000{,}000 + 20{,}000(75) = 500{,}000$$

$$MC = \$100: \quad Q = -1{,}000{,}000 + 20{,}000(100) = 1{,}000{,}000$$

$$MC = \$125: \quad Q = -1{,}000{,}000 + 20{,}000(125) = 1{,}500{,}000$$

C. We note from part b that MC = $100 when Q = 1,000,000. Therefore, when MR = $100, Q = 1,000,000 will be the profit maximizing level of output. More formally:

$$MR = MC$$

$$\$100 = \$50 + \$0.00005Q$$

$$0.00005Q = 50$$

$$Q = 1{,}000{,}000$$

D. Since prices are stable in the industry, P = MR. This means that Shake-n-Shing will supply shakes and shingles at the level of output where:

$$MR = MC$$

and, therefore, that:

$$P = \$50 + \$0.00005Q$$

This is the supply curve for Shake-n-Shing shakes and shingles, where price is expressed as a function of quantity. When quantity is expressed as a function of price, we find:

$$P = \$50 + \$0.00005Q$$

Demand and Supply

$$0.00005Q = -50 + P$$

$$Q = -1{,}000{,}000 + 20{,}000P$$

P4.22 **Industry Supply.** Columbia Pharmaceuticals, Inc. and Princeton Medical, Ltd. supply a generic drug equivalent of an antibiotic used to treat postoperative infections. Proprietary cost and output information for each company reveal the following relations between marginal cost and output:

$$MC_C = \$5 + \$0.001Q_C \qquad (Columbia)$$

$$MC_P = \$6 + \$0.00025Q_P \qquad (Princeton)$$

The wholesale market for generic drugs is vigorously price-competitive, and neither firm is able to charge a premium for its products. Thus, P = MR in this market.

A. Determine the supply curve for each firm. Express price as a function of quantity and quantity as a function of price. (Hint: Set P = MR = MC to find each firm's supply curve.)

B. Calculate the quantity supplied by each firm at prices of $5, $7.50, and $10. What is the minimum price necessary for each individual firm to supply output?

C. Determine the industry supply curve when P < $6.

D. Determine the industry supply curve when P > $6. To check your answer, calculate quantity at an industry price of $10 and compare your answer with Part B.

P4.22 **SOLUTION**

A. Each company will supply output to the point where MR = MC. Since P = MR in this market, the supply curve for each firm can be written with price as a function of quantity as:

Columbia

$$MR_C = MC_C$$

$$P = \$5 + \$0.001Q_C$$

Princeton

$$MR_P = MC_P$$

$$P = \$6 + \$0.00025Q_P$$

When quantity is expressed as a function of price we find:

Columbia

$P = \$5 + \$0.001Q_C$

$0.001Q_C = -5 + P$

$Q_C = -5{,}000 + 1{,}000P$

Princeton

$P = \$6 + \$0.00025Q_P$

$0.00025Q_P = -6 + P$

$Q_P = -24{,}000 + 4{,}000P$

B. The quantity supplied at each respective price is:

Columbia

$P = \$5 \;\; : Q_C = -5{,}000 + 1{,}000(5) = 0$

$P = \$7.50: Q_C = -5{,}000 + 1{,}000(7.50) = 2{,}500$

$P = \$10 \;\; : Q_C = -5{,}000 + 1{,}000(10) = 5{,}000$

Princeton

$P = \$5 \;\; : Q_P = -24{,}000 + 4{,}000(5) = -4{,}000 \Rightarrow 0$

(since $Q < 0$ is impossible)

$P = \$7.50: Q_P = -24{,}000 + 4{,}000(7.50) = 6{,}000$

$P = \$10 \;\; : Q_P = -24{,}000 + 4{,}000(10) = 16{,}000$

For Columbia, MC = \$5 when $Q_C = 0$. Since marginal cost rises with output, Columbia will never supply a positive level of output unless a price in excess of \$5 per unit can be obtained. Negative output is not feasible. Thus, Columbia will simply fail to supply output when P < \$5. Similarly, MC_P = \$6 when $Q_P = 0$. Thus, Princeton will never supply output unless a price in excess of \$6 per unit can be obtained.

C. When P < \$6, only Columbia can profitably supply output. The Columbia supply curve will be the industry curve when P < \$6:

$P = \$5 + \$0.001Q$

Demand and Supply

or

$$Q = -5{,}000 + 1{,}000P$$

D. When P > $6, both Columbia and Princeton can profitably supply output. To derive the industry supply curve in this circumstance, we simply sum the quantities supplied by each firm:

$$\begin{aligned} Q &= Q_C + Q_P \\ &= -5{,}000 + 1{,}000P + (-24{,}000 + 4{,}000P) \\ &= -29{,}000 + 5{,}000P \end{aligned}$$

To check, at P = $10:

$$\begin{aligned} Q &= -29{,}000 + 5{,}000(10) \\ &= 21{,}000 \end{aligned}$$

which is supported by the answer to Part B, since $Q_C + Q_P = 5{,}000 + 16{,}000 = 21{,}000$.

(*Note:* Some of our students mistakenly add prices rather than quantities in attempting to derive the industry supply curve. To avoid this problem, we emphasize that industry supply curves are found through adding up output (horizontal summation), not by adding up prices (vertical summation).)

P4.23 ***Industry Supply.*** *Stanford Plastics, Inc. and Cal-Tech Associates, Inc. supply a generic modular phone jack that connects telephone cords to phone outlets. Proprietary cost and output information for each company reveal the following relations between marginal cost and output:*

$$MC_S = \$1 + \$0.00002Q_S \qquad \text{(Stanford)}$$

$$MC_C = \$1.50 + \$0.000005Q_C \qquad \text{(Cal-Tech)}$$

The wholesale market for modular phone jacks is vigorously price-competitive, and neither firm is able to charge a premium for its products. Thus, P = MR in this market.

116 Chapter 4

A. Determine the supply curve for each firm. Express price as a function of quantity and quantity as a function of price. (Hint: Set P = MR = MC to find each firm's supply curve.)

B. Calculate the quantity supplied by each firm at prices of $1, $1.50, and $2. What is the minimum price necessary for each individual firm to supply output?

C. Determine the industry supply curve when P < $1.50

D. Determine the industry supply curve when P > $1.50. To check your answer, calculate quantity at an industry price of $2 and compare your answer with Part B.

P4.23 SOLUTION

A. Each company will supply output to the point where MR = MC. Since P = MR in this market, the supply curve for each firm can be written with price as a function of quantity as:

Stanford   Cal-Tech

$MR_S = MC_S$ $MR_C = MC_C$

$P = \$1 + \$0.00002Q_S$ $P = \$1.50 + \$0.000005Q_C$

When quantity is expressed as a function of price we find:

Stanford   Cal-Tech

$P = \$1 + \$0.00002Q_S$ $P = \$1.50 + \$0.000005Q_C$

$0.00002Q_S = -1 + P$ $0.000005Q_C = -1.50 + P$

$Q_S = -50{,}000 + 50{,}000P$ $Q_C = -300{,}000 + 200{,}000P$

B. The quantity supplied at each respective price is:

Stanford

$P = \$1 \ : \ Q_S = -50{,}000 + 50{,}000(1) = 0$

Demand and Supply

$$P = \$1.50: Q_S = -50{,}000 + 50{,}000(1.50) = 25{,}000$$

$$P = \$2 : Q_S = -50{,}000 + 50{,}000(2) = 50{,}000$$

Cal-Tech

$$P = \$1 : Q_C = -300{,}000 + 200{,}000(1) = -100{,}000 => 0$$

(since $Q < 0$ is impossible)

$$P = \$1.50: Q_C = -300{,}000 + 200{,}000(1.50) = 0$$

$$P = \$2 : Q_C = -300{,}000 + 200{,}000(2) = 100{,}000$$

For Stanford, $MC_S = \$1$ when $Q_S = 0$. Since marginal cost rises with output, Stanford will never supply a positive level of output unless a price in excess of $\$1$ per unit can be obtained. Negative output is not feasible. Thus, Stanford will simply fail to supply output when $P < \$1$. Similarly, $MC_C = \$1.50$ when $Q_C = 0$. Thus, Cal-Tech will never supply output unless a price in excess of $\$1.50$ per unit can be obtained.

C. When $P < \$1.50$, only Stanford can profitably supply output. The Stanford supply curve will be the industry curve when $P < \$1.50$:

$$P = \$1 + \$0.00002Q$$

or

$$Q = -50{,}000 + 50{,}000P$$

D. When $P > \$1.50$, both Stanford and Cal-Tech can profitably supply output. To derive the industry supply curve in this circumstance, we simply sum the quantities supplied by each firm:

$$\begin{aligned} Q &= Q_S + Q_C \\ &= -50{,}000 + 50{,}000P + (-300{,}000 + 200{,}000P) \\ &= -350{,}000 + 250{,}000P \end{aligned}$$

To check, at $P = \$2$:

$$Q = -350,000 + 250,000(2)$$

$$= 150,000$$

which is supported by the answer to Part B, since $Q_S + Q_C = 50,000 + 100,000 = 150,000$.

(*Note:* Some of our students mistakenly add prices rather than quantities in attempting to derive the industry supply curve. To avoid this problem, we emphasize that industry supply curves are found through adding up output (horizontal summation), not by adding up prices (vertical summation).)

P4.24 **Market Equilibrium.** *Florida Orange Juice is a product of Florida's Orange Growers' Association. Demand and supply of the product are both highly sensitive to changes in the weather. During hot summer months, demand for orange juice and other beverages grows rapidly. On the other hand, hot dry weather has an adverse effect on supply by reducing the size of the orange crop.*

Demand and supply functions for Florida orange juice are as follows:

$$Q_D = 4,500,000 - 1,200,000P + 2,000,000P_S$$

$$+ 3,000Y + 100,000T \qquad \text{(Demand)}$$

$$Q_S = 800,000 + 2,400,000P - 500,000P_L$$

$$- 80,000P_K - 120,000T \qquad \text{(Supply)}$$

where P is the average price of Florida ($ per case), P_S is the average retail price of canned soda ($ per case), Y is income (GNP in $billions), T is the average daily high temperature (degrees), P_L is the average price of unskilled labor ($ per hour), and P_K is the average cost of capital (in percent).

    A.   *When quantity is expressed as a function of price, what are the Florida demand and supply curves if $P = \$11$, $P_S = \$5$, $Y = \$6,000$ billion, $T = 75$ degrees, $P_L = \$6$, and $P_K = 12.5\%$.*

    B.   *Calculate the surplus or shortage of Florida orange juice when $P = \$5$, $\$10$, and $\$15$.*

    C.   *Calculate the market equilibrium price-output combination.*

Demand and Supply

P4.24   SOLUTION

A. When quantity is expressed as a function of price, the demand curve for Florida Orange Juice is:

$$Q_D = 4{,}500{,}000 - 1{,}200{,}000P + 2{,}000{,}000P_S + 3{,}000Y + 100{,}000T$$

$$= 4{,}500{,}000 - 1{,}200{,}000P + 2{,}000{,}000(5) + 3{,}000(6{,}000) + 100{,}000(75)$$

$$Q_D = 40{,}000{,}000 - 1{,}200{,}000P$$

When quantity is expressed as a function of price, the supply curve for Florida Orange Juice is:

$$Q_S = 8{,}000{,}000 + 2{,}400{,}000P - 500{,}000P_L - 80{,}000P_K - 120{,}000T$$

$$= 8{,}000{,}000 + 2{,}400{,}000P - 500{,}000(6) - 80{,}000(12.5) - 120{,}000(75)$$

$$Q_S = -5{,}000{,}000 + 2{,}400{,}000P$$

B. The surplus or shortage can be calculated at each price level:

Price (1)	Quantity Supplied (2)	Quantity Demanded (3)	Surplus (+) or Shortage (-) (4) = (2) - (3)
$5:	$Q_S = -5{,}000{,}000 + 2{,}400{,}000(5)$ = 7,000,000	$Q_D = 40{,}000{,}000 - 1{,}200{,}000(5)$ = 34,000,000	-27,000,000
$10:	$Q_S = -5{,}000{,}000 + 2{,}400{,}000(10)$ = 19,000,000	$Q_D = 40{,}000{,}000 - 1{,}200{,}000(10)$ = 28,000,000	-9,000,000
$15:	$Q_S = -5{,}000{,}000 + 2{,}400{,}000(15)$ = 31,000,000	$Q_D = 40{,}000{,}000 - 1{,}200{,}000(15)$ = 22,000,000	+9,000,000

C. The equilibrium price is found by setting the quantity demanded equal to the quantity supplied and solving for P:

$$Q_D = Q_S$$

$$40{,}000{,}000 - 1{,}200{,}000P = -5{,}000{,}000 + 2{,}400{,}000P$$

$$3{,}600{,}000P = 45{,}000{,}000$$

$$P = \$12.50$$

To solve for Q, set:

Demand: $Q_D = 40{,}000{,}000 - 1{,}200{,}000(12.50) = 25{,}000{,}000$

Supply: $Q_S = -5{,}000{,}000 + 2{,}400{,}000(12.50) = 25{,}000{,}000$

In equilibrium, $Q_D = Q_S = 25{,}000{,}000$.

P4.25 **Market Equilibrium.** Various beverages are sold by roving vendors at Busch Stadium, home of the St. Louis Cardinals. Demand and supply of the product are both highly sensitive to changes in the weather. During hot summer months, demand for ice-cold beverages grows rapidly. On the other hand, hot dry weather has an adverse effect on supply in that it taxes the stamina of the vendor carrying his or her goods up and down many flights of stairs. The only competition to this service may be beverages purchased at kiosks in the stadium.

Demand and supply functions for ice-cold beverages per game are as follows:

$$Q_D = 20{,}000 - 10{,}000P + 20{,}000P_K + 2Y + 500T \quad \text{(Demand)}$$

$$Q_S = 2{,}000 + 60{,}000P - 900P_L - 1{,}000P_C - 200T \quad \text{(Supply)}$$

where P is the average price of ice-cold beverage ($ per beverage), P_K is the average price of beverages sold at the kiosks ($ per beverage), Y is average income (level of baseball fans), T is the average daily high temperature (degrees), P_L is the average price of unskilled labor ($ per hour), and P_C is the average cost of capital (in percent).

A. When quantity is expressed as a function of price, what are the ice-cold beverage demand and supply curves if $P = \$11$, $P_K = \$1.50$, $Y = \$25{,}000$, $T = 80$ degrees, $P_L = \$10$, and $P_C = 12\%$.

B. Calculate the surplus or shortage of ice-cold beverage when $P = \$2, \$3,$ and $\$4$.

C. Calculate the market equilibrium price-output combination.

Demand and Supply

P4.25   SOLUTION

A.   When quantity is expressed as a function of price, the demand curve for ice-cold beverages per game is:

$$Q_D = 20{,}000 - 10{,}000P + 20{,}000P_K + 2Y + 500T$$

$$= 20{,}000 - 10{,}000P + 20{,}000(1.50) + 2(25{,}000) + 500(80)$$

$$Q_D = 140{,}000 - 10{,}000P$$

When quantity is expressed as a function of price, the supply curve for ice-cold beverages per game is:

$$Q_S = 2{,}000 + 60{,}000P - 900P_L - 1{,}000P_C - 200T$$

$$= 2{,}000 + 60{,}000P - 900(10) - 1{,}000(12) - 200(80)$$

$$Q_S = -35{,}000 + 60{,}000P$$

B.   The surplus or shortage can be calculated at each price level:

Price (1)	Quantity Supplied (2)	Quantity Demanded (3)	Surplus (+) or Shortage (−) (4) = (2) − (3)
$2	$Q_S = -35{,}000 + 60{,}000(2)$ = 85,000	$Q_D = 140{,}000 - 10{,}000(2)$ = 120,000	−35,000
$3	$Q_S = -35{,}000 + 60{,}000(3)$ = 145,000	$Q_D = 140{,}000 - 10{,}000(3)$ = 110,000	+35,000
$4	$Q_S = -35{,}000 + 60{,}000(4)$ = 205,000	$Q_D = 140{,}000 - 10{,}000(4)$ = 100,000	+105,000

C.   The equilibrium price is found by setting the quantity demanded equal to the quantity supplied and solving for P:

$$Q_D = Q_S$$

$$140{,}000 - 10{,}000P = -35{,}000 + 60{,}000P$$

$$70{,}000P = 175{,}000$$

$$P = \$2.50$$

To solve for Q, set:

Demand: $Q_D = 140{,}000 - 10{,}000(2.50) = 115{,}000$

Supply: $Q_S = -35{,}000 + 60{,}000(2.50) = 115{,}000$

In equilibrium, $Q_D = Q_S = 115{,}000$.

Chapter 5

DEMAND ANALYSIS

MULTIPLE CHOICE QUESTIONS

Q5.1   All combinations of goods and services that provide the same utility are identified by the:

      A.   law of diminishing marginal utility.
      B.   law of constant marginal utility.
      C.   law of increasing marginal utility.
>   D.   indifference curve.

Q5.2   The increase in overall consumption made possible by a price cut is the:

>   A.   income effect.
      B.   substitution effect.
      C.   income *and* substitution effect.
      D.   consumption effect.

Q5.3   The point advertising elasticity reveals the:

>   A.   percentage change in demand following a change in advertising.
      B.   percentage change in the quantity demanded following a change in advertising.
      C.   percentage change in advertising following a change in the quantity demanded.
      D.   percentage change in advertising following a change in demand.

Q5.4   If $P_1 = \$5$, $Q_1 = 10{,}000$, $P_2 = \$6$ and $Q_2 = 5{,}000$, then at point P_2 the point price elasticity ϵ_P equals:

>   A.   -6.
      B.   -2.5.
      C.   -4.25.
      D.   -0.12.

Q5.5   If $MC = \$25$ and $\epsilon_P = -2.5$, the profit-maximizing price equals:

      A. $25.
      B. $17.86.
>   C. $41.67.
      D. $35.

Q5.6 The concept of cross-price elasticity is used to examine the responsiveness of demand:

>
- A. to changes in income.
- B. for one product to changes in the price of another.
- C. to changes in "own" price.
- D. to changes in income.

Q5.7 When the cross-price elasticity $\epsilon_{PX} = 3$:

>
- A. demand rises by 3% with a 1% increase in the price of X.
- B. the quantity demanded rises by 3% with a 1% increase in the price of X.
- C. the quantity demanded rises by 1% with a 3% increase in the price of X.
- D. demand rises by 1% with a 3% increase in the price of X.

Q5.8 Goods for which $\epsilon_I > 1$ are often referred to as:

>
- A. cyclical normal goods.
- B. noncyclical normal goods.
- C. being relatively unaffected by changing income.
- D. inferrior goods.

Q5.9 If $\epsilon_P = -3$ and $MC = \$1.32$, the profit-maximizing price is:

- A. $3.00.
>
- B. $1.98.
- C. $1.32.
- D. $1.76.

Q5.10 If $MR = \$25,000 - \$300Q$ and $MC = \$5,000 + \$100Q$, the profit-maximizing price is:

- A. $50.
- B. $25,000.
>
- C. $17,500.
- D. $10,000.

Demand Analysis and Estimation

Q5.11 Elasticity is the:

> A. percentage change in a dependent variable, Y, resulting from a one-percent change in the value of an independent variable, X.
> B. change in a dependent variable, Y, resulting from a change in the value of an independent variable, X.
> C. change in an independent variable, X, resulting from a change in the value of a dependent variable, Y.
> D. percentage change in an independent variable, X, resulting from a one-percent change in the value of a dependent variable, Y.

Q5.12 Point elasticity measures elasticity:

> A. over a given range of a function.
> B. at a spot on a function.
> C. along an arc.
> D. before non-price effects.

Q5.13 With elastic demand, a price increase will:

> A. lower marginal revenue.
> B. lower total revenue.
> C. increase total revenue.
> D. lower marginal and total revenue.

Q5.14 With inelastic demand, a price increase produces:

> A. a less than proportionate decline in quantity demanded.
> B. lower total revenue.
> C. lower marginal revenue.
> D. lower marginal and total revenue.

Q5.15 A direct relation between the price of one product and the demand for another holds for all:

> A. complements.
> B. substitutes.
> C. normal goods.
> D. inferrior goods.

Q5.16 A utility function is a descriptive statement that relates total utility to:

    A. income.
    B. the production of goods and services.
>   C. the consumption of goods and services.
    D. prices.

Q5.17 According to the law of diminishing marginal utility:

>   A. as the consumption of a given product rises, the added benefit eventually diminishes.
    B. as the production cost for a given product rises, the added benefit eventually diminishes.
    C. the demand curve for some products is upward-sloping.
    D. as the price of a given product rises, the added benefit eventually diminishes.

Q5.18 Given limited budgets, consumers obtain the most satisfaction if they purchase goods and services that:

    A. provide the highest level of marginal utility.
    B. provide the highest level of total utility.
>   C. provide the highest level of marginal utility per dollar spent.
    D. cost the least.

Q5.19 An indifference curve is a set of market baskets that:

    A. contain the same goods.
>   B. provide the same utility.
    C. have identical marginal rates of substitution.
    D. can be obtained for the same cost.

Q5.20 An increase in the quantity purchased following a price cut is:

    A. unrelated to the law of diminishing marginal utility.
    B. inconsistent with the law of diminishing marginal utility.
    C. inconsistent with utility-maximizing behavior.
>   D. consistent with the law of diminishing marginal utility.

Demand Analysis and Estimation

Q5.21 The marginal rate of substitution is always equal to:

>
- A. the marginal utility of either product.
- B. the total utility of either product.
- C. minus one times the ratio of marginal utilities for each product.
- D. the slope of the budget constraint.

Q5.22 If the quantity of Good X is measured on the horizontal axis and the quantity of Good Y is measured on the vertical axis, the slope of the budget constraint will decrease if the:

>
- A. price of X decreases.
- B. price of Y decreases.
- C. marginal utility of X decreases.
- D. budget decreases.

Q5.23 Income and substitution effects explain change in the quantity of a good consumed that result from a change in:

- A. consumer preferences.
>
- B. price.
- C. price of other goods.
- D. income.

Q5.24 The change to a new indifference curve following a rise in aggregate consumption caused by a price cut is:

- A. a price effect.
>
- B. an income effect.
- C. a substitution effect.
- D. a consumption effect.

Q5.25 The movement along an indifference curve reflecting the substitution of cheaper products for more expensive ones is:

- A. utility effect.
>
- B. a substitution effect.
- C. an income effect.
- D. supply effect.

Q5.26 A consumer will obtain the maximum level of utility if:

    A. $P_x = MU_x$ and $P_y = MU_y$
    B. $B = P_x X + P_y Y$
    C. $\dfrac{MU_x}{MU_y} = \dfrac{P_x}{P_y}$
    D. $MRS = -\dfrac{MU_x}{MU_y}$

For questions 5.22 and 5.23 consider the following:

The demand for peanut butter is linear and defined by the function $P = \$5 - \$0.05Q$.

Q5.27 When $Q = 40$, the point price elasticity of demand for peanut butter is:

    A.   -2/3.
    B.   -3/2.
    C.   -8/3.
    D.   -3/8.

Q5.28 When quantity is increased from $Q_1 = 40$ to $Q_2 = 60$, the arc price elasticity of demand for peanut butter is:

    A.   -1/2.
    B.   -1.
    C.   -4.
    D.   -1/4.

Q5.29 If a decrease in price causes total revenue to increase, the absolute value of the price elasticity of demand is:

    A.   greater than zero but less than one.
    B.   equal to one.
    C.   greater than one.
    D.   equal to zero.

Demand Analysis and Estimation

Q5.30 When the point price elasticity of demand equals -2 and the marginal cost per unit is $5, the optimal price is:

>
- A. $5.
- B. $10.
- C. impossible to determine without further information.
- D. $2.

Q5.31 When marginal revenue is greater than zero the point price elasticity of demand is:

>
- A. greater than zero but less than one.
- B. equal to one.
- C. greater than one.
- D. equal to zero.

Q5.32 The demand for a product tends to be inelastic if:

>
- A. it is expensive.
- B. a small proportion of consumer's income is spent on the good.
- C. consumers are quick to respond to price changes.
- D. it has many substitutes.

Q5.33 Two products are complements if the:

>
- A. cross-price elasticity of demand is less than zero.
- B. cross-price elasticity of demand equals zero.
- C. cross-price elasticity of demand is greater than zero.
- D. price elasticity of demand for each good is greater than zero.

Q5.34 If the income elasticity of demand for a good is greater than one, the good is:

>
- A. a noncyclical normal good.
- B. a cyclical normal good.
- C. neither a normal nor an inferior good.
- D. an inferior good.

Q5.35   A product that enjoys rapidly growing demand over time is likely to be:

>
- **A.** a noncyclical normal good.
- **B.** a cyclical normal good.
- **C.** neither a normal nor an inferior good.
- **D.** an inferior good.

Demand Analysis and Estimation

PROBLEMS & SOLUTIONS

P5.1   **A.**   ***Optimal Consumption.*** Complete the following table that describes the demand for goods:

Price	Units	Total Utility	Marginal Utility	Price/Marginal Utility
$100	1	50		
90	2	90		
80	3	120		
70	4	140		
60	5	150		

B.   Explain your answer to Part A.

C.   What is the optimal level of goods consumption if the marginal utility derived from the consumption of services costs $3 per util?

P5.1   **SOLUTION**

A.

Goods Consumption

Price	Units	Total Utility	Marginal Utility	Price/Marginal Utility
$100	1	50	50	$2.00
90	2	90	40	2.25
80	3	120	30	2.67
70	4	140	20	3.50
60	5	150	10	6.00

B.   The marginal utility derived from goods consumption falls as the number of units consumed increases. This follows from the law of diminishing marginal utility. Indeed, marginal utility is falling so rapidly that the P/MU ratio increases as the number of units consumed expands. Despite falling prices, the marginal cost of utility derived from goods consumption is rising.

C. Three units of goods should be purchased if the marginal cost of utility derived from the consumption of services is $3 per util. The first unit of goods consumed involves a cost of $2 per util. The second and third units of goods consumed involve a cost of $2.25 and $2.67 per util, respectively. All represent relative bargains. However, a fourth unit of goods would involve a price-utility tradeoff of $3.50 per util. At a marginal cost of $3 per util, services consumption would represent the better bargain.

P5.2 A. *Optimal Consumption.* Complete the following table that describes the demand for services:

Price	Units	Total Utility	Marginal Utility	Price/Marginal Utility
$125	1	125		
115	2	225		
105	3	300		
95	4	350		
85	5	375		

B. Explain your answer to Part A.

C. What is the optimal level of services consumption if the marginal utility derived from the consumption of goods costs $2 per util?

P5.2 SOLUTION

A.

Services Consumption

Price	Units	Total Utility	Marginal Utility	Price/Marginal Utility
$125	1	125	125	$1.00
115	2	225	100	1.15
105	3	300	75	1.40
95	4	350	50	1.90
85	5	375	25	3.40

Demand Analysis and Estimation

B. The marginal utility derived from services consumption falls as the number of units consumed increases. This follows from the law of diminishing marginal utility. Indeed, marginal utility is falling so rapidly that the P/MU ratio increases as the number of units consumed expands. Despite falling prices, the marginal cost of utility derived from services consumption is rising.

C. Four units of service should be purchased if the marginal cost of utility derived from the consumption of goods is $2 per util. The first unit of service consumed involves a cost of $1 per util. The second, third and fourth units of service consumed involve a cost of $1.15, $1.40 and $1.90 per util, respectively. All represent relative bargains. However, a fifth unit of service would involve a price-utility tradeoff of $3.40 per util. At a marginal cost of $2 per util, goods consumption would represent the better bargain.

P5.3 *Optimal Consumption.* The following table describes the demand for tickets to the opera, during the two-week season.

Price	Tickets	Total Utility	Marginal Utility	Price/Marginal Utility
$50	1	100		
40	2	180		
30	3	240		
20	4	280		
10	5	300		

A. Complete the table.

B. Explain your answer to Part A.

C. What is the optimal level of opera consumption if the marginal utility derived from the consumption of movie tickets during the same two-week period costs $0.25 per util?

P5.3 **SOLUTION**

A.

Opera Consumption

Price	Tickets	Total Utility	Marginal Utility	Price/Marginal Utility
$50	1	100	100	$0.50
40	2	180	80	0.50
30	3	240	60	0.50
20	4	280	40	0.50
10	5	300	20	0.50

B. The marginal utility derived from opera consumption falls as the number of units consumed increases. This follows from the law of diminishing marginal utility. Despite falling prices, the marginal cost of utility derived from opera consumption remains constant at $0.50.

C. Zero units of opera should be purchased if the marginal cost of utility derived from the consumption of movie tickets is $0.25 per util. Even at the first unit of opera, a price-utility tradeoff of $0.50 per util exists. At a marginal cost of $0.25 per util, movie consumption would represent the better bargain.

P5.4 **Demand Curves.** Paul Ruben is an ardent movie fan. The following table shows the relation between the number of movies he attends per month and the total utility he derives from movie consumption:

Number of Movies per Month	Total Utility
0	0
1	100
2	175
3	225
4	240
5	250

Demand Analysis and Estimation

    A.   Construct a table showing Ruben's marginal utility derived from movie consumption.

    B.   At an average movie ticket price of $5, Ruben is only able to justify three movies per month. Calculate the cost per unit of marginal utility derived from movie consumption at this activity level.

    C.   If the cost-marginal utility tradeoff found in Part B represents the most Ruben is willing to pay for movie consumption, calculate the prices at which he would attend two, three, four, and five movies per month.

    D.   Plot Ruben's movie demand curve.

P5.4   **SOLUTION**

    A.

Number of Movies Per Month	Total Utility	Marginal Utility
0	0	---
1	100	100
2	175	75
3	225	50
4	240	15
5	250	10

    B.   At three movies per month, MU = 50. Thus, at a $5 price per movie ticket, the cost per unit of marginal utility derived from movie consumption is P/MU = $5/50 = $0.1 or 10¢ per util.

    C.   At a maximum acceptable price of 10¢ per util, Ruben's maximum acceptable price varies according to the following schedule:

Number of Movies Per Month	Total Utility	Marginal Utility MU = ΔU	Maximum Acceptable Price at 10¢ per MU
0	0	---	---
1	100	100	$10.00
2	175	75	7.50
3	225	50	5.00
4	240	15	1.50
5	250	10	1.00

D. Ruben's movie demand curve is:

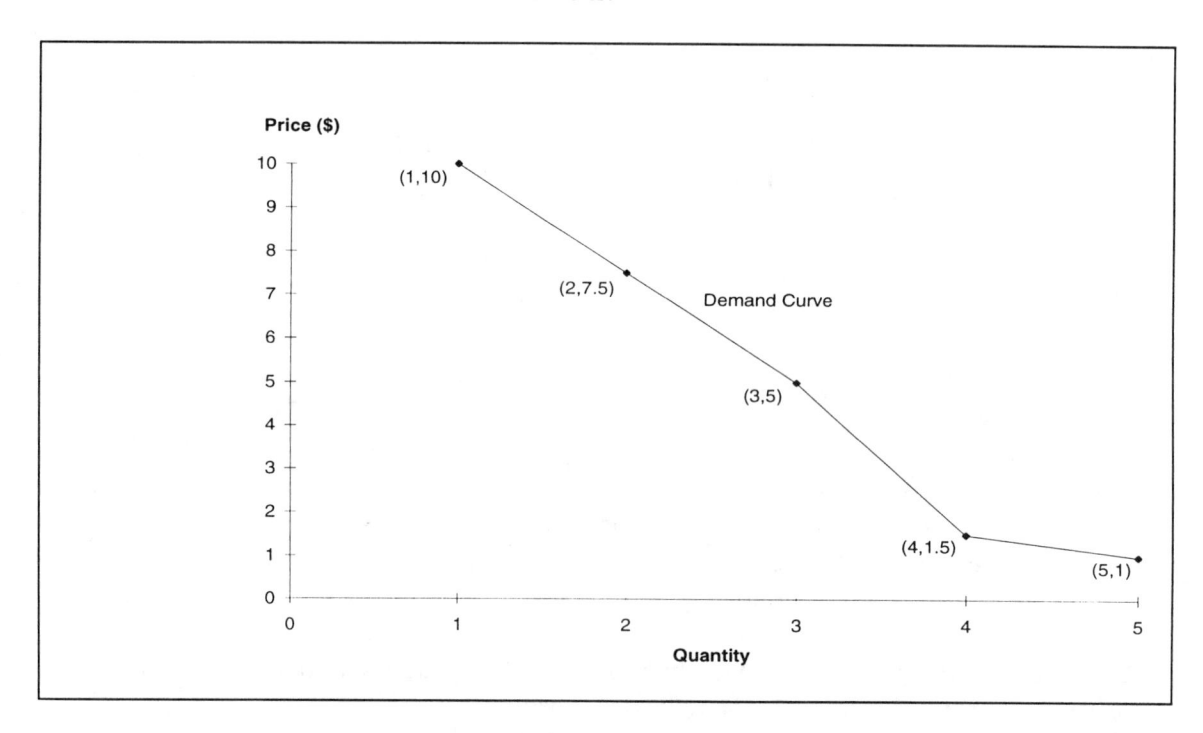

Demand Curve plot with points (1,10), (2,7.5), (3,5), (4,1.5), (5,1); Price ($) on vertical axis, Quantity on horizontal axis.

P5.5 **Demand Curves.** *Baby Hughy enjoys chocolate candy. The following table shows the relation between the pounds of bon-bons eaten per month and the total utility derived from bon-bon consumption:*

Demand Analysis and Estimation

Pounds of Bon-bons per Month	Total Utility
0	0
1	200
2	330
3	420
4	480
5	530

A. Construct a table showing Hughy's marginal utility derived from bon-bon consumption.

B. At an average bon-bon price of $2.50 per pound, Hughy is able to justify five pounds per month. Calculate the cost per unit of marginal utility derived from bon-bon consumption at this activity level.

C. If the cost-marginal utility tradeoff found in Part B represents the most Hughy is willing to pay for bon-bon consumption, calculate the prices of which he would eat one, two, three, four, and five pounds per month.

D. Plot Hughy's bon-bon demand curve.

P5.5 SOLUTION

A.

Pounds of Bon-bons Per Month	Total Utility	Marginal Utility
0	0	---
1	200	200
2	330	130
3	420	90
4	480	60
5	530	50

B. At five pounds of bon-bons per month, MU = 50. Thus, at a $2.50 price per pound of bon-bons, the cost per unit of marginal utility derived from bon-bon consumption is P/MU = $2.50/50 = $0.05 or 5¢ per util.

C. At a maximum acceptable price of 5¢ per util, Hughy's maximum acceptable price varies according to the following schedule:

Pounds of Bon-bons Per Month	Total Utility	Marginal Utility MU = ΔU	Maximum Acceptable Price at 5¢ per MU
0	0	---	---
1	200	200	10.00
2	330	130	6.50
3	420	90	4.50
4	480	60	3.00
5	530	50	2.50

D. Hughy's bon-bon demand curve is:

Demand Analysis and Estimation

Demand Curve

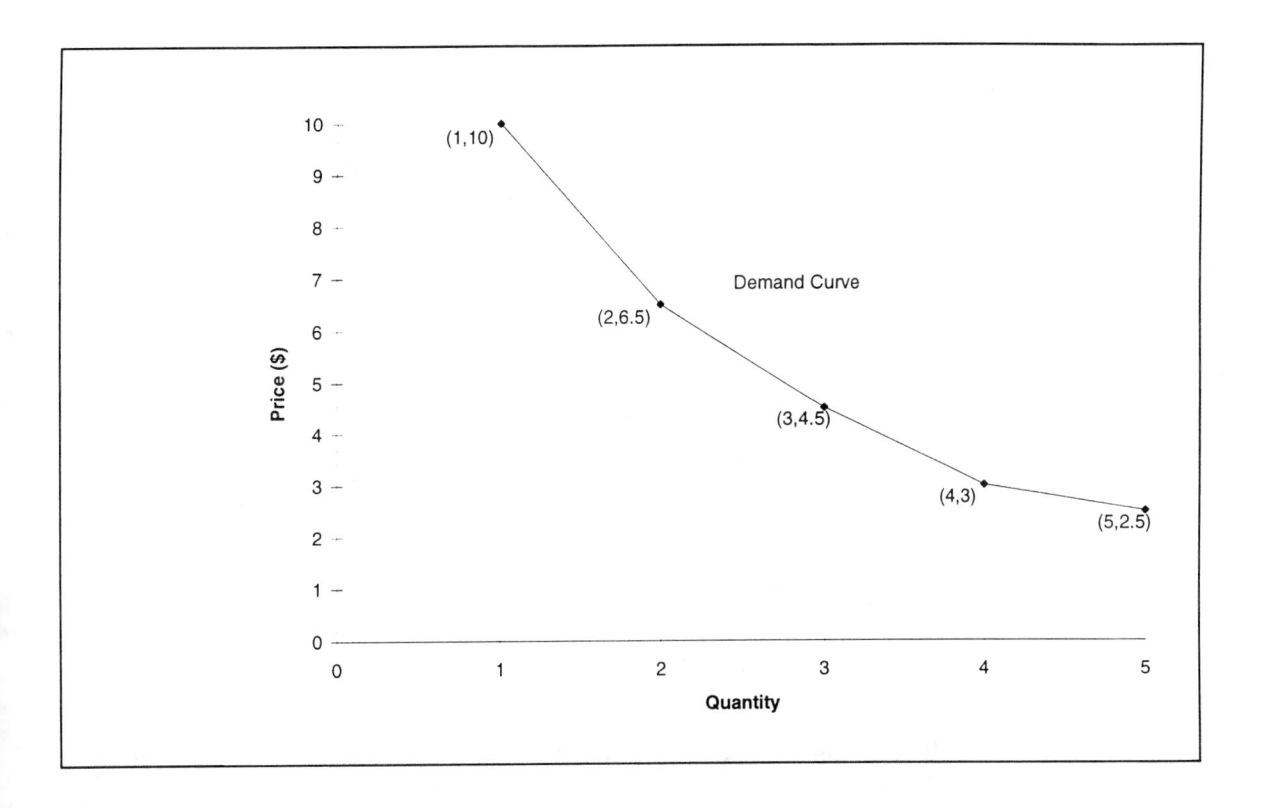

Points: (1,10), (2,6.5), (3,4.5), (4,3), (5,2.5)

P5.6 **Optimal Expenditure.** *Consider the following data:*

Goods (G)		Services (S)	
Units	Total Utility	Units	Total Utility
0	0	0	0
1	150	1	95
2	285	2	185
3	405	3	270
4	480	4	345
5	525	5	400

A. Construct a table showing the marginal utility derived from the consumption of goods and services. Also show the trend in marginal utility per dollar spent (the MU/P ratio) if $P_G = \$30$ and $P_S = \$20$.

140   Chapter 5

B. If two units of goods are consumed, what level of services consumption could also be justified?

C. If four units of services are consumed, what level of goods consumption could also be justified?

D. What is the optimal allocation of a $150 budget? Explain.

P5.6   **SOLUTION**

A.

	Goods (G)				Services (S)		
Units	Total Utility	Marginal Utility	$MU/P_G =$ MU/\$30	Units	Total Utility	Marginal Utility	$MU/P_S =$ MU/\$20
0	0	--	--	0	0	--	--
1	150	150	5.00	1	95	95	4.75
2	285	135	4.50	2	185	90	4.50
3	405	120	4.00	3	270	85	4.25
4	480	75	2.50	4	345	75	3.75
5	525	45	1.50	5	400	55	2.75

B. Two. When 2 units of goods are purchased, the last unit consumed generates 135 utils of satisfaction at a rate of 4.5 utils per dollar. Consumption of 2 units of services could be justified on the grounds that consumption at that level would also generate 4.5 utils per dollar spent on services.

C. Three. When 4 units of services are purchased, the last unit consumed generated 75 utils of satisfaction at a rate of 3.75 utils per dollar. Consumption of 3 units of goods could be justified on the grounds that consumption at that level would generate at least 3.75 utils per dollar spent on goods.

D. G = 3 and S = 3. The optimal allocation of a $150 budget involves spending according to the highest marginal utility generated per dollar of expenditure. In total, $90 would be spent on three units of goods, and $60 dollars would be spent on three units of services.

P5.7   **Optimal Expenditure.** *Consider the following data:*

Demand Analysis and Estimation

	Cola (C)		Orange Juice (O)
12 oz Cans	Total Utility	12 oz Cans	Total Utility
0	0	0	0
1	200	1	500
2	350	2	700
3	450	3	800
4	525	4	850
5	550	5	875

A. Construct a table showing the marginal utility derived from the consumption of cola and orange juice. Also show the trend in marginal utility per dollar spent (the MU/P ratio) if $P_C = \$0.50$ and $P_O = \$1$.

B. If two cans of orange juice are consumed, what level of cola consumption could also be justified?

C. If five cans of cola are consumed, what level of juice consumption could also be justified?

D. What is the optimal allocation of a $3.50 budget? Explain.

P5.7 SOLUTION

A.

	Cola (C)				Orange Juice (O)		
12 oz Cans	Total Utility	Marginal Utility	$MU/P_C =$ MU/$0.50	12 oz Cans	Total Utility	Marginal Utility	$MU/P_O =$ MU/$1
0	0	--	--	0	0	--	--
1	200	200	400	1	500	500	500
2	350	150	300	2	700	200	200
3	450	100	200	3	800	100	100
4	525	75	150	4	850	50	50
5	550	25	50	5	875	25	25

B. Three. When 2 cans of juice are purchased, the last can consumed generates 100 utils of satisfaction at a rate of 100 utils per dollar. Consumption of 3 cans of cola could be justified on the grounds that this consumption level would generate at least 200 utils per dollar spent on cola.

C. Four. When 5 cans of cola are purchased, the last can consumed generated 25 utils of satisfaction at a rate of 50 utils per dollar. Consumption of 4 cans of juice could be justified on the grounds that consumption at that level would generate at least 50 utils per dollar spent on juice.

D. C = 4 and O = 2. The optimal allocation of a $3.50 budget involves spending according to the highest marginal utility generated per dollar of expenditure. In total, two dollars would be spent on four cans of cola, and two dollars would be spent on two cans of orange juice.

P5.8 *Elasticity. The demand for mini cassette players can be characterized by the following point elasticities: price elasticity = -2, cross-price elasticity with AA Alkaline batteries = -1.5, and income elasticity = 3. Indicate whether each of the following statements is true or false, and explain your answer.*

A. *A price increase for cassette players will decrease both the number of units demanded and the total revenue of sellers.*

B. *The cross-price elasticity indicates that a 2% reduction in the price of cassette players will cause a 3% increase in battery demand.*

C. *Demand for cassette players is price elastic and they are cyclical normal goods.*

D. *Falling battery prices will definitely increase revenues received by sellers of both cassette players and batteries.*

E. *A 3% price reduction in cassette players would be necessary to overcome the effects of a 2% decline in income.*

P5.8 **SOLUTION**

A. True. A price increase will always decrease units sold, given a downward sloping demand curve. The negative sign on the price elasticity indicates that this is indeed the case here. The fact that price elasticity equals -2 indicates that demand is elastic with respect to price, and therefore that a price increase will also decrease total revenues.

B. False. The cross-price elasticity indicates that a 2% decrease in the price of batteries will have the effect of increasing cassette player demand by 3%.

Demand Analysis and Estimation 143

C. True. Demand is price elastic (see part a). Since the income elasticity is positive, cassette players are a normal good. Moreover, since the income elasticity is greater than one, cassette player demand is also cyclical.

D. False. A negative cross-price elasticity indicates that cassette players and batteries are compliments. Therefore, falling battery prices will increase the demand for cassette players and resulting revenues for sellers. However, we have no information concerning the price elasticity of demand for batteries, and therefore do not know the effect of falling battery prices on battery revenues.

E. True. A 3% reduction in price will cause a 6% increase in the quantity of cassette players demanded. A 2% decline in income will cause a 6% fall in demand. These changes will be mutually offsetting.

P5.9 *Elasticity.* The demand for Penn's Oil motor oil can be characterized by the following point elasticities: price elasticity = -2.5, cross-price elasticity with Value Lean motor oil = 1.5, and income elasticity = 0.75. Indicate whether each of the following statements is true or false, and explain your answer.

A. A price increase for Penn's Oil will decrease both the number of units demanded and the total revenue of sellers.

B. The cross-price elasticity indicates that a 2% increase in the price of *Value Lean* will cause a 3% increase in Penn's Oil demand.

C. Demand for Penn's Oil is price elastic and the motor oil is a cyclical, normal good.

D. Falling Value's Lean prices will definitely increase revenues received by manufacturers of both brands of oil.

E. A 0.9% price reduction for Penn's Oil would be necessary to overcome the effects of a 3% decline in income.

P5.9 SOLUTION

A. True. A price increase will always decrease units sold, given a downward sloping demand curve. The negative sign on the price elasticity indicates that this is indeed the case here. The fact that price elasticity equals -2.5 indicates that demand is elastic with respect to price, and therefore that a price increase will also decrease total revenues.

B. True. The positive cross-price elasticity indicates that a 2% increase in the price of the substitute good Value's Lean will have the effect of increasing Penn's Oil's demand by 3%.

C. False. Demand is price elastic (see part a). Since the income elasticity is positive, Penn's Oil is a normal good. However, since the income elasticity is less than one, Penn's Oil demand is not cyclical.

D. False. A positive cross-price elasticity indicates that the two motor oils are substitutes. Therefore, falling Value Lean prices will decrease the demand for Penn's Oil and resulting revenues for its manufacturers. However, we have no information concerning the own price elasticity of demand for Value Lean, and therefore do not know the effect of falling prices on its revenues.

E. True. A 0.9% reduction in price will cause a 2.25% increase in the quantity of Penn's Oil demanded. A 3% decline in income will cause a 2.25% fall in demand. These changes will be mutually offsetting.

P5.10 *Demand Analysis.* KRDY-FM is contemplating a T-shirt advertising promotion. Monthly sales data from T-shirt shops marketing the "Listen to KRDY-FM" design indicate that:

$$Q = 3,000 - 500P,$$

where Q is T-shirt sales and P is price.

A. How many T-shirts could KRDY-FM sell at $4 each?

B. What price would KRDY-FM have to charge to sell 2,000 T-shirts?

C. At what price would T-shirt sales equal zero?

D. How many T-shirts could be given away?

E. Calculate the point price elasticity of demand at a price of $4.

Demand Analysis and Estimation

P5.10 **SOLUTION**

A. $Q = 3{,}000 - 500P$

$\quad\quad = 3{,}000 - 500(4)$

$\quad\quad = 1{,}000$

B. $Q = 3{,}000 - 500P$

$2{,}000 = 3{,}000 - 500P$

$500P = 1{,}000$

$P = \$2$

C. $Q = 3{,}000 - 500P$

$0 = 3{,}000 - 500P$

$500P = 3{,}000$

$P = \$6$

D. $Q = 3{,}000 - 500P$

$Q = 3{,}000 - 500(0)$

$Q = 3{,}000$

E. The point price elasticity of demand at a price of $4 is calculated as follows:

$$\epsilon_P = \frac{\Delta Q}{\Delta P} \times \frac{P}{Q}$$

$$= -500 \times \frac{4}{1{,}000}$$

$$= -2 \text{ (elastic)}$$

P5.11 **Demand Analysis.** The San Diego Zoo is contemplating a stuffed panda bear advertising promotion. Annualized sales data from local shops marketing the "Can't Bear it When You're Away" bear indicate that:

$$Q = 50,000 - 1,000P,$$

where Q is Panda bear sales and P is price.

A. How many pandas could the zoo sell at $30 each?

B. What price would the zoo have to charge to sell 25,000 pandas?

C. At what price would panda sales equal zero?

D. How many bears could be given away?

E. Calculate the point price elasticity of demand at a price of $10.

P5.11 SOLUTION

A. $Q = 50,000 - 1,000P$
    $= 50,000 - 1,000(30)$
    $= 20,000$

B. $Q = 50,000 - 1,000P$
    $25,000 = 50,000 - 1,000P$
    $1,000P = 25,000$
    $P = \$25$

C. $Q = 50,000 - 1,000P$
    $0 = 50,000 - 1,000P$
    $1,000P = 50,000$
    $P = \$50$

Demand Analysis and Estimation

D. $Q = 50,000 - 1,000P$

$Q = 50,000 - 1,000(0)$

$Q = 50,000$

E. The point price elasticity of demand at a price of $30 is calculated as follows:

$$\epsilon_P = \frac{\Delta Q}{\Delta P} \times \frac{P}{Q}$$

$$= -1,000 \times \frac{30}{20,000}$$

$$= -1.5 \text{ (elastic)}$$

P5.12 **Demand Analysis.** Lincoln Grade School is contemplating a chocolate bar fund raiser. Weekly sales data from Mrs. Bronellwee's fifth grade class indicate that:

$$Q = 4,000 - 1,000P,$$

where Q is chocolate bar sales and P is price.

A. How many chocolate bars could Lincoln Grade School sell at $2 each?

B. What price would Lincoln Grade School have to charge to sell 2,500 chocolate bars?

C. At what price would Lincoln Grade School sales equal zero?

D. How many chocolate bars could be given away?

E. Calculate the point price elasticity of demand at a price of $2.

P5.12 **SOLUTION**

A. $Q = 4,000 - 1,000P$

$= 4,000 - 1,000(2)$

$= 2,000$

Harcourt Brace & Company

B. $Q = 4,000 - 1,000P$

$2,500 = 4,000 - 1,000P$

$1,000P = 1,500$

$P = \$1.50$

C. $Q = 4,000 - 1,000P$

$0 = 4,000 - 1,000P$

$1,000P = 4,000$

$P = \$4$

D. $Q = 4,000 - 1,000P$

$Q = 4,000 - 1,000(0)$

$Q = 4,000$

E.   The point price elasticity of demand at a price of $2 is calculated as follows:

$$\epsilon_P = \frac{\Delta Q}{\Delta P} \times \frac{P}{Q}$$

$$= -1,000 \times \frac{2}{2,000}$$

$$= -1 \text{ (unitary elastic)}$$

P5.13 **Demand Analysis.** Aspen, Colorado is engaging in a bumper-sticker advertising campaign. Monthly sales data from ski shops selling the "Don't Worry-Be Happy (in Aspen)" bumper-stickers indicate that:

$$Q = 6,000 - 2,000P,$$

where Q is bumper-sticker sales and P is price.

A.   How many bumper-stickers could Aspen sell at $2 each?

Demand Analysis and Estimation 149

    B.   What price would Aspen have to charge to sell 5,000 bumper-stickers?

    C.   At what price would bumper-sticker sales equal zero?

    D.   How many bumper-stickers could be given away?

    E.   Calculate the point price elasticity of demand at a price of $1.

P5.13   **SOLUTION**

    A. $Q = 6{,}000 - 2{,}000P$

                $= 6{,}000 - 2{,}000(2)$

                $= 2{,}000$

    B. $Q = 6{,}000 - 2{,}000P$

            $5{,}000 = 6{,}000 - 2{,}000P$

            $2{,}000P = 1{,}000$

            $P = \$0.50$

    C. $Q = 6{,}000 - 2{,}000P$

            $0 = 6{,}000 - 2{,}000P$

            $2{,}000P = 6{,}000$

            $P = \$3$

    D. $Q = 6{,}000 - 2{,}000P$

            $Q = 6{,}000 - 2{,}000(0)$

            $Q = 6{,}000$

    E.   The point price elasticity of demand at a price of $2 is calculated as follows:

150   Chapter 5

$$\epsilon_P = \frac{\Delta Q}{\Delta P} \times \frac{P}{Q}$$

$$= -2{,}000 \times \frac{2}{2{,}000}$$

$$= -2 \text{ (elastic)}$$

P5.14 **Optimal Price.** Last week, Discount Food Stores, Inc. reduced the average price on the 22 ounce size of Dishwashing Liquid by 1%. In response, sales jumped by 8%.

    A. Calculate the point price elasticity of demand for Dishwashing Liquid.

    B. Calculate the optimal price for Dishwashing Liquid if marginal cost is 70¢ per unit.

P5.14 **SOLUTION**

    A.

$$\epsilon_P = \frac{\text{Percentage change in quantity}}{\text{Percentage change in price}}$$

$$= \frac{0.08}{-0.01}$$

$$= -8 \text{ (elastic)}$$

    B. The optimal price is found setting MC = MR and solving for P where:

$$MC = MR = P\left(1 + \frac{1}{\epsilon_P}\right)$$

$$0.7 = P\left(1 + \frac{1}{-8}\right)$$

$$0.7 = 0.875\,P$$

$$P = 0.8 \text{ or } 80¢$$

P5.15 **Optimal Price.** Last week, Wally's Burgers, Inc. reduced the average price on the 1/2-pound Papa burger by 1%. In response, sales jumped by 2%.

Demand Analysis and Estimation

A. Calculate the point price elasticity of demand for Papa burgers.

B. Calculate the optimal price for Papa burgers if marginal cost is $1 per unit.

P5.15   **SOLUTION**

A.

$$\epsilon_P = \frac{\text{Percentage change in quantity}}{\text{Percentage change in price}}$$

$$= \frac{0.02}{-0.01}$$

$$= -2 \text{ (elastic)}$$

B. The optimal price is found setting MC = MR and solving for P where:

$$MC = MR = P\left(1 + \frac{1}{\epsilon_P}\right)$$

$$1.00 = P\left(1 + \frac{1}{-2}\right)$$

$$1.00 = 0.50 P$$

$$P = \$2$$

P5.16   **Optimal Price.** Last month, Forest Lumber, Inc. reduced the average price on the eight-foot pine 2×4s by 1%. In response, sales jumped by 4%.

A. Calculate the point price elasticity of demand for eight-foot 2×4s.

B. Calculate the optimal price for eight-foot 2×4s if marginal cost is $1.50 per unit.

P5.16   **SOLUTION**

A.

$$\epsilon_P = \frac{\text{Percent change in quantity}}{\text{Percentage change in price}}$$

$$= \frac{0.04}{-0.01}$$

$$= -4 \text{ (elastic)}$$

B.   The optimal price is found setting MC = MR and solving for P where:

$$MC = MR = P\left(1 + \frac{1}{\epsilon_P}\right)$$

$$\$1.50 = P\left(1 + \frac{1}{-4}\right)$$

$$\$1.50 = 0.75P$$

$$P = \$2$$

P5.17   ***Optimal Price.*** *Last month, Rick's Bike Shop, Inc. increased the price on the 24 ounce can of Campynolo bearing grease by 1%. In response, sales dropped by 4%.*

A.   *Calculate the point price elasticity of demand for Campynolo bearing grease.*

B.   *Calculate the optimal price for Campynolo bearing grease if marginal cost is $4.50 per unit.*

Demand Analysis and Estimation

P5.17   SOLUTION

A.

$$\epsilon_P = \frac{\text{Percentage change in quantity}}{\text{Percentage change in price}}$$

$$= \frac{-0.04}{0.01}$$

$$= -4 \text{ (elastic)}$$

B.   The optimal price is found setting MC = MR and solving for P where:

$$MC = MR = P\left(1 + \frac{1}{\epsilon_P}\right)$$

$$4.50 = P\left(1 + \frac{1}{-4}\right)$$

$$4.50 = 0.75P$$

$$P = \$6$$

P5.18   *Elasticity Analysis.* Bloomington's, Inc. is a retailer of distinctive clothing. At the end of the company's fiscal year, you have been asked to evaluate sales of traditional wool suits and classic blazers using the following data:

Month	Number of Suits Sold, Q	Suit Advertising Expenditures A	Suit Price, P	Blazer Price, P_B
July	400	$50,000	$700	$350
August	500	50,000	650	350
September	700	55,000	650	350
October	900	55,000	650	450
November	1,000	65,000	700	450
December	600	65,000	700	350
January	500	60,000	800	350
February	700	60,000	700	350
March	800	60,000	650	300
April	900	63,000	600	300
May	700	57,000	600	300
June	500	57,000	750	300

In particular, you have been asked to estimate relevant demand elasticities. Remember that in order to estimate the required elasticities, you should only consider months when the other important factors considered above have not changed. Note also that by restricting your analysis to consecutive months, changes in any additional factors not explicitly included in the analysis are less likely to affect estimated elasticities. Finally, the average arc elasticity of demand for each factor is simply the average of monthly elasticities calculated over the past year.

A. *Indicate whether there was a change or no change in each respective variable for each month-pair during the past year.*

Month-Pair	Suit Advertising Expentitures, A	Suit Price P	Blazer Price, P_B
July-Aug.			
Aug.-Sept.			
Sept-Oct.			
Oct.-Nov.			
Nov.-Dec.			
Dec.-Jan.			
Jan.-Feb.			
Feb.-March			
March-April			
April-May			
May-June			

B. *Calculate and interpret the average arc advertising elasticity of demand for suits.*

C. *Calculate and interpret the average arc price elasticity of demand for suits.*

D. *Calculate and interpret the average arc cross-price elasticity of demand between suits and blazers.*

Demand Analysis and Estimation 155

P5.18 **SOLUTION**

A.

Month-Pair	Suit Advertising Expentitures, A	Suit Price P	Blazer Price, P_B
July-Aug.	No change.	Change.	No change.
Aug.-Sept.	Change.	No change.	No change.
Sept-Oct.	No change.	No change.	Change.
Oct.-Nov.	Change.	Change.	No change.
Nov.-Dec.	No change.	No change.	Change.
Dec.-Jan.	Change.	Change.	No change.
Jan.-Feb.	No change.	Change.	No change.
Feb.-March	No change.	Change.	Change.
March-April	Change.	Change.	No change.
April-May	Change.	No change.	No change.
May-June	No change.	Change.	No change.

B. In the calculation of the arc advertising elasticity of demand, we only consider consecutive months when there was a change in advertising but no change in the prices of suits and blazers:

$$\underline{\text{Aug.-Sept.}}$$

$$E_A = \frac{\Delta Q}{\Delta A} \times \frac{A_2 + A_1}{Q_2 + Q_1}$$

$$= \frac{700 - 500}{\$55,000 - \$50,000} \times \frac{\$55,000 + \$50,000}{700 + 500}$$

$$= 3.5$$

April-May

$$E_A = \frac{\Delta Q}{\Delta A} \times \frac{A_2 + A_1}{Q_2 + Q_1}$$

$$= \frac{700 - 900}{\$57{,}000 - \$63{,}000} \times \frac{\$57{,}000 + \$63{,}000}{700 + 900}$$

$$= 2.5$$

On average, $E_A = (3.5 + 2.5)/2 = 3$ and demand will rise 3%, with a 1% increase in advertising. Thus, demand appears quite sensitive to advertising.

C. In the calculation of the arc price elasticity of demand we only consider consecutive months when there was a change in the price of suits, but not change in advertising nor the price of blazers:

July-Aug.

$$E_P = \frac{\Delta Q}{\Delta P} \times \frac{P_2 + P_1}{Q_2 + Q_1}$$

$$= \frac{500 - 400}{\$650 - \$700} \times \frac{\$650 + \$700}{500 + 400}$$

$$= -3$$

Jan.-Feb.

$$E_P = \frac{\Delta Q}{\Delta P} \times \frac{P_2 + P_1}{Q_2 + Q_1}$$

$$= \frac{700 - 500}{\$700 - \$800} \times \frac{\$700 + \$800}{700 + 500}$$

$$= -2.5$$

Demand Analysis and Estimation

$$\underline{\text{May-June}}$$

$$E_P = \frac{\Delta Q}{\Delta P} \times \frac{P_2 + P_1}{Q_2 + Q_1}$$

$$= \frac{500 - 700}{\$750 - \$600} \times \frac{\$750 + \$600}{500 + 700}$$

$$= -1.5$$

On average, $E_P = [(-3) + (-2.5) + (-1.5)]/3 = -2.33$. A 1% increase (decrease) in price will head to a 2.33% decrease (increase) in the quantity demanded. The demand for suits is, therefore, elastic with respect to price.

D. In the calculation of the arc cross-price elasticity of demand we only consider consecutive months when there was a change in the price of blazers, but no change in advertising nor the price of suits:

$$\underline{\text{Sept.-Oct.}}$$

$$E_{PX} = \frac{\Delta Q}{\Delta P_X} \times \frac{P_{X2} + P_{X1}}{Q_2 + Q_1}$$

$$= \frac{900 - 700}{\$450 - \$350} \times \frac{\$450 + \$350}{900 + 700}$$

$$= 1$$

$$\underline{\text{Nov.-Dec.}}$$

$$E_{PX} = \frac{\Delta Q}{\Delta P_X} \times \frac{P_{X2} + P_{X1}}{Q_2 + Q_1}$$

$$= \frac{600 - 1{,}000}{\$350 - \$450} \times \frac{\$350 + \$450}{600 + 1{,}000}$$

$$= 2$$

On average, $E_{PX} = (1 + 2)/2 = 1.5$. Since $E_{PX} > 0$, suits and dress blazers are substitutes.

P5.19 **Elasticity Analysis.** Boston's Own, Inc. is a retailer of distinctive men's footwear. At the end of the company's fiscal year, you have been asked to evaluate sales of its traditional business wing-tip and loafer dress shoes using the following data:

Month	Number of Wing-Tips Sold, Q	Wing-Tip Advertising Expenditures, A	Wing-Tips Price, P	Loafer Price, P_I
July	$40,000	$100,000	$100	$70
August	50,000	100,000	90	70
September	60,000	120,000	90	70
October	100,000	120,000	90	90
November	120,000	140,000	100	90
December	80,000	140,000	100	70
January	45,000	125,000	120	70
February	75,000	125,000	100	70
March	85,000	125,000	90	60
April	105,000	130,000	80	60
May	75,000	110,000	80	60
June	45,000	110,000	120	60

In particular, you have been asked to estimate relevant demand elasticities. Remember that in order to estimate the required elasticities, you should only consider months when the other important factors considered above have not changed. Note also that by restricting your analysis to consecutive months, changes in any additional factors not explicitly included in the analysis are less likely to affect estimated elasticities. Finally, the average arc elasticity of demand for each factor is simply the average of monthly elasticities calculated over the past year.

A. Indicate whether there was a change or no change in each respective variable for each month-pair during the past year.

Month-Pair	Wing-Tip Advertising Expenditures, A	Wing-Tip Price P	Loafer Price, P_B
July-Aug.	_____	_____	_____
Aug.-Sept.	_____	_____	_____
Sept-Oct.	_____	_____	_____
Oct.-Nov.	_____	_____	_____
Nov.-Dec.	_____	_____	_____

Demand Analysis and Estimation

Month-Pair	Wing-Tip Advertising Expentitures, A	Wing-Tip Price P	Loafer Price, P_B
Dec.-Jan.	_____	_____	_____
Jan.-Feb.	_____	_____	_____
Feb.-March	_____	_____	_____
March-April	_____	_____	_____
April-May	_____	_____	_____
May-June	_____	_____	_____

B. Calculate and interpret the average arc advertising elasticity of demand for wing-tips.

C. Calculate and interpret the average arc price elasticity of demand for wing-tips.

D. Calculate and interpret the average arc cross-price elasticity of demand between wing-tips and loafers.

P5.19 SOLUTION

A.

Month-Pair	Wing-Tip Advertising Expentitures, A	Wing-Tip Price P	Loafer Price, P_B
July-Aug.	No change.	Change.	No change.
Aug.-Sept.	Change.	No change.	No change.
Sept-Oct.	No change.	No change.	Change.
Oct.-Nov.	Change.	Change.	No change.
Nov.-Dec.	No change.	No change.	Change.
Dec.-Jan.	Change.	Change.	No change.
Jan.-Feb.	No change.	Change.	No change.
Feb.-March	No change.	Change.	Change.
March-April	Change.	Change.	No change.

April-May	Change.	No change.	No change.
May-June	No change.	Change.	No change.

B. In the calculation of the arc advertising elasticity of demand, we only consider consecutive months when there was a change in advertising but no change in the prices of wing-tips and loafers:

Aug.-Sept.

$$E_A = \frac{\Delta Q}{\Delta A} \times \frac{A_2 + A_1}{Q_2 + Q_1}$$

$$= \frac{60,000 - 50,000}{\$120,000 - \$100,000} \times \frac{\$120,000 + \$100,000}{60,000 + 50,000}$$

$$= 1$$

April-May

$$E_A = \frac{\Delta Q}{\Delta A} \times \frac{A_2 + A_1}{Q_2 + Q_1}$$

$$= \frac{75,000 - 105,000}{\$110,000 - \$130,000} \times \frac{\$110,000 + \$130,000}{75,000 + 105,000}$$

$$= 2$$

On average, $E_A = (1 + 2)/2 = 1.5$ and demand will rise 1.5%, with a 1% increase in advertising. Thus, demand appears sensitive to advertising.

C. In the calculation of the arc price elasticity of demand we only consider consecutive months when there was a change in the price of wing-tips, but not change in advertising nor the price of loafers:

Demand Analysis and Estimation

<u>July-Aug.</u>

$$E_P = \frac{\Delta Q}{\Delta P} \times \frac{P_2 + P_1}{Q_2 + Q_1}$$

$$= \frac{50{,}000 - 40{,}000}{\$90 - \$100} \times \frac{\$90 + \$100}{50{,}000 + 40{,}000}$$

$$= -2.5$$

<u>Jan.-Feb.</u>

$$E_P = \frac{\Delta Q}{\Delta P} \times \frac{P_2 + P_1}{Q_2 + Q_1}$$

$$= \frac{75{,}000 - 45{,}000}{\$100 - \$120} \times \frac{\$100 + \$120}{75{,}000 + 45{,}000}$$

$$= -2.75$$

<u>May-June</u>

$$E_P = \frac{\Delta Q}{\Delta P} \times \frac{P_2 + P_1}{Q_2 + Q_1}$$

$$= \frac{45{,}000 - 75{,}000}{\$120 - \$80} \times \frac{\$120 + \$80}{45{,}000 + 75{,}000}$$

$$= -1.25$$

On average, $E_P = [(-2.5) + (-2.75) + (-1.25)]/3 = -2.17$. A 1% increase (decrease) in price will head to a 2.17% decrease (increase) in the quantity demanded. The demand for wing-tips is, therefore, elastic with respect to price.

D. In the calculation of the arc cross-price elasticity of demand we only consider consecutive months when there was a change in the price of loafers, but no change in advertising nor the price of wing-tips:

Sept.-Oct.

$$E_{PX} = \frac{\Delta Q}{\Delta P_X} \times \frac{P_{X2} + P_{X1}}{Q_2 + Q_1}$$

$$= \frac{100{,}000 - 60{,}000}{\$90 - \$70} \times \frac{\$90 + \$70}{100{,}000 + 60{,}000}$$

$$= 2$$

Nov.-Dec.

$$E_{PX} = \frac{\Delta Q}{\Delta P_X} \times \frac{P_{X2} + P_{X1}}{Q_2 + Q_1}$$

$$= \frac{80{,}000 - 120{,}000}{\$70 - \$90} \times \frac{\$70 + \$90}{80{,}000 + 120{,}000}$$

$$= 1.6$$

On average, $E_{PX} = (2 + 1.6)/2 = 1.8$. Since $E_{PX} > 0$, wing-tips and loafers are substitutes.

P5.20 *Income Elasticity.* Deluxe Carpeting, Inc. is a leading manufacturer of stain-resistant carpeting. Demand for Deluxe products is tied to the overall pace of building and remodeling activity and, therefore, is sensitive to changes in national income. The carpet manufacturing industry is highly competitive, so Deluxe's demand is also very price-sensitive.

During the past year, Deluxe sold 28 million square yards (units) of carpeting at an average wholesale price of $16 per unit. This year, GNP per capita is expected to fall from $19,000 to $17,000 as the nation enters a steep recession. Without any price change, Deluxe expects current-year sales to fall to 20 million units.

A. Calculate the implied arc income elasticity of demand.

B. Given the projected fall in income, the sales manager believes that current volume of 28 million units could only be maintained with a price cut of $2 per unit. On this basis, calculate the implied arc price elasticity of demand.

C. Holding all else equal, would a further increase in price result in higher or lower total revenue?

Demand Analysis and Estimation 163

P5.20 **SOLUTION**

A.

$$E_I = \frac{\Delta Q}{\Delta I} \times \frac{I_2 + I_1}{Q_2 + Q_1}$$

$$= \frac{20 - 28}{\$17{,}000 - \$19{,}000} \times \frac{\$17{,}000 + \$19{,}000}{20 + 28}$$

$$= 3$$

B. Without a price decrease, sales this year would total 20 million units. Therefore, it is appropriate to estimate the arc price elasticity from a (before-price-decrease) base of 20 million units:

$$E_P = \frac{\Delta Q}{\Delta P} \times \frac{P_2 + P_1}{Q_2 + Q_1}$$

$$= \frac{28 - 20}{\$14 - \$16} \times \frac{\$14 + \$16}{28 + 20}$$

$$= -2.5 \text{ (elastic)}$$

C. Lower. Since carpet demand is in the elastic range, $E_P = -2.5$, an increase (decrease) in price will result in lower (higher) total revenues.

P5.21 **Income Elasticity.** *Compact, Inc. is a leading manufacturer of powerful personal computers. Demand for Compact computers is tied to the overall pace of the business sales and, therefore, is sensitive to changes in national income. The personal business computer industry is highly competitive, so Compact's demand is also very price-sensitive.*

During the past year, Compact sold 550,000 personal computers at an average wholesale price of $4,000 per unit. This year, GNP per capita is expected to fall from $21,000 to $19,000 as the nation enters a steep recession. Without any price change, Compact expects current-year sales to fall to 450,000 units.

A. *Calculate the implied arc income elasticity of demand.*

B. *Given the projected fall in income, the sales manager believes that current volume of 550,000 units could only be maintained with a price cut of $500 per unit. On this basis, calculate the implied arc price elasticity of demand.*

C. *Holding all else equal, would a further increase in price result in higher or lower total revenue?*

P5.21 **SOLUTION**

A.
$$E_I = \frac{\Delta Q}{\Delta I} \times \frac{I_2 + I_1}{Q_2 + Q_1}$$

$$= \frac{450{,}000 - 550{,}000}{\$19{,}000 - \$21{,}000} \times \frac{\$19{,}000 + \$21{,}000}{450{,}000 + 550{,}000}$$

$$= 2$$

B. Without a price decrease, sales this year would total 450,000 units. Therefore, it is appropriate to estimate the arc price elasticity from a (before-price-decrease) base of 450,000 units:

$$E_P = \frac{\Delta Q}{\Delta P} \times \frac{P_2 + P_1}{Q_2 + Q_1}$$

$$= \frac{550{,}000 - 450{,}000}{\$3{,}500 - \$4{,}000} \times \frac{\$3{,}500 + \$4{,}000}{450{,}000 + 550{,}000}$$

$$= -1.5 \text{ (elastic)}$$

C. Lower. Since personal computer demand is in the elastic range, $E_P = -1.5$, an increase (decrease) in price will result in lower (higher) total revenues.

P5.22 *Metalic Pads (MP), Inc. is a leading manufacturer of automotive brake shoes. Demand for MP's products is tied to the overall pace of new car sales and, therefore, is sensitive to changes in national income. The OEM industry is highly competitive in brake products, so MP's demand is also very price-sensitive.*

During the past year, MP sold 150,000 pairs of brake shoes at an average wholesale price of $13 per pair. This year, GNP per capita is expected to fall from $21,000 to $19,000 as the nation enters a steep recession. Without any price change, MP expects current-year sales to fall to 100,000 units.

A. *Calculate the implied arc income elasticity of demand.*

Demand Analysis and Estimation

B. Given the projected fall in income, the sales manager believes that current volume of 150,000 units could only be maintained with a price cut of $1 per unit. On this basis, calculate the implied arc price elasticity of demand.

C. Holding all else equal, would a further increase in price result in higher or lower total revenue?

P5.22 SOLUTION

A.
$$E_I = \frac{\Delta Q}{\Delta I} \times \frac{I_2 + I_1}{Q_2 + Q_1}$$

$$= \frac{100{,}000 - 150{,}000}{\$19{,}000 - \$21{,}000} \times \frac{\$19{,}000 + \$21{,}000}{100{,}000 + 150{,}000}$$

$$= 4$$

B. Without a price decrease, sales this year would total 100,000 units. Therefore, it is appropriate to estimate the arc price elasticity from a (before-price-decrease) base of 100,000 units:

$$E_P = \frac{\Delta Q}{\Delta P} \times \frac{P_2 + P_1}{Q_2 + Q_1}$$

$$= \frac{150{,}000 - 100{,}000}{\$12 - \$13} \times \frac{\$12 + \$13}{100{,}000 + 150{,}000}$$

$$= -5 \text{ (elastic)}$$

C. Lower. Since brake shoe demand is in the elastic range, $E_P = -5$, an increase (decrease) in price will result in lower (higher) total revenues.

P5.23 Income Elasticity. *Interior Landscapes, Inc. is a leading distributor of potted plants and their maintenance for business environments. Demand for Interior's services is tied to the overall pace of business activity and, therefore, is sensitive to changes in national income. The greenery service sector is highly competitive, so Interior's demand is also very price-sensitive.*

During the past year, Interior's sold 10,500 potted plants at an average wholesale price of $25 per plant. This year, GNP per capita is expected to fall from $19,000 to

$17,000 as the nation enters a steep recession. Without any price change, Interior's expects current-year sales to fall to 7,500 potted plants.

A. Calculate the implied arc income elasticity of demand.

B. Given the projected fall in income, the sales manager believes that current volume of 10,500 plants could only be maintained with a price cut of $5 per unit. On this basis, calculate the implied arc price elasticity of demand.

C. Holding all else equal, would a further increase in price result in higher or lower total revenue?

P5.23 **SOLUTION**

A.

$$E_I = \frac{\Delta Q}{\Delta I} \times \frac{I_2 + I_1}{Q_2 + Q_1}$$

$$= \frac{7,500 - 10,500}{\$17,000 - \$19,000} \times \frac{\$17,000 + \$19,000}{7,500 + 10,500}$$

$$= 3$$

B. Without a price decrease, sales this year would total 7,500 plants. Therefore, it is appropriate to estimate the arc price elasticity from a (before-price-decrease) base of 7,500 plants:

$$E_P = \frac{\Delta Q}{\Delta P} \times \frac{P_2 + P_1}{Q_2 + Q_1}$$

$$= \frac{10,500 - 7,500}{\$20 - \$25} \times \frac{\$20 + \$25}{7,500 + 10,500}$$

$$= -1.5 \text{ (elastic)}$$

C. Lower. Since potted plant demand is in the elastic range, $E_P = -1.5$, an increase (decrease) in price will result in lower (higher) total revenues.

P5.24 **Price Elasticity.** Z-Best Pizza recently decided to raise its regular price on large pizzas from $9 to $12 following increases in the costs of labor and materials. Unfortunately, sales dropped sharply from 8,100 to 4,500 pizzas per month. In an effort to regain lost

Demand Analysis and Estimation

sales, Z-Best ran a coupon promotion featuring $5 off the new regular price. Coupon printing and distribution costs totaled $100, and caused only a modest increase in the typical advertising budget of $2,400 per month. The promotion was judged a success as it proved highly popular with consumers. In the period prior to expiration, coupons were used on 40% of all purchases and monthly sales rose to 7,500 pizzas.

A. Calculate the arc price elasticity implied by the initial response to Z-Best's price increase.

B. Calculate the effective price reduction resulting from the coupon promotion.

C. In light of this price reduction, and assuming no change in the price elasticity of demand, calculate Z-Best's arc advertising elasticity.

D. Why might the true arc advertising elasticity differ from that calculated in Part C?

P5.24 SOLUTION

A.

$$E_P = \frac{\Delta Q}{\Delta P} \times \frac{P_2 + P_1}{Q_2 + Q_1}$$

$$= \frac{4{,}500 - 8{,}100}{\$12 - \$9} \times \frac{\$12 + \$9}{4{,}500 + 8{,}100} = -2$$

B. The effective price reduction is $2, since when X percent of sales are accompanied by a coupon:

$$\Delta P = -\$5(0.4)$$

$$= -\$2$$

or

$$P_2 = \$12 - \$5X$$

$$= \$12 - \$5(0.4)$$

$$= \$10$$

$$\Delta P = \$10 - \$12$$

$$= -\$2$$

C. In order to calculate the arc advertising elasticity, the effect of the $2 price cut implicit in the coupon promotion must first be reflected. With just a price cut, the quantity demanded would rise to 6,500, since:

$$E_P = \frac{Q_* - Q_1}{P_2 - P_1} \times \frac{P_2 + P_1}{Q_* + Q_1}$$

$$-2 = \frac{Q_* - 4{,}500}{\$10 - \$12} \times \frac{\$10 + \$12}{Q_* + 4{,}500}$$

$$-2 = \frac{-11(Q_* - 4{,}500)}{(Q_* + 4{,}500)}$$

$$-2(Q^* + 4{,}500) = -11(Q^* - 4{,}500)$$

$$-2Q^* - 9{,}000 = -11Q^* + 49{,}500$$

$$9Q^* = 58{,}500$$

$$Q^* = 6{,}500$$

Then, the arc advertising elasticity can be calculated as:

$$E_A = \frac{Q_2 - Q_*}{A_2 - A_1} \times \frac{A_2 + A_1}{Q_2 + Q_*}$$

$$= \frac{7{,}500 - 6{,}500}{\$2{,}500 - \$2{,}400} \times \frac{\$2{,}500 + \$2{,}400}{7{,}500 + 6{,}500}$$

$$= 3.5$$

D. It is important to recognize that a coupon promotion can involve more than just the independent effects of a price cut plus advertising as is implied in part C. Synergistic or interactive effects may increase advertising effectiveness when the promotion is accompanied by a price cut. Similarly, price reductions can have a much larger impact when advertised. In addition, a coupon is a price cut for only the most price sensitive (coupon-using) customers, and may spur sales by much more than a dollar equivalent across-the-board price cut.

Synergy between advertising and the implicit price reduction which accompanies a coupon promotion can cause the estimate in part C to overstate the true advertising elasticity. Similarly, this advertising elasticity will be overstated to the extent that targeted price cuts have a bigger influence on the quantity demanded than similar across-the-board price reductions (as seems likely).

P5.25 *Price and Advertising Elasticity.* EZ Auto Wash recently decided to raise its regular price on wash and wax cycles from $5 to $7 following increases in the costs of equipment and materials. Unfortunately, sales dropped sharply from 6,000 to 2,000 washes per month. In an effort to regain lost sales, EZ ran a coupon promotion featuring $4 off the new regular price. Coupon printing and distribution costs totaled $100, and caused only a modest increase in the typical advertising budget of $1,650 per month. The promotion was judged a success as it proved highly popular with consumers. In the period prior to expiration, coupons were used on 25% of all purchases and monthly sales rose to 3,600 washes.

A. Calculate the arc price elasticity implied by the initial response to EZ's price increase.

B. Calculate the effective price reduction resulting from the coupon promotion.

C. In light of this price reduction, and assuming no change in the price elasticity of demand, calculate EZ's arc advertising elasticity.

D. Why might the true arc advertising elasticity differ from that calculated in Part C?

170   *Chapter 5*

P5.25   **SOLUTION**

        A.

$$E_P = \frac{\Delta Q}{\Delta P} \times \frac{P_2 + P_1}{Q_2 + Q_1}$$

$$= \frac{2{,}000 - 6{,}000}{\$7 - \$5} \times \frac{\$7 + \$5}{2{,}000 + 6{,}000}$$

$$= -3$$

        B.   The effective price reduction is $1, since when X percent of sales are accompanied by a coupon:

$$\Delta P = -\$4(0.25)$$
$$= -\$1$$

            or

$$P_2 = \$7 - \$4X$$
$$= \$7 - \$4(0.25)$$
$$= \$6$$
$$\Delta P = \$6 - \$7$$
$$= -\$1$$

        C.   To calculate the arc advertising elasticity, the effect of the $1 price cut implicit in the coupon promotion must first be reflected. With just a price cut, the quantity demanded would rise to 3,200, since:

Demand Analysis and Estimation

$$E_P = \frac{Q_* - Q_1}{P_2 - P_1} \times \frac{P_2 + P_1}{Q_* + Q_1}$$

$$-3 = \frac{Q_* - 2{,}000}{\$6 - \$7} \times \frac{\$6 + \$7}{Q_* + 2{,}000}$$

$$-3 = \frac{-13(Q_* - 2{,}000)}{(Q_* + 2{,}000)}$$

$$-3(Q_* + 2{,}000) = -13(Q_* - 2{,}000)$$

$$-3Q_* - 6{,}000 = -13Q_* + 26{,}000$$

$$10Q_* = 32{,}000$$

$$Q_* = 3{,}200$$

Then, the arc advertising elasticity can be calculated as:

$$E_A = \frac{Q_2 - Q_*}{A_2 - A_1} \times \frac{A_2 + A_1}{Q_2 + Q_*}$$

$$= \frac{3{,}600 - 3{,}200}{\$1{,}750 - \$1{,}650} \times \frac{\$1{,}750 + \$1{,}650}{3{,}600 + 3{,}200}$$

$$= 2$$

D. It is important to recognize that a coupon promotion can involve more than just the independent effects of a price cut plus advertising as is implied in Part C. Synergistic or interactive effects may increase advertising effectiveness when the promotion is accompanied by a price cut. Similarly, price reductions can have a much larger impact when advertised. In addition, a coupon is a price cut for only the most price sensitive (coupon-using) customers, and may spur sales by much more than a dollar equivalent across-the-board price cut.

Synergy between advertising and the implicit price reduction which accompanies a coupon promotion can cause the estimate in part C to overstate the true advertising elasticity. Similarly, this advertising elasticity will be overstated to the extent that targeted price cuts have a bigger influence on the quantity demanded than similar across-the-board price reductions (as seems likely).

Chapter 6

FORECASTING

MULTIPLE CHOICE QUESTIONS

Q6.1 *A panel consensus formed by providing feedback without direct identification of individual positions is called:*

    A. panel consensus.
    B. qualitative analysis.
> C. the Delphi method.
    D. personal insight.

Q6.2 *Unpredictable shocks to the economic system are called:*

> A. random influences.
    B. examples of seasonality.
    C. cyclical fluctuations.
    D. trend reversals.

Q6.3 *A leading economic indicator of business cycle peaks is given by:*

    A. the average duration of unemployment.
    B. the change in prices for consumer services.
    C. personal income minus transfer payments.
> D. an index of stock prices for 500 stocks.

Q6.4 *Qualitative methods and market experiments work best for forecasting product:*

> A. introduction or start-up.
    B. rapid growth.
    C. maturity.
    D. decline and abandonment.

Q6.5 *Economic relations that are hypothesized to be true are called:*

> A. behavioral equations.
    B. identities.
    C. statistical equations.
    D. statistical identities.

Forecasting

Q6.6   A forecast method based on the informed opinion of several individuals is called:

>
    A. personal insight.
    B. panel consensus.
    C. the Delphi method.
    D. qualitative analysis.

Q6.7   A rhythmic annual pattern in sales or profits is called:

    A. cyclical fluctuation.
    B. secular trend.
    C. trend analysis.
>
    D. seasonal variation.

Q6.8   Growth trend analysis assumes:

    A. constant unit change over time.
    B. irregular percentage change over time.
    C. sporadic unit change over time.
>
    D. constant percentage change over time.

Q6.9   Economic relations that are true by definition are called:

    A. behavioral equations.
    B. statistical models.
    C. econometric relations.
>
    D. identities.

Q6.10   Lagging economic indicators include:

    A. personal income.
    B. the change in stock prices.
    C. orders for new plant and equipment.
>
    D. the average duration of unemployment.

Q6.11 The delphi method:

    A. employs interaction among experts in the hope that resulting forecasts embody all available objective and subjective information.
    B. can be influenced by the forceful personality of one or a few key experts.
>   C. employs an independent party to elicit a consensus opinion.
    D. assumes that several experts arrive at forecasts that are inferior to those that individuals generate.

Q6.12 A secular trend is the:

    A. annual pattern in sales or profits caused by weather, habit, or social custom.
    B. predictable shock to the pace of economic activity caused by wars, strikes, natural catastrophes, and so on.
>   C. long-run pattern of increase or decrease in a series of economic data.
    D. rhythmic variation in economic series that is due to expansion or contraction in the overall economy.

Q6.13 Linear trend analysis assumes:

>   A. constant unit change in an important economic variable over time.
    B. arithmetic dollar growth.
    C. geometric dollar growth.
    D. constant percentage change in an important economic variable over time.

Q6.14 The forecasting technique least-suited for short term projection is:

    A. survey analysis.
    B. barometric analysis.
    C. time-series analysis of seasonal variations.
>   D. input-output analysis.

Q6.15 The forecasting method that can be used when market data unavailable is:

    A. time-series analysis.
    B. regression analysis.
    C. input-output analysis.
>   D. qualitative analysis.

Forecasting

Q6.16 Which of the following forecasting methods is not qualitative?

- A. survey techniques.
- > B. barometric method.
- C. expert opinion.
- D. delphi method.

Q6.17 Time-series methods:

- > A. use historical data as the basis for projection.
- B. combine economic theory with mathematical and statistical tools to analyze economic relations.
- C. use interindustry linkages to show how changes in the demand for one industry's output will effect all sectors of the economy.
- D. are based on opinion.

Q6.18 If an economic time series is growing by a constant dollar amount each period, the most accurate forecast model is:

- A. a constant rate of growth model.
- B. an exponential growth model.
- > C. a linear model.
- D. log-linear model.

Q6.19 Social habits that produce an annual pattern in a time series result in:

- A. cyclical fluctuation.
- > B. seasonal variation.
- C. irregular or random influences.
- D. secular trend.

Q6.20 Which of the following is a leading economic indicator?

- A. average prime rate charged by banks.
- B. commercial and industrial loans outstanding.
- > C. change in credit for business and consumer borrowing.
- D. ratio of constant dollar inventories to sales for manufacture and trade.

Q6.21 *Barometric methods that employ leading economic indicators:*

- A. often provide relatively consistent lead times.
- > B. provide little information about the magnitude of the forecast variable.
- C. usually forecast directional changes with 95% accuracy.
- D. always correctly indicate changes in economic variables.

Q6.22 *Econometric methods:*

- > A. combine economic theory with mathematical and statistical tools to analyze economic relations.
- B. project the direction, but not the magnitude of, changes in the variable of interest.
- C. rely solely on historical data as the basis for projection.
- D. use nonmarket data to project the effects of changes in economic variables.

Q6.23 *A diffusion index that registers 40% indicates that:*

- A. leading indicators on average have fallen by 60%.
- B. 40% of the leading indicators have fallen.
- > C. 60% of the leading indicators have fallen.
- D. all leading indicators have risen by 40%.

Q6.24 *Econometric forecasting methods:*

- > A. require explicit assumptions about the relations among economic variables.
- B. can estimate the direction, but not the magnitude, of change for forecasted variables.
- C. can estimate the magnitude, but not the direction, of change for forecasted variables.
- D. always remain the same from period to period.

Q6.25 *The accuracy of an econometric forecast would be most questionable when the:*

- A. stochastic error term is small and randomly distributed.
- B. stochastic error term is large and randomly distributed.
- > C. stochastic error term is large and not randomly distributed.
- D. expected value of the stochastic error term equals zero.

Forecasting

Q6.26　*A dependent variable is also:*

　　A.　an extraneous variable.
　　B.　an exogenous variable.
　　C.　a stochastic variable.
> 　D.　an endogenous variable.

Q6.27　*To predict the effects on a particular industry of changes in other sectors of the economy forecasters should employ:*

　　A.　time series analysis.
> 　B.　input-output analysis.
　　C.　barometric methods.
　　D.　steamroller techniques.

Q6.28　*Which of the following does not indicate the relative accuracy of an economic forecast?*

> 　A.　composite index.
　　B.　sample mean forecast error.
　　C.　stochastic error term.
　　D.　simple correlation coefficient.

Q6.29　*A 5% growth trend with annual compounding:*

　　A.　is a direct estimate of the continuous rate of growth.
> 　B.　will result in lower final-period sales than would a 5% growth trend with continuous compounding.
　　C.　will result in greater final-period sales than would a 5% growth trend with continuous compounding.
　　D.　implies constant period-by-period unit change in an important economic variable over time.

Q6.30　*A roughly coincident indicator of business cycle peaks is given by:*

　　A.　new orders for consumer goods and materials.
　　B.　the rate of change in sensitive materials prices.
　　C.　the rate of change in stock prices.
> 　D.　personal income minus transfer payments.

PROBLEMS & SOLUTIONS

P6.1 ***Annual Compounding.*** *The following table shows annual sales data for Nanotechnology, Inc. over the ten-year 1982-92 period:*

Year	Sales ($ Millions)
1982	$1.0
1983	1.1
1984	1.2
1985	1.2
1986	1.3
1987	1.4
1988	1.5
1989	1.9
1990	2.0
1991	2.5
1992	2.6

A. *Calculate the 1982-92 growth rate in sales using the constant rate of change model with annual compounding.*

B. *Forecast sales for the years 1997 and 2002.*

P6.1 SOLUTION

A.
$$S_t = S_0(1+g)^t$$

$$\$2{,}600{,}000 = \$1{,}000{,}000\,(1+g)^{10}$$

$$2{,}600{,}000/1{,}000{,}000 = (1+g)^{10}$$

$$2.6 = (1+g)^{10}$$

$$\ln(2.6) = 10 \cdot \ln(1+g)$$

$$0.956/10 = \ln(1+g)$$

Forecasting

$$e^{(0.0956)} - 1 = g$$

$$g = 0.100 \text{ or } 10.0\%$$

B. 5-year Sales Forecast

$$S_t = S_0 (1 + g)^t$$

$$= \$2.6 (1 + 0.10)^5$$

$$= \$2.6 (1.611)$$

$$= \$4.2 + u \text{ million}$$

10-year Sales Forecast

$$S_t = S_0 (1 + g)^t$$

$$= \$2.6 (1 + 0.10)^{10}$$

$$= \$2.6 (2.594)$$

$$= \$6.7 + u \text{ million}$$

P6.2 *Annual Compounding.* *The following table shows annual sales data for Landrover, Inc. over the ten-year 1982-92 period:*

Year	Sales ($ Millions)
1982	$ 4.0
1983	4.8
1984	5.6
1985	6.4
1986	7.0
1987	7.6
1988	8.4
1989	9.2
1990	10.2

Year	Sales ($ Millions)
1991	11.2
1992	12.4

A. Calculate the 1982-92 growth rate in sales using the constant rate of change model with annual compounding.

B. Calculate 5-year and 10-year sales forecasts.

P6.2 SOLUTION

A.
$$S_t = S_0(1+g)^t$$

$$\$12{,}400{,}000 = 4{,}000{,}000(1+g)^{10}$$

$$12{,}400{,}000 / 4{,}000{,}000 = (1+g)^{10}$$

$$3.1 = (1+g)^{10}$$

$$\ln(3.1) = 10 \cdot \ln(1+g)$$

$$1.131/10 = \ln(1+g)$$

$$e^{(0.1131)} - 1 = g$$

$$g = 0.12 \text{ or } 12\%$$

B. <u>5-year Sales Forecast</u>

$$S_t = S_0(1+g)^t$$

$$= \$12.4(1+0.12)^5$$

$$= \$12.4(1.762)$$

$$= \$21.9 + u \text{ million}$$

Forecasting

10-year Sales Forecast

$$S_t = S_0 (1 + g)^t$$

$$= \$12.4 (1 + 0.12)^{10}$$

$$= \$12.4 (3.106)$$

$$= \$38.5 + u \text{ million}$$

P6.3 **Annual Compounding.** *The following table shows annual sales data for Stuff Happens, Inc. over the ten-year 1982-92 period:*

Year	Sales ($ Millions)
1982	$2.0
1983	2.2
1984	2.4
1985	2.6
1986	2.8
1987	3.0
1988	3.2
1989	3.5
1990	3.8
1991	4.1
1992	4.3

A. *Calculate the 1982-92 growth rate in sales using the constant rate of change model with annual compounding.*

B. *Forecast sales for the years 1995 and 2000.*

P6.3 **SOLUTION**

A.
$$S_t = S_0 (1 + g)^t$$

$$\$4,300,000 = 2,000,000 (1 + g)^{10}$$

$$4{,}300{,}000/2{,}000{,}000 = (1+g)^{10}$$

$$2.15 = (1+g)^{10}$$

$$\ln(2.15) = 10 \cdot \ln(1+g)$$

$$0.765/10 = \ln(1+g)$$

$$e^{(0.0765)} - 1 = g$$

$$g = 0.08 \text{ or } 8\%$$

B. <u>1995 Sales Forecast</u>

$$S_t = S_0 (1+g)^t$$

$$= \$4.3 (1 + 0.08)^3$$

$$= \$4.3 (1.300)$$

$$= \$5.4 + u \text{ million}$$

<u>2000 Sales Forecast</u>

$$S_t = S_0 (1+g)^t$$

$$= \$4.3 (1 + 0.08)^8$$

$$= \$4.3 (1.851)$$

$$= \$8.0 + u \text{ million}$$

P6.4 ***Annual Compounding.*** *The following table shows annual sales data for Security Watch, Inc. over the ten-year 1982-92 period:*

Year	Sales ($ Thousands)
1982	$100
1983	150
1984	200

Forecasting

Year	Sales ($ Thousands)
1985	220
1986	280
1987	360
1988	480
1989	500
1990	540
1991	580
1992	620

A. *Calculate the 1982-92 growth rate in sales using the constant rate of change model with annual compounding.*

B. *Forecast sales for the years 1995 and 2000.*

P6.4   **SOLUTION**

A.
$$S_t = S_0 (1 + g)^t$$

$$\$620 = \$100 (1 + g)^{10}$$

$$620/100 = (1 + g)^{10}$$

$$6.2 = (1 + g)^{10}$$

$$\ln(6.2) = 10 \cdot \ln(1 + g)$$

$$1.824/10 = \ln(1 + g)$$

$$e^{(0.1824)} - 1 = g$$

$$g = 0.2 \text{ or } 20\%$$

B. 1995 Sales Forecast

$$S_t = S_0(1+g)^t$$

$$= \$620(1+0.2)^3$$

$$= \$620(1.728)$$

$$= \$1{,}071.4 + u \text{ thousand}$$

2000 Sales Forecast

$$S_t = S_0(1+g)^t$$

$$= \$620(1+0.2)^8$$

$$= \$620(4.300)$$

$$= \$2{,}665.9 + u \text{ thousand}$$

P6.5 **Continuous Compounding.** *Nicholas Nickelby, a quality control supervisor for Vinyl Windows, Inc. is concerned about an increase in distribution costs per unit from $10 to $13.80 over the last four years. Nickelby feels that setting up a new direct-sales distribution network at a cost of $17.50 per unit may soon be desirable.*

A. *Calculate the unit cost growth rate using the constant rate of change model with continuous compounding.*

B. *Forecast when unit distribution costs will exceed the current cost of direct-sales distribution.*

P6.5 **SOLUTION**

A.

$$C_t = C_0 e^{gt}$$

$$\$13.80 = \$10 e^{4g}$$

$$13.80/10 = e^{4g}$$

$$1.38 = e^{4g}$$

Forecasting

$$\ln(1.38) = 4g$$
$$g = 0.32/4$$
$$= 0.08 \text{ or } 8\%$$

B.
$$\text{Direct-sales cost} = C_0 e^{gt}$$
$$\$17.50 = \$13.80 e^{(0.08)t}$$
$$17.5/13.8 = e^{(0.08)t}$$
$$1.27 = e^{(0.08)t}$$
$$\ln(1.27) = 0.08t$$
$$t = 0.24/0.08$$
$$= 3 + u \text{ years}$$

P6.6 *Continuous Compounding.* Jack Lawless, a quality control supervisor for Fireball Inserts, Inc. is concerned about an increase in distribution costs per fireplace insert from $40 to $50 over the last five years. Lawless feels that setting up a new direct-sales distribution network at a cost of $58.50 per unit may soon be desirable.

A. Calculate the unit cost growth rate using the constant rate of change model with continuous compounding.

B. Forecast when unit distribution costs will exceed the current cost of direct-sales distribution.

P6.6 SOLUTION

A.
$$C_t = C_0 e^{gt}$$
$$\$50 = \$40 e^{5g}$$
$$50/40 = e^{5g}$$
$$1.25 = e^{5g}$$

$$\ln(1.25) = 5g$$

$$g = 0.22/5$$

$$= 0.04 \text{ or } 4\%$$

B.   Direct-sales cost $= C_0 e^{gt}$

$$\$58.50 = \$50 e^{(0.04)t}$$

$$58.5/50 = e^{(0.04)t}$$

$$1.17 = e^{(0.04)t}$$

$$\ln(1.17) = 0.04t$$

$$t = 0.16/0.04$$

$$= 4 + u \text{ years}$$

P6.7 **Continuous Compounding.** *Tammy Baker, a quality control supervisor for The Armoire Store, Inc. is concerned about an increase in distribution costs per unit from $24.50 to $25 over the last four years. Baker feels that setting up a new direct-sales distribution network at a cost of $27.50 per unit may soon be desirable.*

   A.   Calculate the unit cost growth rate using the constant rate of change model with continuous compounding.

   B.   Forecast when unit distribution costs will exceed the current cost of direct-sales distribution.

P6.7 **SOLUTION**

A.
$$C_t = C_0 e^{gt}$$

$$\$25 = \$24.50 e^{4g}$$

$$25/24.50 = e^{4g}$$

$$1.02 = e^{4g}$$

Forecasting

$$\ln(1.02) = 4g$$
$$g = 0.20/4$$
$$= 0.05 \text{ or } 5\%$$

B.   Direct-sales cost $= C_0 e^{gt}$

$$\$27.50 = \$25 e^{(0.05)t}$$
$$27.5/25 = e^{(0.05)t}$$
$$1.10 = e^{(0.05)t}$$
$$\ln(1.10) = 0.05t$$
$$t = 0.10/0.05$$
$$= 2 + u \text{ years}$$

P6.8   **Continuous Compounding.** *Tom Snyder, a quality control supervisor for California Cotton, Inc. is concerned about an increase in distribution costs per unit from $3 to $3.27 over the last three years. Snyder feels that setting up a new direct-sales distribution network at a cost of $3.56 per unit may soon be desirable.*

A.   *Calculate the unit cost growth rate using the constant rate of change model with continuous compounding.*

B.   *Forecast when unit distribution costs will exceed the current cost of direct-sales distribution.*

P6.8   **SOLUTION**

A. $C_t = C_0 e^{gt}$

$$\$3.27 = \$3 e^{3g}$$
$$3.27/3 = e^{3g}$$
$$1.09 = e^{3g}$$

$$\ln(1.09) = 3g$$

$$g = 0.09/3$$

$$= 0.03 \text{ or } 3\%$$

B. Direct-sales cost $= C_0 e^{gt}$

$$\$3.56 = \$3.27 e^{(0.03)t}$$

$$3.56/3.27 = e^{(0.03)t}$$

$$1.09 = e^{(0.03)t}$$

$$\ln(1.09) = 0.03t$$

$$t = 0.09/0.03$$

$$= 3 + u \text{ years}$$

P6.9 **Sales Forecast Modeling.** The change in the quantity of Product A demanded in any given week is inversely proportional to the change in sales of Product B in the previous week. That is, if sales of B rose by X percent last week, sales of A can be expected to fall by X percent this week.

A. Write the equation for next week's sales of A, using the symbols A = sales of Produce A, B = sales of Product B, and t = time. Assume there will be no shortages of either product.

B. Last week 500 units of A and 250 units of B were sold. Two weeks ago, 200 units of Product B were sold. What would you predict the sales of A to be this week?

P6.9 **SOLUTION**

A. $$A_t = A_{t-1} + \Delta A_{t-1} + u$$

$$A_t = A_{t-1} - \left(\frac{B_{t-1}}{B_{t-2}} - 1\right) A_{t-1} + u.$$

B. For A_t find:

Forecasting

$$A_t = A_{t-1} - \left(\frac{B_{t-1}}{B_{t-2}} - 1\right) A_{t-1} + u$$

$$= 500 - \left(\frac{250}{200} - 1\right) 500 + u$$

$$= 500 - 125 + u$$

$$= 375 + u.$$

P6.10 ***Sales Forecast Modeling.*** *The change in the quantity of MCI service demanded in any given week is inversely proportional to the change in sales by UniBel in the previous week. That is, if sales of UniBel rose by X percent last week, sales of MCI can be expected to fall by 0.5X percent this week.*

- **A.** *Write the equation for next week's sales of MCI, using the symbols MCI = sales of UB = UniBel sales, and t = time. Assume there will be no shortages of either product.*

- **B.** *Last week 200 units of MCI and 450 units of UB were sold. Two weeks ago, 300 units of UB were sold. What would you predict the sales of MCI to be this week?*

P6.10 **SOLUTION**

- **A.** $$MCI_t = MCI_{t-1} + \Delta MCI_{t-1} + u$$

$$MCI_t = MCI_{t-1} - 0.5\left(\frac{UB_{t-1}}{UB_{t-2}} - 1\right) MCI_{t-1} + u.$$

- **B.** For MCI_t find:

$$MCI_t = MCI_{t-1} - 0.5\left(\frac{UB_{t-1}}{UB_{t-2}} - 1\right) MCI_{t-1} + u$$

$$= 200 - 50 + u$$

$$= 150 + u.$$

P6.11 **Sales Forecast Modeling.** The change in the quantity of Cheez Sticks demanded in any given week is inversely proportional to the change in sales of Pretzel Q's in the previous week. That is, if sales of Pretzel Q's fell by X percent last week, sales of Cheez Sticks can be expected to rise by 2X percent this week.

A. Write the equation for next week's sales of Cheez Sticks, using the symbols C = sales of Cheez Sticks, Q = sales of Pretzel Q's, and t = time. Assume there will be no shortages of either product.

B. Last week 600 units of C and 350 units of Q were sold. Two weeks ago, 400 units of Product Q were sold. What would you predict the sales of C to be this week?

P6.11 SOLUTION

A. $$C_t = C_{t-1} + \Delta C_{t-1} + u$$

$$C_t = C_{t-1} - 2\left(\frac{Q_{t-1}}{Q_{t-2}} - 1\right) C_{t-1} + u.$$

B. For C_t find:

$$C_t = C_{t-1} - 2\left(\frac{Q_{t-1}}{Q_{t-2}} - 1\right) C_{t-1} + u.$$

$$= 600 + 150 + u$$

$$= 750 + u.$$

P6.12 **Sales Forecast Modeling.** The change in the quantity of Product C demanded in any given week is inversely proportional to the change in sales of Product D in the previous week. That is, if sales of D rose by X percent last week, sales of C can be expected to fall by X percent this week.

A. Write the equation for next week's sales of C, using the symbols C = sales of Product C, D = sales of Product D, and t = time. Assume there will be no shortages of either product.

B. Last week 750 units of C and 600 units of D were sold. Two weeks ago, 500 units of Product D were sold. What would you predict the sales of C to be this week?

Forecasting

P6.12   **SOLUTION**

A. $C_t = C_{t-1} + \Delta C_{t-1} + u$

$C_t = C_{t-1} - \left(\dfrac{D_{t-1}}{D_{t-2}} - 1\right) C_{t-1} + u.$

B.   For A_t find:

$C_t = C_{t-1} - \left(\dfrac{D_{t-1}}{D_{t-2}} - 1\right) C_{t-1} + u.$

$= 750 - \left(\dfrac{600}{500} - 1\right) 750 + u$

$= 750 - 150 + u$

$= 600 + u.$

P6.13   ***Sales Forecast Modeling.*** *Fashion Plate, Ltd., would like to generate a sales forecast based on the assumption that next year sales are a function of current income, advertising, and advertising by a competing retailer:*

A.   *Write an equation for predicting sales based on the assumption that the percentage change in sales is twice as large as the percentage change in income and advertising; but only one-half as large as, and of the opposite sign of, the percentage change in competitor advertising. Use the symbols S = sales, Y = income, A = advertising, and CA = competitor advertising.*

B.   *During the current year, sales total $500,000, income is $18,900 per capita, advertising is $50,000, and competitor advertising is $100,000. Previous period levels were $18,000 (income), $40,000 (advertising), and $125,000 (competitor advertising). Forecast next year sales.*

P6.13 SOLUTION

A.

$$S_{t+1} = S_t + 2\left(\frac{Y_t}{Y_{t-1}} - 1\right)S_t + 2\left(\frac{A_t}{A_{t-1}} - 1\right)S_t$$

$$- 0.5\left(\frac{CA_t}{CA_{t-1}} - 1\right)S_t + u$$

$$= S_t + 2S_t\left(\frac{Y_t}{Y_{t-1}}\right) - 2S_t + 2S_t\left(\frac{A_t}{A_{t-1}}\right) - 2S_t$$

$$- 0.5S_t\left(\frac{CA_t}{CA_{t-1}}\right) + 0.5S_t + u$$

$$= 2S_t\left(\frac{Y_t}{Y_{t-1}}\right) + 2S_t\left(\frac{A_t}{A_{t-1}}\right) - 0.5S_t\left(\frac{CA_t}{CA_{t-1}}\right) - 2.5S_t + u$$

B.

$$S_{t+1} = 2(\$500{,}000)\left(\frac{\$18{,}900}{\$18{,}000}\right) + 2(\$500{,}000)\left(\frac{\$50{,}000}{\$40{,}000}\right)$$

$$- 0.5(\$500{,}000)\left(\frac{\$100{,}000}{\$125{,}000}\right) - 2.5(\$500{,}000) + u$$

$$= \$850{,}000 + u$$

P6.14 Sales Forecast Modeling. Kids Klothes, Ltd., would like to generate a sales forecast based on the assumption that next year sales are a function of current income, advertising, and advertising by a competing retailer:

A. Write an equation for predicting sales based on the assumption that the percentage change in sales is one-and-a-half as large as the percentage change in income and advertising; but only one-half as large as, and of the opposite sign of, the percentage change in competitor advertising. Use the symbols S = sales, Y = income, A = advertising, and CA = competitor advertising.

B. During the current year, sales total $750,000, income is $20,500 per capita, advertising is $75,000, and competitor advertising is $100,000. Previous period levels were $20,000 (income), $60,000 (advertising), and $80,000 (competitor advertising). Forecast next year sales.

P6.14 SOLUTION

A.

$$S_{t+1} = S_t + 1.5\left(\frac{Y_t}{Y_{t-1}} - 1\right)S_t + 1.5\left(\frac{A_t}{A_{t-1}} - 1\right)S_t - 0.5\left(\frac{CA_t}{CA_{t-1}} - 1\right)S_t + u$$

$$= S_t + 1.5S_t\left(\frac{Y_t}{Y_{t-1}}\right) - 1.5S_t + 1.5S_t\left(\frac{A_t}{A_{t-1}}\right) - 1.5S_t - 0.5S_t\left(\frac{CA_t}{CA_{t-1}}\right) + 0.5S_t + u$$

$$= 1.5S_t\left(\frac{Y_t}{Y_{t-1}}\right) + 1.5S_t\left(\frac{A_t}{A_{t-1}}\right) - 0.5S_t\left(\frac{CA_t}{CA_{t-1}}\right) - 1.5S_t + u$$

B.

$$S_{t+1} = 1(\$750,000)\left(\frac{\$20,500}{\$20,000}\right) + 1.5(\$750,000)\left(\frac{\$75,000}{\$60,000}\right)$$

$$- 0.5(\$750,000)\left(\frac{\$100,000}{\$80,000}\right) - 1.5(\$750,000) + u$$

$$= \$965,625 + u$$

P6.15 *Sales Forecast Modeling.* Lenocks China, Ltd., would like to generate a sales forecast based on the assumption that next year sales are a function of current income, advertising, and advertising by a competing china manufacturer:

A. Write an equation for predicting sales based on the assumption that the percentage change in sales is three times as large as the percentage change in income and advertising; but only one-fourth as large as, and of the opposite sing of, the percentage change in competitor advertising. Use the symbols S = sales, Y = income, A = advertising, and CA = competitor advertising.

B. During the current year, sales total $1,000,000, income is $21,000 per capita, advertising is $90,000, and competitor advertising is $100,000. Previous period levels were $20,000 (income), $80,000 (advertising), and $125,000 (competitor advertising). Forecast next year sales.

P6.15   SOLUTION

A.

$$S_{t+1} = S_t + 3\left(\frac{Y_t}{Y_{t-1}} - 1\right)S_t + 3\left(\frac{A_t}{A_{t-1}} - 1\right)S_t - 0.25\left(\frac{CA_t}{CA_{t-1}} - 1\right)S_t + u$$

$$= S_t + 3S_t\left(\frac{Y_t}{Y_{t-1}}\right) - 3S_t + 3S_t\left(\frac{A_t}{A_{t-1}}\right) - 3S_t - 0.25S_t\left(\frac{CA_t}{CA_{t-1}}\right) + 0.25S_t + u$$

$$= 3S_t\left(\frac{Y_t}{Y_{t-1}}\right) + 3S_t\left(\frac{A_t}{A_{t-1}}\right) - 0.25S_t\left(\frac{CA_t}{CA_{t-1}}\right) - 4.75S_t + u$$

B.

$$S_{t+1} = 3(\$1,000,000)\left(\frac{\$21,000}{\$20,000}\right) + 3(\$1,000,000)\left(\frac{\$90,000}{\$80,000}\right)$$

$$- 0.25(\$1,000,000)\left(\frac{\$100,000}{\$125,000}\right) - 4.75(\$1,000,000) + u$$

$$= \$1,575,000 + u$$

P6.16   Sales Forecast Modeling. *The Record Shack, Ltd., would like to generate a sales forecast based on the assumption that next year sales are a function of current income, advertising, and advertising by a competing retailer:*

A.   *Write an equation for predicting sales based on the assumption that the percentage change in sales is twice as large as the percentage change in income and advertising; but only one-fourth as large as, and of the opposite sing of, the percentage change in competitor advertising. Use the symbols S = sales, Y = income, A = advertising, and CA = competitor advertising.*

B.   *During the current year, sales total $2,000,000, income is $22,000 per capita, advertising is $500,000, and competitor advertising is $300,000. Previous period levels were $20,000 (income), $400,000 (advertising), and $400,000 (competitor advertising). Forecast next year sales.*

Forecasting

P6.16   SOLUTION

A.

$$S_{t+1} = S_t + 2\left(\frac{Y_t}{Y_{t-1}} - 1\right)S_t + 2\left(\frac{A_t}{A_{t-1}} - 1\right)S_t - 0.25\left(\frac{CA_t}{CA_{t-1}} - 1\right)S_t + u$$

$$= S_t + 2S_t\left(\frac{Y_t}{Y_{t-1}}\right) - 2S_t + 2S_t\left(\frac{A_t}{A_{t-1}}\right) - 2S_t - 0.25S_t\left(\frac{CA_t}{CA_{t-1}}\right) + 0.25S_t + u$$

$$= 2S_t\left(\frac{Y_t}{Y_{t-1}}\right) + 2S_t\left(\frac{A_t}{A_{t-1}}\right) - 0.25S_t\left(\frac{CA_t}{CA_{t-1}}\right) - 2.75S_t + u$$

B.

$$S_{t+1} = 2(\$2,000,000)\left(\frac{\$22,000}{\$20,000}\right) + 2(\$2,000,000)\left(\frac{\$500,000}{\$400,000}\right)$$

$$- 0.25(\$2,000,000)\left(\frac{\$300,000}{\$400,000}\right) - 2.75(\$2,000,000) + u$$

$$= \$3,525,000 + u$$

P6.17   Cost Forecast Modeling. Elliot Ness, manager of product packaging at Chicago Tool & Die, Inc., is evaluating the cost effectiveness of the preventive maintenance program in his department. He believes that the monthly downtime of the packaging line due to equipment breakdown is related to the hours spent each month on preventive maintenance.

A.   Write an equation to predict next month's downtime using the symbols D = downtime, M = preventive maintenance, t = time, a_0 = constant term, a_1 = regression slope coefficient, and u = random disturbance and assuming that downtime in the forecast month decreases by the same percentage as preventive maintenance increased during the preceding month.

B.   If 75 hours were spent last month on preventive maintenance and this month's downtime was 50 hours, what should downtime be next month if preventive maintenance this month is 90 hours? Use the equation developed in Part A.

P6.17 **SOLUTION**

A.
$$D_{t+1} = a_0 + a_1 M + u$$

$$= D_t - \Delta D + u$$

$$= D_t - \left(\frac{M_t - M_{t-1}}{M_{t-1}}\right) D_t + u$$

B.
$$D_{t+1} = 50 - \left(\frac{90 - 75}{75}\right) 50 + u$$

$$= 50 - 10 + u$$

$$= 40 + u \text{ hours of downtime}$$

P6.18 **Cost Forecast Modeling.** Phil Berry, manager of bread packaging at RainBo, Inc., is evaluating the cost effectiveness of the preventive maintenance program in his department. He believes that the monthly downtime of the packaging line due to equipment breakdown is related to the hours spent each month on preventive maintenance.

A. Write an equation to predict next month's downtime using the symbols D = downtime, M = preventive maintenance, t = time, a_0 = constant term, a_1 = regression slope coefficient, and u = random disturbance and assuming that downtime in the forecast month decreases by half of the percentage increase in preventive maintenance during the preceding month.

B. If 60 hours were spent last month on preventive maintenance and this month's downtime was 40 hours, what should downtime be next month if preventive maintenance this month is 75 hours? Use the equation developed in Part A.

P6.18 **SOLUTION**

A.
$$D_{t+1} = a_0 + a_1 M + u$$

$$= D_t - \Delta D + u$$

$$= D_t - 0.5 \left(\frac{M_t - M_{t-1}}{M_{t-1}}\right) D_t + u$$

B. $D_{t+1} = 40 - 0.5 \left(\dfrac{75 - 60}{60} \right) 40 + u$

$= 40 - 5 + u$

$= 35 + u$ hours of downtime

P6.19 **Cost Forecast Modeling.** Perry Mason, manager of injection molding at Plastic Toys, Inc., is evaluating the cost effectiveness of the plastic molder training program in his department. Mason believes that the monthly downtime of the packaging line due to equipment breakdown is inversely related to the hours spent each month on molder training.

A. Write an equation to predict next month's downtime using the symbols D = downtime, M = preventive maintenance, t = time, a_0 = constant term, a_1 = regression slope coefficient, and u = random disturbance and assuming that downtime in the forecast month decreases by twice the percentage increase in preventive maintenance during the preceding month.

B. If 40 hours were spent last month on preventive maintenance and this month's downtime was 60 hours, what should downtime be next month if preventive maintenance this month is 50 hours? Use the equation developed in Part A.

P6.19 **SOLUTION**

A. $D_{t+1} = a_0 + a_1 M + u$

$= D_t - \Delta D + u$

$= D_t - 2 \left(\dfrac{M_t - M_{t-1}}{M_{t-1}} \right) D_t + u$

B. $D_{t+1} = 60 - 2 \left(\dfrac{50 - 40}{40} \right) 60 + u$

$= 60 - 30 + u$

$= 30 + u$ hours of downtime

P6.20 **Sales Forecasting.** Samurai, Ltd., must forecast sales for a popular trivia game in order to avoid stockouts or excessive inventory charges during the coming Christmas season. In percentage terms, the company estimates that game sales fall at double the rate of price increases and grow at five times the rate of customer traffic increases. Furthermore, these effects seem to be independent.

   A. Write an equation for estimating the Christmas season sales, using the symbols S = sales, P = price, T = traffic, t = time, and u = a random disturbance term.

   B. Forecast this season's sales if Samurai sold 10,000 games last season at $20 each, this season's price is anticipated to be $25, and customer traffic is expected to rise by 10% over previous levels.

P6.20 **SOLUTION**

   A. $S_{t+1} = S_t + \Delta S + u$

   $= S_t - \Delta S_P + \Delta S_T + u$

   $= S_t - 2(P_{t+1}/P_t - 1)S_t + 5(T_{t+1}/T_t - 1)S_t + u$

   $= -2S_t - 2(P_{t+1}/P_t)S_t + 5(T_{t+1}/T_t)S_t + u$

   B. $S_{t+1} = -2(10,000) - 2(\$25/\$20)10,000 + 5(1.10)10,000 + u$

   $= 10,000 + u$ games

P6.21 **Sales Forecasting.** Toaster Technologies, Inc., must forecast sales for a indoor electric grills in order to avoid stockouts or excessive inventory charges during the coming Christmas season. In percentage terms, the company estimates that electric grill sales fall at triple the rate of price increases and grow at three times the rate of customer traffic increases. Furthermore, these effects seem to be independent.

   A. Write an equation for estimating the Christmas season sales, using the symbols S = sales, P = price, T = traffic, t = time, and u = a random disturbance term.

   B. Forecast this season's sales if Toaster Technologies sold 500,000 indoor electric grills last season at $40 each, this season's price is anticipated to be $45, and customer traffic is expected to rise by 15% over previous levels.

Forecasting

P6.21 SOLUTION

A.
$$S_{t+1} = S_t + \Delta S + u$$
$$= S_t - \Delta S_P + \Delta S_T + u$$
$$= S_t - 3(P_{t+1}/P_t - 1)S_t + 3(T_{t+1}/T_t - 1)S_t + u$$
$$= S_t - 3(P_{t+1}/P_t)S_t + 3(T_{t+1}/T_t)S_t + u$$

B.
$$S_{t+1} = 500{,}000 - 3(\$45/\$40)500{,}000 + 3(1.15)500{,}000 + u$$
$$= 537{,}500 + u$$

P6.22 *Simultaneous Equations.* The Metropolitan Symphony runs a professional symphony in the city of Toledo and has had great success with a "Senior Citizens' Night" promotion. By offering half off its regular $20 admission price, average nightly attendance has risen from 4,000 to 6,000 persons. Beverage (Bev) and other concession (C) revenues tied to attendance have also risen dramatically. Historically, Metropolitan Symphony has found that 75% of all concert goers will buy a $3 beverage, whereas 10% of all concert goers plus 40% of those buying beverages will spend $2 on hors d'oeuvres and other concessions.

A. Write an expression describing total revenue from tickets plus beverage plus other concessions.

B. Forecast total revenues for both regular and special senior citizens' night pricing.

C. If the profit contribution is 25% on concert ticket revenues, and 75% on beverages and other concession revenues, is the pricing promotion profitable?

P6.22 SOLUTION

A. If Q is the number of concert goers, then:

Ticket Revenue = PQ

$$\text{Beverage Revenue} = \$3\text{Bev}$$
$$= 3(0.75Q)$$
$$= \$2.25Q + u$$

$$\text{Other Concession Revenue} = \$2C$$
$$= \$2(0.10Q + 0.40\text{Bev})$$
$$= \$2(0.10Q + 0.40(2.25Q))$$
$$= \$2Q + u$$

Therefore,

$$\text{Total Revenue} = \text{Ticket Revenue} + \text{Beverage Revenue} + \text{Other Concession Revenue}$$
$$= PQ + \$2.25Q + \$2Q$$
$$= PQ + \$4.25Q + u$$

B. <u>Regular Price</u>

$$\text{Total Revenue} = \$20(4,000) + \$4.25(4,000)$$
$$= \$97,000 + u$$

<u>Special Price</u>

$$\text{Total Revenue} = \$10(6,000) + \$4.25(6,000)$$
$$= \$85,500 + u$$

Forecasting

C. Yes. Note that:

Regular Price

Profit Contribution = 0.25($20)(4,000) + (0.75)($4.25)(4,000)

= $32,750 + u

Special Price

Profit Contribution = 0.25($10)(6,000) + 0.75($4.25)(6,000)

= $34,125 + u

Based on these figures, the "Senior Citizens' Night" results in a $1,375 increase in profit contribution. However, calculating the true net profit contribution would involve subtracting any negative sales effects on other nights of the week when full prices would be charged. Thus, $1,375 is a maximum (or upper bound) profit contribution forecast.

P6.23 *Simultaneous Equations.* Buckeye Cinema, Inc., which runs a chain of movie theaters in the state of Ohio, has had great success with a "Tuesday Night at the Movies" promotion. By offering half off its regular $5 admission price, average nightly attendance has risen from 400 to 800 persons. Popcorn (Pop) and other concession (C) revenues tied to attendance have also risen dramatically. Historically, Buckeye Cinema has found that 50% of all movie goers will buy a $2 cup of popcorn, whereas 25% of all movie goers plus 50% of those buying popcorn will spend $1.50 on soda and other concessions.

A. Write an expression describing total revenue from tickets plus popcorn plus other concessions.

B. Forecast total revenues for both regular and special Tuesday-night pricing.

C. If the profit contribution is 25% on movie ticket revenues, and 75% on popcorn and other concession revenues, is the pricing promotion profitable?

P6.23 **SOLUTION**

A. If Q is the number of movie goers, then:

$$\text{Ticket Revenue} = PQ$$

$$\text{Popcorn Revenue} = \$2\text{Pop}$$

$$= 2(0.5Q)$$

$$= \$1Q + u$$

$$\text{Other Concession Revenue} = \$1.50C$$

$$= 1.50(0.25Q + 0.5\text{Pop})$$

$$= 1.50(0.25Q + 0.5(0.5Q))$$

$$= \$0.75Q + u$$

Therefore,

$$\text{Total Revenue} = \text{Ticket Revenue} + \text{Beverage Renvenue} + \text{Other Concession Revenue}$$

$$= PQ + \$1.Q + \$0.75Q$$

$$= PQ + \$1.75Q + u$$

B. <u>Regular Price</u>

$$\text{Total Revenue} = \$5(400) + \$1.75(400)$$

$$= \$2{,}700 + u$$

<u>Special Price</u>

$$\text{Total Revenue} = \$2.50(800) + \$1.75(800)$$

$$= \$3{,}400 + u$$

Forecasting

C. Yes. We note that:

<u>Regular Price</u>

Profit Contribution = 0.25($5)(400) + (0.75)($1.75)(400)

= $1,025 + u

<u>Special Price</u>

Profit Contribution = 0.25($2.50)(800) + 0.75($1.75)(800)

= $1,550 + u

Based upon these figures, the "Tuesday Night Special" results in a $525(= $1,550 - $1,025) increase in profit contribution. However, calculating the true net profit contribution would involve subtracting any negative sales effects on other nights of the week when full prices would be charged. Thus, $525 is a maximum (or upper bound) profit contribution forecast.

P6.24 **Simultaneous Equations.** MBA Industries, based in Seattle, Washington, manufactures a wide range of parts for the aircraft, automotive, and agricultural equipment industries. The company is currently evaluating the merits of building a new plant in order to fulfill a new contract with the federal government. The alternative to expansion is to use additional overtime, reduce other production, or a combination of both. The company will add new capacity only if the economy appears to be expanding. Forecasting the general economic activity of the United States is therefore an important input to the decision making process. The firm has collected data and estimated the following relations for the United States economy:

Last year's total profits (all corporations) P_{t-1} = $500 billion

This year's government expenditures G = $1,600 billion

Annual consumption expenditures C = $400 billion + 0.75Y + u$

Annual investment expenditures I = $750 billion + 0.9P_{t-1} + u$

Annual tax receipts T = 0.2 GDP

National income Y = GDP - T

Gross domestic product GDP $= C + I + G$

Forecast each of the above variables through the simultaneous relations expressed in the multiple equation system. Assume that all random disturbances average out to zero.

P6.24   SOLUTION

A.   Investment

$$I = \$750 + 0.9P_{t-1} + u$$

$$= 750 + 0.9(500) + u$$

$$= \$1{,}200 + u \text{ billion}$$

Gross Domestic Product

$$GDP = C + I + G$$

$$= \$400 + 0.75Y + \$1{,}200 + \$1{,}600$$

$$= 3{,}200 + 0.75(GDP - T)$$

$$= 3{,}200 + 0.75(GDP - 0.2GDP)$$

$$= 3{,}200 + 0.6GDP$$

$$0.4GDP = 3{,}200$$

$$GDP = \$8{,}000 \text{ billion}$$

Forecasting

Consumption

$$C = \$400 + 0.75Y + u$$
$$= 400 + 0.75(GDP - T) + u$$
$$= 400 + 0.75(0.8GDP) + u$$
$$= 400 + 0.6(8,000) + u$$
$$= \$5,200 + u \text{ billion}$$

Taxes

$$T = 0.2GDP$$
$$= 0.2(8,000)$$
$$= \$1,600 + u \text{ billion}$$

National Income

$$Y = GDP - T$$
$$= GDP - 0.2GDP$$
$$= 0.8GDP$$
$$= 0.8(8,000)$$
$$= \$6,400 + u \text{ billion}$$

P6.25 *Simultaneous Equations.* Keystone Equipment, Inc. manufactures a wide range of parts for the agricultural equipment industry. The company is currently evaluating the merits of building a new plant in order to fulfill a new contract with a large export concern. The alternative to expansion is to use additional overtime, reduce other production, or a combination of both. The company will add new capacity only if the regional economy appears to be expanding. Forecasting the general economic activity of the regional economy is therefore an important input to the decision making process. The firm has collected data and estimated the following relations for the regional economy:

Last year's total profits (all corporations) P_{t-1} = $600 billion

This year's government expenditures G = $1,700 billion

Annual consumption expenditures C = $500 billion + $0.8Y + u$

Annual investment expenditures I = $750 billion + $0.75P_{t-1} + u$

Annual tax receipts T = 0.25 GDP

National income Y = GDP - T

Gross domestic product GDP = $C + I + G$

Forecast each of the above variables through the simultaneous relations expressed in the multiple equation system. Assume that all random disturbances average out to zero.

P6.25   SOLUTION

A.   Investment

I = $750 + $0.75P_{t-1} + u$

= $750 + 0.75(600) + u$

= $1,200 + u$ billion

Gross Domestic Product

GDP = $C + I + G$

= $500 + 0.8Y + $1,200 + $1,700

= $3,400 + 0.8(GDP - T)

= $3,400 + 0.8(GDP - 0.25GDP)

= $3,400 + 0.6GDP

0.4GDP = $3,400

Forecasting

GDP = $8,500 billion

Consumption

$$\begin{aligned} C &= \$500 + 0.75Y + u \\ &= 500 + 0.8(\text{GDP} - T) + u \\ &= 500 + 0.8(0.75\text{GDP}) + u \\ &= 500 + 0.6(8{,}500) + u \\ &= 5{,}600 + u \text{ billion} \end{aligned}$$

Taxes

$$\begin{aligned} T &= 0.25\text{GDP} \\ &= 0.25(8{,}500) \\ &= \$2{,}125 + u \text{ billion} \end{aligned}$$

National Income

$$\begin{aligned} Y &= \text{GDP} - T \\ &= \text{GDP} - 0.25\text{GNP} \\ &= 0.75\text{GDP} \\ &= 0.75(8{,}500) \\ &= \$6{,}375 + u \text{ billion} \end{aligned}$$

Chapter 7

PRODUCTION ANALYSIS AND ESTIMATION

MULTIPLE CHOICE QUESTIONS

Q7.1 The maximum output that can be produced for a given amount of input is called a:

- A. discrete production function.
- > B. production function.
- C. continuous production function.
- D. discontinuous production function.

Q7.2 The output effect of a proportional increase in all inputs is called:

- > A. returns to scale.
- B. returns to a factor.
- C. total product.
- D. marginal product.

Q7.3 As the quantity of a variable input increases, the resulting rate of output increase eventually:

- > A. falls.
- B. rises.
- C. becomes constant.
- D. none of these.

Q7.4 Ridge lines identify the:

- A. amount of one input that must be substituted for another to maintain constant output.
- > B. graphic bounds for positive marginal products.
- C. least-cost production of a target level of output.
- D. different input combinations used to efficiently produce a specified output.

Q7.5 Economic efficiency is achieved when all firms equate the marginal:

- A. product and price for all inputs.
- B. cost of all inputs.
- > C. revenue product and price for all inputs.
- D. product of all inputs.

Harcourt Brace & Company

Production Analysis and Estimation 209

Q7.6 A new production function results following:

    A. a new wage agreement following collective bargaining.
    B. a surge in product demand.
    C. a decrease in the availability of needed inputs.
>   D. the successful completion of a training program that enhances worker productivity.

Q7.7 The relation between output and the variation in all inputs taken together is the:

    A. factor productivity of a production system.
    B. law of diminishing returns.
>   C. returns to scale characteristic of a production system.
    D. returns to factor characteristic of a production system.

Q7.8 An irrational employment policy is indicated when the marginal product of X is:

>   A. negative.
    B. positive.
    C. decreasing.
    D. increasing.

Q7.9 When $P_X = \$60$, $MP_X = 5$ and $MP_Y = 2$, relative employment levels are optimal provided:

    A. $P_Y = 16.7¢$.
>   B. $P_Y = \$24$.
    C. $P_Y = \$60$.
    D. $P_Y = \$150$.

Q7.10 When $P_X = \$100$, $MP_X = 10$ and $MR_Q = \$5$, the marginal revenue product of X equals:

    A. $100.
>   B. $50.
    C. $10.
    D. $5.

Q7.11 The returns to scale characteristic of a production system:

A. is measured by the way in which inputs can be varied in an unbroken marginal fashion rather than incrementally.
B. illustrates the distinct, or "lumpy," pattern of input combination.
> C. shows the relation between output and the variation in all inputs.
D. is the relation between output and variation in only one of the inputs employed.

Q7.12 Returns to a factor denotes the relation between the quantity of an individual input employed and the:

A. optimal scale of a firm.
B. optimal size of production facilities.
C. optimal length of production runs.
> D. level of output produced.

Q7.13 The marginal product concept is:

A. used to describe the relation between output and variation in all inputs in a production function.
> B. the change in output associated with a one-unit change in an individual factor.
C. total product divided by the number input units employed.
D. the complete output from a production system.

Q7.14 A production function specifies the:

A. maximum possible output that can be produced given varying degrees of technological progress.
B. minimum cost necessary to produce a given output level.
> C. minimum quantity of inputs necessary to produce a given output level.
D. maximum possible output that can be produced at a given cost.

Q7.15 A production function describes the relation between output and:

A. technical progress.
B. one input.
C. total cost.
> D. all inputs.

Production Analysis and Estimation   211

Q7.16   Total product divided by the number of units of variable input employed equals:

> A. average product.
> B. marginal revenue product.
> C. returns to scale.
> D. marginal product.

Q7.17   Marginal product is the change in output associated with a unit change in:

> A. all inputs.
> B. technology.
> C. scale.
> D. one input factor.

Q7.18   According to the law of diminishing returns, over some range of output:

> A. total product will decrease as the quantity of variable input employed increases.
> B. marginal product will decrease as the quantity of variable input employed increases.
> C. marginal revenue will decrease as the quantity of output increases.
> D. every production function exhibits diminishing returns to scale.

Q7.19   When the slope of the average product curve equals zero:

> A. total product is maximized.
> B. returns to the variable input are increasing.
> C. marginal product equals average product.
> D. marginal product equals zero.

Q7.20   Total output is maximized when:

> A. average product equals zero.
> B. marginal product is maximized.
> C. average product is maximized.
> D. marginal product equals zero.

Q7.21   An isoquant represents:

> A. input combinations that can be employed at the same cost.
> B. input combinations that can efficiently produce the same output.
> C. output combinations that can be efficiently produced using the same input combination.
> D. output combinations that can be produced for the same cost.

Q7.22   Right-angle shaped isoquants reflect inputs that are:

> A. perfect complements.
> B. perfect substitutes.
> C. imperfect substitutes.
> D. inefficient.

Q7.23   The marginal rate of technical substitution is:

> A. the slope of the marginal revenue product curve.
> B. the marginal product of either input.
> C. minus one times the ratio of marginal products for each input.
> D. the slope of an isocost curve.

Q7.24   If the output elasticity equals 0.75, returns to scale are:

> A. constant.
> B. increasing.
> C. cannot be determined without further information.
> D. diminishing.

Q7.25   Marginal revenue product equals:

> A. marginal revenue multiplied by marginal product.
> B. marginal product multiplied by total revenue.
> C. total revenue multiplied by total product.
> D. marginal revenue multiplied by total product.

Production Analysis and Estimation

Q7.26 A firm will maximize profits by employing the quantity of each input where the marginal:

> A. revenue product of each input equals its price.
> B. revenue equals the price of each input.
> C. product of each input is equal.
> D. product of each input equals its price.

Q7.27 If tripling the quantities of all inputs employed doubles the quantity of output produced, the output elasticity:

> A. equals one.
> B. is greater than one.
> C. cannot be determined without further information.
> D. is less than one.

Q7.28 The production function $Q = 0.25X^{0.5}Y$ exhibits:

> A. constant returns to scale.
> B. increasing returns to scale.
> C. increasing and then diminishing returns to scale.
> D. diminishing returns to scale.

Q7.29 For a continuous total product function, marginal product equals the:

> A. inflection point of the total product curve.
> B. inflection point of the average product curve.
> C. slope of the total product curve.
> D. slope of a line drawn from the origin to a point on the total product curve.

Q7.30 The law of diminishing returns:

> A. deals specifically with the diminishing marginal product of fixed input factors.
> B. states that the marginal product of a variable factor must eventually decline as increasingly more is employed.
> C. can be derived deductively.
> D. states that as the quantity of a variable input increases, with the quantities of all other factors being held constant, the resulting output must eventually diminish.

214   Chapter 7

PROBLEMS & SOLUTIONS

P7.1 **Input Combination.** *The following production table provides estimates of the maximum amounts of output possible with different combinations of two input factors, X and Y. (Assume that these are just illustrative points on a spectrum of continuous input combinations.)*

Units of Y Used	Estimated Output per Day				
5	258	360	455	542	620
4	234	332	416	496	542
3	206	294	372	416	455
2	168	248	294	332	360
1	124	168	206	234	258
	1	2	3	4	5
	Units of X Used				

A. Do the two inputs exhibit the characteristics of constant, increasing, or decreasing marginal rates of technical substitution? How do you know?

B. Assuming output sells for $4 per unit, complete the following tables:

X Fixed at 2 Units

Units of Y Used	Total Product of Y	Marginal Product of Y	Average Product of Y	Marginal Revenue Product of Y
1				
2				
3				
4				
5				

Harcourt Brace & Company

Production Analysis and Estimation

	Fixed at 3 units			
Units of X Used	Total Product of X	Marginal Product of X	Average Product of X	Marginal Revenue Product of X
1				
2				
3				
4				
5				

C. Assume the quantity of X is fixed at 2 units. If the output of the production system sells for $4 and the cost of Y is $155 per day, how many units of Y will be employed?

D. Assume that the company is currently producing 258 units of output per day using 1 unit of X and 5 units of Y. The daily cost per unit of X is $155 and that of Y is also $155. Would you recommend a change in the present input combination? Why or why not?

E. What is the nature of the returns to scale for this production system if the optimal input combination requires that X = Y?

P7.1 SOLUTION

A. The inputs exhibit the characteristics of decreasing marginal rates of technical substitution throughout. For decreasing MRTS, the slope of the production isoquants diminishes as one input is increasingly substituted for another. We can also see this point algebraically by holding X or Y constant in the input-output matrix and noting the decline in the relative marginal product of the other input as its usage level grows.

B.

	X Fixed at 2 Units			
Units of Y employed	TP_Y	MP_Y	AP_Y	MRP_Y
	(1)	(2)	(3)	(4) = $4 × (2)
1	168	168	168	$672
2	248	80	124	320
3	294	46	98	184
4	332	38	83	152
5	360	28	72	112

	Y Fixed at 3 Units			
Units of X employed	TP_X	MP_X	AP_X	MRP_X
	(1)	(2)	(3)	(4) = $4 × (2)
1	206	206	206	$824
2	294	88	147	352
3	372	78	124	312
4	416	44	104	176
5	455	39	91	156

C. Three units of Y will be employed. The marginal value of the first three units of Y is greater than their marginal cost. The marginal value of the fourth unit is only $152 or $3 less than its cost, and hence, the firm would employ no more than three units of Y.

D. A change would be in order since the firm could produce 372 units at the same cost using 3 units of each output. That is, the marginal product to price ratios of the two inputs are not equal at the current input proportions. Relatively less Y and more X is needed to provide an optimal combination.

E. The system exhibits constant returns to scale. This is true since a given increase in both inputs causes an increases in output of the same proportion.

X	Y	Output
1	1	124 × 1 = 124
2	2	124 × 2 = 248
3	3	124 × 3 = 372
4	4	124 × 4 = 496
5	5	124 × 5 = 620

P7.2 **Input Combination.** *The following production table provides estimates of the maximum amounts of output possible with different combinations of two input factors, X and Y. (Assume that these are just illustrative points on a spectrum of continuous input combinations.)*

Units of Y Used	Estimated Output per Day				
5	184	265	334	395	440
4	176	248	303	352	395
3	164	216	264	303	334
2	128	176	216	248	265
1	88	128	164	176	184
	1	2	3	4	5

Units of X Used

A. Do the two inputs exhibit the characteristics of constant, increasing, or decreasing marginal rates of technical substitution? How do you know?

B. Assuming output sells for $3 per unit, complete the following tables:

X Fixed at 4 Units

Units of Y Used	Total Product of Y	Marginal Product of Y	Average Product of Y	Marginal Revenue Product of Y
1				
2				
3				
4				
5				

Fixed at 2 units

Units of X Used	Total Product of X	Marginal Product of X	Average Product of X	Marginal Revenue Product of X
1				
2				
3				
4				
5				

C. Assume the quantity of X is fixed at 4 units. If the output of the production system sells for $3 and the cost of Y is $135 per day, how many units of Y will be employed?

D. Assume that the company is currently producing 248 units of output per day using 2 units of X and 4 units of Y. The daily cost per unit of X is $135 and that of Y is also $135. Would you recommend a change in the present input combination? Why or why not?

E. What is the nature of the returns to scale for this production system if the optimal input combination requires that $X = Y$?

P7.2 SOLUTION

A. The inputs exhibit the characteristics of decreasing marginal rates of technical substitution throughout. For decreasing MRTS, the slope of the production isoquants diminishes as one input is increasingly substituted for another. We can also see this point algebraically by holding X or Y constant in the input-output matrix and noting the decline in the relative marginal product of the other input as its usage level grows.

B.

X Fixed at 4 Units

Units of Y employed	TP_Y	MP_Y	AP_Y	MRP_Y
	(1)	(2)	(3)	(4) = $3 × (2)
1	176	176	176	$528
2	248	72	124	216
3	303	55	101	165
4	352	49	88	147
5	395	43	79	129

Y Fixed at 2 Units

Units of X employed	TP_X	MP_X	AP_X	MRP_X
	(1)	(2)	(3)	(4) = $3 × (2)
1	128	128	128	$384
2	176	48	88	144
3	216	40	72	120
4	248	32	62	96
5	265	17	53	51

C. Four units of Y will be employed. The marginal value of the first four units of Y is greater than their marginal cost. The marginal value of the fifth unit is only $129 or $6 less than its cost, and hence, the firm would employ no more than four units of Y.

D. A change would be in order since the firm could produce 303 units at the same cost using 3 units of each output. That is, the marginal product to price ratios of the two inputs are not equal at the current input proportions. Relatively less Y and more X is needed to provide an optimal combination.

E. The system exhibits constant returns to scale. This is true since a given increase in both inputs causes an increases in output of the same proportion.

X	Y	Output
1	1	88 × 1 = 88
2	2	88 × 2 = 176
3	3	88 × 3 = 264
4	4	88 × 4 = 352
5	5	88 × 5 = 440

P7.3 **Production Relations.** *Indicate whether each of the following statements is true or false.*

A. L-shaped isoquants describe production systems where inputs are perfect complements.

B. If the marginal product of capital increases as capital usage grows, the returns to capital are decreasing.

C. Marginal revenue product measures the output gained through expanding input usage.

D. The marginal rate of technical substitution will be affected by a given percentage increase in the marginal productivity of all inputs.

E. Increasing returns to scale and declining average costs are indicated when $\epsilon_Q > 1$.

P7.3 **SOLUTION**

A. True. L-shaped production isoquants reflect a perfect complementary relation among inputs, i.e., no amount of input X can make up for the lack of input Y.

B. False. Returns to the capital input factor are increasing when the marginal product of capital increases as capital usage grows.

Production Analysis and Estimation 221

    C. False. Marginal revenue product is the revenue generated by expanding input usage, and represents the maximum that could be paid to expand usage. Marginal product measures the change in output given a change in an input.

    D. False. The marginal rate of technical substitution is measured by the relative marginal productivity of input factors. This relation is unaffected by a commensurate increase in the marginal productivity of all inputs.

    E. True. When $\epsilon_Q > 1$, the percentage change in output is greater than a given percentage change in all inputs. Thus, increasing returns to scale and decreasing average costs are indicated.

P7.4   **Production Relations.** *Indicate whether each of the following statements is true or false.*

    A. If the marginal product of capital decreases as capital usage grows, the returns to capital are decreasing.

    B. The marginal rate of technical substitution will be affected by a given percentage increase in the marginal productivity of an input.

    C. Marginal revenue product represents the minimum revenue amount required to expand usage.

    D. Linear isoquants describe production systems where inputs are perfect complements.

    E. Decreasing returns to scale and declining average costs are indicated when $\epsilon_Q < 1$.

P7.4   **SOLUTION**

    A. True. Returns to the capital input factor are decreasing when the marginal product of capital decreases as capital usage grows.

    B. True. The marginal rate of technical substitution is measured by the relative marginal productivity of input factors. This relation is affected by an increase in the marginal productivity of a single input.

    C. True. Marginal revenue product is the revenue generated by expanding input usage, and represents the minimum revenue required to expand usage.

D. False. L-shaped production isoquants reflect a perfect complementary relation among inputs, i.e., no amount of input X can make up for the lack of input Y. Linear isoquants reflect perfect substitutability of input X for input Y, and vice versa.

E. False. When $\epsilon_Q < 1$, the percentage change in output is less than the percentage change in all inputs, implying decreasing returns to scale but increasing average costs.

P7.5 **Returns to Scale.** *Determine whether the following production functions exhibit constant, increasing, or decreasing returns to scale.*

A. $Q = 0.25X + 5Y + 30Z$

B. $Q = 4L + 15K + 600$

C. $Q = 9A + 3B + 12AB$

D. $Q = 4L^2 + 6LK + 3K^2$

E. $Q = 2L^{0.2}K^{0.6}$

P7.5 **SOLUTION**

A. Initially, let X = Y = Z = 100, so output is:

$$Q_1 = 0.25(100) + 5(100) + 30(100) = 3{,}525$$

Increasing all inputs by 4% leads to:

$$Q_2 = 0.25(104) + 5(104) + 30(104) = 3{,}666$$

Since a 4% increase in all inputs results in a 4% increase in output (Q_2/Q_1 = 3,666/3,525 = 1.04), the output elasticity is 1 and the production system exhibits constant returns to scale.

B. Initially, let L = K = 100, so output is:

$$Q_1 = 4(100) + 15(100) + 600 = 2{,}500$$

Increasing both inputs by 5% leads to

$$Q_2 = 4(105) + 15(105) + 600 = 2,595$$

Since a 5% increase in both inputs results in a 3.8% increase in output (Q_2/Q_1 = 2,595/2,500 = 1.038), the output elasticity is less than 1 and the production system exhibits diminishing returns to scale.

C. Initially, let A = B = 100, so output is:

$$Q_1 = 9(100) + 3(100) + 12(100)(100) = 21,200$$

Increasing both inputs by 1% leads to:

$$Q_2 = 9(101) + 3(101) + 12(101)(101) = 23,642$$

Since a 1% increase in both inputs results in a 2% increase in output (Q_2/Q_1 = 23,642/21,200 = 1.02), the output elasticity is greater than 1 and the production system exhibits increasing returns to scale.

D. Initially, let L = K = 100, so output is:

$$Q_1 = 4(100^2) + 6(100)(100) + 3(100^2) = 130,000$$

Increasing both inputs by 2% leads to:

$$Q_2 = 4(102^2) + 6(102)(102) + 3(102^2) = 135,252$$

Since a 2% increase in both inputs results in a 4% increase in output (Q_2/Q_1 = 135,252/130,000 = 1.04), the output elasticity is greater than 1 and the production system exhibits increasing returns to scale.

E. Initially, let L = K = 100, so output is:

$$Q_1 = 2(100^{0.2})(100^{0.6}) = 80$$

Increasing both inputs by 4% leads to:

$$Q_2 = 2(104^{0.2})(104^{0.6}) = 82$$

Since a 4% increase in both inputs results in a less than 4% increase in output (Q_2/Q_1 = 82/80 = 1.025), the output elasticity is less than 1 and the production system exhibits decreasing returns to scale.

P7.6 **Returns to Scale.** Determine whether the following production functions exhibit constant, increasing, or decreasing returns to scale.

A. $Q = 25X + 0.5Y + 8Z$

B. $Q = 9L + 5K - 400$

C. $Q = 10A + 7B + 4AB$

D. $Q = 6L^2 + 3LK + 2K^2$

E. $Q = 2L^{0.4}K^{0.6}$

P7.6 **SOLUTION**

A. Initially, let $X = Y = Z = 100$, so output is:

$$Q_1 = 25(100) + 0.5(100) + 8(100) = 3,350$$

Increasing all inputs by 4% leads to:

$$Q_2 = 25(104) + 0.5(104) + 8(104) = 3,484$$

Since a 4% increase in all inputs results in a 4% increase in output (Q_2/Q_1 = 3,484/3,350 = 1.04), the output elasticity is 1 and the production system exhibits constant returns to scale.

B. Initially, let $L = K = 100$, so output is:

$$Q_1 = 9(100) + 5(100) - 400 = 1,000$$

Increasing both inputs by 5% leads to

$$Q_2 = 9(105) + 5(105) - 400 = 1,070$$

Since a 5% increase in both inputs results in a 7% increase in output (Q_2/Q_1 = 1,070/1,000 = 1.07), the output elasticity is greater than 1 and the production system exhibits increasing returns to scale.

C. Initially, let $A = B = 100$, so output is:

Production Analysis and Estimation 225

$$Q_1 = 10(100) + 7(100) + 4(100)(100) = 41{,}700$$

Increasing both inputs by 1% leads to:

$$Q_2 = 10(101) + 7(101) + 4(101)(101) = 42{,}521$$

Since a 1% increase in both inputs results in a 4% increase in output (Q_2/Q_1 = 42,521/41,700 = 1.04), the output elasticity is greater than 1 and the production system exhibits increasing returns to scale.

D. Initially, let L = K = 100, so output is:

$$Q_1 = 6(100^2) + 3(100)(100) + 2(100^2) = 110{,}000$$

Increasing both inputs by 2% leads to:

$$Q_2 = 6(102^2) + 3(102)(102) + 2(102^2) = 114{,}444$$

Since a 2% increase in both inputs results in a 4% increase in output (Q_2/Q_1 = 114,444/110,000 = 1.04), the output elasticity is greater than 1 and the production system exhibits increasing returns to scale.

E. Initially, let L = K = 100, so output is:

$$Q_1 = 2(100^{0.4})(100^{0.6}) = 200$$

Increasing both inputs by 4% leads to:

$$Q_2 = 2(104^{0.4})(104^{0.6}) = 208$$

Since a 4% increase in both inputs results in a 4.0% increase in output (Q_2/Q_1 = 208/200 = 1.04), the output elasticity is 1 and the production system exhibits constant returns to scale.

P7.7 **Returns to Scale.** Determine whether the following production functions exhibit constant, increasing, or decreasing returns to scale.

A. $Q = 2X + 25Y + 5Z$

B. $Q = 3A + 5B - 200$

C. $Q = 5A + 6B + 3AB$

D. $Q = 4L^2 - 3LK + 2K^2$

E. $Q = 4L^{0.4}K^{0.8}$

P7.7 SOLUTION

A. Initially, let $X = Y = Z = 100$, so output is:

$$Q_1 = 2(100) + 25(100) + 5(100) = 3,200$$

Increasing all inputs by 4% leads to:

$$Q_2 = 2(104) + 25(104) + 5(104) = 3,328$$

Since a 4% increase in all inputs results in a 4% increase in output ($Q_2/Q_1 = 3,328/3,200 = 1.04$), the output elasticity is 1 and the production system exhibits constant returns to scale.

B. Initially, let $L = K = 100$, so output is:

$$Q_1 = 3(100) + 5(100) - 200 = 600$$

Increasing both inputs by 5% leads to

$$Q_2 = 3(105) + 5(105) - 200 = 640$$

Since a 5% increase in both inputs results in a 6.7% increase in output ($Q_2/Q_1 = 640/600 = 1.067$), the output elasticity is greater than 1 and the production system exhibits increasing returns to scale.

C. Initially, let $A = B = 100$, so output is:

$$Q_1 = 5(100) + 6(100) + 3(100)(100) = 31,100$$

Increasing both inputs by 1% leads to:

$$Q_2 = 5(101) + 6(101) + 3(101)(101) = 31,714$$

Production Analysis and Estimation

Since a 1% increase in both inputs results in a 1.3% increase in output (Q_2/Q_1 = 31,714/31,300 = 1.02), the output elasticity is greater than 1 and the production system exhibits increasing returns to scale.

D.   Initially, let L = K = 100, so output is:

$$Q_1 = 4(100^2) - 3(100)(100) + 2(100^2) = 30,000$$

Increasing both inputs by 2% leads to:

$$Q_2 = 4(102^2) - 3(102)(102) + 2(102^2) = 31,212$$

Since a 2% increase in both inputs results in a 4% increase in output (Q_2/Q_1 = 31,212/30,000 = 1.04), the output elasticity is greater than 1 and the production system exhibits increasing returns to scale.

E.   Initially, let L = K = 100, so output is:

$$Q_1 = 4(100^{0.4})(100^{0.8}) = 1,005$$

Increasing both inputs by 4% leads to:

$$Q_2 = 4(104^{0.4})(104^{0.8}) = 1,053$$

Since a 4% increase in both inputs results in a 4.8% increase in output (Q_2/Q_1 = 1,053/1,005 = 1.048), the output elasticity is greater than 1 and the production system exhibits increasing returns to scale.

P7.8   **Returns to Scale.** Determine whether the following production functions exhibit constant, increasing, or decreasing returns to scale.

A. $Q = 10X + 4Y + 0.25Z$

B. $Q = 12L + 5K + 500$

C. $Q = 4A + 14B + 3AB$

D. $Q = 5L^2 + 5LK + 5K^2$

E. $Q = 3L^{0.3}K^{0.4}$

P7.8   SOLUTION

A.   Initially, let $X = Y = Z = 100$, so output is:

$$Q_1 = 10(100) + 4(100) + 0.25(100) = 1{,}425$$

Increasing all inputs by 4% leads to:

$$Q_2 = 10(104) + 4(104) + 0.25(104) = 1{,}482$$

Since a 4% increase in all inputs results in a 4% increase in output ($Q_2/Q_1 = 1{,}482/1{,}425 = 1.04$), the output elasticity is 1 and the production system exhibits constant returns to scale.

B.   Initially, let $L = K = 100$, so output is:

$$Q_1 = 12(100) + 5(100) + 500 = 2{,}200$$

Increasing both inputs by 5% leads to

$$Q_2 = 12(105) + 5(105) + 500 = 2{,}285$$

Since a 5% increase in both inputs results in a 3.9% increase in output ($Q_2/Q_1 = 2{,}285/2{,}200 = 1.039$), the output elasticity is less than 1 and the production system exhibits diminishing returns to scale.

C.   Initially, let $A = B = 100$, so output is:

$$Q_1 = 4(100) + 14(100) + 3(100)(100) = 31{,}800$$

Increasing both inputs by 1% leads to:

$$Q_2 = 4(101) + 14(101) + 3(101)(101) = 32{,}421$$

Since a 1% increase in both inputs results in a 2% increase in output ($Q_2/Q_1 = 32{,}421/31{,}800 = 1.02$), the output elasticity is greater than 1 and the production system exhibits increasing returns to scale.

D.   Initially, let $L = K = 100$, so output is:

$$Q_1 = 5(100^2) + 5(100)(100) + 5(100^2) = 150{,}000$$

Production Analysis and Estimation

Increasing both inputs by 2% leads to:

$$Q_2 = 5(102^2) + 5(102)(102) + 5(102^2) = 156{,}060$$

Since a 2% increase in both inputs results in a 4% increase in output (Q_2/Q_1 = 156,060/150,000 = 1.04), the output elasticity is greater than 1 and the production system exhibits increasing returns to scale.

E. Initially, let L = K = 100, so output is:

$$Q_1 = 3(100^{0.3})(100^{0.4}) = 75$$

Increasing both inputs by 4% leads to:

$$Q_2 = 3(104^{0.3})(104^{0.4}) = 77$$

Since a 4% increase in both inputs results in a 2.7% increase in output (Q_2/Q_1 = 77/75 = 1.027), the output elasticity is less than 1 and the production system exhibits decreasing returns to scale.

P7.9 **Optimal Input Mix.** *Medical Devices, Inc., based in Detroit, Michigan, manufactures and distributes prosthetics (artificial limbs) and other medical supplies. Doctor Who, president of Medical Devices, is reviewing the company's sales-force compensation plan. Currently, the company pays its three experienced sales staff members salaries based on the number of years of service. Brian Devlin, a new sales trainee, is paid a more modest salary. Monthly sales and salary data for each employee are as follows:*

Sales Staff	Average Monthly Sales	Monthly Salary
Larry Appleton	$200,000	$8,000
Betty Boop	150,000	6,500
Joe Cartwright	120,000	4,500
Brian Devlin	90,000	3,000

Devlin in particular has shown great promise during the past year, and Dr. Who believes a substantial raise is clearly justified. At the same time, some adjustment to the compensation paid other sales personnel would also seem appropriate. Dr. Who is considering changing from his current compensation plan to one based on a 6%

commission. Dr. Who sees such a plan as fairer to the parties involved and believes it would also provide strong incentives for needed market expansion.

A. Calculate Dr. Who's salary expense for each employee expressed as a percentage of the sales generated by that individual.

B. Calculate monthly income for each employee under a 6% commission-based system.

C. Will a commission-based plan result in efficient relative salaries, efficient salary levels, or both?

P7.9 SOLUTION

A.

Sales Staff	Average Monthly Sales	Monthly Salary	Commission Rate
(1)	(2)	(3)	(4) = (3) ÷ (2)
Larry Appleton	$200,000	$8,000	4.00%
Betty Boop	150,000	6,500	4.33%
Joe Cartwright	120,000	4,500	3.75%
Brian Devlin	90,000	3,000	3.33%

B.

Sales Staff	Average Monthly Sales	6% Commission
(1)	(2)	(3) = (2) × 0.06
Larry Appleton	$200,000	$12,000
Betty Boop	150,000	9,000
Joe Cartwright	120,000	7,200
Brian Devlin	90,000	5,400

C. The commission-based compensation plan will result in more efficient salaries for sales personnel. Under this plan, Dr. Who's sales costs average 6%, irrespective of which member of the sales staff generates a given dollar of sales. Each employee is treated equally under this plan in the sense that all are paid the same rate for generating business.

While a commission-based plan will result in an efficient relative salary structure, a 6% commission may or may not result in an optimal level of compensation being paid to each employee. If 6% of sales represents the net marginal revenue (marginal revenue minus all costs except sales expenses) generated by the sales staff, then optimal levels of compensation would be generated under such a commission-based plan. However, if net marginal revenues are different than this rate, some adjustment in the commission rate would be appropriate.

P7.10 **Optimal Input Mix.** Period Music, Inc., based in Bennington, Vermont, manufactures and distributes recreations of stringed instruments played in the Baroque and Renaissance periods. President Lucy Ricardo is reviewing the company's sales force compensation plan. Currently, the company pays its three experienced sales staff members salaries based on years of service, past contributions to the company, and so on. Jim Ignatowski, a new sales trainee, is paid a more modest salary. Monthly sales and salary data for each employee are as follows:

Sales Staff	Average Monthly Sales	Monthly Salary
Lance Cumson	$100,000	$6,000
Maude Findlay	80,000	5,000
Mary Hartman	60,000	3,450
Jim Ignatowski	45,000	2,475

Ignatowski in particular has shown great promise during the past year, and Ricardo believes a substantial raise is clearly justified. At the same time, some adjustment to the compensation paid other sales personnel would also seem appropriate. Ricardo is considering changing from his current compensation plan to one based on a 7% commission. Ricardo sees such a plan as fairer to the parties involved and believes it would also provide strong incentives for needed market expansion.

A. Calculate Ricardo's salary expense for each employee expressed as a percentage of the sales generated by that individual.

B. Calculate monthly income for each employee under a 7% commission-based system.

C. Will a commission-based plan result in efficient relative salaries, efficient salary levels, or both?

P7.10 SOLUTION

A.

Sales Staff	Average Monthly Sales	Monthly Salary	Commission Rate
(1)	(2)	(3)	(4) = (3) ÷ (2)
Lance Cumson	$100,000	$6,000	6.00%
Maude Findlay	80,000	5,000	6.25%
Mary Hartman	60,000	3,450	5.75%
Jim Ignatowski	45,000	2,475	5.50%

B.

Sales Staff	Average Monthly Sales	7% Commission
(1)	(2)	(3) = (2) × 0.07
Lance Cumson	$100,000	$7,000
Maude Findlay	80,000	5,600
Mary Hartman	60,000	4,200
Jim Ignatowski	45,000	3,150

C.
The commission-based compensation plan will result in more efficient salaries for sales personnel. Under this plan, Ricardo's sales costs average 7%, irrespective of which member of the sales staff generates a given dollar of sales. Each employee is treated equally under this plan in the sense that all are paid the same rate for generating business.

While a commission-based plan will result in an efficient relative salary structure, a 10% commission may or may not result in an optimal level of compensation being paid to each employee. If 10% of sales represents the net marginal revenue (marginal revenue minus all costs except sales expenses) generated by the sales staff, then optimal levels of compensation would be generated under such a commission-based plan. However, if net marginal revenues are different than this rate, some adjustment in the commission rate would be appropriate.

P7.11

Optimal Input Mix. Telephone Systems, Inc., based in St. Louis, Missouri, distributes telephone systems to business customers. President Jack Killian is reviewing the company's sales-force compensation plan. Because of the industry's prior history of

Production Analysis and Estimation 233

regulation, the company currently pays its three experienced sales staff members salaries based on years of service, past contributions to the company, and so on instead of using a commission system. Arthur Dietrich, a new sales trainee, is paid a more modest salary. Annual sales and salary data for each employee are as follows:

Sales Staff	Annual Sales	Annual Salary
Mortica Addams	$600,000	$30,000
Peg Bundy	500,000	26,000
Beaver Cleaver	400,000	25,000
Arthur Dietrich	300,000	18,000

Dietrich in particular has shown great promise during the past year, and Killian believes a substantial raise is clearly justified. At the same time, some adjustment to the compensation paid other sales personnel would also seem appropriate. Killian is considering changing from his current compensation plan to one based on a 8% commission. Killian sees such a plan as fairer to the parties involved and believes it would also provide strong incentives for needed market expansion.

A. Calculate Killian's salary expense for each employee expressed as a percentage of the sales generated by that individual.

B. Calculate monthly income for each employee under a 8% commission-based system.

C. Will a commission-based plan result in efficient relative salaries, efficient salary levels, or both?

P7.11 **SOLUTION**

A.

Sales Staff	Annual Sales	Annual Salary	Commission Rate
(1)	(2)	(3)	(4) = (3) ÷ (2)
Mortica Addams	$600,000	$30,000	5.00%
Peg Bundy	500,000	26,000	5.20%
Beaver Cleaver	400,000	25,000	6.25%
Arthur Dietrich	300,000	18,000	6.00%

B.

Sales Staff	Annual Sales	8% Commission
(1)	(2)	(3) = (2) × 0.08
Mortica Addams	$600,000	$48,000
Peg Bundy	500,000	40,000
Beaver Cleaver	400,000	32,000
Arthur Dietrich	300,000	24,000

C. The commission-based compensation plan will result in more efficient salaries for sales personnel. Under this plan, Killian's sales costs average 8%, irrespective of which member of the sales staff generates a given dollar of sales. Each employee is treated equally under this plan in the sense that all are paid the same rate for generating business.

While a commission-based plan will result in an efficient relative salary structure, an 8% commission may or may not result in an optimal level of compensation being paid to each employee. If 8% of sales represents the net marginal revenue (marginal revenue minus all costs except sales expenses) generated by the sales staff, then optimal levels of compensation would be generated under such a commission-based plan. However, if net marginal revenues are different than this rate, some adjustment in the commission rate would be appropriate.

P7.12 *Optimal Input Mix.* Miami Devices, Inc., based in Miami, Florida, manufactures and distributes fetal monitors and other medical supplies. President Chris Cagney is reviewing the company's sales-force compensation plan. Currently, the company pays its three experienced sales staff members salaries based on years of service, past contributions to the company, and so on. Sonny Crockett, a new sales trainee, is paid a more modest salary. Annual sales and salary data for each employee are as follows:

Sales Staff	Annual Sales	Annual Salary
Flo Castleberry	$400,000	$28,000
Dianne Chambers	350,000	22,750
Cliff Clavin	325,000	21,125
Sonny Crockett	290,000	17,400

Production Analysis and Estimation

Crockett in particular has shown great promise during the past year, and Cagney believes a substantial raise is clearly justified. At the same time, some adjustment to the compensation paid other sales personnel would also seem appropriate. Cagney is considering changing from the current compensation plan to one based on a 9% commission. Cagney sees such a plan as fairer to the parties involved and believes it would also provide strong incentives for needed market expansion.

A. Calculate Cagney's salary expense for each employee expressed as a percentage of the sales generated by that individual.

B. Calculate monthly income for each employee under a 9% commission-based system.

C. Will a commission-based plan result in efficient relative salaries, efficient salary levels, or both?

P7.12 SOLUTION

A.

Sales Staff	Annual Sales	Annual Salary	Commission Rate
(1)	(2)	(3)	(4) = (3) ÷ (2)
Flo Castleberry	$400,000	$28,000	7.00%
Dianne Chambers	350,000	22,750	6.50%
Cliff Clavin	325,000	21,125	6.50%
Sonny Crockett	290,000	17,400	6.00%

B.

Sales Staff	Annual Sales	9% Commission
(1)	(2)	(3) = (2) × 0.09
Flo Castleberry	$400,000	$36,000
Dianne Chambers	350,000	31,500
Cliff Clavin	325,000	29,250
Sonny Crockett	290,000	26,100

C. The commission-based compensation plan will result in more efficient salaries for sales personnel. Under this plan, Cagney's sales costs average 9%, irrespective of which member of the sales staff generates a given dollar of sales. Each employee is treated equally under this plan in the sense that all are paid the same rate for generating business.

While a commission-based plan will result in an efficient relative salary structure, a 9% commission may or may not result in an optimal level of compensation being paid to each employee. If 9% of sales represents the net marginal revenue (marginal revenue minus all costs except sales expenses) generated by the sales staff, then optimal levels of compensation would be generated under such a commission-based plan. However, if net marginal revenues are different than this rate, some adjustment in the commission rate would be appropriate.

P7.13 **Optimal Input Mix.** *Hydraulics Ltd. has designed a pipeline that provides a throughput of 70,000 gallons of water per 24-hour period. If the diameter of the pipeline were increased by 1 inch, throughput would increase by 4,000 gallons per day. Alternatively, throughput could be increased by 6,000 gallons per day using the original pipe diameter with pumps that had 100 more horsepower.*

A. *Estimate the marginal rate of technical substitution between pump horsepower and pipe diameter.*

B. *Assuming the cost of additional pump size is $600 per horsepower and the cost of larger diameter pipe is $200,000 per inch, does the original design exhibit the property required for optimal input combinations? If so, why? If not, why not?*

P7.13 SOLUTION

A. The marginal rate of technical substitution is calculated by comparing the marginal products of "diameter," MP_D, and "horsepower," MP_H:

$$MP_D = \Delta Q/\Delta D = 4,000/1 = 4,000 \text{ gal.}$$

$$MP_H = \Delta Q/\Delta H = 6,000/100 = 60 \text{ gal.}$$

So,

$$MRTS_{DH} = \frac{MP_D}{MP_H} = \frac{4,000}{60}$$

Production Analysis and Estimation

$$\frac{\Delta Q/\Delta D}{\Delta Q/\Delta H} = -66.67$$

$$\frac{\Delta H}{\Delta D} = -66.67$$

This implies $\Delta H = -66.67\Delta D$ or $\Delta D = -0.015\Delta H$. This means, for example, that output would remain constant following a one inch reduction in pipe diameter provided that horsepower were increased by 66.67.

B. No. The rule for optimal input proportions is:

$$\frac{MP_D}{P_D} = \frac{MP_H}{P_H}$$

In this instance the question is:

$$\frac{MP_D}{P_D} \stackrel{?}{=} \frac{60}{\$600}$$

$$\frac{4{,}000}{\$200{,}000} \stackrel{?}{=} \frac{60}{\$600}$$

$$0.02 \neq 0.10$$

Here the additional throughput provided by the last dollar spent on more horsepower (0.10 gallons/day) is five times the gain in output resulting from the last dollar spent to increase the pipe diameter (0.02 gallons/day). Thus, horsepower and pipe diameter are not being employed in optimal proportions in this situation.

P7.14 *Optimal Input Mix.* Electron Specialties, Inc. has designed an electric feeder cable that provides a throughput of 2,000 ampere hours (aH) per 24-hour period. If the diameter of the cable were increased by 1/2 inch, throughput would increase by 500 aH per day. Alternatively, throughput could be increased by 1,000 aH per day using the original cable diameter with an additional 100 mf of capacitance electronics designed by the firm.

A. Estimate the marginal rate of technical substitution between capacitance electronics and cable diameter.

B. *Assuming the cost of additional capacitance electronics is $50 per mf and the cost of larger diameter cable is $20,000 per 1/2 inch, does the original design exhibit the property required for optimal input combinations? If so, why? If not, why not?*

P7.14 **SOLUTION**

A. The marginal rate of technical substitution is calculated by comparing the marginal products of "diameter," MP_D, and "capacitance," MP_C:

$$MP_D = \Delta Q/\Delta D = 500/0.5 = 1{,}000 \text{ aH}.$$

$$MP_C = \Delta Q/\Delta C = 1{,}000/100 = 10 \text{ aH}.$$

So,

$$MRTS_{DF} = \frac{MP_D}{MP_C} = -\frac{1{,}000}{10}$$

$$\frac{\Delta Q/\Delta D}{\Delta Q/\Delta C} = -100$$

$$\frac{\Delta C}{\Delta D} = -100$$

This implies $\Delta C = -100\Delta D$ or $\Delta D = -0.01\Delta C$. This means, for example, that output would remain constant following a one-half inch reduction in cable diameter provided that capacitance were increased by 100.

B. No. The rule for optimal input proportions is:

$$\frac{MP_D}{P_D} = \frac{MP_C}{P_C}$$

In this instance the question is:

$$\frac{MP_D}{P_D} \;?\; \frac{MP_C}{P_C}$$

Production Analysis and Estimation 239

$$\frac{1,000}{\$20,000} \stackrel{?}{=} \frac{10}{\$80}$$

$$0.05 \neq 0.125$$

Here the additional throughput provided by the last dollar spent on additional capacitance (0.125 aH) is two and one-half times the gain in power output resulting from the last dollar spent to increase the cable diameter (0.05 aH). Thus, capacitance electronics and cable diameter are not being employed in optimal proportions in this situation.

P7.15 **Optimal Input Mix.** Boch, Ltd., has designed a fuel injector for oil fired generators that provides a throughput of 3 gallons of oil per minute. If the diameter of the industrial injector nozzle were increased by 1 centimeter, throughput would increase 1 gallon per minute. Alternatively, throughput could be increased by 2 gallons per minute using the original injector diameter with fuel pumps that had 50 more pounds of pressure (psi).

A. Estimate the marginal rate of technical substitution between pump psi and injector diameter.

B. Assuming the cost of additional fuel pump size is $10 per psi (due to changing of the pump and fuel supply peripheral), and the cost of larger diameter fuel injector is $400 per centimeter (due to machining of combustion units), does the original design exhibit the property required for optimal input combinations? If so, why? If not, why not?

P7.15 **SOLUTION**

A. The marginal rate of technical substitution is calculated by comparing the marginal products of "diameter," MP_D, and "psi," MP_P:

$$MP_D = \Delta Q/\Delta D = 1/1 = 1 \text{ gal.}$$

$$MP_P = \Delta Q/\Delta P = 2/50 = 0.04 \text{ gal.}$$

So,

$$MRTS_{DP} = \frac{MP_D}{MP_P} = \frac{1}{0.04}$$

Harcourt Brace & Company

$$\frac{\Delta Q/\Delta D}{\Delta Q/\Delta P} = -25$$

$$\frac{\Delta P}{\Delta D} = -25$$

This implies $\Delta P = -25\Delta D$ or $\Delta D = -0.04\Delta P$. This means, for example, that output would remain constant following a one centimeter reduction in injector diameter provided that psi were increased by 25.

B. No. The rule for optimal input proportions is:

$$\frac{MP_D}{P_D} = \frac{MP_P}{P_P}$$

In this instance the question is:

$$\frac{MP_D}{P_D} \stackrel{?}{=} \frac{MP_P}{P_P}$$

$$\frac{1}{\$400} \stackrel{?}{=} \frac{0.04}{\$10}$$

$$0.0025 \neq 0.004$$

Here the additional throughput provided by the last dollar spent on more psi (0.004 gallons/minute) is about 1.6 times the gain in output resulting from the last dollar spent to increase the output diameter (0.02 gallons/minute). Thus, psi and injector diameter are not being employed in optimal proportions in this situation.

P7.16 *Optimal Input Mix.* Third World Solutions, Inc., has designed a manual water pump that attains a flow rate of 5 gallons per minute using 1 manpower. If the diameter of the pump were increased by 1 inch, throughput would increase 4 gallons per minute. Alternatively, throughput could be increased by an additional 8 gallons per minute using the original pump diameter with one hydraulic chamber.

A. Estimate the marginal rate of technical substitution between hydraulic chambers and pump diameter.

Production Analysis and Estimation

B. *Assuming the cost of additional hydraulic chamber size is $5 per chamber and the cost of a larger pump diameter is $2.50 per inch, does the original design exhibit the property required for optimal input combinations? If so, why? If not, why not?*

P7.16 SOLUTION

A. The marginal rate of technical substitution is calculated by comparing the marginal products of "diameter," MP_D, and "hydraulic chambers," MP_H:

$$MP_D = \Delta Q/\Delta D = 4/1 = 4 \text{ gal.}$$

$$MP_H = \Delta Q/\Delta H = 8/1 = 8 \text{ gal.}$$

So,

$$MRTS_{DH} = \frac{MP_D}{MP_H} = -\frac{4}{8}$$

$$\frac{\Delta Q/\Delta D}{\Delta Q/\Delta H} = -0.50$$

$$\frac{\Delta H}{\Delta D} = -0.50$$

This implies $\Delta H = -0.5\Delta D$ or $\Delta D = -2\Delta H$. This means, for example, that output would remain constant following a one-half inch reduction in pump diameter provided that the number of hydraulic chambers were increased by 1.

B. No. The rule for optimal input proportions is:

$$\frac{MP_D}{P_D} = \frac{MP_H}{P_H}$$

In this instance the question is:

$$\frac{MP_D}{P_D} \stackrel{?}{=} \frac{MP_H}{P_H}$$

$$\frac{4}{\$2.50} \stackrel{?}{=} \frac{8}{\$5}$$

$$1.60 \stackrel{\checkmark}{=} 1.60$$

Here the additional throughput provided by the last dollar spent on more hydraulic chamber (1.60 gallons/minute) is the same as the gain in output resulting from the last dollar spent to increase the pump diameter (1.60 gallons/minute). Thus, hydraulic chambers and pump diameter are being employed in optimal proportions in this situation.

P7.17 **Optimal Input Level.** Tarboro Furniture, Inc., sells hardwood chairs, in both kits and fully assembled forms. Customers who assemble their own chairs benefit from the lower kit price of $35 per chair. "Full-service" customers enjoy the luxury of an assembled chair, but pay a higher price of $60 per chair. Both kit and fully assembled chair prices are stable. The company has observed the following relation between the number of assembly workers employed per day and assembled chair output:

Number of Workers per day	Finished Chairs
0	0
1	5
2	9
3	12
4	14
5	15

A. Construct a table showing the net marginal revenue product derived from assembly worker employment.

B. How many assemblers would Tarboro Furniture employ at a daily wage rate of $75?

C. What is the highest daily wage rate Tarboro Furniture would pay to hire four assemblers per day?

Production Analysis and Estimation

P7.17 **SOLUTION**

A. Since the market for hardwood chairs is perfectly competitive, the $25 price premium for fully assembled chairs versus kits is stable. Thus, the net marginal revenue product of assembler labor (sometimes referred to as the value of marginal product) is:

Number of Assemblers per Day (1)	Fully Assembled Output (2)	Marginal Product of Labor (3)	Net Marginal Revenue Product of Labor (4)=(3)×$25
0	0	--	--
1	5	5	$125
2	9	4	100
3	12	3	75
4	14	2	50
5	15	1	25

B. From the table above, we see that employment of three assemblers could be justified at a daily wage of $75 since $MRP_{A=3}$ = $75. Employment of a fourth attendant could not be justified since $MRP_{A=4}$ = $50 < $75.

C. From the table above, the $MRP_{A=4}$ = $50. Thus, a daily wage of $50 per assembler is the most Tarboro Furniture would be willing to pay to hire a staff of 4 assemblers.

P7.18 *Optimal Input Level.* Do-It-Yourself, Inc., sells budget-priced stereo receivers, in both kit and fully-assembled forms. Customers who assemble their own receivers benefit from the lower kit price of $100 per receiver. "Full-service" customers enjoy the luxury of an assembled receiver, but pay a higher price of $150 per receiver. Both kit and fully assembled receiver prices are stable. The company has observed the following relation between the number of assembly workers employed per day and assembled receiver output:

Number of Workers per day	Finished Receivers
0	0
1	8
2	14
3	18
4	20
5	21

A. Construct a table showing the net marginal revenue product derived from assembly worker employment.

B. How many assemblers would Do-It-Yourself employ at a daily wage rate of $120?

C. What is the highest daily wage rate Do-It-Yourself would pay to hire four assemblers per day?

P7.18 SOLUTION

A. Since the market for budget receivers is perfectly competitive, the $50 price premium for fully assembled receivers versus kits is stable. Thus, the net marginal revenue product of assembler labor (sometimes referred to as the value of marginal product) is:

Number of Assemblers per Day (1)	Fully Assembled Output (2)	Marginal Product of Labor (3)	Net Marginal Revenue Product of Labor (4)=(3)×$50
0	0	--	--
1	8	8	$400
2	14	6	300
3	18	4	200
4	20	2	100
5	21	1	50

B. From the table above, we see that employment of three employees could be justified at a daily wage of $120 since $MRP_{A=3} = \$200 > \$120$. Employment of a fourth could not be justified since $MRP_{A=4} = \$100 < \$120$.

C. From the table above, the $MRP_{A=4} = \$100$. Thus, $100 is the most Do-It-Yourself would be willing to pay to hire a staff of 4 assemblers.

P7.19 Optimal Input Level. Just Bikes, Inc., sells tricycles, in partially-assembled and fully assembled forms. Parents who assemble their own tricycles benefit from the lower price of $40 per tricycle. "Full-service" customers enjoy the luxury of an assembled tricycle, but pay a higher price of $60 per tricycle. Both partially and fully assembled tricycle prices are stable. The company has observed the following relation between the number of assembly workers employed per day and assembled tricycle output:

Number of Workers per day	Finished Tricycles
0	0
1	8
2	14
3	18
4	21
5	23

A. Construct a table showing the net marginal revenue product derived from assembly worker employment.

B. How many assemblers would Huffee Bikes employ at a daily wage rate of $100?

C. What is the highest daily wage rate Huffee Bikes would pay to hire three assemblers per day?

P7.19 SOLUTION

A. Since the market for tricycles is perfectly competitive, the $20 price premium for fully assembled versus partially assembled tricycles is stable. Thus, the net marginal revenue product of assembler labor (sometimes referred to as the value of marginal product) is:

Number of Assemblers per Day (1)	Fully Assembled Output (2)	Marginal Product of Labor (3)	Net Marginal Revenue Product of Labor (4)=(3)×$20
0	0	--	--
1	8	8	$160
2	8	6	120
3	14	4	80
4	20	3	60
5	23	2	40

B. From the table above, we see that employment of two assemblers could be justified at a daily wage of $100 since $MRP_{A=2} = \$120 > \$100$. Employment of a third assembler could not be justified since $MRP_{A=3} = \$80 < \$100$.

C. From the table above, the $MRP_{A=3} = \$80$. Thus, $80 is the most Huffee Bikes would be willing to pay to hire a staff of 3 assemblers.

P7.20 *Nonprice Competition.* Tickets, Inc., uses mall intercept promotion services to promote concerts and sporting events. The St. Louis firm uses a team of ten students to hand-deliver flyers at shopping malls and other high traffic centers, where every hour increment of flyer advertising costs $130. Over the past year, the following relation between advertising and ticket sales per event has been observed:

$$\text{Sales (units)} = 7{,}000 + 200A - 0.6A^2$$

and

$$\Delta \text{Sales}/\Delta A = 200 - 1.2A$$

Here A represents one hour of flyer distribution, and sales are measured in numbers of tickets.

Niki Martin, manager for the St. Louis firm, has been asked to recommend an appropriate level of advertising. In thinking about this problem, Martin noted its resemblance to the optimal resource employment problem she had studied in a managerial economics course that was part of her MBA program. The advertising-sales relation could be thought of as a production function with advertising as an input and sales as the output. The problem is to determine the profit-maximizing level of employment for the input, advertising, in this "production" system. Martin recognized

Production Analysis and Estimation 247

that to solve the problem she needed a measure of output value. After consultation with associates, she determined that the value of output is $2 per ticket, the net marginal revenue earned (price minus all marginal costs except flyer advertising).

A. Continuing with Martin's production analogy, what is the "marginal product" of advertising?

B. What is the rule for determining the optimal amount of a resource to employ in a production system? Explain the logic underlying this rule.

C. Using the rule for optimal resource employment, determine the profit-maximizing number of flyer distribution hours.

P7.20 **SOLUTION**

A. The marginal product of advertising is given by the expression:

$$MP_A = \Delta S/\Delta A$$

$$= 200 - 1.2A$$

B. The rule for determining the optimal amount of a resource to employ is:

$$MRP_A = P_A$$

The logic of this rule can be best understood by simply dissecting the above relations:

$$MRP_A = P_A$$

$$MP_A \times MR_Q = P_A$$

$$\frac{\Delta Q}{\Delta A} \times \frac{\Delta TR}{\Delta Q} = \frac{\Delta TC}{\Delta A}$$

$$\frac{\Delta TR}{\Delta A} = \frac{\Delta TC}{\Delta A}$$

$$\Delta TR = \Delta TC$$

$$\text{Inflow} = \text{Outflow}$$

C. The optimal advertising level is found where:

$$MRP_A = P_A$$

$$MP_A \times MR_Q = P_A$$

$$(200 - 1.2A) \times \$2 = \$130$$

$$400 - 2.4A = 130$$

$$2.4A = 270$$

$$A = 112.5$$

or 115 one-hour segments of flyer advertising.

P7.21 **Nonprice Competition.** Top Gun Marketing, Inc., offers overhead banner fly-by promotion services using their Cessna aircraft and banner creation facilities. The Padres Island firm specializes in restaurant promotion via fly-bys at outdoor events and other high traffic centers, where each 10 minute increment of advertising costs $300. Over the past year, the following relation between fly-by advertising and incremental restaurant guests per month has been observed:

$$Sales\ (units) = 5,200 + 50A - 0.5A^2$$

and

$$\Delta Sales/\Delta A = 50 - A$$

Here A represents a 10-minute fly-by advertisement, and sales are measured in numbers of restaurant guests.

Pete Mitchel, manager for the Padres Island firm, has been asked to recommend an appropriate level of advertising. In thinking about this problem, Act noted its resemblance to the optimal resource employment problem he had studied in a managerial economics course that was part of his MBA program. The advertising-sales relation could be thought of as a production function with advertising as an input and sales as the output. The problem is to determine the profit-maximizing level of employment for the input, advertising, in this "production" system. Ace recognized that to solve the problem he needed a measure of output value. After consultation with the restaurant, he determined that the value of output is $10 per guest, the net marginal revenue earned by the client (price minus all marginal costs except fly-by advertising).

Production Analysis and Estimation 249

    A. Continuing with Mitchel's production analogy, what is the "marginal product" of advertising?

    B. What is the rule for determining the optimal amount of a resource to employ in a production system? Explain the logic underlying this rule.

    C. Using the rule for optimal resource employment, determine the profit-maximizing number of 10-minute ads.

P7.21 SOLUTION

    A. The marginal product of advertising is given by the expression:

$$MP_A = \Delta S/\Delta A$$

$$= 50 - A$$

    B. The rule for determining the optimal amount of a resource to employ is:

$$MRP_A = P_A$$

The logic of this rule can be best understood by simply dissecting the above relations:

$$MRP_A = P_A$$

$$MP_A \times MR_Q = P_A$$

$$\frac{\Delta Q}{\Delta A} \times \frac{\Delta TR}{\Delta Q} = \frac{\Delta TC}{\Delta A}$$

$$\frac{\Delta TR}{\Delta A} = \frac{\Delta TC}{\Delta A}$$

$$\Delta TR = \Delta TC$$

$$\text{Inflow} = \text{Outflow}$$

    C. The optimal advertising level is found where:

$$MRP_A = P_A$$

$$MP_A \times MR_Q = P_A$$

$$(50 - A) \times \$10 = \$300$$

$$500 - 10A = 300$$

$$10A = 200$$

$$A = 20$$

or 20 10-minute increments of fly-by advertising.

P7.22 **Optimal Input Level.** Laboratory Testing, Inc., provides routine drug tests for employers in the Los Angeles metropolitan area. Tests are supervised by skilled technicians using equipment produced by two leading competitors in the medical equipment industry. Records for the current year show an average of 24 tests per hour performed on the A-1, and 51 tests per hour on a new machine, the Caltec. The A-1 is leased for $16,000 per month, and the Caltec is leased at a rate of $34,000 per month. On average, each machine is operated 25 eight-hour days per month. Labor and all other costs are fixed.

A. Does company usage reflect an optimal mix of testing equipment?

B. At a price of $5 per test should the company lease more machines?

P7.22 **SOLUTION**

A. The rule for an optimal combination of A-1 (A) and Caltec (C) equipment is:

$$\frac{MP_A}{P_A} = \frac{MP_C}{P_C}$$

Of course, marginal products and equipment prices must both be in the same relevant time frame, either hours or months.

On a per hour basis, the relevant question is:

$$\frac{24}{\$16,000/(25 \times 8)} \stackrel{?}{=} \frac{51}{34,000/(25 \times 8)}$$

Production Analysis and Estimation

$$0.3 \stackrel{\checkmark}{=} 0.3$$

On a per month basis, the relevant question is:

$$\frac{24 \times (25 \times 8)}{\$16,000} \stackrel{?}{=} \frac{51 \times (25 \times 8)}{\$34,000}$$

$$0.3 \stackrel{\checkmark}{=} 0.3$$

In both instances, the last dollar spent on each machine increased output by the same 0.3 units indicating an optimal mix of testing machines.

B. Yes, expansion would be profitable. The rule for optimal input employment is:

$$MRP = MP \times MR_Q = \text{Input Price}$$

In this instance, for each machine hour:

A-1

$$MRP_A = MP_A \times MR_Q \stackrel{?}{=} P_A$$

$$24 \times \$5 \stackrel{?}{=} \$16,000/(25 \times 8)$$

$$\$120 > \$80$$

Caltec

$$MRP_C = MP_C \times MR_Q \stackrel{?}{=} P_C$$

$$51 \times \$5 \stackrel{?}{=} \$34,000/(25 \times 8)$$

$$\$255 > \$170$$

Or, in per month terms:

$$MRP_A = MP_A \times MR_Q \stackrel{?}{=} P_A$$

$$24 \times (25 \times 8) \times \$5 \stackrel{?}{=} \$16,000$$

$$\$24,000 > \$16,000$$

$$MRP_C = MP_C \times MR_Q \stackrel{?}{=} P_C$$

$$51 \times (25 \times 8) \times \$5 \stackrel{?}{=} \$34,000$$

$$\$51,000 > \$34,000$$

In both cases, we see that each machine returns more than its marginal cost (price), and expansion would be profitable.

P7.23 ***Optimal Input Level.*** Smokey's Garage, Inc., provides routine auto diagnostics for customers in the Atlanta, Georgia, metropolitan area. Tests are supervised by skilled mechanics using equipment produced by two leading competitors in the auto test equipment industry. Records for the current year show an average of 4 tests per hour performed on the Sunny Tune System (STS), and 6 tests per hour on a new machine, the Car Care Tower (CCT). The STS is leased for $8,000 per month, and the CCT is leased at a rate of $12,000 per month. On average, each machine is operated 25 eight-hour days per month. Labor and all other costs are fixed.

A. Does company usage reflect an optimal mix of testing equipment?

B. At a price of $15 per test should the company lease more machines?

P7.23 SOLUTION

A. The rule for an optimal combination of STS and CCT equipment is:

$$\frac{MP_{STS}}{P_{STS}} = \frac{PM_{CCT}}{P_{CCT}}$$

Of course, marginal products and equipment prices must both be in the same relevant time frame, either hours or months.

On a per hour basis, the relevant question is:

$$\frac{4}{\$8,000/(25 \times 8)} \stackrel{?}{=} \frac{6}{\$12,000/(25 \times 8)}$$

$$0.1 \stackrel{\checkmark}{=} 0.1$$

On a per month basis, the relevant question is:

$$\frac{4 \times (25 \times 8)}{\$8,000} \stackrel{?}{=} \frac{6 \times (25 \times 8)}{\$12,000}$$

In both instances, the last dollar spent on each machine increased output by the same 0.1 units indicating an optimal mix of testing machines.

B. Yes, expansion would be profitable. The rule for optimal input employment is:

$$MRP = MP \times MR_Q = \text{Input Price}$$

In this instance, for each machine hour:

$$\text{STS} \qquad\qquad \text{CCT}$$

$$MRP_{STS} = MP_{STS} \times MR_Q \stackrel{?}{=} P_{STS} \qquad MRP_{CCT} = MP_{CCT} \times MR_Q \stackrel{?}{=} P_{CCT}$$

$$4 \times \$15 \stackrel{?}{=} \$8{,}000/(25 \times 8) \qquad 6 \times \$15 \stackrel{?}{=} \$12{,}000/(25 \times 8)$$

$$\$60 > \$40 \qquad\qquad \$90 > \$60$$

Or, in per month terms:

$$\text{STS} \qquad\qquad \text{CCT}$$

$$MRP_{STS} = MP_{STS} \times MR_Q \stackrel{?}{=} P_{STS} \qquad MRP_{CCT} = MP_{CCT} \times MR_Q \stackrel{?}{=} P_{CCT}$$

$$4 \times (25 \times 8) \times \$15 \stackrel{?}{=} \$8{,}000 \qquad 6 \times (25 \times 8) \times \$15 \stackrel{?}{=} \$12{,}000$$

$$\$12{,}000 > \$8{,}000 \qquad\qquad \$18{,}000 > \$12{,}000$$

In both cases, we see that each machine returns more than its marginal cost (price), and expansion would be profitable.

P7.24 ***Optimal Input Level.*** Communications Consultant Services, Inc., advises small to medium-sized businesses on telephone equipment and network configurations. The primary resources CCS employs are skilled network consultants and computers. Currently, CCS employs 16 consultants at a cost of $70 per hour (wage plus fringes and variable overhead), and purchases 160 hours of computer time each week at a time-sharing cost of $280 per hour. Each consultant works a 40-hour week. This level of employment allows CCS to complete 213 communications analyses per week for which the firm receives $300 each.

A. Assuming that both returns to factors and returns to scale are constant, what are the marginal products for: (1) communication consultants and, (2) computer time (up to the full capacity level)?

B. Is CCS employing labor and computers in an optimal ratio, assuming that substitution of the resources is possible? Explain.

C. *Determine the marginal revenue products for consultants and for the computer services employed by CCS. (Assume constant returns to factors in Part A.)*

D. *Is CCS employing an optimal (profit-maximizing) quantity of labor and computer time? Explain.*

P7.24 SOLUTION

A. Since returns to factors and returns to scale are constant for CCS' current operations, the marginal and average products for each input will be equal. Thus,

$$MP_L = AP_L \text{ and } MP_C = AP_C$$

Where,

$$MP_L = \frac{213 \text{ communication analyses}}{40 \text{ hours} \times 16 \text{ consultants}}$$

$$= 0.33 \text{ analyses per planner hour}.$$

$$MP_C = \frac{213 \text{ communication analyses}}{160 \text{ computer hours}}$$

$$= 1.33 \text{ analysis per computer hour}.$$

B. Yes. For CCS to be using inputs in their optimal ratios, then:

$$\frac{MP_L}{MP_C} = \frac{P_L}{P_C}$$

In this problem:

$$\frac{MP_L}{MP_C} = \frac{P_L}{P_C}$$

$$\frac{0.33}{1.33} \stackrel{?}{=} \frac{\$70}{\$280}$$

$$0.25 \stackrel{\checkmark}{=} 0.25$$

Yes. CCS is employing consultants and computers in the optimal ratio.

Production Analysis and Estimation   255

    C. $MRP_L = MP_L \times MR_Q = 0.33 \times \$300 = \$100$

           $MRP_C = MP_C \times MR_Q = 1.33 \times \$300 = \$400$

        This means that an additional hour of consultant time will increase CCS revenue by $100, and an additional hour of computer time will increase revenue by $400.

    D.   No. If CCS were employing a profit maximizing quantity of labor and computer time, then MRP = P for both inputs.

           $MRP_L \overset{?}{=} P_L$ $MRP_C \overset{?}{=} P_C$

           $\$100 \neq \$70$ $\$400 \neq \$280$

        Therefore, CCS is not employing a profit maximizing level of inputs and should expand its operation.

P7.25   **Optimal Input Level.** Sunshine Pest Control, Inc., provides exterminator services to residences in the Miami area. The primary resources SPC employs are skilled exterminators and large dome/air pumps used to cover the homes, pump in insecticide, and minimize leakage to the environment. Currently, SPC employs 10 exterminators at a cost of $15 per hour, employs 2,000 hours of pump time each week at a cost of $3 per hour. Each exterminator works a 40-hour week. This level of employment allows SPC to complete 100 treatments per week for which the firm receives $100 each.

    A.   Assuming that both returns to factors and returns to scale are constant, what are the marginal products for (1) exterminators and (2) gallons of chemicals?

    B.   Is SPC employing labor and domes in an optimal ratio, assuming that substitution of the resources is possible? Explain.

    C.   Determine the marginal revenue products for exterminators and for the domes/pumps employed by SPC. (Assume constant returns to factors in Part A.)

    D.   Is SPC employing an optimal (profit-maximizing) quantity of labor and computer time? Explain.

P7.25 SOLUTION

A. Since returns to factors and returns to scale are constant for SPC's current operations, the marginal and average products for each input will be equal. Thus,

$$MP_L = AP_L \text{ and } MP_D = AP_D$$

Where,

$$MP_L = \frac{100 \text{ treatments}}{40 \text{ hours} \times 10 \text{ exterminators}}$$

$$= 0.25 \text{ treatments per exterminator}$$

$$MP_D = \frac{100 \text{ treatments}}{2,000 \text{ dome-pump hours}}$$

$$= 0.05 \text{ treatments per dome-pump hour.}$$

B. Yes. For SPC to be using inputs in their optimal ratios, then:

$$\frac{MP_L}{MP_D} = \frac{P_L}{P_D}$$

In this problem:

$$\frac{MP_L}{MP_D} = \frac{P_L}{P_D}$$

$$\frac{0.25}{0.05} \stackrel{?}{=} \frac{\$15}{\$3}$$

Yes. SPC is employing exterminators and dome pumps in the optimal ratio.

C. $MRP_L = MP_L \times MR_Q = 0.25 \times \$100 = \$25$

$MRP_D = MP_D \times MR_Q = 0.05 \times \$100 = \$5$

Production Analysis and Estimation

This means that an additional hour of exterminator time will increase SPC revenue by $25, and an additional hour of dome pump time will increase revenue by $5.

D. No. If SPC were employing a profit maximizing quantity of labor and computer time, then MRP = P for both inputs.

$$MRP_L \stackrel{?}{=} P_L \qquad MRP_D \stackrel{?}{=} P_D$$

$$\$25 > \$15 \qquad \$5 > \$3$$

Therefore, SPC is not employing a profit maximizing level of inputs and should expand its operation.

Chapter 8

COST ANALYSIS AND ESTIMATION

MULTIPLE CHOICE QUESTIONS

Q8.1　　The amount paid under prevailing market conditions is:

　　　　A.　historical cost.
　　　　B.　opportunity cost.
> 　　　C.　current cost.
　　　　D.　replacement cost.

Q8.2　　The change in cost caused by a given managerial decision is:

　　　　A.　implicit cost.
> 　　　B.　incremental cost.
　　　　C.　explicit cost.
　　　　D.　opportunity cost.

Q8.3　　Costs that do not vary across decision alternatives are:

　　　　A.　implicit.
　　　　B.　explicit.
> 　　　C.　sunk.
　　　　D.　economic.

Q8.4　　A cost-output relation for a specific plant and operating environment is the:

> 　　　A.　short-run cost curve.
　　　　B.　long-run total cost curve.
　　　　C.　long-run marginal cost curve.
　　　　D.　long-run average cost curve.

Q8.5　　The output level at which short-run average costs are minimized is:

　　　　A.　minimum efficient scale.
　　　　B.　where multiplant economies of scale equal one.
　　　　C.　where multiplant economies of scale exceed one.
> 　　　D.　capacity.

Harcourt Brace & Company

Cost Analysis and Estimation

Q8.6 The foregone value associated with the current rather than next-best use of a given asset is called:

    A. current cost.
    B. replacement cost.
    C. historical cost.
>   D. opportunity cost.

Q8.7 Unlike the marginal cost concept, the incremental cost concept:

    A. does not focus on individual managerial decisions.
    B. is not relevant for optimal output determination.
    C. embodies sunk costs.
>   D. can involve multiple units of output.

Q8.8 In the long run, the:

    A. availability of at least one input is fixed.
    B. firm's operating decisions are typically constrained by prior capital expenditures.
    C. availability of all but one input is fixed.
>   D. firm has complete flexibility with respect to input use.

Q8.9 When $\epsilon_C < 1$:

    A. decreasing returns to all factors are implied.
>   B. increasing returns to scale are implied.
    C. decreasing returns to scale are implied.
    D. constant returns to scale are implied.

Q8.10 Learning involves:

    A. movements along a single LRAC curve.
    B. movements along a single SRAC curve.
    C. shifts in SRAC curves over time.
>   D. shifts in LRAC curves over time.

Q8.11 The amount that must be paid for an item under prevailing market conditions is:

    A. historical cost.
    B. replacement cost.
    C. incremental cost.
>   **D.** current cost.

Q8.12 The foregone value associated with the current rather than next-best use of a given asset is:

    A. replacement cost.
    B. implicit cost.
    C. explicit cost.
>   **D.** opportunity cost.

Q8.13 Incremental cost is the change in:

>   **A.** total cost caused by a given managerial decision.
    B. noncash expenses caused by a given managerial decision.
    C. out-of-pocket costs caused by a given managerial decision.
    D. variable cost caused by a given managerial decision.

Q8.14 Noncash expenses are:

    A. explicit costs.
    B. sunk costs.
    C. incremental costs.
>   **D.** implicit costs.

Q8.15 In the decision process, management should ignore:

    A. implicit costs.
    B. historical costs.
>   **C.** sunk costs.
    D. incremental costs.

Cost Analysis and Estimation

Q8.16 In the decision process, management should always consider:

> A. relevant costs.
> B. sunk costs.
> C. implicit costs only.
> D. historical costs.

Q8.17 The long-run is a period of time:

> A. during which at least one input is variable.
> B. during which at least one input is fixed.
> C. sufficient to vary all inputs in the production process.
> D. greater than one year.

Q8.18 Fixed costs include:

> A. variable labor expenses.
> B. output-related energy costs.
> C. output-related raw material costs.
> D. variable interest costs for borrowed capital.

Q8.19 Marginal cost equals:

> A. average variable cost at its maximum point.
> B. the change in total fixed cost divided by the change in quantity.
> C. the change in total variable cost divided by the change in quantity.
> D. total cost divided by quantity.

Q8.20 If the productivity of variable factors is decreasing in the short-run:

> A. marginal cost must increase as output increases.
> B. average cost must decrease as output increases.
> C. average cost must increase as output increases.
> D. marginal cost must decrease as output increases.

Q8.21 If the slope of a long-run total cost function decreases as output increases, the firm's underlying production function exhibits:

  A. constant returns to scale.
  B. decreasing returns to scale.
  C. decreasing returns to a factor input.
> D. increasing returns to scale.

Q8.22 If a total product curve exhibits increasing returns to a variable input, the cost elasticity is:

  A. equal to one.
  B. greater than one.
> C. unknown, without further information.
  D. less than one.

Q8.23 Each point on a long-run average cost curve is the minimum:

  A. point on the short-run marginal cost curve.
> B. short-run average cost of production.
  C. long-run average cost of production.
  D. point on the short-run average cost curve.

Q8.24 A firm's capacity is the output:

  A. maximum that can be produced in the long-run.
> B. level where short-run average costs are minimized.
  C. level where long-run average costs are minimized.
  D. maximum that can be produced in the short-run.

Q8.25 Minimum efficient scale is the output level where:

> A. long-run average cost is first minimized.
  B. long-run marginal cost is first minimized.
  C. long-run total cost is first minimized.
  D. short-run average cost is first minimized.

Cost Analysis and Estimation 263

Q8.26 Minimum efficient scale will increase if:

> **A.** fixed costs increase.
> **B.** transportation costs increase in relation to production costs.
> **C.** transportation costs decrease in relation to production costs.
> **D.** variable costs decrease.

Q8.27 With the opportunity for beneficial learning, a firm's learning curve is:

> **A.** downward sloping.
> **B.** horizontal.
> **C.** vertical.
> **D.** upward sloping.

Q8.28 The percentage change in profit that results from a 1% change in units sold equals:

> **A.** the cost elasticity.
> **B.** the returns to scope economies.
> **C.** marginal profit.
> **D.** the degree of operating leverage.

Q8.29 Sunk costs:

> **A.** typically involve multiple units of output.
> **B.** do not vary across decision alternatives.
> **C.** come into play when judging the costs of adding a new product line, advertising campaign, production shift, or organization structure.
> **D.** play a role in determining the optimal course of action.

Q8.30 In the long run, the:

> **A.** firm has complete flexibility with respect to input use.
> **B.** availability of all inputs is fixed.
> **C.** operating period is longer than the planning period.
> **D.** availability of at least one input is fixed.

PROBLEMS AND SOLUTIONS

P8.1 *Cost Concepts.* Answer each of the following as true or false.

    A. If $\epsilon_c > 1$, increasing returns to scale and decreasing average costs are indicated.

    B. Average cost exceeds marginal cost at the minimum efficient scale of plant.

    C. When total fixed cost and price are held constant, a reduction in average variable cost will typically cause a reduction in the breakeven activity level.

    D. An increase in total fixed cost will always increase the degree of operating leverage for firms making a positive net profit.

    E. When long-run average cost is decreasing, it can pay to operate smaller plants at their peak efficiency rather than larger plants with some excess capacity.

P8.1 SOLUTION

    A. False. When $\epsilon_c > 1$, the percentage change in cost exceeds a given percentage change in output. This describes a situation of increasing average costs and diminishing returns to scale.

    B. False. The point of minimum average cost identifies the minimum efficient scale of plant. By definition, average and marginal costs are equal at this point.

    C. True. The breakeven activity level is where $Q = TFC/(P - AVC)$. As an average variable cost (AVC) decreases, this ratio and the breakeven activity level will also decrease.

    D. True. The degree of operating leverage is defined $DOL = Q(P - AVC)/[Q(P - AVC) - TFC)]$. Therefore, when total fixed costs rise, DOL will increase as well.

    E. False. When long-run average costs are declining, it can pay to operate larger plants with some excess capacity rather than smaller plants at their peak efficiency.

P8.2 *Cost Analysis.* Demand and supply conditions in the market for unskilled labor are an important concern to business and government decision makers. Consider the case of a federally-mandated minimum wage set above the equilibrium or market clearing wage level. Some of the following factors have the potential to influence the demand or quantity demanded of unskilled labor. Influences on the supply or quantity supplied can

Cost Analysis and Estimation

also result. Holding all else equal, describe these influences as increasing or decreasing, and indicate the direction of the resulting movement along or shift in the relevant labor demand and/or supply curve(s). Will wage rates rise or fall?

A. *An increase in the popularity of self-service restaurants, gas stations, and so on.*

B. *A rise in welfare benefits.*

C. *A decrease in the quality of secondary education.*

D. *A rise in interest rates.*

E. *An increase in the minimum wage.*

P8.2 SOLUTION

A. "Self-service" gas stations, restaurants, car washes, and so on, involve a substitution of the consumer's own labor for hired unskilled labor. As self-service increases in popularity, a decrease or leftward shift in the demand for unskilled labor occurs. Wage rates will *fall*.

B. A rise in welfare benefits makes not working more attractive, and will cause a decrease or leftward shift in the supply of unskilled labor. Wage rates will *rise*.

C. A decrease in the quality of secondary education has the effect of decreasing worker productivity and will cause a decrease or leftward shift in the demand for unskilled labor. To the extent that the disadvantages of a decrease in the quality of education are recognized by students, fewer will stay in school and a secondary effect of an increase or rightward shift in the supply of unskilled labor will also be observed. Wage rates will *fall*.

D. Holding all else equal, a rise in interest rates will decrease the attractiveness of capital relative to labor. Employers can be expected to substitute labor for the now relatively more expensive capital. An increase or rightward shift in the demand for unskilled labor will result. Wage rates will *rise*.

E. An increase in the minimum wage will have the effect of decreasing the quantity demanded of unskilled labor, while at the same time increasing the quantity supplied. The first involves an upward movement along the demand curve, while the second involves an upward movement along the supply curve. Wage rates will *rise*.

P8.3 ***Incremental Costs.*** Electron Control, Inc., manufactures voltage regulators that it sells to other manufacturers, who then customize and distribute the products to quality assurance labs for their sensitive test equipment. The yearly volume of output is 15,000 units. The selling price and cost per unit are shown below:

Selling price		$200
Costs:		
Direct material	$35	
Direct labor	50	
Variable overhead	25	
Variable selling expenses	25	
Fixed selling expenses	_15_	_150_
Unit profit before tax		$50

Management is evaluating the alternative of performing the necessary customizing to allow Electron Control to sell its output directly to Q/A labs for $275 per unit. Although no added investment is required in productive facilities, additional processing costs are estimated as:

Direct labor	$25 per unit
Variable overhead	$15 per unit
Variable selling expenses	$10 per unit
Fixed selling expenses	$100,000 per year

A. Calculate the incremental profit Electron Control would earn by customizing its instruments and marketing directly to end users.

P8.3 SOLUTION

A. This problem should be answered by using incremental profit analysis. The analysis deals only with the incremental revenues and costs associated with the decision to engage in further processing.

Cost Analysis and Estimation

Incremental revenue per unit ($275 - $200)	$75
Incremental variable cost per unit ($25 + $15 + $10)	-50
Incremental profit contribution per unit	$25
Yearly output volume in units	×15,000
Incremental variable profit per year	$375,000
Incremental fixed cost per year	-100,000
Yearly incremental profit	$275,000

Since the incremental profit is positive, the decision to engage in further processing would be more profitable than continuing the present operating policy.

P8.4 **Incremental Costs.** *Fluff Rite, Inc., manufactures stove top popcorn poppers that it sells to distributors, who then customize and distribute the products to retailers as house-brand poppers. The yearly volume of output is 100,000 units. The selling price and cost per unit are shown below:*

Selling price		$20
Costs:		
Direct material	$2	
Direct labor	5	
Variable overhead	2	
Variable selling expenses	2	
Fixed selling expenses	1	13
Unit profit before tax		$7

Management is evaluating the alternative of performing the necessary customizing to allow Fluff Rite to sell its output directly to retailers for $26 per unit. Although no added investment is required in productive facilities, additional processing costs are estimated as:

Direct labor	$2 per unit
Variable overhead	$1 per unit
Variable selling expenses	$1 per unit
Fixed selling expenses	$50,000 per year

A. *Calculate the incremental profit Fluff Rite would earn by customizing its poppers and marketing directly to retailers.*

P8.4 SOLUTION

A. This problem should be answered by using incremental profit analysis. The analysis deals only with the incremental revenues and costs associated with the decision to engage in further processing.

Incremental revenue per unit ($26 - $20)	$6
Incremental variable cost per unit ($2 + $1 + $1)	-4
Incremental profit contribution per unit	$2
Yearly output volume in units	× 100,000
Incremental variable profit per year	$200,000
Incremental fixed cost per year	-50,000
Yearly incremental profit	$150,000

Since the incremental profit is positive, the decision to engage in further processing would be more profitable than continuing the present operating policy.

P8.5 ***Incremental Costs.*** *Infinite Audio, Inc., manufactures car speakers which it sells to other resellers, who then customize and distribute the products to retailers which sell hi-fi auto equipment. The yearly volume of output is 300,000 pairs. The selling price and cost per unit are shown below:*

Selling price		*$150*
Costs:		
Direct material	*$25*	
Direct labor	*45*	
Variable overhead	*20*	
Variable selling expenses	*15*	
Fixed selling expenses	*10*	*115*
Unit profit before tax		*$35*

Management is evaluating the alternative of performing the necessary customizing to allow Infinite Audio to sell its output directly to car stereo retailers for $200 per unit under an in-house marquee. Although no added investment is required in productive facilities, additional processing costs are estimated as:

Cost Analysis and Estimation

Direct labor	$20 per unit
Variable overhead	$15 per unit
Variable selling expenses	$10 per unit
Fixed selling expenses	$300,000 per year

A. Calculate the incremental profit Infinite Audio would earn by customizing its instruments and marketing directly to end users.

P8.5 **SOLUTION**

A. This problem should be answered by using incremental profit analysis. The analysis deals only with the incremental revenues and costs associated with the decision to engage in further processing.

Incremental revenue per unit ($200 - $150)	$50
Incremental variable cost per unit ($20 + $15 + $10)	-45
Incremental profit contribution per unit	$ 5
Yearly output volume in units	× 300,000
Incremental variable profit per year	$1,500,000
Incremental fixed cost per year	-300,000
Yearly incremental profit	$1,200,000

Since the incremental profit is positive, the decision to engage in further processing would be more profitable than continuing the present operating policy.

P8.6 **Breakeven Analysis.** Glow Plug Pros, Inc., is a repair facility specializing in the maintenance and repair of diesel engines just outside of Carlisle, Pennsylvania -- one of the largest trucking hubs in the U.S. Todd Moore, business manager for GPP, has been asked by the owners to prepare a financial analysis of the potential of a 24-hour repair operation. Opening such a center would require remodeling the facility and the hiring of some additional staff. Estimated first year expenses for the Glow Plug Pros diesel service center are:

Support staff salary expense	$ 15,000
Mechanic Salary expense	80,000
Supplies	4,000
Equipment	5,000
Remodeling	10,000
Electricity, heat, and taxes	<u>8,000</u>
Total expenses	$122,000

Mechanic and staff salary expenses are estimated on an hourly basis, reflecting additional salary and overtime costs. Supplies and remodeling expenses are above and beyond those required for normal facility operations. Equipment costs represent a prorated share of the centers fixed equipment-leasing costs. Electricity costs of $2,000 reflect additional anticipated usage, whereas heat and taxes of $6,000 reflect an allocated share of fixed expenses.

A.   Calculate breakeven revenue for the proposed 24-hour GPP diesel service center.

P8.6   **SOLUTION**

A.   The incremental breakeven revenue level for the GPP's proposal is the revenue level that would just cover estimated incremental costs.

Incremental costs:	
Support staff salary expense	$ 15,000
Mechanic staff salary expense	80,000
Supplies	4,000
Remodeling	10,000
Electricity	<u>2,000</u>
Total incremental costs and revenue breakeven level	$111,000

Equipment, heat and tax expenses are fixed, and irrelevant to the decision of opening a 24 hour diesel service center.

P8.7   **Breakeven Analysis.** *Melba Joe's Boutique, Inc., is a beauty salon specializing in full-service beauty treatments: facials, manicures, waxes and tanning booths. The business manager for Melba Joe's has been asked by the owner to prepare a financial analysis*

Cost Analysis and Estimation 271

of the potential of an extended hours operation. Such a move would require remodeling the facility and the hiring of additional staff. Estimated first year expenses for an extended hours operation are:

Support staff salary expense	$ 12,000
Beautician salary expense	90,000
Beauty supplies	8,000
Equipment	10,000
Remodeling	24,000
Electricity, heat, and taxes	25,000
Total expenses	$179,000

Beautician and staff salary expenses are estimated on an hourly basis, reflecting additional salary and overtime costs. Supplies and remodeling expenses are above and beyond those required for normal facility operations. Equipment costs represent a prorated share of the centers fixed equipment-leasing costs. Electricity costs of $4,000 reflect additional anticipated usage, whereas heat and taxes of $5,000 reflect an allocated share of fixed beauty shop expenses.

A. Calculate breakeven revenue for the proposed extended hours operation.

P8.7 SOLUTION

A. The incremental breakeven revenue level is the revenue level that would just cover estimated incremental costs.

Incremental costs:	
Support staff salary expense	$12,000
Beautician staff salary expense	90,000
Beauty supplies	8,000
Remodeling	24,000
Electricity	4,000
Total incremental costs and revenue breakeven level	$138,000

Equipment, heat and tax expenses are fixed, and irrelevant to the decision of opening a 24 hour diesel service center.

P8.8 **Breakeven Analysis.** The Midtown Filling Station is a gasoline retailer and minor tune-up specialty shop in Denton, Texas. Louie DePalma, the proprietor of MFS, has decided to prepare a financial analysis of the potential of a 24-hour convenience store operation. Opening such a center would require remodeling the filling station and the hiring of additional cash register attendants, but mechanics would still work only from 8am to 5pm. Estimated first year expenses for the Midtown's service and convenience center are:

Cash register attendant salary expense	$ 30,000
Mechanic salary expense	80,000
Supplies	8,000
Equipment	10,000
Remodeling	45,000
Electricity, heat, and taxes	15,000
Total expenses	$188,000

Mechanic and attendant salary expenses are estimated on an hourly basis, reflecting any additional salary and overtime costs. Supplies and remodeling expenses are above and beyond those required for normal facility operations. Equipment costs represent a prorated share of the centers fixed equipment-leasing costs. Electricity costs of $3,000 reflect additional anticipated usage, whereas heat and taxes of $2,000 reflect an allocated share of fixed clinic expenses.

A. Calculate breakeven revenue for the proposed 24 hour service and convenience center.

P8.8 SOLUTION

A. The incremental breakeven revenue level is the revenue level that would just cover estimated incremental costs.

Cost Analysis and Estimation

    Incremental costs:

Support staff salary expense	$30,000
Supplies	8,000
Remodeling	45,000
Electricity	3,000
Total incremental costs and revenue breakeven level	$86,000

Equipment, mechanic salary, heat and tax expenses are fixed, and irrelevant to the decision of opening a 24 hour service and convenience center.

P8.9   **Opportunity Costs.** *Three graduate business students are considering operating a tofu burger stand in the Dalles, Oregon, windsurfing resort area during their summer break. This is an alternative to summer employment with a local fruit cannery where they would earn $5,000 each over the three-month summer period. A fully equipped facility can be leased at a cost of $8,000 for the summer. Additional projected costs are $2,000 for insurance, and 25¢ per unit for materials and supplies. Their tofu burgers would be priced at $1.50 per unit.*

    A.   *What is the accounting cost function for this business?*

    B.   *What is the economic cost function for this business?*

    C.   *What is the economic breakeven number of units for this operation? (Assume a $1.50 price and ignore interest costs associated with the timing of the lease payments.)*

P8.9   **SOLUTION**

    A.   The accounting cost function is:

$$\text{Total Accounting Cost} = TC_A = \text{Fixed leasing plus insurance costs} + \text{Variable materials plus supplies costs}$$

$$= \$8,000 + \$2,000 + \$0.25Q$$

$$= \$10,000 + \$0.25Q$$

    B.   The economic cost function is:

$$\text{Total Economic Cost} = \text{Summer employment opportunity cost} + TC_A$$

$$= 3(5{,}000) + \$10{,}000 + \$0.25Q$$

$$= \$25{,}000 + \$0.25Q$$

C. The economic breakeven point is reached when:

$$Q = \frac{TFC}{P - AVC}$$

$$= \frac{\$25{,}000}{\$1.50 - \$0.25}$$

$$= 20{,}000 \text{ units}$$

P8.10 **Opportunity Costs.** Two graduate business students are considering opening a full-service car wash in the Kansas City, Missouri, after graduation. This is an alternative to employment with a local manufacturing firm where they would each earn $25,000 per year. A fully equipped facility can be leased at a cost of $35,000 for the year. Additional projected costs are $15,000 for overhead, and $5 per automobile for materials and supplies. Full detail automobile cleaning would be priced at $25.

A. What is the accounting cost function for this business?

B. What is the economic cost function for this business?

C. What is the economic breakeven number of units for this operation? (Assume a $25 price and ignore interest costs associated with the timing of the lease payments.)

P8.10 **SOLUTION**

A. The accounting cost function is:

$$\text{Total Accounting Cost} = TC_A = \text{Fixed leasing plus overhead costs} + \text{Variable materials plus supplies costs}$$

$$= \$35{,}000 + \$15{,}000 + \$5Q$$

$$= \$50{,}000 + \$5Q$$

Cost Analysis and Estimation

B. The economic cost function is:

$$\text{Total Economic Cost} = \text{Employment opportunity cost} + TC_A$$

$$= 2(\$25,000) + \$50,000 + \$5Q$$

$$= \$100,000 + \$5Q$$

C. The economic breakeven point is reached when:

$$Q = \frac{TFC}{P - AVC}$$

$$= \frac{\$100,000}{\$25 - \$5}$$

$$= 5,000 \text{ automobiles}$$

P8.11 **Opportunity Costs.** *Three University of Florida engineering students are considering operating a mobile car clinic in Gainesville, Florida, during their summer break. This is an alternative to summer employment stacking plastic cups at a local injection molding manufacturer where they would earn $6,000 each over the three-month summer period. A van equipped for such service can be leased at a cost of $4,500 for the summer from an owner taking a long vacation in the Bahamas. Additional projected costs are $2,500 for insurance, and $5 per service call for materials and supplies. Their service calls would be priced at $30 per unit, plus any parts costs (parts will not be inventoried, but purchased from local parts outlets.*

A. What is the accounting cost function for this business (ignoring parts)?

B. What is the economic cost function for this business?

C. What is the economic breakeven number of units for this operation? (Assume a $30 price and ignore interest costs associated with the timing of the lease payments.)

P8.11 **SOLUTION**

A. The accounting cost function is:

$$\text{Total Accounting Cost} = TC_A = \text{Fixed leasing plus insurance costs} + \text{Variable materials plus supplies costs}$$

$$= \$4{,}500 + \$2{,}500 + \$5Q$$

$$= \$7{,}000 + \$5Q$$

B. The economic cost function is:

$$\text{Total Economic Cost} = \text{Summer employment opportunity cost} + TC_A$$

$$= 3(6{,}000) + \$7{,}000 + \$5Q$$

$$= \$25{,}000 + \$5Q$$

C. The economic breakeven point is reached when:

$$Q = \frac{TFC}{P - AVC}$$

$$= \frac{\$25{,}000}{\$30 - \$5}$$

$$= 1{,}000 \text{ calls}$$

P8.12 ***Profit Contribution Analysis.*** Fisherman's Wharf Cotton, Inc., (FWC) sells souvenir T-shirts on San Francisco's Pier 9 at a price of $10. Of this amount, $6 is profit contribution. FWC is considering an attempt to differentiate its product from several other competitors by using higher quality T-shirts. Doing so would increase FWC's unit cost by $1 per shirt. Current monthly profits are $5,000 on 2,500 unit sales.

A. Assuming average variable costs are constant at all output levels, what is FWC's total cost function before the proposed change?

B. What will the total cost function be if higher quality t-shirts are used?

C. Assume shirt prices remain stable at $10. What percentage increase in sales would be necessary to maintain current profit levels?

Cost Analysis and Estimation

P8.12 SOLUTION

A. From the definition of profit contribution we know that on a per unit basis:

$$\text{Profit contribution} = P - AVC$$

$$\$6 = \$10 - AVC$$

$$AVC = \$4 \text{ per unit}$$

Total fixed cost for FWC can be calculated as follows:

$$\pi = TR - TC$$

$$= TR - TVC - TFC$$

$$= (P \times Q) - (AVC \times Q) - TFC$$

$$\$5,000 = \$10(2,500) - \$4(2,500) - TFC$$

$$\$5,000 = \$15,000 - TFC$$

$$TFC = \$10,000$$

Therefore, the total cost function is:

$$TC = TFC + (AVC \times Q)$$

$$TC = \$10,000 + \$4Q$$

B. By using higher quality T-shirts, FWC's variable cost would increase by $1 while its fixed costs remain the same. FWC's new total cost function would be:

$$TC = \$10,000 + \$4Q + \$1Q$$

$$TC = \$10,000 + \$5Q$$

C. The new number of T-shirt sales necessary to maintain current profit levels would be:

$$\pi = (P \times Q) - (AVC \times Q) - TFC$$

Harcourt Brace & Company

$$\$5,000 = \$10Q - \$5Q - \$10,000$$

$$5Q = 15,000$$

$$Q = 3,000$$

$$\text{Percentage increase in Q} = \frac{3,000 - 2,500}{2,500} = 0.2 \text{ or } 20\%.$$

Thus, a 20% increase in deliveries would be needed to maintain current profit levels.

P8.13 **Profit Contribution Analysis.** Rodriques' Rugs, Inc., sells hand-made cotton rugs to tourists at a price of $50. Of this amount, $40 is profit contribution. RR is considering an attempt to differentiate his product from several other competitors by using high quality natural herb dyes. Doing so would increase RR's unit cost by $15 per rug. Current annual profits are $35,000 on 1,000 rug sales.

A. Assuming average variable costs are constant at all output levels, what is RR's total cost function before the proposed change?

B. What will the total cost function be if high quality natural herb dyes are used?

C. Assume rug prices remain stable at $50. What percentage increase in sales would be necessary to maintain current profit levels?

P8.13 **SOLUTION**

A. From the definition of profit contribution we know that on a per unit basis:

$$\text{Profit contribution} = P - AVC$$

$$\$40 = \$50 - AVC$$

$$AVC = \$10 \text{ per unit}$$

Total fixed cost for RR can be calculated as follows:

Cost Analysis and Estimation

$$\pi = TR - TC$$
$$= TR - TVC - TFC$$
$$= (P \times Q) - (AVC \times Q) - TFC$$
$$\$35{,}000 = \$50(1{,}000) - \$10(1{,}000) - TFC$$
$$\$35{,}000 = \$40{,}000 - TFC$$
$$TFC = \$5{,}000$$

Therefore, the total cost function is:

$$TC = TFC + (AVC \times Q)$$
$$TC = \$5{,}000 + \$10Q$$

B. By using high quality natural herb dyes, RR's variable cost would increase by $15 while its fixed costs remain the same. RR's new total cost function would be:

$$TC = \$5{,}000 + \$10Q + \$15Q$$
$$TC = \$5{,}000 + \$25Q$$

C. The new number of rug sales necessary to maintain current profit levels would be:

$$\pi = (P \times Q) - (AVC \times Q) - TFC$$
$$\$35{,}000 = \$50Q - \$25Q - \$5{,}000$$
$$25Q = 40{,}000$$
$$Q = 1{,}600$$

$$\text{Percentage increase in Q} = \frac{1{,}600 - 1{,}000}{1{,}000} = 0.6 \text{ or } 60\%.$$

Thus, a 60% increase in rug sales would be needed to maintain current profit levels.

P8.14 ***Profit Contribution Analysis.*** *Kathy's Bakery is a local full-service bakery in Omaha, Nebraska. Kathy sells loaves of wheat bread for $3 a loaf. Of this amount, $1.50 is profit contribution. She is considering an attempt to differentiate her shop from several other competitors by only producing a special rice bread for customers allergic to wheat. Doing so would increase her unit cost by 50¢ per rice loaf. Current monthly profits are $400 on 800 unit sales.*

    A. Assuming average variable costs are constant at all output levels, what is Kathy's total cost function before the proposed change?

    B. What will the total cost function be if rice loafs are produced?

    C. Assume rice loaf prices remain stable at $3. What percentage increase in sales would be necessary to maintain current profit levels?

P8.14 SOLUTION

    A. From the definition of profit contribution we know that on a per unit basis:

$$\text{Profit contribution} = P - AVC$$

$$\$1.50 = \$3 - AVC$$

$$AVC = \$1.50 \text{ per unit}$$

Total fixed cost for Kathy's can be calculated as follows:

$$\pi = TR - TC$$

$$= TR - TVC - TFC$$

$$= (P \times Q) - (AVC \times Q) - TFC$$

$$\$400 = \$3(800) - \$1.5(800) - TFC$$

$$\$400 = \$1{,}200 - TFC$$

$$TFC = \$800$$

Therefore, the total cost function is:

Cost Analysis and Estimation

$$TC = TFC + (AVC \times Q)$$

$$TC = \$800 + \$1.50Q$$

B. By producing rice loafs, Kathy's variable cost would increase by 50¢ while its fixed costs remain the same. Kathy's new total cost function would be:

$$TC = \$800 + \$1.50Q + \$0.50Q$$

$$TC = \$800 + \$2Q$$

C. The new number of loaves necessary to maintain current profit levels would be:

$$\pi = (P \times Q) - (AVC \times Q) - TFC$$

$$\$400 = \$3Q - \$2Q - \$800$$

$$Q = 1,200$$

$$\text{Percentage increase in Q} = \frac{1,200 - 800}{800} = 0.50 \text{ or } 50\%.$$

Thus, a 50% increase in rice loaves over wheat loaves would be needed to maintain current profit levels.

P8.15 **Degree of Operating Leverage.** *DynaLinear, Ltd., produces digital-to-analog converters for compact disk players used by radio stations and audio enthusiasts. It is contemplating an expansion into the moderately-priced home audio market by producing a CD player that would sell at a price of $300. The production of each CD player would require $100 in materials, and 7.5 hours of labor at the rate of $10 per hour for wages and fringe benefits plus variable overhead tied to labor. Energy, supervisory and other variable overhead costs would amount to $50 per unit. The accounting department has derived an allocated fixed overhead charge of $25 per CD player (at a projected volume of 14,000 units) to account for the expected increase in fixed costs.*

A. *What is DynaLinear's breakeven sales volume (in units) for home audio CD players?*

B. *Calculate the degree of operating leverage at a projected volume of 14,000 units and explain what the DOL means.*

P8.15   **SOLUTION**

A.   The breakeven level of output is

$$Q = \frac{TFC}{P - AVC}$$

$$= \frac{\$25(14,000)}{\$300 - (\$100 + \$10(7.5) + \$50)}$$

$$= \frac{350,000}{75}$$

$$= 4,667 \text{ units}$$

B.   The equation for calculating the degree of operating leverage is:

$$DOL = \frac{Q(P - AVC)}{Q(P - AVC) - TFC}$$

where DOL is the degree of operating leverage, Q is output, and all other variables are as before. Therefore, DOL at Q = 14,000 is:

$$DOL = \frac{14,000(\$300 - \$225)}{14,000(\$300 - \$225) - \$350,000}$$

$$= \frac{1,050,000}{700,000}$$

$$= 1.5$$

A DOL of 1.5 means that following a 1% change in output, profits would be expected to change by 1.5%.

P8.16   ***Degree of Operating Leverage.*** Heat Tamers, Inc., of Bend, Oregon produces special heat-resistant boots used primarily by firefighters, smoke-jumpers and steelworkers. It is contemplating an expansion into the heat resistant leather market charging a price of $150 per pair of boots. The production of each pair of boots would require $60 in materials, and 2 hours of labor at the rate of $15 per hour. Energy, supervisory and other variable overhead costs would amount to $25 per unit. The accounting

Cost Analysis and Estimation

department has derived an allocated fixed overhead charge of $30 per pair of boots (at a projected volume of 280,000 pairs) to account for the expected increase in fixed costs.

A. What is Heat Tamers' breakeven sales volume (in pairs) for heat-resistant boots?

B. Calculate the degree of operating leverage at a projected volume of 280,000 units and explain what the DOL means.

P8.16 **SOLUTION**

A. The breakeven level of output is

$$Q = \frac{TFC}{P - AVC}$$

$$= \frac{\$30(280,000)}{\$150 - (\$60 + \$15(2) + \$25)}$$

$$= \frac{8,400,000}{35}$$

$$= 240,000 \text{ units}$$

B. The equation for calculating the degree of operating leverage is:

$$DOL = \frac{Q(P - AVC)}{Q(P - AVC) - TFC}$$

where DOL is the degree of operating leverage, Q is output, and all other variables are as before. Therefore, DOL at Q = 280,000 is:

$$DOL = \frac{280,000(\$150 - \$115)}{280,000(\$150 - \$115) - \$8,400,000}$$

$$= \frac{9,800,000}{1,400,000}$$

$$= 7$$

A DOL of 7 means that following a 1% change in output, profits would be expected to change by 7%.

P8.17 **Degree of Operating Leverage.** Ion Generating, Inc., produces ion generators and control (detection) devices for industrial applications such as chemical labs. It is contemplating an expansion into the home security market by producing a smoke detector based off of the same technology that would sell at a price of $50. The production of each smoke detector would require $20 in materials, and 0.5 hours of labor at the rate of $20 per hour. Energy, supervisory and other variable overhead costs would amount to $10 per unit. The accounting department has derived an allocated fixed overhead charge of $7.50 per smoke detector (at a projected volume of 300,000 units) to account for the expected increase in fixed costs.

A. What is Ion Generating's breakeven sales volume (in units) for smoke detectors?

B. Calculate the degree of operating leverage at a projected volume of 300,000 units and explain what the DOL means.

P8.17 **SOLUTION**

A. The breakeven level of output is

$$Q = \frac{TFC}{P - AVC}$$

$$= \frac{\$7.50(300,000)}{\$50 - (\$20 + \$20(0.5) + 10)}$$

$$= \frac{2,250,000}{10}$$

$$= 225,000 \text{ units}$$

B. The equation for calculating the degree of operating leverage is:

$$DOL = \frac{Q(P - AVC)}{Q(P - AVC) - TFC}$$

where DOL is the degree of operating leverage, Q is output, and all other variables are as before. Therefore, DOL at Q = 14,000 is:

Cost Analysis and Estimation

$$DOL = \frac{300,000(\$50 - \$40)}{300,000(\$50 - \$40) - 2,250,000}$$

$$= \frac{3,000,000}{750,000}$$

$$= 4$$

A DOL of 4 means that following a 1% change in output, profits would be expected to change by 4%.

P8.18 **Multiplant Operation.** Tasty Snacks, Inc., a regional snack foods company (corn chips, potato chips, etc.) in the northeast, is considering two alternative proposals for expansion into southeastern states. Alternative 1: Construct a single plant in Chattanooga, Tennessee with a monthly production capacity of 250,000 cases, a monthly fixed cost of $265,000, and a variable cost of $45 per case. Alternative 2: Construct three plants, one each in Birmingham, Alabama, Tallahassee, Florida, and Charlotte, North Carolina, with capacities of 100,000, 80,000 and 70,000, respectively, and monthly fixed costs of $180,000, $150,000, and $135,000 each. Variable costs would be only $44 per case because of lower distribution costs. To achieve these cost savings, sales from each smaller plant would be limited to demand within its home state. The total estimated monthly sales volume of 175,000 cases in these three southeastern states is distributed as follows: 70,000 cases in Florida, 60,000 cases in North Carolina, and 45,000 cases in Alabama.

A. Assuming a wholesale price of $50 per case, calculate the breakeven output quantities for each alternative.

B. At a wholesale price of $50 per case in all states, and assuming sales at the projected levels, which alternative expansion scheme provides Tasty Snacks with the highest profit per month?

C. If sales increase to production capacities, which alternative would prove to be more profitable?

P8.18 **SOLUTION**

A. The breakeven output quantity for the single plant alternative is:

$$Q = \frac{F}{P - AVC}$$

$$= \frac{\$265,000}{\$50 - \$45}$$

$$= 53,000 \text{ cases per month}$$

The breakeven output quantities for the multiple plant alternative is:

$$Q_{Birmingham} = \frac{\$180,000}{\$50 - \$44}$$

$$= 30,000 \text{ per month}$$

$$Q_{Tallahassee} = \frac{\$150,000}{\$50 - \$44}$$

$$= 25,000 \text{ cases per month}$$

$$Q_{Charlotte} = \frac{\$135,000}{\$50 - \$44}$$

$$= 22,500 \text{ cases per month}$$

Thus, the firm-level breakeven quantity for the multiple plant alternative would be:

$$Q = 30,000 + 25,000 + 22,500$$

$$= 77,500 \text{ cases per month}$$

provided that demand was distributed among the states in amounts equal to the breakeven quantities for each individual plant.

B. Single plant alternative:

Cost Analysis and Estimation

$$\pi = TR - TC$$
$$= PQ - TFC - AVC(Q)$$
$$= \$50(175,000) - \$265,000 - \$45(175,000)$$
$$= \$610,000$$

Multiple plant alternative:

$$\pi = TR - TC$$
$$= PQ - TFC_B - TFC_T - TFC_C - AVC(Q)$$
$$= \$50(175,000) - \$180,000 - \$150,000 - \$135,000 - \$44(175,000)$$
$$= \$585,000$$

Management would prefer the single plant alternative because of its greater profitability.

C. Single plant at full capacity:

$$\pi = TR - TC$$
$$= PQ - TFC - AVC(Q)$$
$$= \$50(250,000) - \$265,000 - \$45(250,000)$$
$$= \$985,000$$

Multiple plants at full capacity:

$$\pi = TR - TC$$
$$= PQ - TFC_B - TFC_T - TFC_C - AVC(Q)$$
$$= \$50(250,000) - \$180,000 - \$150,000 - \$135,000 - \$44(250,000)$$
$$= \$1,035,000$$

At peak capacity, management would prefer the multiple plant option because of its greater profitability.

P8.19 **Multiplant Operation.** Nature's Green, Inc., a manufacturer of alfalfa tablets sold in health-food stores, currently operates in the Kaw Valley, just outside of Meno, California. Nature's Green is considering two alternative proposals for expansion, because it has run out of acreage to grow its organically-farmed alfalfa. It has found the following sites where farmers are willing to supply organic alfalfa: Alternative 1: Construct a single plant in Big Cabin, Oklahoma with a monthly production capacity of 50,000 cases, a monthly fixed cost of $275,000, and a variable cost of $100 per case. Alternative 2: Construct three plants, one each in Eudora, Kansas, Springfield, Missouri, and Tonkawa, Oklahoma, with capacities of 25,000, 20,000 and 15,000, respectively, and monthly fixed costs of $200,000, $175,000, and $160,000 each. Variable costs would be only $95 per case because of lower distribution costs. To achieve these cost savings, sales from each smaller plant would be limited to demand within its home state. The total estimated monthly sales volume of 49,000 cases in these three southeastern states is distributed as follows: 20,000 cases in Kansas, 15,000 cases in Missouri, and 14,000 cases in Oklahoma.

A. Assuming a wholesale price of $120 per case, calculate the breakeven output quantities for each alternative.

B. Assuming sales at the projected levels, which alternative expansion scheme provides Nature's Green with the highest profit per month?

C. If sales increase to production capacities, which alternative would prove to be more profitable?

P8.19 **SOLUTION**

A. The breakeven output quantity for the single plant alternative is:

$$Q = \frac{F}{P - AVC}$$

$$= \frac{\$275,000}{\$120 - \$100}$$

$$= 13,750 \text{ cases per month}$$

The breakeven output quantities for the multiple plant alternative is:

Cost Analysis and Estimation

$$Q_{Eudora} = \frac{\$200,000}{\$120 - \$95}$$

$$= 8,000 \text{ cases per month}$$

$$Q_{Springfield} = \frac{\$175,000}{\$120 - \$95}$$

$$= 7,000 \text{ cases per month}$$

$$Q_{Tonkawa} = \frac{\$160,000}{\$120 - \$95}$$

$$= 6,400 \text{ cases per month}$$

Thus, the firm-level breakeven quantity for the multiple plant alternative would be:

$$Q = 8,000 + 7,000 + 6,400$$

$$= 21,400 \text{ cases per month}$$

provided that demand was distributed among the states in amounts equal to the breakeven quantities for each individual plant.

B. Single plant alternative:

$$\pi = TR - TC$$

$$= PQ - TFC - AVC(Q)$$

$$= \$120(49,000) - \$275,000 - \$100(49,000)$$

$$= \$705,000$$

Multiple plant alternative:

$$\pi = TR - TC$$

$$= PQ - TFC_E - TFC_S - TFC_T - AVC(Q)$$

$$= \$120(49{,}000) - \$200{,}000 - \$175{,}000 - \$160{,}000 - \$95(49{,}000)$$

$$= \$690{,}000$$

Management would prefer the single plant alternative because of its greater profitability.

C. Single plant at full capacity:

$$\pi = TR - TC$$

$$= PQ - TFC - AVC(Q)$$

$$= \$120(50{,}000) - \$275{,}000 - \$100(50{,}000)$$

$$= \$725{,}000$$

Multiple plants at full capacity:

$$\pi = TR - TC$$

$$= PQ - TFC_E - TFC_S - TFC_T - AVC(Q)$$

$$= \$120(60{,}000) - \$200{,}000 - \$175{,}000 - \$160{,}000 - \$95(60{,}000)$$

$$= \$965{,}000$$

At peak capacity, management would prefer the multiple plant option because of its greater profitability.

P8.20 **Learning Curve.** *Fashionable Designs, Ltd., plans to produce and market a new sports blazer. Based on information provided by the accounting department, the company estimates fixed costs of $40,000 per year and average variable costs at:*

$$AVC = \$1 + \$0.001Q$$

Cost Analysis and Estimation

where AVC is average variable cost (in dollars) and Q is output measured in cases of output per year.

A. Calculate total cost and average total cost for the coming year at a projected volume of 12,000 units.

B. An increase in worker productivity due to greater experience or learning during the course of the year resulted in a substantial cost saving for the company. Calculate the effect of learning on average total cost if actual total cost was $250,000 at an actual volume of 15,000 units.

P8.20 SOLUTION

A. The total variable cost function for the coming year is:

$$TVC = AVC \times Q$$
$$= (\$1 + \$0.001Q)Q$$
$$= \$1Q + \$0.001Q^2$$

At a volume of 12,000 units, estimated total cost is:

$$TC = TFC + TVC$$
$$= \$40,000 + \$1Q + \$0.001Q^2$$
$$= \$40,000 + \$1(12,000) + \$0.001(12,000^2)$$
$$= \$196,000$$

Estimated average cost is:

$$AC = TC/Q$$
$$= \$196,000/12,000$$
$$= \$16.33 \text{ per unit}$$

B. Without learning, estimated total cost and average total cost at a volume of 15,000 units are:

$$TC = \$40,000 + \$1(15,000) + \$0.001(15,000^2)$$

$$= \$280,000$$

$$AC = TC/Q$$

$$= \$280,000/15,000$$

$$= \$18.67 \text{ per unit}$$

Since estimated average cost (without learning) has risen between 12,000 and 15,000 units (see part a), the company is operating in a range of decreasing returns to scale.

If actual total costs were $250,000 at a volume of 15,000 units, actual average total costs were:

$$AC = TC/Q$$

$$= \$250,000/15,000$$

$$= \$16.67 \text{ per unit}$$

Therefore, greater experience or learning has resulted in an average cost saving of $2 per unit since:

$$\text{Learning effect} = \text{Actual AC - Estimated AC}$$

$$= \$16.67 - \$18.67$$

$$= (\$2) \text{ per unit}$$

Alternatively,

$$\text{Learning rate} = \left(1 - \frac{AC_2}{AC_1}\right) \times 100$$

$$= \left(1 - \frac{\$16.67}{\$18.67}\right) \times 100$$

$$= 11.7\%$$

Cost Analysis and Estimation

P8.21 **Learning Curve.** Teddy Bear, Inc., a rapidly growing manufacturer of high fashion children's shoes, plans to open a new production facility in Bethesda, Maryland. Based on information provided by the accounting department, the company estimates fixed costs of $500,000 per year and average variable costs at:

$$AVC = \$5 + \$0.0001Q$$

where AVC is average variable cost (in dollars) and Q is output measured in cases of output per year.

- **A.** Calculate total cost and average total cost for the coming year at a projected volume of 50,000 pairs of shoes.

- **B.** An increase in worker productivity due to greater experience or learning during the course of the year resulted in a substantial cost saving for the company. Calculate the effect of learning on average total cost if actual total cost was $1,080,000 at an actual volume of 60,000 pairs of shoes.

P8.21 SOLUTION

- **A.** The total variable cost function for the coming year is:

$$TVC = AVC \times Q$$
$$= (\$5 + \$0.0001Q)Q$$
$$= \$5Q + \$0.0001Q^2$$

At a volume of 50,000 units, estimated total cost is:

$$TC = TFC + TVC$$
$$= \$500,000 + \$5Q + \$0.0001Q^2$$
$$= \$500,000 + \$5(50,000) + \$0.0001(50,000^2)$$
$$= \$1,000,000$$

Estimated average cost is:

$$AC = TC/Q$$
$$= \$1{,}000{,}000/50{,}000$$
$$= \$20 \text{ per pair}$$

B. Without learning, estimated total cost and average total cost at a volume of 60,000 pairs are:

$$TC = \$500{,}000 + \$5(60{,}000) + \$0.0001(60{,}000^2)$$
$$= \$1{,}160{,}000$$

$$AC = TC/Q$$
$$= \$1{,}160{,}000/60{,}000$$
$$= \$19.33 \text{ per pair}$$

Since estimated average cost (without learning) has fallen between 50,000 and 60,000 units (see part a), the company is operating in a range of increasing returns to scale.

If actual total costs were $1,080,000 at a volume of 60,000 pairs, actual average total costs were:

$$AC = TC/Q$$
$$= \$1{,}080{,}000/60{,}000$$
$$= \$18 \text{ per pair}$$

Therefore, greater experience or learning has resulted in an average cost saving of $1.33 per pair since:

$$\text{Learning effect} = \text{Actual AC - Estimated AC}$$
$$= \$18 - \$19.33$$
$$= (\$1.33) \text{ per pair}$$

Alternatively,

Cost Analysis and Estimation

$$\text{Learning rate} = \left(1 - \frac{AC_2}{AC_1}\right) \times 100$$

$$= \left(1 - \frac{\$18}{\$19.33}\right) \times 100$$

$$= 6.9\%$$

P8.22 **Economies of Scale.** Tucson Timing, Inc., has just completed a study of weekly production costs during the past year for its premium quality, automotive strobe timing light, the Flash Gun II. By regressing total variable costs on output the firm estimated the following equation.

$$TVC = \$30 + \$125Q - \$1Q^2$$
$$(15) \quad (3) \quad (0.5)$$

$$R^2 = 0.90, \text{ S.E.E.} = 10$$

Here total variable cost (TVC) is expressed in thousands of dollars and Q is in thousands of strobe timing lights (units) produced per week. Numbers in parentheses are the standard errors of the coefficients.

A. Estimate total variable cost and average variable cost per week for the coming year at a projected volume of 10,000 units per week.

B. During this period, the company experienced an unexpected interruption in supplier deliveries, and unexpected increases in the cost of labor and materials. If actual average variable costs were $100 per unit at an average actual volume of 15,000 units per week, calculate the separate influences on average variable cost of lost economies of scale and the unexpected input cost increases.

P8.22 **SOLUTION**

A. Estimated total variable cost and average variable cost at a projected volume of 10,000 units are:

$$T\hat{V}C = \$30 + \$125Q - \$1Q^2$$

$$= \$30 + \$125(10) - (10^2)$$

$$= \$1{,}180(000) \text{ per week}$$

$$A\hat{V}C = TVC/Q$$

$$= \$1{,}180/10$$

$$= \$118 \text{ per unit}$$

B. Estimated total variable cost and average variable cost at a volume of 15,000 units are:

$$T\hat{V}C = \$30 + \$125(15) - \$1(15^2)$$

$$= \$1{,}680(000) \text{ per week}$$

$$A\hat{V}C = TVC/Q$$

$$= \$1{,}680/15$$

$$= \$112 \text{ per unit}$$

Thus, the projected AVC decrease due to increased economies of scale as output rose from 10,000 to 15,000 per week is $6 since:

$$\text{Increased economies of scale effect} = A\hat{V}C \text{ @ 10,000 units} - A\hat{V}C \text{ @ 15,000 units}$$

$$= \$118 - \$112$$

$$= \$6 \text{ per unit}$$

Since actual AVC = $100 at a volume of 15,000 units per week, decreases in the cost of labor and materials caused AVC to decrease by $12 over the projected level:

Cost Analysis and Estimation

$$\underset{\text{decrease effect}}{\text{Input cost}} = \text{Projected A}\hat{\text{V}}\text{C} - \text{Actual AVC}$$

$$= \$112 - \$100$$

$$= \$12 \text{ per unit}$$

Therefore, the overall $18 AVC decrease reflects the effects of both increased economies of scale ($6) and the decrease in input costs ($12).

P8.23 **Economies of Scale.** Windy Manes, Inc., has just completed a study of weekly production costs during the past year for its compact hand-held hair dryer. By regressing total variable costs on output the firm estimated the following equation.

$$TVC = \$15 + \$5Q - \$0.01Q^2$$
$$(4) \quad (2) \quad (0.005)$$

$$R^2 = 0.80, \text{ S.E.E.} = 18$$

Here total variable cost (TVC) is expressed in thousands of dollars and Q is in thousands of hand-held hair dryers (units) produced per week. Numbers in parentheses are the standard errors of the coefficients.

A. Estimate total variable cost and average variable cost per week for the coming year at a projected volume of 50,000 units per week.

B. During this period, the company experienced an unexpected interruption in supplier deliveries, and unexpected increases in the cost of labor and materials. If actual average variable costs were $4.30 per unit at an average actual volume of 75,000 units per week, calculate the separate influences on average variable cost of lost economies of scale and the unexpected input cost increases.

P8.23 **SOLUTION**

A. Estimated total variable cost and average variable cost at a projected volume of 50,000 units are:

$$T\hat{V}C = \$15 + \$5Q - \$0.01Q^2$$

$$= \$15 + \$5(50) - \$0.01(50^2)$$

$$= \$240(000) \text{ per week}$$

$$A\hat{V}C = TVC/Q$$

$$= \$240/50$$

$$= \$4.80 \text{ per unit}$$

B. Estimated total variable cost and average variable cost at a volume of 75,000 units are:

$$T\hat{V}C = \$15 + \$5(75) - \$0.01(75^2)$$

$$= \$333.75(000) \text{ or } (\$333,750) \text{ per week}$$

$$A\hat{V}C = TVC/Q$$

$$= \$333.75/75$$

$$= \$4.45 \text{ per unit}$$

Thus, the projected AVC increase due to increased economies of scale as output rose from 50,000 to 75,000 per week is $0.35 since:

$$\begin{array}{c}\text{Increased economies of}\\ \text{scale effect}\end{array} = \begin{array}{c}A\hat{V}C @\\ 50{,}000 \text{ units}\end{array} - \begin{array}{c}AVC @\\ 75{,}000 \text{ units}\end{array}$$

$$= \$4.80 - \$4.45$$

$$= \$0.35 \text{ per unit}$$

Since actual AVC = $4.30 at a volume of 75,000 units per week, decreases in the cost of labor and materials caused AVC to decrease by $0.15 over the projected level:

Cost Analysis and Estimation

$$\text{Input cost decrease effect} = \text{Projected A}\hat{\text{V}}\text{C} - \text{Actual AVC}$$

$$= \$4.45 - \$4.30$$

$$= \$0.15 \text{ per unit}$$

Therefore, the overall $0.50 AVC decrease reflects the effects of both increased economies of scale ($0.35) and the decrease in input costs ($0.15).

P8.24 **Cost Estimation.** *Natural Gas, Inc., has just completed a cost study of its natural gas production operation. By regressing total variable costs (in $000) per week on gas output, the following equation was estimated:*

$$\text{Total variable cost} = \$6{,}500 + \$0.25Q - \$0.000125Q^2$$
$$(5{,}000) \quad (0.12) \quad (0.00005)$$

Here Q is natural gas production in thousand cubic feet (units) and the numbers in parentheses are the standard errors of the coefficients. The R^2 for the equation is 0.85, and the standard error of the estimate is 50 for the weekly observations over a two-year period.

A. *Interpret the coefficient of determination (R^2).*

B. *If volume averages 8,000 units per week, calculate the range within which we would expect to find actual total variable and average variable costs with 95% confidence.*

C. *Calculate and interpret relevant t-statistics.*

D. *Are Natural Gas' average variable costs per unit increasing as output expands?*

P8.24 **SOLUTION**

A. Coefficient of determination = R^2 = 0.85, meaning that 85% of total variable cost variation is explained by the quadratic cost model. The remaining 15% of cost variation is unexplained.

B. With an average volume of 8,000 units per week, the estimated value for total variable costs is:

$$T\hat{V}C = \$6{,}500 + \$0.25Q - \$0.000125Q^2$$

$$= \$6{,}500 + \$0.25(8{,}000) - 0.000125(8{,}000^2)$$

$$= \$500(000)$$

With a standard error of the estimate = S.E.E. = 50, the 95% confidence interval for actual TVC is:

$$TVC = T\hat{V}C \pm 2\,(S.E.E.)$$

$$= \$500 \pm 2(\$50)$$

$$= \$400(000) \text{ to } \$600(000)$$

Given these data, the relevant estimate for average variable cost is:

$$A\hat{V}C = T\hat{V}C$$

$$= \$500(000)/8{,}000(000)$$

$$= \$0.0625 \text{ or } 6.25¢ \text{ per unit}$$

And the relevant 95% confidence interval is:

$$A\hat{V}C = \frac{\$400\,(000)}{\$8{,}000\,(000)} \text{ to } \frac{\$600\,(000)}{\$8{,}000\,(000)}$$

$$= \$0.05 \text{ to } \$0.075$$

C. We note that $6,500 is not an estimate of fixed costs per month since the analysis included only variable costs. T-statistics for each output variable can also be calculated to test:

$$H_0{:}b_1 = 0; \text{ and } H_0{:}b_2 = 0.$$

$$\text{For } b_1{:}\ t = \frac{0.25}{0.12} = 2.08$$

$$\text{For } b_2{:}\ t = \frac{0.000125}{0.00005} = 2.5$$

Cost Analysis and Estimation

Therefore, both coefficients are statistically significant at the 95% confidence level (i.e., t > 2), and a quadratic total variable cost function is suggested.

D. No. Given the negative sign and statistical significance of the quadratic variable coefficient, average variable costs are falling as output expands. Since average fixed costs always decline as output expands, average total costs for Natural are also declining as output expands. This implies that Natural is currently enjoying increasing returns to scale and the elasticity of cost with respect to output will be less than one, $\epsilon_C < 1$.

P8.25 *Cost Estimation. Hampshire Textiles, Inc., has just completed a cost study of its moire taffeta production facility. By regressing total variable costs per week on cloth output, their economists estimated the following equation:*

$$\text{Total variable cost} = \$30{,}000 + \$4Q - \$0.002Q^2$$
$$(20{,}000) \quad (1.5) \quad (0.0008)$$

Here Q is moire taffeta cloth production in square yards and the numbers in parentheses are the standard errors of the coefficients. The R^2 for the equation was 0.80, and the standard error of the estimate was 150 for the weekly observations over a two-year period.

A. *Interpret the coefficient of determination (R^2).*

B. *If volume averages 2,500 yards per week, calculate the range within which we would expect to find actual total variable and average variable costs with 95% confidence.*

C. *Calculate and interpret relevant t-statistics.*

D. *Are Hampshire Textiles' average variable costs per unit increasing as output expands?*

P8.25 **SOLUTION**

A. Coefficient of determination = R^2 = 0.80, meaning that 80% of total variable cost variation is explained by the quadratic cost model. The remaining 20% of cost variation is unexplained.

B. With an average volume of 2,500 yards per week, the estimated value for total variable costs is:

$$T\hat{V}C = \$30,000 + \$4Q - \$0.002Q^2$$

$$= \$30,000 + \$4(2,500) - 0.002(2,500^2)$$

$$= \$27,500$$

With a standard error of the estimate = S.E.E. = 150, the 95% confidence interval for actual TVC is:

$$TVC = T\hat{V}C \pm 2 \text{ (S.E.E.)}$$

$$= \$27,500 \pm 2(\$150)$$

$$= \$27,200 \text{ to } \$27,800$$

Given these data, the relevant estimate for average variable cost is:

$$A\hat{V}C = T\hat{V}C/Q$$

$$= \$27,500/2,500$$

$$= \$11 \text{ per yard}$$

And the relevant 95% confidence interval is:

$$A\hat{V}C = \frac{\$27,200}{2,500} \text{ to } \frac{\$27,800}{2,500}$$

$$= \$10.88 \text{ to } \$11.12 \text{ per yard}$$

C. We note that $30,000 is not an estimate of fixed costs per month since the analysis included only variable costs. T-statistics for each output variable can also be calculated to test:

$$H_0 : b_1 = 0; \text{ and } H_0 : b_2 = 0.$$

$$\text{For } b_1: t = \frac{4}{1.5} = 2.67$$

$$\text{For } b_2: t = \frac{(0.002)}{(0.0008)} = 2.5$$

Cost Analysis and Estimation

Therefore, both coefficients are statistically significant at the 95% confidence level (i.e., t > 2), and a quadratic total variable cost function is suggested.

D. No, given the negative sign and statistical significance of the quadratic variable coefficient, average variable costs are falling as output expands. Since average fixed costs always decline as output expands, average total costs for Hampshire are also declining as output expands. This implies that Hampshire is currently enjoying increasing returns to scale and the elasticity of cost with respect to output will be less than one, $\epsilon_C < 1$.

Chapter 9

LINEAR PROGRAMMING

MULTIPLE CHOICE QUESTIONS

Q9.1 The original statement of a LP problem is called the:

> A. primal.
> B. dual.
> C. shadow price.
> D. constraint condition.

Q9.2 The feasible space is a graphical region that is:

> A. economically feasible but excludes the optimal LP solution.
> B. technically feasible but excludes the optimal LP solution.
> C. technically and economically feasible and includes the optimal LP solution.
> D. technically and economically feasible but excludes the optimal LP solution.

Q9.3 If slack exists in the solution of the primal LP, the dual shadow price variable is:

> A. zero.
> B. positive.
> C. negative.
> D. none of these.

Q9.4 When some capacity constraints are binding, while others are nonbinding:

> A. the shadow price for new capacity is positive.
> B. the shadow price for output is positive.
> C. the marginal revenue product for new capacity is positive.
> D. the marginal product of new capacity is positive.

Q9.5 The cost of capacity subject to constraints is:

> A. variable.
> B. sunk.
> C. semi-variable.
> D. nonzero.

Linear Programming 305

Q9.6 *When an LP objective function is to maximize profits:*

> A. resource constraints must be of the ≤ variety.
> B. resource constraints must be of the ≥ variety.
> C. all input costs must be variable.
> D. the total revenue function must not be linear.

Q9.7 *If X > 0 in the primal solution:*

> A. the marginal value of inputs just equals the marginal value of output in X production.
> B. the marginal value of inputs exceeds the marginal value of output in X production.
> C. $L_X > 0$ in the dual solution.
> D. $L_X < 0$ in the dual solution.

Q9.8 *When the primal LP problem is to maximize revenue subject to various input constraints, the shadow prices of inputs in the dual constraints:*

> A. equal the marginal revenue product of each input.
> B. are positive for inputs with excess capacity.
> C. equals zero for fully utilized inputs.
> D. equal the marginal product of each input.

Q9.9 *If the primal objective function is to minimize cost subject to output constraints, the dual objective function is to maximize:*

   A. revenue.
   B. profits.
   C. output.
> D. the value of inputs employed.

Q9.10 *For managerial decision problems analyzed using the LP approach:*

> A. some input costs must be fixed.
> B. all input costs must be fixed.
> C. increasing returns to scale must predominate.
> D. returns to each factor input must be constant.

Q9.11 Linear programming is an analytical technique used to:

> A. solve constrained optimization problems.
> B. project trends.
> C. increase worker productivity.
> D. estimate linear demand functions.

Q9.12 Linear programming assumes:

> A. falling input prices.
> B. increasing returns to each factor input.
> C. straight-line objective and constraint functions.
> D. monopolistic competition.

Q9.13 For costs to be a linear function of output:

> A. returns to each factor input must be constant.
> B. input prices must change at a constant rate.
> C. product prices must be constant.
> D. returns to scale must be constant.

Q9.14 Along a production ray:

> A. inputs are combined in fixed proportions.
> B. outputs are produced in varying proportions.
> C. output is constant.
> D. inputs are combined in varying proportions.

Q9.15 To determine the quantity to be produced by each production process at varying points along an isoquant, managers could use:

> A. the point-slope method.
> B. slack variable method.
> C. the relative distance method.
> D. the relative cost method.

Linear Programming

Q9.16   When the costs of all inputs rise by a given percentage, the isocost line:

>
A. slope decreases.
B. slope is unaffected.
C. and objective function intersection will be unaffected.
D. slope increases.

Q9.17   Output will be maximized subject to input constraints when the firm employs:

>
A. the greatest quantity of feasible inputs.
B. the combination of inputs in the feasible space tangent to the greatest possible isoquant.
C. the combination of inputs at any corner of the feasible space.
D. any input combination included in the feasible space.

Q9.18   Profit contribution equals:

>
A. total revenue minus variable cost.
B. total revenue minus fixed cost.
C. total profit.
D. total revenue minus total cost.

Q9.19   Net profits equals profit contribution minus:

A. variable costs.
B. total costs.
C. average total costs.
> D. fixed costs.

Q9.20   An objective function:

A. is a function formulated without predisposition or bias.
B. describes any functional relation to be analyzed.
C. defines the boundary of the feasible space.
> D. expresses the goal of a linear programming problem.

Q9.21 Combinations of products that generate the same level of profit are shown graphically by:

    A. an isocost curve.
> B. an isoprofit curve.
    C. an isoquant curve.
    D. a feasible space.

Q9.22 When the objective function coincides with the boundary of the feasible space:

    A. an optimal solution cannot be determined.
    B. there is only one optimal solution.
> C. there are many possible optimal solutions.
    D. an optimal solution does not exist.

Q9.23 Slack variables:

    A. allow constraint equations to be expressed as inequalities.
> B. measure excess capacity.
    C. never equal zero.
    D. in some cases have negative values.

Q9.24 A negative value for a given slack variable implies:

    A. no excess capacity.
> B. use of more resources than are available.
    C. none of the above.
    D. excess capacity.

Q9.25 If a linear programming problem involves the minimization of advertising costs subject to audience marital status and income constraints, the objective function is:

    A. the marital status constraint.
    B. the individual income constraint.
    C. none of the above.
> D. the advertising cost function.

Linear Programming

Q9.26 Unit costs are constant if:

    A. input prices are constant.
    B. the total cost function is linear.
    C. constant returns to scale are operative.
> **D.** input prices are constant *and* the total cost function is linear.

Q9.27 Profits rise in a linear fashion with output if:

    A. profit contribution is constant.
> **B.** both output prices *and* unit costs are constant.
    C. unit costs are constant.
    D. output prices are constant.

Q9.28 If the labor slack variable = 0, then:

> **A.** the shadow price on labor is > 0.
    B. the marginal product of labor = 0.
    C. the marginal revenue product of labor = 0.
    D. excess labor capacity exists.

Q9.29 Constrained profit maximization requires:

    A. no excess capacity.
    B. excess capacity.
    C. a linear profit function.
> **D.** constrained maximization of the total profit contribution.

Q9.30 If $Q_A > 0$, then the marginal value of inputs employed:

> **A.** equals the marginal value of output.
    B. is less than the marginal value of output.
    C. equals current input prices.
    D. exceeds the marginal value of output.

310 Chapter 9

PROBLEMS & SOLUTIONS

P9.1 ***Linear Programming Concepts.*** *Indicate whether each of the following statements is true or false. Defend your answer.*

    A. Linear programming can be used for solving any type of constrained optimization problem where the relations involved can be approximated by linear equations.

    B. Linear revenue, cost and profit relations will be observed when output prices, input prices, and average variable costs are constant.

    C. Equal distances along a given production process ray in a linear programming problem always represent an identical level of output

    D. At isoquant segment midpoints, each adjacent production process must be used to produce 50% of output efficiently.

    E. Maximizing a LP profit contribution objective function always results in also maximizing total net profits.

P9.1 **SOLUTION**

    A. True. Linear programming can be used for solving any type of constrained optimization problem where the relations involved can be approximated by linear equations.

    B. True. Linear revenue, cost and profit relations will be observed when output prices, input prices, and average variable costs are constant.

    C. True. Equal distances along a given production process ray always represent an identical level of output. This stems from the fact that constant returns to scale must be operative in any linear programming problem.

    D. True. The closer a point is to a given process ray, the greater the relative share of output produced using that production process. Conversely, the farther a point is from a given process ray, the smaller the relative share of output produced using that process. At isoquant segment midpoints, for example, each adjacent process will be used to produce 50% of output.

    E. True. Profit contribution is the difference between total revenues and total variable costs. Profit, on the other hand, is the difference between total revenues and total

Linear Programming 311

variable plus fixed costs. Since fixed costs do not vary with output, either maximizing profit contribution or profit with respect to output will always identify a unique activity level.

P9.2 **LP Basics.** *Indicate whether each of the following statements is true or false and why.*

A. *In profit maximization linear programming problems, negative values for slack variables are impossible.*

B. *Binding constraints indicate positive slack variables at the optimum solution.*

C. *Points not on process rays represent unattainable technologies.*

D. *Constant input prices is the only requirement for a total cost function to be linear.*

E. *Changing input prices will not alter the slope of a given isoquant line.*

P9.2 **SOLUTION**

A. True. Slack variables can never take on negative values. For example, in output, revenue, or profit maximization linear programming problems this would imply that the amount of the resource used exceeds the amount available. Thus, slack variables are included in the general non-negativity requirements for all problems.

B. False. Binding constraints are those constraints which intersect at the optimum solution, and therefore take on a value of zero (ne excess of the input).

C. False. Points in between explicit process rays represent feasible production using a linear combination of multiple production technologies.

D. False. Constant returns to scale, and constant input prices result in a linear total cost function.

E. False. The slope of an isocost line is given by the ratio of input prices (e.g., $Y = C_0/P_Y + (P_X/P_Y)X$). Therefore, if individual input prices rise or fall by a given percentage, then the isocost line slope will be affected.

P9.3 **Fixed Input Relations.** *Tubular Tubing, Inc. assembles bicycle frames at a plant in Lexington, Massachusetts. The plant uses labor (L) and capital (K) in an assembly line process to produce output (Q) where:*

$$Q = 0.01L^{1/2}K^{1/2}$$

$$MP_L = \frac{0.005K^{1/2}}{L^{1/2}}$$

$$MP_K = \frac{0.005L^{1/2}}{K^{1/2}}$$

A. Calculate how many units of output can be produced with 25 units of labor and 400 units of capital, and with 225 units of labor and 3,600 units of capital. Are returns to scale increasing, constant, or diminishing?

B. Calculate the change in the marginal product of labor as labor grows from 25 to 36 units, holding capital constant at 400 units. Similarly, calculate the change in the marginal product of capital as capital grows from 400 to 625 units, holding labor constant at 25 units. Are returns to each factor increasing, constant, or diminishing?

C. Assume now and throughout the remainder of the problem that labor and capital must be combined in the ratio 25L:400K. How much output could be produced if Kein Tubing has a constraint of $L = 25,000$ and $K = 500,000$ during the coming production period?

D. What are the marginal products of each factor under the conditions described in Part c?

P9.3   SOLUTION

A.   With $L = 25$ and $K = 400$ available:

$$Q = 0.01L^{1/2}K^{1/2}$$
$$= 0.01(25^{1/2})(400^{1/2})$$
$$= 1$$

With $L = 225$ and $K = 3,600$ available:

Linear Programming

$$Q = 0.01(225^{1/2})(3{,}600^{1/2})$$

$$= 9$$

Thus, a four-fold increase in inputs has led to a four-fold increase in output and constant returns to scale are evident.

B. The change in MP_L is:

At $L = 25$, $K = 400$ At $L = 36$, $K = 400$

$$MP_L = \frac{0.005\, K^{1/2}}{L^{1/2}} \qquad MP_L = \frac{0.005\, K^{1/2}}{L^{1/2}}$$

$$= \frac{0.005\,(400^{1/2})}{25^{1/2}} \qquad = \frac{0.005\,(400^{1/2})}{36^{1/2}}$$

$$= 0.02 \qquad \text{to} \qquad = 0.0167$$

Thus,

$$\Delta MP_L = 0.0167 - 0.02 = -0.003$$

The change in MP_K is:

At $L = 25$, $K = 400$ At $L = 25$, $K = 625$

$$MP_K = \frac{0.005\, L^{1/2}}{K^{1/2}} \qquad MP_K = \frac{0.005\, L^{1/2}}{K^{1/2}}$$

$$= \frac{0.005\,(25^{1/2})}{(400^{1/2})} \qquad = \frac{0.005\,(25^{1/2})}{(625^{1/2})}$$

$$= 0.00125 \qquad \text{to} \qquad = 0.001$$

Thus,

$$\Delta MP_K = 0.001 - 0.00125 = -0.00025$$

Since the marginal product of each input is diminishing as usage grows, the returns to each factor are diminishing.

C. If L = 25,000 is available, and each unit of output requires 25 units of labor, Kein Tubing has enough labor to produce Q = 25,000/25 = 1,000 units of output -- provided sufficient complementary capital is also available. If K = 500,000 is available, and each unit of output requires 400 units of capital, Kein Tubing has enough capital to produce Q = 500,000/400 = 1,250 units of output -- provided sufficient complementary labor is also available.

Given that labor and capital must be combined in the fixed ratio 25L:400K, and a constraint of L = 25,000 and K = 500,000; Kein Tubing is only able to produce Q = 1,000 and labor becomes a binding constraint. At that production level, only 400,000 units of capital are employed and the remaining 100,000 units are surplus.

D. One additional unit of labor could be combined with 16 units of surplus capital to produce 0.04 units of output. Thus, the $MP_L = 0.04$. Since surplus capital is already available, an increase in capital would have no effect on production. Given the assumptions of part c, the $MP_K = 0$.

P9.4 **Return Maximization.** *The American Balanced Fund is an open-end investment company (mutual fund) designed to meet the needs of investors planning for future retirement. ABF seeks to provide current income plus capital growth by investing in a diversified portfolio of high-quality stocks and investment-grade bonds. The fund's bylaws state that at least 30% of the portfolio must be invested in bonds in order to reduce downside risk during bear markets. The fund's growth potential is maintained by a requirement that the share of the portfolio invested in common stocks must be at least as large as the share devoted to bonds. Like most mutual funds, ABF is prohibited from using leverage (borrowing) to enhance investor ABF returns. Without leverage, stock and bond investments cannot exceed 100% of ABF's portfolio. And finally, the fund's investment management committee currently projects an expected return of 10% on stocks and 8% on bonds.*

    A. *Set up and interpret the linear programming problem ABF would use to determine the optimal portfolio percentage holdings in stocks (S) and bonds (B). Use both the inequality and equality forms of the constraint conditions.*

    B. *Use a graph to determine the optimal solution, and check your answer algebraically. Interpret the solution.*

Linear Programming

C. Holding all else equal, how much would the expected return on bonds have to rise before the optimal investment policy determined in part a would change?

D. What is the maximum share of the portfolio that could be converted into cash if management projects a downturn in both stock and bond prices?

P9.4 SOLUTION

A. In this problem, the goal is to maximize expected return, R, subject to the various stock, bond and leverage constraints. The relevant linear programming problem is:

Maximize: $R = 0.1S + 0.08B$

Subject to: $B \geq 0.3$

$S - B \geq 0$ (or $S \geq B$)

$S + B \leq 1$

or, in equality form:

(1) $B - L_B = 0.3$ (Bond constraint)

(2) $S - B - L_S = 0$ (Stock constraint)

(3) $S + B + L_L = 1$ (Leverage constraint)

$S, B, L_S, L_B, L_L \geq 0$

Here, R is expected return, S is the portfolio share in common stocks, B is the portfolio share in bonds. L_S, L_B, and L_L are slack variables, representing excess stock investments, excess bond investments, and "slack leverage" or cash holdings, respectively.

B. From the graph, we see that the bond investment (1) and leverage (3) constraints are binding and, therefore, that $L_B = L_L = 0$ at point X. Thus,

(1) $B - 0 = 0.3$

(2) $S - B - L_S = 0$

(3) $\quad S + B + 0 = 1$

From (1),

(1) $\quad B - 0 = 0.3$

$\quad B = 0.3$

From (3),

(3) $\quad S + 0.3 + 0 = 1$

$\quad S = 0.70$

From (2),

(2) $\quad 0.7 - 0.3 - L_S = 0$

$\quad L_S = 0.4$

And the expected return is:

$$R = 0.1S + 0.08B$$
$$= 0.1(0.7) + 0.08(0.3)$$
$$= 0.094 \text{ or } 9.4\%$$

Solution values can be interpreted as follows:

$S = 0.7$ The optimal portfolio percentage in stocks is 70%.

$B = 0.30$ The optimal share of the portfolio in bonds is 30%.

$L_B = 0$ At optimum, ABF is holding the minimum percentage of bonds.

$L_S = 0.4$ At optimum, ABF is holding a 40% greater share of its portfolio in stocks than the minimum required in light of its bond holdings.

$L_L = 0$ At optimum, ABF is not employing leverage, and the fund is fully invested (holds no cash).

Linear Programming

R = 0.094   Maximum expected return given constraints.

C. The isoreturn line $S = (R_0/R_S) - (R_B/R_S)B$, where R_0 is any return level, and R_S and R_B are returns on stocks and bonds, respectively. The isoreturn line in this problem has a slope equal to $-(R_B/R_S) = -(0.08/0.1) = -0.8$. Holding all else equal, this slope will become more negative as the return on bonds rises (or return on stocks falls). Similarly, this slope will move closer to zero as the return on bonds falls (or return on stocks rises).

Holding all else equal, if R_B falls to slightly less than 10%, the optimal feasible point will shift from point X(0.3B, 0.7S) to point Z(0.5B, 0.5S), since the isoreturn line slope will than be steeper than -1, the slope of the leverage constraint, $S = 1 - B$. Thus, a rise from 7 to more than 10%, or at least 2%, is necessary before the optimal solution derived above would change.

D. The bond investment constraint requires that a minimum of 30% of the overall portfolio be invested in bonds. From the stock constraint, we know that stock investments must be at least as large as bond investments. Therefore, a minimum 60% of the overall portfolio must be invested in stocks (30%) plus bonds (30%), and the maximum share of the portfolio which could be converted into cash is 40% (point Y on the graph).

American Balanced Fund Graph

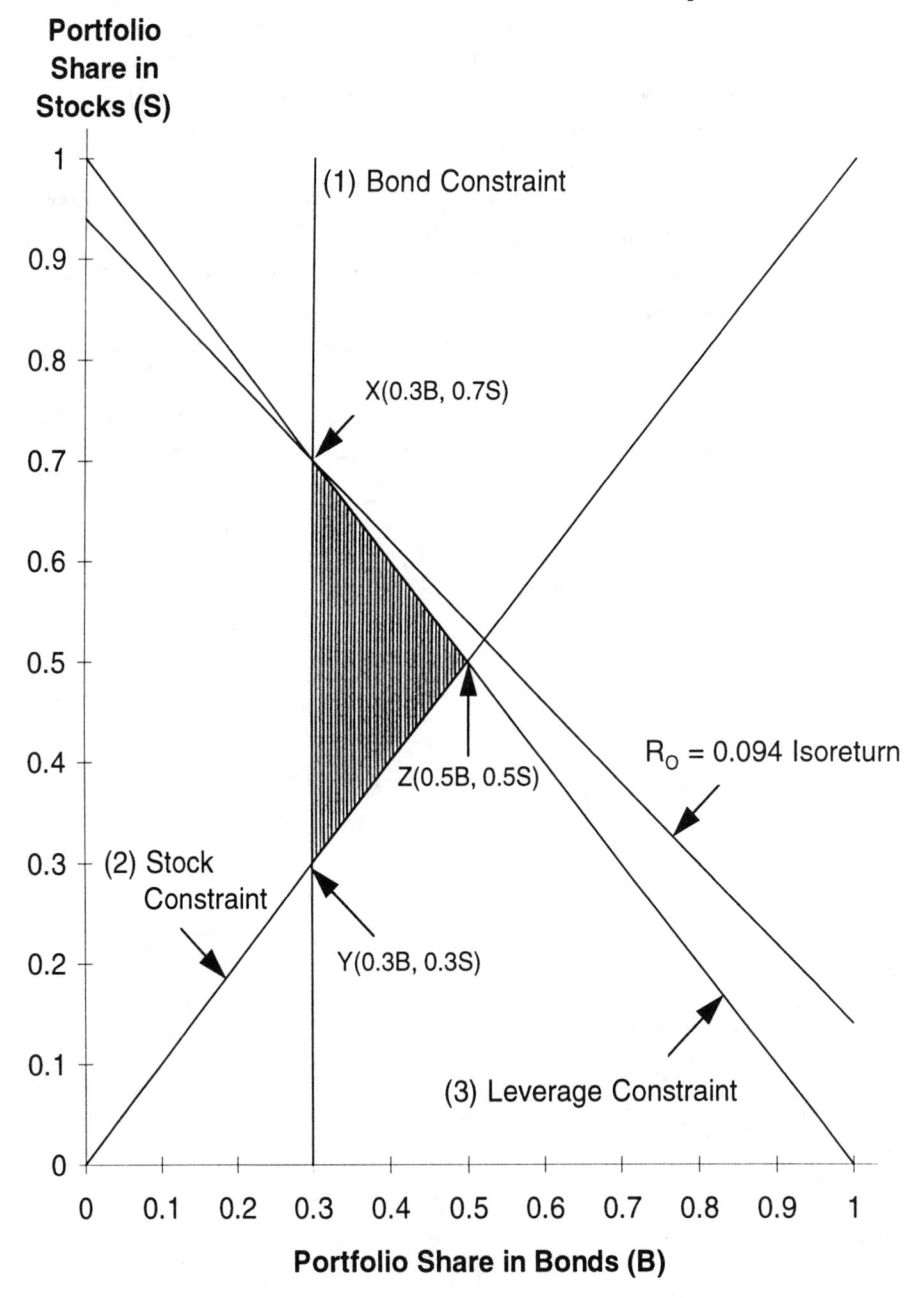

- Portfolio Share in Stocks (S) (vertical axis)
- Portfolio Share in Bonds (B) (horizontal axis)
- (1) Bond Constraint
- (2) Stock Constraint
- (3) Leverage Constraint
- X(0.3B, 0.7S)
- Y(0.3B, 0.3S)
- Z(0.5B, 0.5S)
- $R_O = 0.094$ Isoreturn

Linear Programming

P9.5 ***Optimal Production.*** *Canine Products, Inc., produces and markets a new moist and chewy nugget dog food called "Chowhound" being test marketed in the Minneapolis, Minnesota area. This product is similar to several others offered by CP, and can be produced with currently available equipment and personnel using any of three alternative product methods. Method A requires 6 hours of labor and 1 processing facility hour to produce 100 bags of dog food, Q_A. Method B requires 3 labor and 3 processing facility hours per Q_B. Method C requires 2 labor hours and 4 processing facility hours per unit of Q_C. Because of slack demand for other products CP currently has 15 labor hours and 5 processing facility hours available per week for producing Chowhound.*

 A. *Using the equality form of the constraint conditions, set up and interpret the linear program CP would use to maximize production of Chowhound given currently available resources.*

 B. *Calculate and interpret all solution values.*

P9.5 **SOLUTION**

 A. In determining an optimal use of its resources, CP will seek to maximize output subject to limitations on scarce labor and production facilities. Thus, the relevant linear programming problem can be written, in equality form, as:

  Maximize: $Q = Q_A + Q_B + Q_C$

  Subject to:

  (1) $6Q_A + 3Q_B + 2Q_C + S_L = 15$ (Labor constraint)

  (2) $Q_A + 3Q_B + 4Q_C + S_P = 5$ (Production facility constraint)

  $Q_A, Q_B, Q_C, S_L, S_P \geq 0$

  Here Q_A, Q_B and Q_C represent output from each production method (in hundreds of bags). S_L and S_P represent excess labor and production facility capacity, respectively.

 B. From the graph we see that the maximum output level will be reached on the Q = 3 isoquant where $Q_C = S_L = S_P = 0$. Thus, the primal constraints become a system of two equations and two unknowns that can be solved algebraically.

Take (1) minus (2),

$$(1) \ 6Q_A + 3Q_B + 2(0) + 0 = 15$$
$$-(2) \ \underline{Q_A + 3Q_B + 4(0) + 0 = 5}$$
$$5Q_A = 10$$
$$Q_A = 2(00)$$

From (1),

$$6(2) + 3Q_B = 15$$

$$3Q_B = 3$$

$$Q_B = 1(00)$$

Then, from the objective function:

$$Q = Q_A + Q_B + Q_C$$

$$= 2 + 1 + 0$$

$$= 3(00)$$

Summarizing from above, solutions and an interpretation of these values are as follows:

$Q_A = 2$ 2(00) units of output are produced using process A.

$Q_B = 1$ 1(00) units of output are produced using process B.

$Q_C = 0$ No output is produced using process C.

$S_L = 0$ No excess labor capacity.

$S_P = 0$ No excess production facility capacity.

$Q = 3$ Maximum output given labor and facility resource constraints is 3(00) packages.

Linear Programming 321

Canine Products, Inc. Graph

Labor Hours

- Method 'A' Ray
- (2) Processing Facility Hour
- Method 'B' Ray
- (1) Labor Hour Constraint
- Q*
- $Q_O = 3$ Isoquant
- Method 'C' Ray
- Q = 1 Isoquant

Production Facility Hours

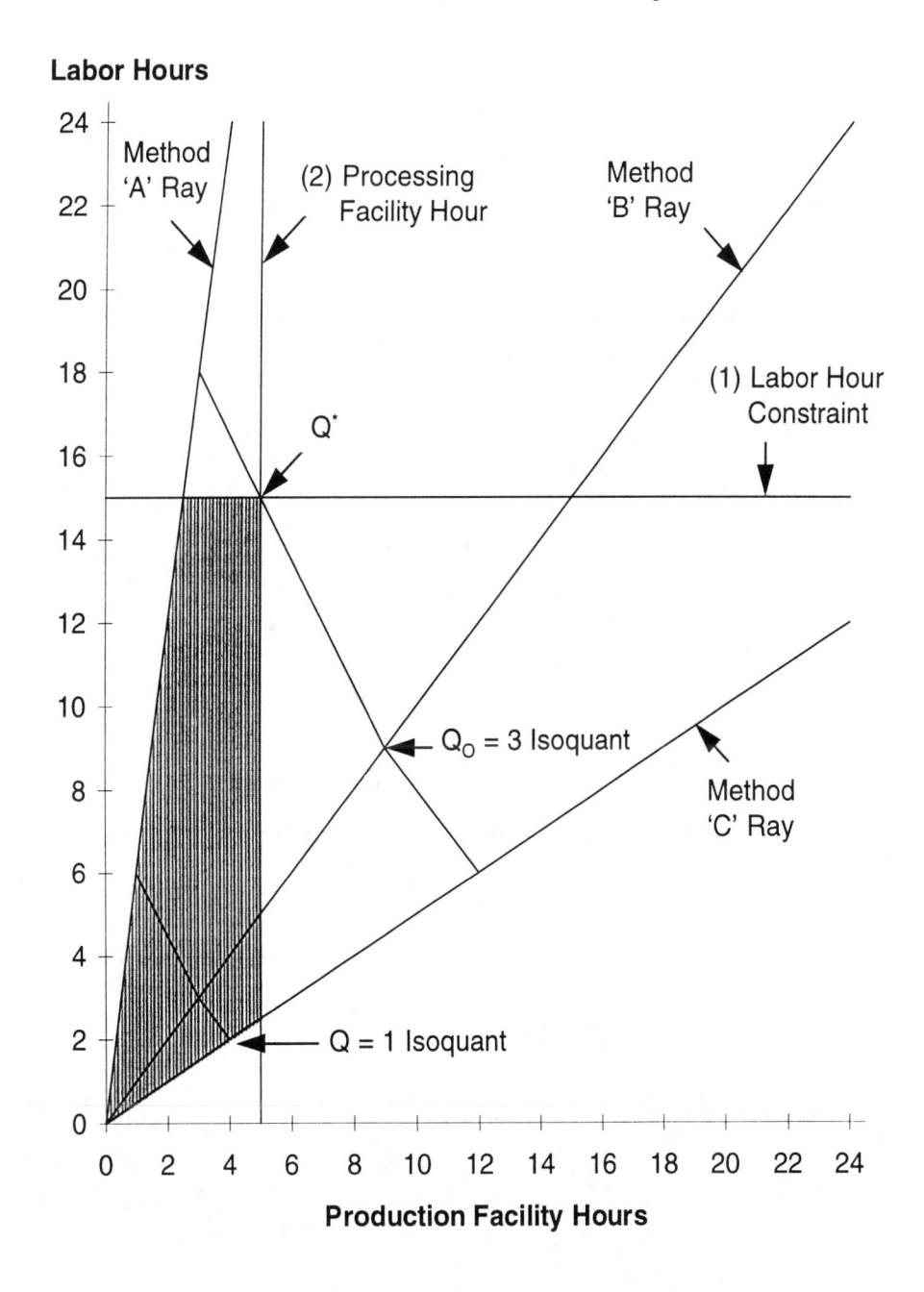

Harcourt Brace & Company

P9.6 **Optimal Production.** Video-Scapes, Inc. (VSI) is a rapidly growing landscaping service in Oakland, California that specializes in merging videos of one's home and property with infinitely changeable computer-generated graphics of various landscape details. VIS offers budget landscaping designs for $1,500 and deluxe designs for $3,000. Both services use scarce computing, creative and consulting resources. Each budget design requires 4 hours of computer time, 2 hours of creative time, and 4 hours of consulting time with the client. Each deluxe design requires 6 hours of computer time, 6 hours of creative time, and 4 hours of consulting time. VSI currently has 60 hours of computer, 42 hours of creative, and 36 hours of consulting time available on a weekly basis.

What output mix would be optimal if VSI wishes to maximize total sales revenue?

A. Using the equality form of the constraint conditions, set up and interpret the linear program that VSI might use to determine an optimal weekly service mix.

B. Solve for and interpret all solution values.

P9.6 SOLUTION

A. In determining an optimal weekly product mix, VSI will seek to maximize sales revenue subject to limitations on scarce drafting, artwork and architectural resources. Thus, the relevant primal linear programming problem can be written:

Maximize: Revenue = $1,500Q_1 + $3,000Q_2

Subject to:

(1) $4Q_1 + 6Q_2 + S_{CO} = 60$ (Computer constraint)

(2) $2Q_1 + 6Q_2 + S_{CR} = 42$ (Creative constraint)

(3) $4Q_1 + 4Q_2 + S_{CS} = 36$ (Consulting constraint)

$Q_1, Q_2, S_{CO}, S_{CR}, S_{CS} \geq 0$

Here Q_1 and Q_2 represent budget and deluxe landscaping designs, respectively. S_{CO}, S_{CR} and S_{CS} represent slack variables and can be interpreted as excess capacity of computing, creativity and consulting inputs, respectively.

B. By graphing the constraints and the highest possible isorevenue line, we find at the optimal point X that $S_{CR} = S_{CS} = 0$.

Linear Programming

Thus,

(1) $\quad 4Q_1 + 6Q_2 + S_{CO} = 60$

(2) $\quad 2Q_1 + 6Q_2 + 0 = 42$

(3) $\quad 4Q_1 + 4Q_2 + 0 = 36$

Taking two times (2) minus (3),

$2\times(2) \quad 4Q_1 + 12Q_2 = 84$

$-(3) \quad \underline{4Q_1 + 4Q_2 = 36}$

$\quad\quad\quad\quad 8Q_2 = 48$

$\quad\quad\quad\quad Q_2 = 6$

From (2),

(2) $\quad 2Q_1 + 6Q_2 = 42$

$\quad\quad 2Q_1 + 6(6) = 42$

$\quad\quad\quad Q_1 = 3$

From (1),

(1) $\quad 4Q_1 + 6Q_2 + S_{CO} = 60$

$\quad\quad 4(3) + 6(6) + S_{CO} = 60$

$\quad\quad\quad S_{CO} = 12$

And finally, from the objective function:

$R = \$1{,}500 Q_1 + \$3{,}000$

$\quad = \$1{,}500(3) + \$3{,}000(6)$

$\quad = \$22{,}500$

Summarizing from above, the solution to the linear programming problem and an interpretation of these values is:

$Q_1 = 3$ Optimal number of budget landscaping designs.

$Q_2 = 6$ Optimal number of deluxe landscaping designs.

$S_{CO} = 12$ 12 hours of excess computer capacity.

$S_{CR} = 0$ No excess creative capacity.

$S_{CS} = 0$ No excess consulting capacity.

$R = \$22,500$ Maximum revenue given input constraints.

Linear Programming

Video-Scapes, Inc. Graph

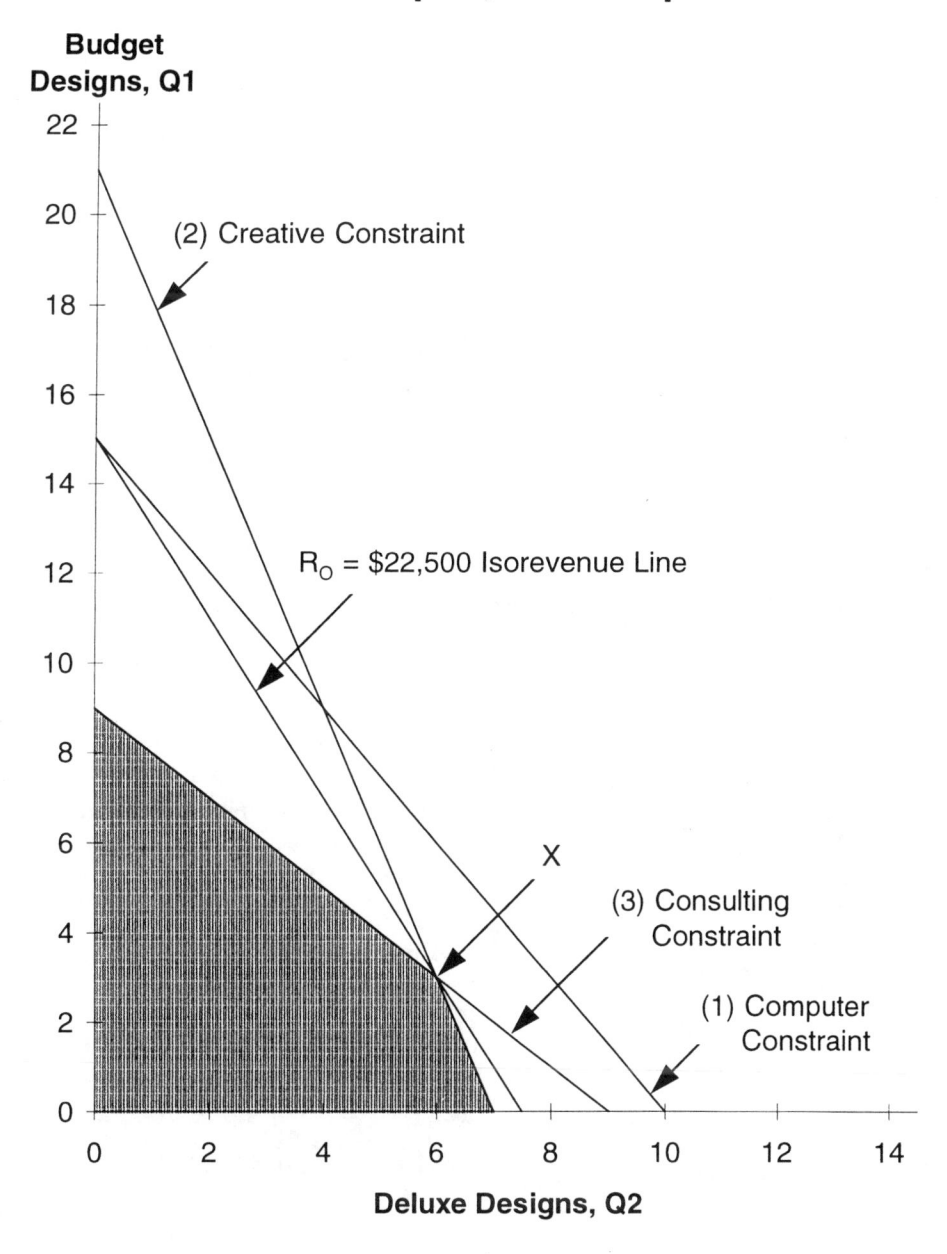

P9.7 **Optimal Lending.** Penny Belton is a senior loan officer with Citrus National Bank in Tampa, Florida. Belton has both corporate and personal lending customers. On average, the profit contribution margin or interest rate spread is 1.75% on corporate loans and 2.25% on personal loans. This return difference reflects the fact that personal loans tend to be riskier than corporate loans. Belton seeks to maximize the total dollar profit contribution earned, subject to a variety of restrictions on her lending practices. In order to limit default risk, Belton must restrict personal loans to no more than 40% of total loans outstanding. Similarly, to ensure adequate diversification against business cycle risk, corporate lending cannot exceed 80% of loaned funds. To maintain good customer relations by serving the basic needs of the local business community, Belton has decided to extend at least 40% of her total credit authorization to corporate customers on an ongoing basis. Finally, Belton cannot exceed her current total credit authorization of $50 million.

A. Using the inequality form of the constraint conditions, set up and interpret the linear programming problem Belton would use to determine the optimal dollar amount of credit to extend to corporate (C) and personal (P) lending customers. Also formulate the LP problem using the equality form of the constraint conditions.

B. Use a graph to determine the optimal solution, and check your solution algebraically. Fully interpret solution values.

P9.7 **SOLUTION**

A. Belton's goal is to maximize the profit contribution earned on loans to corporate (C) plus personal (P) lending customers, subject to a variety of restrictions on her lending practices. The relevant linear programming problem is:

$$\text{Maximize:} \quad \pi = 0.0175C + 0.0225P$$

$$\text{Subject to:} \quad -4C + 6P \leq 0 \text{ or } P \leq 0.4(C + P)$$

$$C - 4P \leq 0 \text{ or } C \leq 0.8(C + P)$$

$$C \geq \$20{,}000{,}000$$

$$C + P \leq \$50{,}000{,}000$$

or, in equality form:

Linear Programming

(1) $-4C + 6P + S_D = 0$ (Default risk constraint)

(2) $C - 4P + S_B = 0$ (Business cycle risk constraint)

(3) $C - S_C = \$20,000,000$ (Corporate lending constraint)

(4) $C + P + S_A = \$50,000,000$ (Credit authorization constraint)

$C, P, S_D, S_C, S_A \geq 0$

Here C and P are the dollars loaned to corporate and personal lending customers. S_D is unused (excess) personal lending capacity, S_B is unused (excess) corporate lending capacity, S_C is (excess) corporate lending above the minimum required to maintain customer relations, and S_A is unused (excess) credit authorization.

B. From the graph, we see that the default risk (1) and credit authorization (4) constraints are binding and, therefore, that $S_D = S_A = 0$ at point X. At this point, our series of constraints is reduced to a system of 4 equations and 4 unknowns that can be solved simultaneously, where:

(1) $-4C + 6P + 0 = 0$

(2) $C - 4P + S_B = 0$

(3) $C - S_C = \$20,000,000$

(4) $C + P + 0 = \$50,000,000$

Adding (1) and four times (4)

(1) $-4C + 6P = 0$

$+ 4 \times$ (4) $\underline{4C + 4P = 200,000,000}$

                       $10P = 200,000,000$

                           $P = \$20,000,000$

From (4),

(4) $\quad C + \$20,000,000 = \$50,000,000$

$$C = \$30,000,000$$

From (2),

(2) $\quad \$30,000,000 - \$4(20,000,000) + S_B = 0$

$$S_B = \$50,000,000$$

From (3),

(3) $\quad \$30,000,000 - S_C = \$20,000,000$

$$S_C = \$10,000,000$$

And finally, from the objective function:

$$\pi = 0.0175C + 0.0225P$$
$$= 0.0175(\$30,000,000) + 0.0225(\$20,000,000)$$
$$= \$975,000$$

Solution values can be interpreted as follows:

C = \$30,000,000		The optimal value of corporate loans is \$30 million.
P = \$20,000,000		The optimal value of personal loans is \$20 million.
S_D = \$0		At optimum, Belton is lending the maximum possible to personal lending customers.
S_B = \$50,000,000		At optimum, given the extent of personal lending, Belton has \$50 million in unused corporate lending capacity.
S_C = \$10,000,000		At optimum, Belton is lending corporate customers \$10 million more than the minimum necessary to meet their basic needs.

Linear Programming

S_A = $0   At optimum, Belton has exhausted her total $50 million credit authorization.

π = $975,000   Maximum profit contribution given constraints is $975 thousand.

Citrus National Bank Graph

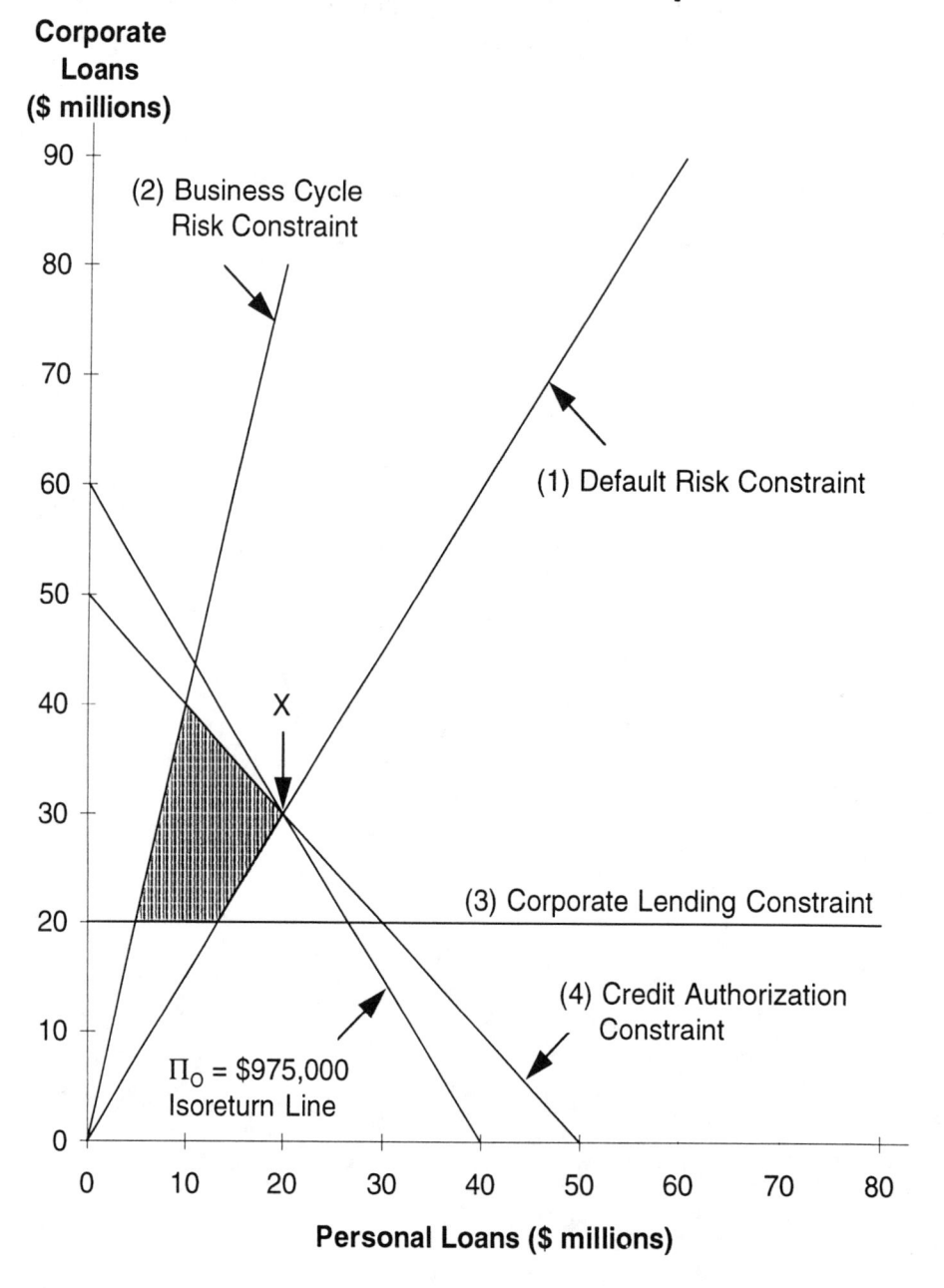

Linear Programming

P9.8 **Optimal Production.** Ozark Telephone, Inc. (OTI) is a small telephone company offering local dial-tone service to its franchised areas in rural southeastern Missouri. A new office park development site is being planned within OTI's territory and John Sample, a network engineer, has to maximize the conversation capacity per line under cost and technology constraints using both traditional copper-wire lines and new fiber-optic lines.

OTI wants to gradually move into the all-digital communication environment possible with fiber-optics, so a company policy has been adopted specifying that at least 3 fiber-optic lines be employed for every 2 copper lines on new installations. To minimize the need to quickly retrain its linemen, OTI wants at least 30% of new telephone lines installed to be copper. No existing telephone facilities run to the development site, and OTI must use its own facilities to carry the traffic (it cannot lease capacity from any other local telephone company). Finally, current costs and technologies dictate that 1 fiber line can carry the equivalent of 5 copper lines at the same cost to OTI. That is, if one copper line can carry one telephone conversation, fiber optic lines can carry five conversations at no cost penalty. Sample's objective is to maximize the capacity per line of the transmissions facilities being built to carry traffic to/from the office park.

A. Using the inequality form of the constraint conditions, set up and interpret the linear programming problem Sample would use to determine the optimal percentage of copper and fiber-optic lines. Also formulate the problem using the equality form of the constraint conditions.

B. With a graph, determine the optimal solution; check your solution algebraically. Fully interpret solution values.

C. Holding all else equal, how much would the capacity of fiber optic lines have to fall to alter the optimal construction mix determined in part b?

D. Calculate the opportunity cost, measured in terms of conversation capacity per line, of OTI's 30% copper line constraint.

P9.8 **SOLUTION**

A. In this problem the goal is to maximize the conversation carrying capacity per line into the development given two different technologies (fiber optic and copper cable). The relevant linear programming problem is:

Maximize: $\quad$ CAP $= 5F + 1C$

Subject to: $\quad 2F - 3C \geq 0$ or $2F \geq 3C$

$$C \geq 0.3$$

$$F + C \leq 1$$

or, in equality form:

(1) $\quad 2F - 3C - L_F = 0 \quad$ (Fiber emphasis constraint)

(2) $\quad C - L_C = 0.3 \quad$ (Copper investment constraint)

(3) $\quad F + C + L_L = 1 \quad$ (Lease constraint)

$F, C, L_S, L_F, L_C \geq 0$

CAP is the expected capacity given technological and cost considerations, F is the line share of fiber optic facilities, C is the share of copper cable facilities, and L_L, L_F, and L_C are slack variables.

Some students may have trouble distinguishing constraint (1) from (2) or (3). The difference, though simple, is important. The fiber emphasis constraint requires that fiber optics be deployed at 3:2 traditional copper cable. The copper investment constraint, for example, requires at least 30% of the telephone lines use copper technology. Likewise, the lease constraint relates to the total distribution investment by the company, and requires that fiber lines plus copper lines percentages be no more than 1(100%).

B. From the graph, we see that the copper investment constraint (2) and lease constraint (3) are binding, and therefore, $L_C = L_L = 0$ at point X ($L_L = 0$ also follows from the assumption that Ozark must use its own facilities and cannot lease capacity). Thus,

(1) $\quad 2F - 3C - L_F = 0$

(2) $\quad C - 0 = 0.3$

(3) $\quad F + C + 0 = 1.0$

Linear Programming

From (2),

$$(2) \qquad C - 0 = 0.3$$
$$C = 0.3$$

From (3),

$$(3) \qquad F + 0.3 + 0 = 1.0$$
$$F = 0.7$$

From (1),

$$(1) \qquad 2(0.7) - 3(0.3) - L_F = 0$$
$$L_F = 0.5$$

And the telephone company can expect a capacity of:

$$CAP = 5(0.7) + 1(0.3)$$

$$= 3.8 \text{ units}$$

Solution values can be interpreted as follows:

$F = 0.7$ — Optimal configuration uses 70% fiber optic lines.

$C = 0.3$ — Optimal configuration uses 30% copper lines.

$L_F = 0.5$ — At optimum, OTI is using 50% greater share of fiber than the minimum required.

$L_C = 0$ — At optimum, OTI is not employing any leased lines; all capacity is owned by the utility.

$CAP = 3.8$ — Maximum expected capacity (voice channels per line) given constraints.

C. The CAP line has a slope of -1/5 (i.e., $CAP = 5F + 1C$ or $F = CAP_0/5 - (1/5)C$). Holding all else equal, the slope becomes more negative ("steeper") as fiber optics carry fewer conversations per line relative to copper cable.

It would take a drop from 5 to at least 1 in the relative capacity of fiber optic cable to move the solution to corner Y from corner X. This would imply new technological developments allowing copper to carry at least as many conversations per line as fiber optic.

D. The optimal conversation capacity per line under the above constraints is 3.8. With 100% versus 70% use of fiber optics, the conversation capacity would be 5 per line. Thus, the opportunity cost of a minimum 30% copper investment is 5 - 3.8 = 1.2 conversations per line.

Linear Programming

Ozark Telephone Graph

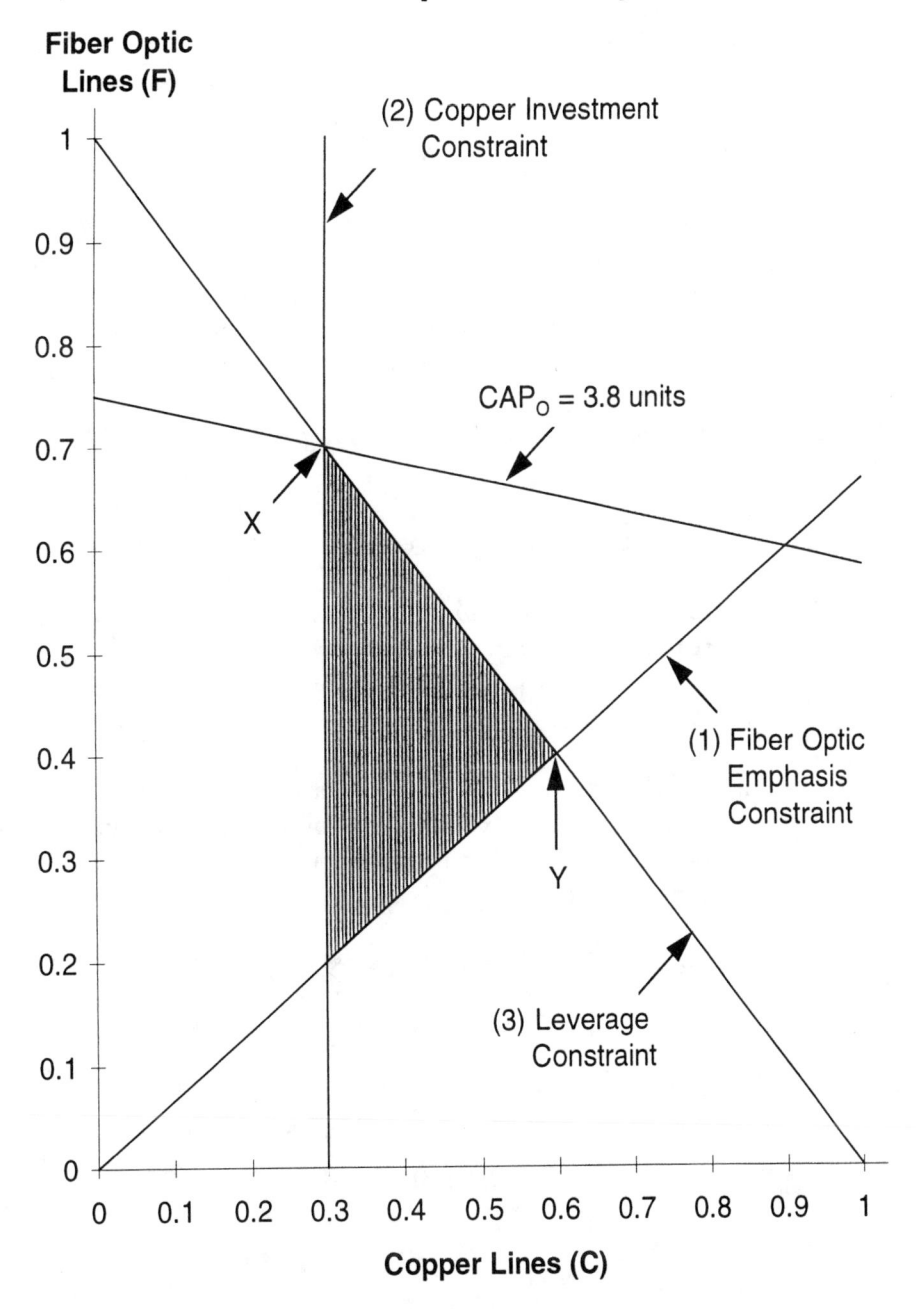

P9.9 **Cost Minimization.** Danbury Chemical, Inc. manufactures surficants used in fertilizers and herbicides (surficants minimize runoff). Danbury uses two manufacturing processes, each having advantages. The Hidex process is more expensive ($0.50 per gallon of Hidex) but produces more surficant and fewer emissions of the pollutant toxide per gallon used. The Lodex process is less efficient in producing surficants but, is less expensive ($0.25 per gallon of Lodex). The Lodex also has the advantage of producing fewer pollutants per gallon used in the production process.

To satisfy contracts with its customers, Danbury must produce at least 240 gallons of surficants per hour. Each gallon of Hidex used in the production process generates 4 gallons of surficant and 10 parts per million (ppm) of toxide. Each gallon of Lodex produces 3 gallons of surficant and 6 ppm of toxide. The EPA limits toxide emissions to 600 ppm per hour. In addition, municipal regulations limit emissions of solids to 180 ppm per hour, and the Hidex process produces solids at a rate of 2 ppm per gallon used and the Lodex process produces 3 ppm per gallon used.

A. Set up and interpret the linear program Danbury Chemical would use to minimize hourly costs.

B. Calculate, graph, and interpret all relevant solution values.

C. Holding all else equal, how much would the price of Lodex have to rise before Hidex would be used exclusively to produce surficants? Explain.

P9.9 **SOLUTION**

A. In this problem, the goal is to minimize Danbury's hourly cost of the primary catalyst (Hidex or Lodex) subject to constraints on output of surficant per hour, emissions of solid waste, and emission of the pollutant toxide per hour. The linear programming problem is:

Minimize: $C = \$0.5H + \$0.25L$

Subject to: $4H + 3L \geq 240$

$10H + 6L \leq 600$

$2H + 3L \leq 180$

Linear Programming

or in equality form:

(1) $4H + 3L - S_Q = 240$ (Output constraint)

(2) $10H + 6L + S_T = 600$ (Toxide constraint)

(3) $2H + 3L + S_S = 90$ (Solids constraint)

$H, L, S_Q, L_T, S_S \geq 0$

Where H is gallons of Hidex, L is gallons of Lodex, S_Q is output of surficant above contractual needs, S_T and S_S are amounts that the two pollutants could rise without violating pollution standards.

B. After construction of the graph, we see that the output and solids constraint are binding at $X(S_Q = S_S = 0)$.

Thus,

(1) $4H + 3L - 0 = 240$

(2) $10H + 6L + S_T = 600$

(3) $2H + 3L + 0 = 180$

Taking (1) minus 2 times (3):

(1) $4H + 3L = 240$

$- 2 \times (3)$ $\underline{-4H - 6L = -360}$

$- 3L = -120$

$L = 40$

Substituting into (1):

(1) $4H + 3(40) = 240$

$H = 30$

Substituting into (2):

(2) $\quad 10(30) + 6(40) + S_T = 600$

$$S_T = 60$$

And minimum costs are:

$$C = \$0.5(30) + \$0.25(40) = \$25$$

Solution values can be interpreted as:

$H = 30$ The optimal number of gallons of Hidex per hour is 30.

$L = 40$ The optimal number of gallons of Lodex per hour is 40.

$S_Q = 0$ Danbury is producing the minimum amount needed to fulfill contracts.

$S_T = 60$ Danbury is emitting 60 ppm per hour less than the regulated maximum.

$S_S = 0$ Solid emissions are at the maximum limit.

$C = \$25$ Minimum hourly catalyst costs for Hidex and Lodex.

C. Holding all else equal, the only thing that changes when the price of Lodex increases is the isocost line, $H = (C_O/P_H) - (P_L/P_H)L$, which becomes steeper. The feasible space remains the same. Thus, to use only Hidex the isocost line must become steeper than the output constraint, $H = 60 - (3/4)L$, intersecting the feasible space at the point Y(0L, 60H).

Linear Programming 339

Danbury Chemical Graph

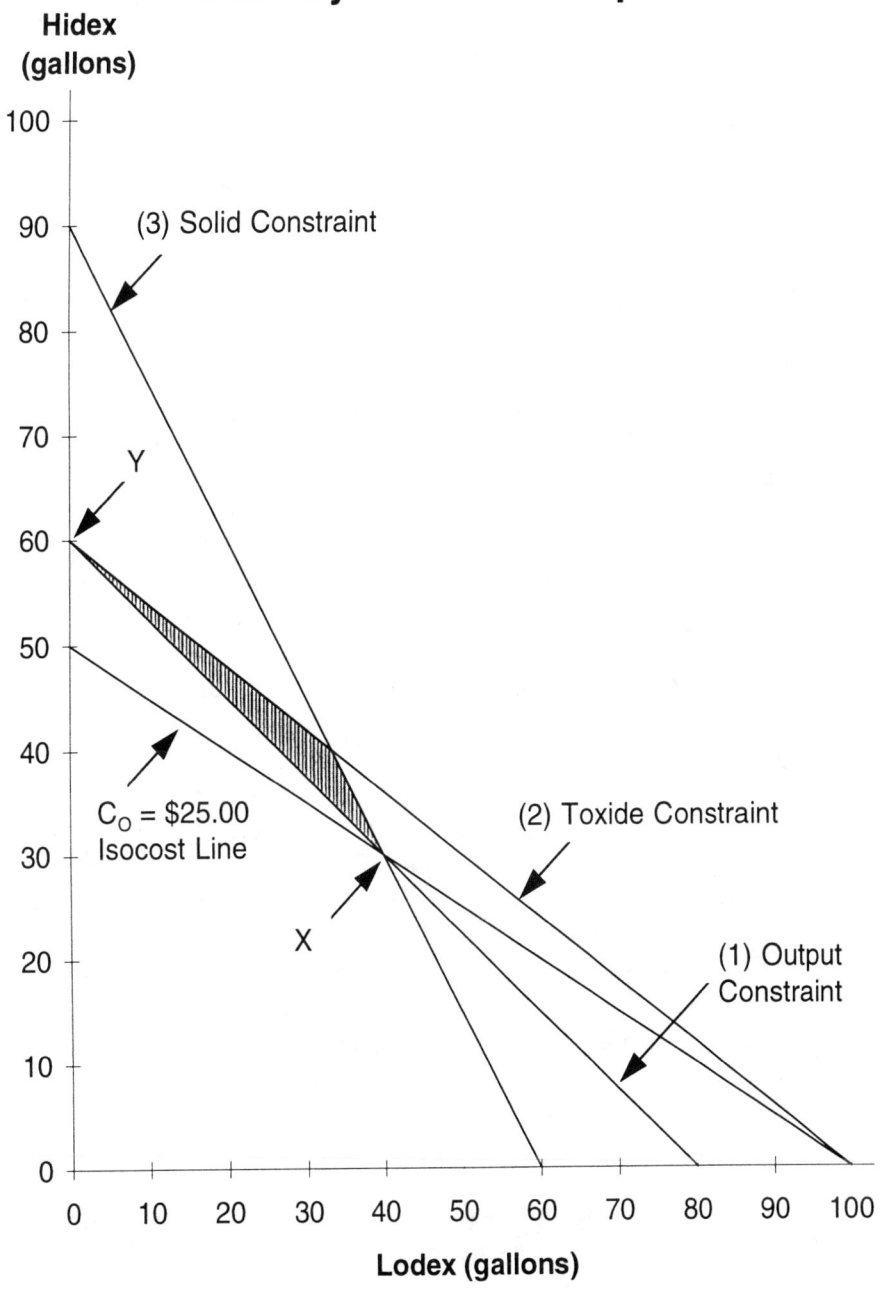

Hidex (gallons) vs **Lodex (gallons)**

- (3) Solid Constraint
- Y
- $C_O = \$25.00$ Isocost Line
- (2) Toxide Constraint
- X
- (1) Output Constraint

Harcourt Brace & Company

P9.10 **Profit Maximization.** Skidmore and Associates, Ltd. is a small architectural firm located in Los Angeles, California, specializing in the preparation of multi-family residential housing complex, R, and commercial retails, C, architectural designs. Prevailing prices in the market are $10,000 for residential housing designs and $25,000 for commercial retail designs.

Six architects run the firm, and work a 50-hour workweek, 50 weeks per year. They are assisted by six drafting personnel and two secretaries, all of whom work a typical 40-hour workweek, 50 weeks per year. The firm must decide how to target its promotional efforts so as to best use its resources during the coming year. Based on previous experience, the firm expects that an average of 150 hours of architect and 100 hours of drafting time will be required for each residential housing complex design, whereas commercial retail design will require an average of 250 architect hours and 200 drafting hours. Fifty hours of secretarial time will also be required for each architectural design. In addition, variable computer and other processing costs are expected to average $1,000 per residential design and $1,500 per commercial retail design.

A. Set up the linear programming problem the firm would use to determine the profit-maximizing output levels for residential and commercial designs. Show both the inequality and equality forms of the constraint conditions.

B. Completely solve and interpret the solution values for the linear programming problem.

C. Calculate maximum possible net profits per year for the firm assuming that architects draw a salary of $100,000 per year, drafting personnel earn $35,000 per year, secretaries are paid $10 per hour, and fixed overhead (including promotion and other expenses) averages $250,000.

D. After considering the above data, one senior architect recommended reducing one drafting personnel to part-time status (adjusting salary accordingly) while retaining the rest of the current staff full-time. What are net profits per year under this suggestion?

P9.10 **SOLUTION**

A. First, the profit contribution for preparing residential, R, and commercial, C, architectural designs must be calculated.

$$\text{Profit contribution per return} = \text{Price} - \text{Variable computer and other processing costs}$$

Linear Programming

Thus,

π_I = $10,000 - $1,000 = $9,000 per residential housing complex design

π_C = $25,000 - $1,500 = $23,500 per commercial retail design

where

OUTPUT	INPUT HOURS PER DESIGN		
	A	D	S
R	150	100	50
C	250	200	50
CAPACITY	15,000	12,000	4,000

This problem requires maximization of profits, subject to limitations on the number of architect hours, draftsmen hours and secretarial hours available. The linear programming problem is:

Maximize: π = $9,000R + $23,500C

Subject to:
$$150R + 250C \leq 15,000$$
$$100R + 200C \leq 12,000$$
$$50R + 50C \leq 4,000$$

or, inequality form:

(1) $150R + 250C + S_A = 15,000$ (Architect constraint)

(2) $100R + 200C + S_D = 12,000$ (Drafting constraint)

(3) $50R + 50C + S_S = 4,000$ (Secretary constraint)

$R, C, S_A, S_D, S_S \geq 0$

Here, R and C are residential complex and commercial retail designs, respectively. S_A, S_D, and S_S are variables representing excess capacity in architect, draftsman and secretary inputs, respectively.

B. By graphing the constraints and the highest possible isoprofit line, we find at the optimal point X that $S_A = S_S = 0$.

Thus,

(1) $\qquad 150R + 250C + 0 = 15{,}000$

(2) $\qquad 100R + 200C + S_D = 12{,}000$

(3) $\qquad 50R + 50C + 0 = 4{,}000$

Then, taking (1) minus three times (3),

$$
\begin{array}{rl}
(1) & 150R + 250C = 15{,}000 \\
-3 \times (3) & \underline{150R + 150C = 12{,}000} \\
& 100C = 3{,}000 \\
& C = 30
\end{array}
$$

From (1),

$$150R + 250(30) = 15{,}000$$
$$R = 50$$

From (2),

$$100(50) + 200(30) + S_D = 12{,}000$$
$$S_D = 1{,}000$$

And the total profit contribution per year is:

$$\pi = \$9{,}000(50) + \$23{,}500(30)$$
$$= \$1{,}155{,}000$$

R = 50   Optimal number of residential housing complex designs.

Linear Programming

$C = 30$ Optimal number of commercial retail designs.

$S_A = 0$ No excess architect capacity at optimal output level.

$S_D = 1{,}000$ 1,000 hours of excess drafting capacity at optimal output level.

$S_S = 0$ No excess secretary capacity at optimal output level.

$\pi = \$1{,}155{,}000$ Maximum weekly profit contribution given constraints.

C. The $1,155,000 maximum annual profit contribution calculated in part b is before fixed labor and overhead costs. Maximum annual net profits can be calculated as:

$$\text{Net Profits} = \text{Profit Contribution} - \text{Labor Expenses} - \text{Over Fixed Overhead}$$

$$= \$1{,}155{,}000 - 6(\$100{,}000) - 6(\$35{,}000) - 4{,}000(\$10) - \$250{,}000$$

$$= \$55{,}000 \text{ per year}$$

D. Given 1,000 hours of excess drafting capacity, if two draftsmen are let go while retaining the rest of present staff, the $R = 120$ and $C = 40$ levels of output will remain optimal. Net profits will rise following the reduction in fixed draftsman labor costs.

$$\text{Net Profits} = \$1{,}155{,}000 - 6(\$100{,}000) - 5.5(\$35{,}000) - 4{,}000(\$10) - \$250{,}000$$

$$= \$72{,}500 \text{ per year}$$

Skidmore and Associates, Ltd. Graph

Residential Designs, R

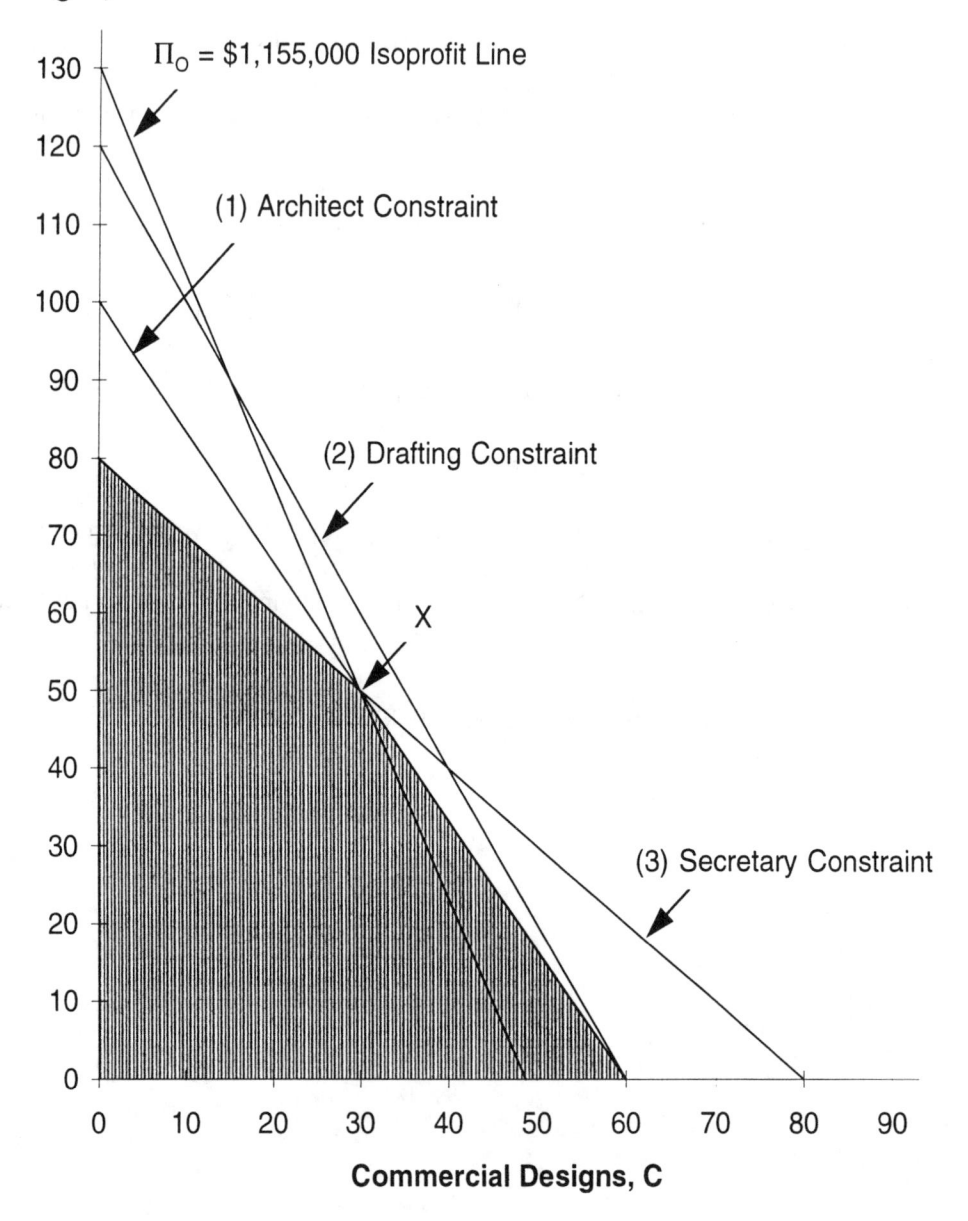

Π_O = $1,155,000 Isoprofit Line

(1) Architect Constraint

(2) Drafting Constraint

X

(3) Secretary Constraint

Commercial Designs, C

Chapter 10

PERFECT COMPETITION AND MONOPOLY

MULTIPLE CHOICE QUESTIONS

Q10.1 Perfect competition is inconsistent with:

    A. economic profits.
    B. economic losses.
    C. barriers to exit.
>   D. hard-to-measure product quality.

Q10.2 Economic profit:

    A. cannot be negative.
>   B. can exceed the risk-adjusted normal rate of return.
    C. is less than the risk-adjusted normal rate of return.
    D. does not reflect the cost of owner-supplied inputs.

Q10.3 Any limit on asset redeployment from one line of business or industry to another is called a:

    A. barrier to mobility.
    B. barrier to entry.
>   C. barrier to exit.
    D. capacity constraint.

Q10.4 A market with one buyer is called:

>   A. monopsony.
    B. monopoly.
    C. perfect competition.
    D. oligopsony.

Q10.5 The labor market confrontation between Major League Baseball and the Players Association is an example of:

    A. natural monopoly.
>   B. countervailing power.
    C. price takers.
    D. market structure.

Q10.6 For a firm in perfectly competitive market equilibrium:

A. MR < AR.
B. P > AC.
C. P > MR.
D. P = MC.

Q10.7 For a firm in perfectly competitive market equilibrium:

A. MC < AC.
B. MR > AR.
C. P < AC.
D. MR = MC.

Q10.8 Above-normal profits in a perfectly competitive industry are caused by:

A. increases in demand that are successfully anticipated.
B. decreases in cost that are successfully anticipated.
C. increases in productivity that are successfully anticipated.
D. luck.

Q10.9 In long-run equilibrium, monopoly prices are set a level where:

A. price exceeds marginal revenue.
B. industry demand equals industry supply.
C. industry demand is less than industry supply.
D. price exceeds average revenue.

Q10.10 For a monopoly in equilibrium:

A. MR = MC.
B. MC ≤ AC.
C. MR ≤ AR.
D. P ≥ AC.

Perfect Competition and Monopoly 347

Q10.11 The level of competition in a given market tends to increase if:

      A. minimum efficient scale of firms increases.
> B. the number of substitutes increase.
      C. significant barriers to exit are imposed.
      D. the number of potential entrants decreases.

Q10.12 A monopsony is a market with:

      A. many sellers.
> B. one buyer.
      C. many buyers.
      D. one seller.

Q10.13 In a perfectly competitive market:

> A. sellers and buyers have perfect information.
      B. entry and exit are difficult.
      C. sellers produce similar, but not identical products.
      D. each seller can affect the market price by changing output.

Q10.14 The demand curve for a unique product without substitutes is:

      A. upward sloping.
      B. downward sloping.
      C. horizontal.
> D. vertical.

Q10.15 The demand curve faced by a single firm in a competitive market is:

      A. upward sloping.
      B. downward sloping.
> C. horizontal.
      D. vertical.

Q10.16 A firm will earn normal profits when price:

> **A.** equals average total cost.
> **B.** equals average variable cost.
> **C.** equals marginal cost.
> **D.** exceeds minimum average total cost.

Q10.17 In the short run, a perfectly competitive firm will shut down and produce nothing if:

> **A.** excess profits equal zero.
> **B.** total cost exceeds total revenue.
> **C.** total variable cost exceeds total revenue.
> **D.** the market price falls below the minimum average total cost.

Q10.18 In the long run, firms will exit a perfectly competitive industry if:

> **A.** excess profits exceed zero.
> **B.** excess profits are less than zero.
> **C.** total profit equals zero.
> **D.** excess profits equal zero.

Q10.19 A monopolist maximizes profits by producing a level of output where:

> **A.** P = AC.
> **B.** P > MC.
> **C.** P < MC.
> **D.** P = MC.

Q10.20 In the short run, a monopolist will:

> **A.** shut down if price equals average total cost.
> **B.** shut down if price is less than average total cost.
> **C.** shut down if price is less than average variable cost.
> **D.** never shut down.

Perfect Competition and Monopoly

Q10.21 In general, a perfectly competitive industry will sell:

- A. less output at lower prices than monopoly.
- B. more output at higher prices than monopoly.
- C. less output at higher prices than monopoly.
- D. more output at lower prices than monopoly.

Q10.22 At the profit maximizing level of output for a monopolist:

- A. P = AR and AR = AC.
- B. P = MC and MR > MC.
- C. P > MC and MR = MC.
- D. P = MR and AC = MC.

Q10.23 Economic agents that have countervailing power in transactions with monopolists are:

- A. other monopolists.
- B. perfect competitors.
- C. monopsonists.
- D. individual consumers.

Q10.24 A monopsony employer facing a perfectly competitive supply of labor would pay a wage:

- A. greater than the perfectly competitive wage.
- B. equal to marginal revenue product.
- C. greater than marginal revenue product.
- D. less than the perfectly competitive wage.

Q10.25 Wages for labor will be highest in labor markets consisting of:

- A. perfectly competitive buyers and a monopolist.
- B. a monopsonist and perfectly competitive sellers.
- C. a monopsonist and monopolist.
- D. perfectly competitive buyers and sellers.

Q10.26 Perfect competition always prevails in markets with:

    A.   few buyers and sellers.
    B.   many buyers and sellers.
>   C.   an even balance of power between sellers and buyers.
    D.   a single buyer.

Q10.27 In monopoly and perfectly competitive markets, profits are maximized when:

    A.   MC = AC.
    B.   P > AC.
>   C.   MR = MC.
    D.   MR = P.

Q10.28 Competition tends to be light when:

>   A.   potential entrants are few.
    B.   capital requirements are nominal.
    C.   standards for skilled labor and other inputs are modest.
    D.   regulatory barriers are modest.

Q10.29 By itself, a reduction in import tariffs (taxes) will:

    A.   reduce quantity demanded.
>   B.   enhance domestic competition.
    C.   enhance the profits of domestic competitors.
    D.   reduce import competition.

Q10.30 Government-mandated wage arbitration for employers can enhance efficiency when the labor market involves:

    A.   monopoly.
    B.   excess seller power.
    C.   perfect competition.
>   D.   monopsony.

Perfect Competition and Monopoly

PROBLEMS & SOLUTIONS

P10.1 **Competition Concepts.** *Indicate whether each of the following statements is true or false and why.*

    A. In long-run equilibrium, every firm in a perfectly competitive industry earns economic profit. Thus, if price falls, all of these firms will still be able to breakeven and survive.

    B. Pure competition exists in a market when firms are price makers as opposed to price takers.

    C. A natural monopoly results when the profit-maximizing output level occurs at a point where long-run average costs are decreasing.

    D. Downward-sloping industry demand curves characterize monopoly markets; horizontal demand curves characterize perfectly competitive markets.

    E. A decrease in the price elasticity of demand would follow an increase in monopoly power.

P10.1 SOLUTION

    A. False. In long-run equilibrium, every firm in a perfectly competitive industry earns zero excess profit. Following a decrease in industry prices, high cost producers will be forced to exit. however, remaining firms will continue to operate and earn a normal rate of return on investment.

    B. False. Pure competition exists in a market when individual firms have no influence over price. Such firms take industry prices as a given.

    C. False. A natural monopoly occurs in a market when the market clearing price, or price where Demand (Price) = Supply (Marginal Cost), occurs at an output level where long-run average costs are declining.

    D. False. Downward sloping demand curves follow from the law of diminishing marginal utility and characterize both perfectly competitive and monopoly market structures. Horizontal demand curves characterize perfectly competitive firms.

    E. True. A decrease in the price elasticity of demand would result following an increase in monopoly power.

P10.2 **Price/Output Determination.** Sun City, Arizona, a retirement community that features full-service living arrangements, is considering two proposals to provide lawn-care to elderly residents. First, a national lawn-care firm has offered to purchase the city's lawn-care equipment at an attractive price in return for an exclusive franchise on residential service. A second proposal would allow several small companies to enter the business without any exclusive franchise agreement or competitive restrictions. Under this plan, individual companies would bid for the right to provide service in a given neighborhood. The city would then allocate business to the lowest bidder.

The city has conducted a survey of Sun City residents to estimate the amount they would be willing to pay for various amounts of lawn service. The city has also estimated the total cost of service per resident. Service costs are expected to be the same whether or not an exclusive franchise is granted.

A. Use the indicated price and cost data to complete the following table.

Hours of Lawn Care per Month	Price per Hour	Total Revenue	Marginal Revenue	Total Cost	Marginal Cost
0	$7.50			$ 0.00	
1	7.25			7.00	
2	7.00			13.50	
3	6.75			19.50	
4	6.50			25.25	
5	6.25			30.75	
6	6.00			35.75	
7	5.75			40.25	
8	5.50			44.00	
9	5.25			50.00	
10	5.00			60.00	

B. Determine price and the level of service if competitive bidding results in a perfectly competitive price/output combination.

C. Determine price and the level of service if the city grants a monopoly franchise.

Perfect Competition and Monopoly

P10.2 **SOLUTION**

A.

Hours of Lawn Care per Month	Price per Hour	Total Revenue	Marginal Revenue	Total Cost	Marginal Cost
0	$7.50	$ 0.00	--	$ 0.00	--
1	7.25	7.25	$7.25	7.00	$ 7.00
2	7.00	14.00	6.75	13.50	6.50
3	6.75	20.25	6.25	19.50	6.00
4	6.50	26.00	5.75	25.25	5.75
5	6.25	31.25	5.25	30.75	5.50
6	6.00	36.00	4.75	35.75	5.00
7	5.75	40.25	4.25	40.25	4.50
8	5.50	44.00	3.75	44.00	3.75
9	5.25	47.25	3.25	50.00	6.00
10	5.00	50.00	2.75	60.00	10.00

B. In a perfectly competitive industry, MR = MC P = AC so the optimal activity level occurs at Q = 8 hours of lawn care per month and MR = MC = $3.75 and P = AC = $5.50. Note for Q > 8, P = MR < MC and losses would be incurred.

C. A monopoly will maximize profits by setting MR = MC. Here, MR = MC = $5.75 at Q = 4 hours of lawn care per month and P = $6.50 per hour.

P10.3 ***Price/Output Determination.*** *Tallahassee Used Cars, Inc., a rapidly expanding new entrant to this metropolitan area, is considering two proposals for the provision of its cosmetic detailing of cars (washing, waxing, polishing, engine cleaning, etc.). First, a large janitorial agency with some experience in the detailing of cars has offered to purchase the business detailing equipment in return for an exclusive franchise. A second proposal would allow several small contractors to enter the business without any exclusive franchise agreement or competitive restrictions. Under this plan, individuals would bid for the right to provide service on groups of cars as they were delivered to the lot, presumably based on how busy they were at the time. The car lot would then allocate business to the lowest bidder.*

TUC has conducted a study of its past sales records and the amount of detailing spent on each car, and the premium over book value recouped in the sale to estimate the amount they would be willing to pay for various amounts of detailing. The car lot has also estimated the total cost of service per car. Service costs are expected to be the same whether or not an exclusive franchise is granted. To incite bidding, TUC guarantees the winner of any bid a minimum per car, whether or not the service is used.

A. Use the indicated price and cost data to complete the following table.

Hours of Detailing per Car	Price per Hour	Total Revenue	Marginal Revenue	Total Cost	Marginal Cost
0	$10.00			$ 0.00	
1	9.25			7.50	
2	9.50			15.00	
3	9.25			22.50	
4	9.00			30.00	
5	8.75			37.50	
6	8.50			45.00	
7	8.25			52.50	
8	8.00			60.00	
9	7.75			67.50	
10	7.50			75.00	

B. Determine price and the level of service if competitive bidding results in a perfectly competitive price/output combination.

C. Determine price and the level of service if the car lot grants a monopoly franchise.

P10.3 SOLUTION

A.

Hours of Detailing per Car	Price per Hour	Total Revenue	Marginal Revenue	Total Cost	Marginal Cost
0	$10.00	$ 0.00	--	$ 0.00	--
1	9.75	9.75	$9.75	7.50	$7.50
2	9.50	19.00	9.25	15.00	7.50

3	9.25	27.75	8.75	22.50	7.50
4	9.00	36.00	8.25	30.00	7.50
5	8.75	43.75	7.75	37.50	7.50
6	8.50	51.00	7.25	45.00	7.50
7	8.25	57.75	6.75	52.50	7.50
8	8.00	64.00	6.25	60.00	7.50
9	7.75	69.75	5.75	67.50	7.50
10	7.50	75.00	5.25	75.00	7.50

B. In a perfectly competitive industry, P = MR so the optimal activity level occurs where P = MC. Here, P = MC = $7.50 at Q = 10 hours of detailing per car, and profits equal zero.

C. A monopoly will maximize profits by setting MR = MC. Here, MR = MC = $7.75 > $7.50 at Q = 5 hours of detailing per car and P = $8.75 per hour. Note that MR < MC when Q > 5.

P10.4 **Price/Output Determination.** The City of Ithica, New York is considering two proposals to provide its city government the service of computer maintenance. First, a national computer maintenance and sales franchise has offered to purchase the city's computer equipment at an attractive price in return for an exclusive franchise on computer maintenance. A second proposal would allow several small companies to provide the service without any exclusive franchise agreement or competitive restrictions. Under this plan, individual companies would bid for the right to provide service in a given department. The city would then allocate business to the lowest bidder.

The city has conducted a survey of its department to estimate the amount they would be willing to pay for various amounts of computer maintenance. The city has also estimated the total cost of service per department. Service costs are expected to be the same whether or not an exclusive franchise is granted.

A. Use the indicated price and cost data to complete the following table.

Hours of Computer Maintenance per Month	Price per Hour	Total Revenue	Marginal Revenue	Total Cost	Marginal Cost
0	$31.00				$20
1	30.00				20

Hours of Computer Maintenance per Month	Price per Hour	Total Revenue	Marginal Revenue	Total Cost	Marginal Cost
2	29.00				20
3	28.10				20
4	27.30				20
5	26.60				20
6	26.10				20
7	25.70				20
8	25.30				20
9	24.90				20
10	24.50				20

B. Determine price and the level of service if competitive bidding results in a perfectly competitive price/output combination.

C. Determine price and the level of service if the city grants a monopoly franchise.

P10.4 SOLUTION

A.

Hours of Computer Maintenance per Month	Price per Hour	Total Revenue	Marginal Revenue	Total Cost	Marginal Cost
0	$30	$ 0	--	$ 0	--
1	29	29	$29	20	$20
2	28	56	27	40	20
3	27	81	25	60	20
4	26	104	26	80	20
5	25	125	21	100	20
6	24	144	19	120	20
7	23	161	17	140	20
8	22	176	15	160	20

Perfect Competition and Monopoly

Hours of Computer Maintenance per Month	Price per Hour	Total Revenue	Marginal Revenue	Total Cost	Marginal Cost
9	21	189	13	180	20
10	20	200	11	200	20

B. In a perfectly competitive industry, P = MR so the optimal activity level occurs where P = MC. Here, P = MC = $20 at Q = 10 hours of computer maintenance per month, and profits equal zero.

C. A monopoly will maximize profits by setting MR = MC. Here, MR = $21 > $20 = MC at Q = 5 hours of computer maintenance per month and P = $25 per hour. Note that Q = 6 could not be justified since $MR_{Q=6} = \$19 < \$20 = MC_{Q=6}$.

P10.5 *Price/Output Determination.* Orange Freight, Inc., (an over-the-road common carrier) is considering two proposals for truck maintenance service. First, a national diesel service franchise has offered to purchase the business' overhaul facilities at an attractive price in return for an exclusive franchise on diesel service. A second proposal would allow several small companies to enter the business without any exclusive franchise agreement or competitive restrictions. Under this plan, individual companies would bid for the right to provide service in a given region. Orange Freight would then allocate business to the lowest bidder.

Orange Freight has conducted a survey of regional service hubs to estimate the amount they would be willing to pay for various amounts of diesel service. Orange Freight has also estimated the total cost of service per truck. Service costs are expected to be the same whether or not an exclusive franchise is granted.

A. Use the indicated price and cost data to complete the following table.

Hours for each Diesel Truck Service per Month	Price per Hour	Total Revenue	Marginal Revenue	Total Cost	Marginal Cost
0	$40				$0
1	39				36
2	38				36
3	37				35

Hours for each Diesel Truck Service per Month	Price per Hour	Total Revenue	Marginal Revenue	Total Cost	Marginal Cost
4	36				34
5	35				33
6	34				30
7	33				27
8	32				34
9	31				45
10	30				65

B. Determine price and the level of service if competitive bidding results in a perfectly competitive price/output combination.

C. Determine price and the level of service if Orange Freight grants a monopoly franchise.

P10.5   SOLUTION

A.

Hours for each Diesel Truck Service per Month	Price per Hour	Total Revenue	Marginal Revenue	Total Cost	Marginal Cost
0	$40	$ 0	--	$ 0	$ 0
1	39	39	$39	36	36
2	38	76	37	72	36
3	37	111	35	107	35
4	36	144	33	141	34
5	35	175	31	174	33
6	34	204	29	204	30
7	33	231	27	231	27
8	32	256	25	265	34
9	31	279	23	310	45

Perfect Competition and Monopoly

Hours for each Diesel Truck Service per Month	Price per Hour	Total Revenue	Marginal Revenue	Total Cost	Marginal Cost
10	30	300	21	375	65

B. In a perfectly competitive industry, P = MR so the optimal activity level occurs where P = MC. Here, equilibrium occurs at Q = 7 hours of diesel truck service per month. Where P = $33 just covers MC = $27. Note that Q = 8 could not be justified since P = MR < MC at that level and beyond. Profits also equal zero at the Q = 7 level.

C. A monopoly will maximize profits by setting MR = MC. Here, MR = $37 > $36 = MC at Q = 3 hours of diesel truck service per month and P = $37 per hour. Note that MR < MC for Q > 3 (except at Q = 7).

P10.6 *Price/Output Determination.* Washington Pulp, Inc., produces bondware, including the imprinted paperware used by fast food franchises. Beverage cups, a major product, is sold in a perfectly competitive market. The following relation exists between the firm's imprinted cup output and total production costs:

Total Output	Total Cost
0	$ 35
1,000	85
2,000	145
3,000	215
4,000	295
5,000	385
6,000	485
7,000	610

A. Construct a table showing Washington Pulp's marginal cost of paper cup production.

B. What is the minimum price necessary for Washington to supply one thousand cups?

C. How many cups would Washington supply at industry prices of $75 and $100 per thousand?

P10.6 SOLUTION

A.

Total Output	Total Cost	Marginal Cost
0	$35	--
1,000	85	$50
2,000	145	60
3,000	215	70
4,000	295	80
5,000	385	90
6,000	485	100
7,000	610	125

B. The minimum marginal cost of bondware cups is $50, so this also represents the minimum price necessary to justify supplying a thousand units of output.

C. In a perfectly competitive market, P = MR. Therefore, Washington Pulp will supply output so long as price at least covers the marginal cost of production. At a price of $75, Q = 3,000 units of output can be justified since P = $75 > $MC_{Q = 3,000}$ = $70. However, production of a fourth unit is not warranted since P = $75 < $MC_{Q = 4,000}$ = $80. Similarly, Q = 6,000 could be justified at a price of $100 since P = $100 = $MC_{Q = 6,000}$.

P10.7 *Firm Supply.* Brooksville Fuse, Inc., produces circuit breakers and fuses for residential electric junction boxes. Fuses, its major product, is sold in a perfectly competitive market. The following relation exists between the firm's fuse output and total production costs:

Total Output	Total Cost
0	$500
10,000	3,500
20,000	7,500

Perfect Competition and Monopoly

30,000	12,500
40,000	18,500
50,000	25,500
60,000	33,500
70,000	45,000

A. Construct a table showing Brooksville Fuse's marginal cost of fuse production.

B. What is the minimum price necessary for Brooksville to supply ten thousand fuses?

C. How many fuses would Brooksville supply at industry prices of $5,500 and $7,000 per ten thousand?

P10.7   SOLUTION

A.

Total Output	Total Cost	Marginal Cost
0	$ 500	--
10,000	3,500	$ 3,000
20,000	7,500	4,000
30,000	12,500	5,000
40,000	18,500	6,000
50,000	25,500	7,000
60,000	33,500	8,000
70,000	45,000	11,500

B. The minimum marginal cost of fuses is $3,000, so this also represents the minimum price necessary to justify supplying ten thousand units of output.

C. In a perfectly competitive market, P = MR. Therefore, Brooksville Fuse will supply output so long as price at least covers the marginal cost of production. At a price of $5,500, Q = 30,000 units of output can be justified since P = $5,500 > $MC_{Q = 30,000}$ = $5,000. However, production of a fourth unit is not warranted since P = $5,500 < $MC_{Q = 40,000}$ = $6,000. Similarly, Q = 50,000 could be justified at a price of $7,000 since P = $7,000 = $MC_{Q = 50,000}$.

P10.8 **Firm Supply.** Baton Rouge Tubing, Inc., produces various diameters of vulcanized tubing for home and industry. Automobile emissions control tubing, a major product, is sold in a perfectly competitive market. The following relation exists between the firm's vulcanized tubing output and total production costs:

Total Output	Total Cost
0	$ 150
1,000	600
2,000	1,060
3,000	1,540
4,000	2,040
5,000	2,565
6,000	3,115
7,000	3,750

A. Construct a table showing Baton Rouge Tubing's marginal cost of tubing production.

B. What is the minimum price necessary for Baton Rouge to supply one thousand feet of tubing?

C. How many feet would Baton Rouge supply at industry prices of $510 and $550 per thousand?

P10.8 **SOLUTION**

A.

Total Output	Total Cost	Marginal Cost
0	$ 150	--
1,000	600	$450
2,000	1,060	460
3,000	1,540	480
4,000	2,040	500
5,000	2,565	525

Perfect Competition and Monopoly

6,000	3,115	550
7,000	3,750	635

B. The minimum marginal cost of vulcanized tubing is $450, so this also represents the minimum price necessary to justify supplying one thousand units of output.

C. In a perfectly competitive market, P = MR. Therefore, Baton Rouge Tubing will supply output so long as price at least covers the marginal cost of production. At a price of $510, Q = 4,000 units of output can be justified since P = $510 > $MC_{Q = 4,000}$ = $500. However, production of a fifth unit is not warranted since P = $510 < $MC_{Q = 5,000}$ = $525. Similarly, Q = 6,000 could be justified at a price of $550 since P = $550 = $MC_{Q = 6,000}$.

P10.9 *Firm Supply.* Miami Felt, Inc., produces feltware: both raw rolled felt and processed goods. Sports and college pennants, a major product, is sold in a perfectly competitive market. The following relation exists between the firm's pennant output and total production costs:

Total Output	Total Cost
0	$ 50
1,000	150
2,000	275
3,000	425
4,000	600
5,000	800
6,000	1,050
7,000	1,350

A. Construct a table showing Miami Felt's marginal cost of pennant production.

B. What is the minimum price necessary for Miami to supply one thousand pennants?

C. How many pennants would Miami supply at industry prices of $180 and $300 per thousand?

P10.9   SOLUTION

A.

Total Output	Total Cost	Marginal Cost
0	$ 50	--
1,000	150	$100
2,000	275	125
3,000	425	150
4,000	600	175
5,000	800	200
6,000	1,050	250
7,000	1,350	300

B.   The minimum marginal cost of pennants is $100, so this also represents the minimum price necessary to justify supplying one thousand units of output.

C.   In a perfectly competitive market, P = MR. Therefore, Miami Felt will supply output so long as price at least covers the marginal cost of production. At a price of $180, Q = 4,000 units of output can be justified since P = $180 > $MC_{Q = 4,000}$ = $175. However, production of a fourth unit is not warranted since P = $180 < $MC_{Q = 5,000}$ = $200. Similarly, Q = 7,000 could be justified at a price of $300 since P = $300 = $MC_{Q = 7,000}$.

P10.10 Industry Supply. An integral part of the reconditioning of any car's brake system is "turning" the rotors (or disks) on a lathe until they become smooth. The technology and labor requirements are very basic, and as a result the market for such services is perfectly competitive. The demand and supply conditions are:

$$Q_S = 2P \qquad \text{(Supply)}$$

$$Q_D = 20 - 0.5P \qquad \text{(Demand)}$$

where Q is thousands of rotor smoothings, and P is the price per rotor.

A.   Graph the industry supply and demand curves.

Perfect Competition and Monopoly 365

B. Determine both graphically and algebraically the equilibrium industry price/output combination.

C. Calculate the level of excess supply if the minimum price is increased to $10 per job.

P10.10 **SOLUTION**

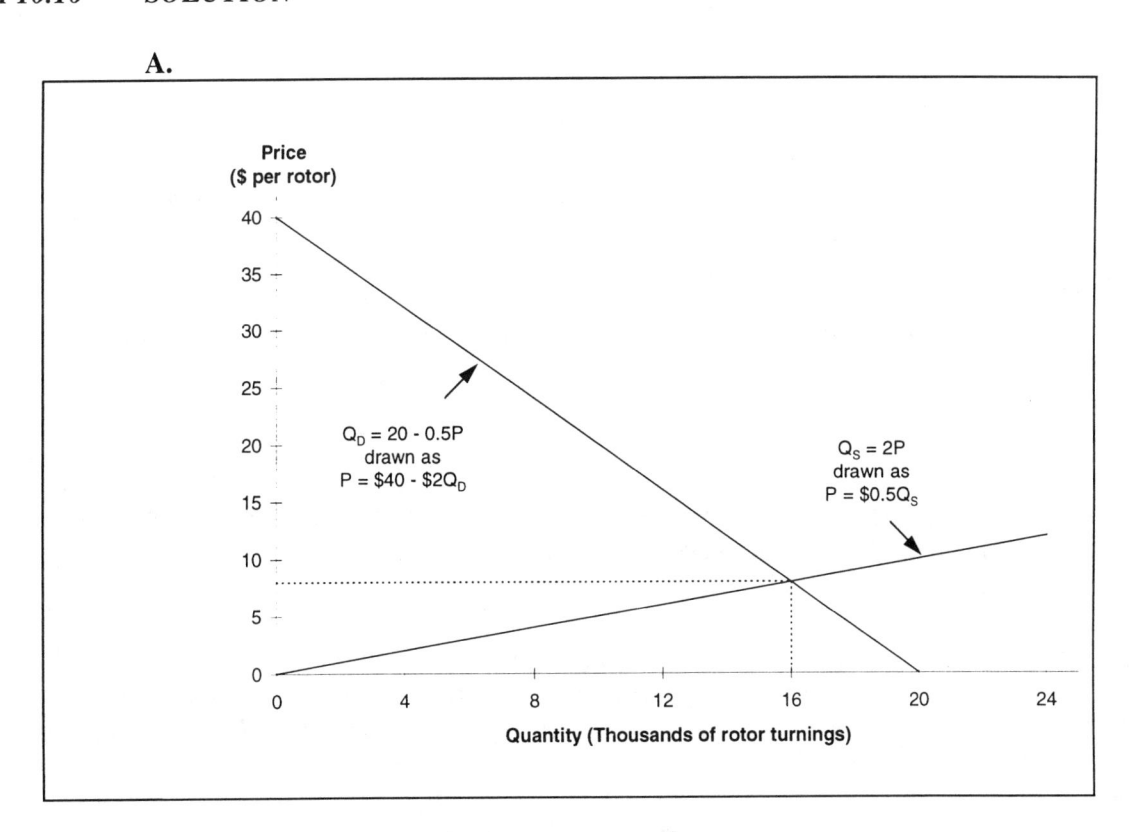

A.

```
Price
($ per rotor)
40
35
30
25
20       Q_D = 20 - 0.5P                          Q_S = 2P
           drawn as                               drawn as
           P = $40 - $2Q_D                        P = $0.5Q_S
15
10
5
0
  0       4       8       12      16      20      24
          Quantity (Thousands of rotor turnings)
```

B. From the graph, we see that $Q_D = Q_S = 16$ at a wage rate of $8 per job. Thus, P = $8 and Q = 16 is the equilibrium price/output combination.

Algebraically,

$$Q_D = Q_S$$

$$20 - 0.5P = 2P$$

$$20 = 2.5P$$

$$20/2.5 = P$$

$$P = \$8$$

Both demand and supply equal 16 since:

Demand: $Q_D = 20 - 0.5(8) = 16(000)$

Supply: $Q_S = 2(8) = 16(000)$

C. At a minimum price of $10, excess supply of 5 units is created since:

Supply: $Q_S =$ $2(\$10) = 20$

minus Demand: $Q_D =$ $\underline{20 - 0.5(\$10) = 15}$

Excess supply $= 5(000)$

Thus, an increase in the minimum price will increase the quantity of investment supplied to the market by 4(000) rotor turning jobs while decreasing the quantity demanded by 1(000). Excess supply of 5(000) rotor turnings will result.

P10.11 *Industry Supply. A necessary step in the rebuilding of any motor is rewinding the coils of copper wire. The technology and labor requirements are very basic, and as a result the market for such services is perfectly competitive. The demand and supply conditions are:*

$Q_D = 75 - 2.5P$ (Demand)

$Q_S = 5P$ (Supply)

where Q is thousands of coil windings, and P is the price per winding.

A. *Graph the industry supply and demand curves.*

B. *Determine both graphically and algebraically the equilibrium industry price/output combination.*

Perfect Competition and Monopoly

C. Calculate the level of excess supply if the minimum price is increased to $12 per winding.

P10.11 SOLUTION

A.

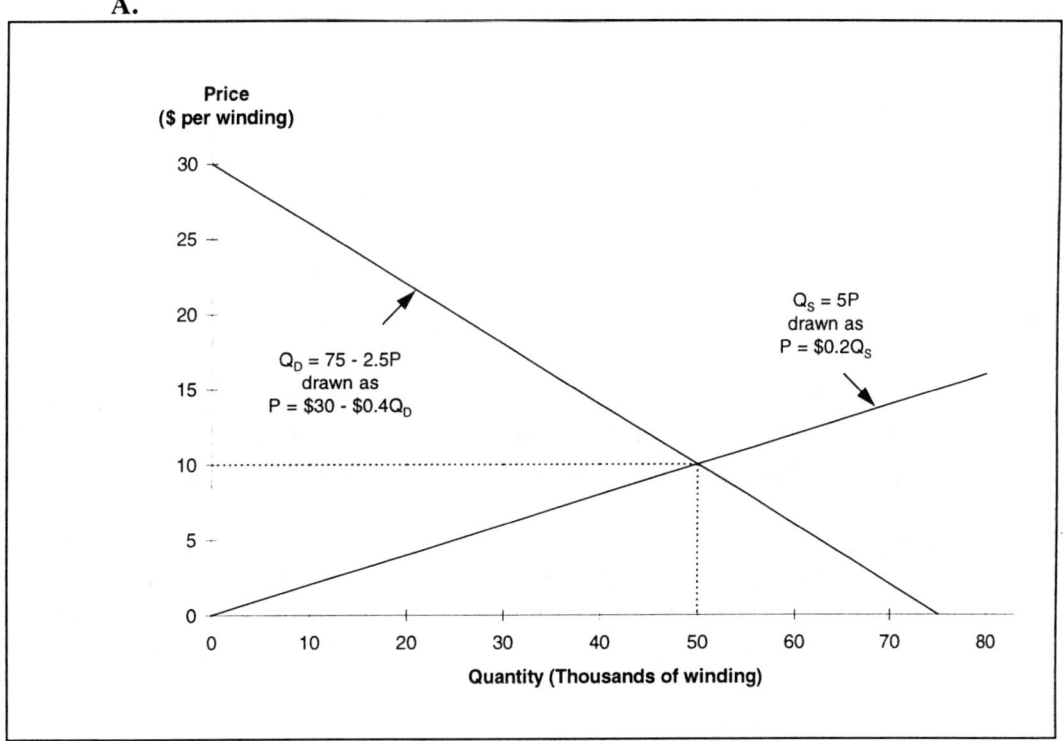

B. From the graph, see that $Q_D = Q_S = 50$ at a wage rate of $10 per winding. Thus, P = $10 and Q = 50 is the equilibrium price/output combination.

Algebraically,

$$Q_D = Q_S$$

$$75 - 2.5P = 5P$$

$$75 = 7.5P$$

$$75/7.5 = P$$

$$P = \$10$$

Both demand and supply equal 50(000) since:

Demand: $Q_D = 75 - 2.5(10) = 50(000)$

Supply: $Q_S = 5(10) = 50(000)$

C. At a minimum price of $12, excess supply of 15 windings is created since:

Supply: $Q_S =$	$5(\$12)$	$= 60$
minus Demand: $Q_D =$	$75 - 2.5(\$12)$	$= 45$
	Excess supply	$= 15(000)$

Thus, an increase in the minimum price will increase the quantity supplied to the market by 10(000) windings while decreasing the quantity demanded by 5(000). Excess supply of 15(000) windings will result.

P10.12 ***Industry Supply.*** *Every maintenance plan for office buildings includes the stripping, waxing, and buffing of ceramic floor tiles. The technology and labor requirements are very basic, and as a result the market for such services is perfectly competitive. The demand and supply conditions are:*

$$Q_S = 16P \quad \text{(Supply)}$$

$$Q_D = 120 - 4P \quad \text{(Demand)}$$

where Q is thousands of hours of floor reconditioning, and P is the price per hour.

A. Graph the industry supply and demand curves.

B. Determine both graphically and algebraically the equilibrium industry price/output combination.

C. Calculate the level of excess supply if the minimum price is increased to $8 per hour.

Perfect Competition and Monopoly

P10.12   **SOLUTION**

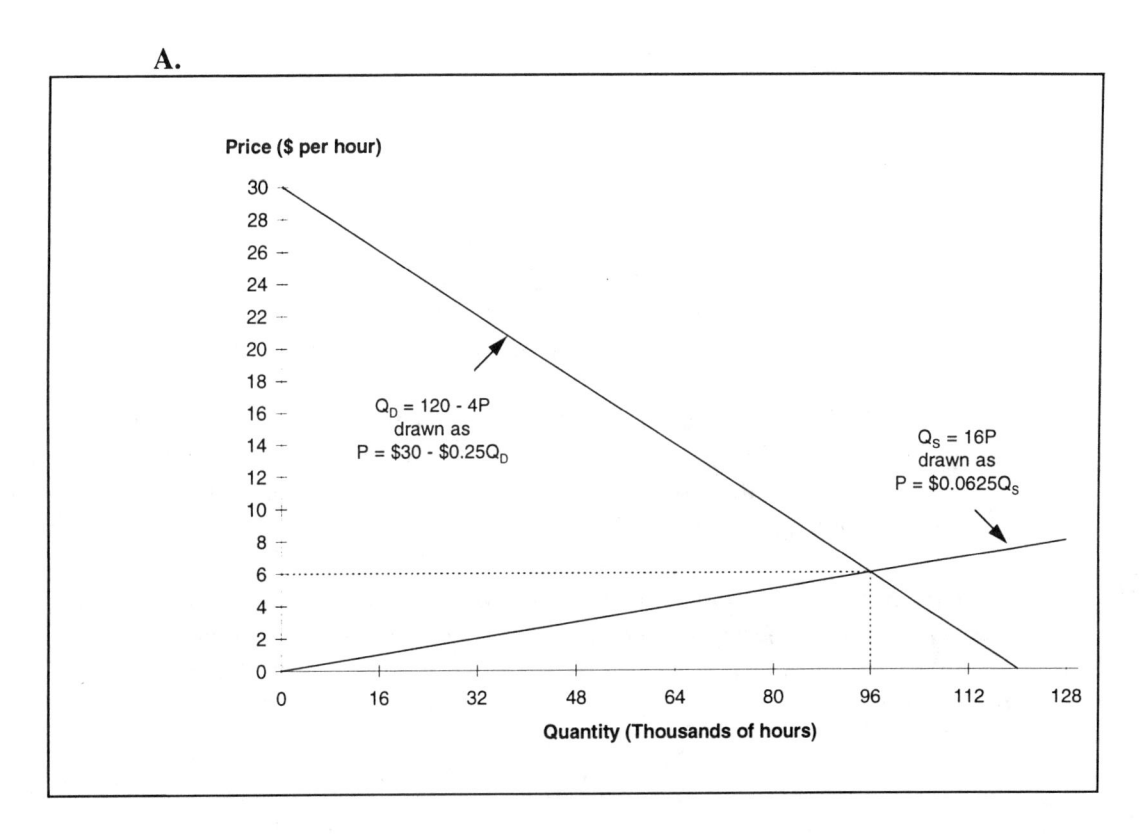

A.

Price ($ per hour)

$Q_D = 120 - 4P$ drawn as $P = \$30 - \$0.25 Q_D$

$Q_S = 16P$ drawn as $P = \$0.0625 Q_S$

Quantity (Thousands of hours)

B. From the graph, see that $Q_D = Q_S = 96$ at a wage rate of $6 per job. Thus, P = $6 and Q = 96(000) is the equilibrium price/output combination.

Algebraically,

$$Q_D = Q_S$$
$$120 - 4P = 16P$$
$$120 = 20P$$
$$120/20 = P$$
$$P = \$6$$

Both demand and supply equal 96(000) since:

Demand: $Q_D = 120 - 4(\$6) = 96(000)$

Supply: $Q_S = 16(\$6) = 96(000)$

C. At a minimum price of $8, excess supply of 40 hours is created since:

$$\text{Supply: } Q_S = 16(\$8) = 128$$
$$\text{minus Demand: } Q_D = 120 - 4(\$8) = 88$$
$$\text{Excess supply} = 40(000)$$

Thus, an increase in the minimum price will increase the quantity supplied to the market by 32(000) hours of floor reconditioning jobs while decreasing the quantity demanded by 12(000). Excess supply of 40(000) hours of floor reconditioning will result.

P10.13 **Industry Supply.** *The move of personnel for any company involves re-cabling of existing office space, for computers, local area networks, and telephone systems. The technology and labor requirements are very basic, and as a result the market for such services is perfectly competitive. The demand and supply conditions are:*

$$Q_S = 2P \qquad \text{(Supply)}$$
$$Q_D = 80 - 2P \qquad \text{(Demand)}$$

where Q is thousands of hours of cabling, and P is the price per hour (excluding cable costs).

A. Graph the industry supply and demand curves.

B. Determine both graphically and algebraically the equilibrium industry price/output combination.

C. Calculate the level of excess supply if the minimum price is increased to $25 per hour.

Perfect Competition and Monopoly

P10.13   **SOLUTION**

A.

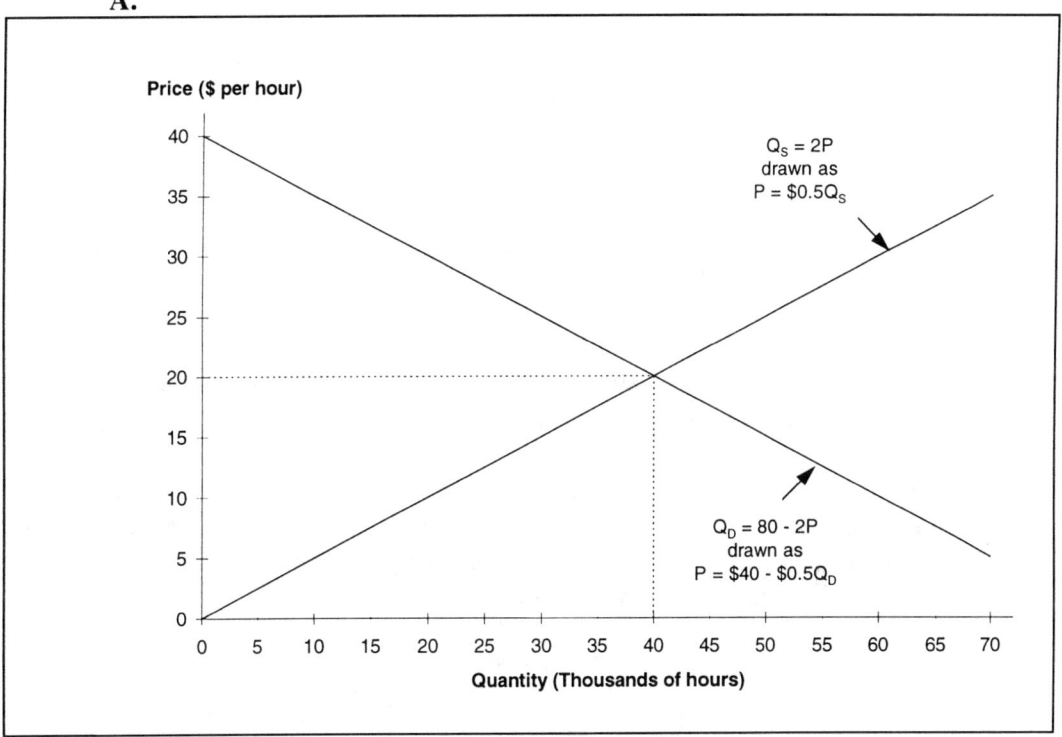

B. From the graph, see that $Q_D = Q_S = 40(000)$ at a wage rate of $20 per job. Thus, P = $20 and Q = 40 is the equilibrium price/output combination.

Algebraically,

$$Q_D = Q_S$$
$$80 - 2P = 2P$$
$$80 = 4P$$
$$80/4 = P$$
$$P = \$20$$

Both demand and supply equal 40(000) since:

$$\text{Demand: } Q_D = 80 - 2(\$20) = 40(000)$$

$$\text{Supply: } Q_S = 2(\$20) = 40(000)$$

C. At a minimum price of $25, excess supply of 5 hours is created since:

Supply: $Q_S =$	$2(\$25)$	$= 50$
minus Demand: $Q_D =$	$80 - 2(\$25)$	$= 30$
	Excess supply	$= 20(000)$

Thus, an increase in the minimum price will increase the quantity supplied to the market by 10(000) hours of cabling while decreasing the quantity demanded by 10(000). Excess supply of 20(000) hours of cabling will result.

P10.14 **Firm Supply.** Nature's Best, Inc., supplies asparagus to canners located throughout the Mississippi River valley. Like several grain and commodity markets, the market for asparagus is perfectly competitive. The company's technology defines a marginal cost per ton of asparagus given by the relation:

$$MC = \$1.50 + \$0.0005Q$$

A. Calculate the industry price necessary for the firm to supply 500, 1,000, and 2,000 pounds.

B. Calculate the quantity supplied by Nature's Best at industry prices of $1.50, $2.25, and $2.75 per ton.

P10.14 **SOLUTION**

A. The marginal cost curve constitutes the supply curve for firms in perfectly competitive industries. Since P = MR, the price necessary to induce supply of a given amount is found by setting P = MC. Therefore, at:

Q = 500:   P = MC = $1.50 + $0.0005(500) = $1.75

Q = 1,000: P = MC = $1.50 + $0.0005(1,000) = $2.00

Q = 2,000: P = MC = $1.50 + $0.0005(2,000) = $2.50

Perfect Competition and Monopoly 373

  B. When quantity is expressed as a function of price, the firms supply curve can be written:

$$P = MC = \$1.50 + \$0.0005Q$$

$$0.0005Q = P - 1.50$$

$$Q = 2{,}000P - 3{,}000$$

Therefore, at:

  P = $1.50: Q = 2,000(1.50) - 3,000 = 0

  P = $2.25: Q = 2,000(2.25) - 3,000 = 1,500

  P = $2.75: Q = 2,000(2.75) - 3,000 = 2,500

P10.15 **Firm Supply.** *Florida's Golden, Inc., supplies oranges to wholesalers located throughout the country. Like several grain and commodity markets, the market for oranges is perfectly competitive. The company's facilities director defines a marginal cost per crate of oranges given by the relation:*

$$MC = \$15 + \$0.0001Q$$

  A. Calculate the industry price necessary for the firm to supply 25,000, 50,000, and 100,000 crates.

  B. Calculate the quantity supplied by Florida's Golden at industry prices of $15, $22.50, and $27.50 per crate.

P10.15 **SOLUTION**

  A. The marginal cost curve constitutes the supply curve for firms in perfectly competitive industries. Since P = MR, the price necessary to induce supply of a given amount is found by setting P = MC. Therefore, at:

Q = 25,000: P = MC = $15 + $0.0001(25,000) = $17.50

Q = 50,000: P = MC = $15 + $0.0001(50,000) = $20

Q = 100,000: P = MC = $15 + $0.0001(100,000) = $25

B. When quantity is expressed as a function of price, the firms supply curve can be written:

$$P = MC = \$15 + \$0.0001Q$$

$$0.0001Q = P - 15$$

$$Q = 10,000P - 150,000$$

Therefore, at:

$P = \$15$: $Q = 10,000(15) - 150,000 = 0$

$P = \$22.50$: $Q = 10,000(22.50) - 150,000 = 75,000$

$P = \$27.50$: $Q = 10,000(27.50) - 150,000 = 125,000$

P10.16 **Firm Supply.** Molten Silicon, Inc., supplies window glass to glaziers located throughout the Northeast. Like several grain and commodity markets, the market for common single-pane glass is perfectly competitive. The company's technology defines a marginal cost per pound of single-pane glass given by the relation:

$$MC = \$1.00 + \$0.0001Q$$

where Q is pounds of single-pane glass.

A. Calculate the industry price necessary for the firm to supply 10,000, 20,000, and 30,000 pounds.

B. Calculate the quantity supplied by Molten Silicon at industry prices of $1.50, $2.50, and $2.50 per pound.

P10.16 **SOLUTION**

A. The marginal cost curve constitutes the supply curve for firms in perfectly competitive industries. Since P = MR, the price necessary to induce supply of a given amount is found by setting P = MC. Therefore, at:

$Q = 10,000$: $P = MC = \$1.00 + \$0.0001(10,000) = \$2$

$Q = 20,000$: $P = MC = \$1.00 + \$0.0001(20,000) = \$3$

Perfect Competition and Monopoly

Q = 30,000:   P = MC = $1.00 + $0.0001(30,000) = $4

B. When quantity is expressed as a function of price, the firm's supply curve can be written:

$$P = MC = \$1.00 + \$0.0001Q$$

$$0.0001Q = P - 1.00$$

$$Q = 10,000P - 10,000$$

Therefore, at:

P = $1.50:   Q = 10,000(1.50) - 10,000 = 5,000

P = $2.50:   Q = 10,000(2.50) - 10,000 = 15,000

P = $3.50:   Q = 10,000(3.50) - 10,000 = 25,000

P10.17 **Industry Supply.** The Gravel & Lime Company is a typical firm in the perfectly competitive crushed rock industry. Its marginal cost of output is described by the relation:

$$MC = \$250 + \$0.05Q$$

where Q is tons of gravel produced per year.

A. Derive the firm's supply curve, expressing quantity as a function of price.

B. Derive the industry supply curve if Gravel & Lime is one of 400 competitors.

C. Calculate industry supply per year at a market price of $300 per ton.

P10.17 **SOLUTION**

A. The perfectly competitive firm will supply output so long as it is profitable to do so. Since P = MR in perfectly competitive markets, the firm supply curve is given by the relation:

$$P = MC = \$250 + \$0.05Q$$

when quantity is expressed as a function of price, the firm supply curve is:

$$P = \$250 + \$0.05Q$$

$$0.05Q = P - 250$$

$$Q_S = -5{,}000 + 20P$$

B. If the company is one of 400 such competitors, the industry supply curve is found by simply multiplying the firm supply curve derived in part a by 400. This is equivalent to a horizontal summation of all 400 individual firm supply curves. When quantity is expressed as a function of price we find:

$$Q_S = 400(-5{,}000 + 20P)$$

$$= -2{,}000{,}000 + 8{,}000P$$

When price is expressed as a function of quantity:

$$Q_S = -2{,}000{,}000 + 8{,}000P$$

$$8{,}000P = 2{,}000{,}000 + Q_S$$

$$P = \$250 + \$0.000125 Q_S$$

C.
$$Q_S = -2{,}000{,}000 + 8{,}000P$$

$$= -2{,}000{,}000 + 8{,}000(\$300)$$

$$= 400{,}000$$

P10.18 *Industry Supply.* Akron Polymers, Inc., is a typical firm in the perfectly competitive crepe rubber industry which is used in the soles of athletic shoes. Its marginal cost of output is described by the relation:

$$MC = \$2.50 + \$0.00025Q$$

where Q is pounds of crepe produced per year.

A. Derive the firm's supply curve, expressing quantity as a function of price.

Perfect Competition and Monopoly

B. Derive the industry supply curve if Akron Polymers is one of 100 competitors.

C. Calculate industry supply per year at a market price of $5 per pound.

P10.18   **SOLUTION**

A. The perfectly competitive firm will supply output so long as it is profitable to do so. Since P = MR in perfectly competitive markets, the firm supply curve is given by the relation:

$$P = MC = \$2.50 + \$0.00025Q$$

when quantity is expressed as a function of price, the firm supply curve is:

$$P = \$2.50 + \$0.00025Q$$

$$0.00025Q = P - 2.50$$

$$Q_S = -10{,}000 + 4{,}000P$$

B. If the company is one of 100 such competitors, the industry supply curve is found by simply multiplying the firm supply curve derived in part a by 100. This is equivalent to a horizontal summation of all 100 individual firm supply curves. When quantity is expressed as a function of price we find:

$$Q_S = 100(-10{,}000 + 4{,}000P)$$

$$= -1{,}000{,}000 + 400{,}000P$$

When price is expressed as a function of quantity:

$$Q_S = -1{,}000{,}000 + 400{,}000P$$

$$400{,}000P = 1{,}000{,}000 + Q_S$$

$$P = \$2.50 + \$0.0000025Q_S$$

378   Chapter 10

C. $Q_S = -1{,}000{,}000 + 400{,}000P$

                              $= -1{,}000{,}000 + 400{,}000(\$5)$

                              $= 1{,}000{,}000$

P10.19 **Industry Supply.** *The Hennepin Novelty Company is a typical firm in the perfectly competitive dime-store balloon industry. Its marginal cost of output is described by the relation:*

$$MC = \$5 + \$0.4Q$$

where Q is thousands of balloons produced per year.

A. Derive the firm's supply curve, expressing quantity as a function of price.

B. Derive the industry supply curve if Hennepin is one of 200 competitors.

C. Calculate industry supply per year at a market price of $25 per thousand balloons.

P10.19 SOLUTION

A. The perfectly competitive firm will supply output so long as it is profitable to do so. Since P = MR in perfectly competitive markets, the firm supply curve is given by the relation:

$$P = MC = \$5 + \$0.4Q$$

when quantity is expressed as a function of price, the firm supply curve is:

$$P = \$5 + \$0.4Q_S$$

$$0.4Q_S = P - 5$$

$$Q_S = -12.5 + 2.5P$$

B. If the company is one of 200 such competitors, the industry supply curve is found by simply multiplying the firm supply curve derived in part a by 200. This is equivalent to a horizontal summation of all 200 individual firm supply curves. When quantity is expressed as a function of price we find:

$$Q_S = 200(-12.5 + 2.5P)$$
$$= -2{,}500 + 500P$$

When price is expressed as a function of quantity:

$$Q_S = -2{,}500 + 500P$$
$$500P = 2{,}500 + Q_S$$
$$P = \$5 + \$0.002Q_S$$

C. $$Q_S = -2{,}500 + 500P$$
$$= -2{,}500 + 500(\$25)$$
$$= 10{,}000$$

P10.20 *Competitive Equilibrium.* Easy-Flo, Inc., supplies standard black printing ink to the nation's offset printing market. Like the output of its competitors, Easy-Flo's ink must meet strict specifications. As a result, the ink supply industry can be regarded as perfectly competitive. Total and marginal cost relations per week for Easy-Flo are:

$$TC = \$2{,}500 + \$5Q + \$0.1Q^2$$
$$MC = \$5 + \$0.2Q$$

where Q is the number of barrels of ink produced.

A. Calculate Easy Flo's optimal output and profits if ink prices are stable at $55 per barrel.

B. Calculate Easy-Flo's optimal output and profits if ink prices rise to $65 each.

C. If Easy-Flow is typical of firms in the industry, calculate the firm's equilibrium output, price, and profit levels.

P10.20 SOLUTION

A. Since the industry is perfectly competitive, P = MR = $55. Set MR = MC to find the profit maximizing activity level.

$$MR = MC$$
$$\$55 = \$5 + \$0.2Q$$
$$0.2Q = 50$$
$$Q = 100$$
$$\pi = TR - TC$$
$$= \$55(100) - \$4,000 - \$5(100) - \$0.1(100^2)$$
$$= \$0$$

B. After a rise in ink prices to $65, the optimal activity level rises to Q = 120 since:

$$MR = MC$$
$$\$65 = \$5 + \$0.2Q$$
$$0.2Q = 60$$
$$Q = 120$$
$$\pi = TR - TC$$
$$= \$65(120) - \$4,000 - \$5(120) - \$0.1(120^2)$$
$$= \$1,760$$

C. In equilibrium, P = AC and MR = MC at the point where average cost is minimized. To find the point of minimum average costs we set:

$$MC = AC = TC/Q$$
$$\$5 + \$0.2Q = (\$4,000 + \$5Q + \$0.1Q^2)/Q$$
$$5 + 0.2Q = \frac{4,000}{Q} + 5 + 0.1Q$$

$$0.1Q = \frac{4{,}000}{Q}$$

$$Q = \sqrt{40{,}000}$$

$$= 200$$

$$P = AC$$

$$= \frac{\$4{,}000}{200} + \$5 + \$0.1(200)$$

$$= \$45$$

$$\pi = TR - TC$$

$$= \$45(200) - \$4{,}000 - \$5(200) - \$0.1(200^2)$$

$$= \$0$$

P10.21 **Competitive Equilibrium.** Extended Metals, Inc., (EMI) of Beaver County, Pennsylvania supplies standard electrical wiring to the construction and renovator markets. Like the output of its competitors, EMI's household AWG-12 wire must meet strict governmental specifications. As a result, the AWG-12 wire supply industry can be regarded as perfectly competitive. Total and marginal cost relations for EMI are:

$$TC = \$3{,}600 + \$5Q + \$0.01Q^2$$

$$MC = \$5 + \$0.02Q$$

where Q is hundreds of feet of wire produced.

A. Calculate EMI's optimal output and profits if AWG-12 wire prices are stable at $20.

B. Calculate EMI's optimal output and profits if AWG-12 wire prices rise to $25 each.

C. If EMI is typical of firms in the industry, calculate the firm's equilibrium output, price, and profit levels.

P10.21 **SOLUTION**

A. Since the industry is perfectly competitive, P = MR = $20. Set MR = MC to find the profit maximizing activity level.

$$MR = MC$$

$$\$20 = \$5 + \$0.02Q$$

$$0.02Q = 15$$

$$Q = 750$$

$$\pi = TR - TC$$

$$= \$20(750) - \$3,600 - \$5(750) - \$0.01(750^2)$$

$$= \$2,025$$

B. After a rise in wire prices to $25, the optimal activity level rises to Q = 1,000 since:

$$MR = MC$$

$$\$25 = \$5 + \$0.02Q$$

$$0.02Q = 20$$

$$Q = 1,000$$

$$\pi = TR - TC$$

$$= \$25(1,000) - \$3,600 - \$5(1,000) - \$0.01(1,000^2)$$

$$= \$6,400$$

C. In equilibrium, P = AC and MR = MC at the point where average cost is minimized. To find the point of minimum average costs we set:

$$MC = AC = TC/Q$$

Perfect Competition and Monopoly

$$\$5 + \$0.02Q = (\$3{,}600 + \$5Q + \$0.01Q^2)/Q$$

$$5 + 0.02Q = \frac{3{,}600}{Q} + 5 + 0.01Q$$

$$0.01Q = \frac{3{,}600}{Q}$$

$$Q^2 = \frac{3{,}600}{0.01}$$

$$Q = \sqrt{360{,}000}$$

$$= 600$$

$$P = AC$$

$$= \frac{\$3{,}600}{600} + \$5 + \$0.01(600)$$

$$= \$17$$

$$\pi = TR - TC$$

$$= \$17(600) - \$3{,}600 - \$5(600) - \$0.01(600^2)$$

$$= \$0$$

P10.22 **Monopoly Equilibrium.** Forked Sticks, Inc., enjoys an exclusive patent on a process to accurately detect water without expensive drilling or core samples. Total and marginal revenue relations for the water detection process are:

$$TR = \$280Q - \$0.005Q^2$$

$$MR = \$280 - \$0.01Q$$

Marginal costs for the process are stable at $100 per test. All other costs have been fully amortized.

    A. As a monopoly, calculate Forked Stick's output, price, and profits at the profit-maximizing activity level.

B. What price and profit levels would prevail following expiration of copyright protection based on the assumption that perfectly competitive pricing would result?

P10.22 SOLUTION

A. Set MR = MC to find the profit maximizing activity level:

$$MR = MC$$

$$\$280 - \$0.01Q = \$100$$

$$0.01Q = 180$$

$$Q = 18{,}000$$

$$P = TR/Q$$

$$= (\$280Q - \$0.005Q^2)/Q$$

$$= \$280 - \$0.005Q$$

$$= \$280 - \$0.005(18{,}000)$$

$$= \$190$$

$$\pi = TR - TC$$

$$= \$190(18{,}000) - \$100(18{,}000)$$

$$= \$1{,}620{,}000$$

B. In a perfectly competitive industry, P = MR = MC in equilibrium. Thus, after expiration of patent protection, P = MC = $100 would result. Since MC = AC, P = MC implies that π = 0.

P10.23 **Monopoly Equilibrium.** Reno Particulate Technologies, Inc., (RPT) enjoys an exclusive patent on a process to atomize gasoline with platinum in combustion engines, producing substantial gains in miles per gallon. Total and marginal revenue relations for the process are:

$$TR = \$250Q - \$0.001Q^2$$

$$MR = \$250 - \$0.002Q$$

Marginal costs for the process are stable at $150 per engine. All other costs have been fully amortized.

A. As a monopoly, calculate RPT's output, price, and profits at the profit-maximizing activity level.

B. What price and profit levels would prevail following expiration of copyright protection based on the assumption that perfectly competitive pricing would result?

P10.23 SOLUTION

A. Set MR = MC to find the profit-maximizing activity level:

$$MR = MC$$

$$\$250 - \$0.002Q = \$150$$

$$0.002Q = 100$$

$$Q = 50,000$$

$$\begin{aligned}
P &= TR/Q \\
&= (\$250Q - \$0.001Q^2)/Q \\
&= \$250 - \$0.001Q \\
&= \$250 - \$0.001(50,000) \\
&= \$200
\end{aligned}$$

$$\begin{aligned}
\pi &= TR - TC \\
&= \$200(50,000) - \$150(50,000) \\
&= \$2,500,000
\end{aligned}$$

B. In a perfectly competitive industry, P = MR = MC in equilibrium. Thus, after expiration of patent protection, P = MC = $150 would result. Since MC = AC, P = MC implies that $\pi = 0$.

P10.24 **Monopoly Equilibrium.** Pile Buffers, Inc., has enjoyed substantial economic profits derived from patents covering the manufacturing of a special shock absorber used in driving piles at construction sites (piles are large I-beams driven vertically into the ground to stabilize a foundation). Market demand and marginal revenue relations for the shock absorber are:

$$P = \$5{,}000 - \$0.05Q$$

$$MR = \$5{,}000 - \$0.1Q$$

Fixed costs are nil, since research and development expenses have been fully amortized during previous periods. Average variable costs are constant at $4,000 per unit.

A. Calculate the profit-maximizing price/output combination and economic profits if Pile Buffers enjoys an effective monopoly on the shock absorber due to its patent protection.

B. Calculate the price/output combination and total economic profits that would result if competitors offer clones that make the pile driver shock absorber market perfectly competitive.

P10.24 **SOLUTION**

A. The profit-maximizing price/output combination is found by setting MR = MC. Since AVC is constant, MC = AVC = $4,000. Therefore:

$$MR = MC$$

$$\$5{,}000 - \$0.1Q = \$4{,}000$$

$$0.1Q = 1{,}000$$

$$Q = 10{,}000$$

Perfect Competition and Monopoly

$$P = \$5{,}000 - \$0.05(10{,}000)$$

$$= \$4{,}500$$

$$\text{Economic Profits} = PQ - AVC \times Q$$

$$= \$4{,}500(10{,}000) - \$4{,}000(10{,}000)$$

$$= \$5{,}000{,}000$$

(*Note*: As a monopolist, Pile Buffers, Inc. is the industry.)

B. In a perfectly competitive market P = MC. In this instance where AVC is constant and, therefore, MC = AVC, perfectly competitive equilibrium will occur when:

$$P = MC = AVC$$

$$\$5{,}000 - \$0.05Q = \$4{,}000$$

$$0.05Q = 1{,}000$$

$$Q = 20{,}000$$

$$P = \$5{,}000 - \$0.05(20{,}000)$$

$$= \$4{,}000$$

$$\text{Economic Profits} = PQ - AVC \times Q$$

$$= \$4{,}000(20{,}000) - \$4{,}000(20{,}000)$$

$$= \$0$$

In words, the transformation of the pile driver buffer industry from a monopoly to perfect competition has brought a $500 reduction in price and a 10,000 unit expansion in output. At the same time, economic profits have been eliminated.

P10.25 *Monopoly Equilibrium.* Sheridan Thermo-Devices, Inc., has enjoyed substantial economic profits derived from patents covering the manufacture of small, quick-reacting thermostats used in household irons that can sense the buildup of heat leading to scorching, and immediately disconnect power to the heating element. Market demand and marginal revenue relations for the thermostats are:

$$P = \$6 - \$0.00005Q$$

$$MR = \$6 - \$0.0001Q$$

Fixed costs are nil, since research and development expenses have been fully amortized during previous periods. Average variable costs are constant at $4 per unit.

A. Calculate the profit-maximizing price/output combination and economic profits if Sheridan Thermo-Devices enjoys an effective monopoly on the thermostats due to its patent protection.

B. Calculate the price/output combination and total economic profits that would result if competitors offer clones that make the thermostat market perfectly competitive.

P10.25 SOLUTION

A. The profit maximizing price/output combination is found by setting MR = MC. Since AVC is constant, MC = AVC = $4. Therefore:

$$MR = MC$$

$$\$6 - \$0.0001Q = \$4$$

$$0.0001Q = 2$$

$$Q = 20{,}000$$

$$P = \$6 - \$0.00005(20{,}000)$$

$$= \$5$$

$$\text{Economic Profits} = PQ - AVC \times Q$$

$$= \$5(20{,}000) - \$4(20{,}000)$$

$$= \$20{,}000$$

Perfect Competition and Monopoly

(*Note*: As a monopolist, Sheridan Thermo-Devices, Inc. is the industry.)

B. In a perfectly competitive market P = MC. In this instance where AVC is constant and, therefore, MC = AVC, perfectly competitive equilibrium will occur when:

$$P = MC = AVC$$

$$\$6 - \$0.00005Q = \$4$$

$$0.00005Q = 2$$

$$Q = 40{,}000$$

$$P = \$6 - \$0.00005(40{,}000)$$

$$= \$4$$

$$\text{Economic Profits} = PQ - AVC \times Q$$

$$= \$4(40{,}000) - \$4(40{,}000)$$

$$= \$0$$

In words, the transformation of the thermostat industry from a monopoly to perfect competition has brought a $1 reduction in price and a 20,000 unit expansion in output. At the same time, economic profits have been eliminated.

Chapter 11

MONOPOLISTIC COMPETITION AND OLIGOPOLY

MULTIPLE CHOICE QUESTIONS

Q11.1 Within a single market the cross-price elasticity of demand is:

> A. positive.
> B. negative.
> C. zero.
> D. irrelevant.

Q11.2 The four-firm concentration ratio will rise following:

> A. a rise in imports.
> B. a fall in imports.
> C. a merger between the two largest firms in the industry.
> D. small firm entry.

Q11.3 A kinked demand curve results from:

> A. different competitor reactions .
> B. competitor price reactions.
> C. an absence of competitor price reactions.
> D. supply imbalance.

Q11.4 A covert, informal agreement among firms in an industry to fix prices and output levels is called:

> A. a cartel.
> B. oligopoly.
> C. monopolistic competition.
> D. collusion.

Q11.5 A perfectly functioning cartel results in:

> A. oligopoly.
> B. monopoly.
> C. perfect competition.
> D. monopolistic competition.

Monopolistic Competition and Oligopoly

Q11.6 For a firm in monopolistically competitive market equilibrium:

    A.   MC ≥ AC.
    B.   MR ≤ AR.
>   C.   MR = MC.
    D.   P ≥ AC.

Q11.7 In oligopoly equilibrium:

    A.   MC = AC.
    B.   MC > AC.
>   C.   MR = MC.
    D.   MC > AC.

Q11.8 A perfectly functioning cartel results in a:

>   A.   monopoly equilibrium.
    B.   oligopoly equilibrium.
    C.   perfectly competitive equilibrium.
    D.   monopolistically competitive equilibrium.

Q11.9 A successfully exploited niche market involves elements of:

    A.   perfect competition.
    B.   monopolistic competition.
>   C.   monopoly.
    D.   monopsony.

Q11.10 A union with an exclusive contract to supply labor enjoys:

    A.   monopsony in the labor market.
>   B.   monopoly in the labor market.
    C.   oligopoly in the labor market.
    D.   oligopsony in the labor market.

Q11.11 In both monopolistic competition and oligopoly market structures;

> A. there is easy entry and exit.
> B. consumers perceive differences among the products of various competitors.
> C. economic profits may be earned in the long run.
> D. there are many sellers.

Q11.12 In a monopolistically competitive industry, firms:

> A. offer products that are not perfect substitutes.
> B. make decisions in light of expected reactions from other firms.
> C. set price equal to marginal cost.
> D. are price takers.

Q11.13 The demand curve faced by a firm in a monopolistically competitive industry is:

> A. the downward sloping industry demand curve.
> B. downward sloping.
> C. more elastic than the perfectly competitive firm's demand curve.
> D. horizontal.

Q11.14 A monopolistically competitive firm will earn short run positive economic profits if it firm can set a price:

> A. equal to minimum average cost.
> B. higher than average cost.
> C. equal to marginal revenue.
> D. higher than minimum average cost.

Q11.15 In long-run equilibrium, the monopolistically competitive firm will set a price equal to:

> A. average cost.
> B. average variable cost.
> C. marginal cost.
> D. minimum long run average cost.

Monopolistic Competition and Oligopoly

Q11.16 A *perfectly functioning cartel leads to a price/output combination identical to an industry that is:*

> **A.** monopolistic.
> **B.** monopolistically competitive.
> **C.** oligopolistic.
> **D.** perfectly competitive.

Q11.17 *Oligopolistic firms:*

> **A.** seldom earn economic profits.
> **B.** always produce differentiated products.
> **C.** always produce homogenous products.
> **D.** make decisions expecting reactions from competitors.

Q11.18 *An informal agreement to set prices and output is called:*

> **A.** collusion.
> **B.** monopolistic competition.
> **C.** kinked demand.
> **D.** a cartel.

Q11.19 *The demand faced by an industry price leader is:*

> **A.** market demand.
> **B.** market demand plus the demand for output by follower firms.
> **C.** market demand less the supply of output by follower firms.
> **D.** kinked.

Q11.20 *The industry supply curve is derived through the horizontal summation of firm:*

> **A.** average cost curves.
> **B.** marginal revenue curves.
> **C.** marginal cost curves.
> **D.** demand curves.

Q11.21 *The kinked demand curve theory of oligopoly assumes that rival firms:*

- A. react to price increases.
- B. react to price increases and decreases.
- C. do not react to price changes.
- D. react to price decreases.

Q11.22 *In equilibrium monopolistic competition results in:*

- A. P > AC and MR = MC.
- B. P = MR and AC = MC.
- C. P < MR and AC < MC.
- D. P = AC and MR = MC.

Q11.23 *Equilibrium in oligopoly markets is characterized by:*

- A. P > AC and MR = MC.
- B. P = MR and AC = MC.
- C. P < MR and AC < MC.
- D. P = AC and MR = MC.

Q11.24 *A firm should increase advertising if the net marginal revenue derived is:*

- A. equal to the marginal cost of advertising.
- B. greater than the marginal cost of advertising.
- C. greater than zero.
- D. less than the marginal cost of advertising.

Q11.25 *Concentration ratios:*

- A. overstate the relative importance of firms in local markets.
- B. ignore potential entrants.
- C. measure the degree of buyer concentration.
- D. understate the relative importance of domestic firms when import competition is important.

Monopolistic Competition and Oligopoly

Q11.26 The vigor of competition always decreases with a fall in:

  A. product differentiation.
  B. barriers to entry.
> C. the level of available information.
  D. the number of competitors.

Q11.27 When prices in monopolistically competitive markets exceed those in a perfectly competitive equilibrium, this difference is the cost of:

  A. information.
  B. market power.
  C. inefficiency.
> D. product differentiation.

Q11.28 Monopolistic competition always entails:

  A. declining LRAC.
> B. vigorous price competition.
  C. increasing LRAC.
  D. constant LRAC.

Q11.29 Monopolistic competition is characterized by:

  A. homogeneous products.
  B. barriers to entry and exit.
> C. perfect dissemination of information.
  D. few buyers and sellers.

Q11.30 Above-normal rates of return in long-run equilibrium require:

  A. homogeneous products.
> B. barriers to entry or exit.
  C. few buyers or sellers.
  D. differentiated products.

PROBLEMS & SOLUTIONS

P11.1 **Competition Concepts.** *Indicate whether each of the following statements is true or false and why.*

- **A.** A high ratio of distribution cost to total cost tends to increase competition by widening the geographic area over which any individual producer can compete.

- **B.** The price elasticity of demand will tend to fall as new competitors introduce substitute products.

- **C.** Equilibrium in monopolistically competitive markets requires that firms be operating at the minimum point on the long-run average cost curve.

- **D.** An increase in product differentiation will tend to decrease the slope of firm demand curves.

- **E.** A perfectly functioning cartel would achieve the perfectly competitive industry price-output combination.

P11.1 **SOLUTION**

- **A.** False. A low ratio of distribution cost to total cost tends to increase competition by widening the geographic area over which any individual producer can compete.

- **B.** False. The price elasticity of demand will tend to rise as new competitors introduce substitute products.

- **C.** False. Stable equilibrium in perfectly competitive markets requires that firms must operate at the minimum point on the long-run average cost curve. In monopolistically competitive markets, however, equilibrium is achieved at a point of tangency between firm demand and average cost curves. This tangency typically occurs at an output level below the point of minimum long-run average costs.

- **D.** False. An increase in product differentiation will tend to increase the slope of individual firm demand curves.

- **E.** False. A perfectly functioning cartel would achieve the monopoly price-output combination.

Monopolistic Competition and Oligopoly 397

P11.2 **Pricing Discretion.** Would the following factors increase or decrease the ability of domestic manufacturers to raise prices and profit margins? Why?

   A.   Elimination of uniform product safety standards.

   B.   Increased import tariffs (taxes).

   C.   Increase import quotas.

   D.   A rising value of the dollar that has the effect of lowering import prices.

   E.   A tax on price advertising.

P11.2 **SOLUTION**

   A. Increase. An elimination of product safety standards will reduce product homogeneity. As product differentiation rises, some increase in the pricing discretion of firms will result.

   B. Increase. An increase in import tariffs (taxes) will increase the price of imports, thus making imports less attractive to buyers. This will reduce the price pressure on domestic manufacturers, and make it easier for them to increase profit margins.

   C. Decrease. As import quotas are increased, more substitutes for domestic automobiles become available. This will increase competition in the industry, and put downward pressure on profit margins.

   D. Decrease. A rising value of the dollar that has the effect of lowering import prices will put downward pressure on the profit margins of domestic manufacturers.

   E. Increase. A tax on price advertising will reduce price competition and thereby increase the ability of firms to raise profit margins.

P11.3 **Monopolistic Competition.** Soft Lens, Inc., has enjoyed rapid growth in sales and high operating profits on its innovative extended-wear soft contact lenses. However, the company faces potentially fierce competition from a host of new competitors as some important basic patents expire during the coming year. Unless the company is able to thwart such competition, severe downward pressure on prices and profit margins is anticipated.

398   Chapter 11

A. Use Soft Lens' current price, output, and total cost data to complete the following table:

Price ($)	Monthly Output (million)	Total Revenue ($million)	Marginal Revenue ($million)	Total Cost ($million)	Marginal Cost ($million)	Average Cost ($million)	Total Profit ($million)
$20	0			$0			
19	1			12			
18	2			27			
17	3			42			
16	4			58			
15	5			75			
14	6			84			
13	7			92			
12	8			96			
11	9			99			
10	10			105			

(Note: Total costs include a risk-adjusted normal rate of return.)

B. If cost conditions remain constant, what is the monopolistically competitive high-price/low-output long-run equilibrium in this industry? What are industry profits?

C. Under these same cost conditions, what is the monopolistically competitive low-price/high-output equilibrium in this industry? What are industry profits?

D. Now assume that Soft Lens is able to enter into restrictive licensing agreements with potential competitors and create an effective cartel in the industry. If demand and cost conditions remain constant, what is the cartel price/output and profit equilibrium?

P11.3   SOLUTION

A.

Price ($)	Monthly Output (million)	Total Revenue ($million)	Marginal Revenue ($million)	Total Cost ($million)	Marginal Cost ($million)	Average Cost ($million)	Total Profit ($million)
$20	0	$0	---	$0	---	---	$0
19	1	19	$19	12	$12	$12.00	7

Monopolistic Competition and Oligopoly

Price ($)	Monthly Output (million)	Total Revenue ($million)	Marginal Revenue ($million)	Total Cost ($million)	Marginal Cost ($million)	Average Cost ($million)	Total Profit ($million)
18	2	36	17	27	15	13.50	9
17	3	51	15	42	15	14.00	9
16	4	64	13	58	16	14.50	6
15	5	75	11	75	17	15.00	0
14	6	84	9	84	9	14.00	0
13	7	91	7	92	8	13.14	-1
12	8	96	5	96	4	12.00	0
11	9	99	3	99	3	11.00	0
10	10	100	1	105	6	10.50	-5

B. The monopolistically competitive high-price/low-output equilibrium is P = AC = $14, Q = 6(000,000), and π = TR - TC = 0. Only a risk-adjusted normal rate of return is being earned in the industry, and excess profits equal zero. Since π = 0 and MR = MC = $9, there is no incentive for either expansion or contraction. Such an equilibrium is typical of monopolistically competitive industries where each individual firm retains some pricing discretion in long-run equilibrium.

C. The monopolistically competitive low-price/high-output equilibrium is P = AC = $11, Q = 9(000,000), and π = TR - TC = 0. Again, only a risk-adjusted normal rate of return is being earned in the industry, and excess profits equal zero. Since π = 0 and MR = MC = $3, there is no incentive for either expansion or contraction. This price/output combination is identical to the perfectly competitive equilibrium. (Note that average cost is rising and profits are falling for Q > 9.)

D. A monopoly price/output and profit equilibrium results if Soft Lens is able to enter into restrictive licensing agreements with potential competitors and create an effective cartel in the industry. If demand and cost conditions remain constant, the cartel price/output and profit equilibrium is at P = $17, Q = 3(000,000), and π = $9(000,000). There is no incentive for the cartel to expand or contract production at this level of output since MR = MC = $15.

P11.4 *Monopolistic Competition.* Merton Labs, Inc., was an early participant in the market of post-heart attack medications. However, the company's market share has quickly eroded from entry of the generic market during the past year as some important basic patents expired. More entry and downward pressure on both prices and profits is expected during the coming year.

A. Use Merton's price, output and total cost data to complete the following table:

Price per unit	Output (000)	Total Revenue ($000)	Marginal Revenue ($000)	Total Cost ($000)	Marginal Cost ($000)	Average Cost ($)
$30	0			$ 6		
28	1			30		
26	2			52		
24	3			72		
22	4			90		
20	5			100		
18	6			108		
16	7			133		

B. Assuming cost conditions remain constant, what is the monopolistically competitive high-price/low-output long-run equilibrium?

C. What is the monopolistically competitive low-price/high-output equilibrium? (Note: this is also the perfectly competitive equilibrium.)

P11.4 SOLUTION

A.

Price	Output (000)	Total Revenue ($000)	Marginal Revenue ($000)	Total Cost ($000)	Marginal Cost ($000)	Average Cost ($)
$30	0	$ 0	--	$ 6	--	--
28	1	28	$28	30	$24	$30
26	2	52	24	52	22	26
24	3	72	20	72	20	24
22	4	88	16	90	18	22.5
20	5	100	12	100	10	20
18	6	108	8	108	8	19
16	7	112	4	133	25	18

B. The monopolistically competitive high price-low output equilibrium is at P = AC = $24, Q = 3(000) and π = TR - TC = 0. No excess profits are being earned, MR = MC = $20, and there would be no incentive for either expansion or contraction.

Monopolistic Competition and Oligopoly

Such an equilibrium is typical of monopolistically competitive industries where each individual firm retains some pricing discretion in the long-run.

C. The monopolistically competitive low price-high output equilibrium is at P = AC = $18, Q = 6(000) and π = TR - TC = 0. No excess profits are being earned, MR = MC = $8, and there would be no incentive for either expansion or contraction. This is similar to the perfectly competitive equilibrium. (Note that average cost is rising for Q > 6.)

P11.5 *Monopolistic Competition.* Plasma Displays was an early innovator in the market for gas plasma "lightning" displays. However, the company's market share has quickly eroded during the past year as some important basic patents expired. Increased competitor entry and downward pressure on both prices and profits is expected during the coming year.

A. Use Plasma Displays price, output and total cost data to complete the following table:

Price per unit	Output (000)	Total Revenue ($000)	Marginal Revenue ($000)	Total Cost ($000)	Marginal Cost ($000)	Average Cost ($)
$625	0			$ 25		
600	1			600		
575	2			1,150		
550	3			1,650		
525	4			2,085		
500	5			2,500		
475	6			2,850		
450	7			3,360		

B. Assuming cost conditions remain constant, what is the monopolistically competitive high-price/low-output long-run equilibrium?

C. What is the monopolistically competitive low-price/high-output equilibrium? (Note: this is also the perfectly competitive equilibrium.)

P11.5 SOLUTION

A.

Price	Output (000)	Total Revenue ($000)	Marginal Revenue ($000)	Total Cost ($000)	Marginal Cost ($000)	Average Cost ($)
$625	0	$ 0	--	$ 25	--	--
600	1	600	$600	600	$575	$600
575	2	1,150	550	1,150	550	575
550	3	1,650	500	1,650	500	550
525	4	2,100	450	2,085	435	520
500	5	2,500	400	2,500	415	500
475	6	2,850	350	2,850	350	475
450	7	3,150	300	3,360	510	480

B. The monopolistically competitive high price-low output equilibrium is at P = AC = $575, Q = 2(000) and π = TR - TC = 0. No excess profits are being earned, MR = MC = $550, and there would be no incentive for either expansion or contraction. Such an equilibrium is typical of monopolistically competitive industries where each individual firm retains some pricing discretion in the long-run.

C. The monopolistically competitive low price-high output equilibrium is at P = AC = $475, Q = 6(000) and π = TR - TC = 0. No excess profits are being earned, MR = MC = $350, and there would be no incentive for either expansion or contraction. This is similar to the perfectly competitive equilibrium. (Note that average cost is rising for Q > 6.)

P11.6

Monopolistic Competition. Rodent Resister, Inc., developed the first electromagnetic device that used a home's electrical wiring to repel rodents instead of exterminate them. However, the company's market share has quickly eroded during the past year as some important basic patents expired. More entry and downward pressure on both prices and profits is expected during the coming year.

A. Use Rodent Resister's price, output and total cost data to complete the following table:

Monopolistic Competition and Oligopoly

Price per unit	Output (000)	Total Revenue ($000)	Marginal Revenue ($000)	Total Cost ($000)	Marginal Cost ($000)	Average Cost ($)
$50	0			$ 600		
48	100			5,000		
46	200			9,200		
44	300			13,200		
42	400			16,700		
40	500			20,100		
38	600			22,800		
36	700			25,200		

B. Assuming cost conditions remain constant, what is the monopolistically competitive high-price/low-output long-run equilibrium?

C. What is the monopolistically competitive low-price/high-output equilibrium? (Note: this is also the perfectly competitive equilibrium.)

P11.6 SOLUTION

A.

Price	Output (000)	Total Revenue ($000)	Marginal Revenue ($000)	Total Cost ($000)	Marginal Cost ($000)	Average Cost ($)
$50	0	$ 0	--	$ 600	--	--
48	100	4,800	$4,800	5,000	$4,400	$50
46	200	9,200	4,400	9,200	4,200	46
44	300	13,200	4,000	13,200	4,000	44
42	400	16,800	3,600	16,700	3,500	41.75
40	500	20,000	3,200	20,100	3,400	40.20
38	600	22,800	2,800	22,800	2,700	38
36	700	25,200	2,400	25,200	2,400	36

B. The monopolistically competitive high price-low output equilibrium is at P = AC = $46, Q = 300(000) and π = TR - TC = 0. No excess profits are being earned,

MR = MC = $4,000, and there would be no incentive for either expansion or contraction. Such an equilibrium is typical of monopolistically competitive industries where each individual firm retains some pricing discretion in the long-run.

C. The monopolistically competitive low price-high output equilibrium is at P = AC = $36, Q = 700(000) and π = TR - TC = 0. No excess profits are being earned, MR = MC = $2,400, and there would be no incentive for either expansion or contraction. This is similar to the perfectly competitive equilibrium. (Note that average cost is rising for Q > 700.)

P11.7 *Price/Output Equilibrium.* Osteopathic Devices, Inc., makes products used in the surgical replacement of degenerated bone material. During recent years, its unique hip joint replacement product has successfully exploited a small but profitable niche in the market. The company's monopoly position in this market niche is now threatened by a competitor's announcement of a new device with capabilities similar to those of the Osteopathic product.

A. Complete the following table based on the Osteopathic product's price, output and costs per month:

Output (00)	Price	Total Revenue ($00)	Marginal Revenue ($00)	Total Cost ($00)	Marginal Cost ($00)
0	$2,500			$ 2,000	
1	2,400			3,000	
2	2,300			4,500	
3	2,200			6,500	
4	2,100			8,400	
5	2,000			10,000	

B. While Osteopathic still enjoys a monopoly position, what is their output, price, and profit at the profit-maximizing activity level?

C. What is the output, price, and profit for this product if a monopolistically competitive equilibrium evolves in this market following the successful introduction of the competitor's product? (Assume identical costs conditions for each firm.)

Monopolistic Competition and Oligopoly

P11.7 SOLUTION

A.

Output (00)	Price ($)	Total Revenue ($00)	Marginal Revneue ($00)	Total Cost ($00)	Marginal Cost ($00)
0	$2,500	$ 0	--	$ 2,000	--
1	2,400	2,400	$2,400	3,000	$1,000
2	2,300	4,600	2,200	4,500	1,500
3	2,200	6,600	2,000	6,500	2,000
4	2,100	8,400	1,800	8,400	1,900
5	2,000	10,000	1,600	10,000	1,600

B. The profit maximizing activity level is found where MR = MC. As a monopoly, MR = MC = $2,000(00) at the Q = 3(00) activity level. This implies P = $2,200 and π = TR - TC = $6,600 - $6,500 = $100(00) per month.

C. The monopolistically competitive equilibrium occurs where MR = MC and zero excess profits are earned, and TR = TC. Here, MR = MC = $1,600(00) and TR = TC = $10,000(00) at Q = 5(00) units per month, with P = $2,000 and π = TR - TC = $0 per month.

P11.8 Price/Output Equilibrium.

RainAway, Inc., makes polymers used to coat the windshields of cars, planes, and boats that makes them slick enough for rain to slide off without wipers. During recent years, its unique windshield coating product has successfully exploited a small but profitable niche in the market. The company's monopoly position in this market niche is now threatened by a competitor's announcement of a new product with capabilities similar to those of the RainAway product.

A. Complete the following table based on the RainAway product's price, output and costs per year:

406 Chapter 11

Case Output (000)	Price	Total Revenue ($000)	Marginal Revenue ($000)	Total Cost ($000)	Marginal Cost ($000)
0	$15			$1	
1	14			13	
2	13			25	
3	12			36	
4	11			44	
5	10			55	

B. While RainAway still enjoys a monopoly position, what is their output, price, and profit at the profit-maximizing activity level?

C. What is the output, price, and profit for this product if a monopolistically competitive equilibrium evolves in this market following the successful introduction of the competitor's product? (Assume similar costs conditions for each firm.)

P11.8   SOLUTION

A.

Case Output (000)	Price	Total Revenue ($000)	Marginal Revenue ($000)	Total Cost ($000)	Marginal Cost ($000)
0	$15	$0	--	$1	--
1	14	14	$14	13	$12
2	13	26	12	25	12
3	12	36	10	36	11
4	11	44	8	44	8
5	10	50	6	55	11

B. The profit maximizing activity level is found where MR = MC. As a monopoly, MR = MC = $12(000) at the Q = 2(000) activity level. This implies P = $13 and π = TR - TC = $26 - $25 = $1(000) per year.

C. The monopolistically competitive equilibrium occurs where MR = MC and zero excess profits are earned, and TR = TC. Here, MR = MC = $8(000) and TR = TC

= $44(000) at Q = 4(000) units per year, with P = $11 and π = TR - TC = $0 per year.

P11.9 *Price/Output Equilibrium.* Enamel Alternatives, Inc., makes tooth enamel bonding kits used in the cosmetic dentistry market. During recent years, its unique bonded enamel tooth process has successfully exploited a small but profitable niche in the market. The company's monopoly position in this market niche is now threatened by a competitor's announcement of a new process with capabilities similar to those of the Enamel Alternatives product.

A. Complete the following table based on the Enamel Alternatives product's price, output and costs per month:

Output (000)	Price	Total Revenue ($000)	Marginal Revenue ($000)	Total Cost ($000)	Marginal Cost ($000)
0	$100			$ 5	
1	90			80	
2	80			150	
3	70			210	
4	60			240	
5	50			260	

B. While Enamel Alternatives still enjoys a monopoly position, what is their output, price, and profit at the profit-maximizing activity level?

C. What is the output, price, and profit for this product if a monopolistically competitive equilibrium evolves in this market following the successful introduction of the competitor's product? (Assume similar costs conditions for each firm.)

P11.9 **SOLUTION**

A.

Output (000)	Price ($)	Total Revenue ($000)	Marginal Revenue ($000)	Total Cost ($000)	Marginal Cost ($000)
0	$100	$ 0	--	$ 5	--
1	90	90	$90	80	$75
2	80	160	70	150	70
3	70	210	50	210	60
4	60	240	30	240	30
5	50	250	10	260	20

B. The profit maximizing activity level is found where MR = MC. As a monopoly, MR = MC = $70(000) at the Q = 2(000) activity level. This implies P = $80 and π = TR - TC = $160 - $150 = $10(000) per month.

C. The monopolistically competitive equilibrium occurs where MR = MC and zero excess profits are earned, and TR = TC. Here, MR = MC = $30(000) and TR = TC = $240(000) at Q = 4(000) units per month, with P = $60 and π = TR - TC = $0 per month.

P11.10 **Price/Output Equilibrium.** Lorrington Mills, Inc., makes stain resistant carpet using a process that locks PTF (aka Teflon) into the fibers. During recent years, its unique carpet has successfully exploited a profitable niche in the market. The company's monopoly position in this market niche is now threatened by a competitor's announcement of a new device with capabilities similar to those of the Lorrington product.

A. Complete the following table based on the Lorrington product's price, output and costs per month:

Monopolistic Competition and Oligopoly 409

Square Yards Output (000)	Price	Total Revenue ($000)	Marginal Revenue ($000)	Total Cost ($000)	Marginal Cost ($000)
0	$30			$0	
1	28			26	
2	26			48	
3	24			68	
4	22			88	
5	20			100	

B. While Lorrington still enjoys a monopoly position, what is their output, price, and profit at the profit-maximizing activity level?

C. What is the output, price, and profit for this product if a monopolistically competitive equilibrium evolves in this market following the successful introduction of the competitor's product? (Assume similar costs conditions for each firm.)

P11.10 SOLUTION

A.

Output (000)	Price ($)	Total Revenue ($000)	Marginal Revenue ($000)	Total Cost ($000)	Marginal Cost ($000)
0	$30	$0	--	$0	--
1	28	28	$28	26	$26
2	26	52	24	48	22
3	24	72	20	68	20
4	22	88	16	88	20
5	20	100	12	100	12

B. The profit maximizing activity level is found where MR = MC. As a monopoly, MR = MC = $20(000) at the Q = 3(000) activity level. This implies P = $24 and π = TR - TC = $72 - $68 = $4(000) per month.

Harcourt Brace & Company

C. The monopolistically competitive equilibrium occurs where MR = MC and zero excess profits are earned, and TR = TC. Here, MR = MC = $12(000) and TR = TC = $100(000) at Q = 5(000) units per month, with P = $0 and π = TR - TC = $0 per month.

P11.11 *Price/Output Equilibrium.* The domestic sewing machine manufacturing industry is highly concentrated with only three active firms. Annual output and the marginal cost of production for "free arm" models produced by each company are as follows:

	Marginal Cost		
Annual Output (million)	Happy Hoffer (H)	Wallace Sewing (W)	Machine Murdock (M)
1	$1,000	$1,200	$1,500
2	900	1,000	1,200
3	800	800	900
4	700	600	600
5	750	750	700
6	850	900	750
7	950	1,000	800

Competition from low-priced imports has been effectively limited by import tariffs (taxes). Given this import protection, domestic firms are able to sell as much output as they wish at the current wholesale market price of $750. However, industry prices haven't risen above $750 because this price triggers a flood of foreign competition.

A. Calculate industry output and the market share of each firm based on the assumptions that prices are stable, and therefore that P = MR = $750, and that MC > AVC.

B. Calculate industry output and the market share of each firm if removal of import restrictions reduces prices such as P = MR = $600. Again assume that MC > AVC.

Monopolistic Competition and Oligopoly 411

P11.11 SOLUTION

A. Each industry participant will produce to the point where MR = MC. Given P = MR = $750, each firm will produce such that MC = MR = $750. A total Q = 16(000,000) units will be produced as follows:

Firm	Output	Market Share
Hoffer (H)	5	31.25%
Wallace (W)	5	31.25%
Murdock (M)	6	37.50%
Total	16	100.00%

B. Following a decrease in industry prices to P = MR = $600, industry output will fall to Q = 8(000,000) distributed as follows:

Firm	Output	Market Share
Hoffer (H)	0	0%
Wallace (W)	4	50%
Murdock (M)	4	50%
Total	8	100%

Note that Hoffer, with a minimum MC = $700 will be unable to justify production when P = MR = $600 and therefore will withdraw from the industry.

P11.12 Cartel Pricing. The domestic silicon wafer manufacturing industry is highly concentrated with only three active firms. Annual output and the marginal cost of production for silicon produced by each company are as follows:

	Marginal Cost		
Annual Output (million)	Corning Glass (C)	Four M (F)	Monsanto (M)
1	$2,300	$2,400	$2,500
2	2,200	2,150	2,300
3	2,050	1,950	2,100
4	1,800	1,800	1,900
5	1,900	2,000	2,000
6	2,000	2,100	2,150
7	2,220	2,300	2,250

Competition from lower-priced imports has been effectively limited by import tariffs (taxes). Given this import protection, domestic firms are able to sell as much output as they wish at the current wholesale market price of $2,000. However, industry prices haven't risen above $2,000 because this price triggers a flood of foreign competition.

A. Calculate industry output and the market share of each firm based on the assumptions that prices are stable, and therefore that P = MR = $2,000, and that MC > AVC.

B. Calculate industry output and the market share of each firm if removal of import restrictions reduces prices such that P = MR = $1,800. Again assume that MC > AVC.

P11.12 SOLUTION

A. Each industry participant will produce to the point where MR = MC. Given P = MR = $2,000, each firm will produce such that MC = MR = $2,000. A total Q = 16(000,000) units will be produced as follows:

Monopolistic Competition and Oligopoly

Firm	Output	Market Share
Corning Glass (C)	6	37.50%
Four M (F)	5	31.25%
Mansanto (M)	5	31.25%
Total	16	100.00%

B. Following a decrease in industry prices to P = MR = $1,800, industry output will fall to Q = 8(000,000) distributed as follows:

Firm	Output	Market Share
Corning Glass (C)	4	50%
Four M (F)	4	50%
Mansanto (M)	0	0%
Total	8	100%

Note that Mansanto, with a minimum MC = $1,900 will be unable to justify production when P = MR = $1,800 and therefore will withdraw from the industry.

P11.13 **Cartel Pricing.** The domestic color separator manufacturing industry is highly concentrated with only three active firms (color separators are used in the production of high-quality images used to produce glossy color, pamphlets, newspapers, etc.). Annual output and the marginal cost of production for production grade models produced by each company are as follows:

Annual Output (thousand)	Houston Graphics (H) — Marginal Cost	Rapid Color (R) — Marginal Cost	Color Purple (C) — Marginal Cost
1	$70,000	$60,000	$80,000
2	50,000	40,000	50,000
3	35,000	20,000	20,000
4	45,000	30,000	35,000
5	55,000	35,000	50,000

6	65,000	55,000	65,000
7	75,000	65,000	75,000

Competition from low-priced imports has been effectively limited by import tariffs (taxes). Given this import protection, domestic firms are able to sell as much output as they wish at the current wholesale market price of $35,000. However, industry prices haven't risen above $35,000 because this price triggers a flood of foreign competition.

A. Calculate industry output and the market share of each firm based on the assumptions that prices are stable, and therefore that P = MR = $35,000, and that MC > AVC.

B. Calculate industry output and the market share of each firm if removal of import restrictions reduces prices such as P = MR = $20,000. Again assume that MC > AVC.

P11.13 SOLUTION

A. Each industry participant will produce to the point where MR = MC. Given P = MR = $35,000, each firm will produce such that MC = MR = $35,000. A total Q = 12(000) units will be produced as follows:

Firm	Output	Market Share
Houston Graphics (H)	3	25.00%
Rapid Color (R)	5	41.67%
Color Purple (C)	4	33.33%
Total	12	100%

B. Following a decrease in industry prices to P = MR = $20,000, industry output will fall to Q = 6(000) distributed as follows:

Monopolistic Competition and Oligopoly 415

Firm	Output	Market Share
Houston Graphics (H)	0	0%
Rapid Color (R)	3	50%
Color Purple (C)	3	50%
Total	6	100%

Note that Houston Graphics, with a minimum MC = $35,000 is unable to justify production when P = MR = $20,000 and therefore will withdraw from the industry.

P11.14 *Cartel Pricing.* The domestic highway asphalt spreader manufacturing industry is highly concentrated with only three active firms. Annual output and the marginal cost of production for standard, 1-lane models produced by each company are as follows:

Annual Output (hundred)	Cat Machinery (C)	John Deer (D)	Harvestor International (H)
1	$230,000	$230,000	$260,000
2	210,000	210,000	240,000
3	190,000	195,000	220,000
4	200,000	180,000	205,000
5	215,000	200,000	180,000
6	230,000	215,000	200,000
7	245,000	225,000	220,000

Marginal Cost

Competition from low-priced imports has been effectively limited by import tariffs (taxes). Given this import protection, domestic firms are able to sell as much output as they wish at the current wholesale market price of $200,000. However, industry prices haven't risen above $200,000 because this price triggers a flood of foreign competition.

A. Calculate industry output and the market share of each firm based on the assumptions that prices are stable, and therefore that P = MR = $200,000, and that MC > AVC.

B. Calculate industry output and the market share of each firm if removal of import restrictions reduces prices such as P = MR = $180,000. Again assume that MC > AVC.

P11.14 SOLUTION

A. Each industry participant will produce to the point where MR = MC. Given P = MR = $200,000, each firm will produce such that MC = MR = $200,000. A total Q = 15 units will be produced as follows:

Firm	Output	Market Share
Cat Machinery (C)	4	26.67%
John Deer (D)	5	33.33%
Harvestor International (H)	6	40.00%
Total	15	100.00%

B. Following a decrease in industry prices to P = MR = $180,000, industry output will fall to Q = 9 distributed as follows:

Firm	Output	Market Share
Cat Machinery (C)	0	0%
John Deer (D)	4	50%
Harvestor International (H)	5	50%
Total	9	100%

Note that Cat Machinery, with a minimum MC = $190,000 will be unable to justify production when P = MR = $180,000 and therefore will withdraw from the industry.

P11.15 **Cartel Pricing.** *An illegal cartel has been formed by three leading residential sanitation (trash pick-up) service companies. Total production costs at various levels of service per month are as follows:*

Monopolistic Competition and Oligopoly

Pick-ups per Month (000)	Alpha Pick-up Ltd. (A)	Beta Service, Inc. (B)	Delta Sanitation, Inc. (D)
	Total Cost ($000)		
0	$2	$4	$0
1	7	10	2
2	11	14	5
3	14	17	9
4	16	22	14
5	25	30	20

A. Construct a table showing the marginal cost of production per firm.

B. From the data in Part A, determine an optimal allocation of output and maximum profits if the cartel sets Q = 10(000) and P = $6.

C. Is there an incentive for individual members to cheat by expanding output when the cartel sets Q = 10(000) and P = $6?

P11.15 **SOLUTION**

A.

Pickups per Day (000)	Alpha (A)	Beta (B)	Delta (D)
	Marginal Cost ($000)		
0	--	--	--
1	$5	$6	$2
2	4	4	3
3	3	3	4
4	2	5	5
5	9	8	6

B. Production should be allocated according to which firm is able to supply output at the lowest marginal cost. When Q = 10(000), total cost is minimized if production is allocated as follows:

Firm	Output	Market Share
Alpha (A)	4	40%
Beta (B)	3	30%
Delta (D)	3	30%
Total	10	100%

$$\text{Profits} = TR - TC_A - TC_B - TC_D$$

$$= \$6(10) - \$16 - \$17 - \$9$$

$$= \$18(000) \text{ per day}$$

C. Yes. At P = $6, both Beta and Delta would have an incentive to expand output. Profits for each firm would grow if they each increased service since the $6 price exceeds their marginal cost of service.

P11.16 *Cartel Pricing.* An illegal cartel has been formed by the three leading catering companies in Colorado Springs, Colorado, large enough to handle parties and food service for groups of over 100 persons. Total production costs for various group sizes are as follows:

Maximum number of guests to serve (000)	Flair for Food Co. (F)	Cater to You, Inc. (C)	Action Catering, Inc. (A)
0	$0	$2	$1
1	8	11	10
2	15	19	17
3	21	25	25
4	26	32	35
5	35	42	46

A. Construct a table showing the marginal cost of production per firm.

B. From the data in Part A, determine an optimal allocation of output and maximum profits if the cartel sets Q = 10(000) and P = $8.

Monopolistic Competition and Oligopoly

C. Is there an incentive for individual members to cheat by expanding output when the cartel sets Q = 10(000) and P = $8?

P11.16 SOLUTION

A.

	Marginal Cost ($000)		
Pickups per Day (00)	Flair for Food (F)	Cater to You (C)	Action Catering (A)
0	--	--	--
1	$8	$9	$9
2	7	8	7
3	6	6	8
4	5	7	10
5	9	10	11

B. Production should be allocated according to which firm is able to supply output at the lowest marginal cost. When Q = 10(000), total cost is minimized if production is allocated as follows:

Firm	Output	Market Share
Flair for Food (F)	4	40%
Cater to Your (C)	4	40%
Action Catering (A)	2	20%
Total	10	100%

Profits = TR - TC_F - TC_C - TC_A

= $8(10) - $26 - $32 - $17

= $5(00) per day

C. Yes. At P = $8, Action Catering would have an incentive to expand output. Profits for the firm would grow if they increased service since the $8 price exceeds their marginal cost of service.

P11.17 **Cartel Pricing.** An illegal cartel has been formed by three leading on-site tractor trailer fleet washing service companies in Harrisburg, Pennsylvania. Total production costs at various levels of service per day are as follows:

Tractor Trailer Washers per Day	On the Job, Inc. (O)	H$_2$O on the Go (H)	Fleet Services (D)
0	$ 50	$ 100	$ 0
25	500	600	450
50	900	1,000	900
75	1,250	1,350	1,450
100	1,550	1,800	2,050
125	2,100	2,400	2,700

Total Cost ($000)

A. Construct a table showing the marginal cost of production per firm.

B. From the data in Part A, determine an optimal allocation of output and maximum profits if the cartel sets $Q = 250$ and $P = \$22$.

C. Is there an incentive for individual members to cheat by expanding output when the cartel sets $Q = 250$ and $P = \$22$?

P11.17 SOLUTION

A.

Tractor Trailer	On the Job, Inc. (O)	H$_2$O on the Go (H)	Fleet Services (D)
0	--	--	--
25	$450	$500	$450
50	400	400	500
75	350	350	550
100	300	450	600
125	550	600	650

Marginal Cost ($000)

B. Production should be allocated according to which firm is able to supply output at the lowest marginal cost. When Q = 250, total cost is minimized if production is allocated as follows:

Firm	Output	Market Share
On the Job, Inc. (A)	100	40%
H_2O on the Go (H)	100	40%
Fleet Services (F)	50	20%
Total	250	100%

$$\text{Profits} = TR - TC_O - TC_H - TC_F$$

$$= \$22(250) - \$1,550 - \$1,800 - \$900$$

$$= \$1,250 \text{ per day}$$

C. Yes. At P = $22, Fleet Services (F) would have an incentive to expand output. Profits for the firm would grow if they increased service since the $22(25) = $550 price exceeds their marginal cost of service for twenty-five additional tractor trailers.

P11.18 *Cartel Pricing.* An illegal cartel has been formed by three leading concrete median divider manufacturing companies. Total production costs at various levels of service per day are as follows:

	Total Cost ($000)		
Median Dividers per Day (000)	Ready Mixes, Inc. (R)	Concrete Products, Inc. (C)	Dyna Molding Inc. (D)
0	$2	$3	$0
1	12	14	8
2	21	23	17
3	29	30	27
4	36	41	38
5	47	53	50

A. Construct a table showing the marginal cost of production per firm.

B. From the data in Part A, determine an optimal allocation of output and maximum profits if the cartel sets Q = 10(000) and P = $10.

C. Is there an incentive for individual members to cheat by expanding output when the cartel sets Q = 10(000) and P = $9?

P11.18   SOLUTION

A.

	Marginal Cost ($000)		
Median Dividers per Day (000)	**Ready Mixes, Inc. (R)**	**Concrete Products, Inc. (C)**	**Dyna Molding Inc. (D)**
0	--	--	--
1	$10	$11	$ 8
2	9	9	9
3	8	7	10
4	7	11	11
5	11	12	12

B. Production should be allocated according to which firm is able to supply output at the lowest marginal cost. When Q = 10(000), total cost is minimized if production is allocated as follows:

Firm	Output	Market Share
Ready Mixes, Inc (R)	4	40%
Concrete Products, Inc. (C)	3	30%
Dyna Molding, Inc. (D)	_3_	_30%_
Total	10	100%

Monopolistic Competition and Oligopoly   423

$$\text{Profits} = TR - TC_R - TC_C - TC_D$$

$$= \$10(10) - \$36 - \$30 - \$27$$

$$= \$7(000) \text{ per day}$$

C. No. At P = $10, none of the three firms would have an incentive to expand output. Profits for each firm would decrease if they each increased service since the $10 price is less than the marginal cost of expanded service.

P11.19 **Kinked Demand.** *Chippewa Pen, Inc., faces the following segmented demand and marginal revenue curves for its mechanical pencils:*

Over the range of 0 to 25(000) units of output:

$$P_1 = \$6 - \$0.04Q$$

$$MR_1 = \$6 - \$0.08Q$$

When output exceeds 25(000) units:

$$P_2 = \$8 - \$0.12Q$$

$$MR_2 = \$8 - \$0.24Q$$

The company's total and marginal cost functions are as follows:

$$TC = \$2.50 + \$1.50Q + \$0.02Q^2$$

$$MC = \$1.50Q + \$0.04Q$$

where P is price (in dollars), Q is output (in thousands), and TC is total cost (in thousands of dollars).

A. *Graph the demand, marginal revenue, and marginal cost curves.*

B. *How would you describe the market structure of this industry? Explain why the demand curve takes the shape indicated above.*

C. Calculate price, output, and profits at the profit-maximizing activity level.

D. How much could marginal costs rise before the optimal price would increase? How much could they fall before the optimal price would decrease?

P11.19 SOLUTION

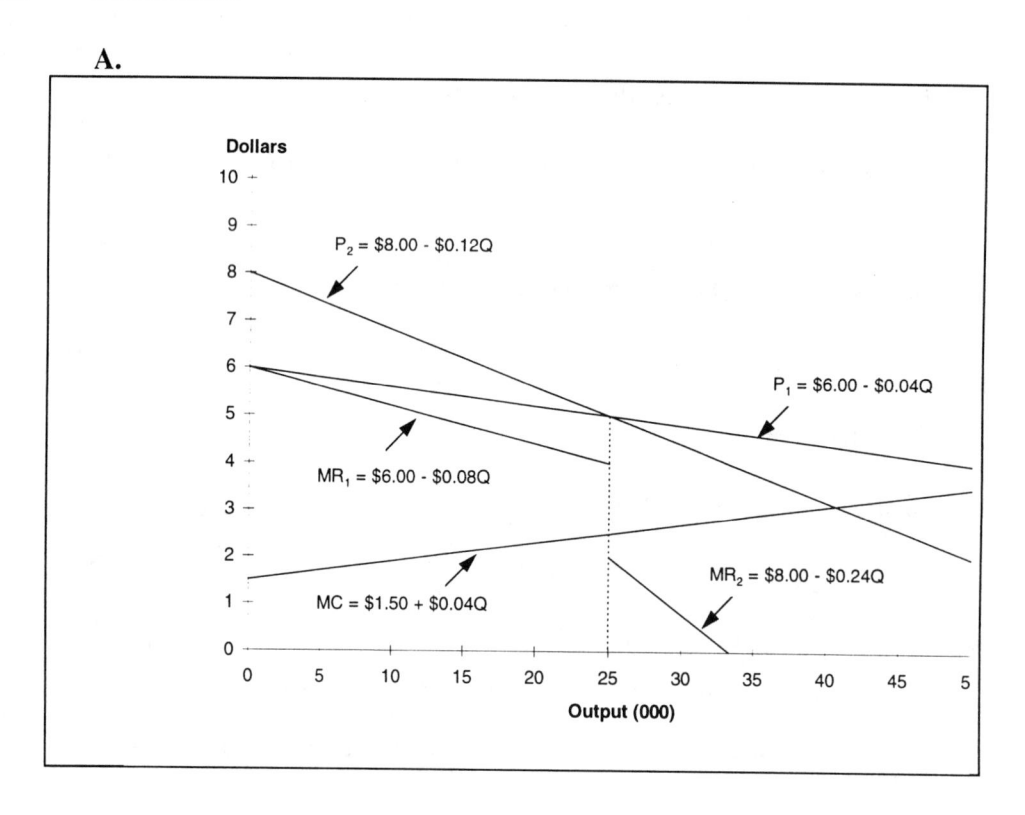

A.

```
Dollars
10 ―

 9 ―
        P₂ = $8.00 - $0.12Q
 8 ―

 7 ―

 6 ―
                                              P₁ = $6.00 - $0.04Q
 5 ―

 4 ―
        MR₁ = $6.00 - $0.08Q
 3 ―

 2 ―
                                      MR₂ = $8.00 - $0.24Q
 1 ―    MC = $1.50 + $0.04Q

 0 ―
   0    5    10   15   20   25   30   35   40   45   5
                    Output (000)
```

B. The firm is in an oligopolistic industry. It faces a kinked demand curve, indicating that competitors will react to price reductions by cutting their own prices and causing the segment of the demand curve below the kink to be highly inelastic. Price increases are not followed, causing the portion of the demand curve above the kink to be very elastic.

C. An examination of the graph indicates that the marginal cost curve passes through the gap in the marginal revenue curve. Graphically, this indicates that optimal P = $5 and Q = 25(000). Analytically,

$$MR_1 = \$6 - \$0.08 \text{ (for Q < 25,000)}$$

Monopolistic Competition and Oligopoly

$$MR_2 = \$8 - \$0.24Q \text{ (for } Q > 25{,}000)$$

$$MC = \$1.50 + \$0.04Q$$

If one solves for the output levels where MR = MC, it is clear that $MR_1 > MC$ over the range $Q < 25(000)$ and $MR_2 < MC$ for the range $Q > 25(000)$. Therefore, CPI will produce 25(000) units of output and market them at a price $P_1 = \$6 - \$0.04Q = \$6 - \$0.04(25) = \$5$. Alternatively, $P_2 = \$8 - \$0.12Q = 4 - \$0.12(25) = \$5$.

At P = $5 and Q = 25:

$$\pi = TR - TC$$

$$= \$5(25) - \$2.50 - \$1.50(25) - \$0.02(25^2)$$

$$= \$72.5(000) \text{ or } 72{,}500$$

D. At Q = 25(000),

$MR_1 = \$6 - \$0.08Q$	$MR_2 = \$8 - \$0.24Q$
$= \$6 - \$0.08(25)$	$= \$8 - \$0.24(25)$
$= \$4$	$= \$2$

This implies that if marginal costs at Q = 25(000) exceed $4, the optimal price would increase. Conversely, if marginal costs at Q = 25(000) fall below $2, the optimal price would decrease. So long as marginal cost at Q = 25(000) is in the range of $2 to $4, CPI will have no incentive to change its price.

P11.20 **Kinked Demand.** *Springform Metals, Inc., faces the following segmented demand and marginal revenue curves for its residential mailboxes:*

Over the range of 0 to 50(000) units of output:

$$P_1 = \$15 - \$0.05Q$$

$$MR_1 = \$15 - \$0.1Q$$

When output exceeds 50(000) units:

$$P_2 = \$22.50 - \$0.2Q$$

$$MR_2 = \$22.50 - \$0.4Q$$

The company's total and marginal cost functions are as follows:

$$TC = \$7.50 + \$1.50Q + \$0.025Q^2$$

$$MC = \$1.50Q + \$0.05Q$$

where P is price (in dollars), Q is output (in thousands), and TC is total cost (in thousands of dollars).

A. Graph the demand, marginal revenue, and marginal cost curves.

B. How would you describe the market structure of this industry? Explain why the demand curve takes the shape indicated above.

C. Calculate price, output, and profits at the profit-maximizing activity level.

D. How much could marginal costs rise before the optimal price would increase? How much could they fall before the optimal price would decrease?

Monopolistic Competition and Oligopoly 427

P11.20 **SOLUTION**

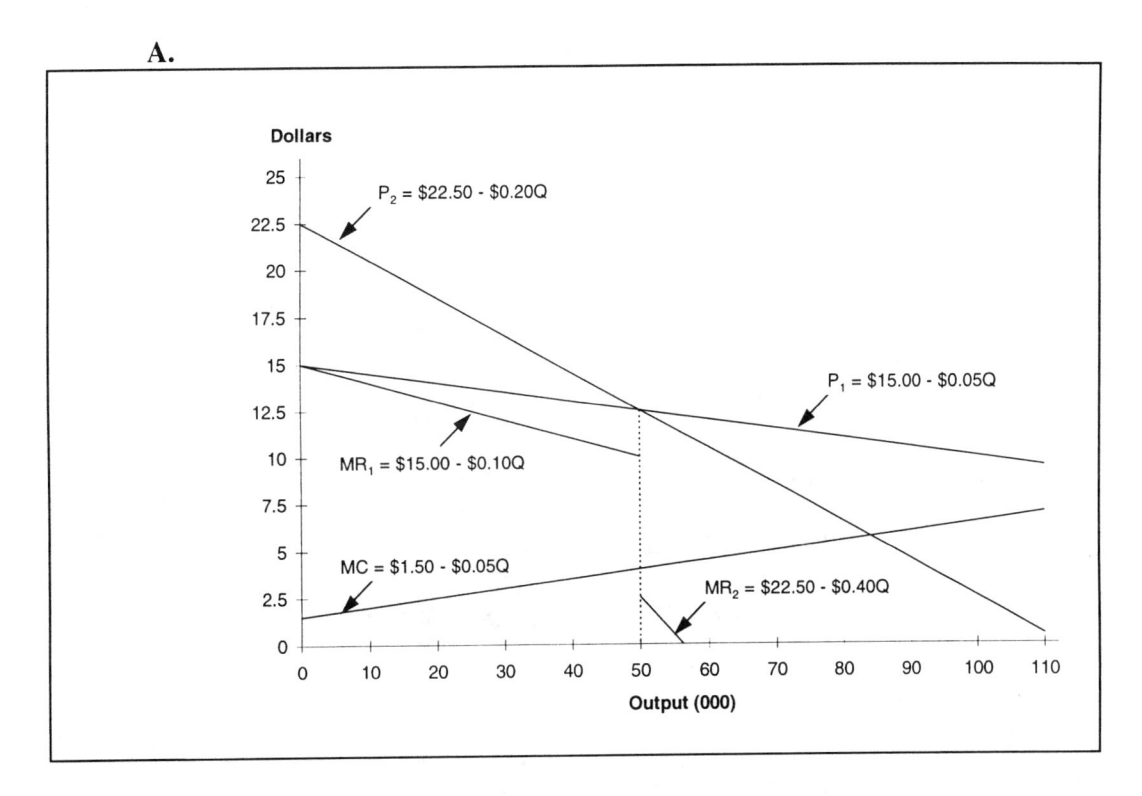

A.

[Graph showing:
- Dollars on y-axis (0 to 25), Output (000) on x-axis (0 to 110)
- $P_2 = \$22.50 - \$0.20Q$
- $P_1 = \$15.00 - \$0.05Q$
- $MR_1 = \$15.00 - \$0.10Q$
- $MR_2 = \$22.50 - \$0.40Q$
- $MC = \$1.50 - \$0.05Q$]

B. The firm is in an oligopolistic industry. It faces a kinked demand curve, indicating that competitors will react to price reductions by cutting their own prices and causing the segment of the demand curve below the kink to be highly inelastic. Price increases are not followed, causing the portion of the demand curve above the kink to be very elastic.

C. An examination of the graph indicates that the marginal cost curve passes through the gap in the marginal revenue curve. Graphically, this indicates that optimal P = $12.50 and Q = 50(000). Analytically,

$$MR_1 = \$15 - \$0.1Q \text{ (for } Q < 50(000)\text{)}$$

$$MR_2 = \$22.50 - \$0.4Q \text{ (for } Q > 50(000)\text{)}$$

$$MC = \$1.50 + \$0.05Q$$

If one solves for the output levels where MR = MC, it is clear that $MR_1 >$ MC over the range Q < 50(000) and MR_2 < MC for the range Q > 50(000). Therefore, SMI will produce 50(000) units of output and market them at a price P_1 = $15 - $0.05Q = $15 - $0.05(50) = $12.50. Alternatively, P_2 = $22.50 - $0.2Q = $22.50 - $0.2Q(50) = $12.50.

At P = $12.50 and Q = 50:

$$\pi = TR - TC$$

$$= \$12.50(50) - \$7.50 - \$1.50(50) - \$0.025(50^2)$$

$$= \$480(000) \text{ or } \$480,000$$

D. At Q = 50(000),

$$MR_1 = \$15 - \$0.1Q \quad MR_2 = \$22.50 - \$0.4Q$$

$$= \$15 - \$0.1(50) = \$22.50 - \$0.4(50)$$

$$= \$10 = \$2.50$$

This implies that if marginal costs at Q = 50(000) exceed $10, the optimal price would increase. Conversely, if marginal costs at Q = 50(000) fall below $2.50, the optimal price would decrease. So long as marginal cost at Q = 50(000) is in the range of $2.50 to $10, SMI will have no incentive to change its price.

P11.21 **Firm Supply.** Iota Facsimile Products, Ltd., and JustheFax, Inc. are domestic suppliers of moderately-priced facsimile machines. Given the vigor of domestic and foreign competition, P = MR in this market. Marginal cost relations for each firm are:

$$MC_I = \$625 + \$0.01Q_I \qquad \text{(Iota Facsimile)}$$

$$MC_J = \$975 + \$0.0025Q_J \qquad \text{(JustheFax)}$$

where Q is output in units, and MC > AVC for each firm.

A. What is the minimum price necessary in order for each firm to supply output?

B. Determine the supply curve for each firm.

Monopolistic Competition and Oligopoly

C. Based on the assumption that $P = P_I = P_J$, determine industry supply curves when $P < \$975$ and $P > \$975$.

P11.21 SOLUTION

A. Profits are maximized when MR = MC. Since P = MR in this market, the supply offered by each company can be determined by setting P = MC. Since $MC_I = \$625$ when $Q_I = 0$ for Iota, this company will supply no output at this price or below. Similarly, JustheFax has a $MC_J = \$975$ when $Q_J = 0$. Thus, JustheFax requires a minimum price of $975 to supply an output to the market.

B. The supply curve for each company is found by setting P = MC:

$$P_I = MC_I = \$625 + \$0.01Q_I$$

or

$$Q_I = -62{,}500 + 100P_I$$

$$P_J = MC_J = \$975 + \$0.0025Q_J$$

or

$$Q_J = -390{,}000 + 400P_J$$

C. When $P < \$975$ only Iota can profitably supply output, so this firm's supply curve becomes the industry supply curve:

$$P = \$625 + \$0.01Q$$

or

$$Q = -62{,}500 + 100P \quad \text{(When } P < \$975\text{)}$$

When $P > \$975$ both firms will be able to profitably supply output and industry supply will be the horizontal summation of individual firm supply:

$$Q = Q_I + Q_J$$

$$= -62{,}500 + 100P - 390{,}000 + 400P$$

$$= -452{,}500 + 500P$$

or

$$P = \$905 + \$0.002Q \quad \text{(When } P > \$975\text{)}$$

P11.22 **Firm Supply.** Wilson Fabricators, Inc., and Johnson City Metalworks, Ltd., are domestic suppliers of backyard basketball goals. Given the vigor of domestic competition, $P = MR$ in this market. Marginal cost relations for each firm are:

$$MC_W = \$25 + \$0.001Q_W \quad \text{(Wilson Fabricators)}$$

$$MC_J = \$75 + \$0.00025Q_J \quad \text{(Johnson City Metalworks)}$$

where Q is output in units, and $MC > AVC$ for each firm.

A. What is the minimum price necessary in order for each firm to supply output?

B. Determine the supply curve for each firm.

C. Based on the assumption that $P = P_W = P_J$, determine industry supply curves when $P < \$75$ and $P > \$75$.

P11.22 SOLUTION

A. Profits will be maximized when $MR = MC$. Since $P = MR$ in this market, the supply offered by each company can be determined by setting $P = MC$. Since $MC_W = \$25$ when $Q_W = 0$ for Wilson, this company will supply no output at this price or below. Similarly, Johnson City has a $MC_J = \$75$ when $Q_J = 0$. Thus, Johnson City requires a minimum price of $75 to supply an output to the market.

B. The supply curve for each company is found by setting $P = MC$:

$$P_W = MC_W = \$25 + \$0.001Q_W$$

or

Monopolistic Competition and Oligopoly

$$Q_W = -25,000 + 1,000P_W$$

$$P_J = MC_J = \$75 + \$0.00025Q_J$$

or

$$Q_J = -300,000 + 4,000P_J$$

C. When P < $75 only Wilson can profitably supply output, so this firm's supply curve becomes the industry supply curve:

$$P = \$25 + \$0.001Q$$

or

$$Q = -25,000 + 1,000P \quad \text{(When P < \$75)}$$

When P > $75 both firms will be able to profitably supply output and industry supply will be the horizontal summation of individual firm supply:

$$Q = Q_W + Q_J$$

$$= -25,000 + 1,000P - 300,000 + 4,000P$$

$$= -325,000 + 5,000P$$

or

$$P = \$65 + \$0.0002Q \quad \text{(When P > \$75)}$$

P11.23 *Firm Supply.* Common Electric Products, Inc., and Lighthouse Manufacturing, Inc., are domestic suppliers of halogen gas light bulbs used in roadside lamps. Given the vigor of domestic and foreign competition, P = MR in this market. Marginal cost relations for each firm are:

$$MC_C = \$15 + \$0.0005Q_C \qquad \text{(Common Electric Products, Inc.)}$$

$$MC_L = \$45 + \$0.000125Q_L \qquad \text{(Lighthouse Manufacturing, Inc.)}$$

where Q is output in units, and MC > AVC for each firm.

A. What is the minimum price necessary in order for each firm to supply output?

B. Determine the supply curve for each firm.

C. Based on the assumption that $P = P_C = P_L$, determine industry supply curves when $P < \$45$ and $P > \$45$.

P11.23 SOLUTION

A. Profits will be maximized when MR = MC. Since P = MR in this market, the supply offered by each company can be determined by setting P = MC. Since $MC_C = \$15$ when $Q_C = 0$ for Common Electric, this company will supply no output at this price or below. Similarly, Lighthouse has a $MC_L = \$45$ when $Q_L = 0$. Thus, Lighthouse requires a minimum price of $45 to supply an output to the market.

B. The supply curve for each company is found by setting P = MC:

$$P_C = MC_C = \$15 + \$0.0005Q_C$$

or

$$Q_C = -30{,}000 + 2{,}000P_C$$

$$P_L = MC_L = \$45 + \$0.000125Q_L$$

or

$$Q_L = -360{,}000 + 8{,}000P_L$$

C. When P < $45 only Common Electric can profitably supply output, so this firm's supply curve becomes the industry supply curve:

$$P = \$15 + \$0.0005Q$$

or

$$Q = -30{,}000 + 2{,}000P \quad \text{(When } P < \$45\text{)}$$

When P > $45 both firms will be able to profitably supply output and industry supply will be the horizontal summation of individual firm supply:

Monopolistic Competition and Oligopoly 433

$$Q = Q_C + Q_L$$

$$= -30,000 + 2,000P - 360,000 + 8,000P$$

$$= -390,000 + 10,000P$$

or

$$P = \$39 + \$0.0001Q \quad \text{(When } P > \$45\text{)}$$

P11.24 **Price Leadership.** *Leading People Magazine is a dominant price leading firm in the popular celebrity news magazine market. Moonlighting and National Inquest are competing news magazines that address the same audience. Total and marginal cost relations for each magazine are:*

Leading People

$$TC_L = \$12,500 - \$1Q_L + \$0.000005Q_L^2$$

$$MC_L = -\$1 + \$0.00001Q_L$$

Moonlighting

$$TC_M = \$10,000 + \$0.5Q_M + \$0.00005Q_M^2$$

$$MC_M = \$0.5 + \$0.0001Q_M$$

National Inquest

$$TC_N = \$50,000 + \$1.25Q_N + \$0.000025Q_N^2$$

$$MC_N = \$1.25 + \$0.00005Q_N$$

and the industry demand curve is:

$$Q_D = 170,000 - 20,000P$$

Assume throughout this problem that Moonlighting and National Inquest are perfect substitutes for Leading People magazine.

A. Determine the supply curves for the Moonlighting and National Inquest magazines, assuming the firms operate as price takers.

B. What is the demand curve faced by Leading People?

C. Calculate Leading People profit maximizing price and output levels. (Hint: Leading People's total revenue and marginal revenue functions are $TR_L = \$4Q_L - \$0.00002Q_L^2$ and $MR_L = \$4 - \$0.00004Q_L$.)

D. Calculate the profit maximizing output levels for the Moonlighting and National Inquest magazines.

E. Is the market for these three magazines in short-run equilibrium?

P11.24 SOLUTION

A. Because price followers take prices as given, they operate where individual marginal cost equals price. Therefore, the supply curves for *Moonlighting* and *National Inquest* are:

Moonlighting

$$P_M = MC_M = \$0.5 + \$0.0001Q_M$$

$$0.0001Q_M = -0.5 + P_M$$

$$Q_M = -5,000 + 10,000P_M$$

National Inquest

$$P_N = MC_N = \$1.25 + \$0.00005Q_N$$

$$0.00005Q_N = -1.25 + P_N$$

$$Q_N = -25,000 + 20,000P_N$$

B. As the industry price leader, *Leading People* demand equals industry demand minus following firm supply. Remember that $P = P_L = P_M = P_N$ since *Leading People* is a price leader for the industry.

Monopolistic Competition and Oligopoly

$$Q_L = Q - Q_M - Q_N$$
$$= 170,000 - 20,000P + 5,000 - 10,000P + 25,000 - 20,000P$$
$$= 200,000 - 50,000P_L$$
$$P_L = \$4 - \$0.00002Q_L$$

C. To find *Leading People*'s profit maximizing price and output level, set MR = MC_L.

$$MR = MC_L$$
$$\$4 - \$0.00004Q_L = -\$1 + \$0.00001Q_L$$
$$5 = 0.00005Q_L$$
$$Q_L = 100,000 \text{ units}$$
$$P_L = \$4 - \$0.00002Q_L$$
$$= \$4 - \$0.00002(100,000)$$
$$= \$2$$

D. Since *Leading People* is a price leader for the industry,

$$P_L = P_L = P_M = P_N = \$2$$

Optimal supply for *Moonlighting* and *National Inquest* magazines are:

$$Q_M = -5,000 + 10,000P_M$$
$$= -5,000 + 10,000(2)$$
$$= 15,000$$

$$Q_N = -25,000 + 20,000P_N$$

$$= -25,000 + 20,000(2)$$

$$= 15,000$$

E. Yes, the industry is in short-run equilibrium since the total quantity demanded is equal to total supply. The total industry demand at a price of $2 is:

$$Q_D = 170,000 - 20,000P$$

$$= 170,000 - 20,000(2)$$

$$= 130,000$$

The total industry supply is:

$$Q_S = Q_L + Q_M + Q_N$$

$$= 100,000 + 15,000 + 15,000$$

$$= 130,000 \text{ units}$$

Thus, the industry is in short-run equilibrium.

P11.25 **Price Leadership.** *Biking Magazine is a dominant price leading firm in the popular bicycle magazine market. Wheel Deal and Free Wheel are competing magazines that address the same audience. Total and marginal cost relations for each magazine are:*

Biking

$$TC_B = \$17,500 - \$0.50Q_B + \$0.000005Q_B^2$$

$$MC_B = -\$0.50 + \$0.00001Q_B$$

Wheel Deal

$$TC_W = \$15,000 + \$2Q_W + \$0.00005Q_W^2$$

$$MC_W = \$2 + \$0.0001Q_W$$

Monopolistic Competition and Oligopoly

Free Wheel

$$TC_F = \$40{,}000 + \$1.875Q_F + \$0.0000125Q_F^2$$

$$MC_F = \$1.875 + \$0.000025Q_F$$

and the industry demand curve is:

$$Q_D = 305{,}000 - 50{,}000P.$$

Assume throughout this problem that Wheel Deal and Free Wheel are perfect substitutes for Biking magazine.

A. Determine the supply curves for the Wheel Deal and Free Wheel magazines, assuming the firms operate as price takers.

B. What is the demand curve faced by Biking?

C. Calculate Biking profit maximizing price and output levels. (Hint: Biking's total revenue and marginal revenue functions are $TR_B = \$4Q_B - \$0.00001Q_B^2$ and $MR_B = \$4 - \$0.00002Q_B$.)

D. Calculate the profit maximizing output levels for the Wheel Deal and Free Wheel magazines.

E. Is the market for these three magazines in short-run equilibrium?

P11.25 SOLUTION

A. Because price followers take prices as given, they operate where individual marginal cost equals price. Therefore, the supply curves for *Wheel Deal* and *Free Wheel* are:

Wheel Deal

$$P_W = MC_W = \$2 + \$0.0001Q_W$$

$$0.0001Q_W = -2 + P_W$$

$$Q_W = -20{,}000 + 10{,}000P_W$$

Free Wheel

$$P_F = MC_F = \$1.875 + \$0.000025Q_F$$

$$0.000025Q_F = -1.875 + P_F$$

$$Q_F = -75,000 + 40,000P_F$$

B. As the industry price leader, *Biking* demand equals industry demand minus following firm supply. Remember that $P = P_B = P_W = P_F$ since *Biking* is a price leader for the industry.

$$Q_B = Q - Q_W - Q_F$$

$$= 305,000 - 50,000P + 20,000 - 10,000P + 75,000 - 40,000P$$

$$= 400,000 - 100,000P_B$$

$$P_B = \$4 - \$0.00001Q_B$$

C. To find *Biking*'s profit maximizing price and output level, set $MR_B = MC_B$.

$$MR_B = MC_B$$

$$\$4 - \$0.00002Q_B = -\$0.50 + \$0.00001Q_B$$

$$4.50 = 0.00003Q_B$$

$$Q_B = 150,000 \text{ units}$$

$$P_B = \$4 - \$0.00001Q_B$$

$$= \$4 - \$0.00001(150,000)$$

$$= \$2.50$$

D. Since *Biking* is a price leader for the industry,

$$P_B = P_B = P_W = P_F = \$2.50$$

Optimal supply for *Wheel Deal* and *Free Wheel* magazines are:

Monopolistic Competition and Oligopoly

$$Q_W = -20{,}000 + 10{,}000 P_W$$

$$= -20{,}000 + 10{,}000(2.50)$$

$$= 5{,}000$$

$$Q_F = -75{,}000 + 40{,}000 P_F$$

$$= -75{,}000 + 40{,}000(2.50)$$

$$= 25{,}000$$

E. Yes, the industry is in short-run equilibrium since the total quantity demanded equals the total supply. The total industry demand at a price of $2.50 is:

$$Q_D = 305{,}000 - 50{,}000 P$$

$$= 305{,}000 - 50{,}000(2.50)$$

$$= 180{,}000$$

The total industry supply is:

$$Q_S = Q_B + Q_W + Q_F$$

$$= 150{,}000 + 5{,}000 + 25{,}000$$

$$= 180{,}000 \text{ units}$$

Thus, the industry is not in short-run equilibrium, a surplus situation exists.

Chapter 12

PRICING PRACTICES

MULTIPLE CHOICE QUESTIONS

Q12.1 If the optimal markup on price is 50%, the optimal markup on cost is:

> A. 100%.
> B. 75%.
> C. 50%.
> D. 25%.

Q12.2 If the optimal markup on cost is 25%, the optimal markup on price is:

> A. 20%.
> B. 25%.
> C. 50%.
> D. 100%.

Q12.3 If MC = $4 and $\epsilon_P = -2$, the optimal markup on price is:

  A. $8.
> B. $4.
  C. $2.
  D. 33%.

Q12.4 Price discrimination exists when:

  A. prices are set according to the price elasticity of demand.
> B. markups differ.
  C. prices differ.
  D. costs differ.

Q12.5 With price discrimination, lower prices are charged when:

> A. the price elasticity of demand is high.
  B. the price elasticity of demand is low.
  C. the cross-price elasticity of demand is high.
  D. the cross-price elasticity of demand is low.

Pricing Practices 441

Q12.6 A 50% markup on cost is equivalent to a markup on price of:

>
- A. 25%.
- B. 33%.
- C. 50%.
- D. 100%.

Q12.7 A 50% markup on price is equivalent to a markup on cost of:

- A. 25%.
- B. 33%.
- C. 50%.
> D. 100%.

Q12.8 When $\epsilon_P = -2$, the optimal markup on cost is:

> A. 100%.
- B. 67%
- C. 50%.
- D. 33%.

Q12.9 When $\epsilon_P = -1$, the optimal markup on price is:

> A. 100%.
- B. 67%
- C. 50%.
- D. 33%.

Q12.10 Consumers' surplus represents:

- A. total revenues.
- B. total revenues less total costs.
- C. the excess of revenues above and beyond the cost of output to producers.
> D. the value of output to consumers above and beyond the amount paid to producers.

Harcourt Brace & Company

Q12.11 The most prevalent pricing practice employed by business firms is setting price equal to:

　　　　A. average revenue.
　　　　B. average cost.
> 　　　C. average variable cost plus a charge for overhead and profit margin.
　　　　D. marginal revenue.

Q12.12 If a firm charges a price of $6 for a product with a cost of $4, the markup on cost equals:

　　　　A. 67%.
　　　　B. 33%.
　　　　C. 150%.
> 　　　D. 50%.

Q12.13 If a firm charges a price of $5 for a product with a cost of $2, the markup on price equals:

> 　　　A. 60%.
　　　　B. 150%.
　　　　C. 250%.
　　　　D. 40%.

Q12.14 If markup on price equals 20%, markup on cost equals:

> 　　　A. 25%.
　　　　B. 67%.
　　　　C. 400%.
　　　　D. 20%.

Q12.15 Profit margin equals:

　　　　A. marginal cost minus marginal revenue.
　　　　B. average cost minus average revenue.
　　　　C. average cost minus average variable cost.
> 　　　D. price minus cost.

Pricing Practices

Q12.16 During off-peak periods, firms should base their markup pricing on:

> A. fully allocated costs.
> B. incremental costs.
> C. sunk costs.
> D. historical costs.

Q12.17 The optimal markup on price will fall following an increase in:

> A. cost.
> B. revenue.
> C. the price elasticity of demand.
> D. price.

Q12.18 If marginal cost is $20 and the price elasticity of demand is -5, the optimal price is:

> A. $25.
> B. $30.
> C. $100.
> D. $24.

Q12.19 If the price elasticity of demand is -2, the optimal markup on price is:

> A. 50%.
> B. 67%.
> C. 100%.
> D. 20%.

Q12.20 When engaging in short-run incremental analysis, managers should ignore:

> A. fixed costs.
> B. implicit costs.
> C. explicit costs.
> D. effects on the costs of already existing products.

Q12.21 Consumers' surplus is:

- A. the costs consumers would have to pay to produce a product minus the amount paid to sellers.
- B. the consumer's budget minus total expenditures.
- > C. the value of a good to consumers of minus the amount paid sellers.
- D. quantity supplied minus quantity demanded.

Q12.22 Price discrimination exists when:

- A. costs vary among customers.
- > B. markups vary among customers.
- C. markups are constant among customers.
- D. prices vary among customers.

Q12.23 Successful price discrimination requires:

- > A. the ability to prevent transfers among customers in different submarkets.
- B. inelastic demand in each submarket.
- C. constant marginal costs.
- D. identical price elasticities among submarkets.

Q12.24 A firm supplying a single product to two distinct submarkets will maximizes profits by equating:

- A. average revenue in each market to average cost.
- B. average revenue in each market to marginal cost.
- > C. marginal revenue in each market to marginal cost.
- D. price in each market to marginal cost.

Q12.25 When products A and B are produced in fixed proportions, profits will be maximized when marginal cost:

- A. equals marginal revenue of B.
- B. of B equals zero.
- > C. equals marginal revenue of A plus B.
- D. equals marginal revenue of A.

Pricing Practices

Q12.26 If $\epsilon_P = -3$, the optimal markup on price is:

> A. 33%.
> B. 50%.
> C. 300%.
> D. 25%.

Q12.27 If $\epsilon_P = -3$, the optimal markup on cost is:

> A. 33%.
> B. 50%.
> C. 300%.
> D. 25%.

Q12.28 During peak periods:

> A. incremental costs are relevant for pricing purposes.
> B. fully allocated costs are relevant for pricing purposes.
> C. facilities are underutilized.
> D. expansion is not required to further increase production.

Q12.29 A by-product:

> A. has MR = 0.
> B. results from an increase in the production of some other output.
> C. has MC = MC_Q.
> D. is identified in terms of its excess production.

Q12.30 When transferred products can be sold in perfectly competitive external markets, the optimal transfer price is the:

> A. external market price.
> B. marginal revenue of the transferred-to (buying) division.
> C. marginal revenue in the output market.
> D. marginal cost of the transferring (selling) division.

PROBLEMS & SOLUTIONS

P12.1 ***Optimal Markup.*** Ralph Kramden is managing partner of Kramden & Associates, Inc., a New York-based management consulting firm. Kramden has asked you to complete an analysis of profit margins for Ed Norton, Inc., a client firm. Unfortunately, your predecessor on this project was abruptly transferred, leaving only sketchy information on the clients' pricing practices.

A. Use the available data to complete the following table:

Price	Marginal Cost	Markup on Cost	Markup on Price
$1	$0.50	100.0%	50.0%
2	1.60	--	--
5	--	400.0	--
10	--	--	25.0
--	15.00	66.7	--

B. Calculate the optimal markup on cost and optimal markup on price for each product, based on the following estimates of the point price elasticity of demand:

Product	Price Elasticity of Demand, ϵ_P	Optimal Markup on Cost, MOC*	Optimal Markup on Price, MOP*
A	-1.5		
B	-2.0		
C	-2.5		
D	-5.0		
E	-10.0		

Pricing Practices 447

P12.1 **SOLUTION**

A.

Price	Marginal Cost	Markup on Cost	Markup on Price
$1	$0.50	100.0%	50.0%
2	1.60	25.0	20.0
5	1.00	400.0	80.0
10	7.50	33.3	25.0
25	15.00	66.7	40.0

B.

Product	Point Price Elasticity of Demand ϵ_P	Optimal Markup on Cost, $MOC_* = \dfrac{-1}{\epsilon_P + 1}$	Optimal Markup on Price, $MOP_* = \dfrac{-1}{\epsilon_P}$
A	-1.5	200.0%	66.7%
B	-2.0	100.0	50.0
C	-2.5	66.7	40.0
D	-5.0	25.0	20.0
E	-10.0	11.1	10.0

P12.2 ***Optimal Markup.*** *Alan Wright is a summer intern at Wicker Works, Inc., a Boston firm that distributes raw wicker in several grades or categories. Alan has been asked to complete an analysis of profit margins for each grade of wicker. Unfortunately, his predecessor on this project abruptly left the company, leaving only sketchy information his pricing practices.*

A. *Use the available data to complete the following table:*

Harcourt Brace & Company

Wicker Grade	Price per Bundle	Marginal Cost	Markup on Cost	Markup on Price
B	$15			
BB	20			
A	35			
AA	45			
AAA	50			

B. Calculate the optimal markup on cost and optimal markup on price for each grade of wicker, based on the following estimates of the point price elasticity of demand:

Wicker Grade	Price Elasticity of Demand, ϵ_P	Optimal Markup on Cost, MOC*	Optimal Markup on Price, MOP*
B	-1.5		
BB	-2.0		
A	-2.5		
AA	-3.0		
AAA	-5.0		

P12.2 SOLUTION

A.

Wicker Grade	Price per Bundle	Marginal Cost	Markup on Cost	Markup on Price
B	$15	$ 7	114.3%	53.3%
BB	20	10	100.0	50.0
A	35	15	133.3	57.1
AA	45	35	28.6	22.2
AAA	50	37	35.1	26.0

Pricing Practices

B.

Wicker Grade	Point Price Elasticity of Demand ϵ_P	Optimal Markup on Cost, $MOC* = \dfrac{-1}{\epsilon_P + 1}$	Optimal Markup on Price, $MOP* = \dfrac{-1}{\epsilon_P}$
B	-1.5	200.0%	66.7%
BB	-2.0	100.0	50.0
A	-2.5	66.7	40.0
AA	-3.0	50.0	33.3
AAA	-5.0	25.0	20.0

P12.3 *Optimal Markup.* Mary Richards is a pricing manager of Caring Move, Inc., a local visiting nurse firm in the home care market. Richards has been asked to complete an analysis of profit margins for the firm. Unfortunately, her predecessor on this project was abruptly terminated, leaving only sketchy information on existing pricing practices.

A. Use the available data to complete the following table:

Hours of Visiting Nurse Care per Day	Price	Marginal Cost of Service	Markup on Cost	Markup on Price
1	$20	$13	53.8%	35.0%
2	35	26	--	--
3	50	--	28.2	--
4	65	--	--	20.0
5	--	65	23.1	--

B. Calculate the optimal markup on cost and optimal markup on price for each service, based on the following estimates of the point price elasticity of demand:

Hours of Visiting Nurse Care per Day	Price Elasticity of Demand, ϵ_P	Optimal Markup on Cost, MOC*	Optimal Markup on Price, MOP*
1	-20.00		
2	-10.00		
3	-5.00		
4	-1.50		
5	-1.25		

P12.3 SOLUTION

A.

Hours of Visiting Nurse Care per Day	Price	Marginal Cost of Service	Markup on Cost	Markup on Price
1	$20	$13	53.8%	35.0%
2	35	26	34.6	25.7
3	50	39	28.2	22.0
4	65	52	25.0	20.0
5	80	65	23.1	18.8

B.

Hours of Visiting Nurse Care per Day	Point Price Elasticity of Demand ϵ_P	Optimal Markup on Cost, $MOC* = \frac{-1}{\epsilon_P + 1}$	Optimal Markup on Price, $MOP* = \frac{-1}{\epsilon_P}$
1	-20.00	5.3%	5.0%
2	-10.00	11.1	10.0
3	-5.00	25.0	20.0
4	-1.50	200.0	66.7
5	-1.25	400.0	80.0

P12.4 ***Optimal Markup.*** *Darla Wigglesworth is a managing partner of Dry Air, Inc., a New Orleans-based dehumidifier-systems distribution firm. Wigglesworth has been asked to complete an analysis of profit margins for the firm. Unfortunately, her predecessor on*

Pricing Practices

this project was abruptly transferred, leaving little information on the firm's current pricing practices.

A. Use the available data to complete the following table:

Model	Price	Marginal Cost	Markup on Cost	Markup on Price
$ 220	$200	$ 120	66.7%	40.0%
440	375	200	--	--
660	600	--	20.0	--
880	900	--	--	33.3
1,000	--	1,000	20.0	--

B. Calculate the optimal markup on cost and optimal markup on price for each model, based on the following estimates of the point price elasticity of demand:

Model	Price Elasticity of Demand, ϵ_P	Optimal Markup on Cost, MOC*	Optimal Markup on Price, MOP*
200	-2		
440	-3		
660	-4		
880	-5		
1,000	-10		

P12.4 SOLUTION

A.

Model	Price	Marginal Cost	Markup on Cost	Markup on Price
220	$ 200	$ 120	66.7%	40.0%
440	375	200	87.5	46.7
660	600	500	20.0	16.7
880	900	600	50.0	33.3
1000	1,200	1,000	20.0	16.7

B.

Model	Point Price Elasticity of Demand ϵ_P	Optimal Markup on Cost, $MOC = \dfrac{-1}{\epsilon_P + 1}$	Optimal Markup on Price, $MOP = \dfrac{-1}{\epsilon_P}$
220	-2	100.0%	50.0%
440	-3	50.0	33.3
660	-4	33.3	25.0
880	-5	25.0	20.0
1000	-10	11.0	10.0

P12.5 **Optimal Price.** *Japanese Imports, Inc., recently offered rebates of $150 off the regular $10,000 price on Sayonara sport vehicles. Sales responded, rising 12% over the previous month's level.*

A. *Calculate the point price elasticity of demand for Sayonara vehicles.*

B. *If marginal cost per unit is $8,750, was the original $10,000 price optimal?*

P12.5 SOLUTION

A.
$$\epsilon_P = \frac{\text{Percentage change in output}}{\text{Percentage change in price}}$$

$$= \frac{0.12}{(-\$150/\$10,000)}$$

$$= -8$$

B. Yes, the profit-maximizing price can be found as follows:

$$MC = MR$$

$$\$8,750 = P \cdot \left(1 + \frac{1}{\epsilon_P}\right)$$

$$\$8,750 = P \cdot \left(1 + \frac{1}{-8}\right)$$

Pricing Practices 453

$$\$8,370 = 0.875P$$

$$P^* \stackrel{\vee}{=} \$10,000$$

P12.6 **Optimal Price.** *Nikishi Bicycles, Inc., recently offered rebates of $10 off the regular $400 price on Triath model bikes. Sales responded, rising 5% over the previous month's level.*

   A. Calculate the point price elasticity of demand for Triath bicycles.

   B. If marginal cost per unit is $200, was the original $400 price optimal?

P12.6 **SOLUTION**

   A. $$\epsilon_P = \frac{\text{Percentage change in output}}{\text{Percentage change in price}}$$

   $$= \frac{0.05}{(-\$10/\$400)}$$

   $$= -2$$

   B. Yes, the profit-maximizing price can be found as follows:

   $$MC = MR$$

   $$\$200 = P^* \left(1 + \frac{1}{\epsilon_P}\right)$$

   $$\$200 = P^* \left(1 + \frac{1}{-2}\right)$$

   $$\$200 = 0.50P^*$$

   $$P^* \stackrel{\vee}{=} \$400$$

P12.7 **Optimal Price.** *Woofer Audio, Inc., recently offered instant rebates of $25 off the regular $1,000 price on Soundman cassette decks. Sales responded, rising 6.25% over the previous month's level.*

A. Calculate the point price elasticity of demand for Soundman cassette decks.

B. If marginal cost per unit is $600, was the original $1,000 price optimal?

P12.7 **SOLUTION**

A. $\epsilon_P = \dfrac{\text{Percentage change in output}}{\text{Percentage change in price}}$

$= \dfrac{0.0625}{(-\$25/\$1{,}000)}$

$= -2.5$

B. Yes, the profit-maximizing price can be found as follows:

$MC = MR$

$\$600 = P^* \left(1 + \dfrac{1}{\epsilon_P}\right)$

$\$600 = P^* \left(1 + \dfrac{1}{-2.5}\right)$

$\$600 = 0.6 P^*$

$P^* = \$1{,}000$

P12.8 **Optimal Price.** Lean Jeans, Inc., recently offered rebates of $1 off the regular $50 price on their designer jeans. Sales responded, rising 4% over the previous month's level.

A. Calculate the point price elasticity of demand for Lean Jeans.

B. If marginal cost per unit is $20, was the original $50 price optimal?

P12.8 **SOLUTION**

A. $$\epsilon_P = \frac{\text{Percentage change in output}}{\text{Percentage change in price}}$$

$$= \frac{0.04}{(-\$1/\$50)}$$

$$= -2$$

B. No, the profit-maximizing price can be found as follows:

$$MC = MR$$

$$\$20 = P \cdot \left(1 + \frac{1}{\epsilon_P}\right)$$

$$\$20 = P \cdot \left(1 + \frac{1}{-2}\right)$$

$$\$20 = 0.5P^*$$

$$P^* = \$40; \text{ thus } P = \$50 \text{ is not optimal.}$$

P12.9 **Markup on Cost.** King Midas Muffler, Inc., offers automobile muffler replacement at a number of outlets in the greater Boston area. The company recently initiated a policy of matching the lowest advertised competitor price. As a result, King Midas has been forced to reduce the average price for mufflers by 3%, but has enjoyed an 18% increase in customer traffic. Meanwhile, marginal costs have held steady at $24.99 per muffler.

A. Calculate the point price elasticity of demand for mufflers.

B. Calculate King Midas' optimal price and markup on cost.

P12.9 **SOLUTION**

A. $$\epsilon_P = \frac{\text{Percentage change in output}}{\text{Percentage change in price}}$$

$$= \frac{0.18}{-0.03}$$

$$= -6$$

B. Given $\epsilon_P = -6$, the optimal markup on cost is:

$$\text{Optimal Markup on Cost} = \frac{-1}{\epsilon_P + 1}$$

$$= \frac{-1}{-6 + 1}$$

$$= 0.2 \text{ or } 20\%$$

Given MC = $24.99, the optimal price is:

$$\text{Optimal Markup on Cost} = \frac{P - MC}{MC}$$

$$0.2 = \frac{P - \$24.99}{\$24.99}$$

$$\$5 = P - \$24.99$$

$$P = \$29.99$$

P12.10 **Markup on Cost.** Oil-n-Go, Inc., offers automobile oil changes at a number of outlets in the greater Ann Arbor area. The company recently initiated a policy of matching the lowest advertised competitor price. As a result, Oil-n-Go has been forced to reduce the average price for oil changes by 5%, but has enjoyed a 15% increase in customer traffic. Meanwhile, marginal costs have held steady at $15.00 per oil change.

A. Calculate the point price elasticity of demand for oil changes.

B. Calculate Oil-n-Go's optimal price and markup on cost.

Pricing Practices 457

P12.10 SOLUTION

A. $\epsilon_P = \dfrac{\text{Percentage change in output}}{\text{Percentage change in price}}$

$= \dfrac{0.15}{-0.05}$

$= -3$

B. Given $\epsilon_P = -3$, the optimal markup on cost is:

$$\text{Optimal Markup on Cost} = \dfrac{-1}{\epsilon_P + 1}$$

$$= \dfrac{-1}{-3 + 1}$$

$$= 0.5 \text{ or } 50\%$$

Given MC = $15.00, the optimal price is:

$$\text{Optimal Markup on Cost} = \dfrac{P - MC}{MC}$$

$$0.5 = \dfrac{P - \$15.00}{\$15.00}$$

$$\$7.50 = P - \$15.00$$

$$P = \$22.50$$

P12.11 *Markup on Cost.* Chim-Chimery, Inc., offers chimney sweepings in the Montpelier, Vermont area. The company recently initiated a policy of matching the lowest advertised competitor price. As a result, Chim-Chimery has been forced to reduce the average price for chimney cleaning by 4%, but has enjoyed a 8% increase in demand. Meanwhile, marginal costs have held steady at $25 per cleaning.

A. Calculate the point price elasticity of demand for chimney cleaning.

B. Calculate Chim-Chimery's optimal price and markup on cost.

P12.11 SOLUTION

A. $$\epsilon_P = \frac{\text{Percentage change in output}}{\text{Percentage change in price}}$$

$$= \frac{0.08}{-0.04}$$

$$= -2$$

B. Given $\epsilon_P = -2$, the optimal markup on cost is:

$$\text{Optimal Markup on Cost} = \frac{-1}{\epsilon_P + 1}$$

$$= \frac{-1}{-2 + 1}$$

$$= 1 \text{ or } 100\%$$

Given MC = $25, the optimal price is:

$$\text{Optimal Markup on Cost} = \frac{P - MC}{MC}$$

$$1 = \frac{P - \$25}{\$25}$$

$$\$25 = P - \$25$$

$$P = \$50$$

P12.12 *Markup on Cost.* Radon Detectives, Inc., offers radon testing to homeowners in the Bethlehem, Pennsylvania area. The company recently initiated a policy of matching the lowest advertised competitor price. As a result, Radon Detectives has been forced to reduce the average price for radon tests by 1%, but has enjoyed a 3% increase in demand. Meanwhile, marginal costs have held steady at $30 per test.

A. Calculate the point price elasticity of demand for radon tests.

B. Calculate Radon Detectives' optimal price and markup on cost.

Pricing Practices

P12.12 SOLUTION

A. $\epsilon_P = \dfrac{\text{Percentage change in output}}{\text{Percentage change in price}}$

$= \dfrac{0.03}{-0.01}$

$= -3$

B. Given $\epsilon_P = -3$, the optimal markup on cost is:

$$\text{Optimal Markup on Cost} = \dfrac{-1}{\epsilon_P + 1}$$

$$= \dfrac{-1}{-3 + 1}$$

$$= 0.5 \text{ or } 50\%$$

Given MC = $30, the optimal price is:

$$\text{Optimal Markup on Cost} = \dfrac{P - MC}{MC}$$

$$0.5 = \dfrac{P - \$30}{\$30}$$

$$\$15 = P - \$30$$

$$P = \$45$$

P12.13 *Markup on Price.* TLC Tree Service, Inc., provides tree spraying services to residential customers in the Detroit area. The company recently raised its service price from $25 to $30 per tree. As a result, sales fell to 3,900 from 4,900 units in the year earlier period.

A. Calculate the arc price elasticity of demand for TLC service.

B. Assume that the arc price elasticity (from Part A) is the best available estimate of the point price elasticity of demand. If marginal cost is $6 per unit for labor and materials, calculate TLC's optimal markup on price and its optimal price.

P12.13 SOLUTION

A.
$$E_P = \frac{\Delta Q}{\Delta P} \times \frac{P_2 + P_1}{Q_2 + Q_1}$$

$$= \frac{3{,}900 - 4{,}900}{\$30 - \$25} \times \frac{\$30 + \$25}{3{,}900 + 4{,}900}$$

$$= -1.25$$

B. Given $\epsilon_P = -1.25$, the optimal TLC markup on price is:

$$\text{Optimal Markup on Price} = \frac{-1}{\epsilon_P}$$

$$= \frac{-1}{-1.25}$$

$$= 0.8 \text{ or } 80\%$$

Given MC = $6, the optimal price is:

$$\text{Optimal Markup on Price} = \frac{P - MC}{P}$$

$$0.8 = \frac{P - \$6}{P}$$

$$0.8P = P - \$6$$

$$0.2P = \$6$$

$$P = \$30$$

P12.14 **Markup on Cost.** Stinging Pesticides, Inc., provides scorpion control services, to residential and business customers in the El Paso area. The company recently raised

Pricing Practices

its service price from $35 to $40 per annual treatment. As a result, sales fell to 37,500 from 52,500 treatments in the year earlier period.

A. Calculate the arc price elasticity of demand for SPI service.

B. Assume that the arc price elasticity (from Part A) is the best available estimate of the point price elasticity of demand. If marginal cost is $24 per unit for labor and materials, calculate SPI's optimal markup on price and its optimal price.

P12.14 SOLUTION

A.
$$E_P = \frac{\Delta Q}{\Delta P} \times \frac{P_2 + P_1}{Q_2 + Q_1}$$

$$= \frac{37{,}500 - 52{,}500}{\$40 - \$35} \times \frac{\$40 + \$35}{37{,}500 + 52{,}500}$$

$$= -2.5$$

B. Given $\epsilon_P = -2.5$, the optimal SPI markup on price is:

$$\text{Optimal Markup on Price} = \frac{-1}{\epsilon_P}$$

$$= \frac{-1}{-2.50}$$

$$= 0.4 \text{ or } 40\%$$

Given MC = $24, the optimal price is:

$$\text{Optimal Markup on Price} = \frac{P - MC}{P}$$

$$0.4 = \frac{P - \$24}{P}$$

$$0.4P = P - \$24$$

$$0.6P = \$24$$

462   Chapter 12

$$P = \$40$$

P12.15 **Markup on Price.** The Video Van, Inc., provides professional, at-home, VCR cleaning services to residential customers in the Binghampton, New York area. The company recently raised its service price from $21 to $27 per cleaning. As a result, sales fell to 5,000 from 7,000 units in the year-earlier period.

    A. Calculate the arc price elasticity of demand for Video Van service.

    B. Assume that the arc price elasticity (from Part A) is the best available estimate of the point price elasticity of demand. If marginal cost is $6.75 per unit for labor and materials, calculate Video Van's optimal markup on price and its optimal price.

P12.15 **SOLUTION**

A.
$$E_P = \frac{\Delta Q}{\Delta P} \times \frac{P_2 + P_1}{Q_2 + Q_1}$$

$$= \frac{5{,}000 - 7{,}000}{\$27 - \$21} \times \frac{\$27 + \$21}{5{,}000 + 7{,}000}$$

$$= -1.33$$

B. Given $\epsilon_P = -1.33$, the optimal Video Van markup on price is:

$$\text{Optimal Markup on Price} = \frac{-1}{\epsilon_P}$$

$$= \frac{-1}{-1.33}$$

$$= 0.75 \text{ or } 75\%$$

Given MC = $6.75, the optimal price is:

$$\text{Optimal Markup on Price} = \frac{P - MC}{P}$$

$$0.75 = \frac{P - \$6.75}{P}$$

Pricing Practices 463

$$0.75P = P - \$6.75$$

$$0.25P = \$6.75$$

$$P = \$27$$

P12.16 **Markup on Price.** Plan It Right, Inc., provides party planning services for elegant residential parties in the Louisville area. The company recently raised its service price from $112.50 to $137.50 per party. As a result, sales fell to 350 from 450 units in the year earlier period.

    A. Calculate the arc price elasticity of demand for PIR service.

    B. Assume that the arc price elasticity (from Part A) is the best available estimate of the point price elasticity of demand. If marginal cost is $27.50 per unit for labor and materials, calculate PIR's optimal markup on price and its optimal price.

P12.16 SOLUTION

A.
$$E_P = \frac{\Delta Q}{\Delta P} \times \frac{P_2 + P_1}{Q_2 + Q_1}$$

$$= \frac{350 - 450}{\$137.50 - \$112.50} \times \frac{\$137.50 + \$112.50}{350 + 450}$$

$$= -1.25$$

B. Given $\epsilon_P = -1.25$, the optimal PIR markup on price is:

$$\text{Optimal Markup on Price} = \frac{-1}{\epsilon_P}$$

$$= \frac{-1}{-1.25}$$

$$= 0.8 \text{ or } 80\%$$

Given MC = $27.50, the optimal price is:

$$\text{Optimal Markup on Price} = \frac{P - MC}{P}$$

$$0.8 = \frac{P - \$27.50}{P}$$

$$0.8P = P - \$27.50$$

$$0.2P = \$27.50$$

$$P = \$137.50$$

P12.17 ***Incremental Analysis.*** *The Just-for-Kids Daycare Center on Clinton Parkway is considering offering child-care services from 6 to 12 P.M. on weekends. Currently, the center only operates Monday through Friday between the hours of 6 A.M. and 6 P.M. At a price of $10 per night, the Center's manager projects that parents of 20 children would take advantage of the new service. Projected costs for each hour the center is open are:*

Cost Category	Costs (per hour)
Two staff members' salaries (overtime rate)	$10 (each)
Variable overhead (electricity, heat)	5
Allocated fixed overhead (lease expenses, insurance, etc.)	10

A. Would the new weekend service be profitable?

B. Calculate the breakeven price per child for weekend service at a projected attendance of 20 children.

P12.17 SOLUTION

A. Yes, on a per night basis, an analysis of incremental revenues and costs reveals the following:

Pricing Practices 465

Incremental revenue ($10 × 20)	$200
Incremental costs	
Staff salaries (2 × $10 × 6 hours)	$120
Variable overhead ($5 × 6 hours)	30 (150)
Incremental profit per night	$50

(*Note:* Allocated fixed overhead costs are ignored since they are irrelevant.)

B. The breakeven price for weekend service is:

Incremental costs	$150
Projected volume	÷ 20
Breakeven price per child	$7.50

P12.18 **Incremental Analysis.** *The Rainbo Luncheon Deli is considering offering a homestyle dinner menu from 6 to 10 P.M. on weekends. Currently, the deli only operates Monday through Friday between the hours of 10 A.M. and 4 P.M. At an average price of $7 per diner, the deli's manager projects that 100 diners per evening would take advantage of the new service. Projected costs for each night the deli is open are:*

Cost Category	Costs (per hour)
Four waitresses' and busboy's salaries (each)	$ 5
Two cooks salaries (each)	10
Variable overhead (electricity, heat)	15
Allocated fixed overhead (lease expenses, insurance, etc.)	40

A. *Would the new weekend service be profitable?*

B. *Calculate the breakeven price per dinner for evening dining at a projected attendance of 100 dinners.*

P12.18 **SOLUTION**

A. Yes, on a per night basis, an analysis of incremental revenues and costs reveals the following:

Incremental revenue ($7 × 100)	$700
Incremental Costs	
Waitress and busboy salaries (4 × $5 × 4 hours)	$80
Cook salaries (2 × $10 × 4 hours)	80
Variable overhead ($15 × 4 hours)	60 (240)
Incremental profit per night	$460

(*Note:* Allocated fixed overhead costs are ignored since they are irrelevant.)

B. The breakeven price for evening dining is:

Incremental costs	$240
Projected volume	÷100
Breakeven price per dinner	$2.40

P12.19 **Incremental Analysis.** *Sanford & Sons Construction Company is a building contractor serving the Mid-Atlantic region. The company recently bid on construction of a new office building in Richmond, Virginia. Sanford & Sons has incurred bid development and marketing expenses of $50,000 prior to submission of the bid. The bid was based on the following projected costs:*

Bid development and marketing expenses	$ 50,000
Materials	1,750,000
Labor (50,000 hours @ $40)	2,000,000
Variable overhead (40% of direct labor)	800,000
Allocated fixed overhead (8% of total costs)	400,000
Total costs	$5,000,000

A. *What is Sanford & Son's minimum acceptable contract price, assuming the company is operating at peak capacity?*

B. *What is the company's minimum acceptable contract price if an economic downturn has left the company with substantial excess capacity?*

Pricing Practices

P12.19   SOLUTION

    A.   Since the $50,000 bid development and marketing expenses were incurred prior to submission of the bid, they are sunk costs and irrelevant in determining a minimum acceptable contract price.

           When operating at peak capacity, the company is fully employed and able to obtain prices covering fully allocated costs. Thus, assuming the company is operating at peak capacity, all non-sunk costs are relevant and a minimum acceptable bid price is $4,950,000 (=$5,000,000 - $50,000). In particular, note that the 8% fixed overhead charge is relevant as it represents an opportunity cost of turning away other profitable business.

    B.   Assuming an economic downturn has left the company with substantial excess capacity, neither the $50,000 sunk development and marketing expense nor 8% fixed overhead charge are relevant. When operating at less than peak capacity, the minimum acceptable contract price is determined solely by the level of incremental costs. Here, the minimum acceptable contract price off-peak is $4,550,000 (=$5,000,000 - $50,000 - $400,000). Any price above that level will make a positive contribution to overhead and should be accepted.

P12.20   *Incremental Analysis. Wichita Printing Company is a small printer serving the greater metropolitan area. The company recently bid on a government contract for the printing of a new pamphlet explaining phone scams. Wichita Printing has incurred bid development and marketing expenses of $250 prior to submission of the bid. The bid was based on the following projected costs:*

Bid development and marketing expenses	$ 250
Materials	980
Labor (200 hours @ $15)	3,000
Variable overhead (35% of direct labor)	1,050
Allocated fixed overhead (12% of total costs)	720
Total costs	$6,000

    A.   What is Wichita's minimum acceptable contract price, assuming the company is operating at peak capacity?

    B.   What is the company's minimum acceptable contract price if an economic downturn has left the company with substantial excess capacity?

P12.20   SOLUTION

    A.   Since the $250 bid development and marketing expenses were incurred prior to submission of the bid, they are sunk costs and irrelevant in determining a minimum acceptable contract price.

            When operating at peak capacity, the company is fully employed and able to obtain prices covering fully allocated costs. Thus, assuming the company is operating at peak capacity, all non-sunk costs are relevant and a minimum acceptable bid price is $5,750(=$6,000 - $250). In particular, note that the 12% fixed overhead charge is relevant as it represents an opportunity cost of turning away other profitable business.

    B.   Assuming an economic downturn has left the company with substantial excess capacity, neither the $250 sunk development and marketing expense nor 12% fixed overhead charge are relevant. When operating at less than peak capacity, the minimum acceptable contract price is determined solely by the level of incremental costs. Here, the minimum acceptable contract price off-peak is $5,030(=$6,000 - $250 - $720). Any price above that level will make a positive contribution to overhead and should be accepted.

P12.21   ***Incremental Analysis.*** *Unique, Inc., manufactures a hand-held electric hair dryer. Sales have increased steadily during recent years and, because of a recently completed expansion program, annual capacity is now 250,000 units. Production and sales during the coming year are forecast at 150,000 units, and standard production costs have been estimated as:*

Materials	*$3.00*
Direct labor	*2.00*
Variable indirect labor	*0.50*
Fixed overhead	*1.00*
Allocated cost per unit	*$6.50*

    In addition to production costs, Unique incurs fixed selling expenses of 50¢ per unit, and variable warranty repair expenses of 75¢ per unit. Unique currently receives $8.25 per unit from its customers (primarily retail department stores) and expects this price to hold during the coming year.

    After making the above projections, Unique received an inquiry concerning the purchase of a large number of units by a discount department store. The inquiry contained two purchase offers:

Pricing Practices

> - Offer 1: The department store would purchase 100,000 units at $8 per unit. These units would bear the Unique label, and the Unique warranty would cover them.
> - Offer 2: The department store would purchase 150,000 units at $7 per unit. These units would be sold under the buyer's private label and Unique would not provide warranty service.

A. Evaluate the incremental net income from each offer.

B. What other factors should Unique consider in deciding which offer to accept?

C. Which offer (if either) should Unique accept. Why?

P12.21 **SOLUTION**

A. The incremental net income from these offers can be determined as follows:

	Offer 1		Offer 2	
Unit price		$8.00		$7.00
Unit variable costs:				
Materials	$3.00		$3.00	
Direct labor	2.00		2.00	
Variable indirect labor	0.50		0.50	
Variable warranty expense	0.75	6.25	0.00	5.50
Unit incremental profit		1.75		1.50
Units to be sold		× 100,000		× 150,000
Total variable profit on units sold at special price		$175,000		$225,000
Less variable profit lost on regular sales:				
Regular price			$8.25	
Regular variable costs			-6.25	
Regular variable profit			$2.00	
Units that cannot be sold at regular price if offer 2 is accepted			× 50,000	
Opportunity cost of lost regular sales		($0)		($100,000)
Incremental profit		$175,000		$125,000

Thus, both offers would involve a substantial incremental profit, but Offer 1 appears to be more attractive on a simple dollar basis.

B. (i) The image of Unique's quality may be affected by sales of the appliance in the department store chain with a private label.

(ii) Other buyers may demand the reduced price if Unique accepts Offer 1 and the department store undercuts them at the retail price level.

(iii) The sales lost if Unique accepts Offer 2 may affect future orders from regular customers.

C. It depends upon how you evaluate the factors discussed in B. The incremental profits of Offer 1 exceed those of Offer 2, but other long-run concerns might well dictate that it not be accepted.

P12.22 *Price Discrimination.* The Do-Drop-Inn, Inc., provides vacation lodging services to both family and senior citizen customers. Yearly demand and marginal revenue relations for overnight lodging services, Q, are as follows:

Family

$$P_F = \$40 - \$0.0004 Q_F$$

$$MR_F = \$40 - \$0.0008 Q_F$$

Senior Citizens

$$P_S = \$30 - \$0.00025 Q_S$$

$$MR_S = \$30 - \$0.0005 Q_S$$

Average variable costs for labor and materials are constant at $20 per unit.

A. Assuming the company can discriminate in price between family and senior citizen customers, calculate the profit-maximizing price, output, and total profit contribution levels.

B. Calculate point price elasticities of demand for each customer class at the activity levels identified in Part A. Are the differences in these elasticities consistent with your recommended price differential? Explain.

Pricing Practices

P12.22 SOLUTION

A. With price discrimination, profits are maximized by setting MR = MC in each market, where MC = AVC = $20 (since AVC is constant).

<u>Families</u>

$$MR_F = MC$$

$$\$40 - \$0.0008Q_F = \$20$$

$$0.0008Q_F = 20$$

$$Q_F = 25{,}000$$

$$P_F = \$40 - \$0.0004(25{,}000)$$

$$= \$30$$

<u>Senior Citizens</u>

$$MR_S = MC$$

$$\$30 - \$0.0005Q_S = \$20$$

$$0.0005Q_S = 10$$

$$Q_S = 20{,}000$$

$$P_S = \$30 - \$0.00025(20{,}000)$$

$$= \$25$$

The profit contribution earned by the Do-Drop-Inn is:

$$\pi = P_F Q_F + P_S Q_S - AVC(Q_F + Q_S)$$

$$= \$30(25{,}000) + \$25(20{,}000) - \$20(25{,}000 + 20{,}000)$$

$$= \$350{,}000$$

472   Chapter 12

B. Yes, a higher price for Family customers is consistent with the lower degree of price elasticity observed in that market.

<u>Families</u>

$$Q_F = 100{,}000 - 2{,}500 P_F$$

$$\epsilon_P = \Delta Q_F / \Delta P_F \times P_F / Q_F$$

$$= -2{,}500 \times (\$30/25{,}000)$$

$$= -3$$

<u>Senior Citizens</u>

$$Q_S = 120{,}000 - 4{,}000 P_S$$

$$\epsilon_P = \Delta Q_S / \Delta P_S \times P_S / Q_S$$

$$= -4{,}000 \times (\$25/20{,}000)$$

$$= -5$$

P12.23 **Price Discrimination.** *The Fun-Land Amusement Park is a 40-acre fun park full of rides, shows, and shops. Fun-Land's marketing department segments its customer base into two parts: local patrons and tourists. Fun-Land assumes local patrons are more price sensitive than out-of-town tourists. Yearly demand and marginal revenue relations for overnight lodging services, Q, are as follows:*

<u>Locals</u>

$$P_L = \$40 - \$0.0005 Q_L$$

$$MR_L = \$40 - \$0.001 Q_L$$

<u>Tourists</u>

$$P_T = \$50 - \$0.0004 Q_T$$

$$MR_T = \$50 - \$0.0008 Q_T$$

Pricing Practices

Average variable costs for labor and materials are constant at $20 per unit.

A. *Assuming the company can discriminate in pricing between locals and tourist customers through coupons distributed to locals via local shops, calculate the profit-maximizing price, output, and total profit contribution levels.*

B. *Calculate point price elasticities of demand for each customer class at the activity levels identified in Part A. Are the differences in these elasticities consistent with your recommended price differential? Explain.*

P12.23 SOLUTION

A. With price discrimination, profits are maximized by setting MR = MC in each market, where MC = AVC = $20 (since AVC is constant).

Locals

$$MR_L = MC$$

$$\$40 - \$0.001Q_L = \$20$$

$$0.001Q_L = 20$$

$$Q_L = 20{,}000$$

$$P_L = \$40 - \$0.0005(20{,}000)$$

$$= \$30$$

Tourists

$$MR_T = MC$$

$$\$50 - \$0.0008Q_T = \$20$$

$$0.0008Q_T = 30$$

$$Q_T = 37{,}500$$

474   Chapter 12

$$P_T = \$50 - \$0.0004(37,500)$$

$$= \$35$$

The profit contribution earned by the Fun-Land Amusement Park is:

$$\pi = P_L Q_L + P_T Q_T - AVC(Q_L + Q_T)$$

$$= \$30(20,000) + \$35(37,500) - \$20(20,000 + 37,500)$$

$$= \$762,500$$

B. Yes, a higher price for Tourist customers is consistent with the lower degree of price elasticity observed in that market.

<u>Locals</u>

$$Q_L = 80,000 - 2,000 P_L$$

$$\epsilon_P = \Delta Q_L / \Delta P_L \times P_L / Q_L$$

$$= -2,000 \times (\$30/20,000)$$

$$= -3$$

<u>Tourists</u>

$$Q_T = 125,000 - 2,500 P_T$$

$$\epsilon_P = \Delta Q_T / \Delta P_T \times P_T / Q_T$$

$$= -2,500 \times (\$35/37,500)$$

$$= -2.33$$

P12.24 ***Joint Product Pricing.*** *The Frank Boulger Mining Company operates the Million Dollar Mine in Leadville, Colorado. Each ton of mined ore yields one ounce of silver and one pound of lead in a fixed 1:1 ratio. Marginal costs are $8 per ton of ore mined. The demand and marginal revenue curves for silver are:*

$$P_S = \$10 - \$0.00002 Q_S$$

Pricing Practices

$$MR_S = \$10 - \$0.00004Q_S$$

and those for lead are:

$$P_L = \$1 - \$0.000005Q_L$$

$$MR_L = \$1 - \$0.00001Q_L$$

where Q_S is ounces of silver and Q_L is pounds of lead.

A. Calculate profit-maximizing sales quantities and prices for silver and lead.

B. Assume that speculation in the silver market has created a doubling (or 100%) increase in silver demand. Now:

$$P'_S = 2(\$10 - \$0.00002Q_S)$$

$$= \$20 - \$0.00004Q_S$$

$$MR'_S = 2(\$10 - \$0.00004Q_S)$$

$$= \$20 - \$0.00008Q_S$$

and all other relations remain as before.

Calculate optimal sales quantities and prices for both silver and lead under these conditions.

P12.24 SOLUTION

A. Analysis of this problem begins by examining the optimal activity level of Boulger, assuming the firm mines and sells equal quantities of silver and lead.

For profit maximization where $Q = Q_S = Q_L$, set:

$$MC = MR_S + MR_L = MR$$

$$\$8 = \$10 - \$0.00004Q + \$1 - \$0.00001Q$$

$$0.00005Q = 3$$

$$Q = 60{,}000$$

Thus, profit maximization with equal sales of each product requires that the firm mine Q = 60,000 tons of ore. Under this assumption, marginal revenues for the two products are:

$$MR_S = \$10 - \$0.00004(60{,}000) = \$7.60$$

$$MR_L = \$1 - \$0.00001(60{,}000) = \$0.40$$

Since each product is making a positive contribution to marginal costs of $8 per ton, Q = 60,000 is an optimal activity level.
Relevant prices are:

$$P_S = \$10 - \$0.00002(60{,}000) = \$8.80$$

$$P_L = \$1 - \$0.000005(60{,}000) = \$0.70$$

B. A 100% increase in silver demand means that a given quantity could be sold at 2 times the original price. Alternatively, 2 times the original quantity demanded could be sold at a given price.

Now, assuming all output is sold,

$$MC = MR_S + MR_L = MR$$

$$\$8 = \$20 - \$0.00008Q + \$1 - \$0.00001Q$$

$$0.00009Q = 13$$

$$Q = 144{,}444$$

Thus, profit maximization with equal sales of each product requires that the firm mine Q = 144,444 tons of ore. Under this assumption, marginal revenues for the two products are:

$$MR_S = \$20 - \$0.00008(144{,}444) = \$8.44$$

$$MR_L = \$1 - \$0.00001(144{,}444) = -\$0.44$$

Pricing Practices

Even though $MR_S + MR_L = MC = \$8$, the above $Q = 144{,}444$ solution is suboptimal. $MR_S = \$8.44 > \$8 = MC$ implies that a 44¢ profit contribution would be earned on each marginal ton of ore mined when just considering S sales. This means that the firm would like to expand production beyond $Q = 144{,}444$ just in order to sell more S. The negative marginal revenue for L implies that the firm had to reduce price so much (to $P_L = \$0.28$ per pound) in order to sell all 144,444 pounds of L that total revenues fell by $0.44 on the last pound sold. Rather than sell L under such unfavorable conditions, the firm would like to reduce L sales below 144,444 pounds.

The firm would sell L only up to the point where $MR_L = 0$ since, given additional production to sell S, the marginal cost of L is zero. Set:

$$MR_L = MC_L$$

$$\$1 - \$0.00001Q = \$0$$

$$0.00001Q = 1$$

$$Q_L = 100{,}000$$

$$P_L = \$1 - \$0.000005(100{,}000)$$

$$= \$0.50$$

The optimal production and sales level of S is found by setting $MR_S = MC$, since S is the only product sold from the marginal ton of ore being mined.

$$MR_S = MC = MC_S$$

$$\$20 - \$0.00008Q_S = \$8$$

$$0.00008Q_S = 12$$

$$Q_S = 150{,}000$$

and

$$P_S = \$20 - \$0.00004(150{,}000)$$

$$= \$14$$

Therefore, the firm should mine 150,000 tons of ore, and sell all 150,000 ounces of S produced at a price of $14 per ounce. Only 100,000 pounds of lead should be sold at a price of 50¢ per pound, with the remaining 50,000 pounds produced being held off the market.

(*Note:* Despite a doubling in silver demand, prices increase by less than a 100% given the firm's expansion in output.)

P12.25 **Joint Product Pricing.** The Golden State Mining Company operates a small gold and copper mine in a remote region of the Sierra Nevadas. Each ton of mined ore yields one ounce of gold and one pound of copper in a fixed 1:1 ratio. Marginal costs are $450 per ton of ore mined, plus a $30 per ton state land reclamation tax.

The demand and marginal revenue curves for gold are:

$$P_G = \$500 - \$0.001 Q_G$$

$$MR_G = \$500 - \$0.002 Q_G$$

and those for copper are:

$$P_C = \$5 - \$0.00025 Q_C$$

$$MR_C = \$5 - \$0.0005 Q_C$$

where Q_G is ounces of gold and Q_C is pounds of copper.

Calculate profit-maximizing sales quantities and prices for gold and copper.

P12.25 **SOLUTION**

Analysis of this problem begins by examining the optimal activity level of GSMC, assuming the firm mines and sells equal quantities of gold and copper.

For profit maximization where $Q = Q_G = Q_C$, set:

$$MC = MR_G + MR_C = MR$$

$$\$450 + \$30 = \$500 - \$0.002Q + \$5 - \$0.0005Q$$

$$0.0025Q = 25$$

Pricing Practices

$$Q = 10,000$$

Thus, profit maximization with equal sales of each product requires that the firm mine Q = 10,000 tons of ore. Under this assumption, marginal revenues for the two products are:

$$MR_G = \$500 - \$0.002(10,000) = \$480$$

$$MR_C = \$5 - \$0.0005(10,000) = \$0$$

Here, the marginal revenue derived from gold is covering all marginal production costs. At the margin, the company is just breaking even on copper sales. Since each product is making a non-negative contribution to marginal costs of $480 per ton, Q = 10,000 is an optimal activity level.

Relevant prices are:

$$P_G = \$500 - \$0.001(10,000) = \$490$$

$$P_C = \$5 - \$0.00025(10,000) = \$2.50$$

Chapter 13

GOVERNMENT REGULATION OF THE MARKET ECONOMY

MULTIPLE CHOICE QUESTIONS

Q13.1　　Consumer sovereignty reflects:

> A. buyer power.
> B. failure by market structure.
> C. failure by incentive.
> D. externalities.

Q13.2　　Regulatory costs are borne by workers when:

> A. demand is perfectly inelastic.
> B. demand is perfectly elastic.
> C. supply is perfectly inelastic.
> D. none of these.

Q13.3　　Conspiracies in restraint of trade are forbidden under the:

> A. Sherman Act.
> B. Clayton Act.
> C. FTC Act.
> D. Robinson-Pattman Act.

Q13.4　　The view of regulation as a government-imposed means of private-market control is called:

> A. capture theory.
> B. public choice theory.
> C. public interest theory.
> D. none of these.

Q13.5　　Effective competition in the cable television service industry is furnished by:

> A. monopoly providers.
> B. potential entrants.
> C. large numbers of providers in local markets.
> D. none of these.

Government Regulation of the Market Economy 481

Q13.6 An example of failure by market structure is given by:

> A. inferior product quality.
> B. air pollution.
> C. false advertising.
> D. utility price regulation.

Q13.7 A body of law that provides a means for victims of accidents and injury to receive just compensation is called:

> A. the tort system.
> B. antitrust law.
> C. regulatory policy.
> D. the criminal justice system.

Q13.8 Holding supply conditions constant, the costs of regulation fall wholly on producers when:

> A. $\epsilon_p = \infty$.
> B. $\epsilon_p \geq 1$.
> C. $\epsilon_p = 1$.
> D. $\epsilon_p = 0$.

Q13.9 Holding supply conditions constant, the costs of regulation fall wholly on consumers when:

A. $\epsilon_p = \infty$.
B. $\epsilon_p \geq 1$.
C. $\epsilon_p = 1$.
> D. $\epsilon_p = 0$.

Q13.10 The economic cost of a tax is paid at the point of:

> A. tax burden.
> B. tax collection.
> C. tax incidence.
> D. tax assessment.

Q13.11 No externalities exist when:

> A. private costs exceed social costs.
> B. private costs and benefits equal social costs and benefits.
> C. private benefits are less than social benefits.
> D. private benefits exceed social benefits.

Q13.12 A government policy that addresses market failures caused by positive externalities is:

> A. patent grants.
> B. subsidies for pollution reduction.
> C. tax policy.
> D. the establishment of operating controls.

Q13.13 The incidence of a per unit tax will fall primarily on customers when:

> A. the tax is collected from customers.
> B. demand is highly elastic with respect to price.
> C. demand is highly inelastic with respect to price.
> D. the tax is collected from producers.

Q13.14 The burden of a per unit tax on a product will fall primarily on producers when:

> A. the tax is collected from customers.
> B. demand is highly elastic with respect to price.
> C. demand is highly inelastic with respect to price.
> D. the tax is collected from producers.

Q13.15 A per unit tax will cause output prices to increase least when:

> A. marginal cost is constant.
> B. marginal cost is falling.
> C. average cost is falling.
> D. marginal cost is rising.

Government Regulation of the Market Economy 483

Q13.16 A natural monopoly exists if:

    A. marginal revenue is falling as output expands.
    B. price equals average cost.
>   C. average cost falls as output expands.
    D. marginal revenue equals marginal cost.

Q13.17 Government seeks to aid economic efficiency in the case of natural monopoly through:

    A. creating government-financed corporations to compete with the natural monopolist.
    B. subsidizing competitors.
>   C. price regulation.
    D. breaking the natural monopolist up into smaller competitors.

Q13.18 Regulatory commissions seek to set a "fair" price that:

    A. maximizes producer output.
>   B. equals average cost.
    C. equals average revenue.
    D. maximizes consumer surplus.

Q13.19 Windfall profit is economic profit due to:

    A. superior operating efficiency.
    B. innovation.
    C. economies of scale.
>   D. unexpected or unwarranted good fortune.

Q13.20 When the allowed rate of return exceeds the cost of capital:

    A. industry will not grow rapidly enough.
    B. the combinations of inputs employed by the industry will be optimal.
    C. the cost of capital will rise.
>   D. industry will shift to capital intensive methods of production.

Q13.21   The Sherman Act specifically prohibits:

>   A.   monopolizing.
       B.   asset acquisitions that reduce competition.
       C.   price discrimination.
       D.   mergers that reduce competition.

Q13.22   The Clayton Act specifically prohibits:

       A.   monopolies.
       B.   asset acquisitions that reduce competition.
>   C.   price discrimination.
       D.   conspiracies in restraint of trade.

Q13.23   The Celler-Kefauver Act specifically prohibits:

       A.   mergers that reduce competition.
>   B.   asset acquisitions that reduce competition.
       C.   tying contracts that reduce competition.
       D.   conspiracies in restraint of trade.

Q13.24   The F.T.C. enforces antitrust laws by:

       A.   sentencing individuals up to three years imprisonment.
       B.   awarding triple damages.
>   C.   issuing cease and desist orders.
       D.   imposing fines on corporations up to $1 million.

Q13.25   The capture theory states that:

       A.   certain industries must be captured by government regulators to promote economic efficiency.
>   B.   some industries actively seek regulation to limit competition and obtain government subsidies.
       C.   monopoly profits can be captured by society through government regulation.
       D.   natural monopolists tend to capture the entire market.

Government Regulation of the Market Economy   485

Q13.26 To the extent that costs exceed benefits, a given mode of regulation is:

  A. inequitable.
  B. efficient.
> C. inefficient.
  D. fair.

Q13.27 In competitive markets:

> A. high-wage workers tend to be those that are most productive.
  B. companies earn excess profits by better serving customer needs.
  C. fairness is sacrificed in the interest of efficiency.
  D. firms dictate the quantity and quality of goods and services provided.

Q13.28 Failure by market structure can occur when:

  A. joint products are produced in variable proportions.
  B. joint products are produced in fixed proportions.
  C. externalities exist.
> D. few buyers or sellers are present.

Q13.29 Utility price and profit regulation is based on the perception of:

  A. externalities.
  B. diseconomies of scale.
> C. natural monopoly.
  D. consumers' surplus.

Q13.30 Failure by incentive occurs in the production goods and services if:

  A. barriers to entry or exit are prevalent.
> B. a benefit of production is not reflected in the product pricing structure.
  C. all product costs are borne by customers.
  D. social values equal private consumption values.

PROBLEMS & SOLUTIONS

P13.1 **Price Fixing.** On March 12, 1991, The Wall Street Journal (p.B1) carried an article titled, "Colleges Cancel Aid Meetings Under Scrutiny." The article described how a group of 21 elite private colleges canceled meetings that have been under federal antitrust investigation, opening their financial-aid awards to competitive forces for the first time in roughly 35 years. The following is an excerpt from that article:

> The schools, including Harvard University, Princeton University and 19 other Ivy League, liberal arts and historically women's colleges in the Northeast, formed the main body of a formal "overlap group" that has traditionally met to share financial information on common applicants. Two other members of process, Yale University and Barnard College, dropped out of the 23-member group last year.
>
> The move could save the colleges from further legal liability in the U.S. Justice Department inquiry into their tuition, aid and salary setting practices, but might also hamper their attempts to defend against private lawsuits brought by students. In overlap, the colleges met and shared information on financial-aid applicants. The information was often used to set aid awards so that net tuition prices to students would be about the same at different schools where the student was admitted. The effect often was to keep students from getting better financial aid packages than they otherwise might have received.

    A. How would you determine if the "financial-aid overlap" meeting is an example of price fixing?

    B. If price fixing did indeed occur at these meetings, which laws in particular might be violated?

P13.3 **SOLUTION**

    A. According to *The Wall Street Journal* (5/2/89, p.B1);

> Lewis Kaplow, an antitrust-law specialist and Harvard Law School professor, says such activity would be illegal if the parties involved agree to concur on the same family contribution in each case, even if their judgments on the award differ. If, however, they are only agreeing to exchange information to arrive at more informed independent judgments, the activity wouldn't be illegal.
>
> "If, in the end, [two schools] might have a different substantive view, that wouldn't be a problem," Mr. Kaplow says. "If, on the other hand, they had some strong

tendency to make the same offer, that would sound close to an agreement on price and be something that is problematic."

The schools say they are not fixing prices, but just giving one another the option to agree on a family-contribution number. "There's no collusion," says Alfred Quirk, Dartmouth's dean of admissions. Adds Harvard's Mr. Miller: "The purpose of this is the exchange of information -- there's no agreement that we agree."

B. If price-fixing is indeed the intent and logical result of the "financial-aid overlap" meeting, a direct violation Section 1 of the Sherman Act would be involved.

P13.2   *Theory of Regulation. On November 21, 1986, The Wall Street Journal (p. 29) carried a short article titled "It'll Mean Another Two Semesters in the Red, But Who's Counting?" This article described efforts by the American Institute of Certified Public Accountants (AICPA) to require a fifth (graduate) year of study in accounting for joining the institute. The following is an excerpt from that article:*

> *"Technical demands have become so great on accountants that they can't get five pounds of education in a four-pound bag," explains James MacNeil, director of the AICPA's education division. He says the extra year "would help graduates understand such new complexities as leveraged leases and buyouts and new types of securities being devised by Wall Street." (Hawaii, Utah and Florida already require five years of study before taking the CPA exam, and several other states are giving the matter independent consideration.)*

> *Such arguments, however, have failed to sway many educators. "Most of the deans of the nation's 650 business schools oppose going to five years from four," says Charles Hickman, projects director for the American Assembly of Collegiate Schools of Business, based in St. Louis. "The big question raised by most deans is whether another roadblock should be raised to becoming a working accountant." Some opponents point out that since Florida imposed its five-year rule in 1983, the number of applicants for the CPA exam there has declined sharply each year.*

Briefly explain:

A.   *The causes and consequences of regulation according to the "capture" theory of regulation.*

B.   *How the preceding article supports this theory.*

P13.2 SOLUTION

A. According to the "capture" theory of regulation, regulation is imposed by industry, or other politically effective groups, to further the narrow self-interest of the regulated.

B. Lobbying of state legislatures by the accounting profession ("industry") for higher CPA candidate credentials has the effect of raising barriers to entry into the profession. As seen in the state of Florida, by imposing a five-year requirement the number of CPA candidates can be expected to decline sharply. With fewer CPA candidates, fewer CPAs will be accepted into the profession. With fewer CPAs available to certify financial statements, CPA salaries can be expected to rise. Therefore, if a fifth year of accounting study is not necessary in a technical sense, the effect of such a requirement would be to increase CPA incomes -- and provide evidence of state legislatures being "captured" by the accounting "industry."

P13.3 Theory of Regulation.
The Power & Light Company generates electricity, and in the process emits sulfur dioxide into the local atmosphere. As a concerned citizen, you are appalled at the aesthetic and environmental implications of the company's policies, as well as the potential health hazard to the local population.

A. *Pollution is a negative production externality and an example of market failure. What might you cite as reasons why markets fail?*

B. *In analyzing remedies to the current situation, consider two general types of controls to limit pollution:*

> *Regulations -- licenses, permits, compulsory standards, and so on.*
> *Charges -- excise taxes on polluting fuels (coal, oil, and so forth), pollution discharge taxes, and others.*

Review each of these methods of pollution control.

1. *Determine the incentive structure for the polluter under each form of control.*

2. *Decide who pays for a clean environment under each form of control. (Note that each form of control has definite implications about who owns the property rights to the environment.)*

Government Regulation of the Market Economy

3. *Defend a particular form of control on the basis of your analysis, including both efficiency and equity considerations.*

P13.3 SOLUTION

A. Markets can fail due to:

(i) Structural problems: Fewness in the number of buyers and/or sellers.

(ii) Incentive problems: If some product benefit (cost) is not reflected in firm revenues (costs), then non-optimal production quantities and output prices will result due to improper firm incentives.

B. Methods of pollution control:

(i) Incentive structure:

(a) Regulation: Incentive is to avoid regulation, be made a "special case."
(b) Charges: Incentive is to reduce pollution in order to avoid charges.

(ii) Who pays for clean environment?

(a) Regulation: Company (its customers) pays to reduce pollution.
(b) Charges: Company (its customers) pays to reduce pollution. again, society's right to a clean environment is implied.

(iii) Defense of the alternatives:

Efficiency considerations favor charges as a more efficient method of pollution control.
Equity considerations make the choice among pollution control methods less certain.

(a) Regulation: Insures due process, a day in court, for the polluter.
(b) Charges: Polluter should pay full costs of production consumption.

P13.4 **Theory of Regulation.** The New England Power & Light Company generates electricity, and in the process emits sulfur dioxide into the local atmosphere. As a concerned citizen, you are appalled at the aesthetic and environmental implications of the company's policies, as well as the potential health hazard to the local population.

- **A.** Pollution is a negative production externality and an example of market failure. What might you cite as reasons why markets fail?

- **B.** In analyzing remedies to the current situation, consider two general types of controls to limit pollution:

    > Regulations -- licenses, permits, compulsory standards, and so on.
    > Payments -- various types of government aid to help companies install pollution-control equipment. Aid can take the form of forgiven local property taxes, income tax credits, special accelerated depreciation allowances for pollution-control equipment, low-cost government loans, and so on.

    Review each of these methods of pollution control and:

    1. Determine the incentive structure for the polluter under each form of control.

    2. Decide who pays for a clean environment under each form of control. (Note that each form of control has definite implications about who owns the property rights to the environment.)

    3. Defend a particular form of control on the basis of your analysis, including both efficiency and equity considerations.

P13.4 **SOLUTION**

- **A.** Markets can fail due to:

    (i) Structural problems: Fewness in the number of buyers and/or sellers.
    (ii) Incentive problems: If some product benefit (cost) is not reflected in firm revenues (costs), then non-optimal production quantities and output prices will result due to improper firm incentives.

Government Regulation of the Market Economy 491

B. Methods of pollution control:

(i) Incentive structure:

(a) Regulation: Incentive is to avoid regulation, be made a "special case."
(b) Payments: Incentive is to reduce pollution in order to earn subsidy.

(ii) Who pays for clean environment?

(a) Regulation: Company (its customers) pays to reduce pollution.
(b) Payments: Society pays to reduce pollution, implying that the company has a right to pollute.

(iii) Defense of the alternatives:

Efficiency considerations favor payments as more efficient methods of pollution control.
Equity considerations make the choice among pollution control methods less certain.

(a) Regulation: Insures due process, a day in court, for the polluter.
(b) Payments: Avoids penalty to polluters with "sunk" investment costs.

P13.5 *Price Discrimination.* During recent years, national hotel and restaurant chains in the U.S. have charged lower lodging and meal prices to senior citizens in an effort to profitably segment the market for their services. Thus, senior citizens have come to enjoy discounts of 10-25% off the prices paid by other (younger) full-price customers. This two-tier pricing scheme has raised the ire of some consumers who view it as discriminatory and a violation of antitrust laws.

A. Is this pricing scheme discriminatory in the economic sense? What conditions would be necessary for it to be profitable to the hotel and restaurant industry?

B. Carefully describe how price discrimination could violate U.S. antitrust laws and be sure to mention which laws in particular might be violated.

P13.5 **SOLUTION**

    A. Price discrimination exists if the relative prices charged do not reflect relative production and distribution (including transportation) costs. Thus, with price discrimination, markups will vary from one market subgroup to another. In order for price discrimination to be profitable, markets must be separable (no reselling), and have differing elasticities of demand. Both conditions would seem to be met in this case. First lower senior citizen incomes will cause their demand to be more elastic than demand by younger and employed consumers. Second, price differentials can be enforced on the basis of verifiable age information (driver licenses or other sources).

    B. Price discrimination is unlawful under the Robinson-Patman Act only if it results in a substantial lessening of competition. However, this prohibition relates only to firm-firm transactions. Price discrimination between firms and final consumers is perfectly legal, and widely practiced.

P13.6 ***Price Discrimination.*** *During recent years, metropolitan bus service companies in the U.S. have charged lower fares to senior citizens in an effort to profitably segment the market for their services. Thus, senior citizens have come to enjoy discounts of 25-50% off the prices paid by other (younger) full-price customers. This two-tier pricing scheme has raised the ire of some consumers who view it as discriminatory and a violation of antitrust laws.*

    A. Is this pricing scheme discriminatory in the economic sense? What conditions would be necessary for it to be profitable to the bus service industry?

    B. Carefully describe how price discrimination could violate U.S. antitrust laws and be sure to mention which laws in particular might be violated.

P13.6 **SOLUTION**

    A. Price discrimination exists if the relative prices charged do not reflect relative transportation costs. Thus, with price discrimination, markets will vary from one market subgroup to another. In order for price discrimination to be profitable, markets must be separable (no reselling), and have differing elasticities of demand. Both conditions would seem to be met in this case. First lower senior citizen incomes will cause their demand to be more elastic than demand by younger and employed consumers. Second, price differentials can be enforced on the basis of verifiable age information (driver licenses or other sources).

Government Regulation of the Market Economy	493

B.	Price discrimination is unlawful under the Robinson-Patman Act only if it results in a substantial lessening of competition. However, this prohibition relates only to firm-firm transactions. Price discrimination between firms and final consumers is perfectly legal, and widely practiced.

P13.7	**Price Fixing.** *Three leading toxic waste disposal companies have entered into a secret cartel to fix prices and allocate business in the upper Midwest. The marginal costs per unit for toxic waste disposal services are as follows:*

Toxic Waste (000)	Ann Arbor Services, Inc. (A)	BIG Environmental, Ltd. (B)	Chicagoland Disposal, Inc. (C)
1	$10	$10	$5
2	15	10	10
3	20	15	15
4	25	20	20
5	30	25	25

A.	Determine the cartel's optimal allocation of output and maximum profit contribution if it sets $Q = 8(000)$ and $P = \$20$.

B.	Calculate the perfectly competitive industry price for $Q = 8$.

C.	How much output would a perfectly competitive industry supply at $P = \$20$?

D.	Describe the value to society of breaking up the cartel.

P13.7	**SOLUTION**

A.	The cartel would allocate output so as to minimized total production costs. For $Q = 8$, the cost minimizing output allocation is:

Firm	Output
Ann Arbor Services, Inc. (A)	2
BIG Environmental, Ltd. (B)	3
Chicagoland Disposal, Inc. (C)	3
Total	8(000)

494   *Chapter 13*

The maximum total profit contribution would be:

$$\pi = TR - TC_A - TC_B - TC_C$$

$$= 8(\$20) - \$25 - \$35 - \$30$$

$$= \$70(000)$$

B. In a perfectly competitive industry $P = MR$ and $MR = MC$ in equilibrium. Thus, price also equals marginal cost, $P = MC$. At $Q = 8$, $MC = \$15$. Therefore, the perfectly competitive industry price for $Q = 8$ is $P = \$15$.

C. Since $P = MC$ in perfectly competitive equilibrium, firms will continue to supply output up until the point where $MC = \$20$ when $P = \$20$. From the table, we see that output would expand from $Q = 8(000)$ to $Q = 11(000)$ if a perfectly competitive industry were in place:

Firm	Output
Ann Arbor Services, Inc. (A)	3
BIG Environmental, Ltd. (B)	4
Chicagoland Disposal, Inc. (C)	4
Total	11(000)

D. If the cartel were abolished, prices would fall from $P = \$20$ to $P = \$15$ at an activity level of $Q = 8(000)$. This $5 price difference implies a $40(000) (= \$5 \times 8$) cost to society arising in the form of excess profits to cartel members. Alternatively, if prices remained stable at $P = \$20$, output would expand from $Q = 8(000)$ to $Q = 11(000)$. This represents a $60(000) (= \$20 \times 3$) increase in the value of output.

Generally speaking, the benefits to abolishing cartels consist of social improvement in terms of both equity and efficiency considerations. Efficiency is improved when output expands and price converges to marginal cost. Equity is improved when unwarranted excess profits are eliminated.

P13.8   *Price Fixing. Three leading CATV companies have entered into a secret cartel to fix prices and allocate business in rural southeastern markets. The marginal costs per unit for CATV service (basic hook-up) are as follows:*

Government Regulation of the Market Economy

Hook-ups (000)	Able Cable, Ltd. (A)	Buckeye Cable, Inc. (B)	Crimson Tide Cable, Inc. (C)
1	$2	$3	$4
2	4	6	5
3	6	10	6
4	12	14	12
5	15	20	15

A. Determine the cartel's optimal allocation of output and maximum profit contribution if it sets Q = 8(000) and P = $12 per month.

B. Calculate the perfectly competitive industry price for Q = 8.

C. How much output would a perfectly competitive industry supply at P = $12 per month?

D. Describe the value to society of breaking up the cartel.

P13.8 SOLUTION

A. The cartel would allocate output so as to minimized total production costs. For Q = 8, the cost minimizing output allocation is:

Firm	Output
Able Cable, Ltd. (A)	3
Buckeye Cable, Inc. (B)	2
Crimson Tide Cable, Inc. (C)	3
Total	8(000)

The maximum total profit contribution would be:

$$\pi = TR - TC_A - TC_B - TC_C$$

$$= 8(\$12) - \$12 - \$9 - \$15$$

$$= \$60(000)$$

B. In a perfectly competitive industry P = MR and MR = MC in equilibrium. Thus, price also equals marginal cost, P = MC. At Q = 8, MC = $6. Therefore, the perfectly competitive industry price for Q = 8 is P = $6 per month.

C. Since P = MC in perfectly competitive equilibrium, firms will continue to supply output up until the point where MC = $12 when P = $12. From the table, we see that output would expand from Q = 8(000) to Q = 11(000) if a perfectly competitive industry were in place:

Firm	Output
Able Cable, Ltd. (A)	3
Buckeye Cable, Inc. (B)	4
Crimson Tide Cable, Inc. (C)	4
Total	11(000)

D. If the cartel were abolished, prices would fall from P = $12 to P = $6 at an activity level of Q = 8(000). This $6 price difference implies a $48(000)(= $6 × 8) cost to society arising in the form of excess profits to cartel members. Alternatively, if prices remained stable at P = $12, output would expand from Q = 8(000) to Q = 11(000). This represents a $36(000)(= $12 × 3) increase in the value of output.

Generally speaking, the benefits to abolishing cartels consist of social improvement in terms of both equity and efficiency considerations. Efficiency is improved when output expands and price converges to marginal cost. Equity is improved when unwarranted excess profits are eliminated.

P13.9 *Costs of Regulation.* The Montana Coal Company sells coal to electric utilities in the Pacific Northwest. Unfortunately, Montana's coal has high particulate content and, therefore, the company is adversely affected by state and local regulations governing smoke and dust emissions at its customer's electricity-generating plants. Montana's total cost and marginal cost relations are:

$$TC = \$187,500 + \$5Q + \$0.0003Q^2$$

$$MC = \$5 + \$0.0006Q$$

where Q is tons of coal produced per month and TC includes a normal rate of return on investment.

Government Regulation of the Market Economy   497

A. Calculate Montana's profit at the profit-maximizing activity level if prices in the industry are stable at $20 per ton, and therefore P = MR = $20.

B. Calculate Montana's optimal price, output, and profit levels if a new state regulation results in a $5 per ton cost increase that can be fully passed onto customers.

C. Determine the effect on output and profit if Montana is only able to pass onto consumers only $1 of the projected cost increase, and must absorb the remaining $4 per ton cost increase.

P13.9   SOLUTION

A. Set MR = MC to find the profit-maximizing activity level:

$$MR = MC$$

$$\$20 = \$5 + \$0.0006Q$$

$$0.0006Q = 15$$

$$Q = 25{,}000$$

$$\pi = TR - TC$$

$$= \$20(25{,}000) - \$187{,}500 - \$5(25{,}000) - \$0.0003(25{,}000^2)$$

$$= \$0$$

B. If the $5 regulation-induced cost increase can be fully passed onto customers, then MR = $25 = $20 + $5. Therefore, the optimal P = MR = $25 and the optimal activity level is unaffected since:

$$MR + \$5 = MC + \$5$$

$$\$25 = \$10 + \$0.0006Q$$

$$0.0006Q = 15$$

$$Q = 25{,}000$$

$$\pi = TR - TC$$

$$= \$25(25{,}000) - \$187{,}500 - \$10(25{,}000) - \$0.0003(25{,}000^2)$$

$$= \$0$$

C. In the short-run, prices rise to P = MR = $21 = $20 + $1 while marginal costs rise by $4 per ton and Montana will be forced to curtail output and suffer losses:

$$MR = MC + \$4$$

$$\$21 = \$9 + 0.0006Q$$

$$0.0006Q = 12$$

$$Q = 20{,}000$$

$$\pi = TR - TC$$

$$= \$21(20{,}000) - \$187{,}500 - \$9(20{,}000) - \$0.0003(20{,}000^2)$$

$$= -\$67{,}500 \text{ (a loss)}$$

Given these monthly losses, Montana would no longer be earning a normal rate of return on investment, and would eventually be forced out of business.

P13.10 **Costs of Regulation.** *FibreTek, Inc., manufacturers molded plastic products used to improve industrial productivity. Unfortunately, the Occupation Health and Safety Administration (OSHA) has required the firm to enhance the durability of its popular safety helmet at a cost of $10 per unit. Prior to these costs, FibreTek's annual manufacturing costs of this item are:*

$$TC = \$225{,}000 + \$20Q + \$0.001Q^2$$

$$MC = \$20 + \$0.002Q$$

where Q is units produced per year and TC includes a normal rate of return on investment.

A. *Calculate the company's profit at the profit-maximizing activity level if prices in the industry are stable at $50 per unit, and therefore P = MR = $50.*

Government Regulation of the Market Economy 499

B. *Calculate the Company's optimal price, output, and profit levels if the OSHA mandated cost increase can be fully passed onto customers.*

C. *Determine the effect on output and profit if the company is not able to pass onto consumers any of the projected cost increase, and must instead absorb it.*

P13.10 **SOLUTION**

A. Set MR = MC to find the profit-maximizing activity level:

$$MR = MC$$

$$\$50 = \$20 + \$0.002Q$$

$$0.002Q = 30$$

$$Q = 15{,}000$$

$$\pi = TR - TC$$

$$= \$50(15{,}000) - \$225{,}000 - \$20(15{,}000) - \$0.001(15{,}000^2)$$

$$= \$0$$

B. If the $10 regulation-induced cost increase can be fully passed onto customers, then MR = $60 = $50 + $10. Therefore, the optimal P = MR = $60 and the optimal activity level is unaffected since:

$$MR + \$10 = MC + \$10$$

$$\$60 = \$30 + \$0.002Q$$

$$0.002Q = 30$$

$$Q = 15{,}000$$

$$\pi = TR - TC$$

$$= \$60(15{,}000) - \$225{,}000 - \$30(15{,}000) - \$0.002(15{,}000^2)$$

$$= \$0$$

Harcourt Brace & Company

C. In the short-run, prices remain at P = MR = $50 while marginal costs rise by $10 per unit and the company will be forced to curtail output and suffer losses:

$$MR = MC + \$10$$

$$\$50 = \$30 + 0.002Q$$

$$0.002Q = 20$$

$$Q = 10{,}000$$

$$\pi = TR - TC$$

$$= \$50(10{,}000) - \$225{,}000 - \$30(10{,}000) - \$0.001(10{,}000^2)$$

$$= -\$125{,}000 \text{ (a loss)}$$

Given these annual losses, the company would no longer be earning a normal rate of return on investment, and would eventually be forced out of business.

P13.11 **Costs of Regulation.** *Ottawa Construction, Ltd., is a medium-sized housing contractor located in eastern Ontario. The company is adversely affected by new local regulations requiring it to pay $10,000 to cover sewer and water hook-up charges for each home that the company builds. Before such expenses, the company's construction costs are described as:*

$$TC = \$100{,}000 + \$50{,}000Q + \$2{,}500Q^2$$

$$MC = \$50{,}000 + \$5{,}000Q$$

where Q is the number of single family homes built per year and TC includes a normal rate of return on investment.

A. *Calculate Ottawa's profit at the profit-maximizing activity level if prices in the industry are stable at $100,000 per unit, and therefore P = MR = $100,000.*

B. *Calculate Ottawa's optimal price, output, and profit levels if the new regulation-induced cost increase can be fully passed onto customers.*

Government Regulation of the Market Economy 501

C. Determine the effect on output and profit if Ottawa is not able to pass onto consumers any of the projected cost increase.

P13.11 SOLUTION

A. Set MR = MC to find the profit-maximizing activity level:

$$MR = MC$$

$$\$100{,}000 = \$50{,}000 + \$5{,}000Q$$

$$5{,}000Q = 50{,}000$$

$$Q = 10$$

$$\pi = TR - TC$$

$$= \$100{,}000(10) - \$100{,}000 - \$50{,}000(10) - \$2{,}500(10^2)$$

$$= \$150{,}000$$

B. If the $10,000 regulation-induced cost increase can be fully passed onto customers, then MR = $110,000 = $100,000 + $10,000. Therefore, the optimal P = MR = $110,000 and the optimal activity level is unaffected since:

$$MR + \$10{,}000 = MC + \$10{,}000$$

$$\$110{,}000 = \$60{,}000 + \$5{,}000Q$$

$$5{,}000Q = 50{,}000$$

$$Q = 10$$

$$\pi = TR - TC$$

$$= \$110{,}000(10) - \$100{,}000 - \$60{,}000(10) - \$2{,}500(10^2)$$

$$= \$150{,}000$$

C. If prices remain at P = MR = $100,000 while marginal costs rise by $10,000 per unit, Ottawa will be forced to curtail output:

$$MR = MC + \$10,000$$

$$\$100,000 = \$60,000 + \$5,000Q$$

$$5,000Q = 40,000$$

$$Q = 8$$

$$\pi = TR - TC$$

$$= \$100,000(8) - \$100,000 - \$60,000(8) - \$2,500(8^2)$$

$$= \$60,000$$

Since Ottawa is still making an excess profit, the company will continue to operate in the long-run.

P13.12 **Costs of Regulation.** The Appalachian Coal Company sells coal to electric utilities in the southeast. Unfortunately, Appalachian's coal has high particulate content and, therefore, the company is adversely affected by state and local regulations governing smoke and dust emissions at its customer's electricity-generating plants. Appalachian's total cost and marginal cost relations are:

$$TC = \$250,000 + \$5Q + \$0.0002Q^2$$

$$MC = \$5 + \$0.0004Q$$

where Q is tons of coal produced per month and TC includes a normal rate of return on investment.

A. Calculate Appalachian's profit at the profit-maximizing activity level if prices in the industry are stable at $25 per ton, and therefore P = MR = $25.

B. Calculate Appalachian's optimal price, output, and profit levels if a new state regulation results in a $300,000 fixed cost increase that cannot be passed onto customers.

P13.12 SOLUTION

A. Set MR = MC to find the profit-maximizing activity level:

Government Regulation of the Market Economy

$$MR = MC$$

$$\$25 = \$5 + \$0.0004Q$$

$$0.0004Q = 25$$

$$Q = 50{,}000$$

$$\pi = TR - TC$$

$$= \$25(50{,}000) - \$250{,}000 - \$5(50{,}000) - \$0.0002(50{,}000^2)$$

$$= \$250{,}0000$$

B. If the $300,000 regulation-induced cost increase cannot be passed onto customers, then MR = $25 as before. Therefore, the optimal P = MR = $25 and the optimal activity level is unaffected since:

$$MR = MC$$

$$\$25 = \$5 + \$0.0004Q$$

$$0.0004Q = 20$$

$$Q = 50{,}000$$

However, profit is affected since:

$$\pi = TR - TC$$

$$= \$25(50{,}000) - \$550{,}000 - \$5(50{,}000) - \$0.0002(50{,}000^2)$$

$$= -\$50{,}000 \text{ (a loss)}$$

Given these monthly losses, Appalachian would no longer be earning a normal rate of return on investment, and would eventually be forced out of business.

P13.13 ***Costs of Regulation.*** Glove-Box, Inc., produces glove boxes designed to allow workers to safely handle hazardous materials used in a wide variety of products. Market demand and marginal revenue relations for the Glove-Box units are:

$$P = \$500,000 - \$250Q$$

$$MR = \$500,000 - \$500Q$$

Unfortunately, the Occupational Health and Safety Administration (OSHA) has recently ruled that Glove-Box must install expensive new shielding equipment to further guard against worker injuries. This will increase the $200,000 marginal cost of manufacturing by $250,000 per unit. Glove-Box's fixed expenses of $50 million per year, which include a required return on investment, will be unaffected.

A. Calculate Glove-Box's profit-maximizing price/output combination and economic profit level before installation of the OSHA-mandated shielding equipment.

B. Calculate the profit-maximizing price/output combination and economic profit level after Glove-Box has met OSHA guidelines.

C. Compare your answers to Parts A and B. Who pays the economic burden of meeting OSHA guidelines?

P13.13 SOLUTION

A. Glove-Box will maximize profits by setting MR = MC. Before the OSHA-mandated increase in costs, MC = $200,000. Therefore,

$$MR = MC$$

$$\$500,000 - \$500Q = \$200,000$$

$$500Q = 300,000$$

$$Q = 600$$

$$P = \$500,000 - \$250(600)$$

$$= \$350,000$$

$$\text{Total Economic Profits} = PQ - TC$$

$$= \$350,000(600) - \$200,000(600) - \$50,000,000$$

$$= \$40,000,000$$

Government Regulation of the Market Economy 505

    B. After the OSHA-mandated increase in costs, MC = $250,000. Therefore, Glove-Box's optimal activity level changes as follows:

$$MR = MC + \$50{,}000$$

$$\$500{,}000 - \$500Q = \$250{,}000$$

$$500Q = 250{,}000$$

$$Q = 500$$

$$P = \$500{,}000 - \$250(500)$$

$$= \$375{,}000$$

$$\text{Total Economic Profits} = PQ - TC$$

$$= \$375{,}000(500) - \$250{,}000(500) - \$50{,}000{,}000$$

$$= \$12{,}500{,}000$$

    C. In this instance, Glove-Box and its customers share the costs of meeting OSHA guidelines. The number of units sold falls by 16.7% from 600 to 500 in response to the $25,000 price increase from $350,000 to $375,000. Therefore, customers bear some of the regulatory burden due to higher prices and fewer units of output being available. The rest of the burden of this regulation has fallen on Glove-Box stockholders in terms of lost economic profits, and Glove-Box employees in terms of lost employment opportunities due to reduced levels of production.

P13.14   *Costs of Regulation.* Biosystems Technology, Inc., manufacturers equipment used by the biotechnology industry in the analysis of protein and DNA. Market demand and marginal revenue relations for the Biosystems units are:

$$P = \$50{,}000 - \$25Q$$

$$MR = \$50{,}000 - \$50Q$$

    Unfortunately, the Occupational Health and Safety Administration (OSHA) has recently ruled that Biosystems must install expensive new shielding equipment to further guard against worker injuries. This will increase the $10,000 marginal cost of manufacturing by $15,000 per unit. Biosystems' fixed expenses of $15 million per year, which include a required return on investment, will be unaffected.

A. Calculate Biosystems' profit-maximizing price/output combination and economic profit level before installation of the OSHA-mandated shielding equipment.

B. Calculate the profit-maximizing price/output combination and economic profit level after Biosystems has met OSHA guidelines.

C. Compare your answers to Parts A and B. Who pays the economic burden of meeting OSHA guidelines?

P13.14 SOLUTION

A. Biosystems will maximize profits by setting MR = MC. Before the OSHA-mandated increase in costs, MC = $10,000. Therefore,

$$MR = MC$$

$$\$50,000 - \$50Q = \$10,000$$

$$50Q = 40,000$$

$$Q = 800$$

$$P = \$50,000 - \$25(800)$$

$$= \$30,000$$

$$\text{Total Economic Profits} = PQ - TC$$

$$= \$30,000(800) - \$10,000(800) - \$15,000,000$$

$$= \$1,000,000$$

B. After the OSHA-mandated increase in costs, MC = $15,000. Therefore, Biosystems' optimal activity level changes as follows:

$$MR = MC + \$5,000$$

$$\$50,000 - \$50Q = \$15,000$$

$$50Q = 35,000$$

$$Q = 700$$

$$P = \$50,000 - \$25(700)$$

$$= \$32,500$$

Total Economic Profits = PQ - TC

$$= \$32,500(700) - \$15,000(700) - \$15,000,000$$

$$= -\$2,750,000 \text{ (a loss)}$$

    C.   In this instance, Biosystems and its customers share the costs of meeting OSHA guidelines. The number of units sold falls by 12.5% from 800 to 700 in response to the $2,500 price increase from $30,000 to $32,500. Therefore, customers bear some of the regulatory burden due to higher prices and fewer units of output being available. The rest of the burden of this regulation has fallen on Biosystems stockholders in terms of lost economic profits, and Biosystems employees in terms of lost employment opportunities due to reduced levels of production. While the company will continue to operate in the short-run, its long-run survival is threatened given that it is unable to generate a post-regulation required rate of return.

P13.15   ***Costs of Regulation.*** *Microwave Components, Inc., produces microwave and digital electronic components for CATV systems. Market demand and cost revenue relations for the MCI units are:*

$$P = \$5,000 - \$0.25Q$$

$$MR = \$5,000 - \$0.5Q$$

$$TC = \$6,000,000 + \$500Q + \$0.5Q^2$$

$$MC = \$500 + \$1Q$$

    Unfortunately, the Occupational Health and Safety Administration (OSHA) has recently ruled that MCI must install expensive new shielding equipment to further guard against worker injuries. This will increase the marginal cost of manufacturing by $150 per unit. MCI's fixed expenses, which include a required return on investment, will be unaffected.

A. Calculate MCI's profit-maximizing price/output combination and economic profit level before installation of the OSHA-mandated shielding equipment.

B. Calculate the profit-maximizing price/output combination and economic profit level after MCI has met OSHA guidelines.

C. Compare your answers to Parts A and B. Who pays the economic burden of meeting OSHA guidelines?

P13.15 SOLUTION

A. MCI will maximize profits by setting MR = MC. Before the OSHA-mandated increase in costs:

$$MR = MC$$

$$\$5,000 - \$0.5Q = \$500 + \$1Q$$

$$1.5Q = 4,500$$

$$Q = 3,000$$

$$P = \$5,000 - \$0.25(3,000)$$

$$= \$4,250$$

Total Economic Profits = PQ - TC

$$= \$4,250(3,000) - \$6,000,000 - \$500(3,000) - \$0.5(3,000^2)$$

$$= \$750,000$$

B. After the OSHA-mandated increase in costs of $150, MC = $650 + $1Q. Therefore, MCI's optimal activity level changes as follows:

$$MR = MC + \$150$$

$$\$5,000 - \$0.5Q = \$650 + \$1Q$$

Government Regulation of the Market Economy

$$1.5Q = 4,350$$

$$Q = 2,900$$

$$P = \$5,000 - \$0.25(2,900)$$

$$= \$4,275$$

Total Economic Profits $= PQ - TC$

$$= \$4,275(2,900) - \$6,000,000 - \$650(2,900) - \$0.5(2,900^2)$$

$$= \$307,500$$

C. In this instance, MCI and its customers share the costs of meeting OSHA guidelines. The number of units sold falls by 3.3% from 3,000 to 2,900 in response to the $25 price increase from $4,250 to $4,275. Therefore, customers bear some of the regulatory burden due to higher prices and fewer units of output being available. The rest of the burden of this regulation has fallen on MCI stockholders in terms of lost economic profits, and MCI employees in terms of lost employment opportunities due to reduced levels of production.

P13.16 **Tariffs.** The High Volume Shoe Corporation is an importer and distributor of Korean-made children's snow boots. The U.S. Commerce Department recently informed the company that it will be subject to a new 20% tariff on the import cost of rubberized footwear. The company is concerned that the tariff will slow its sales growth, given the highly competitive nature of the footwear market. Relevant market demand and marginal revenue relations are:

$$P = \$6 - \$0.00005Q$$

$$MR = \$6 - \$0.0001Q$$

The company's marginal cost equals import costs of $1 per unit, plus 30¢ to cover transportation, insurance, and related selling expenses. In addition these costs, the company's fixed costs, including a normal rate of return, come to $85,500 per year on this product.

A. Calculate the optimal price/output combination and economic profits prior to imposition of the tariff.

B. Calculate the optimal price/output combination and economic profits after imposition of the tariff.

C. Compare your answers to Parts A and B. Who pays the economic burden of the import tariff?

P13.16 SOLUTION

A. The company will maximize profits by setting MR = MC. Prior to imposition of the tariff, marginal cost reflects import costs plus selling expenses only:

$$MR = MC$$

$$\$6 - \$0.0001Q = \$1 + \$0.3$$

$$0.0001Q = 4.7$$

$$Q = 47,000$$

$$P = \$6 - \$0.00005(47,000)$$

$$= \$3.65$$

$$\text{Total Economic Profits} = PQ - TC$$

$$= \$3.65(47,000) - \$1(47,000) - \$0.3(47,000) - \$85,500$$

$$= \$24,950$$

B. After imposition of the tariff, marginal cost reflects import costs, plus selling costs, plus the import fee:

$$MR = MC + \text{Import fee}$$

$$\$6 - \$0.0001Q = \$1 + \$0.3 + 0.2(\$1)$$

$$0.0001Q = 4.5$$

$$Q = 45,000$$

Government Regulation of the Market Economy 511

$$P = \$6 - \$0.00005(45,000)$$

$$= \$3.75$$

Total Economic Profits $= PQ - TC$

$$= \$3.75(45,000) - \$1(45,000) - \$0.3(45,000)$$

$$- \$0.2(45,000) - \$85,500$$

$$= \$15,750$$

C. The company and its customers share the costs of the import tariff. The number of snow boots sold falls from 47,000 to 45,000 units in response to the 10¢ price increase from $3.65 to $3.75. In addition to this burden borne by its customers, the company and its employees suffer due to lost profits and employment opportunities.

P13.17 **Tariffs.** The Nippon Switch Corporation is an importer and distributor of Japanese-made packet switches, special routing devices that direct data traffic to various computers on a large private telecommunications network for companies like GM, Sears and 3M. The U.S. Commerce Department recently informed the company that it will be subject to a new 35% tariff on the import cost of computer switch devices. The company is concerned that the tariff will slow its sales growth, given the highly competitive nature of the packet switch market. Relevant market demand and marginal revenue relations are:

$$P = \$400 - \$0.035Q$$

$$MR = \$400 - \$0.07Q$$

The company's marginal cost equals import costs of $100 per unit, plus $20 to cover transportation, insurance, and related selling expenses. In addition these costs, the company's fixed costs, including a normal rate of return, come to $250,000 per year on this product.

A. Calculate the optimal price/output combination and economic profits prior to imposition of the tariff.

B. Calculate the optimal price/output combination and economic profits after imposition of the tariff.

C. Compare your answers to Parts A and B. Who pays the economic burden of the import tariff?

P13.17 SOLUTION

A. The company will maximize profits by setting MR = MC. Prior to imposition of the tariff, marginal cost reflects import costs plus selling expenses only:

$$MR = MC$$

$$\$400 - \$0.07Q = \$100 + \$20$$

$$0.07Q = 280$$

$$Q = 4{,}000$$

$$P = \$400 - \$0.035(4{,}000)$$

$$= \$260$$

$$\text{Total Economic Profits} = PQ - TC$$

$$= \$260(4{,}000) - \$100(4{,}000) - \$20(4{,}000) - \$250{,}000$$

$$= \$310{,}000$$

B. After imposition of the tariff, marginal cost reflects import costs, plus selling costs, plus the import fee:

$$MR = MC + \text{Import fee}$$

$$\$400 - \$0.07Q = \$100 + \$20 + 0.35(\$100)$$

$$0.07Q = 245$$

$$Q = 3{,}500$$

$$P = \$400 - \$0.035(3{,}500)$$

$$= \$277.50$$

Total Economic Profits = PQ - TC

= $277.50(3,500) - $100(3,500) - $20(3,500)

- $35(3,500) - $250,000

= $178,750

C. The company and its customers share the costs of the import tariff. The number of switches sold falls from 4,000 to 3,500 units in response to the $17.50 price increase from $260 to $277.50. In addition to this burden borne by its customers, the company and its employees suffer due to lost profits and employment opportunities.

P13.18 *Tariffs.* The Northern Lights Company is an importer and distributor of Scandinavian wool sweaters. The U.S. Commerce Department recently informed the company that it will be subject to a new 20% tariff on the import cost of woolen clothing. The company is concerned that the tariff will slow its sales growth, given the highly competitive nature of the clothing market. Relevant market demand and marginal revenue relations are:

$$P = \$240 - \$0.002Q$$

$$MR = \$240 - \$0.004Q$$

The company's marginal cost equals import costs of $50 per unit, plus $10 to cover transportation, insurance, and related selling expenses. In addition these costs, the company's fixed costs, including a normal rate of return, come to $4 million per year on this product.

A. Calculate the optimal price/output combination and economic profits prior to imposition of the tariff.

B. Calculate the optimal price/output combination and economic profits after imposition of the tariff.

C. Compare your answers to Parts A and B. Who pays the economic burden of the import tariff?

P13.18 **SOLUTION**

A. The company will maximize profits by setting MR = MC. Prior to imposition of the tariff, marginal cost reflects import costs plus selling expenses only:

$$MR = MC$$

$$\$240 - \$0.004Q = \$50 + \$10$$

$$0.004Q = 180$$

$$Q = 45,000$$

$$P = \$240 - \$0.002(45,000)$$

$$= \$150$$

$$\text{Total Economic Profits} = PQ - TC$$

$$= \$150(45,000) - \$50(45,000) - \$10(45,000) - \$4,000,000$$

$$= \$50,000$$

B. After imposition of the tariff, marginal cost reflects import costs, plus selling costs, plus the import fee:

$$MR = MC + \text{Import fee}$$

$$\$240 - \$0.004Q = \$50 + \$10 + 0.2(\$50)$$

$$0.004Q = 170$$

$$Q = 42,500$$

$$P = \$240 - \$0.002(42,500)$$

$$= \$155$$

Total Economic Profits = PQ - TC

= $155(42,500) - $50(42,500) - $10(42,500)

- $10(42,500) - $4,000,000

= -$387,500 (a loss)

C. The company and its customers share the costs of the import tariff. The number of wool sweaters sold falls from 45,000 to 42,500 units in response to the $5 price increase from $150 to $155. In addition to this burden borne by its customers, the company and its employees suffer due to lost profits and employment opportunities. While the company will continue to operate in the short-run, it is not earning a required rate of return on this product, and will discontinue operation in the long-run.

P13.19 **Tariffs.** The Steel Supply Corporation is an importer and distributor of Taiwanese-made, 96 piece hand-tool sets (screw drivers, wrenches, and the like). The U.S. Commerce Department recently informed the company that it will be subject to a new 25% tariff on the import cost of fabricated steel. The company is concerned that the tariff will slow its sales growth, given the highly competitive nature of the hand-tool market. Relevant market demand and marginal revenue relations are:

P = $80 - $0.0001Q

MR = $80 - $0.0002Q

The company's marginal cost equals import costs of $32 per unit, plus $8 to cover transportation, insurance, and related selling expenses. In addition these costs, the company's fixed costs, including a normal rate of return, come to $2,500,000 per year on this product.

A. Calculate the optimal price/output combination and economic profits prior to imposition of the tariff.

B. Calculate the optimal price/output combination and economic profits after imposition of the tariff.

C. Compare your answers to Parts A and B. Who pays the economic burden of the import tariff?

P13.19 **SOLUTION**

A. The company will maximize profits by setting MR = MC. Prior to imposition of the tariff, marginal cost reflects import costs plus selling expenses only:

$$MR = MC$$

$$\$80 - \$0.0002Q = \$32 + \$8$$

$$0.0002Q = 40$$

$$Q = 200{,}000$$

$$P = \$80 - \$0.0001(200{,}000)$$

$$= \$60$$

$$\text{Total Economic Profits} = PQ - TC$$

$$= \$60(200{,}000) - \$32(200{,}000) - \$8(200{,}000) - \$2{,}500{,}000$$

$$= \$1{,}500{,}000$$

B. After imposition of the tariff, marginal cost reflects import costs, plus selling costs, plus the import fee:

$$MR = MC + \text{Import fee}$$

$$\$80 - \$0.0002Q = \$32 + \$8 + 0.25(\$32)$$

$$0.0002Q = 32$$

$$Q = 160{,}000$$

$$P = \$80 - \$0.0001(160{,}000)$$

$$= \$64$$

Government Regulation of the Market Economy   517

$$\text{Total Economic Profits} = PQ - TC$$

$$= \$64(160,000) - \$32(160,000) - \$8(160,000)$$

$$- \$8(160,000) - \$2,500,000$$

$$= \$60,000$$

C. The company and its customers share the costs of the import tariff. The number of hand-tool sets sold falls from 200,000 to 160,000 units in response to the $4 price increase from $60 to $64. In addition to this burden borne by its customers, the company and its employees suffer due to lost profits and employment opportunities.

P13.20 **Monopoly Regulation.** *The Woebegone Telephone Company, a utility serving rural customers in Minnesota, is currently engaged in a rate case with the regulatory commission under whose jurisdiction it operates. At issue is the monthly rate the company will charge for basic hookup service. The demand curve for monthly service is P = $50 - $0.005Q. This implies annual demand and marginal revenue curves of:*

$$P = \$600 - \$0.06Q$$

$$MR = \$600 - \$0.12Q$$

where P is service price in dollars and Q is the number of customers served. Total and marginal costs per year (before investment return) are described by the function:

$$TC = \$100,000 + \$100Q + \$0.04Q^2$$

$$MC = \$100 + \$0.08Q$$

The company has assets of $4 million and the utility commission has authorized a 12.5% return on investment.

A. *Calculate Woebegone's profit-maximizing price (monthly and annually), output, and rate-of-return levels.*

B. *What monthly price should the commission grant to limit Woebegone to a 12.5% rate of return?*

P13.20 SOLUTION

A. To find the profit-maximizing level of output, set MR = MC where:

$$MR = MC$$

$$\$600 - \$0.12Q = \$100 + \$0.08Q$$

$$0.2Q = 500$$

$$Q = 2{,}500$$

$$P = \$50 - \$0.005(2{,}500)$$

$$= \$37.50 \qquad \text{(Monthly price)}$$

$$P = \$600 - \$0.06(2{,}500)$$

$$= \$450 \qquad \text{(Annual price)}$$

$$\pi = TR - TC$$

$$= \$450(2{,}500) - \$100{,}000 - \$100(2{,}500) - \$0.04(2{,}500^2)$$

$$= \$525{,}000$$

If the company has $4 million invested in plant and equipment, its optimal rate of return on investment is:

$$\text{Return on investment} = \frac{\$525{,}000}{\$4{,}000{,}000}$$

$$= 0.13125 \text{ or } 13.125\%$$

(*Note*: Profit is falling Q > 2,500.)

B. With a 12.5% return on total assets, Woebegone would earn profits of:

$$\pi = \text{Allowed return} \times \text{Total assets}$$

$$= 0.125(\$4,000,000)$$

$$= \$500,000$$

To determine the level of output that would be consistent with this level of total profits, consider the profit relation:

$$\pi = TR - TC$$

$$\$500,000 = \$600Q - \$0.06Q^2 - \$100,000 - \$100Q - \$0.04Q^2$$

$$500,000 = -0.1Q^2 + 500Q - 100,000$$

$$0 = -0.1Q^2 + 500Q - 600,000$$

which is a function of the form $aQ^2 + bQ + c = 0$ where $a = -0.1$, $b = 500$ and $c = -600,000$, and can be solved using the quadratic equation.

$$Q = \frac{-b \pm \sqrt{b^2 - 4ac}}{2a}$$

$$= \frac{-500 \pm \sqrt{500^2 - 4(-0.1)(-600,000)}}{2(-0.1)}$$

$$= \frac{-500 \pm \sqrt{10,000}}{-0.2}$$

$$= 2,000 \text{ or } 3,000 \text{ customers}$$

Since public utility commissions generally want utilities to provide service to the greatest possible number of customers at the lowest possible price, the "upper" Q = 3,000 is the appropriate output level. This output level will result in a monthly service price of:

$$P = \$50 - \$0.005(3,000)$$

$$= \$35$$

This $35 per month price will provide Woebegone with a fair rate of return on total investment, while ensuring service to a broad customer base.

P13.21 **Monopoly Regulation.** *The Black Hills Telephone Company, a utility serving rural customers in South Dakota is currently engaged in a rate case with the regulatory commission under whose jurisdiction it operates. At issue is the monthly rate the company will charge for call waiting service. The demand curve for this monthly service is P = $6.25 - $0.00025Q. This implies annual demand and marginal revenue curves of:*

$$P = \$75 - \$0.003Q$$

$$MR = \$75 - \$0.006Q$$

where P is service price in dollars and Q is the number of customers served. Total and marginal costs per year (before investment return) are described by the function:

$$TC = \$108,000 + \$25Q + \$0.002Q^2$$

$$MC = \$25 + \$0.004Q$$

The company has assets of $100,000 used for call waiting services and the utility commission has authorized a 12% return on investment.

A. *Calculate Black Hills' profit-maximizing price (monthly and annually), output, and rate-of-return levels.*

B. *What monthly price should the commission grant to limit Black Hills to an 12% rate of return?*

P13.21 **SOLUTION**

A. To find the profit-maximizing level of output, we must set MR = MC where:

$$MR = MC$$

$$\$75 - \$0.006Q = \$25 + \$0.004Q$$

$$0.01Q = 50$$

$$Q = 5,000$$

Government Regulation of the Market Economy

$$P = \$6.25 - \$0.00025(5{,}000)$$

$$= \$5 \quad \text{(Monthly price)}$$

$$P = \$75 - \$0.003(5{,}000)$$

$$= \$60 \quad \text{(Annual price)}$$

$$\pi = TR - TC$$

$$= \$60(5{,}000) - \$108{,}000 - \$25(5{,}000) - \$0.002(5{,}000^2)$$

$$= \$17{,}000$$

If the company has $100,000 invested in plant and equipment, its optimal rate of return on investment is:

$$\text{Return on investment} = \frac{\$17{,}000}{\$100{,}000}$$

$$= 0.17 \text{ or } 17\%$$

(*Note*: Profit is falling Q > 5,000.)

B. With a 12% return on total assets, Black Hills would earn profits of:

$$\pi = \text{Allowed return} \times \text{Total assets}$$

$$= 0.120(\$100{,}000)$$

$$= \$12{,}000$$

To determine the level of output that would be consistent with this level of total profits, consider the profit relation:

$$\pi = TR - TC$$

$$\$12{,}000 = \$75Q - \$0.003Q^2 - \$108{,}000 - \$25Q - \$0.002Q^2$$

$$12{,}000 = -0.005Q^2 + 50Q - 108{,}000$$

$$0 = -0.005Q^2 + 50Q - 120{,}000$$

which is a function of the form $aQ^2 + bQ + c = 0$ where $a = -0.005$, $b = 50$ and $c = -120{,}000$, and can be solved using the quadratic equation.

$$Q = \frac{-b \pm \sqrt{b^2 - 4ac}}{2a}$$

$$= \frac{-50 \pm \sqrt{50^2 - 4(-0.005)(-120{,}000)}}{2(-0.005)}$$

$$= \frac{-50 \pm \sqrt{100}}{-0.01}$$

$$= 4{,}000 \text{ or } 6{,}000 \text{ customers}$$

Since public utility commissions generally want utilities to provide service to the greatest possible number of customers at the lowest possible price, the "upper" $Q = 6{,}000$ is the appropriate output level. This output level will result in a monthly service price of:

$$P = \$6.25 - \$0.00025(6{,}000)$$

$$= \$4.75$$

This $4.75 per month price for call waiting service will provide Black Hills with a fair rate of return on total investment, while ensuring service to a broad customer base.

P13.22 **Monopoly Regulation.** *The Hoosier Gas Company, a utility serving customers in Bloomington, Indiana, is currently engaged in a rate case with the regulatory commission under whose jurisdiction it operates. At issue is the rate the company will charge per mcf usage of natural gas. The demand curve for monthly service is P = $6.75 - $0.000375Q. This implies annual demand and marginal revenue curves of:*

$$P = \$81 - \$0.0045Q$$

$$MR = \$81 - \$0.009Q$$

Government Regulation of the Market Economy

where P is mcf price in dollars and Q is the units of mcf used, in thousands. Total and marginal costs per year (before investment return) are described by the function:

$$TC = \$36,200 + \$21Q + \$0.0005Q^2$$

$$MC = \$21 + \$0.001Q$$

The company has assets of $1 million and the utility commission has authorized an 11% return on investment.

A. Calculate Hoosier's profit-maximizing price (monthly and annually), output, and rate-of-return levels.

B. What monthly price should the commission grant to limit Hoosier to an 11% rate of return?

P13.22 SOLUTION

A. To find the profit-maximizing level of output, we must set MR = MC where:

$$MR = MC$$

$$\$81 - \$0.009Q = \$21 + \$0.001Q$$

$$0.01Q = 60$$

$$Q = 6,000$$

$$P = \$6.75 - \$0.000375(6,000)$$

$$= \$4.50 \qquad \text{(Monthly price)}$$

$$P = \$81 - \$0.0045(6,000)$$

$$= \$54 \qquad \text{(Annual price)}$$

$$\pi = TR - TC$$

$$= \$54(6,000) - \$36,200 - \$21(6,000) - \$0.0005(6,000^2)$$

$$= \$143,800$$

If the company has $1 million invested in plant and equipment, its optimal rate of return on investment is:

$$\text{Return on investment} = \frac{\$143,800}{\$1,000,000}$$

$$= 0.1438 \text{ or } 14.38\%$$

(*Note*: Profit is falling for Q > 6,000.)

B. With an 11% return on total assets, Hoosier would earn profits of:

$$\pi = \text{Allowed return} \times \text{Total assets}$$

$$= 0.11(\$1,000,000)$$

$$= \$110,000$$

To determine the level of output that would be consistent with this level of total profits, we consider the profit relation:

$$\pi = TR - TC$$

$$\$110,000 = \$81Q - \$0.0045Q^2 - \$36,200 - \$21Q - \$0.0005Q^2$$

$$110,000 = -0.005Q^2 + 60Q - 36,200$$

$$0 = -0.005Q^2 + 60Q - 146,200$$

which is a function of the form $aQ^2 + bQ + c = 0$ where $a = -0.005$, $b = 60$ and $c = -146,200$, and can be solved using the quadratic equation.

Government Regulation of the Market Economy 525

$$Q = \frac{-b \pm \sqrt{b^2 - 4ac}}{2a}$$

$$= \frac{-60 \pm \sqrt{60^2 - 4(-0.005)(-146,200)}}{2(-0.005)}$$

$$= \frac{-60 \pm \sqrt{676}}{-0.01}$$

$$= 3,400 \text{ or } 8,600 \text{ customers}$$

Since public utility commissions generally want utilities to provide service to the greatest possible number of customers at the lowest possible price, the "upper" Q = 8,600 is the appropriate output level. This output level will result in a monthly service price of:

$$P = \$6.75 - \$0.000375(8,600)$$

$$= \$3.525$$

This $3.525 per mcf price will provide Hoosier with a fair rate of return on total investment, while ensuring service to a broad customer base.

P13.23 **Monopoly Regulation.** *The Redwood Cable Company, a CATV utility serving customers in Eugene, Oregon, is currently engaged in a rate case with the regulatory commission under whose jurisdiction it operates. At issue is the monthly rate the company will charge for basic hookup service. The demand curve for monthly service is P = $37.50 - $0.0005Q. This implies annual demand and marginal revenue curves of:*

$$P = \$450 - \$0.006Q$$

$$MR = \$450 - \$0.012Q$$

where P is service price in dollars and Q is the number of customers served. Total and marginal costs per year (before investment return) are described by the function:

$$TC = \$4,275,000 + \$75Q + \$0.0015Q^2$$

$$MC = \$75 + \$0.003Q$$

The company has assets of $1.5 million and the utility commission has authorized a 15% return on investment.

A. *Calculate Redwood's profit-maximizing price (monthly and annually), output, and rate-of-return levels.*

B. *What monthly price should the commission grant to limit Redwood to a 15% rate of return?*

P13.23 **SOLUTION**

A. To find the profit-maximizing level of output, we must set MR = MC where:

MR = MC

$450 - $0.012Q = $75 + $0.003Q

0.015Q = 375

Q = 25,000

P = $37.50 - $0.0005(25,000)

= $25   (Monthly price)

P = $450 - $0.006(25,000)

= $300   (Annual price)

π = TR - TC

= $300(25,000) - $4,275,000 - $75(25,000) - $0.0015(25,000^2)

= $412,500

If the company has $1.5 million invested in plant and equipment, its optimal rate of return on investment is:

$$\text{Return on investment} = \frac{\$412,500}{\$1,500,000}$$

$$= 0.275 \text{ or } 27.50\%$$

(*Note*: Profit is falling for Q > 25,000.)

B. With a 15% return on total assets, Redwood would earn profits of:

$$\pi = \text{Allowed return} \times \text{Total assets}$$

$$= 0.15(\$1,500,000)$$

$$= \$225,000$$

To determine the level of output that would be consistent with this level of total profits, we consider the profit relation:

$$\pi = TR - TC$$

$$\$225,000 = 450Q - \$0.006Q^2 - \$4,275,000 - \$75Q - \$0.0015Q^2$$

$$225,000 = -0.0075Q^2 + 375Q - 4,275,000$$

$$0 = -0.0075Q^2 + 375Q - 4,500,000$$

which is a function of the form $aQ^2 + bQ + c = 0$ where $a = -0.0075$, $b = 375$ and $c = -4,500,000$, and can be solved using the quadratic equation.

$$Q = \frac{-b \pm \sqrt{b^2 - 4ac}}{2a}$$

$$= \frac{-375 \pm \sqrt{375^2 - 4(-0.0075)(-4,500,000)}}{2(-0.0075)}$$

$$= \frac{-375 \pm \sqrt{5,625}}{-0.015}$$

$$= 20,000 \text{ or } 30,000 \text{ customers}$$

Since public utility commissions generally want utilities to provide service to the greatest possible number of customers at the lowest possible price, the "upper" Q = 30,000 is the appropriate output level. This output level will result in a monthly service price of:

$$P = \$37.50 - \$0.0005(30,000)$$

$$= \$22.50$$

This $22.50 per month price will provide Redwood with a fair rate of return on total investment, while ensuring service to a broad customer base.

P13.24 **Pollution Regulation.** Porky Pig, Inc., processes hogs at a large facility in Iowa City, Iowa. Each hog processed yields both pork and a render by-product in a fixed 1:1 ratio. While the render by-product is unfit for human consumption, some can be sold to a local pet food company for further processing. Relevant annual demand and cost relations are:

$P_P = \$125 - \$0.0005 Q_P$ (Demand for pork)

$MR_P = \$125 - \$0.001 Q_P$ (Marginal revenue from pork)

$P_B = \$25 - \$0.001 Q_B$ (Demand for render by-product)

$MR_B = \$25 - \$0.002 Q_B$ (Marginal revenue from render by-product)

$TC = \$1,156,250 + \$75Q$ (Total cost)

$MC = \$75$ (Marginal cost)

Here P is price in dollars, Q is the number of hogs processed (with an average weight of 100 pounds), Q_P and Q_B are pork and rendered by-product per hog, respectively; both total and marginal costs are in dollars. Total costs include a risk-adjusted normal return of 15% on a $2 million investment in plant and equipment.

Currently, the city allows the company to dump excess by-product into its sewage treatment facility at no charge, viewing the service as an attractive means of keeping a valued employer in the area. However, the sewage treatment facility is quickly approaching peak capacity and must be expanded at an expected operating cost of $500,000 per year. This is an impossible burden on an already strained city budget.

Government Regulation of the Market Economy										529

A.	Calculate the profit-maximizing price/output combination and optimal total profit level for Porky.

B.	How much by-product will the company dump into the Iowa City sewage treatment facility at the profit-maximizing activity level?

C.	Calculate output and total profits if the city imposes a $25 per unit charge on the amount of B Porky dumps.

D.	Calculate output and total profits if the city imposes a fixed $500,000-per-year tax on Porky to pay for the sewage treatment facility expansion.

E.	Will either tax alternative permit Porky to survive in the long-run? In your opinion, what should Iowa City do about its sewage treatment problem?

P13.24	SOLUTION

A.	Solution to this problem requires that we look at several production and sales options available to the firm. One option is to produce and sell equal quantities of pork (P) and by-product (B). In this case, the firm sets relevant MC = MR.

$$MC = MR_P + MR_B = MR$$

$$\$75 = \$125 - \$0.001Q + \$25 - \$0.002Q$$

$$0.003Q = 75$$

$$Q = 25{,}000 \text{ hogs}$$

Thus, the profit maximizing output level for production and sale of equal quantities of P and B would 25,000 hogs. However, we must check to determine that the marginal revenues of both products are positive at this sales level before claiming that this is an optimal activity pattern.

Evaluated at 25,000 hogs:

$$MR_P = \$125 - \$0.001(25{,}000)$$

$$= \$100$$

$$MR_B = \$25 - \$0.002(25,000)$$

$$= -\$25$$

Since the marginal revenue for B is negative, and since Porky can costlessly dump excess production, the sale of 25,000 units of B is suboptimal. This invalidates the entire solution developed above because output of P is being held down by the negative marginal revenue associated with B. The problem must be set up in a fashion that recognizes that Porky will stop selling B at the point where its marginal revenue becomes zero since, given production for P, the marginal cost of B is zero.

Set:

$$MR_B = MC_B$$

$$\$25 - \$0.002Q_B = \$0$$

$$0.002Q_B = 25$$

$$Q_B = 12,500 \text{ units}$$

Thus, 12,500 units of B is the maximum that would be sold. Any excess units will be dumped into the city's sewage treatment facility. The price for B at 12,500 units is:

$$P_B = \$25 - \$0.001Q_B$$

$$= \$25 - \$0.001(12,500)$$

$$= \$12.50$$

To determine the optimal production of P (pork), set the marginal revenue of P equal to the marginal cost of producing another unit of the output package:

$$MR_P = MC_P = MC_Q$$

$$\$125 - \$0.001Q_P = \$75$$

$$0.001Q_P = 50$$

Government Regulation of the Market Economy

$$Q_P = 50{,}000 \text{ units}$$

(Remember $Q_P = Q$)

and

$$P_P = \$125 - \$0.0005 Q_P$$
$$= \$125 - \$0.0005(50{,}000)$$
$$= \$100$$

Excess profits at the optimal activity level for Porky will be:

$$\text{Excess profits} = \pi = TR_P + TR_B - TC$$
$$= P_P \times Q_P + P_B \times Q_B - TC_Q$$
$$= \$100(50{,}000) + \$12.50(12{,}500) - \$1{,}156{,}250 - \$75(50{,}000)$$
$$= \$250{,}000$$

Since total costs include a normal return of 15% on a $2 million investment

$$\text{Total profits} = \text{Required return} + \text{Excess profits}$$
$$= 0.15(\$2{,}000{,}000) + \$250{,}000$$
$$= \$550{,}000$$

B. With 50,000 hogs being processed, but only 12,500 units of B sold, dumping of B is:

$$\text{Units B dumped} = \text{Units produced} - \text{Units sold}$$
$$= 50{,}000 - 12{,}500$$
$$= 37{,}500 \text{ units}$$

C. Part A shows that if all P and B produced is sold, an activity level of $Q = 25{,}000$ will result in $MR_B = -\$25$. A dumping charge of $25 per unit of B will cause

Porky to prefer to sell the last unit of B produced (and lose $25) rather than pay a $25 fine. Therefore, this fine, as will any fine greater than $25, eliminates dumping and causes Porky to reduce processing to 25,000 hogs per year. This fine structure would undoubtedly reduce or eliminate the need for a new sewage treatment facility.

While eliminating dumping is obviously attractive in the sense of reducing sewage treatment costs, the $25 fine has the unfortunate consequence of cutting output substantially. Pork prices will rise to P_P = $125 - $0.0005(25,000) = $112.50, and by-product prices will fall to P_B = $25 - $0.001(25,000) = $0. (This means Porky will give the pet food company all of its by-product sludge.) Employment will undoubtedly fall as well. In addition to these obvious short-run effects, long-run implications may be especially serious. At Q = 25,000, Porky's excess profits will be

$$\text{Excess profits} = TR_P + TR_B - TC$$

$$= \$112.5(25,000) + \$0(25,000) - \$1,156,250 - \$75(25,000)$$

$$= -\$218,750 \text{ (a loss)}$$

This means that total profits will be:

$$\text{Total profits} = \text{Required return} + \text{Excess profits}$$

$$= 0.15(\$2,000,000) + (-\$218,750)$$

$$= -\$81,250 \text{ (a loss)}$$

This level of profit is insufficient to maintain investment. Thus, while a $25 dumping charge will eliminate dumping, it is likely to cause the firm to close down or move to some other location. The effect on employment in Iowa City could be disastrous.

D. In the short-run, a $500,000 tax on Porky will have no effect on dumping, output or employment. However, at the Q = 50,000 activity level, a $500,000 tax would reduce Porky's total profits to $50,000 (=$550,000 - $500,000) or $250,000 below the required return on investment. Following imposition of a $500,000 tax, the firm's survival and total employment would be imperiled in the long-run.

E. No, Porky will not be able to bear the burden of either tax alternative. Obviously, there is no single best alternative here. The highest fixed tax the company can

Government Regulation of the Market Economy 533

bear in the long-run is $250,000, the full amount of excess profits. If the city places an extremely high priority on maintaining employment, perhaps a $250,000 tax on Porky plus $250,000 in general city tax revenues could be used to pay for the new sewage system treatment facility.

P13.25 **Pollution Regulation.** Blue Gem, Inc., processes almonds at a large facility in Redding, California. Each pound of almonds processed yields both shelled almonds and shell by-product in a fixed 1:1 ratio. While the by-product is unfit for human consumption, some can be sold to a regional manufacturer of stone-washed denim garments (the shells are crushed and used as abrasives). Relevant annual demand and cost relations are:

P_A = $14.25 - 0.000005Q_A$ (Demand for shelled almonds)

MR_A = $14.25 - 0.00001Q_A$ (Marginal revenue from shelled almonds)

P_B = $4 - 0.00001Q_B$ (Demand for shell by-product)

MR_B = $4 - 0.00002Q_B$ (Marginal revenue from shell by-product)

TC = $3,000,000 + 6.25Q$ (Total cost)

MC = $6.25   (Marginal cost)

Here P is price in dollars, Q is the number of pounds of almonds processed, Q_A and Q_B are shelled almonds and shell by-product per pound of almonds, respectively; both total and marginal costs are in dollars. Total costs include a risk-adjusted normal return of 15% on a $10 million investment in plant and equipment.

Currently, the city allows the company to dump excess by-product into its landfill at no charge, viewing the service as an attractive means of keeping a valued employer in the area. However, the landfill is quickly approaching peak capacity and must be expanded at an expected operating cost of $750,000 per year. This is an impossible burden on an already strained city budget.

A. Calculate the profit-maximizing price/output combination and optimal total profit level for Blue Gem.

B. How much by-product will the company dump into the Redding, California landfill at the profit-maximizing activity level?

C. Calculate output and total profits if the city imposes a $4 per unit charge on the amount of shell by-product Blue Gem dumps.

D. Calculate output and total profits if the city imposes a fixed $750,000-per-year tax on Blue Gem to pay for the landfill expansion.

E. Will either tax alternative permit Blue Gem to survive in the long-run? In your opinion, what should Redding do about its landfill problem?

P13.25 SOLUTION

A. Solution to this problem requires that we look at several production and sales options available to the firm. One option is to produce and sell equal quantities of shelled almonds (A) and shell by-product (B). In this case, the firm sets relevant MC = MR.

$$MC = MR_A + MR_B = MR$$

$$\$6.25 = \$14.25 - \$0.00001Q + \$4 - \$0.00002Q$$

$$0.00003Q = 12$$

$$Q = 400{,}000 \text{ pounds of almonds}$$

Thus, the profit maximizing output level for production and sale of equal quantities of A and B would be 400,000 pounds of almonds. However, we must check to determine that the marginal revenues of both products are positive at this sales level before claiming that this is an optimal activity pattern.

Evaluated at 400,000 pounds of almonds:

$$MR_A = \$14.25 - \$0.00001(400{,}000)$$

$$= \$10.25$$

$$MR_B = \$4 - \$0.00002(400{,}000)$$

$$= -\$4$$

Since the marginal revenue for B is negative, and since Blue Gem can costlessly dump excess production, the sale of 400,000 units of B is suboptimal.

This invalidates the entire solution developed above because output of A is being held down by the negative marginal revenue associated with B. The problem must be set up in a fashion that recognizes that Blue Gem will stop selling B at the point where its marginal revenue becomes zero since, given production for P, the marginal cost of B is zero.

Set:

$$MR_B = MC_B$$

$$\$4 - \$0.00002Q_B = \$0$$

$$0.00002Q_B = 4$$

$$Q_B = 200{,}000 \text{ units}$$

Thus, 200,000 units of B is the maximum that would be sold. Any excess units will be dumped into the city's landfill. The price for B at 200,000 units is:

$$P_B = \$4 - \$0.00001Q_B$$

$$= \$4 - \$0.00001(200{,}000)$$

$$= \$2$$

To determine the optimal production of A (shelled almonds), set the marginal revenue of A equal to the marginal cost of producing another unit of the output package:

$$MR_A = MC_A = MC_Q$$

$$\$14.25 - \$0.00001Q_A = \$6.25$$

$$0.00001Q_A = 8$$

$$Q_A = 800{,}000 \text{ units}$$

(Remember $Q_P = Q$)

and

$$P_A = \$14.25 - \$0.000005Q_A$$

$$= \$14.25 - \$0.000005(800,000)$$

$$= \$10.25$$

Excess profits at the optimal activity level for Blue Gem will be:

$$\text{Excess profits} = \pi = TR_P + TR_B - TC$$

$$= P_A \times Q_A + P_B \times Q_B - TC_Q$$

$$= \$10.25(800,000) + \$2(200,000) - \$3,000,000 - \$6.25(800,000)$$

$$= \$600,000$$

Since total costs include a normal return of 15% on a $10 million investment

$$\text{Total profits} = \text{Required return} + \text{Excess profits}$$

$$= 0.15(\$10,000,000) + \$600,000$$

$$= \$2,100,000$$

B. With 800,000 pounds of almonds being processed, but only 200,000 units of B sold, dumping of B is:

$$\text{Units B dumped} = \text{Units produced} - \text{Units sold}$$

$$= 800,000 - 200,000$$

$$= 600,000 \text{ units}$$

C. Part A shows that if all A and B produced is sold, an activity level of Q = 400,000 will result in $MR_B = -\$4$. A dumping charge of $4 per unit of B will cause Blue Gem to prefer to sell the last unit of B produced (and lose $4) rather than pay a $4 fine. Therefore, this fine, as will any fine greater than $4, eliminates dumping and causes Blue Gem to reduce processing to 400,000 pounds of almonds per year. This fine structure would undoubtedly reduce or eliminate the need for a new landfill.

While eliminating dumping is obviously attractive in the sense of reducing landfill costs, the $4 fine has the unfortunate consequence of cutting output substantially. Almond prices will rise to $P_A = \$14.25 - \$0.000005(400,000) = \$12.25$, and by-product prices will fall to $P_B = \$4 - \$0.00001(400,000) = \$0$. Employment will undoubtedly fall as well. In addition to these obvious short-run effects, long-run implications may be especially serious. At Q = 400,000, Blue Gem's excess profits will be:

$$\begin{aligned}\text{Excess profits} &= TR_P + TR_B - TC \\ &= \$12.25(400,000) + \$0(400,000) - \$3,000,000 - \$6.25(400,000) \\ &= -600,000 \text{ (a loss)}\end{aligned}$$

This means that total profits will be:

$$\begin{aligned}\text{Total profits} &= \text{Required return} + \text{Excess profits} \\ &= 0.15(\$10,000,000) + (-\$600,000) \\ &= \$900,000\end{aligned}$$

This level of profit is insufficient to maintain investment. Thus, while a $4 dumping charge will eliminate dumping, it is likely to cause the firm to close down or move to some other location. The effect on employment in Redding could be disastrous.

D. In the short-run, a $750,000 tax on Blue Gem will have no effect on dumping, output or employment. At the Q = 800,000 activity level, a $750,000 tax would reduce Blue Gem's total profits to $1,350,000, or $150,000 below the $1,500,000 required return on investment. Following imposition of a $750,000 tax, the firm's survival and total employment would be imperiled in the long-run.

E. No, Blue Gem will not be able to bear the burden of either tax alternative. Obviously, there is no single best alternative here. The highest fixed tax the company can bear in the long-run is $600,000 the full amount of excess profits. If the city places an extremely high priority on maintaining employment, perhaps a $600,000 tax on Blue Gem plus $150,000 in general city tax revenues could be used to pay for the new landfill.

Chapter 14

RISK ANALYSIS

MULTIPLE CHOICE QUESTIONS

Q14.1   Uncertainty is present when:

> A. outcomes are unknown.
> B. all possibilities are unknown.
> C. all probabilities are unknown.
> D. all of the above.

Q14.2   The amount of a bet is irrational when it:

> A. exceeds the maximum possible payoff.
> B. is less than the maximum possible payoff.
> C. exceeds the expected return.
> D. is less than the expected return.

Q14.3   When the dispersion of possible returns is irrelevant, the decision maker is said to be:

   A. risk averse.
> B. risk neutral.
   C. risk seeking.
   D. none of these.

Q14.4   A risk seeking decision maker displays:

> A. increasing marginal utility of income.
   B. increasing utility of income.
   C. constant marginal utility of income.
   D. decreasing marginal utility of income.

Q14.5   When $E(R) = \$100,000$, only a risk-seeking investor would make a certain sum investment in an amount:

> A. greater than $100,000.
   B. greater than or equal to $100,000.
   C. of $100,000.
   D. less than $100,000.

Risk Analysis

Q14.6 Under conditions of uncertainty, the outcomes of managerial decisions cannot be predicted with absolute accuracy because:

    A. all possibilities and their associated probabilities are not known.
    B. all possibilities are not known.
    C. outcome probabilities are not known.
>   **D.** none of these.

Q14.7 Economic risk is a situation where only:

    A. outcome possibilities are not known.
    B. outcome probabilities are not known.
>   **C.** both a and b.
    D. none of these.

Q14.8 The chance of loss associated with a given managerial decision is:

    A. market risk.
    B. inflation risk.
    C. credit risk.
>   **D.** business risk.

Q14.9 The difficulty of selling corporate assets at favorable prices under typical market conditions is:

    A. derivative risk.
    B. cultural risk.
>   **C.** liquidity risk.
    D. currency risk.

Q14.10 Following an increase in the risk-free rate, the certainty equivalent adjustment factor α will:

    A. rise for risk adverse investors.
    B. fall for risk adverse investors.
    C. fall for risk seeking investors.
>   **D.** none of these.

Q14.11   Uncertainty exists because managers cannot predict:

    A. outcome probabilities.
    B. possibilities.
    C. expected values.
>   D. outcomes.

Q14.12   Economic risk is the:

    A. variance of total profit.
    B. standard deviation of total profit.
    C. coefficient of variation for total profit.
>   D. chance of loss.

Q14.13   A probability distribution for total profit is a list of:

    A. possible events.
    B. probabilities.
>   C. possible events and probabilities.
    D. occurences.

Q14.14   For two projects with the same cost, the one that is less risky has the:

    A. lowest expected profit.
    B. highest standard deviation.
>   C. lowest standard deviation.
    D. highest expected profit.

Q14.15   A project with a 75% chance of earning $4,000 in profit and a 25% chance of earning $12,000 in profit has an expected value of:

    A. $8,000.
    B. $10,000.
    C. $16,000.
>   D. $6,000.

Risk Analysis

Q14.16 A project with a 50% chance of earning $0 and a 50% chance of earning $100 has a standard deviation of:

> A. $100.
> B. $50.
> C. $75.
> D. $0.

Q14.17 For two projects of differing sizes, the project that is less risky has the:

> A. highest standard deviation.
> B. highest coefficient of variation.
> C. lowest coefficient of variation.
> D. highest expected profit.

Q14.18 If profits are normally distributed with a mean of $12 and a standard deviation of $4, there is a 50/50 chance actual profits will exceed:

> A. $12.
> B. $8.
> C. $16.
> D. $4.

Q14.19 If revenues are normally distributed around a mean of $100 with a standard deviation of $10, the probability of exceeding a cost of $80.40 is:

> A. 0.975.
> B. 0.45.
> C. 0.025.
> D. 0.95.

Q14.20 Risk neutrality implies a:

> A. constant marginal utility of income.
> B. diminishing marginal utility of income.
> C. increasing marginal utility of income.
> D. constant utility of income.

Q14.21   For a risk seeker the marginal utility of money is:

   A.   constant.
> B.   increasing.
   C.   positive.
   D.   diminishing.

Q14.22   An α = 0.8 is consistent with risk:

   A.   neutrality.
> B.   avoidance.
   C.   preference.
   D.   seeking.

Q14.23   If you are indifferent between $1 and a lottery ticket that gives you a 0.001 chance of winning $1,000 you are:

> A.   risk neutral.
   B.   risk averse.
   C.   risk elastic.
   D.   a risk seeker.

Q14.24   To justify an investment that involves an out-of-pocket cost of $100 and a 50/50 chance of payoffs of $0 or $250, the decision maker must have personal certainty equivalent adjustment factor that is:

   A.   α = 0.8.
   B.   α ≤ 0.8.
> C.   α > 0.8.
   D.   α < 0.8.

Risk Analysis

Q14.25 A valuation model that explicitly accounts for risk can be written.

- A. $V = \sum_{\alpha=1}^{N} \frac{\pi_t}{(1+\alpha)^t}$
- B. $V = \sum_{i=1}^{N} \frac{E(\pi_t)}{(1+i)^t}$
- > C. $V = \alpha \sum_{i=1}^{N} \frac{E(\pi_t)}{(1+i)^t}$
- D. $V = \alpha \sum_{i=1}^{N} \frac{\pi_t}{(1+k)^t}$

Q14.26 The risk adjusted discount rate equals the riskless rate of return:

- > A. plus a risk premium.
- B. multiplied by a risk premium.
- C. divided by a risk premium.
- D. less a risk premium.

Q14.27 The maximin criterion involves:

- A. minimization of expected opportunity costs.
- > B. avoidance of the worst-case scenario.
- C. acceptance of the best-case scenario.
- D. maximization of expected returns.

Q14.28 The minimax regret criterion directs the decision maker to select the alternative that:

- A. maximizes opportunity cost.
- B. provides the best outcome in the worse case scenario.
- C. provides the worst outcome in the best case scenario.
- > D. minimizes opportunity loss.

Q14.29 The minimum expected opportunity loss associated with a decision equals the:

- A. worst outcome under the best case scenario.
- > B. cost of uncertainty.
- C. incremental cost.
- D. best outcome under the worst case scenario.

Q14.30 A decision standard that selects the alternative with the best of the worst possible outcomes is:

    A. game theory.
>   **B.** the maximin criterion.
    C. the minimax criterion.
    D. sensitivity analysis.

Risk Analysis 545

PROBLEMS & SOLUTIONS

P14.1 **Risk Attitudes.** Identify each of the following as consistent with risk-averse, risk-neutral, or risk-seeking behavior in investment project selection:

    A. Ignoring risk levels of investment alternatives.

    B. Larger risk premiums for riskier projects.

    C. Valuing equally certain sums and expected risky sums of equal dollar amounts.

    D. Increasing marginal utility of money.

    E. Preference for larger, as opposed to smaller, coefficients of variation.

P14.1 **SOLUTION**

    A. Risk neutrality results in a value being placed on individual projects equal to their expected return, irrespective of the underlying variability in returns.

    B. Risk averse describes those investors who are only willing to accept investment projects with larger risk premiums as project risk levels increase.

    C. Risk neutrality implies that a given decision maker places a value on an investment project that is just equal to the project expected return. Therefore, certain sums and expected risky sums of equal dollar amounts are valued equally.

    D. Risk seeking investors display behavior consistent with an increasing marginal utility of money. Since increases in income or wealth provide more than proportionate increases in well-being, these individuals display very aggressive investment behavior.

    E. Risk seeking investors place a relatively high value on small probabilities of a high payoff. As a result, they prefer a higher standard deviation in project returns, holding expected return constant, and, therefore, higher as opposed to lower coefficients of variation (risk-reward ratios).

P14.2 **Certainty Equivalents.** The certainty equivalent concept can be widely employed in the analysis of personal and business decision making. Identify each of the following statements as true or false and explain why.

Harcourt Brace & Company

A. If previously accepted projects with similar risk have α's in a range from α = 0.4 to α = 0.5, an investment with an expected return of $200,000 is acceptable at a cost of $125,000.

B. A project for which NPV < 0 using a risk-adjusted discount rate will have an implied α factor that is too large to allow project acceptance.

C. The appropriate certainty equivalent adjustment factor α indicates the minimum price in certain dollars that an individual should be willing to pay per risky dollar of expected return.

D. State lotteries that pay out 40% of the revenues they generate require players who place at least a certain $2.50 value on each $1 of expected risky return.

E. An α < 1 implies that a certain sum and a risky expected return of a greater dollar amount provides equivalent utility to a given decision maker.

P14.2 SOLUTION

A. False. If similar projects implicitly involve α's in the range from α = 0.4 to α = 0.5, then the maximum certain sum equivalent of an expected risky $200,000 falls in the range between $80,000 (= 0.4 × $200,000) and $100,000 (= 0.5 × $200,000), since:

$$\alpha = \frac{\text{Certain sum}}{\text{Expected risky amount}}$$

Certain sum = α × Expected risky amount

Therefore, a project cost of $125,000 would not be acceptable.

B. True. A project which has an NPV < 0 using the risk adjusted discount rate approach will have an α factor above the maximum acceptable level. Such a project will not be desirable, since it has a "price per risky dollar" above that necessary to induce investment.

C. False. The certainty equivalent adjustment factor α indicates the maximum price in certain dollars that an individual is willing to pay per risky dollar of expected return.

Risk Analysis

D. True. State lotteries that pay back 50% of the amount bet involve players who have an $\alpha \geq 2$.

E. True. The α factor is the ratio of a certain sum divided by an expected risky amount that are equivalent in terms of utility, but may differ in strict dollar terms, as in the case of $\alpha < 1$ where the equivalent expected return (in utility terms) involves a greater dollar amount.

P14.3 *Expected Return Analysis.* William Mays offers free investment seminars to local PTA groups. On average, Mays expects 1% of seminar participants to purchase $25,000 each in tax sheltered investments, and 2% to purchase $10,000 each in stocks and bonds. Mays earns a 4% net commission on tax shelters, and 1% on stocks and bonds.

A. Calculate Mays' expected net commissions per seminar if attendance averages twenty-five persons.

P14.3 SOLUTION

A. Expected net commission will be the sum of net commissions on tax shelters (TS) and stocks and bonds (S&B).

$$E(NC_{TS}) = \text{Expected Sales} \times \text{Commission Rate}$$

$$= (0.01)(\$25,000)(25) \times (0.04)$$

$$= \$250$$

$$E(NC_{S\&B}) = \text{Expected Sales} \times \text{Commission Rate}$$

$$= (0.02)(\$10,000)(25) \times (0.01)$$

$$= \$50$$

$$E(NC) = E(NC_{TS}) + E(NC_{S\&B})$$

$$= \$250 + \$50$$

$$= \$300$$

P14.4 *Expected Return Analysis.* Alex P. Keaton has just accepted a job as a broker at a major NYSE member firm, and has been asked to develop a list of customers by telephoning medical doctors and other professionals located in the metropolitan area. On average, Keaton expects 1% of those called to purchase $15,000 each in mutual fund investments, and 3% to purchase $10,000 each in stocks and bonds. Keaton earns a 2% net commission on mutual funds and 1% on stocks and bonds.

A. Calculate Keatons expected net commissions if he calls an average of twenty-five persons per day.

P14.4 **SOLUTION**

A. Expected net commission will be the sum of net commissions on mutual funds (MF) and stocks and bonds (S&B).

$$E(NC_{MF}) = \text{Expected Sales} \times \text{Commission Rate}$$

$$= (0.01)(\$15,000)(25) \times (0.02)$$

$$= \$75$$

$$E(NC_{S\&B}) = \text{Expected Sales} \times \text{Commission Rate}$$

$$= (0.03)(\$10,000)(25) \times (0.01)$$

$$= \$75$$

$$E(NC) = E(NC_{MF}) + E(NC_{S\&B})$$

$$= \$75 + \$75$$

$$= \$150$$

P14.5 **Expected Return Analysis.** Stuart Markowitz offers free legal seminars to local YMCA groups. On average, Markowitz expects 10% of seminar participants to purchase customized estate planning services priced at $500 each, and 25% to purchase standard will writing services priced at $100.

A. Calculate Markowitz's expected gross return per seminar if attendance averages ten persons.

P14.5 SOLUTION

A. The expected gross return will be the sum of fees generated from estate planning (EP) and will writing (W) services.

$$E(Fee) = E(Fee_{EP}) + E(Fee_W)$$

$$= 0.1(10)(\$500) + 0.25(10)(\$100)$$

$$= \$750$$

P14.6 *Expected Return Analysis.* Dr. William Huxtable offers health investment seminars to local PTA groups. On average, Huxtable expects 2% of seminar participants to become patients of his HMO organization at a gross billing of $2,500 per patient per year.

A. Calculate Huxtable's expected net return per dollar of gross patient billings if attendance averages fifty persons per seminar, and a first-year net return of $100 must be earned to justify Huxtable's time and effort per seminar.

P14.6 SOLUTION

A. The net return per seminar is found as:

$$E(\pi) = \text{Expected Patient Billings} \times \text{Net Return Percentage}$$

$$= (0.02)(50)(\$2,500) \times \text{Net Return Percentage}$$

$$= \$2,500 \times \text{Net Return Percentage}$$

Thus, to earn a net return of $100 per seminar, the net return percentage is:

$$\$100 = \$2,500 \times \text{Net Return Percentage}$$

Net Return Percentage = .04 or 4%

P14.7 *Probability Analysis.* WD-50, Inc. has just completed development of a new spray lubricant. Preliminary market research indicates two feasible marketing strategies: developing general consumer acceptance through media advertising, or developing distributor acceptance through intensive personal selling by company representatives. The marketing manager has developed the following estimates for sales under each alternative:

	Media Advertising Strategy		Personal Selling Strategy	
Probability	Sales	Probability	Sales
0.1	$125,000	0.3	$250,000
0.4	375,000	0.4	375,000
0.4	625,000	0.3	500,000
0.1	875,000		

A. Assume that the company has a 20% profit margin on sales. Calculate expected profits for each plan.

B. Construct a simple bar graph of the possible profit outcomes for each plan. Which plan appears to be more risky?

C. Assume that management's utility function resembles the one illustrated below. Which strategy should the marketing manager recommend?

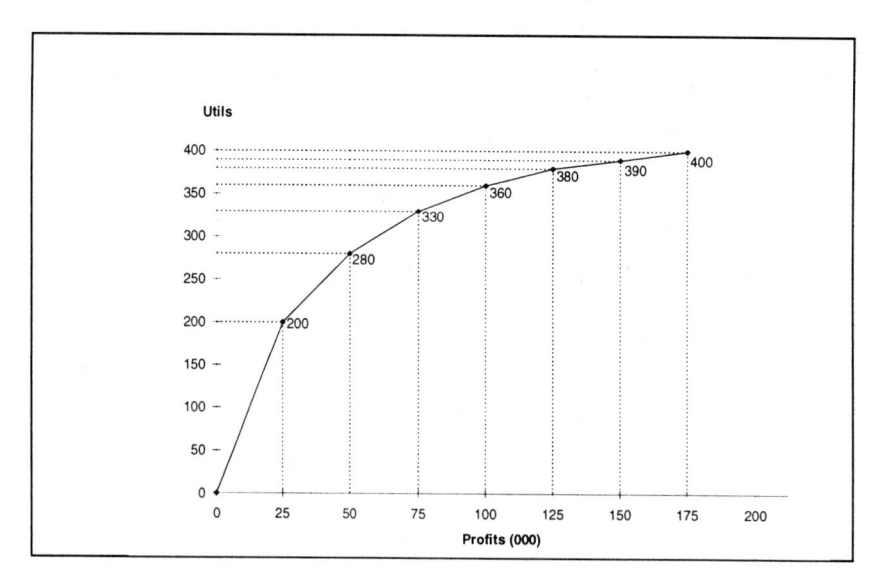

Risk Analysis

P14.7 **SOLUTION**

A.

Media Advertising Strategy

Probability (1)	Sales (2)	Profit (3)=(2)×0.2	(4)=(3)×(1)
0.1	$125,000	$ 25,000	$ 2,500
0.4	375,000	75,000	30,000
0.4	625,000	125,000	50,000
0.1	875,000	175,000	17,500
1.0			$E(\pi_{MA}) = \$100,000$

Personal Selling Strategy

Probability (1)	Sales (2)	Profit (3)=(2)×0.2	(4)=(3)×(1)
0.3	$250,000	$ 50,000	$ 15,000
0.4	375,000	75,000	30,000
0.3	500,000	100,000	30,000
1.0			$E(\pi_{PS}) = \$75,000$

B. The anticipated distribution of profits for the media advertising strategy appears as follows:

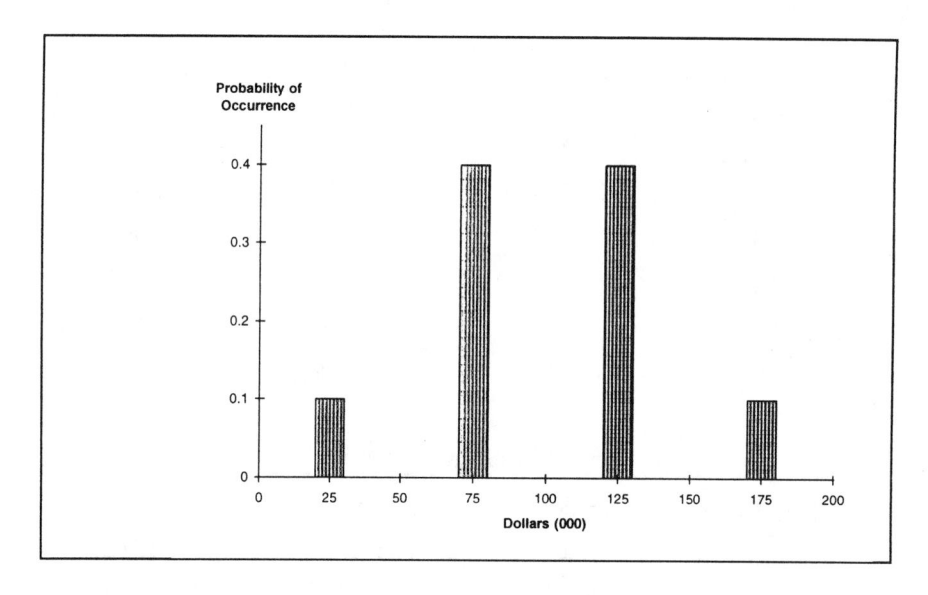

The anticipated distribution of profits for the personal selling strategy appears as follows:

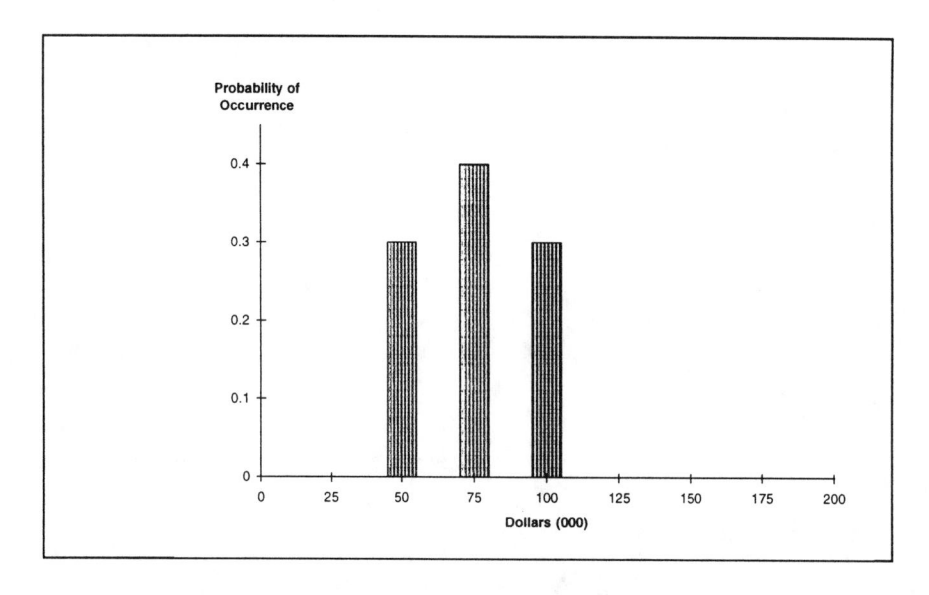

The media advertising strategy is more risky than the personal selling strategy because of the greater variability of possible outcomes.

C.

Media Advertising Strategy

Probability (1)	Profits (2)	Utils (3)	(4)=(3)×(1)
0.1	$ 25,000	200	20
0.4	75,000	330	132
0.4	125,000	380	152
0.1	175,000	400	40
1.0			E(U) = 344

Personal Selling Strategy

Probability (1)	Profits (2)	Utils (3)	(4)=(3)×(1)
0.3	$ 50,000	280	84
0.4	75,000	330	132
0.3	100,000	360	108
1.0			E(U) = 324

The marketing manager should recommend the media advertising strategy because of its higher expected utility. In this instance, the higher expected profit of this strategy more than offsets its greater risk.

P14.8 *Probability Analysis.* Ceramic Tile, Inc. wishes to adopt one of two feasible marketing strategies: developing general consumer acceptance through media advertising, or developing distributor acceptance through intensive personal selling by company representatives. The marketing manager has developed the following estimates for sales under each alternative:

Media Advertising Strategy		Personal Selling Strategy	
Probability	Sales	Probability	Sales
0.3	$ 2,500,000	0.2	$ 5,000,000
0.4	10,000,000	0.6	7,500,000
0.3	17,500,000	0.2	10,000,000

A. Assume that the company has a 10% net profit margin on sales. Calculate expected profits for each plan.

B. Construct a simple bar graph of the possible profit outcomes for each plan. Which plan appears to be more risky?

C. Assume that management's utility function resembles the one illustrated below. Which strategy should the marketing manager recommend?

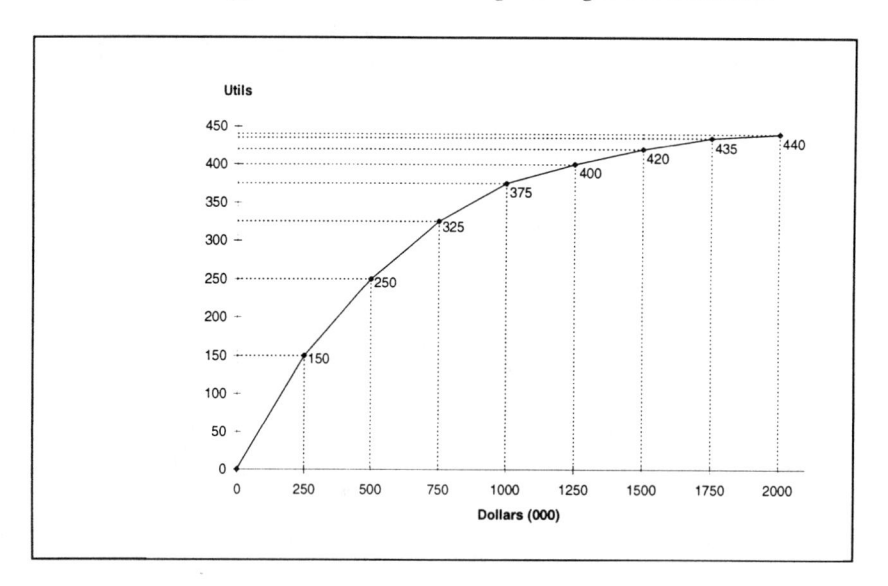

Utils vs. Dollars (000): (250, 150), (500, 250), (750, 325), (1000, 375), (1250, 400), (1500, 420), (1750, 435), (2000, 440)

P14.8 SOLUTION

A.

Media Advertising Strategy

Probability (1)	Sales (2)	Profit (3)=(2)×0.1	(4)=(3)×(1)
0.3	$ 2,500,000	$ 250,000	$ 75,000
0.4	10,000,000	1,000,000	400,000
0.3	17,500,000	1,750,000	525,000
1.0			$E(\pi_{MA})$ = $1,000,000

Risk Analysis

	Personal Selling Strategy		
Probability (1)	**Sales** (2)	**Profit** (3)=(2)×0.1	(4)=(3)×(1)
0.2	$ 5,000,000	$500,000	$100,000
0.6	7,500,000	750,000	450,000
0.2	10,000,000	1,000,000	200,000
1.0			$E(\pi_{PS}) = \$750,000$

B. The anticipated distribution of profits for the media advertising strategy is:

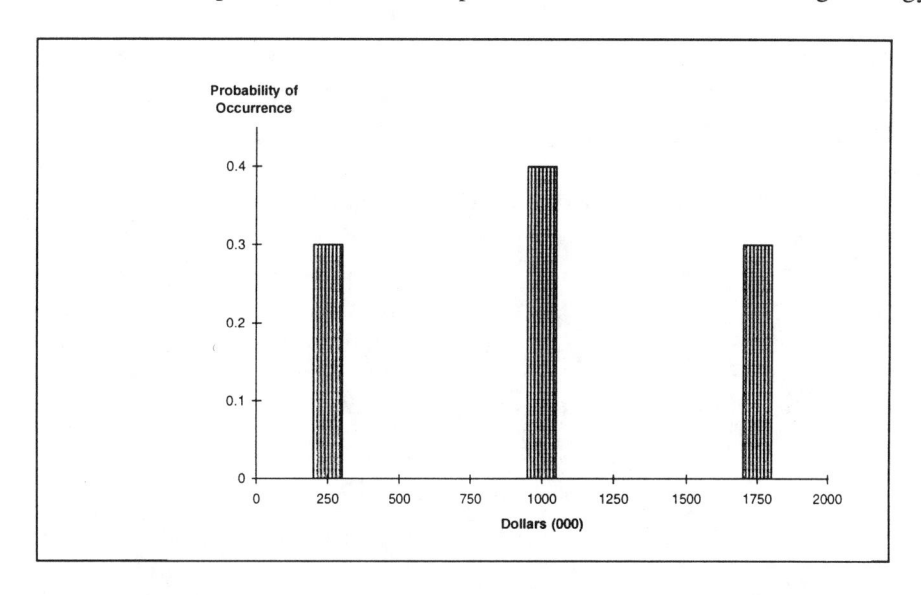

The anticipated distribution of profits for the personal selling strategy is:

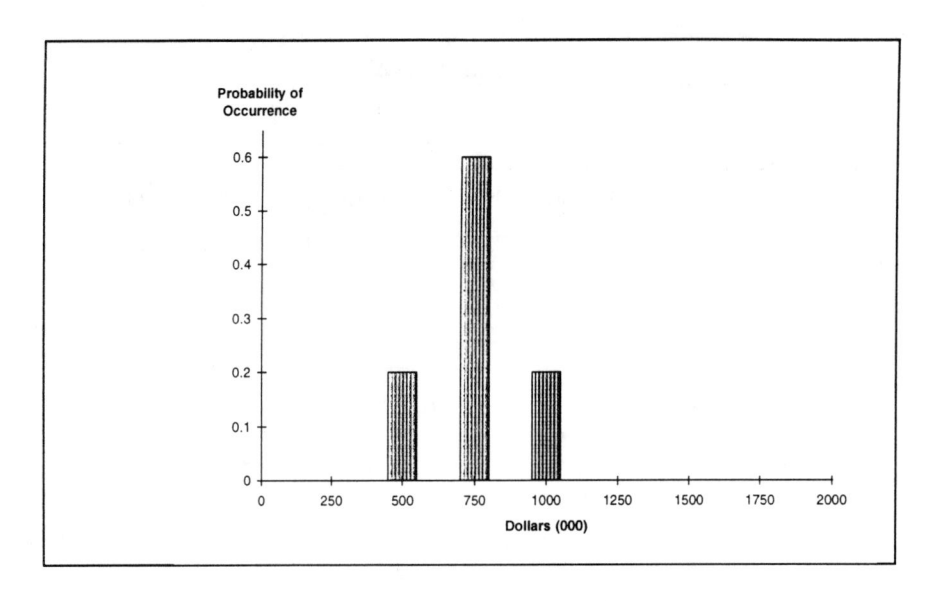

The media advertising strategy appears more risky than the personal selling strategy because of the greater variability of possible outcomes.

C.

Media Advertising Strategy

Probability (1)	Profits(000) (2)	Utils (3)	(4)=(3)×(1)
0.3	$ 250	150	45
0.4	1,000	325	130
0.3	1,750	435	130.5
1.0			E(U) = 305.5

Personal Selling Strategy

Probability (1)	Profits(000) (2)	Utils (3)	(4)=(3)×(1)
0.2	$500	250	50
0.6	750	325	195
0.2	1,000	375	75
1.0			E(U) = 320

Risk Analysis

The marketing manager should recommend the personal selling strategy because of its higher expected utility. In this instance, the lower expected profit of this strategy more than offset by its much lower risk.

P14.9 ***Probability Analysis.*** The Dental Clinic, Inc. is contemplating replacing an obsolete word processing system with one of two innovative lines of equipment. Alternative 1 requires a current investment outlay of $26,022, whereas Alternative 2 requires an outlay of $31,048. The following cash flows (cost savings) will be generated each year over the five-year useful lives of the new systems.

	Probability	Cash Flow
Alternative 1	0.32	$7,000
	0.36	10,000
	0.32	13,000
Alternative 2	0.18	$7,500
	0.64	10,000
	0.18	12,500

A. Calculate the expected cash flow for each investment alternative.

B. Calculate the standard deviation of cash flows (risk) for each investment alternative.

C. The firm will use a discount rate of 15% for the cash flows with higher degree of dispersion and a 12% rate for the less risky cash flows, calculate the expected net present value for each investment. Which alternative should be chosen?

P14.9 **SOLUTION**

A. Expected values of cash flows

	Probability (1)	Cash Flow (2)	(3)=(1)×(2)
Alternative 1	0.32	$7,000	$2,240
	0.36	10,000	3,600
	0.32	13,000	4,160
			$E(CF_1) = \$10,000$

Alternative 2	0.18	7,500	$ 1,350
	0.64	10,000	6,400
	0.18	12,500	2,250
			E(CF$_2$) = $10,000

B. The standard deviations of cash flows are:

	Probability (1)	Deviation (2)	Deviation^2 (3)	(4)=(1)×(3)
Alternative 1	0.32	-$3,000	$9 × 10^6	$2,880,000
	0.36	0	0	0
	0.32	3,000	9 × 10^6	2,880,000
				σ_1^2 = $5,760,000

$$\sigma_1 = \sqrt{\sigma_1^2}$$

$$= \sqrt{\$5,760,000}$$

$$= \$2,400$$

	Probability (1)	Deviation (2)	Deviation^2 (3)	(4)=(1)×(3)
Alternative 2	0.18	-$2,500	$6.25 × 10^6	$1,125,000
	0.64	0	0	0
	0.18	2,500	6.25 × 10^6	1,125,000
				σ_2^2 = $2,250,000

$$\sigma_2 = \sqrt{\sigma_1^2}$$

$$= \sqrt{\$2,250,000}$$

$$= \$1,500$$

Thus, Alternative 2 is the less risky investment.

C. Alternative 1 is riskier because it has the greater variability in its probable cash flows. This is obvious from the inspection of the distributions of possible returns and is verified by calculating the standard deviations. Hence, Alternative 1 is evaluated at the 15% cost of capital, while Alternative 2 requires a 12% cost of capital.

$$NPV = \sum_{t=1}^{5} \frac{\$10,000}{(1.15)^t} - \$26,022$$

$$= \$10,000(PVIFA, N = 5, i = 15\%) - \$26,022$$

$$= \$10,000(3.3522) - \$26,022$$

$$= \$7,500$$

$$NPV = \sum_{t=1}^{5} \frac{\$10,000}{(1.12)^t} - \$31,048$$

$$= \$10,000(PVIFA, N = 5, i = 12\%) - \$31,048$$

$$= \$10,000(3.6048) - \$31,048$$

$$= \$5,000$$

Alternative 1 has the higher risk-adjusted net present value and, therefore, is the more attractive investment.

P14.10 ***Probability Analysis.*** *The True Joist Corporation is a leading manufacturer of wood and steel building joists. The company is considering adoption of one of two innovative lines of production equipment. Alternative 1 requires a current investment outlay of $50,000, whereas Alternative 2 requires an outlay of $75,000. The following cash flows (cost savings) will be generated each year over the five-year useful lives of the new machines.*

	Probability	Cash Flow
Alternative 1	0.245	$10,000
	0.510	15,000
	0.245	20,000

	Alternative 2	0.18	$15,000
		0.64	25,000
		0.18	35,000

A. Calculate the expected cash flow for each investment alternative.

B. Calculate the standard deviation and coefficient of variation of cash flows (risk) for each investment alternative.

C. The firm will use a discount rate of 15% for the cash flows with higher degree of dispersion and a 12% rate for the less risky cash flows, calculate the expected net present value for each investment. Which alternative should be chosen?

P14.10 SOLUTION

A. Expected values of cash flows:

	Probability (1)	Cash Flow (2)	(3)=(1)×(2)
Alternative 1	0.245	$10,000	$ 2,450
	0.510	15,000	7,650
	0.245	20,000	4,900
			$E(CF_1) = \$15,000$
Alternative 2	0.18	15,000	$ 2,700
	0.64	25,000	16,000
	0.18	35,000	6,300
			$E(CF_2) = \$25,000$

B. The standard deviations of cash flows are:

Risk Analysis

	Probability (1)	Deviation (2)	Deviation² (3)	(4)=(1)×(3)
Alternative 1	0.245	-$5,000	25×10^6	$6,125,000
	0.510	0	0	0
	0.245	5,000	25×10^6	6,125,000
			$\sigma_1^2 =$	$12,250,000

$$\sigma_1 = \sqrt{\sigma_1^2}$$

$$= \sqrt{\$12,250,000}$$

$$= \$3,500$$

$$V_1 = \sigma_1/E(CF_1) = \$3,500/\$15,000 = 0.23$$

	Probability (1)	Deviation (2)	Deviation² (3)	(4)=(1)×(3)
Alternative 2	0.18	-$10,000	1.0×10^8	1.8×10^7
	0.64	0	0	0
	0.18	10,000	1.0×10^8	1.8×10^7
			$\sigma_2^2 =$	$36,000,000

$$\sigma_2 = \sqrt{\sigma_1^2}$$

$$= \sqrt{\$36,000,000}$$

$$= \$6,000$$

$$V_2 = \sigma_2/E(CF_2) = \$6,000/\$25,000 = 0.24$$

Since $\sigma_2 > \sigma_1$ and $V_2 > V_1$, Alternative 2 is the more risky investment.

C. Alternative 2 is riskier because it has the greater variability in its probable cash flows. This is obvious from the inspection of the distributions of possible returns and is verified by calculating the standard deviations and coefficients of variation.

Hence, Alternative 1 is evaluated at the 12% cost of capital, while Alternative 2 requires a 15% cost of capital.

$$NPV = \sum_{t=1}^{5} \frac{\$15,000}{(1.12)^t} - \$50,000$$

$$= \$15,000(PVIFA, N = 5, i = 12\%) - \$50,000$$

$$= \$15,000(3.6048) - \$50,000$$

$$= \$4,072$$

$$NPV = \sum_{t=1}^{5} \frac{\$25,000}{(1.15)^t} - \$75,000$$

$$= \$25,000(PVIFA, N = 5, i = 15\%) - \$75,000$$

$$= \$25,000(3.3522) - \$75,000$$

$$= \$8,805$$

Alternative 2 has the higher risk-adjusted net present value and, therefore, is the more attractive investment.

P14.11 ***Probability Analysis.*** *The Seattle HMO, Inc. is considering entering into a data processing contract with a leading consulting firm. Entering into such an agreement would require a current investment outlay of $200,000. The following net cash flows (cost savings) will be generated each year over the ten-year life of the management contract:*

Probability	Cash Flow
0.32	$25,000
0.36	50,000
0.32	75,000

A. *Calculate the expected cash flow.*

B. *Calculate the standard deviation and coefficient of variation of cash flows (risk).*

Risk Analysis

C. Calculate the expected net present value for the investment if the firm uses a discount rate of 20%. Should the investment be undertaken?

P14.11 SOLUTION

A. Expected value of cash flows:

Probability (1)	Cash Flow (2)	(3)=(1)×(2)
0.32	$25,000	$ 8,000
0.36	50,000	18,000
0.32	75,000	24,000
		E(CF) = $50,000

B. The standard deviation of cash flows is:

Probability (1)	Deviation (2)	Deviation^2 (3)	(4)=(1)×(3)
0.32	-$25,000	$6.25 × 10^8	$2.0 × 10^8
0.36	0	0	0
0.32	25,000	6.25 × 10^8	2.0 × 10^8
			σ^2 = $4.0 × 10^8

$$\sigma = \sqrt{\sigma^2}$$

$$= \sqrt{\$400,000,000}$$

$$= \$20,000$$

$$V = \sigma/E(CF) = \$20,000/\$50,000 = 0.4$$

C. Evaluated at a 20% cost of capital, the risk-adjusted NPV is:

$$NPV = \sum_{t=1}^{10} \frac{\$50,000}{(1.2)^t} - \$200,000$$

$$= \$50,000(PVIFA, N = 10, i = 20\%) - \$200,000$$

$$= \$50,000(4.1925) - \$200,000$$

$$= \$9,625$$

Thus, the investment has a positive risk-adjusted net present value and, therefore, is an attractive investment.

P14.12 **Certainty Equivalent Method.** Saddie Hawkins, a management analyst with Mobile Telephone Services, Inc., has collected the following information about three investment projects undertaken by the firm during the past six month period. Hawkins wishes to use this information as a backdrop against which to evaluate the attractiveness of a recent investment proposal put forth by the quality control department. In that proposal, dubbed Project X, the quality control department proposes to spend $100,000 to modify transmission equipment at the Colorado Springs, Colorado facility. Annual expected cost savings of $25,000 per year over the 10-year 1996-2005 period have been projected, and verified as reasonable by Hawkins.

Expected Cash Flows Per Year

Year	Project X	Project Y	Project Z
1996	$25,000	$50,000	$7,500
1997	25,000	45,000	12,500
1998	25,000	40,000	17,500
1999	25,000	35,000	22,500
2000	25,000	30,000	27,500
2001	25,000	25,000	32,500
2002	25,000	20,000	37,500
2003	25,000	15,000	42,500
2004	25,000	10,000	47,500
2005	25,000	5,000	52,500
PV of Cash Flow @ 8%	?	$205,620	$180,210
1995 Investment:	$100,000	$100,000	$100,000

Risk Analysis

A. *Calculate the present value of anticipated cost savings using an 8% discount rate as a reasonable estimate of the risk-free cost of capital.*

B. *In light of the $100,000 investment required for each of these projects, and the discounted present value of future benefits, calculate the certainty equivalent adjustment factor α implicit in the decision to fund each of these investment projects.*

C. *Assume that the α's implicit in the decisions to fund Projects Y and Z represent the upper limits for investment projects of this type. Would a decision to fund Project X be consistent or inconsistent with the firm's decision to fund Projects Y and Z?*

P14.12 SOLUTION

A. The present value of anticipated benefits from Project X can be calculated using the Present Value of an Annuity interest factor table from the Appendix. Using an 8% discount rate as a reasonable estimate of the risk-free cost of capital plus a 10-year horizon, the $\text{PVIFA}_{.08,10} = .67101$.

Therefore, the discounted present value of future benefits anticipated from Project X is:

$$\text{PV of Benefits} = \$25,000 \times \text{PVIFA} \, (i = 0.08, N = 10),$$

$$= \$167,752.50.$$

B. The $100,000 investment required for each of these projects, and the discounted present value of future benefits, can be used to calculate the certainty equivalent adjustment factor α implicit in the decision to fund each of these investment projects. In making each investment decision, the firm reveals a certainty equivalent adjustment factor of at least $\alpha = 0.49$ for Project Y, and $\alpha = 0.55$ for Project Z since:

$$\alpha = \frac{\text{Certain Sum}}{\text{Expected Risky Sum}}$$

$$= \frac{\text{Certain Investment Amount Foregone}}{\text{Expected PV of Future Benefits}}$$

Project X

$$\alpha_X = \frac{\$100,000}{\$167,752}$$

$$= 0.60$$

Project Y

$$\alpha_Y = \frac{\$100,000}{\$205,620}$$

$$= 0.49$$

Project Z

$$\alpha_Z = \frac{\$100,000}{\$180,210}$$

$$= 0.55$$

In words, each risky dollar of expected profit contribution from Project X must be "worth" at least (valued as highly as) 60¢ in certain dollars to justify investment. For each of the projects already undertaken, each risky dollar must be worth at least 49¢ in certain dollars to justify Project Y, and each risky dollar must be worth at least 55¢ in certain dollars to justify Project Z.

C. If the α's implicit in the decisions to fund Projects Y and Z represent the upper limits for investment projects of this type, then an investment in Project X cannot be justified. A decision to fund Project X would be *inconsistent* with the firm's decision to fund Projects Y and Z. At a "price" of 60¢ for each dollar of discounted expected risky return, Project X is too costly when compared with the previously acceptable price range of 49¢ to 55¢ implicit in the acceptance of Projects Y and Z.

P14.13 **Probability Analysis.** *Tex-Mex, Inc. is a rapidly growing chain of Mexican-food restaurants. The company has a limited amount of capital for expansion, and must carefully weigh available alternatives. Currently, the company is considering opening restaurants in Phoenix and/or Tucson, Arizona. Projections for the two potential outlets are:*

Risk Analysis

City	Outcome	Annual Profit Contribution	Probability
Phoenix	Failure	$200,000	0.5
	Success	$300,000	0.5
Tucson	Failure	$100,000	0.5
	Success	$500,000	0.5

Each restaurant would involve a capital expenditure of $1.5 million, plus land acquisition costs of $500,000 for Phoenix and $1,050,000 for Tucson. The company uses the 10% yield on riskless U.S. Treasury bills to calculate the risk-free annual opportunity cost of investment capital.

A. Calculate the expected value, standard deviation, and coefficient of variation for each outlet's profit contribution.

B. Calculate the minimum certainty equivalent adjustment factor for each restaurant's cash flows that would justify investment in each outlet.

C. Assuming the management of Tex-Mex is risk averse, and uses the certainty equivalent method in decision making, which is the more attractive outlet? Why?

P14.13 SOLUTION

A. Phoenix

$$E(\pi_P) = \$200,000(0.5) + \$300,000(0.5) = \$250,000$$

$$\sigma_P = \sqrt{(\$200,000 - \$250,000)^2(0.5) + (\$300,000 - \$250,000)^2(0.5)}$$

$$= \$50,000$$

$$V_P = \sigma_P/E(\pi_P) = 0.2$$

Tucson

$$E(\pi_T) = \$100,000(0.5) + \$500,000(0.5) = \$300,000$$

$$\sigma_T = \sqrt{(\$100,000 - \$300,000)^2(0.5) + (\$500,000 - \$300,000)^2(0.5)}$$

$$= \$200,000$$

$$V_T = \sigma_T/E(\pi_T) = 0.\overline{6}$$

B. To justify each investment alternative, the company must have a certainty equivalent adjustment factor of at least $\alpha = 0.8$ for the Phoenix project and $\alpha = 0.85$ for the Tucson project since:

$$\alpha = \frac{\text{Certain Sum}}{\text{Expected Risky Sum}}$$

$$= \frac{\text{Certain Flow Foregone per year (Opportunity cost)}}{\text{Expected Profit contribution per year } (E(\pi))}$$

Phoenix

$$\alpha_P = \frac{0.1(\$2,000,000)}{\$250,000}$$

$$= 0.8$$

Tucson

$$\alpha_T = \frac{0.1(\$2,550,000)}{\$300,000}$$

$$= 0.85$$

In words, each risky dollar of expected profit contribution from the Phoenix outlet must be "worth" at least (valued as highly as) 80¢ in certain dollars to justify investment. For the Tucson outlet, each risky dollar must be worth at least 85¢ in certain dollars.

C. Given managerial risk aversion, Phoenix is the more attractive outlet since it has a lower risk, $\sigma_P < \sigma_T$ and $V_P < V_T$, and is also less expensive in terms of the "price" of each risky dollar of expected profit contribution. A risk averse management wouldn't pay 85¢ for each risky dollar of expected profit contribution from a Tucson outlet, when less risky expected returns from a Phoenix outlet "cost" only 80¢.

Risk Analysis

P14.14 **Certainty Equivalents.** Tofu-Tofu, Inc. is a rapidly growing chain of health food restaurants. The company has a limited amount of capital for expansion, and must carefully weigh available alternatives. Currently, the company is considering opening restaurants in Fresno and/or Pasadena, California. Projections for the two potential outlets are:

City	Outcome	Annual Profit Contribution	Probability
Fresno	Failure	$300,000	0.5
	Success	$500,000	0.5
Pasadena	Failure	$250,000	0.5
	Success	$750,000	0.5

Each restaurant would involve a capital expenditure of $2.5 million, plus land acquisition costs of $500,000 for Fresno and $1.5 million for Pasadena. The company uses the 10% yield on riskless U.S. Treasury bills to calculate the risk-free annual opportunity cost of investment capital.

A. Calculate the expected value, standard deviation, and coefficient of variation for each outlet's profit contribution.

B. Calculate the minimum certainty equivalent adjustment factor for each restaurant's cash flows that would justify investment in each outlet.

C. Assuming the management of Tofu-Tofu is risk averse, and uses the certainty equivalent method in decision making, which is the more attractive outlet? Why?

P14.14 **SOLUTION**

A. Fresno

$E(\pi_F)$ = $300,000(0.5) + $500,000(0.5) = $400,000

σ_F = $\sqrt{(\$300,000 - \$400,000)^2(0.5) + (\$500,000 - \$400,000)^2(0.5)}$

= $100,000

V_F = $\sigma_F/E(\pi_F)$ = 0.25

Pasadena

$$E(\pi_P) = \$250,000(0.5) + \$750,000(0.5) = \$500,000$$

$$\sigma_P = \sqrt{(\$250,000 - \$500,000)^2(0.5) + (\$750,000 - \$500,000)^2(0.5)}$$

$$= \$250,000$$

$$V_P = \sigma_P/E(\pi_P) = 0.5$$

B. To justify each investment alternative, the company must have a certainty equivalent adjustment factor of at least $\alpha = 0.75$ for the Fresno project and $\alpha = 0.8$ for the Pasadena project since:

$$\alpha = \frac{\text{Certain Sum}}{\text{Expected Risky Sum}}$$

$$= \frac{\text{Certain Flow Foregone per year (Opportunity cost)}}{\text{Expected Profit contribution per year } (E(\pi))}$$

Fresno

$$\alpha_F = \frac{0.1(\$3,000,000)}{\$400,000}$$

$$= 0.75$$

Pasadena

$$\alpha_P = \frac{0.1(\$4,000,000)}{\$500,000}$$

$$= 0.8$$

In words, each risky dollar of expected profit contribution from the Fresno outlet must be "worth" at least (valued as highly as) 75¢ in certain dollars to justify investment. For the Pasadena outlet, each risky dollar must be worth at least 80¢ in certain dollars.

C. Given managerial risk aversion, Fresno is the more attractive outlet since it has a lower risk, $\sigma_F < \sigma_P$ and $V_F < V_P$, and is also less expensive in terms of the "price"

Risk Analysis

of each risky dollar of expected profit contribution. A risk averse management wouldn't pay 80¢ for each risky dollar of expected profit contribution from a Pasadena outlet, when less risky expected returns from a Fresno outlet "cost" only 75¢.

P14.15 **Certainty Equivalents.** Pier-4, Inc. is a rapidly growing chain of sea-food restaurants. The company has a limited amount of capital for expansion, and must carefully weigh available alternatives. Currently, the company is considering opening restaurants in Providence, Rhode Island and/or Glouchester, Massachusetts. Projections for the two potential outlets are:

City	Outcome	Annual Profit Contribution	Probability
Providence	Failure	$500,000	0.5
	Success	$750,000	0.5
Glouchester	Failure	$500,000	0.5
	Success	$1,000,000	0.5

Each restaurant would involve a capital expenditure of $2.5 million, and the company uses the 10% yield on riskless U.S. Treasury bills to calculate the risk-free annual opportunity cost of investment capital.

A. Calculate the expected value, standard deviation, and coefficient of variation for each outlet's profit contribution.

B. Calculate the minimum certainty equivalent adjustment factor for each restaurant's cash flows that would justify investment in each outlet.

P14.15 **SOLUTION**

A. <u>Providence</u>

$E(\pi_P) = \$500{,}000(0.5) + \$750{,}000(0.5) = \$625{,}000$

$\sigma_P = \sqrt{(\$500{,}000 - \$625{,}000)^2(0.5) + (\$750{,}000 - \$625{,}000)^2(0.5)}$

$= \$125{,}000$

$V_P = \sigma_P/E(\pi_P) = 0.2$

Glouchester

$$E(\pi_G) = \$500,000(0.5) + \$1,000,000(0.5) = \$750,000$$

$$\sigma_G = \sqrt{(\$500,000 - \$750,000)^2(0.5) + (\$1,000,000 - \$750,000)^2(0.5)}$$

$$= \$250,000$$

$$V_G = \sigma_G/E(\pi_G) = 0.\overline{3}$$

B. To justify each investment alternative, the company must have a certainty equivalent adjustment factor of at least $\alpha = 0.4$ for the Providence project and $\alpha = 0.\overline{3}$ for the Glouchester outlet since:

$$\alpha = \frac{\text{Certain Sum}}{\text{Expected Risky Sum}}$$

$$= \frac{\text{Certain Flow Foregone Per Year}}{\text{Annual Expected Profit Contribution}}$$

Providence

$$\alpha_P = \frac{0.1(\$2,500,000)}{\$625,000}$$

$$= 0.4$$

Glouchester

$$\alpha_G = \frac{0.1(\$2,500,000)}{\$750,000}$$

$$= 0.\overline{3}$$

In words, each risky dollar of expected profit contribution from the Providence outlet must be "worth" at least (valued as highly as) 40¢ in certain dollars to justify investment. For the Glouchester outlet, each risky dollar must be worth at least 33¢ in certain dollars.

P14.16 *Certainty Equivalents. Rajun Cajun's, Ltd. is a rapidly growing chain of cajun-style cuisine restaurants. The company has a limited amount of capital for expansion, and*

Risk Analysis

must carefully weigh available alternatives. Currently, the company is considering opening restaurants in Montgomery, Alabama and/or Pensacola Beach, Florida. Projections for the two potential outlets are:

City	Outcome	Annual Profit Contribution	Probability
Montgomery	Failure	$150,000	0.5
	Success	$350,000	0.5
Pensacola Beach	Failure	$200,000	0.5
	Success	$400,000	0.5

Each restaurant would involve a capital expenditure of $1.5 million, and the company uses the 10% yield on riskless U.S. Treasury bills to calculate the risk-free annual opportunity cost of investment capital.

A. Calculate the expected value, standard deviation, and coefficient of variation for each outlet's profit contribution.

B. Calculate the minimum certainty equivalent adjustment factor for each restaurant's cash flows that would justify investment in each outlet.

P14.16 SOLUTION

A. Montgomery

$E(\pi_M) = \$150,000(0.5) + \$350,000(0.5) = \$250,000$

$\sigma_M = \sqrt{(\$150,000 - \$250,000)^2(0.5) + (\$350,000 - \$250,000)^2(0.5)}$

$= \$100,000$

$V_M = \sigma_M/E(\pi_M) = 0.4$

Pensacola Beach

$$E(\pi_p) = \$200{,}000(0.5) + \$400{,}000(0.5) = \$300{,}000$$

$$\sigma_P = \sqrt{(\$200{,}000 - \$300{,}000)^2(0.5) + (\$400{,}000 - \$300{,}000)^2(0.5)}$$

$$= \$100{,}000$$

$$V_P = \sigma_P/E(\pi_p) = 0.3$$

B. To justify each investment alternative, the company must have a certainty equivalent adjustment factor of at least $\alpha = 0.6$ for the Montgomery outlet and $\alpha = 0.5$ for the Pensacola Beach outlet since:

$$\alpha = \frac{\text{Certain Sum}}{\text{Expected Risky Sum}}$$

$$= \frac{\text{Certain Flow Foregone Per Year}}{\text{Annual Expected Profit Contribution}}$$

Montgomery

$$\alpha_M = \frac{0.1(\$1{,}500{,}000)}{\$250{,}000}$$

$$= 0.6$$

Pensacola Beach

$$\alpha_P = \frac{0.1(\$1{,}500{,}000)}{\$300{,}000}$$

$$= 0.5$$

In words, each risky dollar of expected profit contribution from the Montgomery outlet must be "worth" at least (valued as highly as) 60¢ in certain dollars to justify investment. For the Pensacola Beach outlet, each risky dollar must be worth at least 50¢ in certain dollars.

P14.17 *Decision Trees.* Atlanta Corporation has been supplying Raleigh Manufacturing, Inc. with electronic control systems, and Raleigh is satisfied with their performance.

Risk Analysis

However, Raleigh has just received a competing bid from Brahmin, Inc., a firm that is aggressively marketing its products. Brahmin has offered to supply systems for a price of $237,500, or $12,500 below the $250,000 price for the Atlanta system. In addition to an attractive price, Brahmin offers a money-back guarantee. That is, if Brahmin's systems do not match Atlanta's quality, Raleigh can reject them and return them for a full refund. However, if it must reject the machines and return them to Brahmin, Raleigh will suffer a manufacturing delay costing the firm $50,000.

A. Construct a decision tree for this problem and determine the maximum probability Raleigh can assign to rejection of the Brahmin system before it would reject the offer, assuming it decides on the basis of minimizing expected costs.

B. Assume that Raleigh assigns a 40% probability of rejection of the Brahmin controls. Would Raleigh be willing to pay $5,000 for an assurance bond that would cover manufacturing delay costs if the Brahmin controls fail the quality check? (Use the same objective as in Part a above.) Explain.

P14.17 SOLUTION

A. The decision tree for this situation is as follows:

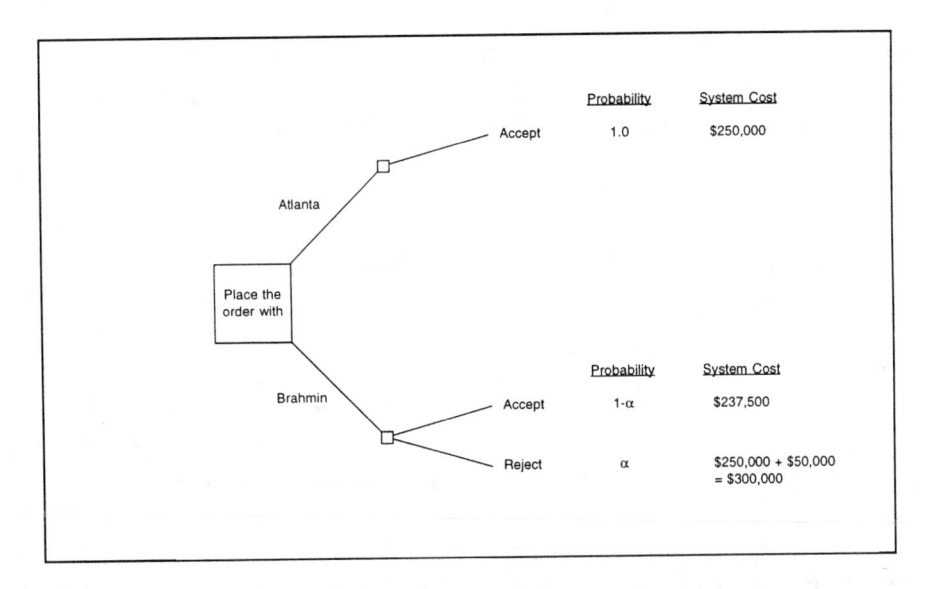

Place the order with	Outcome	Probability	System Cost
Atlanta	Accept	1.0	$250,000
Brahmin	Accept	$1-\alpha$	$237,500
Brahmin	Reject	α	$250,000 + $50,000 = $300,000

The maximum probability of rejection that could be assigned to the Brahmin control system is the probability that makes the expected cost equal for the two alternatives.

$$\text{Expected Brahmin Cost} = \text{Atlanta Cost}$$

$$(1 - \alpha)\$237{,}500 + \alpha(\$300{,}000) = \$250{,}000$$

$$\$237{,}500 - \$237{,}500\alpha + \$300{,}000\alpha = \$250{,}000$$

$$\$62{,}500\alpha = \$12{,}500$$

$$\alpha = 0.2$$

If there is greater than 20% probability of Brahmin's control systems failing to pass the quality control inspection, then Raleigh would choose the bid from Atlanta.

B. Yes. Solution of this problem requires comparing the lower cost alternatives with and without the insurance policy. Without the assurance bond, expected costs are:

$$E(C_A) = \$250{,}000$$

$$E(C_B) = 0.6(\$237{,}500) + 0.4(\$300{,}000) = \$262{,}500$$

Without the assurance bond, purchasing from Atlanta has the lower expected cost. If the bond is purchased, only the expected cost of purchase from Brahmin changes. This expected cost would now be calculated as:

$$E(C_B) = \$5{,}000 + 0.6(\$237{,}500) + 0.4(\$250{,}000) = \$247{,}500$$

Thus, we see that ordering the control from Brahmin with the assurance bond has the lower expected cost.

P14.18 **Decision Trees.** Arnie Becker, an attorney with Dewey, Cheetum & Howe in Los Angeles, California, must serve a subpoena to an individual in New York, New York by 10:00 a.m. tomorrow morning. If the subpoena is delivered late, Becker stands to lose $5,000 in fees. The subpoena can be delivered by mail at a cost of $25, or by courier at a cost of $225. Based on passed experience, Becker assigns a 99% change of on-time delivery using the courier service. Since Express Mail is a relatively new service, Becker does not know the probability of on-time delivery using this service.

A. Construct a decision tree for this problem and calculate the minimum probability of on-time delivery for Express Mail that would make Becker indifferent to the two delivery services.

Risk Analysis

P14.18   SOLUTION

A.   The decision tree for this problem is as follows:

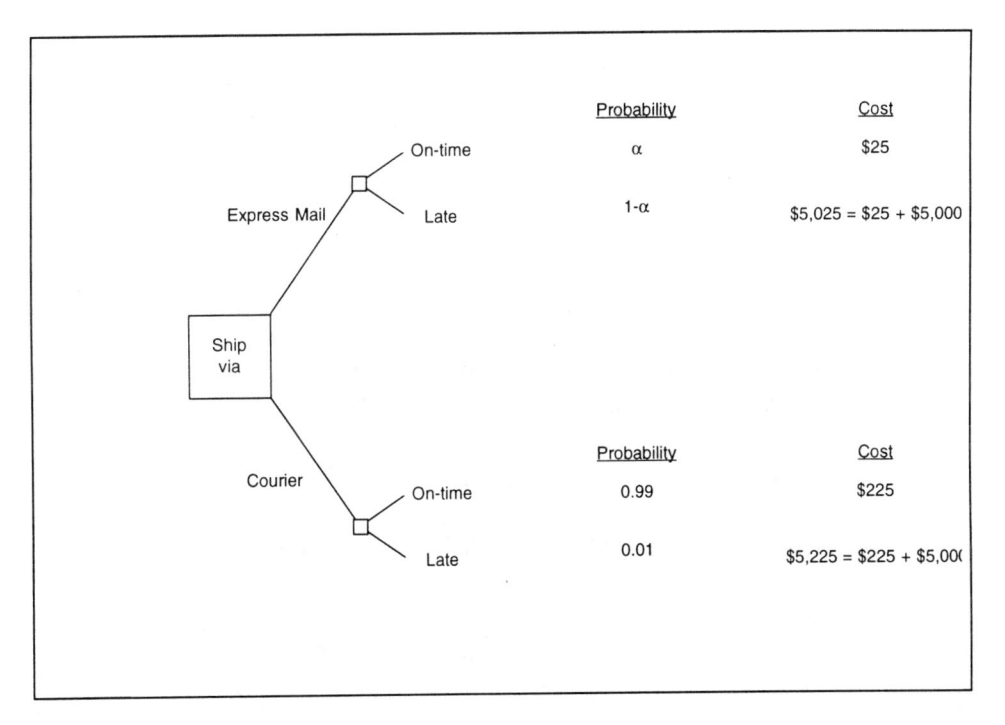

```
                                          Probability          Cost

                        On-time              α                 $25
          Express Mail
                        Late                 1-α               $5,025 = $25 + $5,000

    Ship
    via

          Courier                         Probability          Cost

                        On-time              0.99              $225

                        Late                 0.01              $5,225 = $225 + $5,000
```

The minimum acceptable probability of on-time arrival by Express Mail is the probability that makes the expected cost equal for the two alternatives.

$$EC(\text{Express Mail}) = EC(\text{Courier})$$

$$\$25\alpha + \$5{,}025(1-\alpha) = \$225(0.99) + \$5{,}225(0.01)$$

$$\$25\alpha + \$5{,}025 - \$5{,}025\alpha = \$275$$

$$\$5{,}000\alpha = \$4{,}750$$

$$\alpha = 0.95$$

Therefore, a 95% probability of on-time delivery using Express Mail would make Becker indifferent between that and the courier service. If there is greater than 95% probability of on-time delivery by Express Mail, then Becker would use the Express Mail delivery service.

P14.19 **Standard Normal.** *A leading company in the freight forwarding business offers Overnight Letter delivery service with a record of on-time delivery for 99% of shipped parcels. The price of this service is $15. Express Mail, offered by a leading competitor for $10, has an on-time delivery record of 95%.*

A. *Calculate the cost incurred due to late delivery that would make shippers indifferent to these deliver service alternatives.*

B. *Which delivery alternative is preferred if a $100 cost would be incurred due to late delivery?*

P14.19 **SOLUTION**

A. Shippers will be indifferent to the delivery alternatives if the expected cost is equal for the two alternatives:

$$EC(\text{Overnight Letter}) = EC(\text{Express Mail})$$

$$0.99(\$15) + 0.01(\$15 + X) = 0.95(\$10) + 0.05(\$10 + X)$$

$$\$14.85 + \$0.15 + 0.01X = \$9.50 + 0.50 + 0.05X$$

$$0.04X = 5$$

$$X = \$125$$

Thus, a cost incurred due to late delivery of $125 would make shippers indifferent to the two delivery alternatives.

B. Express Mail. Given a cost due to late delivery of only $100, the Express Mail service would be preferred given its lower expected cost:

$$EC(\text{Overnight Letter}) = 0.99(\$15) + 0.01(\$15 + \$100) = \$16$$

$$EC(\text{Express Mail}) = 0.95(\$10) + 0.05(\$10 + \$100) = \$15$$

P14.20 **Standard Normal.** *Personal Business Cards, Inc. supplies customized business cards to commercial and individual customers. While paper, ink, and other costs cannot be determined precisely, Personal anticipates that costs will be normally distributed around a mean of $15 per unit (each 500-card order) with a standard deviation of $2 per unit.*

Risk Analysis

A. What is the probability that Personal would make a profit at a price of $15 per unit?

B. Calculate the unit price necessary to give Personal a 95% chance of making a profit on the order.

C. If Personal submits a successful bid of $18.20 per unit, what is the probability that it will make a profit?

P14.20 SOLUTION

A. If printing costs are normally distributed around a mean of $15 per unit, there is a 50/50 or 50% chance that actual costs will be above or below that amount. This means that there is a 50-50 or 50% chance that revenues will exceed costs and, therefore, that Personal will make a profit at a price of $15.

B. In order to have a 95% chance of making a profit, 95% of the area under the normal curve describing the distribution of costs per unit must lie to the left of price. Graphically,

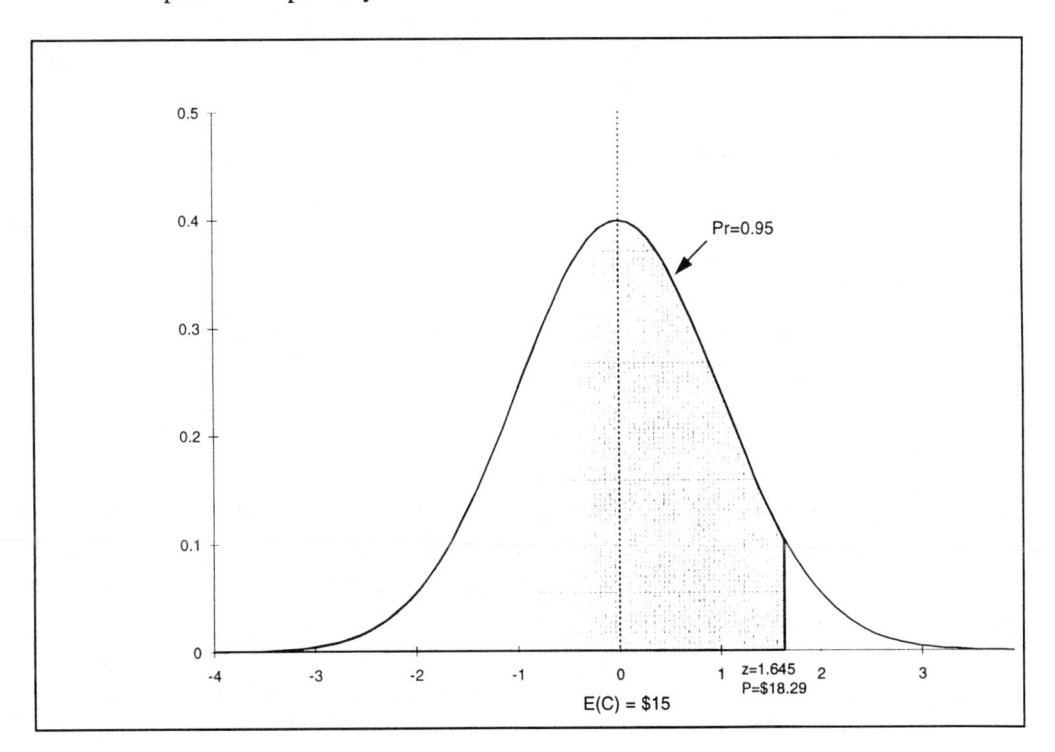

Using the formula for the standardized normal, this occurs at a z-value of 1.645. This implies a price of $18.29 since:

$$z = \frac{x - u}{\sigma}$$

$$1.645 = \frac{P - \$15}{\$2}$$

$$\$3.29 = P - \$15$$

$$P = \$18.29$$

C. With a price of $18.20, Personal's winning bid is 1.6(=$3.20/$2) standard deviations higher than expected costs. From the normal distribution, there is a 0.5 + 0.4452 = 94.42% probability that Personal will be able to make a profit at a price of $18.20 per unit.

P14.21 **Standard Normal.** Chips Technologies, Inc. supplies DRAM computer chips to industrial customers. While labor and material costs cannot be determined precisely, CTI anticipates that costs will be normally distributed around a mean of $3 per unit with a standard deviation of 20¢ per unit.

A. What is the probability that CTI would make a profit at a price of $3 per unit?

B. Calculate the unit price necessary to give CTI a 95% chance of making a profit on the order.

C. If CTI signs a contract to supply chips at a price of $3.20 per unit, what is the probability that it will make a profit?

P14.21 **SOLUTION**

A. If printing costs are normally distributed around a mean of $3 per unit, there is a 50/50 or 50% chance that actual costs will be above or below that amount. This means that there is a 50-50 or 50% chance that revenues will exceed costs and, therefore, that CTI will make a profit at a price of $3.

B. In order to have a 95% chance of making a profit, 95% of the area under the normal curve describing the distribution of costs per unit must lie to the left of price. Graphically,

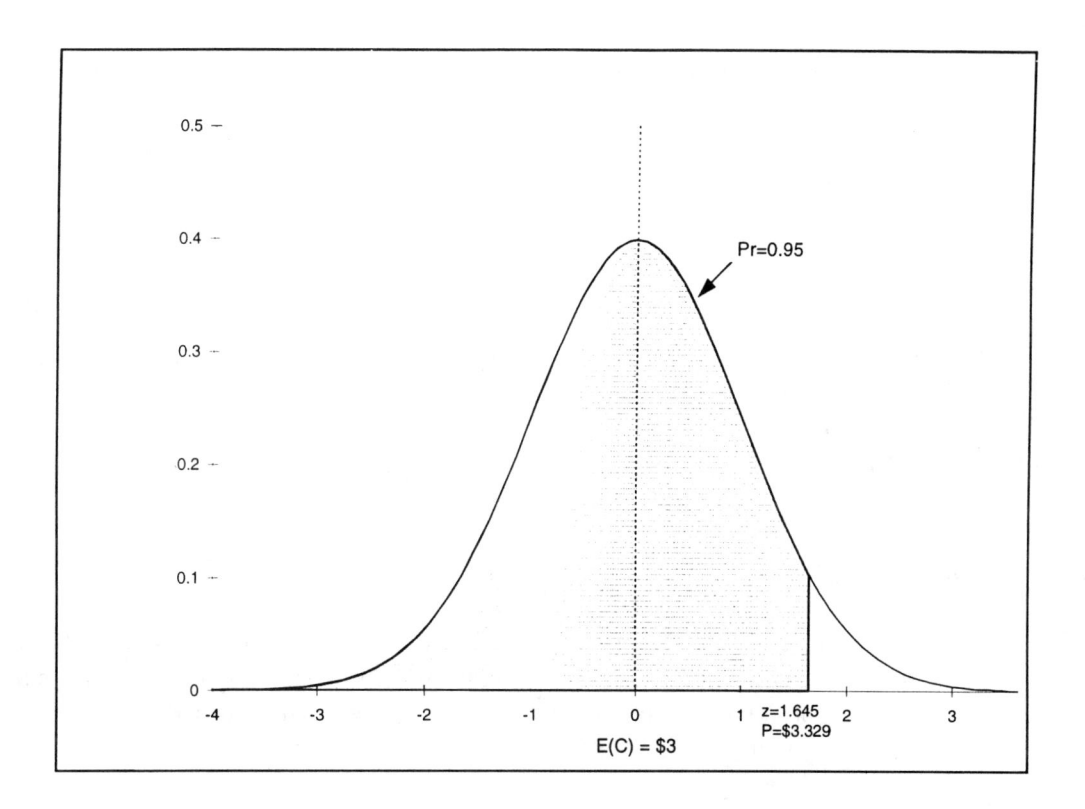

Using the formula for the standardized normal, this occurs at a z-value of 1.645. This implies a price of $3.329 since:

$$z = \frac{x - u}{\sigma}$$

$$1.645 = \frac{P - \$3}{\$0.20}$$

$$\$0.329 = P - \$3$$

$$P = \$3.329$$

C. With a price of $3.20, CTI's winning bid is only 1.0(=$0.20/$0.20) standard deviations higher than expected cost. From the normal distribution, there is a 0.5 + 0.3413 = 84.13% probability that CTI will be able to make a profit at a price of $3.20 per unit.

P14.22 **Standard Normal.** University Savings, Inc offers personal checking accounts to commercial and individual customers. While unit costs cannot be determined precisely, University anticipates that monthly costs will be normally distributed around a mean of $5 per unit with a standard deviation of $1 per unit.

    A. What is the probability that University would make a profit at a checking price of $5 per unit?

    B. Calculate the unit price necessary to give University a 90% chance of making a profit on an individual checking account.

    C. If University offers its accounts at a price of $6, what is the probability that it will make a profit?

P14.22 SOLUTION

    A. If costs are normally distributed around a mean of $5 per unit, there is a 50/50 or 50% chance that actual costs will be above or below that amount. This means that there is a 50-50 or 50% chance that revenues will exceed costs and, therefore, that University will make a profit at a price of $5 per month.

    B. In order to have a 90% chance of making a profit, 90% of the area under the normal curve describing the distribution of costs per unit must lie to the left of price. Graphically,

Risk Analysis

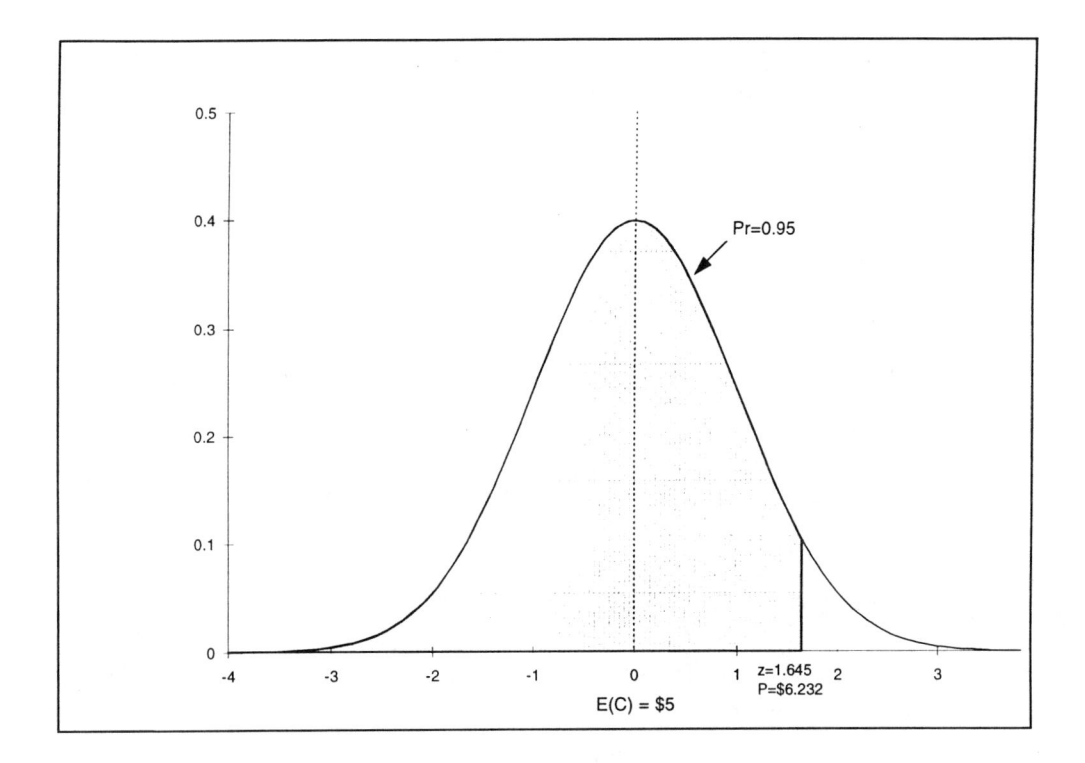

[Graph: Normal distribution curve with E(C) = $5, showing Pr=0.95 at z=1.645, P=$6.232]

Using the formula for the standardized normal, this occurs at a z-value of 1.232. This implies a price of $6.232 since:

$$z = \frac{x - u}{\sigma}$$

$$1.232 = \frac{P - \$5}{\$1}$$

$$\$1.232 = P - \$5$$

$$P = \$6.232$$

C. With a price of $6, University's price is one standard deviation higher than expected cost. From the normal distribution, there is a 0.5 + 0.3413 = 84.13% probability that University will be able to make a profit at a price of $6 per unit.

P14.23 **Game Theory.** Catskill Mountain Bike, Inc. is a producer and wholesaler of rugged bicycles designed for mountain touring. The company is considering upgrading its current line by making standard high-grade chromalloy frames. Of course, the market response to this upgrade in product quality would depend on the competitor response, if any. The company's comptroller projects the following annual profits (payoffs) following resolution of the upgrade decision.

	States of Nature	
Catskill's Decision Alternatives	Competitor Upgrade	No Competitor Upgrade
Upgrade	$2,500,000	$3,500,000
Don't upgrade	$1,500,000	$5,000,000

A. Which decision alternative would Catskill choose given a maximin criterion? Explain.

B. Calculate the opportunity loss or regret matrix.

C. Which decision alternative would Catskill choose given a minimax regret criterion? Explain.

P14.23   SOLUTION

A. The maximin decision strategy is to choose the decision alternative with the "best" worst outcome in order to avoid even the possibility of the worst state of nature being encountered. In this problem, the no upgrade decision involves the possibility of a $1,500,000 payoff under the worse case scenario. This worse case outcome can be avoided with an upgrade decision, the maximin strategy.

B. The opportunity loss or regret matrix is:

Decision Alternatives	1. Competitor Upgrade	2. No Competitor Upgrade
A. Upgrade Decision	$0 (=$2,500,000 -$2,500,000)	$1,500,000 (=$5,000,000 -$3,500,000)
B. No Upgrade Decision	$1,000,000 (=$2,500,000 -$1,500,000)	$0 (=$5,000,000 -$5,000,000)

Risk Analysis 585

C. The minimax decision strategy is to choose the decision alternative that will minimize the maximum opportunity loss or regret. In this problem, the maximum possible regret of $1,500,000 is associated with the upgrade decision. This maximum possible regret can be avoided by choosing the no upgrade decision, the minimax strategy.

P14.24   *Game Theory.* Jessica's, a local retailer of women's clothing is considering adoption of new Sunday hours between 12:00 noon and 6:00 PM. Jessica's is closed on Sundays. Of course, the consumer response to this extension in hours depends on the competitor response, if any. The following annual profit contributions (payoffs) are expected:

| | States of Nature ||
Jessica's Decision Alternatives	Competitor Open	Competitor Closed
Open Sundays	$75,000	$100,000
Closed Sundays	$50,000	$150,000

A. Which decision alternative would Jessica's choose given a maximin criterion? Explain.

B. Calculate the opportunity loss or regret matrix.

C. Which decision alternative would Jessica's choose given a minimax regret criterion? Explain.

P14.24   **SOLUTION**

A. The maximin decision strategy is to choose the decision alternative with the "best" worst outcome in order to avoid even the possibility of the worst state of nature being encountered. In this problem, the "Closed" decision involves the possibility of a $50,000 payoff under the worse case scenario. This worse case outcome can be avoided with an "Open" decision, the maximin strategy.

B. The opportunity loss or regret matrix is:

Decision Alternatives	1. Competitor Upgrade	2. No Competitor Upgrade
A. Open Sundays	$0	$50,000
	(=$75,000-$75,000)	(=$150,000-$100,000)
B. Closed Sundays	$25,000	$0
	(=$75,000-$50,000)	(=$150,000-$150,000)

C. The minimax decision strategy is to choose the decision alternative that will minimize the maximum opportunity loss or regret. In this problem, the maximum possible regret of $50,000 is associated with the "Open" decision. This maximum possible regret can be avoided by choosing the "Closed" decision, the minimax strategy.

P14.25 **Game Theory.** F&M Manufacturing, Inc., a diversified manufacturer of packaging products, is considering upgrading its current line by making available a new line of coated paper products. Of course, the market response to this upgrade in product quality would depend on the competitor response, if any. The company's comptroller projects the following annual profits (payoffs) following resolution of the upgrade decision.

F&M's Decision Alternatives	States of Nature Competitor Upgrade	No Competitor Upgrade
Upgrade	$5 million	$7.5 million
Don't upgrade	$4 million	$8 million

A. Which decision alternative would F&M choose given a maximin criterion? Explain.

B. Calculate the opportunity loss or regret matrix.

C. Which decision alternative would F&M choose given a minimax regret criterion? Explain.

Risk Analysis

P14.25 SOLUTION

A. The maximin decision strategy is to choose the decision alternative with the "best" worst outcome in order to avoid even the possibility of the worst state of nature being encountered. In this problem, the no upgrade decision involves the possibility of a $4 million payoff under the worse case scenario. This worse case outcome can be avoided with an upgrade decision, the maximin strategy.

B. The opportunity loss or regret matrix is:

Decision Alternatives	1. Competitor Upgrade	2. No Competitor Upgrade
A. Upgrade Decision	$0 (=$5,000,000 -$5,000,000)	$500,000 (=$8,000,000 -$7,500,000)
B. No Upgrade Decision	$1,000,000 (=$5,000,000 -$4,000,000)	$0 (=$8,000,000 -$8,000,000)

C. The minimax decision strategy is to choose the decision alternative that will minimize the maximum opportunity loss or regret. In this problem, the maximum possible regret of $1 million is associated with the no upgrade decision. This maximum possible regret can be avoided by choosing the upgrade decision, the minimax strategy.

Chapter 15

CAPITAL BUDGETING

MULTIPLE CHOICE QUESTIONS

Q15.1   The crossover discount rate only equates the:

    A.   NPV for two or more investments.
    B.   IRR for two or more investments.
    C.   present value payback period for two or more investments.
>   **D.**   all of these.

Q15.2   When NPV is positive, the IRR:

    A.   is less than the cost of capital.
    B.   equals the cost of capital.
>   **C.**   exceeds the cost of capital.
    D.   none of these.

Q15.3   The risk-free rate of return is the investor reward for:

    A.   risk-taking.
>   **B.**   postponing consumption.
    C.   relative stock-price variability.
    D.   absolute stock-price variability.

Q15.4   The cost of capital is the:

    A.   component cost of debt.
    B.   component cost of equity.
    C.   both a and b.
>   **D.**   discount rate.

Q15.5   The beta coefficient is:

>   **A.**   a relative measure of stock-price variability.
    B.   an absolute measure of stock-price variability.
    C.   equal to the standard deviation divided by covariance.
    D.   none of these.

Capital Budgeting

Q15.6 The cost of capital is:

- A. the marginal cost of a dollar of equity financing.
- B. the marginal cost of a dollar of debt financing.
- > C. the marginal cost of a composite dollar of debt and equity financing.
- D. none of these.

Q15.7 Holding all else equal, the profitability index will fall following an increase in the:

- > A. cost of capital.
- B. benefit-cost ratio.
- C. IRR.
- D. NPV.

Q15.8 The discount rate that equates present value of cash inflows and outflows is called the:

- A. component cost of capital.
- B. weighted average cost of capital.
- C. after-tax weighted average cost of capital.
- > D. IRR.

Q15.9 Acceptance of investment projects where IRR > MCC:

- > A. will increase the value of the firm.
- B. will decrease the value of the firm.
- C. have no impact on the value of the firm.
- D. none of these.

Q15.10 Acceptance of new investment projects will increase the value of the firm provided that:

- A. IRR > ROE.
- B. ROE < IRR.
- C. ROE = IRR.
- > D. none of these.

Q15.11 The change in net cash flows due to an investment project is called:

- A. marginal profit.
- B. marginal revenue.
- > C. incremental cash flow.
- D. marginal cash flow.

Q15.12 Examples of mandatory nonrevenue-producing investments are provided by:

- A. cost reduction projects.
- B. expansion projects.
- C. replacement projects.
- > D. safety and environmental projects.

Q15.13 Net present value is the:

- > A. current-dollar difference between marginal revenues and marginal costs.
- B. change in net cash flows due to an investment project.
- C. change in before-tax cash flows due to an investment project.
- D. change in net after-tax cash flows due to an investment project.

Q15.14 The profitability index is:

- > A. a benefit-cost ratio.
- B. the number of years required to recover an initial investment.
- C. the discount rate that equates the present value of cash inflows and outflows.
- D. a discount rate.

Q15.15 Capital budgeting is the process of planning investment expenditures when returns are expected to:

- A. be earned at any time in the future.
- B. be earned within one year.
- C. extend beyond one generation.
- > D. extend beyond one year.

Capital Budgeting

Q15.16 Firms should budget capital for investments when their internal rates of return are:

- A. equal to the average cost of capital.
- > B. greater than the marginal cost of capital.
- C. positive.
- D. negative.

Q15.17 When net present value equals zero:

- > A. the internal rate of return equals the cost of capital.
- B. the internal rate of return exceeds the cost of capital.
- C. the internal rate of return is less than the cost of capital.
- D. the internal rate of return equals zero.

Q15.18 The most difficult step in capital expenditure analysis is estimating:

- A. the internal rate of return.
- B. the cost of capital.
- C. the cost of investment.
- > D. project cash flows.

Q15.19 Cash flows should include depreciation:

- > A. to account for taxes effects.
- B. as a cash expense.
- C. if accelerated depreciation is chosen.
- D. to reduce projected cash flows.

Q15.20 Net present value equals:

- A. $\sum_{t=1}^{N} \dfrac{\text{Net cash flow}}{(1+i)^t}$
- > B. $\sum_{t=1}^{N} \dfrac{E(CF_{it})}{(1+k_i)^t} - C_i$
- C. $\sum_{t=1}^{N} \dfrac{E(CF_{it})}{(1+k_i)^t}$
- D. $\sum_{t=1}^{N} \dfrac{E(CF_{it})}{(1+i)^t} - C_i$

Q15.21 The internal rate of return can be calculated by solving for k_i after setting net present value equal to:

> A. zero.
> B. the initial investment cost or outlay.
> C. the cost of capital.
> D. expected cash flows.

Q15.22 Firms should finance a project if its:

> A. expected cash flow is positive.
> B. net cash flow is positive.
> C. internal rate of return is positive.
> D. net present value is positive.

Q15.23 Firms should finance a project if its profitability index is:

> A. equal to zero.
> B. greater than one.
> C. less than one.
> D. greater than the cost of capital.

Q15.24 A firm must choose between two projects, X and Y. Project X has the highest net present value, but project Y has the highest profitability index. The firm should choose project Y if:

> A. the firm is a risk seeker.
> B. the firm is risk averse.
> C. the firm has substantial investment resources.
> D. the firm has limited investment resources.

Q15.25 The first step in most capital budgeting decisions is:

> A. estimating future demand.
> B. determining the operating cost function.
> C. estimating the cost of capital.
> D. determining the optimal level of output and the expected annual cash flows resulting from operation at this level.

Capital Budgeting

Q15.26 If the tax rate is 25% and the prevailing interest rate is 12%, the after tax cost of debt is:

    A.   3%.
> B.   9%.
    C.   16%.
    D.   37%.

Q15.27 The beta coefficient is:

    A.   the rate of return on the market or average stock.
> B.   the index of risk for a particular stock.
    C.   the weighted cost of capital.
    D.   the risk premium on the average stock.

Q15.28 Generally, a firm's estimated component cost of debt:

    A.   accurately estimates the firm's true opportunity cost of debt.
    B.   equals the firm's weighted cost of capital.
> C.   underestimates the firm's true opportunity cost of debt.
    D.   overestimates the firm's true opportunity cost of debt.

Q15.29 An estimate of the firm's cost of equity capital is:

    A.   the market return on common stocks.
    B.   the market return on common stocks multiplied by beta, the firm's risk index.
> C.   expected dividend yield plus projected growth.
    D.   expected dividend yield.

Q15.30 The Pattern of returns for all potential investment projects is the:

> A.   investment opportunity schedule.
    B.   marginal cost of capital.
    C.   optimal capital budget.
    D.   optimal capital structure.

PROBLEMS & SOLUTIONS

P15.1 ***Cost of Capital.*** *Indicate whether each of the following statements is true or false. Explain why.*

    A. In practice, the component costs of debt and equity are independently, determined.

    B. The marginal cost of capital will be more elastic for larger as opposed to smaller firms.

    C. Information costs both increase the marginal cost of capital and reduce the internal rate of return on investment projects.

    D. Investments necessary to replace worn-out or damaged equipment tend to have high levels of risk.

    E. Depreciation expenses, which involve no direct cash outlay, must be incorporated in investment project evaluation.

P15.1 SOLUTION

    A. False. The component costs of debt and equity tend to be jointly as opposed to independently determined. Higher levels of debt, for example, will usually increase the perceived level of risk for debt holders and equity holders alike, and therefore raise the interest rate charged by creditors and the rate of return requirement of stockholders.

    B. True. The marginal cost of capital will tend to be more elastic for larger as opposed to smaller firms. Large firms tend to have easy access to capital markets given their relatively long operating history, and substantial human and other resources. On the other hand, the marginal cost of capital can tend to increase rapidly (be quite inelastic) for smaller firms that, for example, face capital constraints due to scarce managerial talent.

    C. True. The need to gather information concerning the creditworthiness of borrowers increases the interest rates charged by creditors. Similarly, the task of information gathering in the investment project evaluation process reduces the IRR from those projects.

    D. False. Investments necessary to replace worn out or damaged equipment have highly predictable returns and low levels of risk.

Capital Budgeting

      E.   True. Even though depreciation expenses involve no direct cash outlay, they must be explicitly considered in investment project evaluation because they affect corporate cash outlays for income tax payments.

P15.2   *NPV Analysis.* The net present value (NPV), profitability index (PI), and internal rate of return (IRR) methods are often employed in project valuation. Indicate whether each of the following statements is true or false and explain why.

      A.   A PI < 1 describes a project with IRR < k.

      B.   Selection solely according to the PI criterion will tend to favor smaller as opposed to larger investment projects.

      C.   Use of the NPV criterion is especially appropriate for larger firms with easy access to capital markets.

      D.   The IRR method can tend to overstate the relative attractiveness of investment projects when the opportunity cost of cash flows is below the IRR.

      E.   When NPV > 0, the IRR exceeds the cost of capital.

P15.2   **SOLUTION**

      A.   True. The PI = PV Cash Flows/Cost, and the IRR is the interest rate that equates the PV of cash flows with the investment cost of a project. Therefore, when PV Cash Flows < Cost, PI < 1 and IRR < k., where k is the cost of capital.

      B.   True. Selection according to the PI criterion will tend to favor smaller as opposed to larger investment projects so as to maximize the return per dollar invested.

      C.   True. Larger firms with easy access to capital markets will maximize the value of the firm through the capital budgeting process by selecting projects according to the NPV criterion. Smaller firms, that face capital budget constraints forcing rejection of some NPV > 0 projects, can best employ scarce capital through use of the PI criterion.

      D.   True. The IRR method, which implicitly assumes reinvestment of net cash flows during the life of the project at the IRR, will overstate the relative attractiveness of superior investment projects when the opportunity cost of cash flows is below the IRR. For example, if a project has a projected IRR = 22%, but cash flows "thrown off" during the life of the project can only be reinvested at, say, 15%, then the true project IRR will be less than 22% and the relative attractiveness of the project will be overstated using the IRR method.

E. True. The IRR is the interest rate that equates the PV cash flows with the investment cost of a project. NPV = PV cash flows with the investment cost of a project. NPV = PV Cash Flows - Cost, when cash flows are discounted at an appropriate risk-adjusted cost of capital, k. Therefore, when IRR > k, NPV > 0.

P15.3 **Cost of Capital.** Determine whether each of the following would increase or decrease the firm's cost of capital for investment project evaluation. Explain.

A. The company's stock price suffers a sharp decline, but no decline in the company's earnings potential is perceived.

B. A merger with a leading competitor increases the company's stock price substantially.

C. The company's home state increases the corporate state income tax.

D. In an effort to spur business activity, Congress cuts corporate income taxes.

P15.3 **SOLUTION**

A. Increase. As stock prices fall, the required return per dollar of equity capital will rise. This will force upward the weighted average cost of capital used in investment project evaluation.

B. Decrease. Holding all else equal, an increase in the stock price for a company will reduce the component cost of equity and the weighted average cost of capital.

C. Increase. As state corporate income taxes rise, the after-tax component cost of debt will fall and decrease the relative attractiveness of equity financing. The firm's weighted average cost of capital will rise, however, as the after-tax returns available to debt plus equity holders will decrease from a given stream of cash flows, and cause aggregate bond and stock prices to fall.

Of course, average state tax rates are fairly modest compared with federal tax rates, and the effect of changing state tax rates on the weighted average cost of capital can be expected to be similarly modest. Still, on balance and holding all else equal, we would expect the weighted average cost of capital to be marginally less for firms headquartered in Florida (a no income tax state) versus Wisconsin (a relatively high income tax state).

Capital Budgeting

D. Decrease. As federal corporate income tax rates fall, the after-tax returns available to debt plus equity holders will rise, and the weighted average cost of capital will decrease. On a relative basis, debt will become less preferred to equity financing. (Also see part C answer.)

P15.4 **Rate-of-Return Analysis.** New York City licenses taxicabs in two classes: (1) for operation by companies with fleets, and (2) for operation by independent driver-owners who have only one cab. It also fixes the rates that taxis charge. For many years, no new licenses have been issued in either class. In the unofficial market for licenses (medallions), their market value is currently more than $100,000.

A. Does the $100,000 medallion price indicate that operators of New York taxicabs are earning only normal profits?

B. What factors would determine whether a change in the fare fixed by the city would raise or lower the value of a license?

C. Cab drivers, whether hired by companies or as owners of their own cabs, seem unanimous in opposing any increase in the number of cabs licensed. They argue that an increase in the number of cabs would increase competition for customers, and drive down what they regard as an already unduly low return to drivers. Is their economic analysis correct? Who would benefit and who would lose from an expansion in the number of licenses issued at a nominal fee?

P15.4 SOLUTION

A. No, the price of a medallion will be determined by the above-normal or economic profits that can be obtained in the taxicab industry. More precisely, the price of a medallion will equal the discounted present value of all future profits over and above those necessary to attract and maintain the capital necessary to operate in the industry. For example, if one expected the current licensing arrangements to continue in perpetuity, and if opportunity costs for investments of this type were 10%, then the $100,000 medallion price indicates an expected economic profit of $10,000 (= 0.1 × $100,000) per year.

B. The primary determining factor would be the elasticity of demand. With an inelastic demand for cab service, fare increases lead to higher profits, and, hence, higher medallion prices. Fare reductions, on the other hand, would reduce the value of a medallion. With elastic demand, one would have to examine both the added revenues and costs associated with fare reductions (or revenue losses and cost reductions associated with fare increases) in order to answer this question.

C. The $100,000 price of a medallion is a tangible indicator that excess or economic profits exist in the industry. It is impossible for the return to be "unduly low" with such a premium being offered for the license to operate. The obvious losers from an expansion of licenses at a nominal cost would be the holders of current medallions. They would lose the $100,000 current value of their medallions. The purchasers of cab services and potential entrants into the industry would both benefit. Customers would benefit through more service at lower fares. New entrants would benefit through lower capital costs and generally easier entry.

P15.5 *NPV Analysis.* The Santa Catalina Passenger Ferry Company is contemplating leasing an additional ferryboat to expand service to Santa Monica or Newport Beach. Financial analysis resulted in the following projections for a five-year planning horizon:

	Santa Monica	Newport Beach
Cost	$300,000	$200,000
PV of expected cash flow @k = 15%	$375,000	$270,000

A. Calculate the net present value for each service. Which is more desirable according to the NPV criterion?

B. Calculate the profitability index for each service. Which is more desirable according to the PI criterion?

C. Under what conditions would either or both of the services be undertaken?

P15.5 SOLUTION

A.

Santa Monica

NPV_{SM} = PV Cash Flow - Cost

= $375,000 - $300,000

= $75,000

Capital Budgeting

Newport Beach

$$NPV_{NB} = \text{PV Cash Flow - Cost}$$

$$= \$270{,}000 - \$200{,}000$$

$$= \$70{,}000$$

Since $NPV_{SM} > NPV_{NB}$ the Santa Monica service would be ranked ahead of the Newport Beach alternative, using the NPV criterion. However, since NPV > 0 for each service, both are acceptable and would be profitable.

B.

Santa Monica

$$PI_{SM} = \frac{\text{PV Cash Flow}}{\text{Cost}}$$

$$= \$375{,}000/\$300{,}000$$

$$= 1.25$$

Newport Beach

$$PI_{NB} = \text{PV Cash Flow - Cost}$$

$$= \$270{,}000/\$200{,}000$$

$$= 1.35$$

Since $PI_{NB} > PI_{SM}$, the Newport Beach service would be ranked ahead of the Santa Monica alternative using the PI criterion. However, since PI > 1 for each service, both are acceptable and would be profitable.

C. Should the company have relatively abundant capital resources, or at least $500,000 available for investment, both services would be initiated. However, when capital resources are scarce, use of the PI criterion, and initiation of the Newport Beach service first, would result in scarce funds being used where their relative impact on value is greatest.

P15.6 **NPV Analysis.** Nocando, Ltd. is contemplating leasing additional retail space to expand its distribution network in northeastern markets. Financial analysis resulted in the following projections for a five-year planning horizon:

	Stand-Alone Stores	*Shopping Mall Outlets*
Cost	$2 million	$5 million
PV of expected cash flow @k = 12%	$2.5 million	$6 million

A. Calculate the net present value for each type of retail space. Which is more desirable according to the NPV criterion?

B. Calculate the profitability index for each. Which is more desirable according to the PI criterion?

C. Under what conditions would either or both of the leasing options be undertaken?

P15.6 **SOLUTION**

A.

Stand-Alone

NPV_S = PV Cash Flow - Cost

= $2,500,000 - $2,000,000

= $500,000

Mall Outlets

NPV_M = PV Cash Flow - Cost

= $6,000,000 - $5,000,000

= $1,000,000

Since $NPV_M > NPV_S$ the Mall outlets would be ranked ahead of the Stand-Alone stores alternative, using the NPV criterion. However, since NPV > 0 for each, both are acceptable and would be profitable.

B.

Stand-Alone

$$PI_S = \frac{PV\ Cash\ Flow}{Cost}$$

$$= \$2{,}500{,}000/\$2{,}000{,}00$$

$$= 1.25$$

Mall Outlets

$$PI_M = PV\ Cash\ Flow - Cost$$

$$= \$6{,}000{,}000/\$5{,}000{,}000$$

$$= 1.2$$

Since $PI_S > PI_M$, the Stand-Alone stores would be ranked ahead of the Mall Outlets alternative using the PI criterion. However, since PI > 1 for each service, both are acceptable and would be profitable.

C. Should the company have relatively abundant capital resources, or at least $7 million available for investment, both services would be initiated. However, when capital resources are scarce, use of the PI criterion, and initiation of the Stand-Alone stores first, would result in scarce funds being used where their relative impact on value is greatest.

P15.7 *NPV Analysis. Travel Services, Inc., is contemplating purchase of a number of seats on regularly scheduled airlines for resale to leisure and business customers. The company projects the following costs and revenues for each type of service:*

	Leisure	Business
Cost	$200,000	$75,000
PV of expected cash flow	$250,000	$100,000

A. Calculate the net present value for each service. Which is more desirable according to the NPV criterion?

B. Calculate the profitability index for each service. Which is more desirable according to the PI criterion?

C. Under what conditions would either or both of the services be undertaken?

P15.7 SOLUTION

A.

Leisure

$$NPV_L = PV\ Cash\ Flow - Cost$$

$$= \$250,000 - \$200,000$$

$$= \$50,000$$

Business

$$NPV_B = PV\ Cash\ Flow - Cost$$

$$= \$100,000 - \$75,000$$

$$= \$25,000$$

Since $NPV_L > NPV_B$ the Leisure travel service would be ranked ahead of the business travel service alternative, using the NPV criterion. However, since NPV > 0 for each service, both are acceptable and would be profitable.

B.

Leisure

$$PI_L = \frac{PV\ Cash\ Flow}{Cost}$$

$$= \$250,000/\$200,000$$

$$= 1.25$$

<u>Business</u>

$$PI_B = \text{PV Cash Flow} - \text{Cost}$$

$$= \$100,000/\$75,000$$

$$= 1.33$$

Since $PI_B > PI_L$, the business travel service would be ranked ahead of the leisure travel alternative using the PI criterion. However, since PI > 1 for each service, both are acceptable and would be profitable.

C. Should the company have relatively abundant capital resources, or at least $275,000 available for investment, both services would be initiated. However, when capital resources are scarce, use of the PI criterion, and initiation of the business travel service first, would result in scarce funds being used where their relative impact on value is greatest.

P15.8 *NPV Analysis.* Computer-aided Manufacturing, Inc., is contemplating purchase of additional computer hardware equipment and software programming. Financial analysis resulted in the following projections for a three-year planning horizon:

	Hardware	Software
Cost	$500,000	$200,000
PV of expected cash flow @k = 20%	$750,000	$500,000

A. Calculate the net present value for each. Which is more desirable according to the NPV criterion?

B. Calculate the profitability index for each. Which is more desirable according to the PI criterion?

C. Under what conditions would either or both investments be undertaken?

P15.8   **SOLUTION**

A.

<u>Hardware</u>

$$NPV_H = \text{PV Cash Flow - Cost}$$

$$= \$750{,}000 - \$500{,}000$$

$$= \$250{,}000$$

<u>Software</u>

$$NPV_S = \text{PV Cash Flow - Cost}$$

$$= \$500{,}000 - \$200{,}000$$

$$= \$300{,}000$$

Since $NPV_S > NPV_H$, software would be ranked ahead of the hardware alternative, using the NPV criterion. However, since NPV > 1 for each investment, both are acceptable and would be profitable.

B.

<u>Hardware</u>

$$PI_H = \frac{\text{PV Cash Flow}}{\text{Cost}}$$

$$= \$750{,}000/\$500{,}000$$

$$= 1.5$$

<u>Software</u>

$$PI_S = \text{PV Cash Flow - Cost}$$

$$= \$500{,}000/\$200{,}000$$

$$= 2.5$$

Capital Budgeting

Since $PI_S > PI_H$, the software alternative would be ranked ahead of the hardware alternative using the PI criterion. However, since $PI > 1$ for each service, both are acceptable and would be profitable.

C. Should the company have relatively abundant capital resources, or at least $700,000 available for investment, both investments would be initiated. However, when capital resources are scarce, use of the PI criterion, and commitment to the software investment first, would result in scarce funds being used where their relative impact on value is greatest.

P15.9 *NPV Analysis.* The Health Maintenance Organization, Ltd., is considering offering extended service hours during weekday and weekend periods. The company has the following projections for a two-year planning horizon:

	Weekday	Weekend
Cost	$150,000	$100,000
PV of expected cash flow @k = 8%	$125,000	$125,000

A. Calculate the net present value for each service. Which is more desirable according to the NPV criterion?

B. Calculate the profitability index for each service. Which is more desirable according to the PI criterion?

C. Under what conditions would either or both of the services be undertaken?

P15.9 SOLUTION

A.

Weekday

NPV_{WD} = PV Cash Flow - Cost

= $125,000 - $150,000

= -$25,000 (a loss)

Weekend

$$\text{NPV}_{WE} = \text{PV Cash Flow - Cost}$$

$$= \$125{,}000 - \$100{,}000$$

$$= \$25{,}000$$

Since $\text{NPV}_{WE} > 0$ the weekend service would be desirable according to the NPV criterion. However, since $\text{NPV}_{WD} < 0$ for weekday service, it is unacceptable and would not be profitable.

B.

Weekday

$$\text{PI}_{WD} = \frac{\text{PV Cash Flow}}{\text{Cost}}$$

$$= \$125{,}000/\$150{,}000$$

$$= 0.83$$

Weekend

$$\text{PI}_{WE} = \text{PV Cash Flow - Cost}$$

$$= \$125{,}000/\$100{,}000$$

$$= 1.25$$

Since $\text{PI}_{WE} > 1$, the weekend service would be desirable according to the PI criterion. However, since $\text{PI}_{WD} < 1$ for weekday extended service, It would be unacceptable and would not be profitable.

C. Should the company have $100,000 available for investment, weekend service would be initiated. Extended service hours for weekday service would not be profitable and should not be initiated.

P15.10 *NPV Analysis. QED Exploration, Ltd., is contemplating on-shore and off-shore oil and gas exploration projects. Financial analysis resulted in the following projections for a ten-year planning horizon:*

Capital Budgeting

	On-shore	Off-shore
Cost	$5 million	$3 million
PV of expected cash flow @k = 30%	$7 million	$4 million

A. Calculate the net present value for each investment. Which is more desirable according to the NPV criterion?

B. Calculate the profitability index for each investment. Which is more desirable according to the PI criterion?

C. Under what conditions would either or both investments be undertaken?

P15.10 SOLUTION

A.

On-shore

$$NPV_{On} = PV\ Cash\ Flow - Cost$$

$$= \$7,000,000 - \$5,000,000$$

$$= \$2,000,000$$

Off-shore

$$PV_{Off} = PV\ Cash\ Flow - Cost$$

$$= \$4,000,000 - \$3,000,00$$

$$= \$1,000,000$$

Since $NPV_{On} > NPV_{Off}$ the On-shore investment would be ranked ahead of the Off-shore alternative, using the NPV criterion. However, since NPV > 0 for each investment, both are acceptable and would be profitable.

B.

$$\text{On-shore}$$

$$PI_{On} = \frac{\text{PV Cash Flow}}{\text{Cost}}$$

$$= \$7,000,000/\$5,000,000$$

$$= 1.4$$

$$\text{Off-shore}$$

$$PI_{Off} = \text{PV Cash Flow - Cost}$$

$$= \$4,000,000/\$3,000,000$$

$$= 1.33$$

Since $PI_{On} > PI_{Off}$, the On-shore investment alternative would also be ranked ahead of the Off-shore alternative using the PI criterion. However, since PI > 1 for each investment, both are acceptable and would be profitable.

C. Should the company have relatively abundant capital resources, or at least $8 million available for investment, both investments would be initiated. However, when capital resources are scarce, use of the PI criterion, and initiation of the On-shore investment first, would result in scarce funds being used where their relative impact on value is greatest.

P15.11 **Expected Return.** Sunnyvale Technology, Inc., is considering two alternative capital budgeting projects. Project A is an investment of $300,000 to renovate production facilities. Project B is an investment of $600,000 to expand distribution facilities. Relevant cash flow data for the two projects over their expected two-year lives are as follows:

Capital Budgeting

	Year 1		Year 2	
Pr.	Cash Flow	Pr.	Cash Flow	
Project A				
0.18	$ 0	0.08	$ 0	
0.64	100,000	0.84	100,000	
0.18	200,000	0.08	200,000	
Project B				
0.50	$ 0	0.125	$ 0	
0.50	400,000	0.75	200,000	
		0.125	400,000	

A. Calculate the expected value, standard deviation, and coefficient of variation of cash flows for each project.

B. Calculate the risk-adjusted NPV for each project, using a 12% cost of capital for the more risky project and 10% for the less risky one. Which project is preferred using the NPV criterion?

C. Calculate the PI for each project, and rank them according to their PIs.

D. Calculate the IRR for each project, and rank them according to their IRRs.

E. Compare your answers to Parts B, C, and D, and discuss any differences.

P15.11   **SOLUTION**

    A.   <u>Project A</u>

        <u>Year 1</u>:

$$E(CF_{A1}) = \$0(0.18) + \$100,000(0.64) + \$200,000(0.18)$$

$$= \$100,000$$

$$\sigma_{A1} = \sqrt{(\$0 - \$100{,}000)^2(0.18) + (\$100{,}000 - \$100{,}000)^2(0.64)}$$

$$\overline{+ (\$200{,}000 - \$100{,}000)^2(0.18)}$$

$$= \$60{,}000$$

$$V_{A1} = \sigma_{A1}/E(CF_{A1}) = 0.6$$

<u>Year 2:</u>

$$E(CF_{A2}) = \$0(0.08) + \$100{,}000(0.84) + \$200{,}000(0.08)$$

$$= \$100{,}000$$

$$\sigma_{A2} = \sqrt{(\$0 - \$100{,}000)^2(0.08) + (\$100{,}000 - \$100{,}000)^2(0.84)}$$

$$\overline{+ (\$200{,}000 - \$100{,}000)^2(0.08)}$$

$$= \$40{,}000$$

$$V_{A2} = \sigma_{A2}/E(CF_{A2}) = 0.4$$

<u>Project B</u>

<u>Year 1:</u>

$$E(CF_{B1}) = \$0(0.5) + \$400{,}000(0.5)$$

$$= \$200{,}000$$

$$\sigma_{B1} = \sqrt{(\$0 - \$200{,}000)^2(0.5) + (\$400{,}000 - \$200{,}000)^2(0.5)}$$

$$= \$200{,}000$$

$$V_{B1} = \sigma_{B1}/E(CF_{B1}) = 1$$

Capital Budgeting

Year 2:

$$E(CF_{B2}) = \$0(0.125) + \$200,000(0.75) + \$400,000(0.125)$$

$$= \$200,000$$

$$\sigma_{B2} = \sqrt{(\$0 - \$200,000)^2(0.125) + (\$200,000 - \$200,000)^2(0.75)}$$

$$\overline{+ (\$400,000 - \$200,000)^2(0.125)}$$

$$= \$100,000$$

$$V_{B2} = \sigma_{B2}/E(CF_{B2}) = 0.5$$

B. Project B has a higher standard deviation and coefficient of variation in project returns and is, therefore, the more risky of the two investment projects. Project B returns will therefore be discounted using a 12% cost of capital, whereas Project A returns will be discounted using a 10% cost of capital.

The net present value of each project is:

$$NPV_A = \$100,000(PVIFA, N=2, i=10\%) - \$150,000$$

$$= \$100,000(1.7355) - \$150,000$$

$$= \$23,550$$

$$NPV_B = \$200,000(PVIFA, N=2, i=12\%) - \$300,000$$

$$= \$200,000(1.6901) - \$300,000$$

$$= \$38,020$$

Since the $NPV_B > NPV_A$, Project B would be chosen when using the NPV criterion.

C. The profitability index for each project is:

$$PI_A = \text{PV Cash Flows/Cost} = \$173,550/\$150,000 = 1.16$$

$$PI_B = \text{PV Cash Flows/Cost} = \$338,020/\$300,000 = 1.13$$

Harcourt Brace & Company

Since $PI_A > PI_B$, Project A would be chosen using the PI criterion.

D. The IRR is the interest rate that produces an NPV equal to zero.
For Project A set:

$$NPV_A = \$100{,}000(PVIFA, N = 2, i = X\%) - \$150{,}000 = 0$$

This IRR can be easily calculated using many types of hand-held calculators, or by trial and error with various interest rates in the preceding equation. In order for $NPV_A = 0$ in the above equation, we must find the interest rate associated with $PVIFA(N = 2) = 1.5$.
Using the appendix in the back of the book, one finds:

Interest Rate	PVIFA(N = 2)	NPV_A
20%	1.5278	$2,780
24%	1.4568	-4,320

Therefore, $20\% < IRR_A < 24\%$ (or exactly, 21.6%).
Similarly, for Project B set:

$$NPV_B = \$200{,}000(PVIFA, N = 2, i = X\%) - \$300{,}000 = 0$$

Obviously, $NPV_B = 0$ when $PVIFA(N = 2) = 1.5$. As before, $IRR_A = IRR_B = 21.6\%$ and the company would be indifferent between Projects A and B according to the IRR criterion.

E. Both projects have an internal rate of return above the risk-adjusted cost of capital, and would therefore increase the value of the firm after adoption. In the event of capital scarcity, however, Project A would be preferred since it has a greater return per dollar of investment than does Project B. This preference for Project A would be reinforced for risk averse management who would note that despite being riskier, Project B has an IRR that is no greater than the less risky Project A.

P15.12 **Expected Return.** *Manhattan Transfer, Inc. is considering two alternative capital budgeting projects. Project A is an investment of $225,000 to renovate warehouse facilities. Project B is an investment of $450,000 to expand distribution facilities. Relevant annual cash flow data for the two projects over their expected five-year lives are as follows:*

Capital Budgeting

	Project A		Project B	
Pr.	Cash Flow	Pr.	Cash Flow
0.18	$50,000	0.245	$100,000
0.64	75,000	0.510	150,000
0.18	100,000	0.245	200,000

A. Calculate the expected value, standard deviation, and coefficient of variation of cash flows for each project.

B. Calculate the risk-adjusted NPV for each project, using a 15% cost of capital for the more risky project and 12% for the less risky one. Which project is preferred using the NPV criterion?

C. Calculate the PI for each project, and rank them according to their PIs.

D. Calculate the IRR for each project, and rank them according to their IRRs.

E. Compare your answers to Parts B, C, and D, and discuss any differences.

P15.12 **SOLUTION**

A. <u>Project A</u>

$E(CF_A)$ = $50,000(0.18) + $75,000(0.64) + $100,000(0.18)

= $75,000

σ_A = $\sqrt{(\$50,000 - \$75,000)^2(0.18) + (\$75,000 - \$75,000)^2(0.64)}$

$\overline{+ (\$100,000 - \$75,000)^2(0.18)}$

= $15,000

V_A = $\sigma_A / E(CF_A) = 0.2$

Project B

$$E(CF_B) = \$100,000(0.245) + \$150,000(0.510) + \$200,000(0.245)$$

$$= \$150,000$$

$$\sigma_B = \sqrt{(\$100,000 - \$250,000)^2(0.245) + (\$150,000 - \$150,000)^2(0.510)}$$

$$\overline{+ (\$200,000 - \$150,000)^2(0.245)}$$

$$= \$35,000$$

$$V_B = \sigma_B/E(CF_B) = 0.23$$

B. Project B has a higher coefficient of variation in project returns and is, therefore, the more risky of the two investment projects. Project B returns will therefore be discounted using a 15% cost of capital, whereas Project A returns will be discounted using a 12% cost of capital.

The net present value of each project is:

$$NPV_A = \$75,000(PVIFA, N = 5, i = 12\%) - \$150,000$$

$$= \$75,000(3.6048) - \$225,000$$

$$= \$45,360$$

$$NPV_B = \$150,000(PVIFA, N = 5, i = 15\%) - \$450,000$$

$$= \$150,000(3.3522) - \$450,000$$

$$= \$52,830$$

Since the $NPV_B > NPV_A$, Project B would be chosen when using the NPV criterion.

C. The profitability index for each project is:

$$PI_A = \text{PV Cash Flows/Cost} = \$270,360/\$225,000 = 1.20$$

Capital Budgeting 615

PI_B = PV Cash Flows/Cost = $502,830/$450,000 = 1.12

Since $PI_A > PI_B$, Project A would be chosen using the PI criterion.

D. The IRR is the interest rate that produces an NPV equal to zero.
For Project A set:

NPV_A = $75,000(PVIFA,N = 5, i = X%) - $225,000 = 0

This IRR can be easily calculated using many types of hand-held calculators, or by trial and error with various interest rates in the preceding equation. In order for $NPV_A = 0$ in the above equation, we must find the interest rate associated with PVIFA(N = 5) = 3.
Using the appendix in the back of the book, we find:

Interest Rate	PVIFA(N = 5)	NPV_A
18%	3.1272	$9,540
20%	2.9906	-750

Therefore, 18% < IRR_A < 20% (or exactly, 19.86%).
Similarly, for Project B set:

NPV_B = $150,000(PVIFA,N = 5, i = X%) - $450,000 = 0

Obviously, $NPV_B = 0$ when PVIFA(N = 5) = 3. As before, $IRR_A = IRR_B$ = 19.86% and the company would be indifferent between Projects A and B according to the IRR criterion.

E. Both projects have an internal rate of return above the risk-adjusted cost of capital, and would therefore increase the value of the firm after adoption. In the event of capital scarcity, however, Project A would be preferred since it has a greater return per dollar of investment than does Project B. This preference for Project A would be reinforced for risk averse management who would note that despite being riskier, Project B has an IRR that is no greater than the less risky Project A.

P15.13 **Expected Return.** *Cherry Electrical Products, Inc., is considering two alternative capital budgeting projects. Project A is an investment of $800,000 to replace technologically obsolete production equipment. Project B is an investment of $750,000* to upgrade existing production facilities. Relevant annual cash flow data for the two projects over their expected seven-year lives are as follows:

	Project A			Project B	
Pr.	Cash Flow		Pr.	Cash Flow	
0.50	$	0	0.045	$	0
0.50		500,000	0.910		200,000
			0.045		400,000

A. Calculate the expected value, standard deviation, and coefficient of variation of cash flows for each project.

B. Calculate the risk-adjusted NPV for each project, using a 20% cost of capital for the more risky project and 15% for the less risky one. Which project is preferred using the NPV criterion?

C. Calculate the PI for each project, and rank them according to their PIs.

D. Calculate the IRR for each project, and rank them according to their IRRs.

E. Compare your answers to Parts B, C, and D, and discuss any differences.

P15.13 **SOLUTION**

A. Project A

$$E(CF_A) = \$0(0.5) + \$500{,}000(0.5)$$

$$= \$250{,}000$$

$$\sigma_A = \sqrt{(\$0 - \$250{,}000)^2(0.5) + (\$500{,}000 - \$250{,}000)^2(0.5)}$$

$$= \$250{,}000$$

$$V_A = \sigma_A/E(CF_A) = 1$$

Project B:

$$E(CF_B) = \$0(0.045) + \$200,000(0.910) + \$400,000(0.045)$$
$$= \$200,000$$

$$\sigma_B = \sqrt{(\$0 - \$200,000)^2(0.045) + (\$200,000 - \$200,000)^2(0.910)}$$
$$\overline{+ (\$400,000 - \$200,000)^2(0.045)}$$
$$= \$60,000$$

$$V_B 2 = \sigma_B/E(CF_B) = 0.3$$

B. Project A has a higher standard deviation and coefficient of variation in project returns and is, therefore, the more risky of the two investment projects. Project A returns will therefore be discounted using a 20% cost of capital, whereas Project B returns will be discounted using a 10% cost of capital.

The net present value of each project is:

$$NPV_A = \$250,000(PVIFA, N = 7, i = 20\%) - \$800,000$$
$$= \$250,000(3.6046) - \$800,000$$
$$= \$101,150$$

$$NPV_B = \$200,000(PVIFA, N = 7, i = 15\%) - \$750,000$$
$$= \$200,000(4.1604) - \$750,000$$
$$= \$82,080$$

Since the $NPV_A > NPV_B$, Project A would be chosen when using the NPV criterion.

C. The profitability index for each project is:

$$PI_A = \text{PV Cash Flows/Cost} = \$901,150/\$800,000 = 1.13$$

$$PI_B = \text{PV Cash Flows/Cost} = \$832,080/\$750,000 = 1.11$$

Since $PI_A > PI_B$, Project A would be chosen using the PI criterion.

D. The IRR is the interest rate that produces an NPV equal to zero.
For Project A set:

$$NPV_A = \$250,000(PVIFA, N = 7, i = X\%) - \$800,000 = 0$$

This IRR can be easily calculated using many types of hand-held calculators, or by trial and error with various interest rates in the preceding equation. In order for $NPV_A = 0$ in the above equation, we must find the interest rate associated with $PVIFA(N = 7) = 3.2$.

Using the appendix in the back of the book, we find:

Interest Rate	PVIFA(N = 7)	NPV_A
24%	3.2423	$10,575
28%	2.9370	-65,750

Therefore, $24\% < IRR_A < 28\%$ (or exactly, 24.52%).

Similarly, for Project B set:

$$NPV_B = \$200,000(PVIFA, N = 7, i = X\%) - \$750,000 = 0$$

Obviously, $NPV_B = 0$ when $PVIFA(N = 7) = 3.75$. Using the appendix at the back of the book, we find,

Interest Rate	PVIFA(N = 7)	NPV_B
18%	3.8115	$12,300
20%	3.6046	-29,080

Therefore, $18\% < IRR_B < 20\%$ (or exactly 18.58%).

E. Both projects have an internal rate of return above the risk-adjusted cost of capital, and would therefore increase the value of the firm after adoption. In the event of capital scarcity, however, Project A would be preferred since it has a greater return per dollar of investment than does Project B. This preference for Project A would be reinforced for risk averse management who would note that Project A has an IRR that is greater than the more risky Project B.

Capital Budgeting

P15.14   ***Incremental Analysis.*** Cunningham's Drug Store, a medium-sized drug store located in Milwaukee, Wisconsin, is owned and operated by Richard Cunningham. Cunningham's sells pharmaceuticals, cosmetics, toiletries, magazines, and various novelties. Cunningham's most recent annual net income statement is as follows:

Sales revenue		$2,000,000
Total costs		
Cost of goods sold	$1,250,000	
Wages and salaries	100,000	
Rent	120,000	
Depreciation	100,000	
Utilties	40,000	
Miscellaneous	<u>40,000</u>	
Total		<u>1,650,000</u>
Net profit before tax		$ 350,000

Cunningham's sales and expenses have remained relatively constant in the past few years and are expected to continue unchanged in the near future. To increase sales, Cunningham is considering using some floor space for a small soda fountain. Cunningham would operate the soda fountain for an initial five-year period, and then reevaluate its profitability. The soda fountain requires an incremental investment of $25,000 to lease furniture, equipment, utensils, and so on. This is the only capital investment required during the initial five-year period. At the end of that time, additional capital would be required to continue operating the soda fountain and no capital would be recovered if it were dropped. The soda fountain is expected to have sales of $125,000 and food and materials expenses of $30,000 per year. The soda fountain is also expected to increase wage and salary expenses by 8% and utility expenses by 5%. Since the soda fountain will reduce the floor space available for display of other merchandise, sales of nonsoda fountain items are expected to decline by 10%.

A.   Calculate net incremental cash flows for the soda fountain.

B.   Assume that Cunningham has the capital necessary to install the soda fountain and places a 12% before-tax opportunity cost on those funds. Should the soda fountain be installed? Why or why not?

P15.14   SOLUTION

　　A.　The relevant annual cash flows from the proposed soda fountain are:

Incremental revenue:		$125,000
Increment cost:		
Food and materials	$30,000	
Wages and salaries ($100,000 × 0.08)	8,000	
Utilities ($40,000 × 0.05)	2,000	
Opportunity Cost: Profit contribution lost on regular sales = 0.1($2,000,000 - $1,250,000)	75,000	
Total incremental cost		115,000
Net incremental annual cash flow		$ 10,000
Incremental investment		$ 25,000

　　B.　Yes, the NPV for the proposed soda fountain should be calculated to determine the economic viability of the project.

$$\text{NPV} = (\text{Incremental annual cash flow})(\text{PVIFA}, N = 5, i = 12\%) - \$25,000$$

$$= \$10,000(3.6048) - \$25,000$$

$$= \$11,048$$

Since NPV > 0, Cunningham should undertake the soda fountain investment project.

P15.15   Incremental Analysis. *Fonzi's is a medium-sized restaurant located in Denver, Colorado, is owned and operated by Anthony Fonzarelli. Fonzi's currently offers elegant dining to luncheon and dining customers. The restaurant's most recent annual net income statement is as follows:*

Sales revenue:		$5,000,000
Total costs:		
Cost of goods sold	$1,500,000	
Wages and salaries	2,500,000	
Rent	180,000	
Depreciation	250,000	
Utilities	75,000	
Miscellaneous	20,000	
Total		4,525,000
Net profit before tax		$ 475,000

Luncheon and dining customer sales and expenses have remained relatively constant in the past few years and are expected to continue unchanged in the near future. To increase sales, Fonzi's is considering offering a new Sunday buffet brunch service. Fonzi's would offer Sunday brunch for an initial two-year period, and then reevaluate its profitability. Offering a Sunday brunch would require an initial outlay of $10,000 to cover new buffet equipment and utensils. This is the only capital investment required during the initial two-year period. At the end of that time, additional capital would be required to continue operation, and no capital would be recovered if the buffet were dropped. Buffet sales of $300,000 are anticipated, and the share of revenues devoted to cost of goods sold expenses are expected to represent the same as previously. Wage and salary expenses are expected to increase by 8% and utility expenses by 5%. No other incremental costs are expected.

A. Calculate net incremental cash flows for the Sunday buffet.

B. Assume that Fonzi's has the necessary capital and places a 20% before-tax opportunity cost on those funds. Should the buffet service be offered? Why or why not?

P15.15 **SOLUTION**

A. The relevant annual cash flows from the proposed soda fountain are:

Incremental revenue:		$300,000
Increment cost:		
Food and materials ($300,000 × 0.3)	$ 90,000	
Wages and salaries ($2,500,000 × 0.08)	200,000	
Utilities ($75,000 × 0.05)	3,750	
Total incremental cost		293,750
Net incremental annual cash flow		$ 6,250
Incremental investment		$ 10,000

B. No. The NPV for the proposed Sunday buffet brunch must be calculated to determine the economic viability of the project.

$$NPV = (\text{Incremental annual cash flow})(PVIFA, N = 2, i = 20\%) - \$10,000$$

$$= \$6,250(1.5278) - \$10,000$$

$$= \$451.25 \text{ (a loss)}$$

Since NPV < 0, Fonzi's should not undertake the proposed investment project.

P15.16 **Incremental Analysis.** *Career Woman Clothes, Ltd., is contemplating opening a new outlet in a suburban shopping mall. Projections for an initial 10-year period for the potential outlet are:*

Sales revenue:		*$2,000,000*
Total costs:		
Advertising	*$500,000*	
Cost of goods sold	*750,000*	
Wages and salaries	*350,000*	
Rent	*75,000*	

Capital Budgeting

Depreciation	25,000
Utilities	75,000
Miscellaneous	25,000
Total	1,800,000
Projected Net profit before tax	$ 200,000

A. Calculate the NPV for the proposed outlet assuming that an initial investment of $750,000 is required and the cost of capital is k=20%.

B. Given the proposed outlet's projected net profit before tax, calculate the maximum initial investment that could be justified when k=20%.

P15.16 SOLUTION

A. The NPV for the proposed outlet is calculated as follows:

NPV = (Incremental annual cash flow)(PVIFA,N = 10, i = 20%) - $750,000

= $200,000(4.1925) - $750,000

= $88,500

B. From Part A, note that the PV of $200,000 per year in annual projected net profit before tax at k=20% is $838,500(= $200,000 × 4.1925). Therefore, this is the maximum initial investment that could be justified for the project. (*Note:* An investment of this amount would result in a NPV = 0 since k=i.)

P15.17 Cash Flow Analysis. The Gulf States Press, Inc., is analyzing the potential profitability of three printing jobs put up for bid by the State Department of Transportation:

	Job A	Job B	Job C
Projected winning bid (per unit)	$7.00	$9.00	$11.00
Direct cost per unit	$6.00	$6.00	$8.00
Annual unit sales volume	1,000,000	500,000	550,000
Annual distribution costs	$120,000	$90,000	$75,000
Investment required to produce annual volume	$5,000,000	$4,500,000	$4,000,000

Assume that: (1) The company's marginal state plus federal tax rate is 40%, (2) each job is expected to have a ten-year life, (3) the firm uses straight-line depreciation, (4) the average cost of capital is 10%, (5) the jobs have the same risks as the firm's other business, and (6) the company has already spent $100,000 on developing the preceing data. This $100,000 has been capitalized and will be amortized over the life of the job chosen, if any.

A. What is the expected net cash flow each year? (Hint: Cash flow equals net profit after taxes plus depreciation and amortization charges.)

B. What is the net present value of each job? On which job, if any, should Gulf States bid?

C. Suppose that Gulf States' primary business is quite cyclical, improving and declining with the economy, which Job B is expected to be counter cyclical. Might this have any bearing on your decision?

P15.17   SOLUTION

A. The $100,000 spent on job cost development is a sunk cost. This cost must, however, be accounted for in the tax calculation. The Net Annual Cash Flow calculations are:

	Job A	Job B	Job C
Projected winning bid (per unit)	$7.00	$9.00	$11.00
Deduct direct cost per unit	- 6.00	- 6.00	- 8.00
Profit contribution per unit	$1.00	$3.00	$3.00
Times annual unit sales volume	× 1,000,000	× 500,000	× 550,000
Profit contribution per year	$1,000,000	$1,500,000	$1,650,000
Deduct annual distribution costs	- 120,000	- 90,000	- 75,000
Cash flow before amortization, depreciation and taxes	$880,000	$1,410,000	$1,575,000
Deduct amortization charges	- 10,000	- 10,000	- 10,000
Cash flow before depreciation and taxes	$870,000	$1,400,000	$1,565,000
Deduct depreciation	- $500,000	- $450,000	- $400,000
Cash flow before taxes	$370,000	$950,000	$1,165,000
Deduct taxes	- 148,000	- 380,000	- 466,000
Cash flow	$222,000	$570,000	$699,000
Add back depreciation plus amortization	510,000	460,000	410,000
Net annual cash flow	$732,000	$1,030,000	$1,109,000
Investment required to produce annual volume	$5,000,000	$4,500,000	$4,000,000

Capital Budgeting

Job cost development	$100,000
Job life (years)	10
Tax rate	40%

B. The NPV calculations are:

	Job A	Job B	Job C
Net annual cash flow	$732,000	$1,030,000	$1,109,000
Times PVIFA	× 6.1446	× 6.1446	× 6.1446
Present value of annual net cash flows	$4,497,823	$6,328,904	$6,814,325
Deduct initial investment cost	- 5,000,000	- 4,500,000	- 4,000,000
Net present value (NPV)	-$502,177	$1,828,904	$2,814,325
Relevant discount rate		10%	
Job life (years)		10	

Job C is the most profitable, and therefore is the most attractive since $NPV_C > NPV_B > NPV_A$. However, because $NPV_B > 0$ and $NPV_C > 0$, both of these jobs are attractive. Since $NPV_A < 0$, this job is unattractive and should not be pursued.

C. Risk for the firm is reduced through diversification. If Job B is counter cyclical, then it is least risky, other things being equal, and could be preferred on the basis of its risk, rather than return, characteristics.

P15.18 **Cash Flow Analysis.** The Printing Press, Inc., (PPI) is analyzing the potential profitability of three printing jobs put up for bid by a national textbook publisher:

	Job A	Job B	Job C
Projected winning bid (per unit)	$25.00	$35.00	$50.00
Direct cost per unit	$5.00	$15.00	$10.00
Annual unit sales volume	10,000	20,000	7,500
Annual distribution costs	$150,000	$200,000	$50,000
Investment required to produce annual volume	$500,000	$400,000	$250,000

Assume that: (1) The company's marginal city-plus-state-plus-federal tax rate is 35%, (2) each job is expected to have a five-year life, (3) the firm uses straight-line depreciation, (4) the average cost of capital is 15%, (5) the jobs have the same risks as the firm's other business, and (6) the company has already spent $10,000 on developing the preceing data. This $10,000 has been capitalized and will be amortized over the life of the job chosen, if any.

A. What is the expected net cash flow each year? (Hint: Cash flow equals net profit after taxes plus depreciation and amortization charges.)

B. What is the net present value of each job? On which job, if any, should PPI bid?

C. Suppose that PPI's primary business is quite cyclical, improving and declining with the economy, which Job B is expected to be counter cyclical. Might this have any bearing on your decision?

P15.18 SOLUTION

A. The $10,000 spent on job cost development is a sunk cost. This cost must, however, be accounted for in the tax calculation as a non-cash expense. The Net Annual Cash Flow calculation is:

	Job A	Job B	Job C
Projected winning bid (per unit)	$25.00	$35.00	$50.00
Deduct direct cost per unit	- 5.00	- 15.00	- 10.00
Profit contribution per unit	$20.00	$20.00	$40.00
Times annual unit sales volume	× 10,000	× 20,000	× 7,500
Profit contribution per year	$200,000	$400,000	$300,000
Deduct annual distribution costs	- 150,000	- 200,000	- 50,000
Cash flow before amortization, depreciation and taxes	$50,000	$200,000	$250,000
Deduct amortization charges	- 2,000	- 2,000	- 2,000
Cash flow before depreciation and taxes	$48,000	$198,000	$248,000
Deduct depreciation	- 100,000	- 80,000	- 50,000
Cash flow before taxes	-$52,000	$118,000	$198,000
Deduct taxes	- (18,200)	- 41,300	- 69,300
Cash flow	-$33,800	$76,700	$128,700
Add back depreciation plus amortization	102,000	82,000	52,000
Net annual cash flow	$68,200	$158,700	$180,700
Investment required to produce annual volume	$500,000	$400,000	$250,000
Job cost development	$10,000		
Job life (years)	5		
Tax rate	35%		

Capital Budgeting

B. The NPV calculations are:

	Job A	Job B	Job C
Net annual cash flow	$68,200	$158,700	$180,700
Times PVIFA	× 3.3522	× 3.3522	× 3.3522
Present value of annual net cash flows	$228,617	$531,987	$605,734
Deduct initial investment cost	- 500,000	- 400,000	- 250,000
Net present value (NPV)	-$271,383	$131,987	$355,734
Relevant discount rate	15%		
Job life (years)	5		

Job C is the most profitable, and therefore is the most attractive since $NPV_C > NPV_B > NPV_A$. However, since $NPV_A < 0$, Job A is unattractive and should not be bid on.

C. Risk for the firm is reduced through diversification. If Job B is counter cyclical, then it is least risky, other things being equal, and could be preferred on the basis of its risk, rather than return, characteristics.

P15.19 *Cash Flow Analysis.* Biometric Devices, Inc., is analyzing the potential profitability of three potential new testing devices:

	Product X	Product Y	Product Z
Projected market price (per unit)	$100.00	$250.00	$300.00
Direct cost per unit	$25.00	$50.00	$75.00
Annual unit sales volume	12,000	15,000	5,000
Annual selling expenses	$150,000	$250,000	$125,000
Investment required to produce annual volume	$1,200,000	$900,000	$750,000

Assume that: (1) The company's marginal city-plus-state-plus-federal tax rate is 40%, (2) each product is expected to have a three-year life, (3) the firm uses straight-line depreciation, (4) the average cost of capital is 20%, (5) the products have the same risks as the firm's other business, and (6) the company has already spent $25,000 on research and development (R&D) for these products. This $250,000 has been capitalized and will be amortized over the life of the product chosen, if any.

A. What is the expected net cash flow each year? (Hint: Cash flow equals net profit after taxes plus depreciation and amortization charges.)

B. What is the net present value of each product? Which product, if any, should BDI introduce?

P15.19 SOLUTION

A. The $250,000 spent on R&D is a sunk cost. This cost must, however, be accounted for in the tax calculation as a non-cash expense. The Net Annual Cash Flow calculation is:

	Product X	Product Y	Product Z
Projected market price (per unit)	$100.00	$250.00	$300.00
Deduct direct cost per unit	- 25.00	- 50.00	- 75.00
Profit contribution per unit	$75.00	$200.00	$225.00
Times annual unit sales volume	× 12,000	× 15,000	× 5,000
Profit contribution per year	$900,000	$3,000,000	$1,125,000
Deduct annual selling expenses	- 150,000	- 250,000	- 125,000
Cash flow before amortization, depreciation and taxes	$750,000	$2,750,000	$1,000,000
Deduct amortization charges	- 83,333	- 83,333	- 83,333
Cash flow before depreciation and taxes	$666,667	$2,666,667	$916,667
Deduct depreciation	- 400,000	- 300,000	- 250,000
Cash flow before taxes	$266,667	$2,366,667	$666,667
Deduct taxes	- 106,667	- 946,667	- 266,667
Cash flow	$160,000	$1,420,000	$400,000
Add back depreciation plus amortization	483,333	- 383,333	- 333,333
Net annual cash flow	$643,333	$1,803,333	$733,333
Investment required to produce annual volume	$1,200,000	$900,000	$750,000
Research and development expense	$250,000		
Product life (years)	3		
Tax rate	40%		

B. The NPV calculation is:

Capital Budgeting

	Product X	Product Y	Product Z
Net annual cash flow	$643,333	$1,803,333	$733,333
Times PVIFA	× 2.1065	× 2.1065	× 2.1065
Present value of annual net cash flows	$1,355,170	$3,798,688	$1,544,753
Deduct initial investment cost	- 1,200,000	- 900,000	- 750,000
Net present value (NPV)	$155,170	$2,898,688	$794,753
Relevant discount rate	20%		
Product life (years)	3		

Product B is the most profitable, and therefore is the most attractive since $NPV_B > NPV_C > NPV_A$. However, NPV > 0 for each job and each product is attractive.

P15.20 **Cash Flow Analysis.** Dick Tracy has acquired a franchise to sell one of three designs of a novelty watch in the Gotham City Market:

	Design X	Design Y	Design Z
Projected wholesale price (per unit)	$2.00	$4.00	$5.00
Direct cost per unit	$0.50	$1.50	$2.25
Annual unit sales volume	350,000	250,000	100,000
Annual advertising expenses	$10,000	$20,000	$15,000
Investment required to produce annual volume	$1,200,000	$900,000	$750,000

Assume that: (1) The company's marginal city-plus-state-plus-federal tax rate is 50%, (2) each product is expected to have a four-year life, (3) the firm uses straight-line depreciation, (4) the average cost of capital is 12%, (5) the products have the same risk as the firm's other business, and (6) the company has already spent $250,000 on franchise acquisition costs. This $250,000 has been capitalized and will be amortized over the life of the design chosen.

A. What is the expected net cash flow each year? (Hint: Cash flow equals net profit after taxes plus depreciation and amortization charges.)

B. What is the net present value of each product? Which design, if any, should Tracy sell?

P15.20 SOLUTION

A. The $250,000 spent on franchise acquisition costs is a sunk cost. This cost must, however, be accounted for in the tax calculation as a non-cash expense.

	Design X	Design Y	Design Z
Projected wholesale price (per unit)	$2.00	$4.00	$5.00
Deduct direct cost per unit	- 0.50	- 1.50	- 2.25
Profit contribution per unit	$1.50	$2.50	$2.75
Times annual unit sales volume	× 350,000	× 250,000	× 100,000
Profit contribution per year	$525,000	$625,000	$275,000
Deduct annual advertising expenses	- 10,000	- 20,000	- 15,000
Cash flow before amortization, depreciation and taxes	$515,000	$605,000	$260,000
Deduct amortization charges	- 62,500	- 62,500	- 62,500
Cash flow before depreciation and taxes	$452,500	$542,500	$197,500
Deduct depreciation	- $300,000	- $225,000	- $187,500
Cash flow before taxes	$152,500	$317,500	$10,000
Deduct taxes	- 76,250	- 158,750	- 5,000
Cash flow	$76,250	$158,750	$5,000
Add back depreciation plus amortization	362,500	287,500	250,000
Net annual cash flow	$438,750	$446,250	$255,000
Investment required to produce annual volume	$1,200,000	$900,000	$750,000
Franchise acquisition costs	$250,000		
Franchise life (years)	4		
Tax rate	50%		

B. The NPV calculation is:

	Design X	Design Y	Design Z
Net annual cash flow	$438,750	$446,250	$255,000
Times PVIFA	× 3.0373	× 3.0373	× 3.0373
Present value of annual net cash flows	$1,332,637	$1,355,417	$774,524
Deduct initial investment cost	- 1,200,000	- 900,000	- 750,000
Net present value (NPV)	$132,637	$455,417	$24,524
Relevant discount rate	12%		
Franchise life (years)	4		

Capital Budgeting

Design Y is the most profitable, and therefore is the most attractive since $NPV_Y > NPV_X > NPV_Z$. However, NPV > 0 for each desgin and each is attractive.

P15.21 ***Crossover Discount Rates.*** Sally Rogers is the chief financial officer for Popular Productions, Inc., producers of The Allan Brady Show, a hit comedy series. Rogers is considering the desirability of purchasing one of two alternative forms of post-production equipment used in the tape editing process. Rogers has discovered that a serious problem can arise when using the NPV method of project valuation because projects sometimes differ significantly in terms of the magnitude and timing of cash flows. When the size or pattern of alternative project cash flows differs greatly, each project's NPV can react quite differently to changes in the discount rate. Changes in the appropriate discount rate can sometimes lead to reversals in project rankings. Rogers discovered this problem when considering the following before-tax cash flow data:

		Expected Net Cash Flow		Difference
	Year	Project X	Project Y	Project X - Y
	1995	($700,000)	($1,750,000)	$1,050,000
	1996	150,000	500,000	(350,000)
	1997	150,000	450,000	(300,000)
	1998	150,000	400,000	(250,000)
	1999	150,000	350,000	(200,000)
	2000	150,000	300,000	(150,000)
	2001	150,000	250,000	(100,000)
	2002	150,000	200,000	(50,000)
	2003	150,000	150,000	0
	2004	150,000	100,000	50,000
	2005	150,000	50,000	100,000
Net Cash Flow		$800,000	$1,000,000	($200,000)
IRR		16.95%	13.18%	7.99%
NPV @ 7.99%		$306,966	$306,878	$88

A. Conceptually describe how ranking reversals can occur at the crossover discount rate.

B. Which investment project is preferred at a relevant cost of capital that is below the crossover discount rate? Why?

C. Which investment project is preferred at a relevant cost of capital that is above the crossover discount rate? Why?

P15.21 SOLUTION

A. Ranking reversals can occur at various NPV discount rates. Given higher nominal dollar returns, Project Y is preferred when very low discount rates are used in the NPV calculation. Given a higher IRR, the Project X alternative is preferred when very high discount rates are used in the calculation of NPV. Between very high and low discount rates is an interest rate where NPV is the same for both projects. A reversal of project rankings occurs at the crossover discount rate, where NPV is equal for two or more investment alternatives.

B. Project Y is preferred when using the NPV criterion and a discount rate k that is less than the crossover discount rate of roughly 7.99%. Project Y has the greater net cash flows of the two investment projects, and the advantage of greater net cash flow is compelling at very low discount rates.

C. Project X is preferred when using the NPV criterion and a discount rate k that is greater than the crossover discount rate of roughly 7.99%. Cash flows obtained from this project are received sooner than the cash flows received from investment in Project Y. The advantage of quick rather than slow receipt of such funds is most important when very high discount rates are appropriate. The ranking reversal problem illustrated in this problem is typical of situations in which investment projects differ greatly in terms of their underlying NPV profiles.

P15.22 *Cost of Capital.* Chock Full O'Coffee, Inc., processes and markets a leading brand of coffee. A security analyst's report issued by a national brokerage firm indicates that debt yielding 9%, comprises 60% of the company's overall capital structure. Furthermore, both earnings and dividends are expected to grow at a rate of 4% per year.

Currently, common stock in the company is priced at $20, and it should pay $1.40 per share in dividends during the coming year. This yield compares favorably with the 8% return currently available on risk-free securities and the 14% average for all common stocks, given the company's estimated beta of 0.5.

A. Calculate the component cost of equity using both the capital asset pricing model and the dividend yield plus expected growth model.

Capital Budgeting

B. *Assuming a 50% marginal federal plus state income tax rate, calculate the company's weighted average cost of capital.*

P15.22 SOLUTION

A. In the capital asset pricing model (CAPM) approach, the required return on equity is:

$$k_e = R_F + b(k_M - R_F)$$

where k_e is the cost of equity, R_F is the risk-free rate, b is stock price beta, and k_M is the return on the market as a whole. Therefore,

$$k_e = 8 + 0.5(14 - 8)$$

$$= 11\%$$

In the dividend yield plus expected growth model approach, the required return on equity is:

$$k_e = \frac{D}{P} + g$$

Where D is the expected dividend during the coming period, P is the current price of the firm's common stock, and g is the expected growth rate.
Therefore,

$$k_e = \frac{\$1.40}{\$20} + 0.04$$

$$= 0.11 \text{ or } 11\%$$

B. Given a 50% state plus federal income tax rate, the after-tax component cost of debt is:

$$\text{After tax component cost of debt, } k_d = \text{Interest rate} \times (1.0 - \text{tax rate})$$

$$= 0.09 \times (1.0 - 0.5)$$

$$= 0.045 \text{ or } 4.5\%$$

Therefore,

$$\text{Weighted average cost of capital} = \text{Debt percentage} \times k_d + \text{Equity percentage} \times k_e$$

$$= 0.6(0.045) + 0.4(0.11)$$

$$= 0.071 \text{ or } 7.1\%$$

P15.23 *Cost of Capital.* Northwest Bankshares, Inc., is a rapidly growing chain of commercial banks in north central states. A security analyst's report issued by a national brokerage firm indicates that debt yielding 15%, comprises 25% of Northwest's overall capital structure. Furthermore, both earnings and dividends are expected to grow at a rate of 25% per year.

Currently, common stock in the company is priced at $25, and is not expected to pay dividends during the coming year. This yield compares favorably with the 10% return currently available on risk-free securities and the 16% average for all common stocks, given the company's estimated beta of 2.5.

A. Calculate Northwest's component cost of equity using both the capital asset pricing model and the dividend yield plus expected growth model.

B. Assuming a 40% marginal federal plus state income tax rate, calculate Northwest's weighted average cost of capital.

P15.23 SOLUTION

A. In the capital asset pricing model (CAPM) approach, the required return on equity is:

$$k_e = R_F + b(k_M - R_F)$$

where k_e is the cost of equity, R_F is the risk-free rate, b is stock price beta, and k_M is the return on the market as a whole. Therefore,

$$k_e = 10 + 2.5(16 - 10)$$

$$= 25\%$$

In the dividend yield plus expected growth model approach, the required return on equity is:

Capital Budgeting

$$k_e = \frac{D}{P} + g$$

Where D is the expected dividend during the coming period, P is the current price of the firm's common stock, and g is the expected growth rate.

Therefore,

$$k_e = \frac{\$0}{\$25} + 0.25$$

$$= 0.25 \text{ or } 25\%$$

B. Given a 40% state plus federal income tax rate, the after-tax component cost of debt is:

$$\text{After tax component cost of debt, } k_d = \text{Interest rate} \times (1.0 - \text{tax rate})$$

$$= 0.15 \times (1.0 - 0.4)$$

$$= 0.09 \text{ or } 9\%$$

Therefore,

$$\text{Weighted average cost of capital} = \text{Debt percentage} \times k_d + \text{Equity percentage} \times k_e$$

$$= 0.25(0.09) + 0.75(0.25)$$

$$= 0.21 \text{ or } 21\%$$

P15.24 *Cost of Capital.* Marine Transport, Ltd., operates a fleet of oil and chemical tankers. A security analyst's report issued by a national brokerage firm indicates that debt yielding 13%, comprises 50% of Marine's overall capital structure. Furthermore, both earnings and dividends are expected to grow at a rate of 10% per year.

Currently, common stock in the company is priced at $40, and it should pay $2 per share in dividends during the coming year. This yield compares favorably with the 10% return currently available on risk-free securities and the 15% average for all common stocks, given the company's estimated beta of 1.

A. Calculate Marine's component cost of equity using both the capital asset pricing model and the dividend yield plus expected growth model.

B. Assuming a 50% marginal federal plus state income tax rate, calculate Marine's weighted average cost of capital.

P15.24 SOLUTION

A. In the capital asset pricing model (CAPM) approach, the required return on equity is:

$$k_e = R_F + b(k_M - R_F)$$

where k_e is the cost of equity, R_F is the risk-free rate, b is stock price beta, and k_M is the return on the market as a whole. Therefore,

$$k_e = 10 + 1(15 - 10)$$

$$= 15\%$$

In the dividend yield plus expected growth model approach, the required return on equity is:

$$k_e = \frac{D}{P} + g$$

Where D is the expected dividend during the coming period, P is the current price of the firm's common stock, and g is the expected growth rate.
Therefore,

$$k_e = \frac{\$2}{\$40} + 0.1$$

$$= 0.15 \text{ or } 15\%$$

B. Given a 50% state plus federal income tax rate, the after-tax component cost of debt is:

Capital Budgeting

$$\text{After tax component cost of debt, } k_d = \text{Interest rate} \times (1.0 - \text{tax rate})$$

$$= 0.13 \times (1.0 - 0.5)$$

$$= 0.065 \text{ or } 6.5\%$$

Therefore,

$$\text{Weighted average cost of capital} = \text{Debt percentage} \times k_d + \text{Equity percentage} \times k_e$$

$$= 0.5(0.065) + 0.5(0.15)$$

$$= 0.1075 \text{ or } 10.75\%$$

P15.25 **Cost of Capital.** Dartmouth Systems, Inc., is a leading supplier of sorters and collators to the copier and computer printer market. A security analyst's report issued by a national brokerage firm indicates that debt yielding 8%, comprises 50% of Dartmouth's overall capital structure. Furthermore, both earnings and dividends are not expected to grow during coming years.

Currently, common stock in the company is priced at $75, and it should pay $7.50 per share in dividends during the coming year. This yield compares favorably with the 7% return currently available on risk-free securities and the 13% average for all common stocks, given the company's estimated beta of 0.5.

    A. Calculate Dartmouth's component cost of equity using both the capital asset pricing model and the dividend yields plus expected growth model.

    B. Assuming a 40% marginal federal plus state income tax rate, calculate Dartmouth's weighted average cost of capital.

P15.25 **SOLUTION**

    A. In the capital asset pricing model (CAPM) approach, the required return on equity is:

$$k_e = R_F + b(k_M - R_F)$$

where k_e is the cost of equity, R_F is the risk-free rate, b is stock price beta, and k_M is the return on the market as a whole. Therefore,

$$k_e = 7 + 0.5(13 - 7)$$

$$= 10\%$$

In the dividend yield plus expected growth model approach, the required return on equity is:

$$k_e = \frac{D}{P} + g$$

Where D is the expected dividend during the coming period, P is the current price of the firm's common stock, and g is the expected growth rate.
Therefore,

$$k_e = \frac{\$7.50}{\$75} + 0$$

$$= 0.10 \text{ or } 10\%$$

B. Given a 40% state plus federal income tax rate, the after-tax component cost of debt is:

$$\text{After tax component cost of debt}, k_d = \text{Interest rate} \times (1.0 - \text{tax rate})$$

$$= 0.08 \times (1.0 - 0.4)$$

$$= 0.048 \text{ or } 4.8\%$$

Therefore,

$$\text{Weighted average cost of capital} = \text{Debt percentage} \times k_d + \text{Equity percentage} \times k_e$$

$$= 0.5(0.048) + 0.5(0.1)$$

$$= 0.074 \text{ or } 7.4\%$$

Chapter 16

PUBLIC MANAGEMENT

MULTIPLE CHOICE QUESTIONS

Q16.1   All public goods involve:

> A. nonrival consumption.
> B. the nonexclusion concept.
> C. both a and b.
> D. none of these.

Q16.2   When it is impossible or prohibitively expensive to confine the benefits of consumption to paying customers:

> A. the free rider problem emerges.
> B. the hidden preferences problem emerges.
> C. both a and b.
> D. none of these.

Q16.3   An example of a public good subject to nonrival consumption is given by:

> A. national defense.
> B. local trash pickup.
> C. a municipal swimming pool.
> D. a municipal softball diamond.

Q16.4   An example of a public good subject to the nonexclusion concept that is provided by the private sector in the U.S. is:

> A. radio broadcasts.
> B. cable television services.
> C. communicable disease inoculations.
> D. college education.

Q16.5   An example of a public good subject to the nonexclusion concept that is provided by the public sector in the U.S. is:

> A. national defense.
> B. local trash pickup.
> C. a municipal swimming pool.
> D. a municipal softball diamond.

Q16.6 A philosophy of how government decisions are made and implemented is given by:

    A. public choice theory.
    B. public interest theory.
    C. capture theory.
>   D. all of these.

Q16.7 The tendency of consumers to avoid making any contribution towards covering the costs of public goods is called:

    A. the public good problem.
>   B. the free-rider problem.
    C. the hidden preferences problem.
    D. the nonrival consumption problem.

Q16.8 If investment in a public project makes at least one individual better off and no one worse off, the result is called:

>   A. pareto satisfactory.
    B. pareto optimal.
    C. a potential pareto improvement.
    D. none of these.

Q16.9 Expenses that are not directly borne by producers or their customers are called:

>   A. marginal external costs.
    B. marginal social costs.
    C. marginal private costs.
    D. opportunity costs.

Q16.10 A method used to determine how to best employ resources in a given social program or public-sector investment project is called:

    A. social net present value analysis.
    B. social benefit-cost ratio analysis.
    C. social internal rate of return analysis.
>   D. cost-effectiveness analysis.

Public Management

Q16.11 Any change in incentives that result from the purchase of insurance is called the:

- A. free rider problem.
- B. hidden preferences problem.
- C. crowding out phenomenon.
- > D. moral hazard problem.

Q16.12 If use by certain individuals does not reduce availability for others, then a good or service is said to display:

- > A. the nonrival consumption concept.
- B. the nonexclusion concept.
- C. positive net social benefits.
- D. the private good concept.

Q16.13 When an anticipated program or project involves positive net benefits it is:

- A. pareto satisfactory.
- B. pareto optimal.
- > C. a potential pareto improvement.
- D. of benefit to at least one individual, and hurts no one.

Q16.14 When government-run enterprise is sold to the private sector, this process is known as:

- > A. privatization.
- B. liquidation.
- C. nationalization.
- D. deregulation.

Q16.15 One important difference between private and public institutions is:

- A. that private sector institutions involve exploitation.
- B. the existence of discrimination in the private sector.
- > C. the power of compulsion or coercion.
- D. the importance of self-interest in the private sector.

Q16.16 Adam Smith's belief that the pursuit of self-interest by individuals leads to social betterment is called the:

- A. public good.
- B. elimination of externalities.
- > C. invisible hand.
- D. private good.

Q16.17 It is not generally considered to be an appropriate function of government to:

- A. produce public goods.
- > B. alter individual preferences.
- C. eliminate externalities.
- D. stabilize the economy.

Q16.18 Market failure refers to a situation where:

- A. nothing useful is produced.
- B. markets fail to bring about an equality between losses and gains.
- > C. economic efficiency is not achieved.
- D. scarcity is not eliminated.

Q16.19 The stabilization function of government refers to attempts to control the problems of:

- > A. unemployment and inflation.
- B. negative and positive externalities.
- C. externalities and public goods.
- D. business failures and unemployment.

Q16.20 Air and water pollution are examples of:

- A. positive externalities.
- > B. negative externalities.
- C. public goods.
- D. public bads.

Public Management 643

Q16.21 Social costs refer to costs borne by:

> A. the government.
   B. third-party individuals
   C. foreign consumers.
   D. public sector producers.

Q16.22 Which of the following is the best example of a public good?

   A. a pizza.
> B. a radio broadcast.
   C. a bottle of soda.
   D. a video cassette.

Q16.23 One of the characteristics of a public good is that the:

   A. costs are imposed on individual producers.
   B. benefits accrue to individuals.
   C. payers can be excluded.
> D. nonpayers cannot be excluded.

Q16.24 Market failure refers to:

   A. an unequal division between private and public sector uses.
   B. a market process that does not yield useful outcomes.
> C. an inefficient use of scarce resources.
   D. a situation where markets fail to generate profitable market-clearing prices.

Q16.25 The notion that individuals know what is in their own best interest is:

> A. consumer sovereignty.
   B. paternalism.
   C. rational ignorance.
   D. the invisible hand.

Q16.26   All of the following influence exports except:

   A.   prices of foreign goods.
   B.   prices of domestic goods.
   C.   incomes in foreign countries.
> D.   the marginal propensity to import.

Q16.27   Policies that are designed to reduce barriers to international trade are known as:

   A.   trade deficit policies.
> B.   free trade policies.
   C.   protectionist policies.
   D.   import quotas.

Q16.28   Any social program or public-sector investment project should be undertaken when:

   A.   SIRR > k and B/C ratio < 1.
   B.   SIRR < k and B/C ratio > 0.
> C.   SIRR > k and B/C ratio > 1.
   D.   SIRR < k and B/C ratio = 1.

Q16.29   At the socially efficient price-output level:

   A.   external costs equal zero.
   B.   marginal social benefit equals marginal private benefit.
   C.   marginal social cost equals marginal private cost.
> D.   social marginal benefit equals social marginal cost.

Q16.30   Social marginal cost is the cost borne by:

> A.   all individuals in the economy.
   B.   individuals with no direct role in a given transaction.
   C.   all firms in the economy.
   D.   the government.

PROBLEMS & SOLUTIONS

P16.1 **External Social Benefits.** Publicly-funded primary and secondary education is typical throughout the world. This support is usually justified on the basis that there are significant external social benefits to having an articulate and well-educated populace. Some of the external benefits associated with a more highly educated populace include higher income tax revenues, reduced crime, higher voter participation, and so on.

A. Describe the nonrival consumption concept as it pertains to publicly-funded primary and secondary education.

B. Describe the nonexclusion consumption concept as it pertains to publicly-funded primary and secondary education.

C. In terms of the external social benefits of education argument, is the public support basis for college education as strong as it is for primary and secondary education?

P16.1 SOLUTION

A. The distinguishing characteristic of public goods is the concept of nonrival consumption. In the case of public goods, use by certain individuals does not reduce availability for others. However, primary and secondary education cannot be provided at zero marginal cost. This is despite the fact that many of the costs of schooling are fixed and marginal costs are very small, so long as some excess capacity exists, following a very modest increases in the number of students. Thus, publicly-funded primary and secondary education is not a good example of a public good in the sense of the nonrival consumption concept.

B. The concept of nonrival consumption must be distinguished from the nonexclusion concept. A good or service is characterized as nonexclusionary if it is impossible or prohibitively expensive to confine the benefits of consumption to paying customers. While nonrival consumption and nonexclusion often go hand in hand, theory defines public goods only in terms of the nonrival consumption concept.

Because student attendance and access to primary and secondary education can be limited, such education does *not* represent a type of public good from the perspective of the nonrival consumption concept. This is despite the fact that primary and secondary education have important external social benefits that can be used to support a public funding argument.

C. In terms of the external social benefits of education argument, the public support basis for college education may or may not be as strong as it is for primary and secondary education. On the one hand, elementary literacy, computational skills, good citizenship and other external benefits of basic education are achieved at the primary and secondary education levels, well before college. This would suggest that the basic *external* social benefits to primary and secondary education may in fact be greater than those from college education.

To be sure, college education has an enormous economic payoff in terms of increased lifetime income for college graduates. However, this tremendous economic benefit is largely earned by college graduates themselves; it is an *internal* benefit of a college education. Still, the internal benefit of increased lifetime income for college graduates translates into increased income tax receipts over the lifetime of college graduates, and one might argue that it constitutes something of an external benefit that might justify public funding for college education.

P16.2 ***External Social Benefits.*** *During the 1990s, professional sports have enjoyed an unprecedented boom all across the U.S. and Canada. Team revenues have skyrocketed with growing fan interest and attendance, thriving broadcast revenues, and flourishing corporate sponsorship support. At the same time, major and minor league teams in baseball, football, basketball, and hockey have come to increasingly rely upon public funding to cover construction costs and maintenance expenses for sport facilities.*

A. *Describe the nonrival consumption concept as it applies to publicly-funded sport facilities.*

B. *Describe the nonexclusion consumption concept as it applies to publicly-funded sport facilities.*

C. *In terms of the external social benefits concept, is the equity argument in favor of public support for sport facilities as strong as it is for industrial development in general?*

P16.2 SOLUTION

A. The distinguishing characteristic of public goods is the concept of nonrival consumption. In the case of public goods, use by certain individuals does not reduce availability for others. However, professional sports entertainment cannot be provided at zero marginal cost. This is despite the fact that many of the costs of sports exhibition are fixed and marginal costs are very small, so long as some excess capacity exists, following a very modest increases in the number of fans.

Public Management

Thus, publicly-funded professional sports facilities are *not* a good example of a public good in the sense of the nonrival consumption concept.

    B.   The concept of nonrival consumption must be distinguished from the nonexclusion concept. A good or service is characterized as nonexclusionary if it is impossible or prohibitively expensive to confine the benefits of consumption to paying customers. While nonrival consumption and nonexclusion often go hand in hand, theory defines public goods only in terms of the nonrival consumption concept.

           Because fan attendance and access to professional sports entertainment can be limited, such entertainment does *not* represent a type of public good from the perspective of the nonrival consumption concept. This is despite the fact that the location of a professional sports franchise in a given city or state have important *local* external social benefits that can be used to support a public funding argument.

    C.   No, in terms of the external social benefits argument, the public support basis for sports facility funding would not appear as strong as it is for industrial development in general. To be sure, both professional sports facilities and general industrial development produce benefits in terms of increased employment opportunities and increased tax receipt income. However, from an *efficiency* basis one might argue that the two are comparable. However, from an *equity* basis it is clear that public funding for professional sports facilities lowers operating costs for team franchises and leads to higher incomes for team owners and players--both among the very most wealthy segments of society. On the other hand, there is no clear reason to suspect that general industrial development funding would focus resulting benefits on very high income individuals. Thus, from an equity standpoint, the public support basis for sports facility funding would not appear to be as strong as it is for industrial development in general.

P16.3   ***Public vs Private Goods.*** *Use the nonrival concept to classify each of the following goods and services as public goods or private goods. Also indicate whether or not the good or service in question can be characterized by the nonexclusion concept. Explain.*

    A.   *Police protection.*

    B.   *Public libraries.*

    C.   *State and local lotteries.*

    D.   *Long-distance phone service.*

    E.   *Yellowstone National Park.*

P16.3 SOLUTION

A. Public good that is nonexclusionary. Enjoyment of police protection by one consumer does not reduce its enjoyment by others. Hence, it is nonrival in consumption. It is also nonexclusionary since it would be impossible or prohibitively expensive to confine the benefits of police protection to paying customers.

B. Private good that is not nonexclusionary. In the case of public library service, use by certain individuals can in fact reduce availability for others, especially during the peak periods or for popular items where usage is high. Thus, library service is a private good. Because on-site and loan service is often restricted to local card-holding customers, library service also cannot be described as nonexclusionary.

C. Private good that is not nonexclusionary. In the case of state and local lotteries, enjoyment of winning ticket proceeds by certain individuals does in fact reduce availability for others. Thus, the lotto is a private good. Because lotto tickets are easily restricted to paying customers, playing the lotto cannot be described as nonexclusionary.

D. Private good that is not nonexclusionary. In the case of long-distance telephone service, use by certain individuals can in fact reduce availability for others, especially during peak periods when telephone usage is high. Because long-distance phone service is in fact restricted to paying customers, it cannot be described as nonexclusionary.

E. Private good that is not nonexclusionary. In the case of national or provincial parks, use by certain individuals does in fact reduce the space and quality of space availability for others, especially during summer peak periods. Thus, park service is a type of private good. Because admission is easily restricted to paying customers, park service cannot be described as nonexclusionary.

P16.4 **Public vs Private Goods.** Use the nonrival concept to classify each of the following goods and services as public goods or private goods. Also indicate whether or not the good or service in question can be characterized by the nonexclusion concept. Explain.

A. *Lighthouse signals.*

B. *Small pox vaccinations.*

C. *Criminal justice system.*

Public Management

  D.   Local phone service.

  E.   The Simpsons television program provided on "free" TV.

P16.4   **SOLUTION**

  A.   Public good that is not nonexclusionary. The service provided by such lighthouses is an often-cited classic example of a public good. Once a lighthouse is built, it can send signals to additional cargo ships and pleasure craft at practically zero marginal cost. Because lighthouse signals can be enjoyed equally by more than one cargo ship or pleasure craft at the same point in time, they represent a type of public good. This is despite the fact that lighthouse services do not exhibit the characteristic of nonexclusion since the use of lighthouse services can be restricted, at least somewhat. Lighthouse signals are not exclusive because the light signal could be turned off for ships not paying for the service.

  B.   Private good that is not nonexclusionary. In the case of small pox vaccinations, vaccine use by certain individuals can in fact reduce availability for others. Vaccinations are, therefore, a private good. Since vaccinations can be easily restricted to paying customers, they cannot be described as nonexclusionary.

  C.   Public good that is nonexclusionary. Enjoyment of the benefits of our criminal justice system by one consumer does not reduce its enjoyment by others. Hence, it is nonrival in consumption and a public good. It is also nonexclusionary since it would be impossible or prohibitively expensive to confine the benefits of this system to paying customers.

  D.   Private good that is not nonexclusionary. In the case of local telephone service, use by certain individuals can in fact reduce availability for others, especially during the peak periods when telephone usage is high. It is, therefore, a private good. Because local phone service is in fact restricted to paying customers, it cannot be described as nonexclusionary.

  E.   Public good that is nonexclusionary. When an individual watches a "free" over-the-air (UHF or VHF) broadcast of a popular FOX program such as *The Simpsons*, this does not interfere with the enjoyment of that same FOX program by others. As a result, FOX and all other over-the-air broadcasts are a type of nonexclusionary public good. The enjoyment of TV broadcasts could be, and very well might be in the near future, made exclusive by restricting viewership to cable TV customers.

P16.5 ***The Social Rate of Discount.*** *Assume that the rate of return on long-term government bonds is 10%, a typical after-tax return on investment in the private sector is 12%, the marginal corporate and individual tax rate is 40%, and consumption averages 95% of total income.*

  A. *Based on the information provided, calculate an economically appropriate social rate of discount.*

  B. *Is a decrease in the marginal corporate tax rate likely to increase, decrease, or have no effect on the appropriate social rate of discount?*

P16.5 SOLUTION

  A. The appropriate social rate of discount is a weighted average of the opportunity cost of consumption and investment spending diverted from the private sector to public-sector use.

   Using the assumptions provided, an appropriate average social rate of discount is 10.5%, calculated as follows:

$$\begin{aligned}\text{Social rate of discount} =\ & \left(\begin{array}{c}\text{Percentage of}\\ \text{funds diverted}\\ \text{from private-sector}\\ \text{consumption}\end{array}\right) \times \left(\begin{array}{c}\text{Before-tax}\\ \text{opportunity}\\ \text{cost of}\\ \text{private-sector}\\ \text{consumption}\\ \text{(Govt. bond rate)}\end{array}\right)\\ & + \left(\begin{array}{c}\text{Percentage of}\\ \text{funds diverted}\\ \text{from private-sector}\\ \text{investment}\end{array}\right) \times \left(\dfrac{\text{After-tax}\\ \text{opportunity}\\ \text{cost of}\\ \text{private-sector}\\ \text{investment}}{(1 - \text{Tax rate})}\right)\\ =\ & (95\%) \times (10\%) + (5\%) \times \left(\dfrac{12\%}{1 - 40\%}\right)\\ =\ & 10.5\%\end{aligned}$$

  B. Decrease. A decrease in the marginal corporate tax rate has a simple, or first-order, effect of decreasing the appropriate social rate of discount since it increases the denominator of the second term shown in Part A. This stems from the fact that the average *pretax* rate of return on private-sector investment is a useful estimate of the opportunity cost of funds diverted from private investment. On a simple mathematical basis, as the corporate income tax falls, the required *pretax* rate of return required on social programs or public-sector investment projects also falls.

P16.6 **The Social Rate of Discount.** *Assume that the rate of return on long-term government bonds is 9%, a typical after-tax return on investment in the private sector is 10%, the marginal corporate and individual tax rate is 50%, and consumption averages 95% of total income.*

    A. *Based on the information provided, calculate an economically appropriate social rate of discount.*

    B. *Would a reduction in the Federal deficit that led to a decline in the long-term government bond rate affect the appropriate social rate of discount? If so, how? If not, why not?*

P16.6 **SOLUTION**

    A. The appropriate social rate of discount is a weighted average of the opportunity cost of consumption and investment spending diverted from the private sector to public-sector use.

    Using the assumptions provided, an appropriate average social rate of discount is 9.55%, calculated as follows:

$$\begin{aligned}\text{Social rate of discount} &= \begin{pmatrix}\text{Percentage of} \\ \text{funds diverted} \\ \text{from private-sector} \\ \text{consumption}\end{pmatrix} \times \begin{pmatrix}\text{Before-tax} \\ \text{opportunity} \\ \text{cost of} \\ \text{private-sector} \\ \text{consumption} \\ \text{(Govt. bond rate)}\end{pmatrix} \\ &+ \begin{pmatrix}\text{Percentage of} \\ \text{funds diverted} \\ \text{from private-sector} \\ \text{investment}\end{pmatrix} \times \begin{pmatrix}\text{After-tax} \\ \text{opportunity} \\ \text{cost of} \\ \text{private-sector} \\ \text{investment} \\ \overline{(1 - \text{Tax rate})}\end{pmatrix} \\ &= (95\%) \times (9\%) + (5\%) \times \left(\frac{10\%}{(1 - 50\%)}\right) \\ &= 9.55\%\end{aligned}$$

B. Yes. The average *pretax* rate of return on government securities is a conservative estimate of the opportunity cost of private-sector consumption that is diverted from public use. Thus, any reduction in the Federal deficit that causes the long-run bond rate to decline would have the effect of reducing the opportunity cost of private-sector consumption and, therefore, decrease the appropriate social rate of discount.

P16.7 *The Social Rate of Discount.* Assume that the rate of return on long-term government bonds is 8%, a typical after-tax return on investment in the private sector is 10%, the marginal corporate and individual tax rate is 50%, and consumption averages 94% of total income.

A. Based on the information provided, calculate an economically appropriate social rate of discount.

B. Would an increase in the Federal deficit that led to an increase in the long-term government bond rate affect the appropriate social rate of discount? If so, how? If not, why not?

P16.7 **SOLUTION**

A. The appropriate social rate of discount is a weighted average of the opportunity cost of consumption and investment spending diverted from the private sector to public-sector use.

Using the assumptions provided, an appropriate average social rate of discount is 8.72%, calculated as follows:

$$\text{Social rate of discount} = \begin{pmatrix}\text{Percentage of}\\\text{funds diverted}\\\text{from private-sector}\\\text{consumption}\end{pmatrix} \times \begin{pmatrix}\text{Before-tax}\\\text{opportunity}\\\text{cost of}\\\text{private-sector}\\\text{consumption}\\(\text{Govt. bond rate})\end{pmatrix}$$

$$+ \begin{pmatrix}\text{Percentage of}\\\text{funds diverted}\\\text{from private-sector}\\\text{investment}\end{pmatrix} \times \begin{pmatrix}\text{After-tax}\\\text{opportunity}\\\text{cost of}\\\text{private-sector}\\\text{investment}\\\hline(1 - \text{Tax rate})\end{pmatrix}$$

$$= (94\%) \times (8\%) + (6\%) \times \left(\frac{10\%}{(1 - 50\%)}\right)$$

$$= 8.72\%$$

B. Yes. The average *pretax* rate of return on government securities is a conservative estimate of the opportunity cost of private-sector consumption that is diverted from public use. Thus, any increase in the Federal deficit that causes the long-run bond rate to rise would have the effect of increasing the opportunity cost of private-sector consumption and, therefore, increase the appropriate social rate of discount.

P16.8 ***The Social Rate of Discount.*** Assume that the rate of return on long-term government bonds is 7%, a typical after-tax return on investment in the private sector is 9%, the marginal corporate and individual tax rate is 40%, and consumption averages 94% of total income.

A. Based on the information provided, calculate an economically appropriate social rate of discount.

B. Would an increase in the private-sector savings rate due to a reduction in tax benefits for individual retirement accounts increase, decrease, or have no effect on the appropriate social rate of discount?

P16.8 **SOLUTION**

A. The appropriate social rate of discount is a weighted average of the opportunity cost of consumption and investment spending diverted from the private sector to public-sector use.

Using the assumptions provided, an appropriate average social rate of discount is 7.48%, calculated as follows:

$$\begin{aligned}\text{Social rate of discount} &= \begin{pmatrix} \text{Percentage of} \\ \text{funds diverted} \\ \text{from private-sector} \\ \text{consumption} \end{pmatrix} \times \begin{pmatrix} \text{Before-tax} \\ \text{opportunity} \\ \text{cost of} \\ \text{private-sector} \\ \text{consumption} \\ (\text{Govt. bond rate}) \end{pmatrix} \\ &+ \begin{pmatrix} \text{Percentage of} \\ \text{funds diverted} \\ \text{from private-sector} \\ \text{investment} \end{pmatrix} \times \begin{pmatrix} \text{After-tax} \\ \text{opportunity} \\ \text{cost of} \\ \text{private-sector} \\ \text{investment} \\ \hline (1 - \text{Tax rate}) \end{pmatrix} \\ &= (94\%) \times (7\%) + (6\%) \times \left(\frac{9\%}{(1 - 40\%)} \right) \\ &= 7.48\% \end{aligned}$$

B. The net effect of an increase in the private-sector savings rate on the appropriate social rate of discount is ambiguous. Given the magnitude of relevant savings rates, and the relative after-tax rate of interest on government bonds versus the after-tax rate of return on private-sector investment, an increase in the private-sector savings rate due to new tax benefits for individual retirement accounts could very well increase or decrease the appropriate social rate of discount.

The savings rate affects the appropriate social rate of discount in both arguments of the equation expressed in Part A. Note that as the savings rate increases, the percentage of funds diverted from private-sector consumption falls but the percentage of funds diverted from private-sector investment rises. As a practical matter, savings rates tend to be far less than 50% of private sector income, and the before-tax opportunity cost of private-sector consumption (the risk-free government bond rate) tends to be less than the before-tax opportunity cost of private sector investment. By itself, this would suggest an ambiguous effect of an increase in the private-sector savings rate on the appropriate social rate of discount.

Public Management

Using orders of magnitude that are typical in the U.S. and Canada during the 20th century, an increase in the private-sector savings rate would, by itself, increase the appropriate social rate of discount. However, an increase in private-sector savings might very well have a "second order" effect of decreasing interest rates which are themselves partly determined by the availability or supply of savings.

Thus, on an overall basis, an increase in the private-sector savings rate due to new tax benefits for individual retirement accounts could increase, decrease, or have no effect on the appropriate social rate of discount.

P16.9 **The Social Rate of Discount.** *Assume that the rate of return on long-term government bonds is 5%, a typical after-tax return on investment in the private sector is 7%, the marginal corporate and individual tax rate is 50%, and consumption averages 95% of total income.*

    A. *Based on the information provided, calculate an economically appropriate social rate of discount.*

    B. *Would a decrease in the private-sector savings rate due to new tax benefits for individual retirement accounts increase, decrease, or have no effect on the appropriate social rate of discount?*

P16.9 **SOLUTION**

    A. The appropriate social rate of discount is a weighted average of the opportunity cost of consumption and investment spending diverted from the private sector to public-sector use.

        Using the assumptions provided, an appropriate average social rate of discount is 5.45%, calculated as follows:

$$\begin{pmatrix} \text{Social rate} \\ \text{of discount} \end{pmatrix} = \begin{pmatrix} \text{Percentage of} \\ \text{funds diverted} \\ \text{from private-sector} \\ \text{consumption} \end{pmatrix} \times \begin{pmatrix} \text{Before-tax} \\ \text{opportunity} \\ \text{cost of} \\ \text{private-sector} \\ \text{consumption} \\ (\text{Govt. bond rate}) \end{pmatrix}$$

$$+ \begin{pmatrix} \text{Percentage of} \\ \text{funds diverted} \\ \text{from private-sector} \\ \text{investment} \end{pmatrix} \times \begin{pmatrix} \dfrac{\text{After-tax opportunity cost of private-sector investment}}{(1 - \text{Tax rate})} \end{pmatrix}$$

$$= (95\%) \times (5\%) + (5\%) \times \left(\dfrac{7\%}{(1 - 50\%)} \right)$$

$$= 5.45\%$$

B. The net effect of an increase in the private-sector savings rate on the appropriate social rate of discount is ambiguous. Given the magnitude of relevant savings rates, and the relative after-tax rate of interest on government bonds versus the after-tax rate of return on private-sector investment, an increase in the private-sector savings rate due to new tax benefits for individual retirement accounts could very well increase or decrease the appropriate social rate of discount.

The savings rate affects the appropriate social rate of discount in both arguments of the equation expressed in Part A. Note that as the savings rate increases, the percentage of funds diverted from private-sector consumption falls but the percentage of funds diverted from private-sector investment rises. As a practical matter, savings rates tend to be far less than 50% of private sector income, and the before-tax opportunity cost of private-sector consumption (the risk-free government bond rate) tends to be less than the before-tax opportunity cost of private sector investment. By itself, this would suggest an ambiguous effect of an increase in the private-sector savings rate on the appropriate social rate of discount.

Using orders of magnitude that are typical in the U.S. and Canada during the 20th century, an increase in the private-sector savings rate would, by itself, increase the appropriate social rate of discount. However, an increase in private-sector savings might very well have a "second order" effect of decreasing interest rates which are themselves partly determined by the availability or supply of savings.

Thus, on an overall basis, an increase in the private-sector savings rate due to new tax benefits for individual retirement accounts could increase, decrease, or have no effect on the appropriate social rate of discount.

P16.10 ***Public Management Theory.*** *A traditional rationale for public sector management of economic resources is that there is a fundamental difference in the economic characteristics of two broad categories of goods and services. These two categories are called public goods and private goods.*

A. *Describe the essential characteristic of public goods and cite some examples.*

B. *Describe the essential characteristic of private goods and cite some examples.*

P16.10 SOLUTION

A. If the consumption of a product by one individual does not reduce the amount available for others, the product is referred to as a public good. Once public goods are provided for a single consumer, they become available to all consumers at no additional marginal cost. Classic examples of public goods provided by various levels of government include national defense, police and fire protection. Over-the-air radio and TV broadcasts are typical examples of public goods provided by the private sector in the U.S., though radio and TV programming is provided by the public sector in many foreign countries.

B. A private good is one where consumption by one individual precludes or limits consumption by others. All types of food, clothing and shelter are private goods because the number of potential consumers of a fixed amount is strictly limited.

P16.11 ***Nonrival Consumption Concept.*** *The essential distinguishing characteristic of public goods is the concept of nonrival consumption.*

A. *Explain the nonrival consumption concept.*

B. *Cite some examples of goods that display the nonrival consumption attribute.*

P16.11 SOLUTION

A. The distinguishing characteristic of public goods is that they all share the attribute of nonrival consumption. In the case of public goods, use by certain individuals does not reduce availability for others. For example, when an individual watches a network broadcast of a popular TV program such as *The Simpsons*, this does not interfere with the enjoyment of that same TV program by others. In contrast, if an individual consumes a 12 ounce can of *Diet Coke*, this same can of soda is not available for others to consume.

B. All public goods are identified as goods or services that embody the attribute of nonrival consumption. Classic examples of public goods provided by various levels of government include national defense, police and fire protection. Over-the-air radio and TV broadcasts are typical examples of public goods provided by the private sector in the U.S., though radio and TV programming is provided by the public sector in many foreign countries.

P16.12 ***Nonexclusion Concept.*** *Many public goods display the attribute of being nonexclusionary in consumption.*

A. Explain the nonexclusion concept, and how it differs from the nonrival consumption concept.

B. Does national defense display both the nonrival and nonexclusion attributes?

C. Is an optimal amount of national defense likely to be provided by the private sector?

P16.12 **SOLUTION**

A. The concept of nonrival consumption is properly distinguished from the nonexclusion concept. All public goods share a common nonrival consumption attribute. Goods display the nonrival consumption characteristic if use by certain individuals does not reduce availability for others. A good or service is characterized as nonexclusionary if it is impossible or prohibitively expensive to confine the benefits of consumption to paying customers. While nonrival consumption and nonexclusion often go hand in hand, theory defines public goods only in terms of the nonrival consumption concept.

B. Yes, since national defense can be enjoyed equally by more than one consumer at the same point in time it is a public good that displays the nonrival consumption trait. National defense also exhibits the characteristic of nonexclusion because when it is provided for by taxpayers, nontax paying citizens cannot be excluded from also enjoying the benefits of a strong national defense.

C. No, public goods like national defense that are also nonrival in consumption would not be provided in the optimal amount by the private sector.

Public Management 659

P16.13 **Nonexclusion Concept.** *Many public goods display the attribute of being nonexclusionary in consumption.*

    A.   *Explain the nonexclusion concept.*

    B.   *Do educational TV broadcasts display both the nonrival and nonexclusion attributes?*

    C.   *With the emergence and popularity of cable TV, is an optimal amount of educational TV likely to be provided by the private sector?*

P16.13 **SOLUTION**

    A.   A good or service is characterized as nonexclusionary if it is impossible or prohibitively expensive to confine the benefits of consumption to paying customers.

    B.   No, since TV broadcasts can be enjoyed equally by more than one consumer at the same point in time, they are public goods that display the nonrival consumption trait. However, the enjoyment of educational TV broadcasts can be made exclusive by restricting viewership to cable TV customers. As such, at least since the emergence of cable TV, educational TV broadcasts do not display the trait of being nonexclusionary in consumption.

    C.   Yes, with the emergence and popularity of cable TV, an optimal amount of educational television likely to be provided by the private sector. Given this relatively new technology, and the coming of over-the-air "cable" channels like "Sky cable," TV broadcasts are clearly a type of public good that does not display the nonexclusion characteristic. While public goods that are also nonrival in consumption would not be provided in the optimal amount by the private sector, there is no obvious reason why an optimal amount of educational TV could not now be provided on cable channels.

P16.14 **The Hidden Preferences Problem.** *Public goods that incorporate both the nonrival consumption and nonexclusive attributes involve a number of difficulties in demand estimation.*

    A.   *What is the hidden preferences problem?*

    B.   *How is the hidden preferences problem overcome in practice?*

C. Is the hidden preferences problem relevant for all public goods, or only for those that also display the nonexclusion characteristic?

P16.14 SOLUTION

A. A hidden preferences problem can emerge in the provision of public goods because individuals have no economic incentive to accurately reveal their true demand for public goods. Consumers are reluctant to reveal high demand for public goods because they fear similarly high payment demands. With private goods, the price that consumers are willing to pay provides a credible signal to producers regarding the quantity and quality that should be produced. No such pricing signals are available in the case of new or better public goods and services. As a result, it is virtually impossible to use market forces to determine the optimal amount of public goods that should be provided.

B. The hidden preferences problem is generally overcome when the government initiates a tax on the general public to pay for the provision of important public goods, like national defense. In the private sector, hidden preferences problems are sometimes resolved through group consensus to support local zoning covenants, charitable associations, and so on.

C. The hidden preferences problem is only relevant for public goods that also display the nonexclusion characteristic. As discussed in Part A, when individuals not paying for a certain public good cannot be excluded from consumption, there is a tendency for consumers to avoid payment responsibility.

P16.15 ***Demand Estimation for Public Goods.*** Assume that students and nonstudents have revealed their group demands for secondary education, a public good, in the local school district as follows:

$$P_1 = \$5,000 - Q, \quad \text{(Student demand)}$$

$$P_2 = \$2,500 - Q, \quad \text{(Nonstudent demand)}$$

where P is price and Q is the number of student educated per year in the local school district.

A. Calculate the total or aggregate demand for secondary education.

B. The marginal cost of secondary education is given by the expression:

$$MC = \$500 + \$5Q,$$

where MC is marginal cost and Q is again the number of students.

Determine the socially optimal amount of publicly-supported secondary education in the local school district.

P16.15 SOLUTION

A. Total or aggregate demand for public goods such as secondary education is determined by a vertical summation of individual student and nonstudent demand curves:

$$\text{Total demand} = P_1 + P_2$$
$$= \$5,000 - Q + \$2,500 - Q$$
$$= \$7,500 - \$2Q$$

B. The socially optimal amount of publicly-supported secondary education in the local school district is determined by the intersection of demand and supply:

$$\text{Demand} = \text{Supply}$$
$$P_1 + P_2 = MC$$
$$\$7,500 - \$2Q = \$500 + 5Q$$
$$7Q = 7,000$$
$$Q = 1,000$$

And,

$$P = \$7,500 - \$2(1,000) = \$5,500 \qquad \text{(Demand)}$$
$$P = \$500 + \$5Q(1,000) = \$5,500 \qquad \text{(Supply)}$$

P16.16 *Demand Estimation for Public Goods.* Assume that patients and nonpatients have revealed their group demands for hospital emergency room service, a public good, as follows:

$$Q = 20{,}000 - 50P, \quad \text{(Patients demand)}$$

$$Q = 20{,}000 - 200P, \quad \text{(Nonpatients demand)}$$

where Q is the number of emergency room patients per year at the local hospital and P is the price of emergency room service.

A. Calculate the total or aggregate demand for emergency room service.

B. The marginal cost of emergency room service is given by the expression:

$$MC = \$50 + \$0.02Q,$$

where MC is marginal cost and Q is again the number of patients.

Determine the socially optimal amount of publicly-supported emergency room service.

P16.16 SOLUTION

A. Total or aggregate demand for public goods such as emergency room service is determined by a vertical summation of individual patient and nonpatient demand curves. First, it is necessary to express patient and nonpatient demand in terms of Q as a function of P.

For patient demand:

$$Q = 20{,}000 - 50P$$

$$-50P = Q - 20{,}000$$

$$P = \$400 - \$0.02Q$$

For nonpatient demand:

$$Q = 20{,}000 - 200P$$

$$-200P = Q - 20{,}000$$

$$P = \$100 - \$0.005Q$$

Then,

Total demand = Patient demand + Nonpatient demand

= $400 - $0.02Q + $100 - $0.005Q

= $500 - $0.025Q

B. The socially optimal amount of publicly-supported emergency room service is determined by the intersection of demand and supply:

Demand = Supply

Patient demand + Nonpatient demand = MC

$500 - $0.025Q = $50 + $0.02Q

0.045Q = 450

Q = 10,000

And,

P = $500 - $0.025(10,000) = $250   (Demand)

P = $50 + $0.02(10,000) = $250   (Supply)

P16.17 *Demand Estimation for Public Goods.* Assume that park goers and nonpark goers have revealed their group demands for national park service, a public good, as follows:

Q = 60 - 2P,   *(Park goers demand)*

Q = 50 - 2.5P,   *(Nonpark goers demand)*

where Q is the number of persons that attend national parks (in millions) and P is the price of admission.

A. Calculate the total or aggregate demand for national park service.

B. The marginal cost of national park service is given by the expression:

MC = $1 + $0.08Q,

where MC is marginal cost and Q is again the number of park goers (in millions).

Determine the socially optimal amount of publicly-supported national park service.

P16.17   SOLUTION

A.   Total or aggregate demand for public goods such as national park service is determined by a vertical summation of individual park goers and nonpark goers demand curves:

First, it is necessary to express park goers and nonpark goers demand in terms of Q as a function of P.

For park goers demand:

$$Q = 60 - 2P$$

$$-2P = Q - 60$$

$$P = \$30 - \$0.5Q$$

For nonpark goers demand:

$$Q = 50 - 2.5P$$

$$-2.5P = Q - 50$$

$$P = \$20 - \$0.4Q$$

Then,

$$\text{Total demand} = \text{Park goers demand} + \text{Nonpark goers demand}$$

$$= \$30 - \$0.5Q + \$20 - \$0.4Q$$

$$= \$50 - \$0.9Q$$

B.   The socially optimal amount of publicly-supported national park service is determined by the intersection of demand and supply:

$$\text{Demand} = \text{Supply}$$

$$\text{Park goers demand} + \text{Nonpark goers demand} = MC$$

$$\$50 - \$0.9Q = \$1 + \$0.08Q$$

$$0.98Q = 49$$

$$Q = 50 \text{ (million)}$$

And,

$$P = \$50 - \$0.9(50) = \$5 \quad \text{(Demand)}$$

$$P = \$1 + \$0.08(50) = \$5 \quad \text{(Supply)}$$

P16.18 **Demand Estimation for Public Goods.** *The nonrival consumption concept gives rise to fundamental differences between demand estimation for public goods and demand estimation for private goods.*

    A. *Explain the graphical difference between aggregating individual demand for public goods versus private goods.*

    B. *Can the aggregate value of a given public good ever be less than the maximum value placed upon it by a single individual?*

P16.18 SOLUTION

    A. Since public goods can be enjoyed by more than one consumer at the same point in time, the aggregate or total demand for a public good is determined through the vertical summation of the demand curves of all consuming individuals. This contrasts with the market demand curve for any private good which is determined by the horizontal summation of individual demand curves. This difference between the demand for public and private goods can give rise to significant problems in estimating the demand for public goods.

    B. No, the aggregate value of a given public good can never be less than the maximum value placed upon it by a single individual. Since the aggregate demand for public goods is the *vertical* summation of individual demand curves, aggregate demand is always greater than individual demand.

P16.19 **Size of Government.** *Both unregulated private markets and government-administered resources have their strengths and weaknesses.*

A. Discuss a primary weakness of the unregulated private- sector allocation of economic resources.

B. Discuss a primary weakness of government-administered social programs or public sector investment projects.

P16.19 SOLUTION

A. While perfectly functioning competitive markets yield output prices and quantities that exactly balance marginal social benefits and marginal social costs, market imperfections can yield inefficiencies. When too few buyers or too few sellers are present, or when externalities are operative, competitive markets can fail to provide what consumers desire in a least-cost fashion.

Monopoly profits, low wages due to monopsony in the labor market, and air pollution are but a few examples of the problems engendered by private market failures.

B. A common assumption concerning the proper role of government is that intervention is necessary in the form of taxes, subsidies or regulation to correct market failures and thereby increase social welfare. As experience has shown, however, when markets operate inefficiently, government intervention does not guarantee an improvement in the efficiency of equity of resource allocation.

Both unregulated private markets and government-administered social programs and public-sector investment projects have their strengths and weaknesses. While private markets can identify and be responsive to individual preferences, they are unable to ensure cooperative allocations that maximize social welfare. At the same time, the efficiency and equity of government programs is limited by the fact that enforced allocation by government often ignores individual preferences.

Perhaps the most serious challenge facing public sector management is that it is almost impossible to determine the optimal amount of a public good or service that should be provided. Private-sector competition forces firms to use resources efficiently and to provide the quantity and type of goods and services consumers want. In the public sector, free rider and hidden preferences problems make the efficient and equitable allocation of economic resources extremely difficult.

P16.20 **Public Choice Theory.** *While government intervention may improve the functioning of the economic system in the presence of market failure, political forces can lead to government failure in the selection and implementation of governmental goals. In these situations, public programs can reduce rather than increase social welfare. The theory*

Public Management   667

of public choice helps explain how the political process and government decisions can lead to government policies and programs that do not reflect the public interest.

    A.   Who plays the role of consumers in the public choice theory of government?

    B.   Describe some of the characteristics of these "consumers" that can contribute to government failure.

P16.20   **SOLUTION**

    A.   According to public choice theory, the voters play a role in the public sector much like the role played by consumers in the private sector. Voters elect government representatives who purchase goods and services for the general welfare and make and enforce public policies. Voters tend to elect candidates for public office that will benefit their own self-interest.

    B.   Voting is an imperfect measure of consumer preferences. A decline in government performance can result when voters are less informed about the public goods and services they receive than they are about their own private market choices. Because voters elect officials to purchase public goods for them, there is less of an incentive for many individuals to be fully informed about public choices. In addition, it is often prohibitively costly for individuals to gather information about public choices. For example, it is more difficult to evaluate the benefits and costs of international free trade agreements than it is to compare the relative value of foreign-made and U.S.-made wrenches.

        And finally, under our system of representative government, a voter exercises less influence on public policy than he or she wields on a particular market transaction. Moreover, any citizen's selection of a politician to represent his or her district will not guarantee that person will vote exactly as desired. Since voters often feel they are not directly affected by many public policy decisions, voter apathy leads to low levels of citizen involvement in the political process. Clearly, the general welfare can be compromised when the preferences of large blocks of citizens are not included in political election results.

P16.21   **Public Choice Theory.** Special-interest groups are organized for the purposes of influencing public opinion and electing politicians who support the passage of laws and regulations that support their goals. Many special-interest groups have considerable influence because they are well-funded, well organized and very vocal.

    A.   From a social welfare perspective, what is the problem with special interest groups?

B. According to public choice theory, would an elimination of campaign contributions by special interest groups enhance social welfare?

P16.21 **SOLUTION**

A. From a social welfare perspective, the problem with many special interest groups is that they may wield power in excess of the size of their voting block due to campaign contributions. As a result, their efforts can be in conflict with broader national interests represented by larger but less powerful groups of voters.

For example, during the 1980's, lobbyists for the minerals industry and representatives of Congress successfully defeated administration efforts to eliminate the U.S. Bureau of Mines, considered by many to have outlived it's original purpose. The mineral industry wants to keep the bureau alive for the free services it provides to private companies and as a spokesman for government policies favoring mining. In another case, the country's largest teacher's union, the National Education Association (NEA), has become a potent force in lobbying at both the federal and state levels. In particular, the NEA has become one of the leading contributors to the re-election campaigns of congressional candidates that support NEA policies and programs.

B. No, not necessarily. Despite the problems posed by special interest group involvement in the political process, special interest groups may have a valid role to play. In a sense, there is a demand and supply for government policies, programs and public-sector investment projects. Like voters, special interest groups can play a useful role in articulating the public interest in government. While the intensity of special interest group concerns and focus can sometimes cause problems for the public interest, they do provide a conduit for the articulation of consumer, labor and business interests.

P16.22 **Public Choice Theory.** *Public choice theory argues that political forces make justifying, planning, financing, operating and evaluating public programs a complex and controversial task. Managerial decision making is made even more difficult when the program objectives of public or not-for-profit organizations are designed to meet equity-related objectives such as income redistribution or the care for the sick and unemployed.*

According to public choice theory, public sector managers called bureaucrats play a vital and controversial role in the public-sector management of economic resources.

A. What forces might lead bureaucrats to make suboptimal choices from a social perspective?

Public Management

    B. As a practical matter, how might bureaucrats pursue their own self-interest in public-sector management?

    C. What evidence might you cite as support for the alternate hypothesis that bureaucrats largely act as well-intentioned public servants?

P16.22 SOLUTION

    A. Bureaucrats are managers of public agencies or investment projects who are responsible for implementing the policies and laws enacted by legislative bodies. Since bureaucrats receive annual lump sum appropriations to cover the cost of providing services, they have only limited incentives to minimize operating costs. Moreover, they typically operate under monopoly conditions with little or no competition from other bureaus or private firms. As a result, the financing government of programs can lead to an inefficient allocation of resources from the private to the public sector.

    B. Public choice theory argues that bureaucrats pursue their own self-interest rather than the public interest by attempting to favorably influence the design and implementation of government rules and policies. Maximizing bureaucratic self-interest can be achieved when bureaucrats lobby to increase the scope of bureau responsibilities and funding, and thereby facilitate greater personal power, prestige and salaries.

    C. While voters, politicians, special interest groups and bureaucrats often and understandably operate in their own self-interest, these political participants often make decisions that lead to improvements in the general social welfare. For example, voters have supported income redistribution policies such as progressive taxation and unemployment compensation programs. Some politicians have boldly championed beliefs that threatened their re-election efforts. Some government bureaucrats have even lobbied for the abolition of their own departments, like the Civil Aeronautics Board in the U.S. Many public managers have also been successful in improving the quality of public services. The empirical evidence suggests that it is an exaggeration to claim that bureaucrats pursue narrow self interests to the detriment of the broader public interest.

P16.23 *Benefit-cost Analysis. The economic valuation of human life has consequences for a broad range of management decisions in both the private and public sectors. Since resources are limited for individual companies and for society as a whole, rational decision makers cannot argue that any individual company or society should spend "whatever it takes" to save a human life.*

A. Explain how public sector managers might obtain reliable life value estimates based upon actual economic behavior.

B. Describe some of the limitations of such life value estimates based upon actual economic behavior.

P16.23 **SOLUTION**

A. Public sector managers have the ability to obtain reliable life value estimates based upon actual economic behavior. For example, it might be possible to derive life-value estimates based on people's willingness to pay extra for houses located in areas with lower levels of pollution. Another approach would be to estimate life values from data on the risk versus time tradeoffs connected with automobile seat belt usage (those who buckle up and those who do not). Credible life-value estimates have actually been developed using labor-market data on the relationship between job safety and worker pay. One useful approach is to simply ask the question: How much more pay is required to entice workers to accept risky jobs? The primary advantages of these studies are that they are based on the actual judgments of large numbers of workers that are generally knowledgeable with respect to pay versus safety tradeoffs.

B. A obvious shortcoming of labor-market studies that use actual market behavior to shed light on real-world life-value estimates is that they focus on workers who have chosen to engage in especially dangerous occupations. It is one thing to simply ask the question: How much more pay is required to entice workers to accept risky jobs? It is another to get a "market basket" of responses from risk avers, risk neutral and risk-seeking individuals. Don't just ask race car drivers about their safety preferences if you want a balanced view of social attitudes. Race car drivers and other such individuals may be relatively risk-seeking in their behavior, and therefore not representative of typical workers with respect to risk-reward tradeoffs.

(*Note:* This topic was purposely chosen to be thought provoking. No one can be so presumptuous as to value something so sacred as human life. Nevertheless, everyday public policy decisions are based on set economic values that must be debated and understood.)

P16.24 **Privatization.** *With airline regulation, high prices were eaten away by ever-rising costs for new airplane equipment, fancy meals, and redundant employees. In the post-deregulation period, passenger fares have plummeted as consumers made known their preference for safe and reliable service with cheap airfares. Critics of public sector*

Public Management

management of the U.S. Post Office contend that experience with airline deregulation suggests that privatization of the U.S. Post office would lead to dramatic cost reductions and service improvements.

A. Explain how breaking the U.S. Post Office monopoly could help reduce the cost and improve the quality of first-class mail delivery.

B. Explain why privatizing the U.S. Post Office might not lead to such advantages.

P16.24 SOLUTION

A. Both public-sector and private-sector monopoly have the potential to lead to inefficiency and waste. In the case of first-class mail delivery in the U.S., significant evidence exists to suggest that the U.S. Post Office monopoly on public funding has led to poor quality, inefficiency and waste. By failing to meet the expectations of business and residential customers, the U.S. Post Office has given rise to a wide variety of message delivery mechanisms, including: overnight package delivery by Federal Express and a host of competitors, commercial package delivery by the United Parcel Service, FAX transmission of letters and other correspondence, and a wide variety of electronic message and image delivery systems.

It is worth noting that the explosion of alternative methods for delivering messages, packages and other information that has taken place during the past decade has occurred because mail customers have long sought relief from the inefficiencies of the U.S. Post Office. None of these innovations in information technology have emanated from the U.S. Post Office itself, as one might expect, if indeed that organization were focused on the timely and cost-effective meeting of customer needs.

B. The dilemma faced by public sector managers is that while both public-sector and private-sector monopoly have the potential to lead to inefficiency and waste, they also have the awesome opportunity for scale advantages. In the case of first-class mail delivery in the U.S., and despite significant and well-known problems, the quality of postal service provided still exceeds that offered in many parts of the world. Moreover, the goal of that organization is to simply provide a basic level of message delivery service to all Americans. It was not intended to meet all message and information delivery needs of all customers at all times. Thus it might be unfair to accuse the U.S. Post Office of failing to meet customer demands for overnight package delivery, all forms of commercial package delivery, FAX transmission of letters and other correspondence, and a wide variety of electronic message and image delivery systems.

If the U.S. Postal monopoly were broken to allow regional state and local bidding for the right to deliver first class mail service, as suggested by critics, a veritable onslaught of pressure groups would form to sway or otherwise fix bidding procedures and curry public favor. Whether or not such pressure groups are successful in their private rent-seeking behavior would determine the extent to which privatization of the U.S. Post Office would prove successful for the general public.

P16.25 ***The Economics of Health Care*** *During the 1990s, the share of the income devoted to health care in the U.S. has been growing rapidly. At the same time, more than 35 million Americans lack health insurance. Growing concern about rising expenditures and reduced access to insurance has led to the development of a wide variety of proposals for health care reform, from market-based approaches to calls for government-run national health insurance featuring universal coverage. The potential for success of any of these proposals depends on how well they address the reasons behind the recent increase in expenditures and decline in insurance coverage.*

A vexing problem is the persistence of serious disparities in health across income and race categories. For example, black babies are more than twice as likely as white babies to have low birth weight. While many ascribe these differences in health to differences in the ability to pay for care, evidence from the United States and other countries casts doubt on the belief that health insurance alone can greatly narrow these disparities. Studies in the United Kingdom have found that the gap in mortality between rich and poor has actually increased since the introduction of national health insurance. This result is consistent with evidence showing that increased utilization of medical services has relatively little effect on health.

- **A.** *Explain how tax provisions that exempt employer-provided health insurance from Federal and State income taxes encourage the spread of such insurance.*

- **B.** *Describe some of the alternative means by which employers might voluntarily expand the amount of health insurance provided to employees.*

- **C.** *Explain how government-mandated universal health care coverage might be deemed both fair by proponents and unfair by opponents.*

P16.25 SOLUTION

A. Employees do not pay tax on the share of their compensation that comes to them in the form of employer-paid health insurance. This preferential tax treatment is effectively a government subsidy. The amount of the subsidy depends on the worker's tax rate: the higher the tax rate, the greater the subsidy. The greater the subsidy, the more likely workers are to want a larger part of their compensation in the form of health insurance.

As tax rates have changed over time, so has the proportion of health care expenditures funded by employer payments. In 1965, when the marginal combined Federal tax rate of the median worker (including the Federal income tax and the employee's and employer's shares of the Social Security and medicare tax) was 17%, private employer contributions for private health insurance accounted for 14% of U.S. national health care expenditures. By 1982, when the combined marginal rate reached 38%, 21% of U.S. health expenditures were accounted for by private employer contributions for private insurance. During the 1980s, the marginal combined tax rate of the median worker fell (to 30% in 1990) and the share of national health care expenditures paid for by private employer contributions stopped rising, remaining at about its 1982 level, although the dollar amount of employer health care expenditures continued to increase.

Employer-sponsored insurance is also exempt from State income taxes in most States, but these taxes are not included in the above figures. State income taxes currently range between 0 and 12%, so that for most people the entire tax subsidy is greater than the Federal subsidy.

By not taxing benefits as income, the government is effectively forgoing revenues that could be used to lower tax rates. If all the health insurance benefits expected to be provided in 1993 were counted as part of Americans' taxable income, the Federal Government would collect approximately $65 billion in additional revenues.

B. Firms can increase the generosity of a health insurance package by lowering deductibles (the fixed amounts that policyholders must pay toward bills each year before any insurance payments are made), copayment rates (the share of medical bills that must be paid by policyholders), or the employee's share of premiums. Employers may also expand the range of services included in policies, as they did during the 1980s, when an increasing proportion began to offer vision and home health care benefits. Between 1972 and 1989 the total cost of all deductibles, copayments, and employee-paid insurance premiums remained almost constant as a share of after-tax income, at about 5%, despite the sharp increase in overall health care expenditures.

C. Most proponents of government-mandated universal health care coverage cite access to state-of-the-art health care services as a right to be guaranteed by all modern governments. Their goal in providing universal access to state-of-the-art health care is to wipe out the persistence of disparities in health across income and race categories. As described previously, many ascribe such differences to disparity in the ability to pay for health care.

Unfortunately, evidence from the United Kingdom suggests that the gap in mortality between rich and poor has actually increased since the introduction of national health insurance. This finding is consistent with widespread evidence showing that increased utilization of medical services has relatively little effect on the general health of the overall population. Changes in behavior offer great promise as a way to prevent disease and preventing disease is often less costly than treating it. Many Americans have adopted increasingly healthy lifestyles. For example, during the 1980s, the rate of smoking among adults decreased from 33% to 26%, more Americans exercised regularly, and deaths associated with alcohol abuse declined substantially. Traffic accident deaths per capita have declined by over 30% since 1970, in part because of greater use of seat belts. Consumers buy health care to improve their health and well-being, but recent research suggests that the connection between health care and health is not a simple one.

Opponents of government-mandated universal health care coverage argue that it is unfair to ask responsible citizens to bear the obvious and avoidable health care costs of irresponsible smokers, drinkers, over eaters, and so on.